Women Cross-Culturally: Change and Challenge

World Anthropology

General Editor

SOL TAX

Patrons

CLAUDE LEVI-STRAUSS
MARGARET MEAD
LAILA SHUKRY EL HAMAMSY
M. N. SRINIVAS

MOUTON PUBLISHERS · THE HAGUE · PARIS
DISTRIBUTED IN THE USA AND CANADA BY ALDINE, CHICAGO

Women Cross-Culturally
Change and Challenge

Editor

RUBY ROHRLICH-LEAVITT

MOUTON PUBLISHERS · THE HAGUE · PARIS

DISTRIBUTED IN THE USA AND CANADA BY ALDINE, CHICAGO

General Editor's Preface

What does the human species consist of, if not of both women and men of all ages? And if the subject matter of anthropology is the whole of the species, why have we had a topic within it called "Women, position of" and not one dealing specifically with the position of men in society as well — if it is not that men have dominated anthropology as they have the rest of our society, almost always and almost everywhere. Even exceptions have been only partial, often in new activities like American anthropology in its horse-and-buggy days as opposed to its professionalized, competitive present. This book makes that clear. Doubtless movements for the equality of women have appeared whenever opportunity has arisen, have persisted as long as possible before being overpowered, and then — like rebellions of colonies and of slaves — have submerged to be forgotten by the histories which are also the products of men. It seems over-optimistic to expect that finally, in our lifetime, we are making equality permanent. But at least this is a great moment for learning and for recording — and thus possibly improving the chances for the survival and success of the movement. This book should be considered not only as a symbol and the voice of the scholarly leadership of the emerging "equal" woman, but also as a rare opportunity to begin to unmask our ignorance. It further makes clear the fact that for the first time in history the woman's movement is international. It should not be be surprising, therefore, that a critical ingredient in making so opportune a book was an unusually heterogeneous gathering of scholars.

Like most contemporary sciences, anthropology is a product of the European tradition. Some argue that it is a product of colonialism, with one small and self-interested part of the species dominating the study of the whole. If we are to understand the species, our science needs substantial input from scholars who represent a variety of the world's cultures. It was a deliberate purpose of the IXth International Congress of Anthropological and Ethnological Sciences to provide impetus in this direction. The *World Anthropology* volumes, therefore, offer a first glimpse of a human science in which members from all societies have played an active role. Each of the books is designed to be self-contained; each is an attempt to update its particular sector of scientific knowledge and is written by specialists from all parts of the world. Each volume should be read and reviewed individually as a separate volume on its own given subject. The set as a whole will indicate what changes are in store for anthropology as scholars from the developing countries join in studying the species of which we are all a part.

The IXth Congress was planned from the beginning not only to include as many of the scholars from every part of the world as possible, but also with a view toward the eventual publication of the papers in high-quality volumes. At previous Congresses scholars were invited to bring papers which were then read out loud. They were necessarily limited in length; many were only summarized; there was little time for discussion; and the sparse discussion could only be in one language. The IXth Congress was an experiment aimed at changing this. Papers were written with the intention of exchanging them before the Congress, particularly in extensive pre-Congress sessions; they were not intended to be read at the Congress, that time being devoted to discussions — discussions which were simultaneously and professionally translated into five languages. The method for eliciting the papers was structured to make as representative a sample as was allowable when scholarly creativity — hence self-selection — was critically important. Scholars were asked both to propose papers of their own and to suggest topics for sessions of the Congress which they might edit into volumes. All were then informed of the suggestions and encouraged to rethink their own papers and the topics. The process, therefore, was a continuous one of feedback and exchange and it has continued to be so even after the Congress. The some two thousand papers comprising *World Anthropology* certainly then offer a substantial sample of world anthropology. It has been said that anthropology is at a turning point; if this is so, these volumes will be the historical direction-markers.

As might have been foreseen in the first post-colonial generation, the large majority of the Congress papers (82 percent) are the work of scholars identified with the industrialized world which fathered our traditional discipline and the institution of the Congress itself: Eastern Europe

(15 percent); Western Europe (16 percent); North America (47 percent); Japan, South Africa, Australia, and New Zealand (4 percent). Only 18 percent of the papers are from developing areas: Africa (4 percent); Asia-Oceania (9 percent); Latin America (5 percent). Aside from the substantial representation from the U.S.S.R. and the nations of Eastern Europe, a significant difference between this corpus of written material and that of other Congresses is the addition of the large proportion of contributions from Africa, Asia, and Latin America. "Only 18 percent" is two to four times as great a proportion as that of other Congresses; moreover, 18 percent of 2,000 papers is 360 papers, 10 times the number of "Third World" papers presented at previous Congresses. In fact, these 360 papers are more than the total of ALL papers published after the last International Congress of Anthropological and Ethnological Sciences which was held in the United States (Philadelphia, 1956).

The significance of the increase is not simply quantitative. The input of scholars from areas which have until recently been no more than subject matter for anthropology represents both feedback and also long-awaited theoretical contributions from the perspectives of very different cultural, social, and historical traditions. Many who attended the IXth Congress were convinced that anthropology would not be the same in the future. The fact that the next Congress (India 1978) will be our first in the "Third World" may be symbolic of the change. Meanwhile, sober consideration of the present set of books will show how much, and just where and how, our discipline is being revolutionized.

This was one of a number of books which gained greatly from the set of pre-Congress conferences held at the University of Wisconsin in Oshkosh. The present book is able complemented in this series by Dana Raphael's *Being female: reproduction, power, and change.* Readers will also be interested in other related titles — on youth, migration, population, ethnicity, development, competition, and education.

Chicago, Illinois   SOL TAX
October 11, 1975

Preface

The papers in this volume were written for the session on women's status and women's movements at the IXth International Congress of Anthropological and Ethnological Sciences, held in the United States in the late summer of 1973. The three-day preliminary conference at Oshkosh was particularly significant; women from many different cultures were welded into a solidary group by the nature of their involvement in the subject matter and were able to discuss their diverse findings and viewpoints with both friendliness and frankness.

The papers they wrote are critical evaluations of women's status in gathering-hunting bands, fishing clans, peasant communities, agricultural chiefdoms, and in the developing and developed countries, both capitalist and socialist. They show women as food gatherers, farmers, potters, weavers, traders, chiefs, miners, industrial workers, union organizers, servants, and professionals; as victims of exploitation and as fighters against oppression. What is quite clear is that women everywhere are realizing that only through autonomous movements to change their subordinate status will they achieve societies that are humane and just.

I am grateful to Sol Tax for his stupendous labors under enormous disfficulties in making the Congress possible; to Eleanor Leacock for her suggestions and criticisms of the section introductions and final chapter of conclusions; and to Constance Sutton for her help in organizing both the session and the book. My heartfelt thanks to the women who attended the session and who wrote the papers.

RUBY ROHRLICH-LEAVITT

Table of Contents

SECTION SIX: CONCLUSIONS

SECTION ONE

Women in Islam and Africa

Introduction

Africa and India are linked by Islam which, beginning in the eighth century, spread over much of both these regions. But there is a striking contrast between the status of women in areas that are completely Islamicized and in those parts of Africa that were least affected by both Islam and European colonization. African "cultures have traditionally included freedoms which, in other parts of the world, women have only recently begun to enjoy or aspire to" (Patai 1967:315). Autonomous women's organizations have historically protected and furthered African women's rights, whereas until very recently organizations of Islamic women have counted for little.

Islamic women are among the most oppressed in the world, according to Jahan in "Women in Bangladesh." The institution of *purdah*, symbolized by the veil, thoroughly segregates Muslim women, especially in the rural areas, from the public domain and reduces them to a state of almost complete subordination and dependency. Islamic men, whether in traditional or socialist countries, generally fight ferociously against all attempts to liberate women or even to improve their lot.

Although the network of female relatives and friends among women in Morocco, described by Sutton, et al. in "Women, knowledge, and power" (Section 5), permits the relay of information, exchange of personal services, limited circumvention of male authority, and the expression of common dissatisfactions, it does not get beyond the "gripe" session. Islamic women, with minimal access to knowledge about their own and other cultures, are unable to form a positive self-image, discover the ways in which their society functions to oppress them, and organize to resist their oppression.

In Bangladesh, even the elite women's groups with limited reformist goals who operate within Islamic traditions encounter the intense hostility of the powerful Muslim religious leaders. When Muslim women in the U.S.S.R. tried to assert their legal independence, established by the Communist Party shortly after the Russian Revolution, they were kidnapped, raped, and murdered in a priest-led movement consisting of men of all classes, as described by Rosenthal in her article on women in the U.S.S.R. (Section 4). The recent violation of Bangali women by both Pakistani men (during the war) and Bangali men (in the post-liberation period of lawlessness in Bangladesh), discussed by Jahan, demonstrates the vulnerability of women, even when they are unassertive, within a system in which they are brutalized by men who at the same time pose as their protectors. However, this terrorization of Bangali women has made feminists of some members of the younger generation, who, according to Jahan, are attempting to reach out to the masses of women in Bangladesh.

As Okonjo and Rousseau show in their papers on women in Nigeria, Sierra Leone, and Zaire, women in much of Africa had higher status and greater autonomy than most women in South and East Asia and Europe. Their economic roles as farmers, traders, and craftswomen were crucial to their society, and through their traditional women's organizations they participated fully in a form of political decision-making that was widely dispersed. Leacock, in "Class, commodity, and the status of women" (Section 5), shows that in the nineteenth century, the Balonda, one of the Lunda Bantu peoples of the Congo, had, like many other African tribes, a woman chief.

But the educational system which the Europeans imposed along with other colonial controls was a particularly powerful instrument for the exploitation of human resources and contributed to the deterioration of women's status. Nevertheless, women's organizations persisted throughout the colonial world to provide the framework for women's resistance struggles, and they are becoming increasingly effective in re-establishing the socioeconomic significance of African women.

REFERENCES

PATAI, RAPHAEL, *editor*
1967   *Women in the modern world*. New York: The Free Press.

Women in Bangladesh

ROUNAQ JAHAN

It is difficult to write about the women of Bangladesh. Little published
material is available on women. Statistical data are outdated because the
last census was taken in 1961. The vast majority of Bangladesh's 35 million
women live in *purdah*,[1] and little is being said or written about their problems. This lack of data on women is partially explained by the difficulties that researchers (usually male) face in studying women in a *purdah*-
dominated society. Additionally, as women are nonvisible and unorganized, their problems are not articulated and hence they fail to draw
the attention of researchers.[2] But the fact that nothing is being written
about the problems of women in Bangladesh does not mean that the
problems do not exist. Indeed the women of Bangladesh are among the
most oppressed in the world. This paper attempts to highlight this oppression and to anlyze some of the problems they face today.

The study is divided in three parts. Part 1 describes the lifestyles of
women in Bangladesh. A distinction is made between the various categories of women — rural and urban, traditional and modern, working

I would like to thank the Ford Foundation, which reproduced and made this report
available for discussion in advance of its formal publication. The views expressed are
those of the author and do not necessarily represent views of the Ford Foundation.

[1] *Purdah*, literally meaning the curtain, refers to the system of seclusion of women
prevalent in the Middle East and South Asia. In the strictest sense *purdah* involves
keeping women confined within the four walls of the home and veiling them when they
leave the home. In a wider context, *purdah* refers to women's modesty and restrictions
on their interactions with males who do not fall within the specified categories of those
with whom contact is permitted by the religion.

[2] Usually social scientists are attracted to problems that become controversial and
debated issues.

class and middle class. The divergent lifestyles in these categories are analyzed to illustrate the basic inequity — the great distinction between the elite and the mass — that exists in any developing country. The elite women (who are urban and modern) have a very different lifestyle from the mass of the women in Bangladesh (who are rural and traditional). But while their lifestyles are different, both categories of women are oppressed, though the levels and modes of oppression differ. Part 2 of the paper deals with the legal, economic, political, and social status of women in Bangladesh. The dichotomy between the legal and socio-economic status of women is emphasized to indicate their actual status. Part 3 discusses the gradual evolution of the movement for women's emancipation in Bangladesh. The role of the various women's organizations is analyzed. It is hypothesized that because the women's organizations are highly elitist in nature they play only a marginal role in emancipating the women of Bangladesh.

The study is based on some one hundred open-ended interviews that the author conducted with women in Bangladesh in the spring and summer of 1973. The women interviewed included all categories: urban and rural housewives and career women, students, political workers, and persons active in women's movements and organizations. Some parts of the study, especially Part 1, are based on data derived largely from interviews. However, only Muslim women are discussed in this paper. The observations made are not applicable to the Hindu, Christian, and Buddhist women, who constitute roughly 15 percent of Bangladesh's female population.

1. WOMEN OF BANGLADESH: RURAL AND URBAN

To describe the lifestyles of women in Bangladesh, one has to distinguish between those of rural and urban women. The overwhelming majority of Bangali[3] women are rural; only about 5 percent of the population is urbanized. While most of the rural women can be broadly classified as traditional, not all urban women can be called modern. If modernity is defined in terms of literacy, urbanization, and adoption of a modern occupation, then only a small fraction of Bangali women can be classified as modern. Of 35 million women in Bangladesh, only 1.75 million are urban; of these urban women a mere 32 percent are literate and only about 1.27 percent adopt a modern occupation. As modern women constitute a miniscule minority of Bangali women, it is useful to describe

---

[3]   A Bangladesh national is called a Bangali. It is also spelled Bangalee.

in some detail the lifestyle of rural women who form the mass of the women in Bangladesh. If generalizations are ever to be made about the women of Bangladesh, it has to be done in terms of the rural women.

Rural Women

A brief description of a rural woman's life from birth to death facilitates an understanding of her lifestyle. In the rural areas the birth of a girl is rarely celebrated by parents and relatives, unless she happens to be the first daughter after four or five sons. That usually no *azan* [call for prayer] is given when a girl is born symbolizes the community's disinterest in the girl's arrival.[4] From early childhood on, girls are made fully conscious of the feeling that, unlike their brothers, they are liabilities. Girls are taught the two virtues — patience and sacrifice — of ideal Bangali womenhood.[5] They also learn to accept the essentially inferior status of women in society. As girls grow up they perceive the preferential treatment given to the male members of the family, and they are told that getting less of everything and not complaining about it is the ideal behavior of good women. In a *milieu* of scarcity, whatever is available — food, clothing, or opportunities for education and health care — is offered first to the men. If the family can afford good food, i.e. meat or milk, the father and sons have the first and major share. If the family has enough resources to send children to school, boys get preference over girls, even if the girls are brighter.

From her childhood a girl is trained to fit into the only socially acceptable role, that of wife and mother. By the time a girl reaches the age of five or six, her mother has produced two or three additional children, and the young girl has to look after them. She also helps her mother in other households chores, i.e. cooking, cleaning, sewing, etc. In rural areas few girls are sent to school. According to the 1961 census, only 21.9 percent of rural females between the ages 5 to 14 (compared to 46.7 percent of males) were enrolled in school. Girls are given some schooling only by economically and socially established families. And that schooling usu-

4 After a male child is born, the call for prayer is given welcoming the new addition to the Muslim community. But when a girl is born no *azan* is given. My data show that only in socially established families *azan* is given for girls. One poor woman interviewed in a village in Savar commented, "It is against the *Hadith* to give *azan* when a girl is born."
5 Both the folklore and the religious tradition idolize women who made immense sacrifices for their husbands, e.g. Mahua and Malua (folklore) and Hazera, Sara, Rahima, Khadija, Aisha, and Fatima (religious tradition).

ally consists of learning to read and recite the *Quran* [the Holy Book] and four or five years of formal school attendance. The major purpose of formal schooling is very similar to that of the girl's informal learning at home, i.e. training her to be a good wife and mother. A girl's stock in the marriage market goes up if she has some formal schooling (Ahmad 1966). Educated men prefer wives who can at least read and write letters and keep basic accounts. "Respectable" families[6] in rural areas therefore give their daughters some formal schooling so that they can be married to educated men employed in urban areas.

Village girls usually drop out of school after the fifth or sixth grade. Only 1.7 percent of rural women above the age of fifteen are enrolled in school, compared to 20.8 percent of men. Girls discontinue schooling at an early age for two main reasons. First, by the time a girl is in the fifth or sixth grade, she has completed basic training in reading, writing, and arithmetic, and any further education is regarded as unnecessary, if not harmful, for a happy married life. Second, after she reaches the age of 12 or 13, a girl has to drop out of school for *purdah* considerations. Few villages have high schools for girls, and the village *samaj*[7] frowns upon girls attending coeducational schools after they have reached puberty. Also, because many villages do not have boys' schools, girls' enrollment becomes even more problematic. A woman's *purdah* observance is more rigidly enforced outside her own village (Ahmed 1966). While it is difficult for a girl to study in a boys' high school in her own village, it is nearly impossible for her to go to a neighboring village to study.

In rural areas it is customary for girls to go in *purdah* when they reach puberty. But even before that, a girl is made aware of the two separate worlds of men and women. A woman's world is her home, while the man's world is outside the home. Separation of the two worlds is enforced by the pervasive *purdah* system. Women perform tasks at home (cooking, cleaning, nursing children, sewing, etc.), and men negotiate with the outside world (working in the fields, shopping, etc.). Only in very rare cases does a man help his wife in her household tasks, and few women work in the fields, no matter how poor the family is. Here Muslim society in Bangladesh differs from other Muslim countries, e.g. Indonesia, where women work freely in the field and in the market place. However, Bangali rural women do share in tasks that involve earning family income. Women clean and husk rice, prepare fuel, make sugar, and tend the kitchen garden, but their role in earning family income is never acknowledged.

---

[6]   By respectable families I mean here the *Bhadrolok* class.
[7]   *Samaj* connotes the village power structure. It consists of the village notables who make decisions about the various mechanisms of social control.

Farming is a "two-person" occupation (Papanek 1973)[8] where the wife's role is non-paid and non-recognized. Thus while the two worlds of men and women are interdependent, a woman's world is always regarded as inferior to the man's world.

The rigidity of *purdah* observance, like the extent of schooling, depends very much on the socioeconomic status of the family. An easy index of the rising socioeconomic status of the family is the increasing rigidity of *purdah* observance. Economic status and *purdah* observance are correlated because only prosperous families can afford to put their women in *purdah*. *Purdah* observance involves two kinds of restrictions on women's movements (Papanek 1971). The first is spatial: women are confined within the walls of their homes, a separate women's wing, separate tank for women's bathing and cleaning facilities, and separate toilet facilities for women. The second type of restriction allows a woman to move out of her home, but only if she is veiled in *burqah* [tent-like veiled clothing for women] or travels in veiled transports (carts, boats, or rickshas with heavy curtains drawn around them). To ensure spatial restriction on women's mobility, the family has to be realtively wealthy, so that it can allocate enough living space and separate tanks and tube wells for its women. The second category of restriction also requires money. Only rich farmers can afford to buy *burqah* for their women; average rural women have only one or two saris.

In poorer rural families, the women have to leave their households and go to the houses of rich farmers to fetch water, to bathe, and to work as part-time household help. When leaving their houses, these women cover their heads with their sari to symbolize their *purdah* observance. And when they visit relatives in the neighboring villages, they go walking in the evening and use umbrellas as veils. Thus, while the rigidity of *purdah* observance varies among families, at puberty all girls are required to start observing some *purdah*, whether total seclusion at home or imposition of some restrictions on contact with men.[9]

At puberty, not only are girls put in *purdah* but their marriages are also

---

8 Hanna Papanek describes certain occupations, e.g. foreign service and academic positions, where the wife plays a substantial role in her husband's career though her role is not officially recognized. She hypothesizes that because of the separation of the world of men and women in South Asia, such two-person careers have no future there. However, in farming, weaving, and many other occupations in the rural sector in South Asia women participate actively in their husband's/father's occupations, though their role is taken for granted and hence is unrecognized.

9 After puberty, restrictions are put on a girl's movements, and she can meet members of the opposite sex only with her family's consent. Within the village, girls can see and talk to unrelated (non-kin) men, but they address each other in appropriate kin-terms, i.e. "Bhai-bon", "kaka," "mama," etc.

arranged by their families. In rural areas girls are usually married between the ages of 12 and 15. Girls are married early because by 11 or 12
they complete all the informal and formal training necessary for their
only socially acceptable roles — those of housewife and mother. Furthermore, after a girl reaches puberty she is regarded as "vulnerable,"
needing "shelter," and the safest course open to her family is to arrange
a marriage for her so that she can move into a permanent shelter (Papanek
1871).[10]

Marriages are always arranged, and the father and other male members
of the family have the dominant say in the matter. As the marriage
arrangement requires negotiations with the outside world, it is handled
by the male guardians of the girl (Ahmed 1966). In Muslim marriage, a
girl's consent is mandatory, but the consent is a mere formality.

After her marriage, a girl moves to her husband's household. In the
first few years of marriage, her position is very insecure. In her husband's
house, a bride has to observe a stricter *purdah*, her mobility is even more
curtailed, her work load increases, and the two virtues of Bangali
womanhood — patience and sacrifice — instilled in her as a child, are
put to a hard test. Her position is inferior to that of the other women of
her husband's house, i.e. her mother-in-law and sister-in-law. The only
way she can get security in her husband's household is by producing a
male heir. The more male children she has, the greater is her security and
acceptance.[11]

On the average, a rural woman has eleven or twelve pregnancies. She
may have one or two miscarriages, two or three of her children may die
young, and six or seven children may survive. She has little control over
her body; the decision to have children is totally her husband's. Rarely
does a rural woman practice any form of birth control. A survey in
Comilla indicated that after six years of widespread publicity about family
planning, only about 4 percent of women practiced some measures of
birth control (Stoeckel and Chowdhury 1973). Abortion as a means of
birth control is sometimes practiced by the poorer section of the rural
population but it is considered a sin.

[10]   A good illustration of this anxiety over a girl's "shelter" was found in 1971 during
the Pakistani occupation. As stories spread of Pakistani soldiers' violation of women,
parents became anxious to marry off their single daughters so that the responsibility
for providing shelter for them could be transferred to another family.
[11]   Even in cases of women raped by Pakistani soldiers, it was found that women with
many children had a greater prospect of acceptance by the husbands as compared to
women with one or two children. The typical reaction of husbands who accepted back
wives who had borne them several children was "What can I do? She is the MOTHER of
so many of my children!"

By the time a woman reaches the age of thirty, she is often a grand-mother and is regarded as an old woman. Divorce and remarriage are more frequent in rural areas, especially among poor farmers. According to one study of a village in Comilla, approximately 16.5 percent of all marriages ended in divorce (Peter Bertocci, personal communications). In socially established families, divorce is frowned upon. A divorced woman, if she is young, is usually remarried, because an unattached woman, be she single, widowed, or divorced, has no social standing. Additionally she is a financial burden. Young widows are also remarried, sometimes to their brothers-in-law to keep the family property intact. After a certain age, however, it is difficult for widows and divorced women to get married. *The master survey of agriculture*, published in 1961, listed a sharp increase in the number of widowed females after the age of 34, with no such corresponding increase in the number of widowed males, which only indicates that while Bangali men can and do remarry at all ages, women can not (East Pakistan Bureau of Statistics 1961). If a widow or a divorced woman remains unmarried, she has to live under the guardianship of either her father or brother, or father-in-law or brother-in-law. In short, a woman is never regarded as capable of taking care of herself. Before marriage her father is her guardian, after marriage her husband takes that role, and after her husband's death her son be-comes her guardian.

Urban Women

In urban areas, there are sharp differences in the lifestyles of various categories of women. Here we would distinguish between two: working-class and middle-class women. There is a third group of westernized women, but they are small in number and play a marginal role in society.

The lifestyle of urban working-class women is not very different from that of rural women, the only difference being the relaxation of *purdah* oberservance in an urban setting. The majority of urban working-class women are new migrants to cities and they maintain close rural ties.[12] As in rural areas, the birth of a girl is unwelcome and the early socialization process is very similar. Girls from working-class families are also made aware of the separate worlds of men and women, though their housing is conducive to relaxation of *purdah* observance. From childhood,

[12] When rural women migrate to cities for jobs, they live in slums where they have friends from their own villages. They visit their rural homes frequently and invest in land in the rural areas.

working-class girls are trained to be housewives and mothers. They have to carry the major burden of household chores, including care of baby brothers and sisters, because their mothers go outside to work. The literacy and school enrollment rates among working-class women are low. Most girls leave school after fifth or sixth grade. The drop-out rate is high partly because the family cannot afford to send the children to school and partly because women's education in working-class families is not customary.

Working-class women are married early, ordinarily by the age of 15 or 16. Marriages are usually arranged by parents, but as there is a greater scope for contact between the sexes, some love matches do take place. Divorce and remarriage are frequent. Like rural women, urban working-class women have little say over such a vital matter as the decision to have children. They have nearly as many pregnancies, miscarriages, and surviving children as the rural women.

Working-class women cannot observe strict *purdah*, but they do not repudiate the concept of *purdah*. Indeed, in their minds *purdah* is associated with respectability, and they do observe *purdah* when their economic status becomes more secure. When asked whether they would want their daughters to observe *purdah*, the majority of working-class women answered in the affirmative (personal interview). *Purdah*, in the sense of modesty, restriction on contact between the sexes, and shelter for women, is a universally accepted value in Bangladesh.

Of all the categories of women, only among urban working-class women do we find many women who are their own guardians. Even in cases where there are male guardians, the women are more assertive. This deviant behavior pattern is explained by their being wage earners.[13] Compared to their rual sisters, working-class women are more politically conscious and organized. Working class women constitute the bulk of all the women's processions brought out by political parties. But while their rate of political participation is high, they are not feminists. This will be elaborated in Part 2 of the paper.

"Modern" Bangali women are urban middle-class women, whose lifestyles are visibly different from that of rural women or working-class women. Ostensibly the modern woman has an easier life and more leisure, but like all modern women in a traditional society, she lives in two worlds. While rural women are more blatantly oppressed and discriminated against, the oppression of and discrimination against urban women is subtle.

[13] Interview with some social workers who are organizing women's cooperative projects among urban working-class women.

The birth of a girl is not a happy event even in an urban middle-class family, though her parents quickly become reconciled to a daughter. She is socialized differently from a rural girl. She grows up in a nuclear family; has greater contact with her brothers, father, and other male members of the family; and her opportunities for education are nearly equal to those of her brothers. The informal learning process at home, where she is taught how to cook, clean, sew, and look after babies, does not start as early for an urban girl. And she is expected to finish school before she is married.

Urban middle-class women do not observe rigid *purdah*, but they do live in a separate world of women. Segregation of sexes starts at puberty. Girls may not wear the veil, but restrictions are put on their mobility and on their contact with males. Between the ages of 11 and 17, boys and girls go to separate schools; and though the university is coeducational, contact between male and female students is restricted. Here again, separate space is allocated for women: there are separate reading rooms and lounges and in classrooms women students occupy separate seats (usually the first two or three rows). A woman may spend four years in a coeducational institution and not exchange four sentences with her male classmates. Indeed, the less contact she has with males, the better her reputation as a good woman.[14]

Marriages are arranged for urban middle-class women. Most women are married between the ages of 19 and 24. Only in rare cases does a woman remain single beyond 24. Single women have no social status even in urban areas, and a good marriage is regarded as the ultimate goal of a woman's life. An overwhelming majority of urban, educated women still accept and prefer arranged marriages because there is little opportunity to meet members of the opposite sex. Girls also have little confidence in their own abilities to find established husbands and they trust their fathers' judgment in arranging suitable matches for them. Nearly all the university students who were interviewed showed an anxiety over security and preferred arranged marriages.

A small percentage of urban middle-class women adopt a career. In a recent survey of a part of the Dacca municipal area, about 10 percent of urban women were found to be working, though nearly 34.4 percent of these women are university graduates.[15] Women's career choices are very much determined by the *purdah* society's imperative of two separate worlds. Papanek (1971) argues that teaching and medicine are regarded

[14] Modesty and chastity in women are still higly prized values.
[15] Data are taken from the author's election survey of two constituencies where some 2561 interviews were conducted.

as the two most respectable occupations for women because of the presence of a large female clientele. In a *purdah* society women are preferred as doctors for female patients and as teachers for female students, and hence there is a great demand for women in these occupations. Similarly occupations that bring women in contact with men, e.g. nursing and secretarial work, are regarded as non-respectable. In contrast to the pattern in Western countries, many more women go into medicine than into such women's occupations as nursing and secretarial work.

A women's career choice is also determined by her family. Her father usually will decide whether she should study and what she should study. It is again her father or her husband who decides whether she should have a job and what type of a job she should have.

An urban middle-class woman, if she has a job, has some say in the couple's decision to have babies. She often practices some form of birth-control. Career women usually have fewer children than a housewife, who tends to have five to six children. The notion of a planned family appears to be acceptable only to the younger generation of urban women. Divorce and remarriage are rare among the urban middle class. Divorce brings disrepute to the whole family and hence is looked down upon.

Thus an urban middle-class woman's life is different from a rural woman's in that she has greater opportunities for education and a career. But she can enter a man's world only by exploiting another class of women — maidservants, mothers, and mothers-in-law — who take over her household tasks and thus provide her with the free time needed for outside work. Even in an urban middle-class family the household tasks are not shared by the husband of a career woman, except for the care of babies, in which the younger generation of men show an interest. Men refuse to share in household work because it is regarded as women's work and hence inferior.

That a woman's status should be inferior to a man's is a thesis universally accepted by Bangali men. In a recent survey of two localities — one rural and one urban — 70 percent of rural men and 80 percent of urban men, compared to 39 percent of urban women, agree with the statement that "It is natural and right for women to have inferior status to men" (author's election survey). Interestingly enough, on the question of whether women should participate in politics, 52 percent of urban women approved of women's participation compared to 55 percent of rural men and 64 percent of urban men. Thus the response of urban men is inconsistent. While 64 percent of urban men support women's participation in politics, only about 20 percent of them regard women as equals. Their deep bias against women is obvious.

An urban middle-class woman is considered as vulnerable as a rural woman, as much in need of male protection and shelter. She is rarely her own guardian; almost always a male relative is the guardian. Thus the basic relationship between men and women remains constant in rural and urban areas. An urban woman has greater mobility, but she can achieve and retain that mobility by not challenging the superior social status of men.

2. STATUS OF WOMEN: LEGAL, ECONOMIC, POLITICAL, AND SOCIAL

Much is said and written about the legal status of Muslim women, and indeed, compared to the other South Asian religion, Hinduism, Islamic women are treated more equally by the *sharia* (Islamic personal laws). But there is a great difference between the legal status and the socioeconomic status of women. Their insecure socioeconomic status prevents women from exercising their legal rights.

Legal Status

Three noteworthy legal rights are given to Muslim women by *sharia:* rights regarding marriage, divorce, and inheritance. In Islam marriage is a contract, and the consent of both partners in front of witnesses is required. Because marriage is a contract, divorce is allowed. The marriage contract itself enumerates the conditions under which each partner may inititate divorce proceedings. In the marriage contract provision is made for *Mehr*—a fixed sum of money, part of which is payable to the bride after the wedding ceremony and the rest payable only in case of a divorce. Both the husband and the wife can start divorce proceedings, but it is by far much easier for a husband to divorce his wife. Islamic law allows a man to divorce his wife by simply pronouncing his intention to do so in front of witnesses.[16] A woman is allowed to obtain a divorce by returning the *Mehr*. Such divorces—known as *Khul*—are rarely practiced these days. At the time of divorce, a woman who has minor children can

---

[16] In most Muslim countries civil law interprets *Sharia* law regarding polygamy and divorce in such a way as to restrict the husband's greater facility in initiating divorce. Thus, in Tunisia, civil law prohibits polygamy on the ground that the Quranic precondition for polygamy (i.e. the husband has to treat all the wives equally) is humanly unattainable.

get custody of them, but she can never get their guardianship, which remains with the husband.

Another much publicized legal right of Muslim women is their right to inherit property. After a man's death, his widow inherits one-eighth of his property; and if he dies childless, she inherits one-fourth; daughters inherit one-half of the sons' shares.

But though the law recognizes women's rights in marriage, divorce, and inheritance, in practice women can rarely take full advantage of these rights. As mentioned earlier, a woman's marriage is arranged by her father or other male guardians and she usually consents to such arrangements. Only in rare cases would a woman stand up against the expressed wishes of her guardians.[17]

In cases of divorce, men usually take the initiative. Though the Muslim Family Laws Ordinance, passed in 1961, put a number of restrictions on the male's *sharia* rights regarding polygamy and divorce, in practice prevailing social norms still permit men greater freedom to practice polygamy and initiate divorce.[18] Women initiate divorce only among the poorer sections of population, but here, too, the initiative is taken by the woman's father or other male guardians. Among the poor, *Mehr* is regarded as a bride-price, and the bride's male guardian demands payment of part of the *Mehr* after the wedding ceremony. Often a woman is married several times so that her male guardian can collect more *Mehr*. Among the middle class, the actual payment of *Mehr* is rarely made. Even when a woman is divorced, *Mehr* is renounced because that improves the chances of her remarriage. Men are reluctant to marry divorced women who demand *Mehr* (Ahmed 1966). Few middle-class women initiate divorce, because it involves litigation and is regarded as a disreputable act.

There is a similar gap between a woman's inheritance rights and the actual practice. Widows always demand inheritance, but it is used by their

[17]   Civil registration of marriages, however, does provide an alternative to arranged marriages. In this respect Bangali women are better off then women in some other countries, i.e. Indonesia, where religious courts are the only legally recognized authority regarding marriage and divorce.
[18]   The Muslim Family Laws Ordinance provided regulatory measures and procedures for registration of marriages, polygamy, divorce, maintenance, succession right of children of predeceased father, and child marriage. It empowered the local bodies to deal with these provisions. An evaluation of the workings of the Family Laws Ordinance pointed out that a large number of the marriages in the rural areas were still unregistered, few of the divorces went to the Arbitration Councils, and the councils generally followed the social norms in making decisions regarding polygamy and divorce. The ordinance therefore did not radically change women's status. For details of the evaluation of the ordinance (see Qadir 1968).

sons. If a widow demands inheritance, she is expected to live in her husband's household and not to return to her parents. It is customary for daughters to renounce inheritance in favor of brothers unless the family is either very rich or very poor. Daughters give up inheritance in exchange for *naior* (Ahmad 1966) — the right to visit the father's house once or twice a year after the father's death. Women give up inheritance for a number of reasons. Partly it is a social custom. The majority of women interviewed argued that they gave up inheritance to be on good terms with their brothers. In case of divorce or widowhood, they would need their brothers' assistance, guardian protection, and sometimes they would come back (especially in case of divorce) to live in their natal homestead. So they did not want to strain relations with their brothers by claiming their inheritance, which was their legal due, and thus risk being rejected by their brothers. Additionally, women who give up inheritance in favor of *naior* indicate their preference for mobility. For a woman, *naior* days are the only days of vacation in a year. In her father's house, a woman has greater mobility, *purdah* observance is less strict, and she is relieved of her household chores. Thus, renouncing inheritance for *naior* appears to be a fair exchange, because inheritance is used by the husband but *naior* is a woman's exclusive vacation. In a social system where a woman always needs a guardian, her legal rights are exercised by the guardian on her behalf.

Economic Status

As discussed in Part 1 of the paper, being a wife and a mother is the only goal of a Bangali woman, and few take up a career. Roughly 10 percent of women are in the civilian labor force and only about 1 percent of these adopt a modern occupation. As Table 1 shows, out of 2,553,212 women in the civilian labor force in 1961, only 214,715 were in the nonagricultural labor force; the rest were in the agricultural labor force. Thus the overwhelming majority of working women live in the rural areas. In urban areas, the largest number of women are employed in factories; Table 1 indicates that nearly half of the female nonagricultural labor force were in manufacturing and mechanical occupations. Urban women are employed in such low-paid jobs as factory labor, street cleaning, and construction work, as well as in professional and technical occupations, e.g. teaching, medicine, and nursing. Middle-class women usually enter teaching, nursing, sales work, research and other related professional "women's" occupations. Table 2 shows that very few women enter

Table 1.   Civilian labor force by main occupational groups and sex (12 years and above)

	1951		1961	
	Male	Female	Male	Female
Civilian labor force	11,887,080	999,260	14,317,776	2,553,212
Agricultural labor force	9,899,006	816,461	11,997,999	2,338,497
Non-agricultural labor force	1,988,074	182,799	2,319,777	214,715
Professional, technical, and related occupations	115,713	5,231	180,686	8,195
Managerial, administrative, and and clerical occupations	207,335	666	201,582	944
Transport and communication	115,744	314	145,999	182
Manufacturing and mechanical occupations	410,081	70,137	576,706	118,516
Sales and related occupations	477,452	24,877	504,744	18,513
Agricultural, fishing-trapping, and logging occupations	184,619	10,797	121,862	363
Construction occupations and general laborers	284,665	36,184	240,528	3,806
Service, sports, entertainments	191,456	34,592	230,435	58,013

Source: Adapted from Government of Pakistan (1961:Table 1A, 96–97).

Table 2.   Non-agricultural labor force by occupation and sex, 1961 (ten years and above)

Occupational groups	Both	Male	Female
Non-agricultural labor force	2,570,953	2,350,044	220,909
Professional, technical, and related occupations	189,021	180,800	8,221
Architects, surveyors, and engineers	4,117	4,106	11
Chemist and physical scientists	318	305	13
Physicians, surgeons, dentists, and medical specialists	7,152	6,952	200
Nurses and midwives	3,763	783	2,986
Professional medical workers and medical technicians	29,212	28,286	926
Teachers	100,883	97,342	3,541
Lawyers, judges, and magistrates	4,889	4,879	11
Administrative and managerial, clerical, and related workers	202,730	201,784	946
Proprietors, directors, and managers	30,812	30,627	185
Governmental and public service administrators and officers	2,632	2,612	20
Sales workers	528,308	509,626	18,682
Proprietors and managers and retail traders	15,774	15,707	67

Source: Adapted from Government of Pakistan (1961:Table 2, 98).

traditionally male occupations. In 1961, while there were 3,541 female teachers and 2,986 nurses and midwives, there were only 11 architects and engineers, 13 scientists, 200 physicians, 11 lawyers and judges, and 20 public service administrators. In contrast to women in such South East Asian countries as Burma and Thailand and in East and West Africa, few Bangali women go into business. In 1961, only 185 women, as compared to 30,627 men, were classified as proprietors and managers of industrial and business offices. Only 67 women, versus 15,707 men, were in retail trade, and this number might be even smaller — men often register businesses in their wives' or sisters' or mothers' names to publicly cover the real ownership.

Similar to women's occupational patterns in other countries, the majority of women are employed in low and middle-salaried jobs, with very few women in top administrative or decision-making posts. As the top administrative posts are manned by ex-C.S.P. (Civil Service of Pakistan) and ex-E.P.C.S. (East Pakistan Civil Service) members, organizations where women's participation was restricted, women have little input in decision-making processes. Unlike India, where women compete in the foreign service and administrative service examinations, in Bangladesh women were barred from these jobs during the Pakistani days. There is no woman in the Bangladesh foreign service, or in the higher echelons of the various ministeries and the Planning Commission of the Bangladesh government. Administration and planning in Bangladesh are all-male affairs.

The pyramidal structure of the women's employment pattern is also visible in educational institutions. More women are employed as lecturers than as principals of colleges, chairpersons of departments, or deans of various faculties in the universities. In Dacca University during the 1972–1973 session, of a faculty of 566 there were 86 women. There were 166 male Ph.D.s and only 9 women Ph.D.s; 5 women professors and associate professors, and only two women chairpersons of departments. None of the deans were women.

It is, however, interesting to note that few women feel job discrimination. None of the women interviewed, especially those in middle-class occupations, felt that they were discriminated against on the basis of sex in recruitment, in salary distribution, or in promotion. This is an expected response. In other countries, also, women felt little job discrimination before their consciousness about it was raised. Another reason appears to be that since there are only a few women in various jobs, they are usually not in a competitive position with men and hence do not pose a threat. Additionally, even when a woman takes up a career, she keeps to her place. Except for the time she puts in her job, she remains in the women's world and does not question the socially sanctified superior status of men. A career woman is therefore no threat to a man's ego; rather she is a financial asset, as her income helps balance the family budget. Quite frequently an educated, urban man proudly introduces his wife as "my wife who is an M.A. and a professor," or the like. In a society where education is universally valued,[19] having an educated wife enhances a husband's social status.

In sum, very few Bangali women take up an occupation, especially a modern occupation. But once they are in a job, particularly a middle-class job, they face little discrimination. It is difficult for women to break the barriers of tradition, but after they break them, there is greater acceptance.

Political Status

Bangali women won their basic political right, the right to vote, without a fight. It was granted to them by the British colonial government at the same time as it was granted to Bangali men. In all elections from 1937 on, women constituted nearly half of the country's electorate, but their only political role consisted of casting their ballots. Bangali women's participation in the movement for Pakistan was marginal. In the hierarchy of the Muslim League there was no woman. There was a separate women's wing of the party, and the major function of women in the Muslim League was to recruit the support of Muslim women for electoral purposes. No attempt was made to organize the women on feminist issues or even to get a pledge of the male leadership on such issues.

In a *purdah* society, the ethos of separate worlds for men and women permeates even politics. Thus separate seats are reserved for women in the parliament and in the political parties women work only in the women's wings. The Bangladesh Constitution provides for 15 reserved seats for women in the Parliament. These women are to be elected, not by the female electorate of the country, but by the three hundred male members of parliament. The constitution does not prohibit women from campaigning for general seats. Indeed, two women contested but failed to win general seats in the March, 1973, election. The reserved seats deter political parties from nominating women for the general

---

[19]   In Alex Inkeles' survey of peasants, factory workers, and students, which was conducted in the 1960's, an overwhelming majority of women favored education as good and desirable.

seats, as the prominent party women can easily be accommodated in the reserved seats. Similarly, because of the existence of separate women's wings in the parties, the top post a woman can aspire to in any party hierarchy is that of women's secretary. In only one of the existing political parties does a woman hold the post of organizing secretary (Mrs. Motia Chowdhury of National Awami Party, Muzaffer group). There were no women in the first two cabinets, and the two women ministers of state predictably hold the traditionally female portfolios of education and social welfare.

Women are still far from being politically organized. They played a marginal role in the various political movements of the country in the last two decades. Few women took active part in the national liberation movement. While thousands of young men were recruited in the Mukti Bahini (freedom fighters), only a handful of women took arms training, and a few hundred women worked as nurses and teachers in the freedom fighters' hospitals and refugee camps. Only as the victims of the liberation war did the Bangali women receive world-wide publicity. Soon after Liberation, the government of Bangladesh disclosed that thousands of Bangali women who had been raped by the Pakistani soldiers were then made social outcasts. The failure of the various women's organizations to mobilize public support or, for that matter, women's support for the raped women indicates the weak politicization of Bangali women.

Social Status

A woman's social status is separate from, and inferior to, a man's. The religious community takes little notice of the existence of women. Women do not participate in any congregational prayers — e.g. the Friday prayer, the *I'd* prayer (one of the Muslim holidays), or the funeral prayer. Women are deeply religious, but they practice the various forms of prayer individually and in private. Although the idea of *umma* [community] is important to Muslims, women are excluded from any community celebrations. In some of the Muslim countries of the Middle East, women do participate in separate women's congregational prayers, but Bangali Muslim women do not. *Purdah*, the social imperative of sexual segregation, isolates women and confines them to their individual homes.

Papanek (1971) argues persuasively that because *purdah* society regards women as highly vulnerable, there is a need to "shelter" them and to control their impulses. "Impulse control is achieved with the help of restraining social institutions, in ways which are closer to 'shame' mechanisms of social control than those associated with 'guilt'" (1971: 519). The non-acceptance of raped women in Bangladesh is a good illustration of the operation of the "shame" mechanism. If a woman is raped and it can be kept a secret from her social circle, then she is acceptable. It is not raping *per se*, but the *samaj's* knowledge about it that brings disrepute to the family. When a woman is violated, the family is more concerned about the loss of face than about her physical and mental health. One organization, which worked with the war-affected women in Bangladesh (the National Board of Bangladesh Women's Rehabilitation program), informed the author that it maintained strict secrecy about the cases of violated women because their chances of social acceptance depended on it. Where parents were alive, a violated daughter was always accepted back by the parents. Only in rare cases were women who had been in Pakistani army camps taken back by their husbands. These women were not acceptable because the fact of their violation was known by the *samaj*. But many women whose violations were not publicized were accepted back by their husbands after they underwent secret abortions.[20] The National Board of Bangladesh Women's Rehabilitation in Dacca received 22,500 applications from raped women. Of them 19,500 were illiterate and 3,000 were literate; 15,030 were rural and the rest were urban. The majority of cases were not reported because of the family's desire to maintain secrecy.

This anxiety over secrecy is illustrated by the reluctance of Bangali women to talk about the problem of the women who were violated during the war. The majority of women interviewed stated that, while they were agitated by the problem, they rarely discussed it. The father of the nation reflected the same anxiety when he coined the term "war heroines" for women raped by Pakistani soldiers. The term camouflages the state of these women and is less disreputable and shocking than the term "violated" women. The fate of these war-affected women, together with the failure of the non-affected women to mobilize support for the acceptance of these women, reflects the totally vulnerable social status of women.

---

[20]   Two separate women's organizations working with violated women gave the author two different stories on the question of violated women's acceptability. The National Board stated that in 90 percent of cases women were accepted back by their families. Only women who had no families left stayed back in the institute. Another organization mentioned that only where parents were alive could women go back home. Not a single husband accepted back his wife even if she were the mother of five or six children.

3. WOMEN'S MOVEMENTS AND WOMEN'S ORGANIZATIONS IN BANGLADESH

The movement for the emancipation of Muslim women in Bengal started in the 1920's. The emancipation of women was closely associated with the modernist movement among the Muslims, and it received sympathy and support from the modernist men. In the twenties and thirties, the movement was primarily concerned with women's literacy, and did not raise questions about employment opportunities of the equal status of women. These questions came up only at the later phase of the movement.

Roughly, the movement for women's emancipation in Bengal can be divided into three periods. The first phase (1910–1947) saw the questioning of rigid *purdah* observance and the demand for women's literacy and school enrollment. The 1920's and 1930's were the periods of *Khilafat* movement and the development of Muslim nationalism in India. The movement for the emancipation of Turkish women and other Middle Eastern women at this time inspired Muslim modernists in Bengal to agitate for women's emancipation at home.

The leadership in the first phase belonged to women from traditional landlord families, many of whom were Calcutta-based and nonvernacular but who later achieved fluency in the vernacular. The movement for women's emancipation was started by a woman from a traditional, landlord family who was married to a "modernist" civil servant. Rokeya Sakhawat Hussain (1880–1932) was not only the pioneer of the women's emancipation movement, she was a true feminist. Indeed, she is the only femenist in the leadership of the women's movement. None of the women who came after her could be called feminists. Rokeya Sakhawat Hussain keenly felt the oppression of the rigid *purdah* system. In her father's and husband's houses she lived in *purdah*, and she had to fight against heavy odds to educate herself. Rokeya felt that the only way a woman could be emancipated was through education, which would enable her to achieve economic independence and to renounce strict *purdah*.

Rokeya was both a publicist and an activist. She wrote a number of short stories, articles, and a novel, all of which depict the stultifying life of women in a *purdah* society. In all her writings, she made scathing attacks on the unequal relationship between men and women and propagated the cause of women's emancipation. In *Sultana's dream* (1905) Rokeya portrays a social system where men are kept in seclusion and women handle all the traditionally male jobs.

In 1911, Rokeya established the first Muslim girls' school in Calcutta, which started with eight students. For twenty years she worked in the school despite bitter criticisms from orthodox Muslims. At the time of her death in 1932, the school had 123 students. In 1916, Rokeya also established a women's organization, Anjuman-e-Khawatein-Islam, which was essentially meant to draw out the Muslim women from traditional families.

After Rokeya's death in 1932, there was not a single woman who made the cause of women's emancipation her lifelong interest. In the thirties and forties, there was a small group of Muslim literary women who wrote occasional pieces on women, but these women served more as models for women's emancipation than as active participants in a movement.

The 1947 partition of India and Bengal marked a radical change in women's status and role. The second phase of the women's movement (1947–1970) saw the growth of women's organizations in urban areas. Muslim women took the place of Hindu women in all the women's organizations. In the second phase, though women's organizational activities increased, there was no recognizable movement for the emancipation of women. During this period a large number of women were emancipated, but their emancipation was the result of the general process of modernization and was not due to any feminist movement. There was less of a women's movement in the second phase than there had been in the first.

The most important women's organization that developed during this phase was the All Pakistan Women's Association (APWA). The APWA in Bangladesh was a branch of the central APWA, which had local branches in all the districts and subdivisions. The APWA had very close ties with the government and the power structure of the country. The leaders were the wives of powerful political and administrative figures. In the districts and subdivisions, the wives of district and subdivisional officers were invariably the presidents of the APWA. In Dacca the APWA presidency shifted between the wife of the chief minister and the wife of the governor, depending on the relative power of their husbands in the political system. As the APWA leadership changed with the administration, the organization failed to develop leadership among women. The APWA was very much like a social club of elite women which arranged social and cultural get-togethers. In Dacca APWA women did some voluntary work; they ran schools and managed sewing and handicraft centers. But the APWA's major activities were still confined to the concept of neighborhood women's clubs. The APWA's major role was to act as a meeting place for middle-class Muslim women who had been in strict *purdah* and were not even used to meeting other women in an organization.

Table 3. Enrollment of male and female students in primary and secondary school and university in Bangladesh 1947–1966

Academic year	Primary school		Secondary school		University	
	Male	Female	Male	Female	Male	Female
1947–1948	1,812,330	209,372	418,914	44,106	1,593	27
1948–1949	1,900,916	630,408	504,830	43,786	1,941	44
1949–1950	1,766,040	566,629	470,549	47,253	2,237	67
1950–1951	1,835,244	457,516	472,241	42,271	2,016	67
1951–1952	1,868,431	606,486	434,843	45,014	2,306	85
1952–1953	1,979,744	675,021	412,893	40,548	2,209	95
1953–1954	1,983,314	669,971	398,631	43,818	2,328	103
1954–1955	1,938,329	666,040	410,558	46,739	2,716	142
1955–1956	1,937,730	708,526	425,299	47,821	3,130	219
1956–1957	1,980,263	731,507	443,391	54,208	2,934	191
1957–1958	2,039,041	755,874	431,799	59,246	3,198	252
1958–1959	2,170,915	814,343	435,435	59,600	3,680	282
1959–1960	2,139,111	841,256	465,202	65,283	3,465	301
1960–1961	2,405,194	925,388	466,223	66,679	3,622	348
1961–1962	2,497,333	925,899	503,617	71,250	5,432	385
1962–1963	2,663,472	973,025	563,599	95,746	6,628	512
1963–1964	2,709,397	1,142,925	640,799	104,818	6,885	779
1964–1965	2,830,469	1,213,710	719,298	129,214	8,831	888
1965–1966	2,951,541	1,284,495	794,591	154,895	7,830	1000

Source: Adapted from Government of Pakistan (1947–1967:170–173, 186).

Table 4. Number of women doctors and registered nurses in Bangladesh, 1964–1969

Number of registered medical practitioners in Bangladesh

Year	Female			
	F.R.C.S.	M.B.B.S.	L.M.F.	Total practitioners
1964	Nil	42	170	212
1965	Nil	57	182	239
1966	Nil	67	184	251
1967	Nil	203	311	514
1968	Nil	246	319	565
1969	Nil	301	319	620

Number of registered nurses in Bangladesh

Year	Senior nurses	Junior nurses	Senior midwife	Junior midwife	Lady health visitors
1964	36	15	21	24	22
1965	38	4	60	22	15
1966	25	5	26	16	10
1967	25	1	1	25	11
1968	38	—	31	8	7
1969	208	59	38	9	18

Source: Bangladesh Bureau of Statistics (1970–1971:(7), Tables 14.3 and 14.4, 267–268).

Table 5. Number of male and female primary and secondary school teachers in Bangladesh, 1947–1966

Academic year	Primary		Secondary	
	Male	Female	Male	Female
1947–1948	72,703	2,921	23,418	944
1948–1949	67,932	2,471	23,645	952
1949–1950	64,999	1,822	23,167	880
1950–1951	61,942	2,873	22,452	1,238
1951–1952	60,056	1,898	22,213	887
1952–1953	65,175	1,913	21,017	904
1953–1954	69,988	1,900	20,703	935
1954–1955	69,716	1,761	21,310	979
1955–1956	70,111	1,863	21,848	920
1956–1957	69,566	1,672	22,155	1,005
1957–1958	72,882	1,843	21,820	1,089
1958–1959	75,432	1,691	21,650	1,146
1959–1960	76,843	1,619	22,303	1,268
1960–1961	78,803	1,721	23,097	1,357
1961–1962	80,873	1,604	23,808	1,510
1962–1963	84,767	1,846	25,844	1,666
1963–1964	90,487	1,960	30,782	1,797
1964–1965	92,511	2,019	31,578	2,092
1965–1966	94,390	2,244	33,126	2,529

Source: Adapted from Government of Pakistan (1947–1967:174–175).

The decades of the 1950's and 1960's saw a rapid increase in women's literacy and school enrollment. As Table 3 shows, the rate of increase in female enrollment in schools and universities was much greater than the rate of increase for male students. These rates are of course deceptive, because the base for women was so low at first. The increase in the number of career women was also substantial. As a result, a number of women's organizations developed, especially in the capital, Dacca. In addition to the APWA, nine other women's organizations were established in Dacca at this time. Many were neighborhood women's clubs, e.g. Gandaria Mahila Samity (formed in 1950), Wari Mahila Samity (formed in 1954), and Purana Paltan Ladies Club. All these associations were formed by the "enlightened" ladies (to quote one woman long associated with women's organizations) of these localities, who wanted to improve the socioeconomic condition of lower-middle-class and poor women. Their usual activities included running a neighborhood primary school and sewing or handicraft center. It is interesting to note that these associations were formed in the established and affluent neighborhoods of Dacca in the fifties, e.g. Gandaria, Wari, and Purana Paltan. The motivating force behind these associations was the feeling among the "enlightened" women that they should work FOR and not WITH their less enlightened sisters in the neighborhood. Apart from these three neighborhood associations, which were run by vernacular-speaking Bangali women, there were two organizations for non-Bangali and non-vernacular speaking Bangali women, the Anjuman Falah Muslim Khawateen and Baitul Athfab-e-Sabiyya (orphanage for Muslim girls).

In the 1960's the more westernized women formed a number of women's organizations to achieve specific goals. The Business and Career Women's Club was formed in 1960 to look after the interests of career women, i.e. to establish hostels for working women, childcare centers for working mothers, and programs to encourage and train women from lower-class groups to take up an occupation, etc. The leaders of this organization were mostly non-Bangali women. Bangali women associated with the Career Women's Club were different from the women in the *mahila samity* who were mostly housewives and rarely career women.

In 1960 the House Wives Association was formed for the "meeting of minds and sharing of experiences" by housewives. Here, too, the women were more westernized than were the *samity* women. Two other women's organizations of the 1960's were the Women's Voluntary Association (WVA) and the Zonta club. Foreign women resident in Bangladesh took the initiative in establishing the WVA. Wives of the diplomatic community played an active but less publicized role. WVA's major purpose is social work — to raise funds for specific projects. Unlike the APWA, Samity, or Career Women's club, WVA did not have regular social and cultural get-togethers. Instead duties were assigned to individual members and the group met specifically to discuss projects. The Zonta club is the Dacca branch of an international club, very similar to the Lions and the Rotary clubs. Its major purpose is to motivate women from affluent families to donate voluntary service or money for the poorer section of society.

The modes of operation and the leadership patterns of these various women's organizations differed from each other. Roughly speaking, the leaders of the neighborhood *samities* were Bangali middle-class women, while the APWA and the organizations of the 1960's — the Career Women's club, WVA, and Zonta — were dominated by non-Bangali and upper middle-class women. In many ways the varied women's leadership of the two decades reflected the sociopolitical reality of the country, which saw a transfer of power from Bangali lawyer-type politicians to non-Bangali bureaucrats. The role of the Bangali women in the organizations of the 1960's was that of intermediaries, the same role the Bangali political-administrative leadership was playing in the country. The organizations of the 1950's and the 1960's did not differ fundamentally. Groups were especially involved with girls' schools, women's sewing and handicraft centers, and women's career-trainings programs. While the *samity* women raised funds by organizing cultural evenings at the Begum Club, the APWA, WVA, Zonta women raised funds by organizing *meena bazaars* at the Dacca Club or Grand balls at the *Hotel Inter Continental* and the *Purbani*.

The third phase of the women's movement, in the post-liberation period in Bangladesh, is marked by a growing awareness among the women about women's problems, though no concrete program or organizational leadership has yet come forward. The liberation movement, the fate of the violated and other war-affected women, and the vulnerable position of women in the post-liberation period of lawlessness have led women to raise questions (not publicly) about the stability of the "shelter" provided by men. The women of Bangladesh have found themselves in a state of semi-permanent seige by male aggression — the incidence of abduction and raping of women has increased tremendously since liberation, as have other acts of lawlessness such as robbery and murder, which has severely restricted women's mobility. All this has made feminists of many women of the younger generation, but the women's leadership is lagging far behind. The post-liberation period saw a scramble by Bangali women to move into the positions of organizational leadership left vacant by the departure of non-Bangali women. The APWA was renamed Bangladesh Mahila Samity, and the Awami League women moved into its leadership positions; in the Business and Career Women's club and the WVA, Bangali women are filling the slots left empty by non-Bangali women.

Since 1970, many women have become very active in Mahila Parishad. Its leadership is in the hands of women with leftist (especially pro-Moscow) leanings, and it has branches in various districts outside Dacca. Mahila Parishad leadership partly resembles the old *samity* leadership of middle-class and vernacular Muslim women. In part, it consists of ex-student leaders who were active in student politics or party politics. Of all the women's organizations, Parishad is the most political; it concerns itself with women's problems and it has a systematic program to recruit the support of the larger masses of women.

Still, there is no women's movement in Bangladesh at present. There are no feminist leaders or feminist journals, or feminist writings. The absence of a movement or leadership has not prevented a growing number of Bangali women from seeking their emancipation. However the process is understandably slow since the rate of social change and modernization is slow. Only an active women's movement with a feminist leadership can expedite the emancipation of Bangali women.

To conclude, Bangali women, both rural and urban, traditional and modern, live in a social system that sanctifies an unequal and inferior status for women. *Sharia* laws grant Muslim women a number of limited rights, but prevailing social norms prevent them from taking full advantage of even these limited rights. So far, the women's emancipation movement has concerned itself with such basic issues as literacy and employment for women. The unequal relationship between men and women is not yet questioned. There has been no serious movement to modify the legal system to give women equal rights of inheritance, guardianship, or marriage and divorce. The small number of women who are educated and seek careers can easily be accommodated by the social system, especially because these women do not challenge the basic rules of the system. The elite women can participate and hence there is no dissatisfied elite group to lead a women's movement. In the absence of a movement, consciousness about the oppression of women is low. In Bangladesh the movement for women's emancipation is part of the process of social change and not a revolutionary movement.

REFERENCES

AHMAD, TAHERUNNESSA
  1966 *Palli anganader jemon dekhecki* [Rural women as I saw them]. Comilla: PARD.
BANGLADESH BUREAU OF STATISTICS
  1970–1971 *Statistical digest of Bangladesh.*
EAST PAKISTAN BUREAU OF STATISTICS
  1961 *The master survey of agriculture in East Pakistan.* Sixth Round, Table 2.4 (A), page 18.
GOVERNMENT OF PAKISTAN
  1947–1967 *Twenty years of Pakistan in statistics.* Ministry of Economic Affairs, Central Statistical Office.
  1961 *Census of Pakistan*, volume four. Ministry of Home and Kashmir Affairs (Home Affairs Division).
HUSSAIN, ROKEYA SAKHAWAT
  1905 *Sultana's dream.*
PAPANEK, HANNA
  1971 Purdah in Pakistan: seclusion and modern occupations for women. *Journal of Marriage and the Family.* (August):517–530.
  1973 Men, women and work: reflections on the two-person career. *The American Journal of Sociology* 78 (4):852–872.

QADIR, S. A.
  1968   *Modernization of an agrarian society.* Rural sociology research
         Report 1. Mymensingh: Agricultural University.
STOECKEL, JOHN, MOQBUL A. CHOWDHURY
  1973   Fertility, infant mortality, and family planning in rural Bangladesh.
         Dacca: Oxford.
ZEIDENSTEIN, SONDRA, LAURA ZEIDENSTEIN
  1973   "Observations on the status of women in Bangladesh." Unpublished
         paper. Dacca.

The Role of Women in the Development of Culture in Nigeria

KAMENE OKONJO

Over the last twenty years, researchers have paid more and more attention to the role that women can play in social change and in the transition of a society from a rural agricultural state to a modern industrial one. Associated with such change — which, in a fluid and dynamic society like that of Nigeria, leads to a transformation of the social and economic systems — is culturally a change in which women, in their roles as wives and mothers, play a very important part as innovators and as transmitters of culture. Culture here is to be understood as including not only social institutions and their derivative forms of learned behavior (behavior that is not instinctive, innate, or biologically determined) but also those manifestations of human creativity whereby new and distinctively individual forms are produced within the range of traditional patterns (Herskovits and Bascom 1959: 1, 6).

It is therefore pertinent to examine the traditional roles of women in the development of culture in Nigerian society and the degree to which women in modern Nigerian society transform these roles. This examination is of great importance, as the conventional wisdom in Western liberal circles maintains that women in traditional and modern African societies comprise a deprived group, incapable of giving focus and direction to cultural development, of low status, economically dependent on men, with few legal rights and no political responsibilities. This widely held viewpoint is, of course, a projection on African women of the experience of nineteenth century Western women, a projection that ignores the fundamental differences between the various cultures and the roles that women have played in them.

It should not be surprising, therefore, to find that in Nigeria, as in many other African countries south of the Sahara, women have played and still play a very important role in the cultural process. In fact, as mothers in the nuclear or extended family, their role is central, for they help to conserve those vital elements that make Nigerian culture distinctive. Like women the world over, they are responsible for transmitting the indigenous language to their children. They are also responsible, in great part, for handing down the oral literature and history, especially to children, through the vehicle of moonlight stories. In many parts of Nigeria, after the evening meal women tell stories of heroes and villains, of might and prowess, to their own children and to children from neighboring compounds. These stories feature the traditional norms of society, and through them children unconsciously assimilate the traditions of the societies to which they belong and learn quite early in life what sanctions await them if they do not conform to these norms.

As transmitters of the culture, women also ensure that there is no radical break with the past and that the process of change is gradual. It might be thought, for example, that modern Nigerian women, with Western-type education, would repudiate the bonds that link the nuclear family with its kin. However, these women realize that Western notions of social relations cannot be applied so readily to Nigerian society and that the nuclear family is not in a position to repudiate the obligations of family and kinship (cf. Wilson 1961:111). The Nigerian woman has safeguarded the ties between the nuclear family and its kith and kin by insisting that the husband observe family and kinship obligations (e.g. contributing cash for ritual and ceremonial occasions, education, clothing, and other expenses), even if this stretches to their limits the budget and harmony of the nuclear family.

The attitude of women, no matter how highly educated and modern, toward marriage customs also illuminates the role of Nigerian women in the process of change. For marriages to be accepted as legal in most Nigerian societies, a marriage payment, however small, must be made, and bridal gifts must be exchanged. As field observations[1] have shown, it is usually the women of the elite, not the men, who insist on these payments and gifts in order to ensure that their daughters are PROPERLY married. Recently, a highly educated Western Ibo woman told me that the most important thing that had happened to her in the previous year

---

[1] Observations were made in the course of research on the role of women in social change among the Ibos of Southeastern Nigeria who were living west of the Niger River. The field work lasted from June, 1971, to November, 1972, with 300 interviews of women from the Midwestern Ibo home area as well as women who had migrated to the towns of Benin, Ibadan, and Lagos.

was her husband's decision, after eight years of marriage, to buy her a sewing machine. When I asked her why she herself had not bought the machine if she needed it, as she was a well-paid business executive, her answer was prompt and unexpected: "Custom requires that my husband should, as part of his gift to me during marriage, buy me a sewing machine." Here is a striking example of the role that women play in preserving the distinctiveness of Nigerian culture.

In addition to functioning as the main transmitter of the culture, the Nigerian woman has shown herself to be an innovator in spheres that are ordinarily held to be unrewarding for cultural innovation. These include food preparation, hairdressing, pottery manufacture, cloth weaving, and dressmaking, which in Nigeria are dominated by women. To understand the current cultural significance of these activities it must be remembered that Nigeria, like most other sub-Saharan African countries, has only recently made the transition from colonial to independent status.[2] Under colonialism, one expression of cultural domination by the British metropole was the adoption by the emerging Nigerian elite of Western norms in food, dress, and toiletry. Western foods like potatoes and baked beans were preferred to nutritionally similar but indigenous foods like yams and *ewa*, because the Western foods displayed the degree of Western acculturation of the elite, with the power and prestige that this conferred.

But with the emergence from the colonial situation and the necessity of creating and stressing a national image and personality, the elite were forced to rediscover their roots in the traditions, customs, and practices of their own people. Three spheres in which it was relatively easy to "boycott the boycottables,"[3] to use a slogan current in Nigeria in the early fifties, were those of food preparation, toiletry, and dress. Thanks to the quick response and inventiveness of the womenfolk, Nigerian dishes soon took their proper place at state parties and other functions, albeit with a considerable improvement in their preparation and variety. To the standard dishes of village fare were added new dishes based on traditional foods.

l Plantain crispies took the place of potato crispies; salad was made from ocally grown fruits and vegetables; yam balls (a fried mixture of mashed yam and meat) and *moi moi* (a pudding of bean flour with eggs, beef, pepper, and onions) appeared on the tables of the elite. The distinctively

[2] Nigeria became independent on 1 October, 1960.
[3] The slogan "Boycott the boycottables" was introduced into Nigeria by Mazi Mbonu Ojike, who returned to Nigeria in the early fifties after studying in the United States; he became minister of finance in the East Regional government of Nigeria when Nigeria became a federation in 1954.

Nigerian cuisine that emerged could take its place beside the cuisine of any other nation.

A similar development can also be traced in the evolution of hairdressing among the elite in Nigeria. In the 1930's Sylvia Leith-Ross noted the intricate hairstyles of the Owerri Ibo women, yet from 1940 to 1960 hair straightening by pomades or hot iron combs was the fashion among the women of the elite (Leith-Ross 1965:95). Since then, however, the situation has turned full circle and today, when a primary goal of most developing countries is an accelerated economic growth rate, with the concomitant rapid assimilation of Western technology, traditional hair styles have come back into their own, against the competition of Western styles and wigs. Many women of the elite prefer traditional hairstyles for their durability and beauty. In offices, markets, recreation clubs, and meetings, in streets and homes, in rural and urban areas, women are wearing traditional hair styles, and women hairdressers are hard at work, improving former hairstyles and inventing new ones. Moreover, an important aspect of the yearly Festival of the Arts competition is hairdressing, and traditional hair fashions were decreed as standard for the Second All-Africa Games, which were held recently in Lagos.[4]

Traditionally, pottery manufacture is exclusively a woman's domain. Throughout Nigeria women make pots and other household utensils of various sizes, shapes, and qualities, to suit every taste and purse. Despite the severe competition of imported china and enamel ware, these potters still remain very active. In the rural areas particularly, and to some extent in the semiurban towns, women prepare meals, expecially sauces, in traditional clay pots. Clay pots are also preferred for the storage of water because they keep the water cool in the absence of refrigerators. In some areas, such as Abuja, in Northern Nigeria, the standard of workmanship is so high that the pottery has attracted national and international attention. The governments of the federation have had to take an interest in and give support to such work, as these wares have given Nigeria a craft which is distinctive and of very high aesthetic quality.

Traditional weaving and dyeing, dominated by women, have also lately come into their own, despite the increased and severe competition of foreign machine-made textiles which are dumped on the Nigerian market and which imitate traditional designs and colors. These foreign textiles, however, have only strengthened the traditional homemade

---

[4]   At the Second All-Africa Games held in Lagos, Nigeria, in January, 1973, women ushers were required to wear distinctive traditional Yoruba hairstyles, thus giving an official stamp of national approval to traditional hairstyles. This step has given greater popularity to traditional hairstyles in Nigeria.

textile industry. The demand for the *Akwete* [cloth woven by the Akwete women of East Central Nigeria] by both foreigners and Nigerians has been remarkable and has naturally resulted in a price increase. Almost the same can be said of the *asho oke* [cloth woven by Yoruba men] which is also much sought after and quite expensive. The increased popularity of these traditional cloths can be traced in part to the patronage given them by prominent Nigerian women. But by far the greater part of this popularity is attributable to the imagination and taste that women dress designers like Shade Thomas, trained in Western Europe and North America, have put into their creations, which have won them and these cloths an international reputation.

An equally important role is played by Nigerian women in the dyeing industry. Barth, visiting Kano in the 1830's, remarked that dyeing was by far the most important industry there (Barth 1965:512). The Yoruba woman has brought this art to near perfection, introducing varied patterns in order to achieve an attractive, distinctive effect. Visitors to Nigeria now readily admit that whether the *akwete* is used as an evening or cocktail dress, the *asho oke* as a wedding outfit with the *onilegogoro* head tie to attract attention, or the *adire* [dyed cloth] as a shirt or dress, they all have a charm that is uniquely Nigerian.

Less well known is the important role that women play in the economic activities of Nigeria. In agriculture, which is the main economic activity, farm work in many Nigerian societies is shared by men and women. Some crops, like yams, are produced by men, while others, like cocoyams and cassava, are produced by women. Both men and women provide food for the family, and many an erring husband in the rural areas finds himself being starved into submission when his offended wife refuses to provide her portion of the family meal.

Furthermore, as Green (1964:170–171) has pointed out, the part that women play in Nigeria's economic life has meant that, where they do not occupy public positions, they have much quiet power, because they are often the chief breadwinners, supplying the lion's share of the family food, buying such extras as salt and fish with their own money, and providing their husbands with funds to finance their multifarious activities. This gives women, both individually and collectively, a lever by which they can bring pressure to bear on their men. Thus the notion that women are economically dependent on men, when viewed in the actual operation of Nigerian society, is easily recognized as a myth. The Nigerian woman, whether as mother, tiller of the soil, or trader, has her own quiet dignity and commands respect not only from her husband but also from her family and her community.

Nowhere is this real power better exemplified than in the markets, which are dominated by women whose archetype is the proverbial "market mammy." In the lives of Nigerian women, markets have a central function and have always been important. As Hodder (1961:153–154) points out:

Women rather than men are concerned in rural marketing activities. Rarely will a rural periodic day market contain more than a handful of men... To Yoruba women, moreover, marketing, petty-trading or at least attending a market, forms part of their way of life, and their reward lies as much in the social life offered by the markets as in their cash profits.

In addition to their economic functions, these markets (most of which are periodic day or night markets) act as meeting places and as channels of communication for friends and relatives, where the latest news and gossip can be discussed. The market is also a place for displaying wealth. In many Ibo towns and villages, women who have taken titles come to their local markets accompanied by friends and relatives, to display their *erulu* [coral beads] and *odu* [elephant tusk armbands], local emblems of wealth. Furthermore in some parts of Benin and Ishan divisions, a mother brings her newborn baby to the local market after her obligatory rest period of a few weeks following delivery. Accompanied by friends and relatives, the mother dances around the market, receiving congratulations and presents from the other women.

Markets are also advertising grounds for new dances. Dances — especially women's dances like the age group dances in Eastern Nigeria — are not sanctioned for display to the public until they have been taken through the market and approved by the market women. Even dance competitions, which have recently been encouraged by women's groups to strengthen and develop this aspect of Nigerian culture, take place in these rural towns on market days. In the urban areas, too, women's societies organize and encourage dance festivals and competitions. Girls in secondary schools are encouraged to enter their traditional dances in arts festivals and competitions, which not only consolidate what is traditional and uniquely Nigerian, but also refine and improve dance styles and techniques.

Paradoxically, in the realm of economic attitudes, where men have had the greatest degree of direct acculturative experience, it is the women who have changed most. Among the Afikpo Ibo, for example, although wealth has long been an index of personal importance and distinction for both men and women, the economic aspirations of women have changed in recent years (Ottenberg 1959).

Afikpo men, having achieved a high consumption level — with cars, bicycles, radios, European furniture, and certain European foods and smoking habits — still regard taking titles as the most valid form of investment. While many women believe taking titles represents the best disposition of wealth, a number of them, both literate and illiterate, give first consideration to a standard of living that includes clothing, adequate nutrition, and the education of their children. Thus the number of women taking titles has declined, even when business conditions are good. Instead of living on a near-starvation diet in order to save money for a title, many women now consider it bad "not to eat in one's house" in order to take unnecessary titles. In fact, among women a higher standard of living and better education for children are replacing titles as symbols of status, and sometimes profit, although the principle underlying both the old and the new forms of distinction, achievement, and prestige, have remained the same (Ottenberg 1959:216–217).

However, it is not only in the economic affairs of the nation that women play an important role. They are also a force to be reckoned with in politics. Those who think that Nigerian women are passive, lethargic, and uninterested in the political life of their communities need only be reminded of the role they played in the Women's Riot of 1929–1930.[5]

The British colonial government in Nigeria introduced taxation of men in 1926. In 1929 women in the Owerri and Calabar areas learned that the government was preparing to tax women. The women were, of course, enraged by this, as it ran counter to all culture and tradition. "How can they tax the seed that bears fruit?" they asked. "We cannot buy food or clothes, how shall we get money to pay tax?" (Aba Commission, 11–12). Word spread, especially during market days, when the women had the opportunity to exchange views, and soon the women rose like an army in massive protest against this injustice, looting European trading stores and banks, breaking into prisons to release prisoners, and beating chiefs and court messengers. The British district officers, fearing for their lives and hoping to reestablish law and order, sent for the police and troops. To their eternal disgrace and shame, they actually opened fire and killed or wounded over thirty of these angry but defenseless women (Leith-Ross 1965:23–30). Since then, governments in Nigeria have been extremely chary of taxing women, and it is only within the last twen-

---

[5] For an official account of the Women's Riot of 1929–1930, as reported by the Britsh colonial government of Nigeria, see the Aba Commission Report. For a comprehensive historical study of the Riot and its political impact, see Afigbo (1972: 207–248).

ty years that working women have had to pay tax. As recently as the early 1940's Abeokuta women in Western Nigeria revolted under the leadership of Mrs. Fumilayo Ransome-Kuti, a well-known member of the Nigerian Woman's Union. This uprising protesting the taxation of women led to the temporary self-exile of the *Alake* of Abeokuta, Oba Ademola II, by the Abeokuta Native Authority, which was headed by the *Alake* [king] of Egbaland (Sklar 1963:25, note 52). Thus Nigerian women can and do exercise great political influence.

But in many traditional Nigerian societies women also exercise considerable power and authority, participating fully in decision making at most levels. Among the Ibos of Midwestern Nigeria, for example, the villages and rural towns are ruled jointly by the *obi* [the male king] and the *omu* [the female counterpart of the king]. The *omu* is not the wife of the *obi* and is in no way related to him. The rules for succeeding to the positions of *obi* and *omu* are different. In the case of the *obi*, succession to the throne is hereditary and lies with the eldest male child. A regent is appointed if the child is not yet of age. In the case of the *omu*, succession is not hereditary and the *omu*'s eldest daughter has no claim to her throne. The *omu* is appointed from certain lineages; in some of these lineages she is selected by the *umuaka* [all adult daughters of the lineage]. The *omu* is thus appointed by her kith and kin and she is always a woman past child-bearing age.[6]

The *omu* rules in conjunction with the *obi*. A clear division of functions exists between them, and neither is inferior to the other. The *omu* rules the women just as the *obi* rules the men, and the *omu* has the onerous duty of seeing that the women abide by tradition. With the help of her advisers, she judges cases, metes out punishments in cases of adultery, stealing, or other infractions of local law and custom, and gives advice in the spirit of the age-old traditions. She also presides over and encourages title-taking among the women. Women are thus responsible for maintaining law and order among their own sex, and they participate in making decisions that affect the life of the whole community.

In the local government reforms that swept over Nigeria from 1950 to 1960, very little cognizance was taken of this institution and of the traditional role that women play in government.[7] This is perhaps not too

[6]   Observations were made among the Ibos of Midwestern Nigeria from June 1971 to November 1972 (cf. Thomas 1969:7, 40, 41, 77, 88, 138, 137).
[7]   The years from 1950 to 1960 saw the transfer of political power from the British colonial government to the Nigerians, with independence being declared on October 1960. Accompanying this transfer of power was a series of reforms of the local govern-

surprising, because the designers of the proposals seem to have based their recommendations not on the principle of modernizing the traditional political systems, but rather on that of copying the British local government system, paying deference here and there to local tradition. The result has been that even these recent political adaptations of governmental forms do not exhibit the congruence between political structure and political culture that is expected of a properly functioning political system.[8]

We can thus conclude, with Bohannan, that

African women, by and large, have a high social position: legal rights, religious and political responsibility, economic independence. ... Women in Africa are not, in short, a deprived group as they were in the nineteenth century Western world. (Bohannan and Curtin 1971:107–108).

They are, in fact, a driving force in the search for cultural regeneration and a national identity. In Nigeria women have succeeded in their own way in creating forms and fashions that are uniquely Nigerian and that grow organically from the traditional culture. They have thus helped to lessen the psychological frustration engendered by the colonial and neocolonial experience. They have built up poles of creativity and aesthetic invention which are essentially Nigerian and have thus given purpose and direction in the search for a new Nigerian cultural identity in the postcolonial era.

REFERENCES

ABA COMMISSION
  n.d.   *Report of the Commission of Enquiry Appointed to Inquire into the Disturbances in the Calabar and Owerri Provinces.*
AFIGBO, A. E.
  1972   *The warrant chiefs: indirect rule in South-Eastern Nigeria 1891–1929.* London: Longmans.
AMUCHEAZI, FLOCHUKWU
  1973   Local government and traditional legitimacy: divisional administration in the East Central State. *Quarterly Journal of Administration* 7 (4): 439–450. Ife: University of Ife, Institute of Administration.

---

ment systems in Eastern, Western, and Midwestern Nigeria to make these systems more responsive to local needs and notions of government.

[8] For a discussion of this lack of congruence between political structure and political culture in the East Central State of Nigeria, especially as it relates to women, and the attempts to combat its results (which led to the promulgation by the East Central State government of the Divisional Administration Edict of 1971), see Amuchezai (1973).

BOHANNAN, P., P. CURTIN
  1971   *Africa and Africans.* New York: Doubleday.
BARTH, HEINRICH
  1965   *Travels and discoveries in North and Central Africa (1849–1855)*
          (centenary edition), first volume 444. London: Frank Cass.
GREEN, M. M.
  1964   *Igbo village affairs* (second edition). London: Frank Cass.
HERSKOVITS, M. J., W. R. BASCOM
  1959   "The problem of stability and change in African culture," in *Con-
          tinuity and change in African cultures.* Edited by M. J. Herskovits and
          W. R. Bascom. Chicago: University of Chicago Press.
HODDER, B. W.
  1961   Rural periodic day markets in parts of Yorubaland. *Institute of
          British Geographers Transactions and Papers* 29.
LEITH-ROSS, S.
  1965   *African women* (second edition). London: Routledge and Kegan
          Paul.
OTTENBERG, P. V.
  1959   "The changing economic position of women among the Afikpo Ibo,"
          in *Continuity and change in African cultures.* Edited by M. J. Hersko-
          vits and W. R. Bascom. Chicago: University of Chicago Press.
SKLAR, L. R.
  1963   *Nigerian political parties.* Princeton: Princeton University Press.
THOMAS, NORTHCOTE W.
  1969   *Ibo speaking peoples of Nigeria* (second reprint). New York: Negro
          Universities Press.
WILSON, G.
  1961   "Mombasa — a modern colonial municipality," in *Social change in
          modern Africa.* Edited by A. Southall. London: Oxford University
          Press.

African Women: Identity Crisis?
Some Observations on Education and the
Changing Role of Women in Sierra Leone
and Zaire

IDA FAYE ROUSSEAU

THE BEAST OF BURDEN MYTH

The immediately apparent division of labor according to sex in traditional Africa has been evaluated by many non-Africans as the merciless domination of women by men. It is also felt that if modernization requires that all citizens have opportunities for mobility, the right to participate in economic activities, and a voice in political decision making, there can be no separation in these domains on the basis of sex or any other particularistic criterion. The goals of modernization appear incompatible with such traditional patterns, and education is looked upon as capable of restructuring society while inculcating skills for development. Ostensibly the education of women will particularly cause the emergence of a female presence in the heretofore male-monopolized economic and political structures.

The resulting social reorganization will provide women with alternative roles to marriage and motherhood, thereby elevating the position of African women who "...appear to be esteemed by the [African] not as individuals possessed of sentiment, but as the mere creatures formed to gratify his desires and to minister to his wants..." (Clarke 1843:38–39).

Essentially, however, the foregoing statement reflects an evaluation derived from the Western romantic myth of women which pervades the literature on African women, dwelling on exploitation and subordination. It tells us little about the traditional relationship between women and their work, or between women and men. The reasoning that has been used to perpetuate the "beast of burden" myth is based on an idea of work that is non-African; the women conceptualized are also non-African.

We cannot refute the myth of female exploitation, neither can we understand the role of African women solely in terms of their positions in the
economic and political institutions of the colonial legacy. It is therefore
necessary to investigate the traditional roles of women in Africa. All
illustrations will be drawn from Sierra Leone in West Africa and Zaire
(formerly the Democratic Republic of the Congo) in Central Africa.

Traditionally in Sierra Leone, women fit into societies where:

1.   Political organization and recruitment are based on relationships to
the land. Stratification is based on ancestral prerogatives and primogen-
iture. There are both matrilineal and patrilineal groups.

In the patrilineal groups of Sierra Leone, there are special offices held
by offspring of matrilines within ruling families. Examples of these offices
in Mendeland are: KENYA, the mother's brother who holds a special position within his sister's household; and LAVALIE, the Protocol officer of the
paramount chief who must come from his maternal line. Although these
officeholders are men, the offices represent institutionalized ways in which
women can make their presence felt in both the domestic and jural domains so that claims to ruling rights through ancestry take precedence;
sex is never a determinant. There are adequate examples of female paramount chiefs to give evidence of this fact. In the case of the office of chief,
the deference due is to the office itself, and not to the sex of the officeholder. Thus even in the most rigid patrilineal societies the woman is a
key figure, and certainly not subordinated to men solely because of her
sex.

In Islamicized societies (particularly in the north) which may have been
matrilineal before the influence of Islam, kin from the female line of
chiefs also have structured roles within traditional political institutions.
In Koinadugu (Limba territory) it is only from SESA (matrilineal kin of the
chief) that the most influential political officeholders are chosen. In fact
these officeholders are more permanent than the chief himself. Although
there is no evidence here of the institution of "queen mother," BASARKA is
a woman not from the chief's family who acts as his advisor and who is the
symbol of legitimacy of his office. The chief is both morally and politically
bound to adhere to her advice in judicial matters, particularly those
affecting women, and those concerned with conflicts of interest between
women and men.

2.   Economic organization is in family units with some larger communal
activities. Work is sex-specific and to a lesser extent, age-specific.

The economic organization of Sierra Leone societies follows the principles mentioned above. There are some activities engaged in jointly by

men and women. Some have internal divisions, such as weaving. The preparation of the thread is done by women. Men do the actual tissage, and women do the dyeing either of the thread or the finished cloth. There are also such sex-specific economic activities as masonry and carpentry (men) and potting (women). Within each sex category there are internal age divisions, with small children and the aged often performing similar tasks.

The entire social organization of Sierra Leonean traditional societies is mirrored in the "secret societies" and other task-specific groups. BUNDU or SANDE is the female society. The top-level women in this organization have official positions in HUMOI (which regulates public demeanor) and PORO (the men's "secret society"). The specific political importance of PORO has been discussed by Little (1965), and we can only deny the idea of political exclusion of women with such evidence. Among the Sherbro, TUNTU is an ecology group which regulates fishing and agriculture, sets work standards and structures communal work organization. No distinction is made between men and women in TUNTU.

A symbolic representation of their harmony and integration is seen in WUNDE ceremonials. WUNDE is the military organization of the Kpa Mende in the South. During one ceremony, a battle scene is acted out — between young and old, between strangers. Those who play the role of peacemakers (KAMAKOIS) are men dressed as women. The symbolic message is that women reestablish harmony and continuity in the social structure. The reliance on women, depicted here symbolically, does not convey either subordination or exploitation.

Women in Zaire present much more of a problem in efforts to summarize their traditional position, primarily because Zaire itself has suffered as much from the biases of exclusion in Western scholarship as it has from the colonial act. Another cause is the problem of size and diversity; there are more than fifty major ethnic groups which may be subdivided several times again.

From the information available, however sketchy, we do know that, as in Sierra Leone, economic activities are divided by sex and subdivided by age. Fishing, farming, and marketing are all activities in which both women and men participate, but internal sex divisions exist. This principle of organization in no way implies exploitation.

The social structures of the peoples of Zaire are also similar to those of Sierra Leone. There are matrilineages and patrilineages. The importance of women and maternal kin in patrilineal societies is never denied; and in fact, Vansina (1965) in referring to the Ngbabandi, points out the specific importance of *"toutes les familles issues d'une meme mere"* for regulating peaceful relations between neighboring clans.

There are two well-known matrilineal societies in Zaire where the importance of female ancestors is institutionalized into the formal political structure. The Kongo trace their existence and the nine original Kongo clans to the nine sons of MBANGALA, a woman. This original "matrilineage" is said to account for the transfer of political and judicial power through NKAZI, the representative of the oldest woman of the oldest generation. There is no institutionalized role for a "queen mother," but we can infer the political and judicial importance of women through the fact that Christian missionaries working among the Kongo and other matrilineal peoples set about deliberately to remove women from their positions and place "men in their rightful places at the head..." (Storms 1949). The Lunda also trace their ancestry to a woman — LUEJI (Lueshi), who dominated the political structure of a state that covered parts of what is now southeastern Zaire, Zambia, and Angola. There is among the Lunda an institutionalized female political unit — LUKONKESHA, similar to the "queen mother" of Asante.

The symbolic importance of women is defined in a variety of proverbs which indicate the cooperative and complementary aspects of male and female roles (Makonga 1964). Again, among the Luba of the Katanga and Kasai basin, the MYUOMBA (Nsanga in the Kasai) symbolizes the spirit of the people in much the same way as the sacred stool of the Ashanti. It is placed in a sacred place (Isola) which is the domain of WOMEN ONLY.

For both Sierra Leone and Zaire there are similarities emerging. There is the expected division of labor by sex. There is not, however, any evidence of the exploitation of women. There is participation of women in political decision making, but there is no evidence of women being dominated by men, nor of political structures being completely monopolized by men. The role of women in traditional African societies can best be understood if we conceive of it in terms of the African woman's traditional integrity within a separate but not subordinate female community. It can secondly be conceived of in terms of the mutually interdependent relationship between the male and female communities, an interdependence without which the equilibrium of the natural order upon which traditional societies are based would be destroyed. The role of women, and hence their traditional identity, is always in compatibility with that of men — never in competition. The perception of women is in harmony with men — never in conflict.

The "beast of burden" myth is obviously ficticious in the traditional society, and more specifically, it is the result of the colonial intrusion. The particular aspect of the colonial intrusion which concerns us is European education. A question for consideration is how the traditional harmony in role structure and identity become either disrupted and dysfunctional or translated functionally into the modern sector. The agency for reorganization of society in colonial territories was most deliberately education which was to prepare human resources to fit whatever colonial model the colonizer had in mind.

FEMALE EDUCATION IN SIERRA LEONE AND ZAIRE

Sierra Leone's capital settlement, Freetown, is Britain's oldest African possession, and the history of education dates back to the founding of the settlement for recaptive and liberated African slaves. Female education also dates back to the founding of the colony (1791). Schools were supported by the settlers themselves, by the church through missionary enterprise, and later (1807) by the British government. At no time was the education of girls neglected.

Even greater concern over the education of girls came near the middle of the 19th century when several secondary schools for girls were established in the capital, but there were primary schools for girls and boys in the interior regions. The first girls' school in the interior began as a primary school and became secondary in 1900. Higher education in Freetown also dates back to this period. Fourah Bay College was founded in 1848.

The period immediately preceding World War II was one of general concern about education in Africa. In Sierra Leone, the focus was on the quality of the curriculum. The early schools provided classical and academic education for both boys and girls. After several "commission reports on education," domestic science, clerical, and teacher training options were provided female students in the existing schools; and several technical coeducational institutions were established. There began a steady increase in female students pursuing higher education both in Sierra Leone and abroad. Despite regional inequalities which still exist, educational opportunities in terms of variety in the curriculum for women at all levels has been very comprehensive for several decades.

But the history of education in Sierra Leone cannot be understood without reference to the Creole community, made up of descendants of the original black settlers. The most predominant feature of the settlement was the obvious deliberate attempt by the British founders to prepare the settlers as allies in the British "civilizing mission." They were to be the black standard-bearers to the interior of Sierra Leone, and in fact, to the whole of "British West Africa." This applied to women as well as men. The famous Creole families had their female pioneer educators as well as their male, and it was not uncommon to see women in some distant village of the Protectorate (Lukach 1910). There is no doubt that the Creole community heavily increased the spread and influence of British education for women in Sierra Leone. By the beginning of the 20th century, there existed a cadre of fourth-generation educated African men and women who were involved in the act of education as participants as well as recipients.

The case in Zaire is quite different. Zaire began as the Congo Free State, created by Leopold II in 1865. It remained his personal property until it was annexed as a colony by Belgium in 1908. The atrocities and the exploitation of Africans during the Free State period are a permanent part of the narrative of international immorality. Along with its late entry into the colonial scene and its stormy early history, one of the most striking features of the subsequent development of Zaire is the strict control the Belgians exercised over all aspects of African life. This policy is reflected in the concept of evolution and *mise en valeur* of the colony.

The education of women did not concern the Belgians because women were economically marginal and could not serve any practical function for the Belgians in their enterprise of exploitation. Women did not fit into the trinity of church, state, and commercial firm. Even as far as men were concerned, the Belgian belief in the GRADUAL evolution of the Africans led them to take GRADUAL steps toward realizing that evolution. In the process of this gradual evolution, Belgians were to gain maximum economic utility from their subjects, and Africans were to be of maximum economic utility. Belgian education therefore emphasized skills necessary for the exploitation of resources, the rational organization of work, and the expounding of Christian principles in justification. Women had no role to play here, and where they might have, they were deliberately denied the opportunity (cf. supra, 5). Missionaries did establish some institutions for girls, but their primary function was to ease the missionaries' burden of living in the tropics. The mission schools for boys were devoted primarily to scripture; those for girls (which were few and far between) were devoted to needlecraft, gardening, canning, butter making and soap making. There were church, government, private commercial and parastatal agencies which established schools for boys, giving Zaire the reputation during its colonial period of having the highest MALE literacy rate and the highest MALE primary school enrollment for all colonized areas of the continent. This was achieved for males despite "overwhelming obstacles:

The task of supplying any kind of education to eleven million primitive and in some instances barbarous people distributed in groups of varying numbers over a territory almost a million square miles in extent, cannot be fully appreciated even by a student of education" (Jones 1922:273).

What more can be said? After 1948, there were token secondary academic institutions for boys, but only "concerned discussion" by *evolués* about any type of education for girls. Those men wanted obedient women who would be properly educated in the Belgian tradition. The desires of these *evolués* was more for moral and domestic education for women. They wanted a better selection of wives who would not be an embarrassment to their husbands. The 1950's did not show too much change, and in fact, it was only after independence (1960) that significant changes began being made in the education of women and girls.

There are noticeable contrasts between female education in Zaire and Sierra Leone. In terms of the length and also of the quality of their exposure, Sierra Leonean women are at least four generations ahead of their sisters in Zaire. If we accept the premise that (European) education is to reorganize societies in transition, that the exposure of women to (European) education will enhance the status of women as a CLASS, we would expect Sierra Leonean women to be much further ahead of Zairois women in terms of their participation in the modern sector without adherence to traditional distinctions based on sex.

WOMEN IN THE MODERN SECTOR

Zaire

Not only were women in Zaire excluded from education, but they were severely restricted in terms of their political activities. La Fontaine (1970) notes that there were no women's associations legally allowed during the colonial regime. Coeducational associations were condemned by *evolués* as breeders of moral turpitude. However, there did exist some women's associations, but they were primarily limited to mutual aid, and they had to be clandestine. This policy of excluding women from the spheres of economic activity continued until 1957, when only ONE woman in the entire country ran for the post of *burgemeister* and lost. Emphasized again was the fact that women had no place in public life. The unnaturalness of this kind of participation on the part of women is understandable if we refer to a tradition of separate, complementary spheres of action for women and men, but the effect of colonial policy was to provide NO place for women. The status of women then DETERIORATED from that which they had enjoyed in the traditional social structure.

Aspirations of schoolgirls and the occupations of employed women give us some idea of both the opportunities open to women and how younger women perceive these opportunities. Pons (1956) along with Comhaire (UNESCO 1956:177) note that schoolgirls most often chose occupations such as teaching, needlework, and dressmaking, rather than housework. The aspirations of the schoolgirls is significant when we compare them to the boys who rejected teaching. This shows not that they were lacking hope and opportunity by taking jobs rejected by boys, but that they were reflecting the future NEW occupational roles of women, which by understood tradition must be different from those of men. Another example of an emergent pattern attempting to reestablish the traditional equilibrium of sex roles is that, after the opening of the universities, a significant number of men aspired to become medical doctors. Medical training was offered to women also, and a significant number of them aspired to become nurses (Belgian Congo 1959).

A more recent picture of the emergent role of women in Zaire must be juxtaposed against the slogan for the political, social, and economic "revolution" articulated in 1965: "new man, new woman." The official policy is that opportunities in work, politics, and education be equally open to women as to men.

In terms of individual participation of women, the scene is very impressive; however, in terms of class participation, there is still ambivalence on the part of both men and women, less as to whether or not women should participate in non-domestic affairs, than as to what KIND of participation it should be. There is beginning to emerge a pattern in which women tend to cluster around certain job categories. These categories include teaching, nursing, social work, and, to a lesser extent, clerical and petty administrative. Top-level administrative positions, professional jobs in law, medicine, and post-secondary education, and scientific and technical jobs are not sought after by women. Women are not preparing themselves for these jobs either. Despite official pronouncements, women are voluntarily adhering to separate job categories.

In political life, individual women are also active participants and officeholders. These women, however, are the exception rather than the rule. No specific movements for women only have been formed. No candidate (male) feels it necessary to seek the support of women as a political force. Women are very active in social service centers, but the impact of their activity is limited. Women's lack of participation reinforces the notion that no specific political activities, designated for women only, have yet developed. They have so far only recognized that the contribution they can make is to be different from that of men, but it has not been specified. We refer again here to the colonial period when women were denied the opportunity to organize pre-political groups like those men organized. This partly explains why there has been no carryover of political participation into the modern sector. Social work activities, which are monopolized by women, are a survival of the segmentary clandestine mutual-aid associations. There is still little emphasis on level of education as such in the party structure. The negligible contribution made by university students during the negotiations for independence established a precedent of putting education in second order of priority to experience within the colonial superstructure (Lemarchant, 1964). Women have neither the experience nor the education.

It appears that the policy of female education during the colonial regime had negative effects on the traditional political, economic, and social dimensions of the female role in Zaire. The integral importance of this role atrophied during the colonial period. But now that opportunities are more available, the pattern emerging is to reestablish the traditional equilibrium by women not competing in male spheres. It remains to be determined what those male spheres will be.

Sierra Leone

The colonial period of Sierra Leone is much longer than that in Zaire. The history of women working outside the home dates back to the early days of settlement. Creole women worked as traders and became wealthy shopkeepers. They became influential in settlement politics because they often owned the best properties (Fyfe 1963). Women from the interior also often came to Freetown, made money, and settled there or returned home to follow the example of the Creole women. The Sierra Leonean's general esteem for education, however, led them to encourage second generations to become other than shopkeepers and landlords. Women became post office workers, administrators in foreign commercial enterprises and nursing. Teaching was particularly popular and African women teachers dominated educational institutions especially at the lower levels. The colonial policy of female education in Sierra Leone seems to have been functional in integrating women into the modern sector and hastening their reestablishment of traditional equilibrium between sex roles. There is now and there has been for some time general acceptance of women working. On the other hand, marriage and motherhood are still emphasized.

The greatest participation of women in politics has been through women's participation in voluntary associations. West African women are particularly active in such groups: the church, alumnae associations, cooperatives, market women's associations, and proto-syndicalist guilds. Such women's groups have been active in political compaigns since the first elections at independence. They have played a major supportive role for political office seekers and, if the support is withdrawn, the contesting party has no chance of winning (Kilson 1969). On the other hand, female officeholders have mostly been appointed rather than elected, but they do represent the presence of women because of the importance of women's organizations.

It is interesting to note here that the trends of work in Sierra Leone are seen in embryo in the Zairois case. If Sierra Leonean women voluntarily select themselves out of certain activities, this phenomenon cannot be explained solely in terms of lack of opportunity. How then can it be explained?

CONCLUDING OBSERVATIONS

Future trends in terms of the type of participation of women in political, social, and economic life will more readily reflect traditional values in which sex roles are well defined, than Western values which confuse and distort sex roles. European-type education, even where there has been an exposure of over a century, has not worked to alter the basic commitment of African women to the underlying values of traditional society upon which the conceptualization of sex roles is based. The changes we see taking place can only be understood in terms of these traditional values. The disruptive social forces of the colonial act explain the differences between women in Zaire and women in Sierra Leone. In the case of the latter, There was much less disruption. The introduction of European education aided the transition from traditional to modern and the translation of the traditional content of the female role into a modern content. This transition was inhibited in Zaire.

A closer look at the two societies, however, reveals that the differences we observe are really differences in the magnitude of change, and not in the direction of change. In both cases we can only predict that there will re-emerge the separate yet interdependent categories of action for men and women through designated spheres of economic and political activity for each.

In relation to development proposals and plans for maximum utilization of educated labor power, social policy planners must take into account these trends. In the concern for the identity crisis which African women are allegedly undergoing, the traditional integrity of women must be taken into account within the African perspective, and not be befuddled by Western myths. There must be a more serious consideration of women as an educated working force and political force. There must be more consideration of women as a SEPARATE working force and a SEPARATE political force.

REFERENCES

APTER, DAVID
   1963   *Ghana in transition*. New York: Atheneum.
BELGIAN CONGO AND RUANDA-URUNDI INFORMATION AND PUBLIC RELATIONS OFFICE
   1959   *Belgian Congo*, volume one. Brussels.
CLARKE, ROBERT
   1843   *Sierra Leone*. London: James Ridgeway.
DRAKE, ST. CLAIR
   1960   Traditional authority and social action in former British West Africa. *Human Organization* 19(3):150–158.
EVANS-PRITCHARD, E. E.
   1965   *The position of women in primitive societies and other essays*. London: Faber and Faber.
FYFE, CHRISTOPHER
   1963   *A history of Sierra Leone*. London: Oxford University Press.
JONES, THOMAS J.
   1922   *Education in Africa*. New York: Phelpes-Stokes Fund.
KILSON, MARTIN M.
   1969   *Political change in a West African state*. New York: Atheneum.
LA FONTAINE, J. S.
   1970   *City politics: a study of Leopoldville 1962–1963*. New York: Cambridge University Press.
LITTLE, KENNETH
   1965   "The political function of Poro," *Africa* 25(4):350–365, 26(1):62–70.
LUKACH, HARRY C.
   1910   *A bibliography of Sierra Leone*. Oxford: Clarendon Press.
MAKONGA, BONAVENTURE
   1964   *La Mère Africaine*. Bruxelles: Editions Remarques Africaines.
PONS, VALDO, NELLIE XYDIAS
   1956   "Social effects of urbanization in Stanleyville, Belgian Congo," in *UNESCO*, 229–365.
STORMS, A.
   1949   "Famille Chrétienne et Société Matriarchiale au Katanga," *Zaire* 2 (March):239–248.

UNESCO
  1956   *Social implications of industrialization and urbanization.* London: International African Institute.

VANSINA, JAN
  1965   *Introduction à l'ethnographie du Congo.* Kinshasa: Editions Universitaires du Congo.

SECTION TWO

Women in Latin America

SECTION TWO

Introduction

Latin America is included in a global construct variously termed the "Third World," the "underdeveloped nations," the "developing countries," etc. by the definition-makers in the "First World." In "Female labor and capitalism in the United States and Brazil," Saffioti more accurately describes Latin America as a "peripheral" region controlled by the "central" nations in the international capitalist system. In both the "peripheral" and "central" sectors of this system women function as a huge reserve labor force to serve the needs of the fluctuating economy, according to Saffioti. In each sector the patriarchal techniques used to propel women into, and expel them out of, the labor market differ only in degree, *machismo* in Latin America being a more blunt and overt version of the "feminine mystique" in the United States.

Socialized from the earliest age to view their primary role as that of wife and mother, to function as self-sacrificing servants, women experience ambivalence when they become wage-earners. Even when their earnings raise the family income to a subsistence level, their wage-earning function, depicted as a secondary role, in no way relieves them of the obligations associated with the primary role. Thus they submit to being pushed out of the labor market when the economy contracts and to being limited to their primary unpaid role in the nuclear family, where their socioeconomic dependence is maintained and they cannot easily collaborate with other women to organize liberation movements.

But while women's psychological acceptance of their status as a marginal labor force is a great triumph of patriarchal capitalism, it is subsidiary to the grim reality of the widespread economic discrimination they experience when they attempt to integrate fully into the labor market.

Capitalism, as Saffioti points out, disseminates the ideology that women are increasingly drawn into the economy and polity as a nation undergoes economic development, but this appears to be a myth without foundation. The deterioration of women's former high status in the indigenous cultures of the dominant society as economic development takes place is described by Sánchez and Domínguez in "Women in Mexico," by Elmendorf in "The Mayan woman and change," and by Nash in "Resistance as protest." When these women migrate to the cities, the most highly "developed" areas of Latin America, the vast majority barely eke out a living as domestic servants, factory workers, and prostitutes.

In Lima, Peru, for example, women comprise 90 percent of the servant class, their roles in this category epitomizing the general status of women. Smith shows that they are ruthlessly exploited and controlled by their employers: their workday is almost unlimited and, since they receive room and board, they are paid the lowest possible salaries. Nevertheless they are expected to strive for the love of their exploiters and to obey them without protest. Dispersed among many thousands of individual families, they can organize against their oppression only with great difficulty. However, according to Smith, small groups of Lima servant women have in the last decade been meeting for consciousness-raising, some even defining themselves as radical.

It is the prevalence of women servants that permits women elites to work as professionals in Latin America. In Buenos Aires, Kinzer's sample shows that servants relieve professional women of most of their maternal obligations, so "smotheringly viewed in the United States." Thus child-rearing and domestic labor remain the purview of individual women, whether professionals or servants.

As in the rest of Latin America and throughout the capitalist world, professional women in Buenos Aires are found mainly in the traditional "women's fields," which are extensions of family roles. But Kinzer reports that women also constitute a sizeable proportion — in some occupations, a majority — of professions that are male-dominated in the United States: law, medicine, pharmacy, biochemistry, dentistry, architecture, the natural sciences, and the veterinary sciences.

In Latin American factories, the bulk of the women are textile workers. Piho shows that in Mexico City women textile workers not only support themselves but, whether married or single, care for numerous dependents. Conditioned to place little value on themselves, they are exploited both as workers and women.

Latin American women resist their oppression in a number of ways. Increasingly, women in the lower socioeconomic sectors reject the patrilineal form of marriage and the legal nuclear family which entrap them, as shown by Brown's study of village women in the Dominican Republic and by Piho's finding that among the women textile workers in Mexico City "the majority of the single women felt that marriage caused many problems and that they were better off alone."

In Puerto Rico and in the tin-mining communities of Bolivia, women workers have participated militantly, both in their own organizations and together with men, in labor and political movements. Silvestrini-Pacheco reports that, particularly in the 1930's, Puerto Rican women played a crucial role in exposing the corruption of labor union leaders and the alliance of government, industry, and the Socialist Party to subvert the goals of Puerto Rican labor.

In Bolivia, the Chola are more independent than most of the women in the world and act out of a sense of their own identity with self-respect and courage because the indigenous culture has long recognized and acknowledged the significance of women. But in the last decade the miners, shaken by the hardships and social disruptions in the wake of the massacres of workers and more fully "acculturated" to European patriarchal norms, rarely recognize the support provided by women and do not permit them access to decision-making in the unions and political organizations.

Women's acts of resistance, concludes Nash, shake the roots of the dominance-subordination hierarchy in the patriarchal family system imposed on the indigenous Indian cultures, and the wage slave becomes afraid of "losing his own slave in the house." Thus, as Nash points out, women must organize separately within liberation movements so that they can bring about structural changes in the society that will include their own liberation.

Female Labor and Capitalism in the United States and Brazil

HELEIETH IARA BONGIOVANI SAFFIOTI

> All science would be superfluous if the appearance of things coincided directly with their essence.
>
> KARL MARX

THE POSITION OF WOMEN IN CAPITALIST SOCIETIES

The unifying aspect of this analysis will be the degree and quality of female participation in the occupational structure of the social formations governed by the capitalist mode of production. More explicitly, the condition of women must be examined through the four fundamental social roles, that is, the woman's functions in the domain of PRODUCTION, SEXUALITY, REPRODUCTION, and SOCIALIZATION of the immature generation. While the selection of these four functions is of no surprise, the manner in which they are conceived and interpreted in this study does not coincide with the functionalist viewpoint, which tends to situate the various female roles on an equal plane, and to give them equal weight. Nor does it agree with the classic Marxist position which, being centered in principle on the mechanisms of social production, tends to assimilate the relations between the sexes to the relations among the social classes. We proceed, therefore, to an extreme simplification, in an attempt to explain the woman's position in the capitalist social formations.

The difficulty in this analysis lies in the fact that the relations between the sexes are considered in their intersection with the relations between the classes. Obviously, belonging to a specific social class has much more penetrating consequences for the *Socii* than belonging to a sex category.

Nevertheless, sex has been viewed as a condition that permits carrying out roles in the area of reproduction and sexuality, functions that are not necessarily linked. And the socialization of the immature has been considered the female social assignment. In this framework, sex acts as a mediator in the composition of working women, just as it interferes in the very internal differentiation of the category WOMEN WORKERS. Sex furnishes the elements which the ideological mediations use to regulate degree and quality of absorption of the female labor force by the productive apparatus, according to its needs. Production, then, is the ultimate determining moment for the social condition of women, even though the biological data are apparently often responsible for the particular coordinates which govern the existential situation of women.

From this discussion, we conclude that the social elaboration of the SEX factor cannot be understood simply as an ideological variant without effect on production. The sex factor is a phenomenon whose roots are imbedded in the economic nucleus of the capitalist mode of production, and in this sense is one of its constituent parts. It is an ideological counterpart of the economic base of society, and justifies the changes and differentiations which permit the constant renewal of conditions for reproducing the capitalist mode of production as a whole. The patriarchal ideology is present in all phases of gestation of the capitalist economic social formation and permeates all its levels. In the capitalist mode of production, patriarchy reaches its most refined expression, and increasingly incorporates scientific and pseudo-scientific knowledge.

In this context, one must not seek to explain the female condition by the patriarchal character of capitalist societies. For the patriarchal ideology is simultaneously a reinforcement and an internal differentiation of the class ideology. The differentiation accommodates the human substratum's need to reproduce, according to the capitalist mode of production's historical pattern of achievement. From this factor stems the coexistence of distinct cultural patterns which regulate the participation of female labor in the occupational structure of capitalist societies. That is to say, there is relatively widespread social acceptance of the pattern FEMALE WORKER for the WOMAN ON HER OWN (single, widow, divorced, legally separated, or merely separated from her husband) and also for the married woman without children or with older children, who do not require constant attention. The acceptance has the intensity that the national or international conjuncture permits. There is an almost complete rejection of the pattern FEMALE WORKER for married women with young children, which varies somewhat according to the various conjunctural moments.

In short, we are defending the following thesis: that the capitalist mode of production, based as it is on the extraction of relative surplus value, and therefore, on the incessant effort toward the increasing evolution of work productivity, places itself throughout the capitalist economic social formation as the least propitious historical moment for updating the economic dimension of the social PRAXIS, characteristic of this system of production, not only with regard to women but especially with regard to women. This does not mean that the female members of precapitalist societies have always carried out economic functions of equal importance with those typically performed by the men. The degree of similarity between the economic functions carried out by men, and those performed by women, has varied in each progressive stage of the development of the capitalist economic social formation. Such variations were not that significant in terms of drawing a clear demarcation line between the subordinate tasks reserved for women and those tasks designated for men, because they were either vaguely considered as relevant, or socially defined as such. Even if the division of labor in terms of sex was clear with respect to certain sectors of economic activity, the criteria for assigning functions was not basically defined from the angle of the social importance of the various economic roles. And there were even many activities that were performed equally by men and women. In general, the performance of economic roles by women was viewed as subsidiary, since men retained the decision-making capacity. Evidently, the distribution of decision-making power always occurred more frequently on the dividing line of the society's social classes (or of its embryonic counterparts: caste and estate than on the sex line, since the sex line becomes an operational criterion within the social class.

For this reason, we contend that the use of the female labor force in precapitalistic societies was never unnecessary. Strata of non-workers were made up of men and women who belonged to the privileged social class, while the position of worker, male or female, stemmed from the need to earn a living, a need imposed by their belonging to the underprivileged social class. From another angle, it is not entirely correct to state that the woman's integration in the economic world of the precapitalist societies was accomplished exactly as was the man's. This integration is mediated by an ideological superstructure which situates the woman as socially inferior to the man, especially in judicial and political instances. With regard to the pattern FEMALE WORKER in the specific historical stages of the capitalist mode of production, one finds that what is "pure" is relegated to women. In these phases of the capitalist social formation, the structure is already outlined in the subsidiary nature of the women's economic functions.[1] The burg econo-my,[2] which prepared the advent of capitalism, marks the passage from the historical moment in which the jettison of the female labor force was still an outline, to the latter phase, in which capitalist manipulation of the enormous increase in work productivity would regulate the absorption of labor from racial minorities and women.

In the competitive society, the natural factor, SEX, is socially elaborated to accommodate the needs of the new system of producing goods and services. On the ideological level, however, the woman figures as an ele-ment which, because of deficiencies and physical, mental, and emotional insufficiencies, contributes to obstruct economic and social development. Nevertheless, the intensity with which a society resorts to such prejudices is not uniform; it varies not only according to the woman's family situa-tion (lone woman on her own or married with young or older children), but also according to the economic conjunctures that have occurred.

One must emphasize two diverse phenomena. The first is fundamental to the purpose of this study and concerns the relative reduction of the number of economic functions performed by women in the capitalist mode of production as compared with the precapitalist modes of produc-tion. The second concerns the short term fluctuations of the use of the female labor force with regard to conjunctures, especially the economic ones, and to the long term establishment of the percentage of effective, economically active humans that women represent — a percentage that is always lower than the percentage of men. Except for certain special conjunctures in central capitalist countries, the trend in capitalist social formations places the proportion of women in the total economically

---

[1]   Even if the female labor force were widely used in the productive systems of slave and feudal societies, we obviously cannot pose the question of the woman's economic independence. Given that the family simultaneously constituted the unit of production and consumption, a category for individual economic independence cannot be situated in this context. In fact, its appearance is possible only in the historical context of the individualistic, competitive society; in a word, in capitalism.

[2]   "Na Idade Media, a mulher do povo, que a sociedade esmaga, deve contentar-se com um salario extremamente baixo. As corporacoes opoem-se ao trablho feminino, esforcam-se por suprimir uma concorrencia perigosa, que julgam desleal. Algumas obrigam as mulheres a aderir, interditando-lhes, porem, o acesso a mestria. Outras lhes fecham as portas, alegando o carater muito penoso de suas tarefas. Disto resulta que as mulheres, excluidas das corporacoes, sao submetidas as duras condicoes e aos baixos salarios do trabalho a domicilio. A revolucao industrial do secula XVIII faz entrar na producao um numero crescente de mulheres; mas ao mesmo tempo as novas maquinas sumprimem os trabalhos a mao, tais como a fiacao e a tecelagem, tornando a concorrencia mais acirrada e o desemprego mais frequente, baixando o preco da mao-de-obra feminina" (Freville 1951; translated from French).

active population between 20 percent and 40 percent, as per the figures in Table 1.

Table 1. Percentage of women in the economically active population (International Labor Organization 1967)

Austria	40	United Kingdom	32
Finland	39	Canada	31
Denmark	37	Belgium	31
Fed. Rep. Germany	36	Sweden	30
United States	35	Italy	27
France	35	Ireland	26
Greece	33	Norway	23
		Netherlands	22

These percentages refer to different years in the period 1960–1967, except for the case of France, where the figure refers to 1968 (Institute National de la Statistique et des Etudes Economiques 1969). It must be noted that in the U.S.S.R., where women represented 54 percent of the population, their participation in the economically active contingent was 46 percent in 1962. In 1967, the U.S.S.R. had a figure of 50 percent for female participation, and Byelorussia alone had 51 percent (United Nations 1970). Even today, when U.S. women are exerting considerable pressure to eliminate, or at least diminish, the inequalities between the sexes in the labor market, and when the country is engaged in a war that is greatly consuming its labor power, the United States has not equaled the U.S.S.R.'s figure for female participation. In fact, according to Dianne Feeley (1973), the female representation in the economically active population of the United States is 44 percent.

Even so, within the above-mentioned limits, there have been enormous fluctuations in the percentage of women in the economically active population. In the decade of the 1950's, the proportion of active women workers in relation to the entire economically active population of the different nations was: 38 percent in Austria; 31 percent in Great Britain; 25 percent in Italy; 24 percent in Belgium; 31 percent in the United States; 33 percent in France (where the proportion declined from 36 percent in 1931 to 33 percent in 1954) (Thibert 1961). A great plateau in the evolution of female labor can be observed in France in the period from 1906 to 1946, when the proportion of economically active women, in relation to the entire female population of a productive age, stabilized at around 22 percent (Myrdal and Klein 1962). Yet this period witnessed great fluctuations in female labor. In fact, in the four years between August 1914 and July 1918, the number of women workers in the economically active population grew 142 percent. In the industrial sector, the growth was 242 percent (Guilbert 1966:60–61). After the war, female labor regressed to its previous levels.[3]

During World War II, between 1939 and 1944, the number of economically active women in England rose to 40 percent (Myrdal and Klein 1962:42). The war need had a more or less compulsory effect on female labor. Women were urged to do at least part-time work. This meant great pressure on married women to work. The organization of services, like popularly priced restaurants and nursery schools, was designed to attract married women with pre-school children. The period of hostility over, employers were no longer disposed to divide the workday into shorter periods in order to employ different personnel in each period. Many nursery schools were then forced to close. According to a survey made in 1945 (Myrdal and Klein 1962:53), of 2,000 women workers, mainly middle-aged, two-thirds intended to continue in the economically active population. Notwithstanding, women workers returned to the home, leaving economic positions to the men. Female participation among economically active workers in England would only rise again with the rearmament effort of the 1950's.

WOMEN IN A CENTRAL CAPITALIST SOCIETY: THE UNITED STATES

In the United States, female participation in the economically active population represented only 14 percent in 1901. The wars, as well as the country's economic leadership in the Western World, especially after the last world conflict, were the principal causes of the increased proportion of women workers. The number of active women workers went from 10,880,000 in March 1941, the year in which the country became directly engaged in the war, to 18,030,000 in August 1944 — an increase of almost 66 percent in little more than three years. In December 1944, female participation in the economically active population reached a figure of

---

[3] "Le nombre de femmes exerçant une profession non agricole n'a enregistré, au cours des années qui nous séparent du recensement de 1921, que de légères fluctuations qui paraissent surtout liées à la conjoncture économique: hausse importante en 1931, correspondant à un niveau général élevé d'activité, baisse en 1936 qui traduit les effets de la crise économique, relèvement au lendemain de la deuxième guerre mondiale légère tendance à baisse lors du recensement de 1954. Il subit en définitive une hausse relativement peu importante puisqu'il passe de 4 436 000 en 1921 à 4 714 000 en 1954. La population active totale non agricole ne subit pas non plus de modifications importantes si bien que la proportion des femmes dans cette population reste, elle aussi, relativement stable" (Guilbert 1966:66).

34 percent. Women's unemployment was reduced during this period to less than one-fourth what it had been in 1940 (Sullerot 1968). Considering that the country was at war, this percentage is actually not that high when compared to the figures in certain European countries in periods of peace. At any rate, the United States had never witnessed such significant female participation in the economically active population. Such a proportion, however, was not maintained once the war was over. But the return of women workers to the home was not as strongly felt as in the European countries.

One must remember that the United States shared not only the military victory with the Allies in the Second World War, but it also consolidated its economic leadership in the Western World. As the dominant center of international capitalism, this country could introduce rather profound transformations in the economic system, in order to avoid stagnation and recession. State intervention in the economy, and the broadening and intensification of the U.S. domain in the West had the effect of lessening the 1949 and 1954 recessions, as well as raising the employment level.[4] Even though the proportion of women in relation to the total number of workers fell rapidly to 28 percent at the end of the war, and reached its lowest point in 1947, the figure rose again, as shown in Table 2.

Table 2

Years	Total number of active women	Percentage of women in the economically active population
1947	16,320,000	27.6
1950	18,064,000	29.0
1953	19,296,000	30.0
1955	20,154,000	31.2
1960	23,239,000	33.3
1965	26,108,000	35.0
1968	29,000,000	37.0
1970	31,233,000	38.0
1973		44.0

Sources: United States (1965, 1968b). The 1970 Figure was taken from United States (1971d). The 1973 percentage was taken from Feeley (1973).

[4] "E verdade que os Estados Unidos continuam sendo um pais de desemprego em massa; o numero de desempregados varia de 4 a 5 milhoes de pessoas. Mas e preciso lembrar que nos Estados Unidos, depois da crise dos anos trinta, o emprego alcancou um nivel muito mais alto e que atualmente os Estados Unidos experimentam escassez de mao-de-obra mais qualificada" (Urban 1967).

The increase of women workers in the economically active population is partially due to the role played by the United States in the economic and political world scene. However, extremely important in creating the conditions to achieve this continual increase was the fact that since the last world war the country has lived through limited periods of peace. During the years of the cold war, the war industry grew and the United States became the largest seller of armaments on the world market. These phenomena were highly propitious to the greater absorption of labor power in the economy. In addition, the country was directly involved in the Korean War during 1950–1953, and for the last decade has been making enormous investments in "death weapons," and has sent its men to the Vietnam War. Such "political policies" favor the rise of the employment level much less by the quantity of men mobilized on combat fronts, than by the labor demands of a war economy. In this manner, the United States increased the female participation in the total economically active population of the country by 32 percent in the 1958–1968 period. Female unemployment, calculated at 7.2 percent in 1961, was reduced to 4.8 percent in 1968, while male unemployment fell from 6.4 percent to 2.9 percent during the same period.[5]

Although the prejudices which justify a smaller absorbtion of female than male labor are not completely eliminated even in time of war, when the cooperation of women in the capitalist economy is most solicited, they are necessarily softened to permit a greater mobilization of the female contingents of productive age. However, other factors act as coadjutors, such as a cut in the real salary of the head of the family, a greater or lesser adherence to the ideology of upward social mobility, which includes all forms of increased material and non-material consumption (education, for example), the determination of the family situation to a certain point by the possibility of limiting births, the domestic facilities created by the development of technology, the rise or fall of the average age for women getting married, etc..

In all, these factors seem merely to facilitate the process of absorbing female labor by the economy. In fact, not one of them, nor all of them

---

[5]   Figures taken from United States (1970a). Obviously, the validity of these figures is very problematic. Since the study was not adapted to the female personality, at least to the same extent as it was to the man's, there are many more women prepared to engage in economic activities who do not try to acquire the means to secure these positions than men in the same situation. The percentage of unemployed is calculated using the number of people who effectively seek employment as a base. The question remains as to whether the female unemployment rate would remain the same if the percentage of women seeking employment (calculated against the total female population of productive age) were the same as the male percentage.

together, are capable of reducing the economically inactive female contingents during periods of stagnation or economic recession. Actually, the extremely variable conjunctures of the capitalist economy demand the participation of women in economic activities, a participation achieved through the mediation of ideologies. This occurs not only with respect to quantitative participation of the female labor force, but also in the quality of this labor, as well as its composition. As shown by the following figures, U.S. women represented 20 percent of the effective workers in the country in 1920, and were, on the average, single women, 28 years of age. In 1970, they represented 38 percent, married women predominating, and were on the average 39 years old. In fact, the percentage of married women has continued to grow: 23 percent in 1920; 37 percent in 1940; 60 percent in 1960; 62 percent in 1962; 63.4 percent in 1970.

Notwithstanding the growing number of married women participating in the economically active population, the curve for the figures on female activity in the United States continues to present the shape characteristic of capitalist countries. It reaches its culminating point between 20 and 25 years of age; the lowest point is between 30 and 35 years; and it rises again at 40 years to fall abruptly after fifty years (see Table 3).

In the socialist countries, we observe no lapse of occupational activity on the part of the women, even during the period when children require special care. The difference in the shape of the curve of female activity between capitalist and socialist countries is evident in Tables 3 and 4 below.

Table 3.   Female activity rate, by age, in the U.S. in 1970 (United States 1971e)

Activity rate
(Percent)

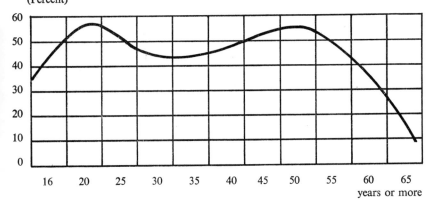

Table 4. Female activity rate, by age, in the U.S.S.R. in 1959 (Sullerot 1968:375)

Activity rate
(Percent)

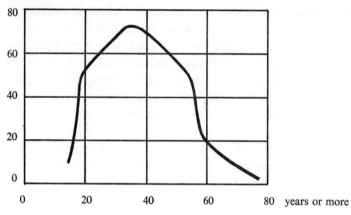

The percentage of married women among effective U.S. workers is extra-ordinary for a capitalist country in time of peace. In time of war, however, when work opportunities for women expand, as is the case of the United States, other factors hinder women from assuming economic functions. In fact, according to official information (United States 1971c), approx-imately half the women who made up the U.S. economically active pop-ulation in March 1970, did so because of absolute economic need. These were single women, widows, divorcees, women separated from their husbands, or women whose husbands earned less than $3,000 per year. Another 5,700,000 women workers, representing 18.4 percent of the economically active female population, were married to men whose annual incomes ranged between $3,000 and $7,000 — incomes which do not meet the criteria established by the U.S. Bureau of Labor Statistics for even a low standard of living for an urban family of four. The data give sufficient evidence that 70 percent of the effective women workers are forced to work through economic need. The inflationary phenomenon, responsible for the drop in the real salary of male workers, has forced many women to work. Another factor to be considered is the extension of life expectancy in this century, especially for women, which has length-ened their productive phase (see Table 5).

Thus, in any group of the U.S. population (whites, all others, or the whole), the woman outlives the man by more than seven years. (7.2 years among whites, 7.7 years among non-whites, and 7.3 years in the popula-tion in general). In 1963, there were nearly 800,000 more women over

Table 5. Life expectancy in years of those born in the United States (National Center for Health Statistics, U.S. Department of Health, Education, and Welfare)

Year	Whites			All others			Total		
	Men	Women	Total	Men	Women	Total	Men	Women	Total
1900	46.6	48.7	47.6	32.5	33.5	33.0	46.3	48.3	47.3
1910	48.6	52.0	50.3	33.8	37.5	35.6	48.4	51.8	50.0
1920	54.4	55.6	54.9	45.5	45.2	45.3	53.6	54.6	54.1
1930	59.7	63.5	61.4	47.3	49.2	48.1	58.1	61.6	59.7
1940	62.1	66.6	64.2	51.5	54.9	53.1	60.8	65.2	62.9
1950	66.5	72.2	69.1	59.1	62.9	60.8	65.6	71.1	68.2
1960	67.4	74.1	70.6	61.1	66.3	63.6	66.6	73.1	69.7
1963	67.5	74.4	70.8	60.9	66.5	63.6	66.6	73.4	69.9
1966	67.6	74.7	71.0	60.7	67.4	64.0	66.7	73.8	70.1
1969	67.9	75.1	71.4	60.7	68.4	64.5	67.0	74.3	70.5

75 than men. The number of women over 75 years of age increased from two million in 1950 to three million in 1960.

Two consequences may be inferred from these factors. The first is the need for a woman to prepare herself for a vocation even if she interrupts her occupational activity for a few years to care for her children; she still has many productive years.[6] The second is the fact that marriage does not mean economic security, especially towards the end of life for women. As the number of women who survive their husbands is enormous, and the social security system is neither satisfactory nor uniform, women, if they do not wish to have a miserable old age, must rely on the

[6] The average woman worker has a productive life-expectancy of 25 years, while the man's is 43 years. The single woman remains, on the average, 45 years in the economically active population of the United States (see United States 1971c). Even in old age, the life expectancy of the woman is greater than the man's.

Life expectancy, at various ages, in the United States (Institute of Life Insurance 1971)

Age in years	1969					
	Whites		Non-whites		Total	
	Men	Women	Men	Women	Men	Women
0	67.9	75.1	60.7	68.4	67.0	74.3
20	54.8	61.7	48.6	56.0	54.1	61.1
40	36.4	42.5	31.7	37.6	35.9	41.9
45	31.8	37.8	27.9	33.3	31.4	37.3
50	27.4	33.2	24.3	29.3	27.1	32.8
55	23.3	28.8	20.8	25.5	23.0	28.4
60	19.5	24.5	17.7	21.8	19.3	24.3
65	16.0	20.5	14.9	18.9	15.9	20.3
70	13.0	16.6	12.5	15.7	13.0	16.5

benefits of their retirement pensions or on interest from private securities.[7]

In fact, in 1962, there were almost 9 million mature women who depended on social security benefits: 6 million elderly women, $2^1/_2$ million widows, and 400 thousand invalids (President's Commission on the Status of Women 1963). In 1970, 80 percent of the persons who lived only on the meager resources of social security were women. Given their greater longevity, this picture will tend to worsen if there is no serious intervention. In 1960, women in the United States outnumbered men by about 3 million; by 1980, the difference will increase to 3.6 million U.S. Bureau of Census). Whether the growing trend of female participation in the U.S. economically active population will continue depends to a great extend on the war production demanded by the correlation of world forces, and on the broadening and /or intensification of the economic-political domain of the United States in its international environment. The sex composition of contingents living on social security will certainly undergo profound alterations. However, the current picture does not permit very optimistic prognostications with regard to the degree of well-being that the U.S. woman worker will be able to enjoy in her old age. In fact, women continue to suffer the effects of hateful discrimination,

[7]   In only eight of the forty-eight American states (excluding Alaska and Hawaii), the goods aquired by a couple during the years they live together belong to a common fund. Even so, the husband has the exclusive authority to administer this fund, and can spend it freely without the consent of his wife:

"In the other forty states of the U.S. the situation is very similar, a wife has no legal right to any part of her husband's earnings or the property saved from the combined efforts of her husband and herself through her housekeeping. She does have a right to be supported, but the husband has the power to make the decisions as to what he will pay for her support and that of the children. If she thinks that he does not allow her sufficient, she may go to court but this is likely to so aggravate him that the marriage would be broken in spirit and probably later by divorce or his desertion. The mother raising children and tending the home usually has insufficient time left to earn much or anything from outside employment. She, therefore, usually becomes economically dependent upon her husband and comes to realize that she must please him even when his demands seem unreasonable in order to receive funds for her own and her children's support...

"Some years ago a Wall Street brokerage concern published a study on the numbers of men and women who held shares in certain leading companies. It stated that women constituted about 56% of the shareholders of American Telephone & Telegraph Co.; 43% of the shareholders of United States Steel Corp.; and 58% of General Motors Corp., etc. and concluded that women own more than half of the leading company shares in in the U.S. There was a big fallacy in this conclusion. The number of shares held by the shareholders was omitted in this study. If the number of shares the shareholders owned were included the result would have been entirely different. If the women shareholders held an average of 10 shares each and the men shareholders held an average of 50 shares each, the men would be holding four or five times as many shares as the women...

"This incorrect statement was a tool to silence U.S. women which is still used today" (Bassett 1971).

despite the great increase in the percentage of women in the economically active population.

We do not intend to make an exhaustive examination of even the principal occupations that would reveal the subordinate character of the functions performed by women, as well as the difference in the salaries of women and men. Some specific sectors will illustrate women's opportunities for earning a living. A document presented to the Human Rights Commission of the City of New York on September 9, 1970 by Doris L. Sassower, former president of the New York Women's Bar Association, provides a sufficiently clear idea of the situation of the U.S. woman worker (Sassower 1970). The first striking feature is the low representation of women in the professions. Women constitute 2 percent of the pharmacists in the U.S., while in the U.S.S.R. they represent 95 percent; 75 percent of the doctors in the U.S.S.R. are women, as opposed to 7 percent in the U.S.; women constitute only 3 percent of the lawyers in this country, and 36 percent in the U.S.S.R. The number of women's degrees in medicine in the U.S. has not increased since 1920. Other professions reveal this same stagnation, and sometimes even a decline. The proportion of women teaching at the college level is smaller now than it was 50 years ago (18 percent in 1965–1966); almost a century ago women constituted more than one-third of the teaching staffs of the institutions of higher learning.

The woman is not only losing ground in the professions, she is also losing positions of prestige within them. In the last twenty years, all the women who left the office of judge, either by death or retirement, were replaced by men. In 1950 women represented 4 percent of the legal profession; today, this figure is 2.5 percent. There is a remarkable difference in salary between men and women in the professions, where women earn 66 percent of men's salaries. However, the difference in other occupations is even greater. For example, women salesclerks earn about 40 percent of the men's salaries. In 1968, the differences in men's and women's salaries in the professions varied from $1,700 per year in the field of anthropology, where the acceptance of women is greater, to $4,500 in chemistry (Bird 1970:74)[8] The top salary for the same job varies enormously according to whether it is filled by a man or a woman. For all full-time workers

[8]   On the same page, the author continues to illustrate the situation: "Unequal pay was even more rampant in business management. The managers of a new manufacturing enterprise in northern New Jersey saved money by hiring a woman to serve as their chief financial officer at $ 9,000 a year. When she left, they had to pay $ 20,000 to get a man to do her job. When he left, they went back to a woman at $ 9,000 and they replaced her with a man at $ 18,000. According to the recruiter, all four employees were good at the job."

who remain in the economically active population for the whole year, the gap between men's and women's salaries has widened continuously. Women's salaries represented 62.2 percent of men's in 1956; in 1966, they represented 56.5 percent (United States 1968b). The figures in Table 6 show the position of men and women in different salary brackets.

Table 6.   Incomes for women and men fourteen years of age and over, 1966, U.S.A. (United States n.d.a.)

Percentage distribution	Total money income		Wage or salary income	
Total in US $	Women	Men	Women	Men
under 1,000	35.9	12.9	32.7	13.7
1,000 to 1,999	19.4	10.1	15.1	6.6
2,000 to 2,999	12.6	8.2	13.5	6.2
3,000 to 3,999	11.6	7.9	14.0	7.5
4,000 to 4,999	8.2	7.8	10.1	8.5
5,000 and over	12.5	53.1	14.7	57.5

Full-time year-round workers

Percentage distribution

	Women	Men	Women	Men
Total wage earners	30.0	60.2	40.5	67.2
Average income in US $	4,026	6,955	3,973	6,848

Women occupy underpaid positions in several professions, and are virtually absent from management, administration in general, and as a rule from the most prestigious positions. This is true even in the occupational sectors where women dominate. Thus, while women are librarians, men are library administrators; in social services, women are house visitors, while men are supervisors; in the educational sector, women are teachers, and men, directors. In academia many more women are assistant professors than associate or full professors. Even in government, women are special assistants and men are agency heads.

According to the latest government study, 60 percent of the women versus 20 percent of the men earned less than $5,000 per year; 28 percent of the men versus 3 percent of the women drew $10,000 or more. In the city of New York only 24 of the 300 highest positions in the municipal government are occupied by women. In short, the professions and the other occupations, as well as the various positions within each of these, have been stereotyped as "masculine" or "feminine."

As a matter of fact, a survey made by the United Nations (1970) confirmed that the eradication of the labor market division into masculine and feminine sectors is a slow, difficult, and burdensome process even in countries where the woman enjoys ample freedom, like Sweden, and in countries-in-transition to socialism, like Poland. The U.N. survey shows that there are few countries where women do not encounter obstacles to high posts, including Communist China, the Philippines, Hungary, Israel, Yugoslavia, the Ukraine, Byelorussia, and the U.S.S.R. in general.

A survey made in 1968, when women represented 51 percent of the U.S. population and nearly 37 percent of the economically active population, showed that in the six largest cities, including New York, only 186 of the 2,700 lawyers employed by the 40 largest firms were women. Male lawyers' salaries are greater than those of female lawyers in almost all cases. Of almost 10,000 judges in the U.S. only 200 are women and almost all serve in the lower courts, of limited jurisdiction. And all this occurs in a country that has had a Women's Bureau as part of the U.S. Department of Labor since 1920; a Commission on the Status of Women, established by President Kennedy in 1961; and a Civil Rights Act, approved in 1964, which prohibits all discrimination on the basis of sex. In a country that describes itself as the "achieving society," where education should function as the principal factor in securing economic-social positions, salaries show variations with regard to sex at certain educational levels (see Table 7).

Table 7. Salaries in US $ (United States 1971a)

Years of schooling	Men	Women	Percentage of women to men
8	7,140	3,970	55.6 %
12	9,100	5,280	58.0 %
16 or 17	13,320	7,930	59.5 %

The Equal Pay Act, first proposed in 1945, was finally approved on October 6, 1963, prohibiting all salary discrimination on the basis of sex. But women's salaries are still seen as a supplementary income to increase material and/or non-material consumption. Actually, however, the salaries permit superfluous consumption for only one-third of women workers (See Table 8).

Table 8. Women in the economically active population in the U.S., March 1970 (United States 1971d)

	All women		Women belonging to ethnic minorities	
	Number	Percentage	Number	Percentage
Total	31,233,000	100.0	3,935,000	100.0
Single	6,965,000	22.3	814,000	20.7
Married (husband present)	18,377,000	58.8	1,986,000	50.5

Husband's income US $ (1969)

Less than 3,000	2,077,000	6.7	348,000	8.8
3,000 to 4,999	2,316,000	7.4	455,000	11.6
5,000 to 6,999	3,400,000	10.9	427,000	10.9
7,000 and over	10,584,000	33.8	756,000	19.2
Married (husband absent)	1,422,000	4.6	527,000	13.4
Widows	2,542,000	8.1	351,000	8.9
Divorcees	1,927,000	6.2	257,000	6.5

These figures show that almost two-third (66.2 percent of the economically active women in the United States) need their salaries to support themselves and their dependents. The minimum annual income, according to the Bureau of Labor Statistics, needed to guarantee a low standard of living for an urban family of four is $6,960. In the non-white population of economically active women, that proportion rises to more than 80 percent. In fact, for only 19.2 percent of these women does their income permit increased consumption. For the rest, these earnings are indispensable for their survival and that of their dependents. For this reason, many non-white women, especially blacks, who have pre-school children, work outside the home, even though in a great number of cases the children do not receive adequate care (see Table 9).

Table 9. Percentage of married women in the 1969 U.S. economically active population, according to their children's ages (Schiffmen 1962)

	Whites	Non-whites
With children under 3 years	17.0	29.0
With children between 3 and 5	25.0	52.5
With children between 6 and 17	40.0	57.0

In the confluence of two prejudices, race and sex, are found the extreme cases of marginalization in a society of mass consumption. These are families headed by women whose earnings reflect their position in a racial minority and in the most exploited sex category. The figures in Table 10 show the incidence of this phenomenon.

Table 10. Confluence of race and sex (United States 1971b)

	All families, 1970			Poor families, 1970		
	All races	Whites	Blacks	All races	Whites	Blacks
Number in millions	51.9	46.5	4.9	5.2	3.7	1.4
Male head	88.5 %	90.6 %	69.4 %	62.9 %	70.4 %	43.3 %
Female head	11.5 %	9.4 %	30.6 %	37.1 %	29.6 %	56.7 %
	100.0 %	100.0 %	100.0 %	100.0 %	100.0 %	100.0 %

The striking fact is that more than half of the black families are headed by women. The percentage of black families, in fact, is almost double the proportion of white families in the same conditions. In 1970, one-third of all families headed by women were living in poverty, as opposed to 7.1 percent of those headed by men. The considerable number of poor black families in the U.S. population reveals the intensified discrimination in the double classification: SEX and RACE (see Table 11).

Table 11. Poor families in the U.S.A. in 1970 (United States 1971b)

| Type of family | Number in millions | | | Percentage in relation to all families | | |
	All races	Whites	Blacks	All races	Blacks	Whites
Total	5.2	3.7	1.4	10.0	8.0	29.3
Male head	3.3	2.6	0.6	7.1	6.2	18.3
Female head	1.9	1.1	0.8	32.5	25.0	54.5

The employment of women who head their own families often pulls them out of poverty. However, the woman often cannot work for health reasons or because she cannot find a job. In 1969, among white families headed by women, the poverty rate was 15 percent when these women were economically active, and 37 percent when they were not. The corresponding percentages for black families headed by women were 38 percent and 69 percent, respectively. The intensity of poverty also varies according to these same natural characteristics, sex and race, which have been chosen to operate as social selectors. In fact, the income deficit in 1970 for poor families headed by men was $995 among whites and $1,109 among blacks. The corresponding figures for poor families headed by women were $1,219 and $1,492. The difference in the average deficit between poor black and white families stems partially from the greater average number of members of the former. This difference is highly accentuated by the gap between the actual income of black families headed by women and the supposed minimum standards for a modest living — for the black woman simultaneously possesses the two characteristics chosen to operate as social selectors.

In relation to the social utilization of SEX and RACE for the purpose of discrimination in the work situation, the evolution of the phenomenon shows a softening of racial prejudice and a reinforcement of prejudices against the category female sex. In fact, taking salary as perhaps the most significant indicator, the situation has evolved in the following manner. In 1939 average earnings of the white man were the highest, the white woman the second, the black man the third, and the black woman the fourth. In 1966, the black man occupied the second position, and the white woman, the third; the white man and the black woman remained in the first and last places (see Table 12).

Table 12.   Salary percentages according to race and sex (United States 1968b)

	1939			1966		
	Black man	White woman	Black woman	White man	White woman	Black woman
White man	45.0	60.8	23.0	63.2	57.9	41.1
White woman	74.0	—	37.8	109.0	—	71.0
Black man	—	135.0	51.0	—	91.4	65.1

These figures clearly reflect the valorization of the black element, man or woman, which has occurred in recent decades. The sex factor actually began to operate more strongly than the race factor, bringing significant disadvantages to the white woman. For the black woman, on whom both types of discrimination fall, the situation, despite a noticeable improvement, is still one of profound injustice.

We must add that at least part of the changes which have occurred in recent years are voided when the growth of the employment level is confronted with the inflation of prices on consumer items. In fact, while unemployment went down from 5.6 percent in 1960 to 3.9 percent in 1969, price inflation for the consumer rose from 1.7 percent to 5.4 percent (United States 1970c). The figures indicate that increased employment was accompanied by a fall in the real value of salaries. Even if the entire increase in the degree of productivity were being distributed, which is not the case according to the falling rate of salaries, it would not be sufficient to cover the increase in prices. In fact, the rate of increased productivity fell from 3.5 percent in 1960 to 1.0 percent in 1969, with rather substantial oscillations in this period. Between 1965 and 1969, the average increase in productivity in the United States was 2.5 percent — rather low when compared to that of other industrial nations: 3.2 percent in Canada, 6.9 percent in France, 6.4 percent in West Germany, 4.2 percent in Italy, 13.4 percent in Japan, 10.6 percent in the Netherlands, 6.7 percent in Sweden and 4.3 percent in the United Kingdom (United States 1970c).

The figures indicate, therefore, that the richest and most developed capitalist country, despite its position of economic and political leadership in the international scene, is quite far from achieving equity for the various races which make up its population, as well as for the two categories of sex. It is also clear that even in time of war the opportunities for earning a living increase for women at the expense of a certain qualitative deterioration of the economic functions which they carry out, and at the expense of the relative reduction of the social product distributed among them. Obviously, the analysis of the data presented is not sufficient to justify the statement that the social condition of women in the United States stems from the domination exerted by men over women. Intensifying sex prejudices, or easing racial prejudice has caused certain observers to lose sight of the division of the U.S. society into social classes. Thus, they attribute excessive importance to the patriarchal ideology when considered as the mediator in realizing the economic structure of the competitive societies.

Neither in theoretical nor in practical terms does the concept of women's liberation through a struggle against the other sex category make sense. The framework in which this liberation is possible is unquestionably that of class struggle. However, a mechanical determinism, often implicit in this position, is rejected. The abolition of the capitalist system of production does not necessarily bring about the liberation of women, as shown by the fact that, until now, no country in the process of constructing socialism has secured equality of the sexes. Obviously, the class perspective is the most inclusive; yet within it the need for the struggle for women's liberation is evident. Like women, and probably even more than women, men are also deceived by the dominant ideology, which gives the role of leadership to them, and transforms them into its most obstinate defenders. Showing the men of the dominated class their role as intermediaries in the preservation of a socioeconomic system that also does not guarantee them the equal opportunities of earning their means of subsistence could be a good means of gaining their support in the women's liberation movement. Within this context, one is not dealing with a movement for women's liberation, but with a movement for the liberation of the human being. It is probably not enough that the man recognize the need for women's liberation for the betterment of the whole family as a unit — no longer for production, yet still for consumption. He must also be willing to undertake together with the woman the task of reconstructing the family.

The feminist movements, in as much as they are situated in a sex perspective and not a class one, tend to obscure class conflicts, and in this manner preserve the capitalist mode of production. In this case, nevertheless, if one were to try to prove Revel's position (1970:11–12),[9] the

[9] Revel characterizes the revolutionary process through the five following conditions which he feels are present in the American society: "(1) Critique of the injustice existing in economic, social, and racial relationships. (2) Critique of management and efficiency.

movements for women's liberation could play a relevant role in transforming U.S. society.

From a certain viewpoint, social contradictions seem to have actually
become so intense that the United States, much more so than the apparently more progressive countries, holds the conditions to promote a great
socioeconomic transformation. In this perspective, the statement made
by the black militant, Eldridge Cleaver, is meaningful:

It is no exaggeration to say that the destiny of the whole human race depends on
the way in which America solves the problems that confront her today. The
number-one question of the contemporary world is: will she go to the Right or
to the Left (Revel 1970).

THE WOMAN IN A PERIPHERAL CAPITALIST SOCIETY:
THE CASE OF BRAZIL

It is mistakenly believed that development of productive forces, including
the human elements, eliminates the utlization of factors of the natural
order to justify the marginalization of enormous human contingents
from either the production system or from the power structure of the
competitive society. Nevertheless, it is possible to distinguish, in the
development of social techniques, the direction of human behavior through
certain channels towards modalities. The behavior, then, is apparently
stamped as voluntary conduct, which conceals non-explicit but active
designs to preserve the rule of the privileged strata. Although it is
often subtle and not easily perceived, there is a highly positive correlation between the development of the productive forces and the rational

---

(3) Critique of political power. (4) Critique of cultures: or morality, religion, accepted
beliefs, customs, philosophy, literature, art, of the ideological attitudes which underlie
these things; of the function of culture and of intellectuals in society; and of the distribution of that culture (education, communication, information). (5) Critique of the
old civilization-as-sanction, or a vindication of individual freedom. This critique is
aimed at the relations between society and the individual. In it, the individual is considered as a sensitive and original being, rather than a citizen; and society is regarded
as a means either of developing or distorting the proper worth of each individual. Such
a critique means, for example, the failure of a society to deal with poverty and the sterility of the human relations it establishes (brotherhood versus aggressiveness); with the
uniformity of the human types it engenders (conformity); in general, with the restraints
with which it burdens its people, and the obstacles which it places in the way of the
development of individual potential and self-identity. In this context, revolution is seen
as the liberation of the creative personality and the awakening of personal initiative, as
opposed to the 'closed horizons', the climate of frustration and despair, which prevail
in progressive societies" (1970: 11–12).

utilization of irrational criteria to legitimize the existing social order. Having revealed its own economic basis, the capitalist economic social formation, then, takes shape in such a way that it must construct the broadest and best designed cover under which to conceal social injustices. Thus, in defending real or supposedly higher values — such as the equilibrium of family relations, the smooth running of domestic services, the preservation of traditional methods of socialization of the young, and the respect for the moral principle of distance between the sexes — one finds the most complete and rational utilization of criteria of an irrational order. Female physical disability, emotional instability, and reduced intelligence are used to imprint on female labor the character of subsidiary labor. The woman, then, becomes the constitutive element, *par excellence*, of the human contingents directly marginalized from productive functions.

Apparently, the developed capitalist countries still are the ones which do most to further the woman and her labor. The changes effected with the advent of industrial capitalism brought to light the economic functions of women engaged in activities outside the home. Yet they obscured the woman's role in agriculture and in the domestic industries, which preceded the system of gigantic factories. The changes simultaneously marginalized a large female contingent from the occupational structure. On a superficial level, the employment of a certain number of women in paid occupations outside the home constitutes sufficient evidence of the "wide acceptance" female labor supposedly enjoys. It supposedly demonstrates the freedom which the class society allows a woman, who through an alleged personal and voluntary determination of her own existence, chooses a professional career or marriage, or a combination of both. The ideological casing of the capitalist societies promotes the belief that the number of economically active women rises with the economic social development of a country.

Actually, one must distinguish between the absorption of a growing number of women by the occupational structure of capitalist societies — an absorption which always varies according to national or international conjunctures and remains short of male absorption — and the fact that this absorption is accomplished with relatively less intensity than that characteristic of precapitalist societies. In other words, one must not lose sight of the fact that the phenomenon, participation of female labor, conducts itself differently in functions of an economic character, when considered simply within the capitalist economic social formation or when it is accompanied by more than one means of production. From this angle, the growing participation of the female labor force in the occupational structure of capitalist societies represents merely an under-utilization of this labor power in relation to the historically previous modes of production. It is evident that carrying out functions in the home also has an economic character, since these functions provide a certain savings to be added to the family budget. In all, the domestic functions, despite their economic nature, inhibit the designation of a woman as the economically independent person that she should be in the individualistic, capitalist, industrial-urban society.

Brazil is a "peripheral area" of the international capitalist system, which since its colonization has been establishing itself as a capitalist society.[10] Although it is an underdeveloped country, one must not expect the female participation in the economically active population, first in the colony, and later in the nation, to present a growing increase. On the contrary, surmounting the "proslavery capitalist" modality — in which the precapitalist relations of production were formally redefined according to the expansion needs of the capitalist mode of production originally located in Western Europe — the modernization of the capitalist historical configuration's new dimensions caused the fragmental expulsion of the female labor force from the occupational structure.

In the competitive societies, be they "central" or "peripheral," the

[10] "As for enlarged reproduction or accumulation, in Marx's diagram the composition of the social product in terms of value is also strictly in proportion to its material forms: the surplus value, or rather that part of it which is earmarked for capitalization, has from the very beginning the form of material means of production and means of subsistence for the workers in a ratio appropriate to the expansion of production on a given technical basis. As we have seen, this conception, which is based upon the self-sufficiency and isolation of capitalist production, falls down as soon as we consider the realisation of surplus value. If we assume, however, that the surplus value is realized outside the sphere of capitalist production, then its material form is independent of the requirements of capitalist production itself. Its material form conforms to the requirements of those non-capitalist circles who help to realise it, that is to say, capitalist surplus can take the form of consumer goods, e.g. cotton fabrics, or means of production, e.g. materials for railway construction, as the case may be. If one department realises its surplus value by exporting its products, and with the ensuing expansion of production helps the other department to realise its surplus value on the home market, then the fact still remains that the social surplus value must yet be taken as realized outside the two departments, either mediately or immediately.... In addition, there is no obvious reason why means of production and consumer goods should be produced by capitalist methods alone.... Between the production of surplus value, then, and the subsequent period of accumulation, two separate transactions take place — that of realising the surplus value, i.e. of converting it into pure value, and that of transforming this pure value into productive capital. They are both dealings between capitalist production and the surrounding non-capitalist world. From the aspect both of realizing the surplus value and of procuring the material elements of constant capital, international trade is a prime necessity for the historical existence of capitalism — an international trade which under actual conditions is essentially an exchange between capitalistic and non-capitalistic modes of production" (Luxemburg 1951).

woman does not cooperate in constructing and developing the economy as merely the labor force in general. She functions as special labor power, which undergoes economic fluctuations, more so than male labor power. She is subject to drawing salaries which correspond to subsidiary work, fundamentally because of her lesser technical qualifications and the lesser development in the female personality of traits characteristic of the worker adjusted to the capitalist production system. The relative lack of overall qualifications of the female labor force functions as a prerequisite for preserving the equilibrium of a society whose economic structure increasingly restrains the participation of women in the occupational structure in relation to the other modes of production. The mere technical qualifications of the labor force, constituted as a *sine qua non* condition for professionalization in certain sectors of activity, are insufficient to impede a woman from seeking direct participation in the occupational structure. Even when aspirations for upward social mobility lie at the base of female mobilization, it is not always the woman who represents the final point in an upward process. In fact, the effective use of female labor power, when determined by the desire for upward social mobility, becomes linked more to concretizing the possibilities for the ascent of the male members of the family than of the woman. For this reason, women's aspiration for promotion on the position scale in the class society take shape much more as masculine aspirations than feminine ones. They acquire, at least, a diverse coloring when one attempts to make them more concrete through paid female labor.

The partial socialization of the women, as a worker, constitutes an effective mechanism which the society seizes upon to mobilize the immense reserves of female labor power, on a greater or lesser scale according to conjunctural needs. The socialization of women in capitalist countries has similar basic components in the basic duality of their social roles, whether in developed or underdeveloped countries. The social function of the feminine mystique is the same in capitalism's different historical settings; even its content is very similar. The rationally developed aspects of the feminine mystique seek to marginalize the woman from the occupational structure. This mystique is essentially constructed in international capitalism's center of dominance, and then projected through the popular distribution of "scientific works" — television soap operas, serial stories, and comic strips — to the secondary economic, social, and cultural areas. Although everything is done in the name of promoting the modernization process, the feminine mystique promoted by the "center" combines with phenomena that are characteristic of the cultural traditions of various underdeveloped countries and gains the status of a national mystique. Under the strong influence of these ideas, it has not been difficult in the peripheral nations of the world capitalist system to reduce labor power, for which there has long been less and less room in the occupational structure despite certain conjunctural fluctuations of a slight increase.

Although the status of women is basically similar in all capitalist countries, two phenomena differentiate their status in the developed countries from that in the underdeveloped countries. On one hand, the peripheral nations, because of the very manner in which they are integrated into the "Western block," are not in a position to resort to the mechanisms for reducing social tensions that the United States had used since the Second World War with respect to reducing the unemployment rate. At most, the governments of some of the peripheral nations of the international capitalist system, through austere economic policies, have managed to promote more or less prolonged surges of economic growth. The historical conditions that would permit a redivision of the world in terms of influential areas and subareas would allow certain "peripheral" countries to redefine their own integration in world capitalism. In this manner, they would gain a certain degree of growth, and/or could establish a development process. Both of these would be simultaneously and individually capable of a short and medium term raising of the female participation in the economically active population. But such a hypothesis implies the intensification of economic stagnation in other peripheral areas. The latter condition would not alter, and would do little to transform, the situation of female labor power in the capitalist national units as a whole.

On the other hand, in the underdeveloped areas in general, and especially in the Latin American nations, the cultural complex of *machismo* ostensibly exposes more vividly the subordinate position of women. This does not mean that the behavior of the "virile" male is responsible for reduced female participation in the economically active population of these countries, but rather that the techniques for dominating women and the justifications for their expulsion from the labor market are more blunt and less refined than in the developed nations. Prejudices are not strong enough to impede a woman from engaging in economic activity, if an opportunity presents itself, when she or her family find themselves in financial need.[11] But they can be effective, and frequently are, in establish-

[11] In Brazil, there has never been a study surveying the total national population with the objective of precisely defining the situation of women and labor. There are some investigations covering restricted empirical fields. In 1970, the Department of Labor

ing a profound ambiguity in the woman's personality, so that she currently hesitates between the extremes of the worker-housewife pattern. This ambivalence, imposed on the woman through the socialization process, which meets the demands of an economy subject to periods of prosperity and periods of recession, is what makes the woman a special worker. She is different from the man, since his personality has been socially molded mainly according to the worker pattern.

It is not uncommon for even legislation to ratify this ambiguity, principally in countries of the Latin tradition. In regulating work, legislation opens special clauses for women, forbidding them, in the name of protection, to execute certain tasks, thus making the woman a financial burden to her employer. Although laws in the non-Latin countries under the pretext of protection actually discriminate against the woman in the work situation,[12] it seems that the tendency to ratify prejudices legally is more frequently manifested in countries where the image of the "virile" male is more highly valued.

The consolidation of labor laws in Brazil prohibits female labor "in underground areas, in underground mines, in quarries, and public or private construction, and in dangerous or unhealthy activities." The obsolete character of this legislation is obvious. It may have already become obsolete, now, in construction work and the beginning of subway operations in the large Brazilian cities. In fact, the "metro" will not be able to employ women in its underground sections. The same law assures the woman a paid leave of absence six weeks before and after childbirth. She is paid on the basis of a calculated average of her entire earnings over the preceding six-month period, which in special cases can be exten-

---

and Administration published the results of a socio-economic survey of the industries, in the city of São Paulo: *Feminine Labor* (*Mão-de-Obra Feminina*). This pilot survey made by the Sectorial Planning Group, reports the same situation as that found in capitalist countries: the majority of women work in order to meet economic needs. In fact, of those interviewed, 93.6 percent worked to support themselves, 2.7 percent, to help their families, 1.6 percent, to have a better life style, and 2.1 percent, to be independent.

[12] The American labor laws prohibit women from working during certain hours of the night in some occupations, just as they set the maximum amount of weight to be lifted or transported by a woman on the job. This obviously constitutes sexual discrimination, for it would be more just to formulate these interdictions according to the personal characteristics of both men and women. On the other hand, only five states and Puerto Rico forbid women to work just before and after childbirth; another state forbids work only in the period immediately after childbirth. Only two states and Puerto Rico have legislation guaranteeing a special paid leave for expectant mothers. Frequently, collective contracts assure the woman the right to return to the same job, after a year's absence due to childbirth, without losing any of the advantages gained during the previous period of service (see United States 1968b).

ded. There are other demands made on the employer by the governing power.

Legislation is meaningful only if the society as a whole is prepared to cope with the burden of motherhood. But from the viewpoint of the capitalist entrepreneur, it is perfectly legitimate to ignore or compromise this legislation, since, on the one hand it counteracts the effort towards greater profits, and on the other the man's salary is supposedly sufficient to produce and reproduce his labor force. The capitalist system is, actually, sufficiently malleable to accomodate the "socialization" aspect of the burden of motherhood. Given the classist character of the state, financing the reproduction of the labor force through tax collections could become an item of public expense, in the same way as state action has for a long time constructed the economic infrastructure which permits the widening of profits for private companies. This hypothesis, however, encounters considerable difficulty, since it probably creates a rise in the birth rate, the direct consequence of which is the growth of a multitude of unemployed workers. It would thus affect the very unemployment level which some countries have managed to reduce at great expense. Furthermore, this measure would remove one of the great obstacles to employing married women, and free them for work.

For it is precisely the capacity to mobilize female labor power according to the demands of the different conjunctures that the capitalist society cannot and does not want to lose. In the ambiguity, working woman/ housewife, lies one of its greatest triumphs — the capacity to maneuver this immense labor supply made up of women.

In Brazil, as in the other underdeveloped countries, it is difficult to measure this phenomenon. First, there has never been a rigorous study of employment in general for both men and women; also there is considerable difficulty in measuring the degree of underemployment.[13] Sec-

---

[13]   The first mission of the International Labor Organization in Colombia, directed by Dusley Seers, 1970, estimated the urban unemployed at 25 percent of the labor force. Such missions are the result of a growing concern that the high level of unemployment in underdeveloped countries has caused politicians, technicians, and intellectuals; these missions are part of the "World Employment Program" of the ILO (1972). A survey made by the Plan for Social Assistance Foundation in 1970, covering the entire state of São Paulo (and excluding the greater São Paulo (city) municipalities) verified the existence of 4,098,000 unemployed; that is 43.3 percent of the population of productive age. The mechanization of agriculture has largely contributed to raising the unemployment figures. Day to day observation leads one to believe that the expulsion of farm labor is growing, and that the city is not able to absorb this work force. The case of the migrant worker clearly shows that the absorption of this manpower, aside from being small, is conjunctural and seasonal. The general situation of the underprivileged strata is worsened further by the heavy drop in the real salary that has occurred since 1965, as the figures distributed by DIESSE (1970) show:

ond, the available data from censuses and from the Nationaı Research through Home Surveys (PNAD) do not concur. Even the censuses are organized according to different criteria, so that a strict comparison is not possible. Comparing census data with the PNAD information seems even more precarious, since the former deal directly with the population, and the latter with surveys. The criteria used in each Brazilian census have been different with regard to the categorization of the various occupational activities, in the computation or non-computation of domestic activities, and in the division of the country into regions. Under these circumstances, the collation of data permits only a rough idea of the evolution of the effective use of female labor power.

In 1872, when the country operated with a system of slave labor (already in advanced stages of deterioration), women made up 45.5 percent of the economically active population. Given the minute differentiation of the Brazilian economy of the time, the economically active women were heavily concentrated in agriculture (35 percent), and in domestic service (33 percent). About 20 percent were seamstresses, 5.3 percent were employed in the textile industry, and 6.7. percent in other activities. Even if the women employed in domestic services at the time were excluded, the participation of women in the economically active population of the country was still rather high, that is, 37.4 percent.

The participation remained practically the same until 1900, when it was 45.3 percent. There were changes then in the distribution of active women throughout the various occupations. At the turn of the century, 52.6 percent were in domestic service; 24.6 percent in agriculture; 14.2 per-

---

Development of the real salary (1958–1969), São Paulo

Average monthly salary (NCr$ –new cruzeiros)

Year	Nominal	Real
1958	8.54	8.54
1959	11.53	8.29
1960	15.86	8.67
1961	23.88	8.99
1962	36.79	9.36
1963	56.23	9.25
1964	121.20	9.61
1965	169.68	8.14
1966	220.58	6.88
1967	275.73	6.49
1968	344.66	6.51
1969	430.83	6.58

cent in the arts and in offices; 4.2 percent in manufacturing activities; and 4.4 percent in business and other activities. Taking the portion of the economically active female population engaged in domestic service as a point of reference, between 1872 and 1900 there was an intense process of expelling women from productive activities and even from commercial and parallel activities. In primary activities, 21.1 percent of the effective labor force was made up of women; while they represented 91.3 percent of the labor power employed in secondary activities. The almost exclusive existence of cloth factories was the factor responsible for the absolute predominance of women in secondary activities. The sectors of domestic service, the arts, and office work diverted a considerable portion of female labor from agriculture. So the situation of almost-equal male and female labor would not endure.

According to the 1920 census, if we exclude those persons who lived on outside incomes, those with undeclared professions, and those having no profession, female participation in the economically active population was reduced to 15.3 percent. Female participation in the area of primary economic activities was reduced to 9.4 percent; in the secondary area it fell to 27.9 percent; and in tertiary activities it fell to 22.2 percent. The war of 1914–1918 permitted an 83.3 percent increase of the working population over a 13 year period,[14] and promoted industrial growth through the wide utilization of female labor in secondary activities.

Although the percentage of female labor effectively employed rose slightly, from 15.3 percent in 1920 to 15.9 percent in 1940,[15] in relation to the total economically active population of the country this increase was not statistically significant. The proportion of women in secondary activities fell to 25.3 percent of the total of persons employed in this branch of the economy. Female participation in primary activities rose to 13.3 percent, and in the tertiary sector it increased only slightly to 22.7 percent. In secondary activities, women represented 22.2 percent of the workers aged 18 or over and 82.3 percent of house workers. Contrary to popular beliefs, the industrial growth of the thirties did not bring about a substantial relative increase in the use of the female labor force. Taking secondary activities exclusively, the female representation among the total of employed persons fell from 91.3 percent in 1900 to 27.9 percent

[14]   The number of laborers was 150,841 in 1907, and 275,512 in 1920. Of this last amount, 182,670 were men and 92,842 were women (*Resultados gerais do censo das industrias* 1924).
[15]   Since the 1940 census includes domestic and teaching activities in the same category, it is impossible to know how many women devoted themselves exclusively to domestic activities.

in 1920, and reached a mere 25.3 percent in 1940, despite the rapid growth of the industrial population in the thirties.

In the fifties, the domestic pattern for women would grow even further in Brazil. Within the category of unpaid domestic activities and student activities, in 1950 women represented 90.3 percent of the workers in a population 10 years of age or over. Their participation in direct economic activities fell to 14.7 percent in relation to the total number of workers. In 1940, women's participation in secondary activities fell again, while there was a substantial increase of female participation in tertiary activities. While the female participation in primary activities was 7.3 percent, it was 17.4 percent in secondary ones, and 32.2 percent in the teriary sector of the national economy. Of the total female population 10 years of age and over, only 10 percent took part in activities outside the home, 84.1 percent took part in domestic and school activities, and 5.9 percent were inactive. Of the entire population engaged in economic activities outside the home, women represented only 11.3 percent.

Due to the industrial growth that occurred between 1955 and 1960, the female representation in the economically active population of the country rose to 17.1 percent. However, the increase in female participation in secondary activities was negligible; the figure rose to 17.9 percent. In the tertiary sector it fell to 30.7 percent, while in primary activities there was a substantial rise to 10 percent. The industrial expansion of 1955–1960 diverted male labor from agriculture to urban activities, freeing occupations in the primary sector for women.

The 1970 census registers female participation in the economically active population at 21 percent. The following percentages reflect women's positions as workers at that time. Women represented 27 percent of the employed, 10 percent of autonomous workers (independents), 4.1 percent of the employers, and 24 percent of unpaid workers. In the first three categories combined, women represented 20 percent of the workers. Thus, the percentage of paid workers is smaller than that of unpaid workers. In the sector of primary activities, female participation was 9.7 percent, while the unpaid workers' figure rose to 24.7 percent. When the three categories are considered together, female participation fell to 6.5 percent. In industrial activities, women represented 12.2 percent of the workers, 12.1 percent of the total paid workers (employees, independents, and employers), and 24.7 percent of the unpaid workers. In the tertiary sector, women constituted 37.8 percent of the effective workers; the figure falls to 23.5 percent among unpaid workers, and rises to 38.3 percent for the total of the other three categories.

Even though there was a certain increase in female participation in the economically active population between 1960 and 1970, the figure remains rather low[16]: 50.5 percent of the population ten years of age or older were women; yet only 13 percent of this contingent were economically active, versus 36 percent of the men in the same group. The figure for male activity almost triples the female figure. Over 52.8 percent of the population fifteen years old and over were women, yet the figure for female activity was 15.7 percent, and the male figure, 43 percent.

The figures for the last forty years show a strong tendency toward the relative establishment of the woman's presence among effectively employed labor in the country.

The use of the potential labor force existing in the diverse modalities of the historical realization of the capitalist economic social formation is regulated by the demand for labor. This, in turn, is linked not only to the interest on invested capital, but also to the nature of the equipment in which a portion of the constant capital is rendered. As the organic composition of capital rises, work productivity undergoes so great an increase that only the expansion of the system and the growing extension of its reproduction can assure the maintenance and even the rise of the labor force demand. This is the crucial point in the differentiation between the "central" and the "peripheral" developments of capitalism. While the societies representing the first modality solve the problem of the growing difficulty of realizing surplus value through the ecological extension of the bases of its operation, and by the growing penetration of precapitalist economies, the societies of the second modality are penetrated from the outside by the capitalist mode of production. Thus, in the latter case the imbalance between the demand and supply of the labor force is sharper. Given their high rate of population growth and their low extension capacity, the "peripheral" societies generate an enormous excess in labor which live within the "peripheral" capitalist system, yet remain as suppliers for the labor force without attaining their incorporation into the system in a definite and stable way. The "periphery" of the international capitalist system presents a chronically weak labor force demand, which causes it to be known for excluding immense manpower reserves.

On the basis of these facts, it is obviously inaccurate to affirm that female participation in the economically active population rises with

[16]   The figures from the 1960 census refer to the resident population, while the 1940, 1950, and 1960 censuses refer to the population present in the country. Those who were seeking employment for the first time, when the 1970 census was made (September 1, 1970), were computed as being economically active. Those included in the economically active classification were: students, those retired or living on pensions, prisoners, invalids, those living on outside incomes, and those engaged in unpaid domestic activities.

the social and economic development. This statement is not valid, even within certain limits, except for "central" capitalist countries. With regard to the precapitalist modes of production, capitalism, even in its "central" achievements, absorbs a relative surplus amount of labor. If we consider only the capitalist mode of production, we can detect the existence of mechanisms capable of reducing the contingents of unemployed in its "central" realizations at the expense of raising the unemployment rate in its "peripheral" realizations. The populations of the societies where capitalist "peripheral" realizations are located are greater than those of societies where its "central" realizations occur. Thus the intensified inability of capitalism, as a system encompassing the members of many societies, to absorb the available labor force has become increasingly apparent.

In addition, certain results of the imbalance created in the "peripheral" capitalist areas are transferred by the working of imperialism to the capitalist "central" areas in a process for "internalizing" tensions produced outside the central areas' geo-political limits. An example of this phenomenon is found in the migration of relatively large numbers of Mexicans and Cubans to the United States, espcially to Florida and California. Because of the uncertainty, or the total absence of qualifications of this labor force, and the fact that it is foreign, having come from underdeveloped countries, their level of employment will be lower than that of the North Americans. These groups, then, constitute permanent focal points of tension, whose intensity the American government must control.

The marginalization of women from the occupational structure has been one of the means frequently used to reduce the number of male unemployed from these two underdeveloped countries. In the areas most affected by the large number of Cubans and Mexicans seeking employment, no attempt is made to disguise discrimination against women. In dealing with foreign women, the government department in charge of distributing working papers refuses them to those who are married, declaring, without even the suggestion of pretext, that since they have husbands to support them, they should leave the jobs to men. Working papers for married foreign women have been systematically denied, especially in the Miami area. Government power, as concerns the employer, has proceeded in the same manner with U.S. women. This example illustrates the contradictions of an economy which presents the need for expansion as an inherent trait, which at the same time permits the rise of the unemployment rate within its geo-political boundaries and increases unemployment in the "peripheral" areas, thus internalizing a portion of these unemployed or underemployed.

The balance of this contradiction is positive, however, for the countries where capitalism's "central" realizations are located. From this angle, it is correct to affirm that the economic-social development is accompanied by a growing utilization of the female labor force. Such an assertion is meaningful only in the present theoretical context, that is, when viewing the capitalist system from a market perspective, as a mode of production which is realized, partially or totally, in each of its constituent geopolitical units. On the other hand, this standpoint implies accepting the above statement within the "central" realizations of the capitalist mode of production as correct. In the final analysis, this statement is acceptable only if the possibilities for developing the "peripheral" areas of the world capitalist system are envisioned outside the system. Given the capitalist regime's unique manner of operation, and more specifically, its increasing difficulty in obtaining surplus value, there is no place for a hypothesis stating that, in a near or distant future, the societies in which capitalism's "peripheral" realizations occur today will reach development (when development is understood as a macro-structural type realization, toward which these societies lean).

If Brazil is successful in its attempt to establish itself as the leading Latin American nation, it will probably gain certain possibilties for reducing its unemployment rate. This does not mean that the path to economic-social development will be opened, but merely that Brazil will establish itself as the most important link in the chain of domination which is established between "central" capitalism, the United States, and "peripheral" capitalism, in this case the Latin American countries. In other words, using this hypothesis, Brazil would be the base for "central" capitalist operations, and consequently would gain certain opportunities to reduce its internal unemployment rate. But the probabilities of accomplishing this are still remote, since they depend directly on the success attained by the leading center of the international capitalist system in controlling social tensions which occur within its own geopolitical limits. And, notwithstanding capitalism's enormous malleability, there is evidence that the use of mechanisms to ease these tensions is reaching its maximum limit. In other words, the exploitation of this method is leading rapidly to a breaking point. Under these circumstances, it is difficult, if not impossible, for the absorption of the female labor force by the occupational structure of the capitalist societies to reach the same levels which characterize the utilization of male labor. This holds true with regard to capitalism's "central" or "peripheral" realizations, but especially in the latter case.

For the time being, the Brazilian woman continues to suffer a high

duction, and the socialization of the young, on one hand, and production, on the other. A flexible definition of feminine roles in the first three areas offers a wide margin for maneuvering immense contingents, integrated by women, according to the variation of the LABOR FORCE DEMAND. We are not stating that the woman's activities as sexual partner, reproducer, and socializer of the young interfere in any way with her roles as a worker. The concrete possibility of unlinking the practice of sexuality from the phenomenon of reproduction, in limiting and planning births, and of resorting to specialized child care institutions will unquestionably bring about certain changes in the life of the working woman. Through a variable rate in the labor force demand, production must ultimately direct the absorption of labor power from socially and politically fragile groups. Of these, quantitatively speaking, women constitute the most important contingent.

REFERENCES

BASSETT, MARION
1971 "Property of women," in *Women speaking*. Pittsburgh: KNOW.
BIRD, C.
1970 *Born Female*. New York: David McKay.
DIESSE
1970 *DIESSE in review* 4 (3). São Paulo.
FEELEY, D.
1973 The case for an equal rights amendment. *International Socialist Review* 4:6–9, 34–37.
FREVILLE, J.
1951 "La femme et le communisme," in *La Femme et le communisme*. Paris: Editions Sociales.
GUILBERT, M.
1966 *Les fonctions des femmes dans l'industrie*. Paris and The Hague: Mouton.
INSTITUT NATIONAL DE LA STATISTIQUE ET DES ÉTUDES ÉCONOMIQUES
1969 *Économie et statistiques*. INSEE 2, Paris.
INSTITUTE OF LIFE INSURANCE
1971 *Life insurance fact book*.
INTERNATIONAL LABOR ORGANIZATION
1967 *Annuaire des statistiques du travail*. Geneva: International Labor Organization.
1972 *Folha de São Paulo*. June 18.
LOPES, J. C., J. PASTORE
1971 *A mão de obra especializada na indústria*. São Paulo: IPE.
LUXEMBURG, R.
1951 *The accumulation of capital*. New Haven: Yale University Press.

MYRDAL, A., V. KLEIN
1962   *Women's two roles.* London: Routledge and Kegan Paul.
PRESIDENT'S COMMISSION ON THE STATUS OF WOMEN
1963   *American women.* Report of the President's Commission on the Status of Women.
Resultados gerais do çenso das industrias
1924   Río de Janeiro.
REVEL, J. F.
1970   *Without Marx or Jesus.* Garden City: Doubleday.
SASSOWER, D.
1970   *Women in the professions. Sixteen reports on the status of women in the professions.*
SCHIFFMEN, J.
1962   *Marital and family characteristics of workers.* U.S. Dept. of Labor, Bureau of Labor Statistics, Special Labor Force Report 26. Washington.
SULLEROT, E.
1968   *Histoire et sociologie du travail féminin.* Paris: Gonthier.
THIBERT, M.
1961   L'évolution du travail féminin. *Esprit* (May): 724–741.
UNITED NATIONS
1970   *Participación de las mujeres en el desarollo económico y social de sus países.* Geneva: United Nations.
UNITED STATES
1965   *Handbook on women workers.* Women's Bureau Bulletin 290, U.S. Department of Labor.
1968a   *American women 1963–1968.* Report of the Interdepartmental Committee on the Status of Women.
1968b   *Handbook on women workers.* Women's Bureau Bulletin 294, U.S. Department of Labor.
1970a   *Automation and women workers.* Women's Bureau, U.S. Department of Labor.
1970b   *Feminine labor (Mão-de-obra feminina).* Department of Labor and Administration.
1970c   *U.S. manpower in the 1970's.* Washington: U.S. Department of Labor.
1971a   *Equal pay.* WHD Publication 1320. U.S. Department of Labor.
1971b   *Fact sheet on the American family in poverty.* Women's Bureau, U.S. Department of Labor.
1971c   *The myth and the reality.* Women's Bureau, U.S. Department of Labor.
1971d   *Why women work.* Women's Bureau, U.S. Department of Labor.
1971e   *Women workers today.* Women's Bureau, U.S. Department of Labor.
n.d.a. *Current population reports.* U.S. Department of Commerce, Bureau of Census, P–60, Number 53.
n.d.b   *Interim revised projections of the population of the United States by age and sex: 1975 and 1980.* Current Population Reports. U.S. Bureau of Census.
URBAN, L.
1967   "Modicaficoes an estrutura economica do capitalismo de pos-guerre," in *Tendencias do capitalismo contemporaneo.* Edited by M. Dobb, et al, 85–109.

Women in Mexico

AURELIA GUADALUPE SÁNCHEZ and ANA E. DOMÍNGUEZ

Mexico is a country of many cultures so to talk about Mexican women as a whole is quite a complicated task. Any generalization could lead to a a misunderstanding of the whole, which is the sum of a wide variety of parts. This whole is a mosaic with pieces that differ because of ethnic characteristics, social classes, geographical regions, the degree of socio-economic-political integration into an urban society, and many other factors. This paper seeks to describe several representative bits of the mosaic as the Mexican women express and experience it.

Generalities about Mexican women are totally misleading. Often they are made by those who believe that a study of a village in the State of Morelos, such as Tepoztlán, is a model for all rural areas, but this is a distorted view of the typical rural Mexican. Nor do the studies about *colonias* surrounding Mexico City provide adequate material about the urban Mexican. Even worse is the assumption that the impaired image of the Mexican living in the northern border states is applicable to the whole.

In his book *The labyrinth of solitude*, Octavio Paz says: "The history of Mexico is the history of man seeking his parentage, his origins... He wants to go back beyond the catastrophe he suffered... to return to the center of that life from which he was separated one day..." (1961). Perhaps this is why some Indian communities have not been assimilated into the "national culture."

The national culture consists of a group of individual cultures which are related and interacting in a geographic area and which coexist under a centralized power, such as the Aztecs and Mayas who have become completely acculturated and who have almost disappeared. But the marginal cultures exist almost without any contact or relation to the rest of the country, as in the case of the Lacandones and Seris peoples.

There are also "indiocolonial" groups who have changed their language and dress but who have conserved their Indian institutions; and the rural mestizo communities, which are very conservative and far from being industrialized. In Mexico it is still possible to step back into prehistory and find people who live by hunting and gathering wild seeds and fruits. There are still 53 living indigenous languages which have, surprisingly, survived, besides the dozens of cultures which show a great internal vitality, and which are still determining Mexican history and appear to be far from final liquidation.

This panorama has made Mexico a "paradise" for the anthropologist, as well as for adventurers who often hide behind fellowhips and degrees and whose writings lack seriousness and scientific exactness. We know of anthropological and/or sociological studies where generalizations are made on the basis of observations of one person or very small groups, whose values and lifestyles are often misunderstood. They are written by foreigners who have spent some months touring around without the slightest change in their own cultural habits and who after a short stay have thought they penetrated the core of Mexican culture. They have not taken into consideration the fact that the persons they considered as objects of study and who know they are being studied protect themselves in various ways. For example, they may attempt to disorient the researcher.

On a visit to a small village of Mazahua Indians, some mestizos, and a few foreigners, it was noteworthy that no one invited the visitors into their homes, a Mexican sign of welcome. Instead they inquired with some mistrust "Have you come to study us?" Later it was discovered that their fear and their rejection of the idea of being objects of research were related to their frequent exposure to visitors representing foundations, universities, and/or linguistic institutes.

It is true that to be scientific one has to observe, analyze, and systematize, but a contribution to science loses its significance and honesty if it is used to gain personal prestige, or to obtain money from the publication of books, corporation fellowships, university degrees, etc. The only acceptable reason for making people an object of study even temporarily would be to make available the information for the benefit of those being studied so that it could be used to help them reach a better human status. This is particularly the case with women.

Some of the differences among Mexicans are closely related to the geographical variants throughout the country: jungle and desert, mountain and plateau, and an extensive seacoast. The corresponding climates, which are not always pleasantly tropical, often make survival difficult and do not provide the best conditions for food production. The 50 million inhabitants of Mexico live in a number of different ways. Economic development is unequal so that many people live in big, modern cities that compete with those of any part of the world, while others still live in the pretechnological era, in small villages scattered throughout miles of empty lands.

Mexico is a complex of cultures. There is a large indigenous population; approximately 50 percent of the total population are peasants; and a significant percentage is completely urban. Among the Indian groups, the Taharahumaral Indian in the north has a different culture from the Tzeltal in the south, or the Otomi in the central part. This is also true of the peasants and the urban populations living in different geographical areas. One has to be aware of this complexity in order to recognize the limitations of our knowledge about the realities of Mexico as given in statistics and figures. Nor can we forget that people are in process, not static, and are therefore changeable. Exact sciences have a contribution to make, but they study people who are capable of exercising creativity, freedom, responsibility, and criticism. This is why even census and statistical data have only a relative value, since the figures for 1970 will not show the reality for 1973 or 1975.

SOME HISTORICAL CULTURAL EVENTS

Most important to understand the social status of the Mexican women are historical events which have left very deep impressions.

At the time of the violent invasion of the Spanish conquerors, Indian communities were organized in many different ethnic groups under the imperialist rule of the Central Aztec kingdom. This was a very important fact, for it permitted cultural relationships and communication between the groups, and at the same time it enabled the Spanish to make use of the tensions created by the internal conflicts between the Aztec Empire and its tributary subjugated neighbors. It was so important that several authors think that Mexicans were conquered by themselves, since Cortes and his small number of troops could only have won with the help and alliances of dissident groups (Kirkpatrick 1958:55–56, 70).

Also Cortes used his mistress, Malintzin, an Indian woman, as an official translator, ambassador, and counsellor, because of her brilliant mind and wide knowledge of the Mexican reality of the time. In spite of all her good qualities, Mexicans consider Malintzin a traitor: her name is used as an insult. Was she voluntarily helping the conqueror;

was she given to him as a present; was she sold to him, as is still the custom of some Indian groups, to be used as a guide, informant, translator, as well as sexual object? She never was his official wife; for that role a lady was brought from Europe (Ramírez 1970:50).

Of course the conqueror was imitated, and many women were taken in the same way or simply violated. This was a very bitter experience that created anxiety and left a strong impact on a society where virginity and chastity were noble virtues for both man and woman. This historical fact, in the opinion of many authors, is one of the factors contributing to the degradation of the feminine imgage and to the fact that women have been considered intrinsically as traitors and unworthy of confidence (Ramírez 1970:48–51).

Judging by the social participation and the importance of Indian women at that time, it would seem that they were still in a matrilineal society or at least in a transitional stage, in contrast with the culture of the conquerors where the patriarchy was fully established. Many aspects of the life of Indian women help to support this theory.The new wife was taken by her mother or an older female family member to her husband's home where she was received and fed by her mother-in-law and welcomed by the female relatives of the boy who could send her back if they disapproved of her. Women had many religious and social duties related to the de- livery and reception of newborn babies. Most important, women devel- oped plant cultivation and animal domestication.

Some studies of matrilineal societies have shown that the important thing was to know "who the mother was" in terms of inheritance and group identification. Women had some economic power and their participation in government, justice, and war-making were very impor- tant. The most important virtues for women were strength, decency and honesty, religious devotion and piety, knowledge and skill in handi- crafts, chastity (important for both boys and girls), and modesty (Hell- bom 1967:247).

From the time of the Conquest to the present the dominant cultural patterns, both in rural and urban areas, have been patriarchal and male- oriented. The human dignity of women has seriously deteriorated because of the *macho* violations which have converted Mexican women into concubines and servants.

An important time in our history was 1910, when the people's insur- rection disrupted all social structures and opened up new possibilities for women. Their active participation was recorded in a number of songs and stories, but at the same time the most famous women soldiers also had to be very special lovers or the love objects of every one.

La Adelita, Juana Gallo, La Valentian, and many anonymous women, such as la Jesusa Palancares, (Poniatowska 1971:69) fought side by side with men. La Valentain, recently interviewed at the age of 79, lives alone and forgotten. She remembers how at 16, she decided to fight and went to the battlefront dressed as a man. After five months of service her sex was discovered and she was discharged because she was a woman (Leyzaola 1973:36–37).

This moment of history has been exploited in many ways by the Mexican movies and other mass media. For example, in the 1940's they created a different feminine image, no longer the very sad and suffering prostitute or the cabaret girl but the domineering female, the cold love-priestess who lends her body but never gives it. The myth was incarnated in Maria Félix, the female model who knows she is used as an erotic object, but whose weapon is her cold beauty. When the myth was enacted she was presented as the central figure of a folklorized Revolution in the role of a *guerrillera* soldier or as a general, a woman who lived with the soldiers in the battlefields. From silk and velvet dresses she changed to campaign boots, rifles, and bullet belts. Her language was crude and she insolently entered into every field traditionally reserved for men. However, she eventually surrendered herself to love, and then went back to "normalcy," to her traditional feminine role. Later, to continue as a movie star, this woman had to forget her "womanhood" and take on male characteristics, even outside her films (De La Colina 1973:34–35).

After the Revolution ended, around 1917, education for women became possible as a result of industrialization.

The machine began to take economic activity out of the home and into the factory, replacing the labor power of women and children especially in the textile industries. Though many women are leaving the home to work in factories, the traditional reaction is that they should ONLY work when there is a real economic need, e.g. with widows or some divorcees.

In our society it is now axiomatic that it is men who are to work outside of the home. At the beginning of the Industrial Revolution most men and women worked together cultivating the land, making handicrafts and sharing some of the domestic tasks. However, this was not seen as sufficient justification for women to accompany the men into industry.

WOMEN IN RURAL MEXICO

Ethnic Differences

THE INDIGENOUS RURAL WOMAN   Luis González, a Mexican anthropologist with the National Center for Indigenous Pastoral Care, lists four criteria for distinguishing the differences among rural women: somatic or physical; psychological; linguistic; and cultural (lifestyles, relationships, social organization, traditions).

According to the 1970 national census, which used only the linguistic criteria, there were 29 different indigenous groups in Mexico making up a total of 3,100,000 people. Using the four criteria listed above, there were at this time about sixty different groups totalling between 10 and 15 million people.

THE MESTIZO RURAL WOMAN   The mixing of races increased throughout the seventeenth century and then began to decrease. This resulted in a great variety of mestizo groups, depending on the degree of Iberian influence in an area and on the groups making up the mixtures. In addition, the Africans, brought in at a later period, also played their part in the racial mixture in some areas, and we cannot overlook the Anglo-Saxon influence in some parts of the country.

Cultural Differences

There are distinct cultural differences not only between indigenous groups, but also between groups of mestizos. The strongest prehispanic cultures in Mexico were concentrated in the central and southern regions, where the Spanish Conquest began. Its influence in the north came later and was of a lesser degree. Furthermore, in the north the indigenous groups were still nomads or semi-nomads and were also influenced by the Anglo-Saxon culture.

Social Differences

Social classes adopt different customs not only in the urban and rural settings, but from region to region. In some areas social classes are still determined by wealth, as for example, in Monterrey. In other areas, classes are determined by an "aristocratic lineage," as, for example, in Puebla. As a result of the Agrarian Reform, a new class appeared, the *ejidatarios*, the landowners who are the beneficiaries of the land reform. In many cases they have become the oppressors of the landless, the day laborer who works the land while the new owner rests or gets drunk. The wife of the new landowner is on a different level from the wife of the laborer, as in the *ejidos*, the former public lands, of Paso del Rio, Colima.

WOMEN AND WORK INSIDE AND OUTSIDE THE HOME IN PASO DEL RIO, COLIMA.

From January to October, 1971, a team made up of a social science graduate, two social workers, a teacher, and a secretary carried out a socioreligious survey in the *ejido* area of Paso del Rio, Colima. The rural men and women in Paso del Rio were interviewed on the question of work inside and outside of the home as part of research on the family which included man-woman relations, parent-child relations, extra-familial relations of the sexes, etc. ("Estudio socio-religioso de Paso del Rio" 1971:129–210). This is a community made up of four sub-communities: The collective *ejido* de Cofradia Juárez; the individual *ejido* of Periquillo; Rincón de López, an *ejido* in process of integration; and a community made up of small landowners, small merchants, employees, and laborers. The team defined communities as "groups conditioned by the norms and customs of a traditional society...." A traditional society is generally accepted as one which is structured on generalized Western sociocultural presuppositions (Díaz Guerrero, 1970, of the Autonomous National University of Mexico), which supports the image of man as strong, domineering, conquering, and of woman as dependent, conformist, routinized, timid.
It is a society in which to be a man is synonymous with being privileged, while to be a woman means to have a series of limitations which can only be overcome with the help of a man.

The team found that the women of Paso del Rio, especially those of Cofradia Juárez and Periquillo, were not happy with their social status at the time of the study.

Women and Work Outside the Home

The questionnaire included two questions to detect the attitudes of both men and women with respect to the activities of women inside the home and gainful employment outside the home.

Contrary to what might be expected, in Rincón de López, the group that we would expect to be the most traditional because it was the most isolated, the work of the women was accepted by a larger percentage than in Periquillo and Cofradia Juárez. In Periquillo 68.4 percent of the men were opposed to women working; in Cofradia Juárez, 64 percent;

and in Rincón de López, only 30.7 percent. As far as the women were concerned, the larger percentage of those who still thought that "women's place is in the home" were in Periquillo, with 16.7 percent; while in Cofradía Juárez it was 11.9 percent, and in Estación, only 4.2 percent. However in Rincón de López 100 percent of the women were in favor of women working.

Favorable opinions about women working do not necessarily indicate ideas favoring some degree of liberation. The reason given most often by both men and women for accepting the work of women outside the home is the need for financial help in the home. Women's work becomes the answer to a need. If the need did not exist she would not have to work, according to the male response of 4 percent in Cofradía Juárez, of 7.17 percent in Rincón de López, and of 5.9 percent of Estación. These men were willing to accept the work of woman only if she were single, or a widow, or if her husband were ill.

Only 10.5 percent, 15.4 percent and 5.9 percent of the men in Periquillo, Rincón de López, and Estación would leave some initiative to women in the decision to work so that they could buy some personal things for themselves. The idea that women might dispose of their own money is still unacceptable to the great majority of the population: 16.7 percent and 14.3 percent of the women in Periquillo and Rincón de López gave this same response.

Of the 88.1 percent of the women of Cofradía Juárez who agreed that women should work outside the home, 42% gave an interesting reason: "So that the woman would be valued for her own self." Woman wants to be valued for what she is, she wants to occupy the place in the home and in society which rightfully belongs to her, she wants to move from being an OBJECT to being a SUBJECT.

This desire to be valued for her own self would indicate that at the present this is not the case. One of the reasons given by men for women not working was: "She is not capable." If she is not considered capable, can she be given a place in the family, in society?

A small percentage of men admit that "every human being should work." This response was also given by 2.4. percent of the women in Cofradía Juárez. In Rincón de López a response was given that did not appear in the other communities — the conceding of a right: "Women have the right to earn money." This response was given by 15.4 percent of the men, but curiously by no woman.

In Estación, possibly because of the influence from the city of Tecomán, a response was made which it would be difficult to conceive of in Periquillo and Cofradía Juárez, and perhaps a bit easier to understand in Rincón de López, "Woman has the right to progress." This reply was given by 25 percent of the women but only 5.9 percent of the men.

Why Don't Women Work Outside the Home?

All the women who do not accept the idea of women working give as their only reason: "Women should be in the home." Among the men, the majority gave this reason and the reason that "Women are not capable of working."

Four percent of the men of Cofradía Juárez said that "Woman was born for the kitchen." Of the men of Pariquillo 10.5 percent and of Rincón de López 15.4 percent do not accept the idea of women working because "It is not decent" for a woman to work. They want her to go out of the home "clean": these are the exact words used. Why should work defile a woman while it ennobles a man? Because, according to the traditional family stereotypes, woman must be submissive and dependent because she is inferior to man. Man must protect her because she is weak and cannot defend herself. The women of Paso del Rio, at least a good percentage of them, did not accept this role. They wanted not only to have more, but to be more.

Women and Work in the Home

According to a large percentage of the population, women should be in the home. But what should she do in it? Much has been said about men and women sharing in the various activities of the family. How was this viewed in Paso del Rio?

The family is considered "the socializing group." The advancement of its members with a view to their integration in the society depends largely on the family. The internal organization of the family may have different characteristics according to the concept it has of the roles of men and women and children. The traditional family is characterized by a complete separation of the work which the man and the woman do in the bosom of the family, while in the modern family there tends to be a sharing of the work by all.

A question was included in the study to see if the man collaborated in the domestic duties of the home or if he held them in contempt, considering them as "woman's work." In Cofradía Juárez the larger percentage of the men listed household tasks as "woman's work," but

40.5 percent of the women wanted the men to help take care of the children at least. It was here that there was the largest number of children per family. Among the most conservative women on this point were those of Rincón de López. This was contrary to what was expected, since 100 percent of them accepted the fact that women may work outside the home.

Household tasks, according to traditional standards, are predominantly woman's responsibility. The fact that a group of men at least accepted the idea of sharing in this work is a sign of some lessening of the contempt in which women are held.

The tensions which are provoked by the traditional thinking about women and the present social evolution demand that women have a new consciousness of their status and that society assume responsibility for giving them their rightful place. It is obvious from the studies that the education of rural women must be revised, and the cooperation of all will be necessary if they are to be stimulated to assume their responsibilities with a new sense of involvement. A much greater preparation is needed than that which sufficed in a traditional society, for example, in the concept of motherhood, which has been one of the most important factors in creating a distorted concept of the meaning of being a woman. If the rural woman in particular is not prepared for greater social cooperation she runs the risk of being enslaved rather than liberated, by a consumer society in which human values count for little.

The Urban Context

The main urban centers are Monterrey and Chihuahua in the north; Guadalajara and Morelia on the Pacific coast; Jalapa, Veracruz, and Merida on the Gulf coast; Puebla, San Luis, and Toluca in the Central part; and the macropolis, Mexico City.

Several problems related to our underdevelopment are easily seen in population concentration. This is a result of the growing rural migration to urban centers that are thought of as a paradise of possiblities and a magic panacea for every social, economic, and political problem. Of course the reality is quite different. This internal migration is making cities into typical underdeveloped centers. Angela Alessio Robles (Alessi Robles), an engineer working for the urban planning office of the Mexico City government recently wrote that our urbanization process shows exactly the opposite effects to those in industrialized countries:

1. Accelerated population growth due to rural migration creates mar-

ginal groups, similar to the prehistoric nomads, which become sort of "modern urban hunters."

2. The migration rate is so high that instead of increased urbanization, what actually results is a "ruralization of the big city."

3. Housing and living space are minimal and lead to promiscuity and other social problems. According to the last census, due to the influence of the consumer society, meager economic resources are invested in buying superfluous apparatus and clothes rather than in housing improvement or family savings.

4. Health and sanitary agencies are insufficient to prevent growing pollution and conditions for widespread epidemics.

How does this kind of urbanization, or city ruralization, affect women? In the first place internal migration creates transitional "rural-urban" groups in the multiplying misery belts around cities. It makes Mexican suburbia the poorest and most marginated areas. Here the women are servants, factory workers, and very often prostitutes.

Birth rates have been more or less constant during the last 40 years, but there is a decrease in the number of young women and an increase in older women. On the other hand, although the natural rural growth has been greater than the natural urban growth, internal migration has contributed to an unnatural urban growth, three to four times greater than the rural growth. This migration consists mainly of young people, of whom a majority are women.

Migration affects the labor market, and although Mexico is not a fully industrialized country, it is suffering all the illnesses of one and has a disproportionately large working force.

A recent study (*Perfil de México en 1980* [1972] of the Autonomous University of Mexico) of social research analyzed the occupational margination by sex in the working population from 21 to 60 years of age as seen in Table 1.

The women are mostly employed in services and their salaries are always lower than men's, very often for the same kind of work, and sometimes for harder work. This makes women the most marginal of the marginal. Recent studies show that in migrant groups only 27 percent of the men, but 64 percent of the women are marginals.

They belong to a "culture of silence," a situation in which one is not allowed to express an opinion, creating auto-repression. They are modern slaves who are given the hardest jobs that nobody else will do. They are fatalists ("everything we suffer is God's will"), personally insecure, with inferiority complexes and submissive attitudes. All of this prevents them from making decisions even about their own bodies and lives.

Table 1.   Occupation by Sexes

Marginal occupational groups are (1) street vendors; (2) non-qualified workers in service; (3) unskilled factory workers; (4) unskilled construction workers; (5) agricultural workers.

Group	1	2	3	4	5
Percent men	59.8	28.2	78.3	100	94.2
Percent women	40.2	71.8	21.7	0.0	5.8

Monthly income (in Mexican pesos)

Men	1251.00	1012.00	1109.00	810.00
Women	907.00	446.00	881.00	

Almost 70 percent of Mexican women are living this way.

Attitudes Towards The Work of Women in Urban Areas

In her contribution to the book, *Women that speak out*, Guadalupe Zentina comments about her studies on married women's work (1971: 165):

Out of a group of working women she found that the motivation for working for 62 percent was economic, and for some 29 percent it was also economic but related to a "better" education for children. Only 2 percent saw work as a means of increasing their personal growth. There is also a correlation between work motivation and education: 13.8 percent of the group had no formal schooling, 32.8 percent had not finished elementary school, and only 5.1 percent had attended universities.

Since it is assumed that married women should not work, it follows that they will become economically unproductive and dependent. Only under special circumstances are they allowed to work. In 1968, 20 percent of the married women were employed, mainly in services. Traditionally the role of the woman has been related almost exclusively to her role as a mother. Maternity functions are still considered most important, so most of her productive life is dedicated to child birth and care. Thus factories, banks, and other employing agencies are reluctant to hire married women. The resulting economic dependence creates extreme subordination, psychologically and socially.

Several studies in Mexico City by a team of IMES and a group of social workers in 1970 showed that 23 percent of the men accepted the fact that their wives could work in the following occupations: 40 percent, as a dressmaker; 31.4 percent, as a servant; 8.5 percent as a factory worker; 6 percent, as a nurse. The acceptance of dressmaking had to do with the fact that the wife would not have to go out and could still take care of everything at home (Instituto Mexicano de Estudios Sociales 1969).

One of the cultural taboos against women working is the belief that manhood is proved by the ability to earn the money to meet the family needs. If the man is not able to earn a sufficient income or if he is unwilling to give her all he makes, the wife must adapt or make "magic economics" with any amount she receives, even if it means a miserable survival.

A study in Monterrey showed that 87 percent of the women workers were single; 3.6 percent, single mothers; 3.6 percent, widows or divorced, and only 2.3 percent were married (Estudio Socio-religioso de Ntra. Sra. de Lourdes, 1970). Most of these working women are part of the migrant population and suffer very severe culture shock in the cities, especially when they come from Indian groups.

Indian women are accustomed to working with their husbands in agricultural tasks. However, in non-rural areas women are excluded from sharing the work of their husbands, especially in developed areas using machines.

When women are rejected as workers, they are confined at home with their dependent children and the tedious slavery of housework. This means that it is easier for them to be reached by consumer advertising through radio and television. It is painful to see how the mass media reinforce and perpetuate old cultural patterns which limit women's participation in collective production and life. In a consumer society women have a most important role but only as consumers who want all the items which the producers advertise.

According to the 1970 census, out of 15 million working women (12 to 60 years old) twelve and a half million are housemaids. Young girls learn their duties through a rather hard "training"; without previous preparation they are expected to learn the use of electrical aparatus when they come from places where there is no electricity. They are poorly paid and badly exploited. There is no time limit on their work in the evening and they must be ready to begin again at six in the morning. They must take care of the children and do the cooking and all the work in the house. If, after some time, the girl isn't able to do everything, she may be sent away without notice. This causes a tremendous trauma for most of them. They find themselves in the hostile environment of the big cities without knowing how to deal with it. Many of these girls end up in prostitution either because of ignorance and naiveté or because they aren't able to make a living any other way.

The general attitude towards women, the cultural shock experienced by girls coming to the cities, their lack of preparation for technical activities, and general unemployment, very often result in their being pushed into prostitution, which is frequently entered as the last recourse for survival.

A study made in 1970 in one of the Mexican border cities, which are some of the most important prostitution markets, shows that 90 percent of a group of five thousand women came from rural areas or small cities. They are exploited mainly by American men who cross the border any time they wish. This situation is repeated in Ciudad Juárez, Tijuana, Reynosa, Matamoros, and other places.

Middle-class women are slightly better off, but in 1970 they made up only about 9.5 percent of the total population and their numbers seem to be decreasing.

Women are expected to leave their jobs when they get married so they can devote all their time to the house and children. All of this means a great change in their economic possibilities and personal development. This is true with slight variations for every social group from the popular sector to the highest classes. They are always economically, psychologically, and emotionally dependent. The traditional image of the woman in urban areas is that of the mother, a woman with as many children as possible, loving and self-denying, ready to give everything without getting anything but the recognition of being a good wife and, above all, a model as a mother.

FINAL CONSIDERATIONS

For millennia woman has been enslaved, exploited, or at least marginated and subordinated by man. Man has appropriated for himself the ruler's scepter, the center of the world, and the prerogative of giving it form, organizing it, orienting it. Woman has had to accept the masculine patterns of thought and action, in the family, in education, and in recreation, as well as in politics, in the economy, and even in religion. Women have had to live by masculine standards in abnegation and fidelity, the qualities which man has "generously" assigned to woman as the exclusive privilege of being feminine.

In order to maintain the many forms of slavery or exploitation, of subordination or margination, man has invented for woman a series of qualties, all of which are a counterbalance for his faults and vices. Woman must be self-denying so that man can be irrational; chaste and faithful, to make up for his degeneracy and infidelity; tender and gentle, so that he can behave like a beast. Man has also created the myth of the weaker sex without which the other myth, the myth of the stronger sex which implies "supremacy," would not be possible.

But woman no longer moves only in the closed circle of her family. Her home is no longer the four walls of a house. It is the street culture, public life. Woman should conscientiously contribute to the development of her country, but this will require a new mentality, a change for which woman herself is not prepared.

A woman economist, former Director of the School of Economics at the Autonomous University of Mexico recently wrote:

Neither biology nor tradition can impose procreation on women as their only possible destiny. Today women combine these essential functions with economic, political, and social tasks of their choice which permit the development of their potentialities as human beings and their contribution through a full giving of themselves (Navarrete 1969:35, 104).

The fulfillment of woman does not come only with her participation in the decision-making process at all levels, although that is essential. It does not have to do so much with HAVING MORE as with BEING MORE. The fulfillment of woman will come when she is free, when women and men are equal, and when they make effective use of their freedom for the whole of society.

REFERENCES

ALESSIO ROBLES, ANGELA
1973 "*Urbe típica del subdesarrollo.*" *Excelsior.* July 18. Mexico.
BENÍTEZ, FERNANDO
1972 *Los Indios de México.* Editorial Era.
DE LA COLINA, JOSÉ
1973 "Aventuras y tribulaciones del cine mexicano." *Revista de Revistas.* July 25. México.
DÍAZ GUARRERO, ROGELIO
1970 *Estudios de psicología del mexicano* (reprinted edition). Editorial Trillas.
ELU DE LEÑERO, MA. DEL CARMEN
1969 *Hacia dónde va la mujer mexicana.* Instituto Mexicano de Estudios Sociales.
Estudio socio-religioso de Ntra. Sra. de Lourdes
1970 Unpublished private study. Monterrey, Nuevo Leon, Mexico.
Estudio socio-religioso de Paso del Río
1971 Unpublished private study. Colima, Mexico.

HELLBOM, ANNA BRITTA
1967   *La participación cultural de las mujeres indias y mestizas en el México precortesiano y postrevolucionario.* Stockolm: The Ethnolographical Museum.

INSTITUTO MEXICANO DE ESTUDIOS SOCIALES
1969   "Estudio sociográfico de la colonia Cailos, Cd. México." Unpublished mimeograph.

KIRKPATRICK, F. A.
1958   *Los conquistadores españoles* (sixth edition). Espasa Calpe. Argentina.

LEYZAOLA, MARGARITA
1973   "Valentina, Valentina..." *Revista de Revistas.* July 18. Mexico.

MORA, ANTONIA
1973   *Del oficio* Mexico: Editorial Samo S.A.

NAVARRETE, IFIGENIA
1969   *La mujer y los derechos sociales.* México: Ediciones Oasis.

PARROQUIA AGUILAS
1970   "Estudio sociográfico." Mexico: Instituto Mexicano de Estudios Sociales. Unpublished manuscript.

PAZ, OCTAVIO
1961   *The labyrinth of solitude.* New York: Grove Press.
Perfil de México en 1980
1972   Volumes two and three. Mexico: Editorial Siglo XXI.

PONIATOWSKA, ELENA
1971   *Hasta no verte Jesús mío* (seventh edition). México: Editorial Era.

POZAS, RICARDO, ISABEL H. POZAS
1971   *Los indios en las clases sociales de México.* Mexico: Editorial Siglo XXI.

RAMÍREZ, SANTIAGO
1970   *El mexicano, psicología de sus motivaciones* (sixth edition). México: Editorial pax.

RAMOS, SAMUEL
1962   *Profile of man and culture in Mexico.* University of Texas Press.

ROJAS AVENDAÑE, MARIO
1973   "Los mercados de sirvientas en la región de los Tuxtlas, Ver." July 22. Mexico: Excelsior.

ZETINA, GUADALUPE
1971   *Mujeres que hablan.* Mexico: IMES.

The Mayan Woman
and Change

M. L. ELMENDORF

For the past half century or more, anthropologists, economists, sociologists, psychologists, and others have been examining peasant societies
in an effort to arrive at satisfactory theories of development, progress,
and modernization. All too rarely, however, have their studies taken into
account the roles of women in these processes. In most of the studies
cited above, the word "peasant" — even though itself of neutral gender —
usually implies a male. Women peasants appear in the literature as sex
partners of the men, as mothers of the children or as helpers, rarely if
ever as individuals with hopes, abilities, and functions of their own in the
society. As Beverly Chiñas said:

Up to now, one might accurately state, I think, that ethnology has been rather
completely male-oriented and male-dominated, making the cross-cultural investigation of women's roles and how these may interrelate with, affect,
influence, and be influenced by the total system, difficult (Chiñas 1971: 22).

In a time of unprecedented change throughout the world, peasant
societies are increasingly impinged upon by the "necessities" of progress.
It is crucial to learn about the roles which women have played and will
play as their societies face change. But, in considering women's potential
role in any society, we must first understand what her current or actual
role is. As Elise Boulding says in a recent unpublished paper, "The social
invisibility of women makes it difficult to document their roles in any
society, in whatever stage of industrialization" (Boulding 1970: 1).

How do the roles of women change? Where and how might one find
new evidence about the relationships of these roles to change, either as
the women effected change or were affected by it? This study will focus
on a single group of peasant women who are living in a society which has

been undergoing change and which faces still more drastic modernization. It will undertake a direct investigation of the nature of women's roles as it is perceived by themselves, by others in their community, and by the writer, a trained woman observer who herself becomes part of the process she is studying by assuming the role of "activist observer."

In the interests of economy of effort, as well as accuracy of findings, I decided that the ideal community would be one which had been thoroughly studied by competent scholars over a relatively long period of time, for which present data could be effectively integrated into preceding data, so that the nature and extent of change could be measured, its effects studied, and the role of women in the whole process examined in historical perspective.

I wanted very much to find out if the beauty and the rhythm, the enjoyment and the dignity which I had felt in my years of working with Mexican peasant women, was only due to sentimentality on my part. Were my eyes really as blinded, as Oscar Lewis and some of my friends once felt? Was I really caught into dignifying the "noble savage?" Or was there something nearer the truth than the "culture of poverty" which Oscar Lewis has so extensively described? Were all the women morose, timid, and male-dominated, as he had projected them? Was a traditional society more "life-centered" than a *mestizo* [mixed Indian-Spanish] community? Were the women there more satisfied with their lives? Was work more "spiritually satisfying" than in the *mestizo* village where Erich Fromm and Michael Maccoby found that "work is seen by all but the most productive individuals as a necessary evil and as a means for gain" (1970: 120). In this study of *Social character in a Mexican village*, they have suggested:

Both in medieval society and among the Mayan peasants described by Redfield, work is meant to be spiritually satisfying. The art, folklore and handicrafts of both the Mayan and the medieval peasant suggest a higher level of productiveness and a greater enjoyment of life than in the village we have studied (Fromm and Maccoby 1970: 120).

In my decade of fieldwork I had spent many days and nights visiting isolated villages of all kinds, and working closely with the community leaders, men and women. However, I had always been an outsider, a community development expert, a change agent, nearly always within an operational framework. Would I see things differently if I lived in a traditional subsistence agricultural village? If possible, I wanted to find this out as it was felt by the people who were living it, and not by the ones of us who were observing it. Being a small Mayan village of about one hundred families, Chan Kom thus filled two of my requirements — excel-

lent previous studies over a long period of time and broad agreement as
to the traditional nature of its culture. It was also facing a time of serious
change, in connection with the building of a new highway. I decided to
concentrate on the women of one of the leading families in Chan Kom.
I did not want to use a large questionnaire, or do a macro-study. I wanted
to have the women share their life-stories with me.

During my early talks with these women I asked each if she would like
to have a taped interview answering some questions I was interested in.
All of them agreed. For these first interviews I used selected parts of the
revised Fromm-Maccoby questionnaire, adding specific questions which
would give information on individuation covering the nine variables
Boulding used: age of marriage; freedom of marriage choice; property
rights; inheritance rights; divorce rights; range of movement from hearth;
handler of money and/or food provider; freedom to be traders and/or
business women; tribal positions of authority.

I was especially interested in knowing how the women felt about themselves, how much individuation or individualism in the Riesman and
Fromm sense they had and felt that they had. I wanted to learn their
capacity to discover and realize themselves as they lived and were. Mind-
ful of Fromm's statement that this type of "freedom and individualism is
bound up with economic and social changes that will permit the individual
to become free in terms of realization of self" (Fromm 1946: 234), I
wondered how much the people of Chan Kom might lose or gain with the
opening of the new road.

During my first visit the women seemed shy, perhaps embarrassed by
my questions relating to sex and personal life. On my second visit, however, they had grown to trust me and were eager to talk. It seemed that
all of the pent-up emotions and questions came pouring out of them. I
was someone with whom they could talk about their concerns. I could
hardly stop them to ask questions of my own.

I came into Chan Kom as a foreigner. I wanted to avoid imposing
views from an alien culture, but I found that I could not remain a completely passive observer. It seemed extremely important to understand
and be sensitive to the local situation in order to work there in a culturally
non-polluting, but human, way. I agree very much with Freire, who says:

...to impose one ideology or prove a theory is another form of cultural oppression, and "creative dialogue between researcher and object-subject turns into a
process of mutual learning (Freire 1971).

Partly because of these convictions, and partly because I found that I
learned most when I let the women lead the conversation, I put aside my

original research design, including the carefully translated questionnaires, the schedules, the collection of data for comparison and statistical analysis. I decided instead to gather the substance of my study from "creative dialogues" (see Elmendorf 1972).

I made five separate field trips to Chan Kom between March, 1971 and July, 1972, averaging ten days each. I talked at length with the wife, daughters, and daughters-in-law of one of the leaders of the community. It was through these women and their networks of friends that I have been able to get some feeling for the life of the Mayan woman. They range in age from seventeen to sixty-five. In fact, with children and grand-children, grandmothers and aunts, cousins and friends, I reached many other age groups.

Let me introduce briefly each of these women whom I came to know so well, and tell you how I got to know them and their friends as I tried to understand their roles in daily life as they faced potentially imminent change.

First there was Luz, wife of the village leader. She was not only my host-ess, but also my guide to the past, particularly in regard to Mayan rituals such as the *loh casa* [ceremonial cleansing of a new thatched hut] (see Redfield and Villa 1934: 146) on my first night there, and on later visits, the handwashing ceremony and the *Pib* [ceremonial cooking in an earth oven]. She is *curandera* [healer] for Chan Kom and neighboring *rancherías* [small ranches]. If I got up early enough in the morning I could watch her having office hours in the kitchen, giving different kinds of herbal medi-cines. Luz was my first introduction to the rhythm of life in Chan Kom — she is up with the sun, and seems to pray as it sets. She is a key figure in Chan Kom, and not just because of her status as Don Trini's wife.

As we talked we were joined in the kitchen by a lovely looking young woman. "This is Ana, the wife of my son Jorge, who eats with us but lives on the corner where the *nixtamal* [corn-grinding mill] is." Ana is twenty-four, and runs one of the four *molinos* [mills] in town, a key position. She has more time for this than most women because she has only one child. She is intelligent about business matters, and also sells people the right to use her well, fruit and vegetables, sewing, and so forth. I see her as natu-rally beautiful; she is quiet and very domestic, vain and independent. She is at once child-like and astute. She says she sees no threat in moderniza-tion, but some of her dreams can be interpreted as showing fear. As she moved through stages of cure from *h-men* [shaman, or Mayan priest] to the herbalist, and finally to the doctor in town, she seemed a transitional figure. It was she who shared her dreams so freely with me, and who, by dreaming of me, followed my direction to the clinic to see the doctor. She is ambitious for her little son and seeks outside contacts because of him.

As I watched Ana and Luz making more tortillas and ate my beans and eggs, a very different looking woman came in — taller, heavier, and dressed in modern clothes. This was Flora, the wife of Antonio whom I had just met, and the mother of all the other children who seemed to flow in and out of the hut. She sat down with a handsome baby nursing at her breast and an older baby leaning against her, and joined the other two making tortillas. She, her husband, and their six children, three of whom are loaned to relatives, are interwoven in the network — and will, I predict, be the earliest marginal family, lost between tradition and urbanization.

While we talked, first Antonio joined me at the table, then Jorge, and finally Don Trini. There seemed to be no specific time or order for their meal that I could observe, but the making of tortillas went on for several hours during which all of the extended family were fed, with the women eating last around the hearth where they had fed the children.

Just before sunset the children and adults started appearing, all looking well-scrubbed. Seeing Ana come back fresh, obviously from a bath, I suddenly felt tired and dusty and asked if I might have a bath too. Doña Luz took me ceremoniously across the plaza to the house of Gabriela, Don Trini's daughter. She said that this house had a "bathroom which would be better" for me. Gabriela became another key person in my understanding of Chan Kom, as the only widow in the village that I got to know well. Don Trini had forced her to marry her first cousin, who died later, and unlike most of the other widows in the village, she had never remarried. Gabriela and the others in the village believe that her husband's death was the punishment for marrying so close in the family. In spite of having extensive property, her family seems to be one of the poorest in the village. Her sons work as day laborers for relatives, painting and building walls. Everything which she owns — her house and her farm land — were given to her by her husband's father. Although as a widow she has a right to *ejido* [communal] property, she has not claimed a share, nor have her sons. Don Trinidad, as Comisario Ejidal, has done nothing to help her. She works her own *milpa* [cornfield] "like a man," the others say. Her sons and daughters help and they raise bees, too, and sell the honey.

Later we went to the corner store, run by Don Trini's son, Eduardo, with a great deal of help from his seventeen-year-old daughter, Felicia. Amparo, Eduardo's wife, bakes bread professionally with the help of her daughters. This is an extremely close, tightly knit family; they think of themselves as a cooperative. The family is very literate, in contrast to the others in the village, and Amparo wants each of her daughters to have a profession. In fact, they may go to live with their aunt in Mérida in order to learn. She is extremely religious; she has a beautiful shrine to Fátima in her home and is close to the priest. As a mother of eight, Amparo is always busy, but never frantic; warm and adaptable, she is a strong personality.

Then Don Trini took me to meet another son, Alvaro, who is mayor of Chan Kom for the third time. He is married to Victoria, who, I later found out, was a sister of both Amparo and Flora. She is a hearty, vigorous person who loves sewing and works almost compulsively. She is quick-tempered and bossy, but she has a good sense of humor and enormous curiosity. She considers herself an artist because of the intricate designs she weaves into her *huipiles* [shifts], and indeed she does beautiful work. Victoria and Alvaro have no living children of their own, but have two sons of Flora's living with them. On my second visit Victoria invited me to live in her upstairs room after she accepted me as a fellow artist when she saw me sketching the houses on the square.

From then on during my field trips to Chan Kom I lived as a member of an extended family; sleeping in my hammock in a vacant room at Victoria's; eating in Luz's community kitchen with Flora and her children; doing my laundry in a hollow log near Ana's well; having my daily bath, which is practically a ceremony there, at Gabriela's; and buying the few things I needed from Felicia. I found a natural living network in which I moved without plan from one part of the day to another — without appointments, without timing, but still without feeling that I had disturbed the lovely rhythm which I felt was such a real part of their lives. When they would see me coming they would know what framework I was coming in, for what need.

Now my network included a key family on each of the four sides of the village square, and I joined the parade of people crossing and recrossing this commons. Soon I had met the other children of Don Trini and their households. First was Anita, the second wife of Demetrio, Don Trinidad's oldest son. My first impression of Anita was that she was aggressive; also, her children seemed to be less well-cared for than the others I saw. As I got to know her better, it seemed to me that this was a reflection of her attitudes toward many things, that she was just easy-going, and wanted her children to feel free and happy. She would let them run around unkempt, throwing pebbles, playing in the mud. She liked them to dress as they pleased or not dress at all. She herself is as unselfconscious as her children. She is talkative, exuberant, and much less reserved than the other women.

And then there was Marta, another daughter of Don Trini, who was living in a grass hut on a side street. She is fat, happy, and has an earthy, almost raucous laugh. "My father made me get married when I was just thirteen. I was in tears because I was afraid to leave my mother. I didn't know the boy well, but now I love my husband very much. I wouldn't trade him for anyone," she said. She told me that Mayan women have it easy compared to the men — they get to stay in the cool houses with their children, swinging in their hammocks and sewing. Her husband raises corn in the ancient slash-burn method, still using a planting stick. She and the children help him in the fields. Their front room was piled high with corn when I stopped by in November, and I was shown the fullness of the ears, the beauty of the grain. It was like a flower arrangement.

But we wouldn't have the family picture complete unless we included Beatriz, the oldest daughter of Don Trinidad who married one of the young Mayans who had worked with Morley on the original excavation at Chichén Itzá. When I called on her in her modern home in Mérida, the capital of Yucatán, after making an appointment by telephone, I was very curious. How had she changed? Had she rejected the past after leaving Chan Kom? Even though she was in city clothes I could see a strong family resemblance; and as we talked, there was great warmth in her voice as she spoke of her family and her old home. "I married when I was just seventeen. My father arranged everything, but I have been very happy. My daughters married much later than I did, though, one at twenty-one and one at twenty-five. And they chose their own husbands. I am happy here, but I still like to go back to Chan Kom." We talked for a long time, and I came to the conclusion that, as I had been told in the village, this was truly a half-way station between the village and city.

Although not a close member of the extended family group on which I was concentrating, Berta was drawn to my attention because she is the first and only female member of the town council. Later I learned her father was Don Trinidad's half-brother who had Castillianzied his name. Her husband, Juan, the town clerk, spoke proudly of her to me and invited me to interview her. I was immediately struck by how different their home was in comparison to the other homes in Chan Kom. It seemed to belong to another part of Mexico — *mestizo* Mexican, not Mayan. They actually cooked in the masonry house, not in a grass hut out back where nearly everyone else prepared their meals. She served me lemonade in a real glass rather in the *jícara* [gourd container]. Berta and her family wore modern clothes also, dresses rather than *huipiles*, factory made trousers, and plastic shoes. Why such a difference, I wondered. I began to find answers to my questions. Her father had been a member of the first Rural Cultural Mission to come to Chan Kom, and many of her ideas and attitudes were greatly influenced by him. When we began our discussions, I had asked that the children leave so we might talk privately. But when Berta told me that her greatest pleasure was in having the whole family together, learning and sharing, I immediately asked that they come back in. They returned, quietly but eagerly, and all pulled their chairs up close to hear the conversation. They are quite industrious. Even the little four-year-old boy was busy making henequen *margaritas* [daisies] on a frame while he listened to us talk. Berta was very proud that theirs was the only family in Chan Kom who sent their children away to a good school in Mérida. Other families, including Don Trini's, I had learned, actually prevented their children from leaving if they wanted to study somewhere else. Berta said all her children were doing well in school, and her greatest wish for them all was to get a good education so that they could get good jobs. We spoke also of her unique position as the town council secretary. She also helps her husband with his job as *registro civil* [town clerk] and is capable of taking over for him when he leaves town. "I have a key to the office," she told me, smiling. On one occasion, however, I noticed that the other men on the council had perhaps not totally accepted her. There was an important meeting on the arrival of the governor going on one day, and I noticed that Berta wasn't there. "That's right, she should be here," said one member. Had she been forgotten? Had she been left out on purpose? Which and why? And during the state governor's visit she was not sitting at the table with the rest of the committee members, even though the new women teachers, who had been in town less than a week, were invited. Instead she was helping the other women prepare the food. I asked her about this later. "When the governor came back to thank us, I told him I was the secretary of the council, and he congratulated me!"

Another woman who impressed me greatly as a key figure in Chan Kom is Concepción, the midwife who is married to Ramón, the bonesetter of the village. She is also sister of the local *h-men* [shaman and priest] and their father was a shaman before he died. At Luz's invitation, I had attended the *Pib*, the handwashing, and other Mayan ceremonies at Concepcion's house. As she spoke only Mayan, my interview with her was conducted through her eldest son. I originally asked that a daughter translate for us, but Concepción smiled and said that her son would do. "He helped his wife when their two children were born, as do most Mayan fathers," she added. Concepción told me that no one had taught her to be a midwife, not even as a child. She simply had dreams which told her how to do the various things, dreams about each woman she took care of. She is, to me, a beautiful, dignified-looking woman, with a completely professional attitude toward her job. She and Doña Luz seem to me to be the most respected women in Chan Kom. Their power and influence are not obvious, but they form a pervasive undercurrent in the life of the village. These two relate most closely to the Mayan past, with their knowledge of medicine, of herbs, and secrets.

Chan Kom is not a typical Mayan village and these women were not necessarily typical of Chan Kom. Even though most of the women who were more deeply involved in this study were related to the leading family, and as such held positions where they potentially may claim more "status through wealth" than others when modernization gives it more impor- tance, I felt a great similarity between them and the other women of the community. They wore the same clothing, ate the same food, drew water from the same wells, had children in the same school. Every family has a home plot and a right to *ejido* land. There are no peons. Everyone is a peasant! Even though all of these women have masonry houses, most of their daily life — and sleeping for many, including the family patriarch and his wife—takes place in the *jacales* [thatched huts]. Alfonso Villa Rojas once said, "As wives of leaders, as members of the leading family, these women are setting the trend." They are at the pressure-point of change.

How do these women feel about their lives? Are they happy? One of the questions I had asked various people was suggested to me by Erich Fromm: "How do you feel about your life? — are you very satisfied, a little satis- fied, dissatisfied?" Unanimously the answer was "*muy satisfecha* [very sat- isfied]." What were the happiest times? Two of the wives said the happiest times in their lives had been when they were living in the bush raising corn with their husbands. They thought they might move out to the country again if the road brought noise and crime and problems. They all feel they are happy, they say they are happy, they look happy, they sound happy. All of them except the oldest seem happy with their husbands, in spite of the fact that all except two had married the men who had been chosen for them by their father.

It is probably often true that the modern-day Maya marry without love in the conventional American sense. It seems rather a matter of routine. The boy wants a home and children of his own, and either his parents or a matchmaker simply arranges for this marriage with a suitable girl.

In Chan Kom I met one twenty-one-year-old girl who was very happy not to be married and enjoyed being a *soltera* [unmarried woman]. Mar- ried women seem happy in the married state, and do not question it; they seem to feel for their daughters that this is the only way a woman would want to live.

Alfonso Villa Rojas said that he had noticed in Quintana Roo, and I had felt the same in Chan Kom, that couples are very stable and usually pass their lives together in congenial and tranquil companionship.

Quarrels are very rare and the small disagreements which do occur are brief and inconspicuous. During the course of his time in Quintana Roo only once did he see an instance when a man struck his wife, and in no instance did a wife strike a husband (Villa Rojas 1945: 89).

In Chan Kom I found one wife who said that her husband struck her during their early years of marriage, but she blamed herself as being young and inexperienced. "He is *muy delicado* [very touchy], but now I know how to handle him."

Of the ten couples that I got to know well in Chan Kom, eight seemed to be "loving partners," in the Fromm/Maccoby sense. In their village, Las Cuevas, they found very few husbands and wives who could fit the definition, and those few were considered by the others as "remarkable, admirable, but exceptional" (Fromm and Maccoby 1970: 149).

But then they also found strong *machismo* feelings among the men, as is common throughout Mexico. "Machismo indicates an attitude of male superiority, a wish to control women and keep them in an inferior position" (Fromm and Maccoby 1970: 166). In Chan Kom I found very little of this attitude. While the village is set up as a patriarchy, and the men hold the positions of power, they treat their wives and children with loving concern, and respect. As one observer noted. "In the years in Yucatan I have never seen, a Mayan man kiss a woman." I should go on and say neither did I; in fact I never saw even an overt sign of affection, not even an arm around a shoulder or a hand touching. Husband and wife would pass each other on the plaza without speaking. There may have been signals I didn't understand, or passing in the plaza may be rather like meeting in the hall of one's home. In their homes there is a very warm interpersonal relationship. Husbands and wives sit together around the hearth on low stools, talking, drinking chocolate or cola. When tortillas are being made, the woman continues doing this while her husband and children eat. There doesn't seem to be the rigid segregation of males and females at meals in the nuclear family, as is often reported.

All of these women but Victoria have children. When asked how many children people had and how many they wanted, all the women except one countered by asking me how many children I had. When I said two, they asked why I only had two children and how Americans know how not to have more. This seemed to be an interest of theirs which, as I came to know them as women, we could discuss freely and in depth. All but one said they hoped to go to a nearby village to visit a Mayan doctor whom I knew, one trained by Planned Parenthood in birth control methods, including IUDs. One of the mothers said she wished I had taken her to the doctor when I was there the time before. "Now it is too late," she said. "I'm pregnant again." Since then, she has had a serious miscarriage. Her husband went for the doctor, but could not get him to come to help her in time.

In one of my early visits, the village leader suggested that I talk with the women about birth control. His understanding and the freedom with which he discussed such matters with me seemed rare. He seemed pleased but surprised when I told him that most of them had already asked me for information. Alfonso Villa Rojas had reported that "proudly they turned down the use of contraceptives" in the thirties when he suggested to the men that there were protective devices that they could use so as to have fewer children (González 1970: 288).

One wife of thirty, with five living children, one dead, said that she had never had more than one menstrual period between her children in all her thirteen years of married life.

"I've always wanted to ask my sister-in-law how she managed to have only one," she confided, "but I never could ask somehow." She eagerly took the address of the Mayan doctor, saying that she hoped she could see him in time — she had just had her first menstrual period after the last baby, and if she could manage not to have any more children, she would be so happy. "I could take better care of the children," she said. "I could make more hammocks, and maybe buy a sewing machine so I could make *huipiles* to sell. I can teach my daughter." Her whole world would be expanded.

Another young woman of twenty-four who has had only one son after five years of marriage wanted to speak with the doctor too because she is afraid to have another baby. She almost died in childbirth and her husband, too, is afraid for her life. According to her this has meant that they have not had intercourse ("slept in separate hammocks") since their son's birth; her husband told me on my last visit that they had the midwife fix her to prevent any further children.

It was this same woman who had described her curing by the shaman on my previous visit. As her illness soon returned, I invited her to come with me to the clinic in town on my way back home. On my last day in the village her husband got up and left before I had breakfast, unusual since we had always eaten together. I was very upset, fearing that I had caused trouble between them by inviting her to come with me. She told me when I left that her husband did not wish her to go to the clinic; hence I left worrying about her and about them.

On my third visit, the first person I met was her husband. He greeted me warmly and said that he knew I was coming because his wife was weaving my colors into the hammock she was working on that morning. When I arrived at their home, I found the hammock woven in the blue and white design of the dress I had lived in during my last trip there. She told me that after I left she had a dream every night for a week in which I was standing on the road, pointing the way to the clinic for her. Finally, she told her husband that if he would not take her there she would use her own money and go alone. So he sold two pigs and took her to the clinic for two weeks. He left her there with her mother and son, coming to visit her every third day. Now she trusts the doctor there and told me that she may go back soon with her husband to learn about birth control devices.

This incident, along with others I observed made me realize that the women do have more freedom to control their lives than I had thought or read about previously. The property which they own or the things which they can sell do in fact give them money which is theirs to spend as they wish, and they take real pride in the freedom this gives them.

The question of "freedom" in the context of Chan Kom is one with several dimensions. One of the questions which I raised was, "Whose life is harder (*mas duro*) that of a man or a woman?" Every woman told me that the men's work was much harder, except the childless wife who said she felt men's and women's work was equal. The others said, "We get to stay inside the cool houses, be with our children, embroider — 'paint with needles', we call it — while the men have to work out in the hot sun." The women carry up to forty pails of water a day drawn from deep wells, but they say that the water isn't heavy.

The men, on the other hand, told me they thought that the women's life was harder. "They have to stay home and cook and wash and be with the children. They can't go out to the fields or the city alone." One element involved in this apparent contradiction seems to be that men perceive women's work as being confining, limited to the house and yard, while theirs is free of that confining element. Women, on the other hand, see men's work as being harsh, physically exhausting, and therefore not as free as theirs, since men do not have the opportunity to take advantage of free moments in the hammock in the coolness of the home. What we have then is a reverse pair of concepts, one involving freedom TO and the other freedom FROM. There would appear to be little difference in the value assigned by the women to their freedom to enjoy what the men perceive as limiting factors and that which the men assign to their freedom of movement, in turn seen by the women as limiting or negative factors. Thus, both men and women FEEL freer and consequently live in a value system which is more comfortable for them, using their freedoms in ways which enhance their respective joy in life and hence the overall harmony of their lives together.

Another dimension of the relative freedom of men and women in Chan Kom may derive from the phenomenon commented on by Oscar Lewis. "In general," he says, "women's work is less rigidly defined than men's" I have commented elsewhere in this paper on the almost random AP-PEARANCE of structure in the daily routines of the women, their occasional "hammock-breaks," their sporadic turns at the loom or at embroidery and their unscheduled lives, with little other than the preparation of meals to demand a specific action at a specific time and even that not tied down to an hour. But there is some evidence that activities which were once the exclusive domain of the men, activities which do indeed demand a more rigid structure, are increasingly becoming open to the women of Chan Kom. Among these tasks are the baking of bread for sale, keeping shop, and even the singing of sacred songs, once the exclusive role of the *maestro cantor* [male singer], now being assumed by the *rezoneras* [female singers] (Redfield and Villa Rojas 1934: 70).

In summary, there is much more feeling of independence on the part of these women than I have sensed among many suburban women in the United States. Dorothy Lee has said, "Self-esteem is paramount and rests on freedom and self dependence" (Lee 1959: 160). The women of Chan Kom derive self-esteem from their essential skills and knowledge, and from their private income, possessions, livestock, and real property. The combination of these assets places them in an integral position in the functioning of the village economy and brings them prestige and power in the community and in their homes.

The important thing really is that each sex feels the other has an important job, a hard job, and in this community in which life is divided in such a way that man and woman depend on each other, an interdependence is tied to subsistence living based on a corn culture. Life is still related to the corn god and the rain god, the two Mayan gods for whom ancient ceremonies are still held. In fact, according to local legend, God made the first people from corn.

The most salient conclusion I have drawn from this study relates to change. Mayan women do accept change; they will initiate and even agitate for change — even against the wishes of their husbands and school teachers, who are highly respected — if it seems to be in their own best interests or those of their children. Mayan women are not frightened by a new language, either literal or metaphorical, since they are already bilingual — linguistically, culturally, and "ceremonially," as Redfield put it. They are strangely sophisticated peasants who have somehow absorbed from the Spanish culture what they wanted from it, without, in the process, losing much which they value from the traditional pre-Columbian culture, above all the corn culture. Even though they appear not to have realized that the old culture is passing, that matters beyond their control have made the old concept, "to make *milpa* is to live," an anachronism, perhaps even a myth, they still cling to the value system of the *milpa*, even while changing in many other ways.

The facts speak for themselves. Don Trinidad no longer cultivates his *milpa*. Of his six sons, only two made *milpa* last year. In contrast, when we check on his daughters, we find that both of them in Chan Kom are still tied closely to the life of the *milpa*. The widow, Gabriela, physically works with her sons in the fields, and the only source of income for Marta and her husband Rufino is their earnings from the corn they raise and from produce and household animals they sell.

But unless something drastic happens, I foresee the approaching end of the corn culture and with it the relationship to the Mayan Gods and the *milpa*-based intertwining of the lives of the men and women. It may be that the family with whom I was living is in the process of repeating history. They may be on the verge of returning to the combination cattle and maize culture in hacienda complexes which had been introduced earlier by the Spaniards (Strickon 1965: 46–47). This resulted in an extension of the pure corn agricultural patterns of the earliest Mayans without disturbing basic life patterns. These cattle ranches, in turn, were supplanted by huge sugar and henequen plantations. These "factories in the field," as Strickon and Mintz have called them, were highly destructive of village life and cultural patterns, and it was from them that many people fled to renew their traditional way of life. Many, in fact, fought for their old ways in the War of the Castes. Now again, the people of Chan Kom appear to be adding cattle as a source of income, which is compatible with their ways of life and value systems. Hopefully this new development will prevent SOME of the possible dehumanization effects which the new road forbodes and help Chan Kom avoid some of the problems of the consumer society.

I see the cattle and the increase in the production of handicrafts (and their sale) by women and children as supplements to the corn economy, as ways to increase their monetary wealth in order to purchase the medicines and other new commodities which they will desire without destroying their present life styles. With these changes, corn will remain central as food for people, for cattle, chickens, etc. so the cultural patterns of the village will not be destroyed.

A village leader said to me just before the highway opened, "I wonder what will happen to Chan Kom when the highway comes — when the smell of gasoline is like it is on the streets of Mérida? Will the community be so crowded that people push each other off the streets? Will the noise be so great that I will want to go back up to the bush and live in a thatched hut?" There is both hope for modernization and fear of it, which I felt among women as well. Two of the wives had said that the happiest times in their lives had been when they were living in the bush raising corn with their husbands. They felt they might move back out if the road brought noise, crime, and pollution.

Some of the fears that were often mentioned were pollution, smells, noise, and dirt as in the city. And as I looked around me on my first visit I had a strange feeling of being in a balanced aquarium. In the thatched hut where I ate and chatted I never saw a fly, never was there an ant. In spite of the setting turkey in the corner, the hens and chickens, and the innumerable pigs and dogs in the yard, I never once stepped in filth, not even in the dark. This strange cleanliness — this exciting ecological equilibrium — continued to amaze me everywhere until I was there my last trip.

When the road opened, when the fiesta commenced, when the festive meals of chicken and pig began, when the outsiders started arriving, all at once there were flies — in the corner store, in my room, in the plaza — and I saw three scorpions in one day. Maybe it was just coincidence, but I felt that the aquarium was already out of balance. But this is just a part; the bigger thing is the feeling of harmony with nature — with earth and sky and wind and water — with the feeling that all essentials are really there. As Landa reported charmingly, even the dishes were provided by God. They merely picked them from the trees, where God had provided them (the *jícaras*). The women of Chan Kom see the new road as a way to bring things they want into the village, things like better medical care, electricity, and markets for their products. They do not see it as an escape, a way out. But, one wonders, will they be able to resist the road out which has entrapped so many peasants into changing their lives from the rural, farming subsistence economy to the meager existence of the urban culture of poverty? These and other questions are real. One way out does lead to the pockets of poverty which clutter the *barrios* around Latin American cities and our own United States cities. In this move out, many are in culture shock, but the women often suffer the most.

They leave a subsistence economy where they have been part of a mutually dependent relationship with their husbands for an urban pocket of poverty where their role is undefined, uncertain, and undignified, and which at best it is rarely, if ever, possible to redefine in a culturally meaningful way. Often there are fewer opportunities for employment, or those which do seem tempting turn out to have much less status than the traditional role in the village. And one key role, that of map-builder and guide for the young, is lost. No longer does the woman have either self-respect or the respect of her children, her husband, or her community. No longer is she tied into those communications networks, these half-hidden but very real ones which work so well in the village. Admittedly the problem is a complex one. "At one end of the scale is the peasant community in which all work is essential for survival and thus all work has dignity. The man and woman exist in an interdependent relationship in which each has status, but neither is free to change" (Elmendorf 1971: 18).

I left Chan Kom with ambivalent feelings this time. From the huge Coca-Cola advertisement painted on the multi-colored store, once all white, to the mini-skirted schoolteachers, it was obvious that Chan Kom was turning away from its past and beginning a new stage of existence. We can only guess at the range of these changes. The men and women might remain contented with their lives, each believing the other's job to be more difficult — or the exposure that the road will bring might make them feel "backward," "underdeveloped," and soon discontent to live the lives in which they have had such joy and pride. Will the road bring in the many benefits of modernization, or will the changes overwhelm them, sending those still able to leave back up into the peaceful bush country? Will the women have any part in making the choices that affect their lives, or might they see, as many have seen before, their role as women and as mothers particularly minimized as they come into contact with a civilization to which their past experience does not relate?

REFERENCES

BOULDING, ELISE
  1970   "Women as role models in industrializing societies: a macro-system of socialization for civic competence." Mimeographed manuscript, University of Colorado.
CHIÑAS, BEVERLY
  1971   "Women as ethnographic subjects," in *Women in cross-cultural perspective*. Compiled by S. E. Jacobs, 21–31. Chicago: University of Illinois Press.
DE LANDA, DIEGO
  1566   "Relación de las cosas de Yucatán." Unpublished manuscript, Madrid.
ELMENDORF, MARY
  1971   "Role of women as agents for peaceful social change." Mimeographed manuscript, Society for International Development, Ottawa.
  1972   *The Mayan woman and change.* Cuernavaca, Mexico: CIDOC Dossier 81.

FREIRE, PAULO
  1971   *Pedagogy of the oppressed.* New York: Herder and Herder.
FROMM, ERICH
  1946   *The fear of freedom.* London: Keeger Paul, French, Turner.
FROMM, ERICH, MICHAEL MACCOBY
  1970   *Social character in a Mexican village: a socio-psychoanalytic study.* Englewood Cliffs, New Jersey: Prentice-Hall.
GONZÁLEZ N. MOISES
  1970   *Raza y tierra.* Mexico City: El Colegio de México.
JACOBS, SUE ELLEN
  1971   *Women in cross-cultural perspective.* Illinois: University of Illinois Press.
LEE, DOROTHY
  1959   *Freedom and culture.* Englewood Cliffs, New Jersey: Prentice-Hall.
REDFIELD, ROBERT, ALPHONSO VILLA ROJAS
  1934   *Chan Kom, a Maya village.* Washington: Carnegie Institute.
REDFIELD, ROBERT
  1950   *A village that chose progress: Chan Kom revisited.* Chicago: University of Chicago Press.
STEGGERDA, MORRIS
  1941   *Maya Indians of Yucatán.* Washington: Carnegie Publication 531.
STRICKON, ARNOLD
  1965   Hacienda and plantation in Yucatan. *América Indígena* 25:35–63. Mexico: Instituto Indigenista Interamericano.
TOZZER, ALFRED M.
  1941   Eight edition of Landa's *Relación de las cosas de Yucatán.* Papers of the Peabody Museum, Volume 18. Cambridge: Harvard University.
VILLA ROJAS, ALFONSO
  1945   *The Maya of east central Quintana Roo.* Washington: Carnegie Publication 559.

Marital Status and Sexual Identity: The Position of Women in a Mexican Peasant Society

DOREN L. SLADE

This paper discusses women's and men's roles in Chignautla, an Indian community in the Central Mexican Highlands.[1] My specific purpose is to describe the ways in which women are implicated on a number of levels in the political process. But in order to discuss their involvement, it is necessary to analyze men's roles as well, since a woman's status is determined by her relationship with men and particularly her husband. Consistent with the fact that women's status derives from men's status, both sexes have differential access to formal positions of authority in the household and in public life. Men's access is far greater than women's, yet their assumption of formal positions of authority is not independent of their relationship to women. By approaching women's and men's roles developmentally, I will show how their statuses are interlinked and how this affects the activities of both women and men alike.

Chignautla is a community of the type typically associated with agriculturally-based peasant society. It is a patricentered system, in which men control the fundamental productive resources which are only irregularly available to women. Interaction is largely kin-based and patrilineal

[1] Two years were spent in Chignautla gathering data upon which this analysis was based, although my focus was not women's roles nor was my study of religious politics carried out from a woman's perspective. Some of the ideas presented here were first conceptualized in a short paper given at the meeting of the Northeastern Anthropological Association in 1974. I would like to thank Sue Makiesky for that opportunity and Judith Mendell for pointing out the difference between a male and female perspective in the first draft. I am also indebted to Ruby Rorlich-Leavitt for her painstaking editorial assistance and to Constance Sutton for guidance in conceptualization without which my ideas would have remained obscure. I owe the women of the New York Women's Anthropology Caucus much, mainly for their help in my own transition from an asexual graduate student to a woman anthropologist.

descent results in patrilocal residence and patrilineal inheritance, both of which favor men. However, it is in societies of this type, that are patrilineal and where kinship is the basic principle articulating most social activities, that the cultural conceptualization of sex roles for women and men is tied to marital roles.[2] But, while marital roles are pivotal in determining the statuses of each sex, they have different implications for women than they do for men. Marriage for men initiates the assumption of their jural adulthood; for women it places them jurally in the status of dependent minors. And because marital roles are basic to social identity, it is the marital role that constrains the range of activities in which women can engage, resulting in role conflict where women have alternatives to dependency on their husbands.

The position of women in Chignautla is by no means unique. But what is of interest is that women do have crucial roles in the larger political processes precisely because they affect men's status in public life as well as help initiate their entrance into it. Women contribute to the definition of male status and the man who does not marry is limited in what he can do in public life. In contrast, an unmarried woman is less limited in the roles she can play publicly. This points not only to the functional interdependence of marital and sexual identities in this community but also indicates the asymmetry of sex roles, an asymmetry which is reserved for adult women and men who do not marry.

THE COMMUNITY

Some 7,500 Indians live in Chignautla, a *municipio* located in the Nahuat-speaking enclave of northern Puebla. Just four kilometers from Teziutlán, the region's largest market center, Chignautla's economy is open and competitive. The importance of agriculture makes land the most valued good and the majority of Indians own from $1/2$ to 2 hectares in fee simple. Most arable land is devoted to *milpa* (corn agriculture), grown for home consumption, and the cultivation of fruit and vegetables for the market. Wage labor in agriculture in the fields of nonrelated Chignautecos, or semi-skilled occupations for local artisans or in businesses in Teziutlan, is now commonplace. Indian households are regularly scattered among the fields to form hamlets which Chignautecos call "barrios".

---

[2]   I am suggesting that the configuration in women's roles and the interdependence of sexual and marital statuses would be quite different in a society in which kinship is matrilineal, and I feel that the importance of marriage in relation to these processes would not be as marked as it is in a patrilineal society like Chignautla.

Barrio membership is inherited from father and maintained by residence within the barrio, all barrios representing well-defined areas of the community. Women do not change their names at marriage nor do they become members in their husbands' agnatic descent group, identified by a common paternal surname and generally localized within a barrio. Barrios are preferentially and largely endogamous, and barrio membership defines rights to sponsor certain images in Chignautla's parish church.

The care and sponsorship of an annual fiesta for an image is the main ritual obligation associated with a hierarchy of religious offices called the "cargo" system in Mesoamerica. These ritual offices or cargos are ranked in authority and sanctity which determine the influence a cargo-holder has in public affairs. In actuality, these cargos represent informal political positions since cargo systems are the institutions through which political processes are carried out.[3]

The fewer, higher cargos at the top levels of the hierarchy comprise the formal authority for church affairs. Men holding these top positions have final say in decisions regarding recruitment to cargos, which change hands every one to three years. Once each year every cargo-holder pays for a mass and provides a ritual meal in his house to honor the image he represents.[4] These fiestas, called *mayordomías*, are elaborate events with expenses consistent with the cargo's rank, those on top costing more in overall expenditures. A certain amount of cash is always needed, but the most crucial economic good is corn used to feed anywhere from 50 to over 1,000 people who come to the *mayordomía*. Even if a man has sufficient cash income to purchase corn, he will not easily receive a cargo without also having sufficient land in *milpa*, a bias reflecting the traditional ritual relationship between subsistence, culture, and the supernatural. Thus, level of participation in the cargo system depends upon control of this fundamental productive resource.

[3]   The *municipio* of Chignautla covers an area of 105 square kilometers but only about one-third is settled. Some 1200 mestizos live in Chignautla's one village and head town and have an independent religious cargo system quite distinct from that of the Indians, although they share the same church. Also, the religious cargo system is entirely separate from the Ayuntamiento Municipal, the local civil administration, and today Indians do not hold civil office but are almost always dominated by the wealthier mestizos who either hold office themselves or who dominate Indian office-holders informally. Indians rarely involve themselves with civil politics and generally consider the civil authority as illegitimate and corrupt. A detailed description of the political economy of Chignautla may be found in Slade (1973).

[4]   Not all cargos are that of *mayordomo*, the cargo traditionally sponsoring images and involved in the *mayordomía*, but in Chignautla, regardless of the type of cargo, all cargo-holders have the opportunity to assume the role of *mayordomo* in fiesta and mass sponsorship *vis-à-vis* an image with which they are associated.

Cargo sponsorship is voluntary and ideally open to all adult men of the community. In fact, though, not only must a man have a certain amount of *milpa* matching the level required for the cargo he wants to hold, he must also be married and hold the position of household head. These requisites are interdependent: men must reside in their own households to be household head, and to support a family a man must control land which in turn is possible only after he marries. He then is able to move out of his father's house and become a household head himself.

A second unstated factor in recruitment is barrio membership. Since all barrios monopolize certain cargos for their members, a man holds a cargo by virtue of his barrio membership. Membership, of course, relates equally to descent and residence, since residence subsumes descent in defining rights in a barrio.[5] Recruitment by descent is further reinforced by a principle of ritual association between agnates, individuals who "share the same blood." Sons of men who held high cargos begin their careers in the church with a cargo similar in rank to the last one held by their fathers, while sons of men who held only minor cargos, or who never served at all, must begin at the bottom of the hierarchy. Few men reach the top but few men do not serve in some capacity at least once in their lives. Men who never serve, and these are few, have little impact on the social system and are seen by others as ineffectual.

There is one more point worth mentioning in regard to recruitment. This is the behavior of cargo holders. For men who serve, there is a personal and social injunction to act not only within the limits of normal behavior but as close to the ideal as possible. Inappropriate behavior, such as becoming unruly while drunk, being disrespectful to church officials or parents, or committing more grave deviations, such as adultery (that is found out), theft, murder, rape or cheating, etc., is seen as a transgression against God. Such behavior is inappropriate for a man who serves God or society, a man of ritual rank to whom others defer in all matters, sacred or secular, God created ideals and norms for human behavior, Chignautecos believe, and no one is ever excused from obeying the moral order. The cargo system is in essence a moral system, stipulating binding rules for behavior backed by the authority of God. However,

---

[5]   Individuals may hold membership in two barrios simultaneously or change affiliation from the barrio in which they are born by taking up residence in the other barrio and contributing to that barrio's projects and fiestas. However, since descent is an important principle in defining rights in a barrio, men at times may manipulate an agnatic genealogical connection in order to gain access to the cargos associated with the barrio where their agnatic ancestors originally came from. Since women do not generally hold cargos, barrio membership is less important as a point of conflict between competing interest groups.

this does not mean that all Chignautecos comply with the dictates of Catholicism, for they do not. Rather, church "rules" are distinguished from the broad-based ethics of religion permeating Chignauteco life and representing to the Indians the norms of social life as created by the same supernatural force which creates society. And it is through the cargo system that individuals participate dually in society and the moral order upon which it is based.

Cargos are sacred trusts, held among individuals, the group, and the supernatural. Through service in the church, the individual enters into a union with the supernatural, since having the ability to pass cargos is tantamount to confirming the individual's on-going relationship with God. This union or reconciliation establishes an individual's ritual rank, because holding a cargo effects a permanent change in the cargo-holder's nature, creating a sacredness that becomes a permanent attribute of a man's social identity which increases with each higher-ranking cargo he holds. Men who have passed cargos are not only considered good men deserving of trust and respect from members of the community, but they are seen as men who are particularly favored by God, who helped them to acquire the capacity to serve Him in the first place. It is this conceptualization of sacredness that underlies the ritual power of men who have obtained a ritual rank defined by the ritual value of the cargos they hold or held in the past.

Cargo systems, then, produce men of importance in the community. These men are powerful first because of the formal authority of the cargo they hold and second because of their enduring ritual rank. It is precisely because ritual rank is associated with the man and not the office that these individuals are able to influence decisions regarding public life, in secular as well as ritual contexts. But this power should not be confused with coercive power even though the authority of men in office is compelling, since these men may apply sanctions in the form of disenfranchising individuals from the ritual system by denying them access to cargos. Chignautecos listen to men of ritual rank whenever they speak because they are convinced of the value and legitimacy of the status these men have gained in the community. The people have faith that the person will live up to the respect his cargo merits, and they must respect him as the cargo holder must respect them, and avoid abusing the position in which he is placed by his ritual rank. Men who commit social and moral wrongs while in office are greatly feared because they have no respect for God and will therefore behave without regard for supernatural punishment. Trust, then, is essential for granting ritual power. Recruitment for cargos is a carefully-conducted and often laborious process and their public image becomes a preoccupation of men who intend to move up in society. In effect, the divine authority of God underlies the social norms of this society, and cargo-holders whose behavior falls below the general level of approval undermine their service to God and the community and are likely to receive supernatural punishment in the form of illness, misfortune, or even death. Individuals will also be ostracized for asocial acts, for while God forgives, the community never forgets.

In Chignautla, reciprocating God for favors received is an important principle of religious participation, and interbarrio competition for cargos is a common cause of conflict, each barrio attempting to retain a cargo distribution favorable to its members. Barrios are able to exert pressure on the church authority through their influential members, the mechanism being a carefully-controlled use of gossip about contending individuals from other barrios. Because Chignautla is a small-scale society, gossip focusing on misconduct readily becomes politicized slander disastrous to a career in public life.

The function of gossip as a mechanism of social control is quite common in societies like Chignautla, where the distinction between what one does in public and in one's home is quite sharp. Chignautecos are aware of this distinction and act accordingly. Most notably, there is strong pressure for women to act deferentially to their husbands in public while they may be more demonstrative to these same men at home. Similarly, a man might ignore his wife at a public gathering but he will consider his wife's opinions in making decisions. It is true that a wife cannot accept or reject a cargo if notification arrives at the house while her husband is away, but a husband will never make a decision to pass a cargo without first consulting his wife, for he cannot in fact meet ritual obligations without her. Women always accompany their husbands to meetings of cargo holders either in the church or in the barrio and women have access to all the ritual knowledge men have, although there are many ritual occasions where men are the primary and sole ritual actors.

In fact, there is no facet of life in Chignautla from which women are excluded and women just as easily as men could serve as informants about ritual, agriculture, and politics, even though these spheres of activity are considered important in male behavior. And similarly women do not normally hold cargos but since men must be married to serve, what results is participation by couples and whole households rather than by individuals. However, a woman who is not sufficiently retiring and submissive in the presence of others detracts from her husband's ascribed maleness and tarnishes her own reputation for not living up to the culturally assigned role expectations of a wife. Overly aggressive women and overly passive men are the objects of ridicule, but these traits do not contribute to eliminating a man from holding office, as the more grave breaches of conduct would. It is also important to point out that if a man is too aggressive he will be judged unfit, just as it will indeed be difficult, though not impossible, for a man to receive a cargo if his wife or immediate agnates deviate too blatantly from customary behavior. It is a wife's duty to uphold the reputation of her husband and it will be the wife who is blamed if he falls below normal standards in what he does.

Aside from the role of guardian of a man's public image, women do take part in the ritual process. More than half the days of the year are spent in fiestas or preparations for them and there are some 270 cargos of importance. And while women may not be the primary ritual actors, they do participate by virtue of their relationship to men. Women play an important role in sponsoring *mayordomías* although their obligations reflect the tasks that are normally assigned to women in the household. It is a man's wife, the *mayordoma*, with the assistance of her agnatic kinswomen, who makes ready the lavish ritual meal of the *mayordomía*, often requiring two weeks of preparation. Women must greet the officers of the hierarchy when they accompany the *mayordomo* to his house after the mass on the day of the fiesta. A wife must accompany her husband when he attends the *mayordomías* of other cargo-holders, since it is the wife who carries away the special ritual portion served before the ritual food is actually consumed at the fiesta. A wife will also complete the obligations of office if her husband should die while serving, and a widow may request a cargo on behalf of her deceased husband if he did not fulfill a vow to hold a fiesta for an image made years before his death.

All decisions concerning religious fiestas and ritual action are made by a man and his wife, and it is the married couple who appear at the various events forming part of the obligations of office. Nor can a household head accept a cargo without first consulting his wife. This not only characterizes ritual participation, but also secular affairs. It is uncommon for husbands to make a financial investment in land or animals without discussing the negative and positive aspects of the venture with their wives, even though it is the husband who will buy the land, cultivate it, and control the profits from it. A man is dependent upon his wife and therefore must accept her suggestions, support, or refusals in whatever he does. Wives enter actively in the political actions taken by their husbands regarding barrio interests, and I have never met a woman who did not know exactly what was happening behind closed doors in the *mayordomo*'s chamber in the church or in a more open meeting of the civil officials. It is the wife who will put a check on her husband's ambitious desire to enter public office if he is not really ready financially to meet cargo expenses in a manner that will bring approval from neighbors, just as it is the wife who will insist that her husband request a cargo if he becomes so pretentious about his economic success that he no longer feels dependent upon God's help. After all, women know that men who do not repay God for His favors are not likely to receive favors in the future, and if ill luck befalls the household, it will most likely affect her more than anyone else.

In ritual situations a wife receives respect from others in accordance with the ritual rank of her husband, However, unlike men who are under great pressure to behave well in and out of ritual contexts, women have far more freedom in their actions and must conform to rigid etiquette only during ritual events when they accompany their husbands. A wife's misconduct will reflect back on her husband's ability to maintain authority over her. Daughters also have ascribed ritual rank gained from their fathers and they seek husbands who are sons of men of similar rank. Thus, unlike descent group membership and patrimonial rights which do not pass equally to women of the descent group, ritual rank is retained through marriage. Women only stand to gain from maintaining their husband's interest in a career in the church since a wife's status improves as her husband's does. What men have in the ritual sphere women do not lose in marriage, as they do in other sectors of life in Chignautla.

Thus it is clear that women have a secondary but complementary role in the ritual system in this community. But it is also clear that a man cannot enter public life without a wife. Aside from the tasks that a wife carries out, she also contributes to the conceptualization of male adulthood. Without a wife a man would not be judged mature and responsible enough to fulfill the obligations of sacred office. Indeed, the Chignauteco conceptualization of the temperamental attributes of females and males indicates a central role for women precisely because of the contrasting, ascribed temperament of women and men. Men are considered incurable romantics, proud to extremes, overly sensitive, and given to hesitancy in situations in which they are intensely self-conscious. It is the woman who has endurance and emotional stability. Women, and not men, are pragmatic, ambitious, and resourceful. For a man, a wife is comfort and strength in an indifferent and hostile world. Chignautecos believe that women reach maturity by the time they arrive at puberty; men do not "mature" until they marry. In effect, a woman becomes an adult when she reaches a certain age. But unlike our jural adulthood where age is the main criterion, as it is for women in Chitnautla, for men it is marital status that grants them jural majority and precipitates their entrance into public life. In obtaining a wife, a man gains access to cargos, but obtaining a husband serves to undermine a woman's jural status so that she is not eligible for public office. However, marriage for a woman as her husband's partner is not without its rewards. By encouraging her husband to enter the religious system, a woman decreases the likelihood that he will drink too much, enter an adulterous union, or be so lazy that household resources would be depleted to the point that holding a cargo would be impossible. In gaining these secondary benefits, marriage also makes it impossible for a woman to assert herself outside the context of defending her husband's interests.

HOUSEHOLD AND FAMILY

In Chignautla, as in most peasant societies, the household is a multifunctional unit operating as a collectivity in economics and ritual and in relating to the local civil administration. Households are discrete social and territorial units and members relate to the larger society through the household head. Households are actually house compounds with dwellings, kitchens, animals, and animal pens all surrounded by a fence with one entranceway to the street. A house compound may contain one or more domestic units distinguished from each other by independence in production and consumption manifested in a separate corn supply, cooking hearth, and religious altar. Nearly half the households contain only one domestic unit; that is, they have one expense budget to which members contribute and from which members draw according to need and allotment by the household head.

Household heads are usually males who have the titles to the house. Men living in households owned by their wives are nominal heads who, like *de jure* heads, fulfill the quotas imposed on households by the community. When a man reaches the age when he can no longer be active economically, or serve in office, he will transfer ownership to the son who has remained after marriage. This son may now hold cargos, while other sons do not until they have moved out and established a household of their own.

All material goods of the household are individually owned and owners have sole control of their use, just as individuals, female or male, have an inalienable right to dispose of gains from their productive efforts. Even as household head and ultimate authority in the residential kin group, a man cannot, for example, use a pig owned by his wife or son without permission. A wife has the duty to obey her husband and do what she can to make the household a viable unit, just as husbands are under obligation to invest their earnings in household needs before investing in individual benefits. Since women do not usually own productive resources, a wife is expected to contribute her labor as her share in household maintenance while men will often contribute only as much labor as necessary to avoid criticism. Parents have liens on whatever is earned by dependent off-spring. Husbands and wives are co-owners of household property only when they are civilly married. Even today, though, civil marriage is not customary among the Indians because they are aware that it undermines the solidarity of the agnatic descent group and destroys the continuity of the patrimony. Women, however, will attempt to convince their husbands to marry civilly.

Nearly half the households are patrilocal, extended families of three generations. The rest are mainly independent nuclear family households, which quickly become extended when sons begin to bring women in to live with them as a prelude to marriage. Living in an extended family has good and bad features for both the women and men. For women who are already mothers and formally married, it lightens the burdens because they share domestic chores with other co-resident women. Infant care, though, has never stopped a woman from engaging in extra-domestic activities since she carries her child on her back wrapped in the shawl all women wear. Besides, by the time women are wives of residentially in-dependent men, at least one of her children is old enough to take care of the others.

Men do not do chores that are culturally assigned to women, such as cooking, cleaning, food preparation, etc., nor do women work in the *milpa*. But these tasks are complementary and not necessarily distinguished on the basis of any inherent sexual inability; in emergencies tasks are com-pletely interchangeable. If wives or husbands become incapacitated, each will do the work of the other. I have never seen individuals criticized for doing so; instead, they are pitied. Women find agricultural work onerous, and men sulk when they must do housework. If a husband mistreats his wife, the wife has few means to make him change his ways; I have seen Indian women going about the streets on Sunday searching for their husbands who spent their week's earnings on drink and were too drunk to return at night to the house. These are women who live in the house-hold owned by their husbands, by and large the vast majority. Women who own households, on the other hand, will not hesitate to throw a husband out and they will not be criticized for doing so. Property owner-ship underlies power in interpersonal relationships and provides a basis for male domination in Chignautla, since property comes normally to men through inheritance. However, an inheritance might be long in coming and control of property will come to men through their residential independence, a social process mobilized by formal marriage or its informal counterpart, free union.

Both sexes attempt to establish conjugal unions by the age of 19 or 20, and roughly 80 percent of all conjugal unions begin as free unions when men still hold the status of dependent sons in the household of their fathers. A woman moves into her fiancé's house and becomes subject to the authority of her future mother-in-law. Women expect to suffer at this stage and they find solace in constant visits to the household of their fathers where they have more freedom to do as they wish in helping their mothers. Fathers and daughters, and mothers and sons, have a close, affectionate relationship in Chignautla, which is in marked contrast to the restraint characterizing the relationship between fathers and sons. But in public life, a daughter who is still dependent receives her social identity from her father and is known as the daughter of so-and-so. Daughters of men of high ritual rank see themselves as special and are treated deferentially by peers. These young women spend more time at public gatherings than daughters of men of lower social standing. It is this type of young woman who will view a conjugal relationship with a dependent son as a drop in her social standing; many marry and do not enter free unions at all, which is possible because of the boy's father's wealth.

When a woman enters a conjugal relationship her identity changes from that of her father to that of her sexual partner. She will be known as the woman of the son of so-and-so, a dependent status through which she must enter society. Women are expected to be ambitious, but for the men upon whom they depend, not for themselves. Having children creates a binding tie between two young adults and legitimizes a woman's ambitions for her fiancé. A young mother may then prod her fiancé to ask his father for the wedding that will make them both adults. Once married, a son has the right to ask his father for his portion of the patrimony.

Mutual obligations characterize the relationship between sons and fathers which involves control and transfer of land. Fathers are obliged to provide their sons with a wedding, land to work, and help in building a house. How and when these obligations are met depend upon a father's willingness to let his sons out. Household heads stand to gain from maintaining as long as possible a large residential labor force. Chignautla has the type of economy where cultivation and wage labor are exploited more profitably by this type of residential group. *Milpa* agriculture is not labor-intensive, but no matter how much land a man has, without laborers to work it the harvest will be limited. Men who are heads of independent

nuclear family households face this problem, for they rarely have sufficient cash to hire workers. A son does not receive pay from his father
while he lives with him. At this point in his life a man is also interested in
helping a father's cargo career since his career will determine the sons's
point of entry into the system once he is a household head. But when sons
have families of their own their interests become focused around their
own careers and ultimately co-resident men are bound to come into conflict over their share of household resources. A household head will put
off the expensive weddings of his sons as long as he can, since in the years
these ceremonies are held, there will be little money or corn left to invest
in a cargo.

Conflict between co-resident men is multifaceted. Because there is no
cultural stipulation as to which son remains to inherit a father's house,
brothers are placed into competition with each other for their father's
affection. But again, the father's authority prohibits competition from
coming into the open, just as a son's resentment over his father's control
will not be expressed for fear of consequences except when both are ine-
briated. For this reason, a typical stage in the developmental cycle of the
household is the division of one domestic unit into separate domestic
units for each son before pressure can be exerted on the father to sponsor
the weddings of one son after another. Again sons wait until tensions
within the household reach the point when the only solution seen is
having a married son move out, since conflict will focus mainly around
this son and his wife and children. Most sons retain the land given them
when they established independent domestic units within their father's
house compound, land divided off from father's estate and held in usu-
fruct by the son until titles are transferred usually at father's death. Residential independence follows the wedding and from this time on a son's
wife will be dependent upon her husband's interests in his household.
It is during this period that husbands encourage their young wives to be
active economically in any way they can, since sons who leave their
father's house in anger do not have the help ideally forthcoming to build
a house.

Relationships surrounding the transfer of property are ambivalent.
Sons owe fathers respect and obedience; brothers owe each other reciprocal aid once each has a house of his own; wives owe husbands support
often against their sons; and daughters-in-law owe their mothers-in-law
respect while they owe their new husband and children allegiance. But
only the potential for conflict in relationships between co-resident men is a
common theme in Chignauteco culture, elaborated in myths and folklore,
the most striking references involving the condemnation of sons who

commit patricide. And it is precisely these relationships that are characterized by the most stylized and binding respect.

Sons are most likely not to resort to direct petitions of independence
although they are motivated to do so. In Chignautla, it is the men who
must be covertly political, while women are allowed to express dissatisfaction in defense of the interests of the men upon whom they depend. And
even though mothers and sons have a close and warm relationship, and
mothers will protect their sons from an irate father, it is untenable that a
woman will side with a son over her husband. After all, the wife of a
mayordomo is a *mayordoma* while the mother of a *mayordomo* is just the
mayordomo's mother.

It is not surprising then that co-resident women who openly cause disruptions within the household are those who are the sexual partners of
men who compete but are restrained from coming into open conflict with each other, e.g. sisters-in-law, and mother and daughters-in-law.
Sisters and daughters and mothers rarely come into conflict, nor do wives
of men who compete openly. It is therefore incorrect to view domestic
quarrels between women as motivated by their pursuit of personal gain, as
suggested by Lamphere (1974) and Collier (1974) in articles examining the
politics of domestic quarrels.[6] It is the woman in a dependent relationship
to a man who is disadvantaged and who will quarrel to the point that life
within the household becomes unpleasant if the husband is unable to
take action himself. And the woman who stands to gain most by complain-

---

[6] This paper was originally written before the Rosaldo and Lamphere volume,
Woman, culture and society appeared in print (1974). My analysis resembles the articles
of Jane Collier and Louise Lamphere, both of whom deal with women's political roles,
although our interpretations differ on a number of essential points. Both writers focus
on strategies of women which have a political cast, those strategies acted out within the
domestic domain since women do not participate in public life formally but use strategies
directed toward public goals. Both Collier and Lamphere assert that women must work
through men in order to secure their interests by influencing men who hold authority.
Collier contends that the actions of young mothers which cause partition in domestic
groups politically important to men are essentially accomplished through sons rather
than husbands, while husbands use "woman's nature" to maintain their control over
household resources and public office. While there is a typical pattern to domestic quarrels between women, I believe that it is incorrect to label "domestic goals" as political
goals or to suggest that mothers manipulate sons when competition must involve those
who control resources and the individuals who are dependent upon them, i.e. wives and
husbands. If political clout rests on a large residential group, a woman stands to gain
more from helping her husband than from helping her son, who inevitably divides his
father's resources and leaves his mother when he takes a wife. I would also question the
validity of assuming that men actually believe that woman's nature prevents them from
holding public office or whether these male rationalizations about domestic quarrels
between women are the means by which men defend their own actions ultimately causing
domestic group fission, especially if men have power derived from their control of resources and women must resort to influence since they themselves have no power basis.

ing is the mother of a dependent son's children, an adult because of her motherhood but a minor because of her position within her fiancé's household. Thus, it is the relationship between women tied to men concerned in the transfer of productive property that produces the now classic pattern of domestic conflict in patricentered societies. Ultimately, a dependent son's sexual partner creates a situation whereby her husband-to-be is compelled to press for his independence even though it is the man who stands to gain more, obtaining residential independence once married. Marriage becomes an illusion of freedom for a woman after her years of residence in her husband's household. But it is only an illusion since the marital role of women in this society places the men a position where their independence can only bring conflict to the marriage and loss of self-esteem in the eyes of society.

PRODUCTION

Women do not customarily receive land as an inheritance. Land is scarce and the relation of women to their agnatic descent group is undermined by their marriage and transfer of their interests to men of another and competing descent group, even though a woman's membership is never lost. If a man is wealthy he will give his daughters a portion of the patrimony. These women are then free to pass their land to a daughter as well as a son. If a woman with land marries a man who is able to amass enough property for himself, she will reserve her inheritance for her daughters. Women also receive land when they have no male siblings and the household head seeks a son-in-law to help with agricultural work. Daughters, though, do not press for an inheritance and settle for a dowry in household articles and animals to be received upon their marriage. Daughters who press for an inheritance will be labeled *ambiciosa* (greedy) by women and men alike. I have heard women comment that a betrothed woman does not need her own land since her husband will provide for her once they have formally married. The assumption is that women should not attempt to compete with the productive monopoly of their husbands for it can only lead to the type of role reversals that are the subject of jokes and cruel gossip.

When women inherit land, they own it in their own right. Roughly 18 percent of households are built by men on land belonging to their wives, and roughly 20 percent of all households have in-marrying men who were orphans, sons of land-poor men or sons who for one reason or another broke with their fathers and lost their inheritance. It is rare for men to seek a wife for instrumental reasons — e.g. that she is the only daughter of a rich man or because her brothers have good connections in the church — since in-marrying men never become the owners of their wives' property unless they marry civilly. Ritual rank does not transfer from one descent group to another, and marrying for love is an important ideal. A man living matrilocally is said to be "making *atole* in the house of his wife," a derogatory comment since the preparation of *atole*, a corn gruel, is women's work. The "maleness" of men who live with their wives is always in question; without property ownership there are doubts about a husband's capacity to act like a man in assuming a dominant position in the household. Unless in-marrying men work independently on their own land, it is unlikely that they will be given a cargo even though they act as household heads in representing the household to the community.

Male and female marital roles are clearly spelled out and those individual women and men who do not live up to expectations are held in low esteem and not trusted for important responsibilities. Economic independence or property ownership by women threatens a man's self-image, for as her status goes up, his is bound to drop. Because of pressure from without, given the preoccupation individuals have with their public image, couples adopt a number of solutions to reduce role conflict in the household when positions are reversed. For example, if a woman owns land and her husband works it, he will be paid for his labor unless the profits are invested in household maintenance. If a woman wants to control the profits she may easily hire laborers to cultivate her land if she has the money to do so.

Entering economic production is problematic for women. It is not common for a woman to have either land or cash which could be used to expand investment possibilities. Woman's labor in Chignautla has use rather than exchange value and any work a woman might find would pay very little and be demeaning. Although a woman may easily hire men to work for her if the workman is her husband, people will say that she has "stolen his pants." On the other hand, men cannot hire women to work for them because they will be said to have "lost their pants" to another man's wife. Thus, without land and capital, the most common economic activity women enter is that of *regatón* (broker). *Regatones* buy fruit and vegetables from individual producers and then bulk and sell to buyers either in Teziutlán or to men who come from as far away as Puebla (the state capital) and Mexico City. Women who make profits at this trade keep them for personal use. Only a small percentage of women have become sucessful *regatonas* because economic success fosters the type of independence

which conflicts with a husband's dominance within the marital relationship. Role conflict usually suffices to constrain women from becoming
economic actors apart from their market participation, which represents
small-scale earnings made irregularly and used to purchase needed items
for the house. Women may compete with other women or even other men
in the market, but husbands and wives cannot compete with each other.
As household heads, men far more easily than women transfer their position in the household to positions of authority in high-level institutions
which only serve to strengthen their jural status in the community. What
men gain as jural adults women lose in becoming wives for there can be
only one household head.

POLITICS OF PUBLIC LIFE

Much of the power of men derives from their jural status, a status impossible to obtain without a woman. Some men do become household
heads without marrying but do not participate in public life in the same
capacity as men who are also heads of families in their own household.
Women contribute to the definition of men's adult status in such a way
that only husbands are considered as candidates for cargo sponsorship.
Men in other statuses are similarly barred from office: unmarried, dependent sons are jural minors; unmarried men living in free union with a
woman in a household of their own can not serve because they are "living
in sin"; and unmarried adult men living alone would not be able to meet
the ritual obligations of office without a wife to complete the range of tasks
forming a *mayordomía*. And while widows may request and hold cargos
for their deceased husbands, utilizing the help of sons, widowers cannot
hold a cargo until they marry again. In fact, men who never marry or
marry very late in life rarely have any type of role in public life or in
making decisions within their barrios. Without a wife these men are
forced to remain peripheral members of society, while unmarried women
often become successful merchants and because of their wealth have a
relatively greater influence than married women who must remain in
their husbands' shadows.

My point is that men do not *ipso facto* gain positions of authority in
public life simply because they are men, nor are women prohibited from
holding office solely because they are women. The vast majority of women
and men do marry and thereby perpetuate the customary pattern of male
dominance by removing the possibility for women to become jural adults
by heading a domestic unit. Even a widowed mother who has become

legal owner of her husband's house must take a back seat to the son with whom she lives. In the past it was not possible for women to live alone but today women who inherit property need not marry in order to gain access to male labor since a woman may have her house built, her fields cultivated, and her contributions to local corvés carried out for her by men she will pay in cash or in corn. In other words, a woman need not buy into a dependency role in order to survive, but a woman attempting to "make it on her own" will inevitably suffer in her relations with other women and men and within herself from the role strain she fosters by her freedom and independence. However, if such a woman gained a certain level of wealth and had an appropriate agnatic genealogy of service in the church, she too could serve God as men do who are also household heads.

Just three years ago, a top-level cargo was held by an unmarried woman who met all the traditional and unstated requirements for holding a cargo. With the help of relatives and neighbors she carried out all the obligations of office but she did not participate in activities where she felt that as a woman she would be disadvantaged. These activities involve heavy drinking and are occasions where religious politics are played out. However this "female *mayordomo*" still had political clout since recruitment decisions could not be made without her vote. Much of the politicking revolving around change of officers is carried out informally and she could participate informally, as wives do.

It is clear that women have secondary ritual roles in Chignautla's cargo system. Women attend church more than men do but they cannot actively relate to God as a cargo-holder. But because marital roles bind husbands and wives to each other, what women do affects their husbands. Wives play an active part in defending their husband's interests just as they did when their husbands were still dependent minors in the household of their fathers. The inequality, yet interlinking, of marital roles is seen in Chignauteco conceptualizations about the nature of personal-supernatural relations. Women have access to the supernatural through their husbands but husbands do not relate to the supernatural through their wives. An even more striking contrast is the belief that if a man acts against the supernatural order, his wife is the most likely recipient of supernatural punishment befalling the household, e.g. her illness or even death. The converse is never true, though a woman may cause her husband to lose respect, diminishing his chances for holding office. Husbands also recognize that wives contribute to their success by giving support and affirmation of their worth through their actions and defense. The most important defensive strategy of a woman is her ability to speak for her husband in situations where he is constrained from speaking on his own behalf in an effort to secure a cargo.

In much the same manner that dependent sons fear to ask their fathers for independence, household heads fear rejections from the men of the church authority if they request a cargo. Instead of "putting themselves through this embarassment," as they say, men prefer to be appointed. But in order for an appointment to arrive at the house in the hands of a sexton a man must make his intentions known to those involved in the recruitment process. Knowing also that there is often competition for cargos a man must carefully plan the appropriate time for leaking this information. A man will inform his wife several years in advance when he is aware that a cargo is about to be released or contended. The wife then carries this information to other women who will in turn inform their husbands who are already holding cargos or who are in a position to influence men currently in office. By and by, a man is able to assess his chances on the basis of the information returned to him through his wife in an on-going process of selecting the best candidate for the cargo in question. It is here that a woman actively enters the politics of religion. Women are in stratigic positions to distribute information damaging to men whose request becomes public in this informal manner. Less constrained than men outside of ritual contexts, when women meet at the mill or in the market in Teziutlán, it is relatively easy for them to learn of the behavior of individuals in the general flow of information disseminated through gossip. Thus, just as a desire to serve becomes known, facts eliminating a man from serving become known by interested parties, while all persons involved have lived up to the standards of proper conduct outside the home.

The role of women in transmitting information through gossip is not in itself unusual and it would be incorrect to say that men do not also gossip for one reason or another, But what is of interest is the discernible pattern of gossip in Chignautla. The slight changes interjected in rumors are not random. They are changes useful to and consistent with barrio interests. Once they become public, whether or not they are true, a man's reputation is ruined. It is this type of politicized slander used by women that permits men to use their ability to control the distribution of cargos. Women are expected to be protective and ambitious for their husbands, and no one would criticize a woman for doing what she could to make sure her husband receives the cargo she feels he deserves, a cargo he is unable to obtain by his own efforts.

CONCLUDING REMARKS

In this paper I have described the role of women in the political process of an Indian community, one similar to other rural communities in Meso-america. Social life in Chignautla is articulated through kinship which is patricentric, producing a typical configuration in which males are dom-inant. However, within the household women are active in decision-making processes and in establishing men in positions having public rec-ognition and use. I have also shown that women are active in the politics of religion which determines acquiring positions of power within the bar-rios. Though women are important to men's gaining public office, men normally hold the formal positions of authority within the household and in the public domain, positions they hold largely by virtue of their con-trol over productive resources. It is the status of wife that defines for men their social identity in a jurally significant way, allowing them to partici-pate as primary actors in the higher-level institutions of the community.

Recent work in the anthropology of women has taken a critical view of the way in which the contribution of women to processes in society has been submerged in discussions that focused on the roles and activities of men. While there are a few discussions of women which do not mention men, the reverse is seldom the case. This paper is offered as a partial corrective of this bias, and I have aimed at the more general problem of trying to discuss the role of one sex without showing relationship to the other sex. Specifically, I have shown that for this community, not only would analysis be incomplete if it were to omit the ways in which women's positions affects men's activities and the positions they hold in public life, but this type of omission would represent a denial of the complemen-tary nature of sex roles even though they may be strongly asymmetrical. On the one hand, women in Chignautla derive their status from the men upon whom they are dependent and they strongly identify with them. On the other hand, male dominance in Chignautla does not extend to the point where men engage in important activities independent of the approval and cooperation of women. The basic sex role identity in this kin-based society is tied to the role of husband and wife. It is in these statuses that the sexual identities of women and men are most clearly delineated.

The structural implications of marriage for sexual status are evident in many societies. That these societies are usually characterized by sexual asymmetry when they are patricentered is obvious, for the literature is replete with descriptions of men playing roles deemed critical for social functioning in such societies. But what has been obscured, and what I have tried to show in this case study, is the essential role of women in defining men's social identity and in determining their public functioning. It is in this type of kin-based social system that the interlocking of marital and community roles becomes apparent. At the same time, the asymmetry of the system is also revealed when departures from the norm of marriage are examined: for the man this entails a loss of status in the public domain, while it allows the woman to gain status in the same arena.

REFERENCES

COLLIER, JANE F.
  1974   "Women in politics," in *Woman, culture and society*. Edited by M. Rosaldo and L. Lamphere. Stanford: Stanford University Press.
LAMPHERE, L.
  1974   "Strategies, cooperation and conflict among women in domestic groups," in *Woman, culture and society*. Edited by M. Rosaldo and L. Lamphere. Standford: Standford University Press.
ROSALDO, M., L. LAMPHERE
  1974   *Woman, culture and society*. Stanford: Stanford University Press.
SLADE, D. L.
  1973   "The Mayordomos of San Mateo: Political economy of a religious system." Unpublished doctoral dissertation, University of Pittsburgh. Ann Arbor: University Microfilms.

Lower Economic Sector Female Mating Patterns in the Dominican Republic: A Comparative Analysis

SUSAN E. BROWN

Most Caribbean ethnographies and sociological treatises have emphasized topics related to domestic organization. Household cycle and composition, mating patterns, domestic functions, and the like have been of primary concern. Most especially, the divergent multiple partner mating patterns, and their ensuing forms of domestic organization which are found among the lowest economic sector have continued to draw attention. Recent studies of low income North American blacks have detailed patterns of domestic organization similar to those of low income Carribbean populations.

Among the lowest economic sectors of both Caribbean and North American black populations such characteristics as unstable marital unions, high illegitimacy rates, male marginality within the households, and high instances of matrifocal families continually reappear (Blake 1961; Clark 1966; Frazier 1939; Gonzalez 1969; Hannerz 1969; Henriques 1953; Herskovits 1941; Lewis 1966; Liebow 1967; Matthews 1953; Moynihan 1965; Otterbein 1966; Rainwater 1970; Rodman 1971; Simey 1946; M. G. Smith 1962; R. T. Smith 1956; Stack 1970; Valentine 1968; Whitten and Szwed 1970).

Much of this literature, however, reflects the ethnocentrism of dominant sectors in both the society under investigation and that of the investigator. Since Frazier (1939), there have been those who see such characteristics of lower economic sector domestic organization in both Caribbean and North American black societies as signifying states of social disorganization and breakdown. Welfare-oriented research typically takes this perspective (Blake 1961; Henriques 1953; Matthews 1953; Moynihan 1965; Simey 1946). Others have tried to explain variant forms of domestic organization in different ways. Otterbein (1966) explains mating patterns in terms of sex ratios. M. G. Smith (1962) argues that differences in family structure are due to differences in mating systems. Moynihan (1965) regards the divergent low economic sector black family structure as the causal factor for most all of the ills that the North American black family suffers.

On the other hand, many investigators have proposed that forms of domestic organization found in populations of the lowest economic sector are positive mechanisms by which the people manage to cope under the conditions forced upon them (Clark 1966; Gonzalez 1969; Hannerz 1969; Valentine 1968; Whitten and Szwed 1970). It should be noted that many of these mentioned researchers refer to the studied low economic sector forms of domestic organization as "adaptive mechanisms" or "means of adapting to" given stressful circumstances.[1] It is suggested here, however, that the mechanisms involved are coping rather than adaptive ones. In this light, coping, defined as individual behavior aimed at continuance under given stressful circumstances, is distinguished from adaptation, which implies a successful behavior passed on from generation to generation at the expense of less beneficial behaviors. Returning then to the brief literature review, it must be said that various researchers have suggested the coping function of these divergent, low economic sector forms of domestic organization. In none of these former studies, however, has quantitative analysis been carried out to test if within a given economic sector one form of domestic organization provides for better coping mechanisms than another. The novelty of this study concerns the presentation and analysis of such quantitative data.

The object of this paper is to outline the major findings of research recently conducted on lower economic sector female mating patterns and domestic organization in a rural village of the Dominican Republic. Fieldwork was carried out during a three year period. May through August, 1969, 1970, and 1971 were spent in the Dominican Republic. Participant observation and scheduled interviews were the major methods of data gathering. These have been compiled in Brown (1972).

The village studied, comprised of 916 inhabitants residing among 162 households, lies in the fertile northern valley region known as the Cibao. Dominicans believe the entire region to be one of relatively prosperous small landholding peasants. However, 30 percent of all village households own no land at all, and 40 percent hold less than one acre. At the same

---

[1] Among those to employ "adaptation" in this manner are Lewis (1966:xliv), Rainwater (1970:397), Rodman (1968:759), Stack (1970:311), Whitten and Szwed (1970:40).

time, the nine largest landholders (6 percent of all households) own more than half of approximately 250 acres of cultivable land of the village.

Although considered to be an agricultural area, agriculture accounts for the main source of income in only 57 percent of all households: 18 percent of all households receive their major income from non-agricultural self employment; 15 percent receive it from non-agricultural wage labor; 6 percent are retired and mainly supported by their children; and 4 percent of the households live mainly by male migrant wage labor. In short, the economy is one in transition. The vast majority of villagers are not able, either through agricultural or wage labor pursuits, to obtain sufficient funds to allow them to participate fully in the industrial society upon which they have been made dependent.

As recently as thirty years ago, these villagers were relatively successful peasants living within an UNDEVELOPED society, today they are UNDERDEVELOPED participants in the economy of a capitalistic metropolis-satellite economy. As is demonstrated in this study by use of such quantitative data as household budgets, daily diets, shelter quality, and health indices, the vast majority of villagers suffer from underconsumption and live in constant debt. It should be noted, however, that compared with other areas of the country most of the workers enjoy a relatively prosperous existence. For example, although their diet may not be nutritionally adequate, rarely do these villagers suffer the hunger common to other Dominican areas. All villagers, however, do not live under the same economic conditions, and various distinguishable economic sectors exist. In this study, for example, three broad village economic sectors are recognized: the highest sector containing about 8 percent of all households; the middle sector with 70 percent; and the lowest sector with about 22 percent of all households.

The major concern of this analysis is the two female mating patterns found among the lowest economic sector. These two mating patterns, shown to be best understood as patterned means of dealing with and existing under the stress-laden socioeconomic circumstances, are comparatively analyzed in terms of their relative coping ability within the lowest economic sector. These female mating patterns represent more than just types of sexual behavior, they designate different life styles, different patterns of domestic organization, and are different means of coping within the lowest economic sector. Briefly defined the two lowest economic sector female mating patterns are:

(1) the single mate form by which a woman has only one mate during her lifetime (except for rare cases of widow re-marriage). The typical domestic organization associated with this single mate pattern is the male-headed

Table 1.   Characteristics of the two female life styles as distinguished by mating patterns

	Single mate pattern	Multiple partner pattern	Community held ideal pattern
Type of union	Formal marriage (usually within the Catholic Church)	Informal free and visiting unions[a]	Formal marriage (usually within the Catholic Church)
Duration of union	Permanent	Temporary	Permanent
Post-martital residence	Patrilocal, i.e. on land of or near husband's family	Matrilocal, i.e. on land of or near woman's family	Neolocal, i.e. independent of both families
Household composition	Nuclear, i.e. husband, wife, and children	Nonnuclear, i.e. a woman and her children	Nuclear
Household headship	Male	Female	Male
Child-rearing responsibilities	Within the nuclear household	Children often "farmed out," especially to maternal kin	Within the nuclear household
Major income provider	Male head of household	Female head of household	Male head of household
Most likely mutual aid interaction	With husband's kin	With woman's kin	With husband's kin

[a] A free or consensual union is one in which a couple lives together without the sanction of religious or civil authority. A visiting union is one which not only lacks formal sanction but also differs from a free union in that no coresidence is involved; instead, one party (in these cases the male) visits the household of the other.

nuclear household. Furthermore, the marriage union is usually an official and permanent one; offspring are legitimate; the husband is the major authority figure as well as the major economic provider for the household and so on (see Table 1). This pattern represents the community held, middle class, ideal behavior and is by far the majority pattern for the community at large.[2]

(2) the multiple mate form whereby a woman has more than one mate, usually more than two, and has them serially. Characteristics of this pattern are such features as unstable marital unions, high illegitimacy rates, male marginality within the household, high instances of matrifocal and woman headed households and so on. These latter characteristics are those noted as common to low economic sector Caribbean and North American black population. This second pattern, limited to the lowest economic

[2]   Within the village as a whole (total = 162 households) only twelve women (heads or co-heads of households) were found to have had multiple mates. Within the rest of the households the women, head or co-head of the household, were found to follow the single partner mating pattern.

sector of the village, is held as deviant behavior by the community at large.

The major hypothesis of this study contains two parts, (X) and (Y); both parts pertain exclusively to the lowest economic sector sample households (N = 18, 9 of the single mate pattern and 9 of the multiple mate pattern).[3] Part (X) of the hypothesis proposes the following: Women following the ideal single mate pattern are better off in terms of traditional measures of wealth (land, income, and capital) than women who follow the deviant multiple mate pattern. Part (Y) of the hypothesis, on the other hand, states that women following the deviant multiple mate pattern do better than the women following the ideal single mate pattern in terms of various indices of well-being, including reproduction success, shelter size and quality, quality and quantity of food consumption, and psychological well-being. Standard non-parametric tests for statistical significance are carried out for both parts of the hypothesis.

Part (X): The data analyzed support Part (X) of the hypothesis which states that women following the ideal single mate pattern are better off in terms of traditional measures of wealth (income, land, and capital) than those who follow the deviant multiple mate pattern. The differences between the two groups' mean distributions for income is significant at the .05 level (using the Mann-Whitney "U" test) (see Table 2). Differences in landholding, while not statistically significant, support the predicted trend and point up important differences in access to this resource between the two groups (see Table 3). Furthermore, capital differences, in totals and means, favor those of the single mate group (see Table 4). Part (Y) of the

Table 2. Estimated income figures for sample low economic sector grouped by mating pattern (calculated in U.S. dollars)

Single mate pattern		Multiple mate pattern	
Household number	Dollars	Household number	Dollars
1	340	1	250
2	460	2	200
3	270	3	750
4	380	4	900
5	650	5	150
6	920	6	360
7	475	7	190
8	370	8	130
9	450	9	350

[3] While the entire village contained 162 households, only the three largest extended families (comprising a total of 64 households) were studied in detail. In turn, for this analysis of the low economic female mating patterns, all low economic sector households found to exist within the 64 households studied were included in the sample, (total = 18).

Table 3.   Landholding figures for sample low economic sector grouped by mating
pattern (in Tareas)

Single mate pattern		Multiple mate pattern	
Household number	Tareas	Household number	Tareas
1	7	1	0
2	12	2	0
3	0	3	0
4	2	4	0
5	0	5	0
6	7	6	0
7	10	7	0
8	1	8	30
9	0	9	20
Total 39		Total 50	
M = 4.3		M = 5.5	

Table 4.   Livestock ownership figures for sample low economic
sector grouped by mating pattern (per household)

Pigs			
Single mate pattern		Multiple mate pattern	
Household number	Quantity	Household number	Quantity
1	3	1	4
2	10	2	2
3	1	3	0
4	10	4	3
5	10	5	3
6	3	6	3
7	1	7	0
8	0	8	2
9	0	9	2
Total 38		Total 19	
M = 4.2		M = 2.1	

Chickens			
Single mate pattern		Multiple mate pattern	
Household number	Quantity	Household number	Quantity
1	12	1	9
2	8	2	6
3	10	3	1
4	20	4	2
5	10	5	2
6	16	6	12
7	7	7	7
8	1	8	1
9	1	9	15
Total 85		Total 52	
M = 9.5		M = 5.8	

hypothesis suggests that although those households belonging to the single partner female mating pattern group do better than those of the multiple partner mating pattern, in terms of various traditional indices of wealth, households belonging to the multiple partner female pattern, to the contrary, do better in terms of the various indices of well-being. These indices (reproductive success, shelter conditions, and food quality) can be seen as reflections of different ways of coping with the life circumstances of the low economic sector. In the majority of cases significant differences are shown to exists between the two female mating groups in the direction predicted by part (Y) of the hypothesis. As a whole, sample women of the single mate pattern group had 18 percent more occurrence of prenatal and post-natal mishaps than did women of the multiple partner group. Women of the latter group also managed to raise significantly larger numbers of children beyond the age of five (7.95 per woman), than women of the single mate group (4.8 per woman) (see Table 5). In regard to shelter

Table 5.   Reproductive success figures for sample low economic sector grouped by mating pattern

	Single mate	Multiple mate
Average number of pregnancies per woman	7.25	9.05
Average occurrence per woman of combined pregnancy and early childhood mishaps (spontaneous abortions, still births, and infant mortality under five years of age)	2.40	1.35
Average number of children raised beyond five years of age (per woman)	4.80	7.95

conditions, households of the single mate pattern contained an average of 2.0 persons per room, while households of the multiple mate pattern had only 1.1 persons per room. As for mean scores, the first group exhibits an average of 4.1 rooms per house, while the respective figure for the second group is 5 rooms per house. As for other shelter indices, statistical analysis shows the differences between the two groups for the quality of walls and roofs to be significant (using Fisher Exact 2×2 Contingency Tables at, respectively, .025 and .041 levels of significance). The third feature, floors, while not statistically significant, differs considerably in the predicted direction (see Table 6). In regard to the quality of food consumed (measured in terms of food items of higher protein content consumed per week) the hypothesis that those households of the multiple mate pattern have a significantly greater intake of higher protein items than do those of the single mate pattern is tested with the K-S (one-tailed) Test. Although the initial ratio D is not significant, obvious differences exist between the two groups in the predicted direction. Numerical analysis does support

Table 6. Statistical procedures used to analyze household construction for the low economic sector sample grouped by mating pattern

Fisher exact 2×2 contingency tables

		Zinc	Cana	
Roof material	MD-I	0	9	9
	MD-II	4	5	9

Significant at the .041 level

		Wood or Concrete	Palma	
Wall material	MD-I	3	6	9
	MD-II	9	0	9

Significant at the .025 level

		Cement or wood	Earth	
Floor material	MD-I	3	6	9
	MD-II	6	3	9

Not Significant at the .05 level

Table 7. Statistical procedure used to analyze higher protein consumption for the low economic sector sample grouped by mating pattern

One-tailed Kolomogorov – Smirnov test for "D maximum"

		(—1)	1	3	3
Consumption of higher protein	MP-I	3/9	6/9	8/9	9/9
items for week	MP-II	0	4/9	8/9	9/9

D Max = 3/9 that is, not significant at the .05 level

the hypothesis; no household of the multiple mate group consumes less than one high protein item per week, while one-third of the households in the single partner group have such an intake only once every two weeks (see Table 7). Beyond all this, it is our opinion that women following the multiple rate pattern manifest greater personal contentment and are psychologically better adjusted to their life circumstances within the low economic sector than are women belonging to the single mate group. This implies, of course, that women following the deviant multiple mate pattern, though "poorer" according to traditional measures of wealth, in reality "do better" within conditions of the low economic sector than women following the ideal single mate pattern who are "better off" in terms of traditional wealth indices. In other words, the multiple mate pattern as a constellation of behavioral characteristics offers certain measurable advantages over the ideal single mate pattern as a constellation of behavioral characteristics for persons of the lowest economic sector.

There are many reasons why the single mate pattern, while viable elsewhere, might not represent the most advantageous form of domestic organization for life within the poverty sector. Among other things, in adhering to the single mate pattern a woman becomes predominantly dependent upon her spouse, a situation little advantageous in the poverty sector.

The division of labor and responsibility by sex implied in the single mate pattern is much more viable among the more affluent middle and high economic sectors and among more properous peasants than in the poverty sector. Typically, men of the more affluent economic sectors are most able to adequately support a household. A woman, under such circumstances, can afford to work exclusively within the household while depending upon her husband for the wherewithal to run the household. Similarly, within landholding peasant households, where subsistence may be more meager, the daily labor of both men and women is imperative. The husband and wife work as a team to provide for the household. The man works the fields, cares for the livestock, maintains the necessary tools and the like, while the woman spends her day with the tasks of food preparation, household maintenance, child care, and so on. So necessary is this male-female combination within the peasant household that in peasant societies where one or the other sex is scarce, one often finds households made up of consanguineal kin such as brothers and sisters.[4]

Life within the poverty sector, however, provides different economic circumstances which, as a whole, deny the necessity and viability of the ideal single mate pattern and in turn favor the multiple mate pattern. Under these conditions, the single mate female pattern is less advantageous for the women involved. Poor women who take on multiple mates can provide for themselves and their children more efficiently than poor women who maintain the standard of a single mate.

With respect to type and duration of unions, women of both mating pattern groups verbalize the advantages of the more flexible free and visiting unions as follows: "Once married, a woman is subject to her husband; not only can he dispose of his own resources as he sees fit but also he has access to the wife's resources." A woman living in a free union vividly explained why she preferred it to marriage:

---

[4]   Such consanguineal household arrangements have been described in the Carribbean as well as in other areas. Among those to describe such households within the Carribbean are Clark (1966), Gonzalez (1969) and Otterbein (1966).

I would rather not marry the man with whom I live. If I marry him I will not be free to move about and find the employment I choose and, anyway, he would have some control over the money I earn. As it stands now, if he fails to provide adequately for me and my children, or if he abuses me (which is more likely to cause a break-up as most men do not provide adequately), or if he turns *gallero* and spends all his money on cock-fights, women and alcohol, then I would leave him. I would leave the children with my mother (who already lives with her), and go, as I have gone before, to Santo Domingo to work.

Regarding household residence and composition, living in proximity with one's mother allows greater interchange and mutual aid in such chores as food procurement and preparation, child care, and assistance in times of illness or emergency. The strong mother-daughter dyad, also, for example, allows for greater flexibility in personal mobility. A woman, in time of need, may leave her children with her mother and seek employment elsewhere. She returns to the village only intermittently, and in the meantime sends money to her mother for the children's care.

The question of household headship is also an important one. The head has most control over the household resources, and thus a common complaint among women of the single partner pattern concerns their husband's management of household funds. All too often it seems that men dispose of household resources in ways the wife considers inappropriate. For example, expenditures on cock fighting, other women, and alcohol, while highly valued among a man's peers, are deplored by the wife. Women of the multiple mate pattern, on the other hand, are the heads of their own households and thus have more direct control over household resources and are free to dispense them as they see most fit.

Recognition of the importance of women having only one mate at a time and of having children is imperative to an understanding of the female mating patterns. Even though a woman might have various mates during her lifetime she has them one at a time. In accordance with the prevalent *macho* complex men tend to demand exclusive rights to the women with whom they unite. While male infidelity is common and widely tolerated, more than one village union has been broken by men who felt that their women had been unfaithful; and there are other considerations. Imagine the difficulty a woman would have knowing and proving the paternity of her child, and thus the person presumably in part responsible for the child's upbringing, if she has been having sexual relations with more than one man during the same period of time.

In all sectors of village society it is important to have children. A woman must marry and have children for it is one's children who will take care of one in their old age. It is explained that, of course, not all one's children turn out to be as they should; many forget their parents when they leave to make a life of their own. Perhaps one or two children, however, will turn out to be "good" children and remember their mother in her old age. Within a society where there exists little chance for savings and no old age insurance, it is one's children to whom one looks in old age. Children are important; they are especially important to women living in poverty.[5]

Poor women want and need children but often encounter difficulty in supporting their children adequately. While women of the single mate pattern generally raise all of their children within the nuclear household, women of the multiple mate pattern often avail themselves of child-shifting procedures which place their children temporarily in other households. While living in another household, the child, in exchange for room, board, a small wage, clothing, and medical attention if required, is expected to help in household chores. Girls to assist in the "female" chores of laundering, cleaning, food preparation, and child care are highly valued and thus are involved in these child-shifting arrangements more often than boys. These arrangements, common to the multiple mate pattern, provide obvious benefits for the women involved. They allow, for example, a woman to bear and raise more children than she could otherwise afford. If a child is loaned out only temporarily, which is usually the case, the child retains loyalty to the mother and eventually returns to her or his natal household. In the meantime, the child has been cared for and the mother has obtained an additional, however small, income from the household to which the child was lent. Also important are the alliances this child-shifting procedure establishes between more powerful and less powerful families. A child is usually shifted into a household that is better-off than its natal household. Even after the child no longer works there, the child's family may expect to receive, upon request, goods such as garden products from the household where the child was shifted.[6]

Everything considered, the constellation of features associated with the multiple mate pattern thus allows for greater flexibility; it allows, so to speak, a better chance for maximizing one's meager resources. In cases where the male fails to fulfill his role as major household provider, the woman may leave this mate and take on another who might provide better for her, even if only for a short period of time. On the other hand, a woman

[5] The fact that women need and desire children has been reported repeatedly in Latin America as well as in other "underdeveloped" areas. Among Carribbean scholars reporting such findings are Clark (1966), Gonzalez (1969), and Lewis (1966).
[6] Although little has been published on cross-cultural arrangements of child shifting, the topic represents an area of actual concern. For example, at the 1972 American Anthropological Association meetings in Toronto a symposium was presented on "Transactions in Parenthood."

might decide to live alone with her children or to return with her children to live with her mother. Beyond these and other options the multiple mate pattern is associated with wider mutual aid networks than the ideal single pattern. It seems that women of the multiple mate pattern remain more closely aligned with their own mothers. For example, one village woman, Carmen, would not go live in the village of her third mate saying that she could not leave her mother (with whom she and her children lived) alone. Carmen's relationship with her mother was obviously more important than her relationship with her third mate. She anticipated, and so it occurred, that this mate was to be but another transitional partner for her. Unlike women following the ideal single pattern, Carmen ran her own household as she saw most fit. During the harvest months she worked in the local tobacco warehouse and with her earnings she gradually repaired the house in which they lived. Although at this time Carmen's fourth mate lived with them and contributed to the household maintenance, Carmen was the household head. As head of her own household Carmen saw fit to "lend-out" some of her children to neighborhood and kin families. Thus she was relieved of having all seven children in the small house all at once. At the same time her household received a few dollars monthly for each child living in another household. If financial complications were to develop and Carmen needed additional money, she would, as she has done in the past, go to work in Santo Domingo, leaving the children with her mother.

A woman following the single mate pattern does not have all these options. She must make the best of what her mate provides for her. Even the possibility of her supplementing the household income with her own outside work is subject to her husband's approval. Social customs and considerations of what is "proper behavior" deny to these women of the single mate pattern many of the more beneficial mechanisms by which poor Dominican women have come to cope with poverty. For example, it is not considered "proper" for a woman to participate in free or visiting unions, to "lend-out" some of her children, to be the head of her own household, to make decisions about household economics, to represent the household in extra-household affairs, to be the major provider for the household, and so on.

Relatively speaking for a majority of village inhabitants economic conditions are getting worse. If they continue to deteriorate, more women will be searching for ways to maximize the meager resources available to them — more women will be forced to weigh the benefits of the "ideal" single mate pattern against those of the multiple mate pattern. And, in fact, because of the advantages it offers for life under poverty, it appears that as time passes more Dominican women will take on the multiple mate pattern with its ensuing form of domestic organization and constellation of behavioral features. In this final sense it is being suggested that the multiple partner female mating pattern not only provides better coping mechanism for life within the studied low economic sector, but that also it is evolutionarily adaptive under these circumstances while the single mate pattern is not. That is to say, as the multiple mate pattern and its ensuing form of domestic organization provide for a better existence under given stressful economic conditions, they can be expected to be increasingly followed and in turn passed on to succeeding low economic sector women at the expense of less efficient coping mechanisms such as the single mate pattern.

REFERENCES

BLAKE, JUDITH
  1961   *Family structure in Jamaica.* New York: Free Press.
BROWN, SUSAN E.
  1972   Unpublished doctoral dissertation, University of Michigan.
CLARK, EDITH
  1966   *Land tenure and the family in four selected communities in Jamaica.* London: George Allen and Unwin.
FRAZIER, E. FRANKLIN
  1939   *The Negro family in the United States.* Chicago: University of Chicago Press.
GONZÁLEZ, NANCIE L.
  1969   *Black Carib household structure.* Seattle: Univ. of Washington Press.
HANNERZ, ULF
  1969   *Soulside: inquiries into ghetto culture and community.* New York: Columbia University Press.
HENRIQUES, FERNANDO
  1953   *Family and colour in Jamaica.* London: Eyre and Spottiswoode.
HERSKOVITS, M.
  1941   *The myth of the Negro past.* New York.
LEWIS, OSCAR
  1966   *La vida: A Puerto Rican family in the culture of poverty — San Juan and New York.* New York: Random House.
LIEBOW, ELLIOT
  1967   *Tally's corner: a study of Negro streetcorner men.* Boston: Little, Brown.
MATTHEWS, BASIL
  1953   *The crisis of the West Indian family.* Mona, Jamaica: University College of the West Indies.
MOYNIHAN, DANIEL P.
  1965   *The Negro family: the case for national action.* Washington: Govern-Printing Office.

OTTERBEIN, KEITH F.

1966 *The Andros Islanders: a study of family organization in the Bahamas.* Lawrence: University of Kansas Press.

RAINWATER, LEE

1970 *Behind ghetto walls: black family life in a federal slum.* Chicago: Aldine.

RODMAN, HYMAN

1968 Family and social pathology in the ghetto. *Science* 61:756–762.

1971 *Lower class families: the culture of poverty in Negro Trinidad.* New York: Oxford Press.

SIMEY, T. S.

1946 *Welfare and planning in the West Indies.* Oxford: Clarendon Press.

SMITH, M. G.

1962 *West Indian family structure.* Seattle: University of Washington Press.

SMITH, RAYMOND T.

1956 *The Negro family in British Guiana.* London: Routledge and Kegan Paul.

STACK, CAROL

1970 "The kindred of Viola Jackson: residence and family organization of an urban black family," in *Afro-American anthropology.* Edited by J. Szwed and N. Whitten, 303–311. New York: Free Press.

VALENTINE, CHARLES

1968 *Culture and poverty.* Chicago: University of Chicago Press.

WHITTEN, NORMAN, JOHN SZWED, *editors*

1970 *Afro-American anthropology.* New York: Free Press.

The Female Domestic Servant and Social Change: Lima, Peru

MARGO L. SMITH

In spite of their large numbers and their high degree of visibility, domestic servants in the large urban centers of Latin America generally have been ignored by social scientists and other observers of the urban scene. Servants and the servitude complex in which they live are presented most frequently in a peripheral sense: in supporting roles in novels (Donoso 1965, 1967); as a small part of contemporary urban life (Lewis 1959); as a part of the historical record (Lockhart 1968; Carrio de la Vandera 1966; Prado 1941; Von Tschudi 1966); and as a part of either the "Indian problem" or one of the major "social problems" of the urban arena. It is within the context of defining servants as a contemporary "problem" that most of the recent social science-oriented research on servants in Peru has been framed (Helfer 1966; Pascual 1968; Flores 1961; Vasquez 1969; and numerous journalistic exposés) and that servants have become a main topic for investigation. In these studies, servants also are presented as passive members of a tradition-oriented and essentially static social context.[1]

When the topic of this study was originally suggested to me[2] the op-

The fieldwork on which this article is based was conducted in Lima, Peru, and the Peruvian provinces, in 1967 and 1968–1970. Financial support was provided by Indiana University, the Alpha Gamma Delta social fraternity, and the Department of Health, Education and Welfare (Fulbright-Hays).

[1] Nett (1966), for example, depicts servants in the Ecuadorean capital city as survivals from the colonial period. However, the situation in Quito is not directly comparable to that in Lima. Although both are national capitals, Quito is a highland city whereas Lima is a coastal city. Contrasts between domestic service in the highlands and on the coast are striking and worthy of consideration in another essay.

[2] Nora S. Kinzer merits the author's appreciation for mentally prodding her along new lines of thinking, but shares none of the responsibility for the ideas expressed here.

portunity to view the Lima servant from a different perspective was presented. To examine the servant within the context of social change, three general areas of scrutiny come to mind: changes which take place at the individual level among servants and their employers; changes which are taking place within the institution of urban servitude; and changes which can be seen taking place on a broader national scope. An initial view of the Lima servant shows servants to be most visible, in their distinctive uniforms, peering out at the street from the windows or roofs of the houses of their employers, running errands, making purchases in the market, sweeping the sidewalks, walking a few paces behind their employers and carrying all the packages, supervising the out-of-doors play of their employer's children, or chatting with fellow servants on the sidewalk or in the park. Once out of uniform and on their own time, servants melt into the anonymity of the vast urban lower class. This hardly suggests a social context much different from that of twenty years ago. However, a close scrutiny of the Lima servant and her world reveals factors both stimulating and inhibiting changes on all three of the levels mentioned. But before discussing these factors, it will be useful to provide a profile of the women working as servants in metropolitan Lima and a summary of the urban institution of which they, along with their employers, are the most integral members.[3]

Precise enumeration of the total number of servants in Lima has not been made. Women completely dominate the servant scene; they comprise 88 percent of all Lima servants (Centro Arguideocesano de Pastoral, CAP, 1967). Extrapolating from the Fifth and Sixth Peruvian National Census (Ministerio de Hacienda y Comercio, MHC, 1940, 1961) in which 26,200 and 66,100 women, respectively, were recorded as domestics (representing an increase in the servant segment of economically active females from 25 to 30 percent), a reasonable "questimate" of the number of women employed as servants in 1970 approaches 90,000. If women who have ever worked as servants, but who have managed to extricate themselves from that occupational niche, were to be included in this group as well, the total number of women living in contemporary Lima who have been involved personally in the servitude complex as subordinate members might approach 250,000. There are at least several thousand additional women who have worked as servants in Lima for some time before dropping out and returning to the Peruvian provinces to live.

The author also thanks Richard Schaedel, Robert Myhr, and the other seminar participants for their insightful comments.
[3]   A detailed view of the Lima servant and urban servitude is presented in Smith (1971).

The servant population is not a homogeneous, monolithic group; rather it reflects the widest spectrum of the lower class Peruvian population. Yet domestics "typically" represent a relatively narrow band of that spectrum. They are uniformly categorized by their employers as Indians or, at best, *cholas*,[4] categories with both racial and ethnic connotations. In actuality, an estimated 95 percent should be lumped, on the basis of their phenotype, into the *mestizo* category. The remainder of the servants are of Negro ancestry (descendants of African slaves brought to work as agricultural laborers on the Peruvian coast).

The majority of servants are older adolescents and young adults; 58 percent range in age from fifteen to twenty-four years (CAP 1967). Most of them are unmarried (some 90 percent according to CAP 1967), not an unexpected finding in light of the young age of the servants and their residence in the homes of their employers. One-quarter of the servants admit to having children; of these, slightly more than half have only one child (MHC 1965: Table 201). Not unexpectedly, as servants become older, they are more likely to have children, and also more likely to have more children (MHC 1965: Table 201). Although the Lima stereotype of servants as unwed mothers is not supported, the largest percentage of servant mothers are, in fact, unwed (CAP 1967).

Servants have completed very little formal education; a mere 8 percent have continued beyond elementary school (CAP 1967). However, few are illiterate and most have had at least some primary education. *Muchachas*, to employ the derogatory term often used in referring to these female servants, have less formal schooling than either male servants in Lima (CAP 1967), all women migrants to Lima from the provinces 1965: Table 3c), or women born in Lima (MHC 1966:60). Nearly one-third of the servants are of school age (under nineteen years of age) and literally thousands of them, along with their less-educated older counterparts, attend school while they are employed. Additional servants seek employment with this most highly desired fringe benefit.

Servant women are almost exclusively migrants from provincial areas outside of metropolitan Lima (91 percent according to CAP 1967). Nearly 57 percent of them are from the ten highland Andean areas; some 30 percent claim coastal origins; and only about 3 percent are migrants from the jungle areas (CAP 1967). Of these migrants, approximately 40 percent had come from provincial places with a population of 5,000 or more, and approximately 44 percent had come from places with

---

[4] The urbanized lower class woman, a social rank one important step above the lowest rung of Indian.

a population of 1,000 or more (MHC 1965; Table 11). This certainly does not support another tenet of the servant stereotype: that servants are born and raised in the most remote and isolated corners of the provinces. None of the author's servant informants had been raised in a provincial setting so isolated that some kind of public transportation was not easily accessible.

Nevertheless, the town environment in which the servants were raised and their family backgrounds are a far cry from the cosmopolitan bustling metropolis of the capital city to which servants have to adjust, often on their first job. They come from predominantly agricultural, poorly-educated families. Two-thirds of the servants' fathers are employed as agriculturalists or laborers ("Encuesta de la Parroquia" 1967:5). However, servants do not tend to come from the poorest or lowest ranking (in socioeconomic terms) families. Three-quarters of their fathers are landowners, and few of the servants' mothers, if living, are employed outside of the home (Escuela Municipal, 1965-1966). Illiteracy is high among servants' families; half of the fathers are unable to read and write, and, given the generally inferior level of educational achievement of Peruvian women relative to that of men, it can be assumed that an even greater percentage of the servants' mothers also are illiterate. However, the occupational category of the largest percentage of servants' siblings (approximately one-third, according to Escuela Municipal 1965-1966 is that of student. The "typical" servant is one of 5.6 siblings in the family, and has a better than even chance of being either the oldest or the youngest.

Numerous conditions bring about a young woman's move to Lima. The overwhelming majority of them move directly from their home towns to the capital. Most make the move willingly and on their own initiative, some only because they are brought or sent, and a few are brought to the capital very much against their wishes. Specifically servants mention being motivated to move to the capital by a desire to get ahead (*superación*); the search for a job, or to earn money to buy goods such as clothing or a radio; a desire to see what the capital city is like; a desire to continue her education; or in response to a family situation. Once in Lima, they find that servitude is the only or the best means within their power of supporting themselves and getting what they want out of urban life.[5]

The largest segment of migrant servant women are relatively recent

[5] Domestic service shelters, in addition to young migrants, some orphans, husbandless young women with a child to support, offspring of the poorest families, and older lower-class widows with numerous children to support.

arrivals in the capital, adolescents at the time of their migration, and previously unemployed. Nearly half of them have been in Lima for four and one-half years or less (CAP 1967). Two-thirds of them were between the ages of ten and nineteen years at the time of their migration (CAP 1967). More than half had not been habitually employed in the provinces, but of those who had worked, the largest number had been domestics there also (MHC 1965: Table 3a).

The institutionalized social and occupational niche of servant into which nearly two-thirds of employed migrant women find themselves in Lima is a highly structured context which continues to reinforce the rigid socioeconomic hierarchy. Domestics are among those who occupy the lowest rung on the urban socioeconomic scale (Delgado 1968; and Plan regional 1959). They are completely dominated, exploited, and controlled by groups ranking above them.

Servants are employed almost exclusively on a live-in basis, a pattern preferred by both servants and employers: by the former for the room and board received; and by the latter for the convenience of having the servant on call twenty-four hours a day and for the increased ease of controlling the servant's nonworking activities. Because servants are employed almost exclusively by middle and upper class families, they are most densely concentrated in the residential neighborhoods of their employers, rather than in the lower class residential neighborhoods of the servants' relatives. Most servants find that they are the only servants working in the households of their employers and that they are responsible for all general household tasks. However, the more servants are employed by the households the more likely they are to be specialized (the most frequently encountered specialties include two types of nursemaid, cook, and cleaning woman) and also expected to perform any number of strictly personal services for the various members of the employer's family.

A servant's career tends to follow a distinct seven-year pattern. Upon her arrival in Lima, she seeks out relatives or friends from her home town, with whom she spends her first few months. After this initial period of acculturation to the city, these relatives or friends are instrumental in placing her in her first job, usually sought by looking for *se necesita muchacha* (servant wanted) placards placed in the windows of houses and apartments in commercial neighborhoods. As the only servant in the household, she receives on-the-job training in a wide variety of household tasks in return for a low salary and few fringe benefits. After six months to a year, the servant moves on to a better job with a higher salary, fringe benefits, and more affluent employers living in a higher-ranking residential neighborhood. This and subsequent jobs are located by means of an employment agency (of which there are thirty in the metropolitan area), want ads in the newspaper, or the recommendation of friends or relatives. She begins to focus on one of the servant specialities and improves her position within the servant hierarchy as she passes from one job to the next. Each job generally lasts from six months to two years.

It is likely that she will have six different jobs during her tenure as a domestic. During this time, her salary and fringe benefits will range from only room and board; to an average salary of S/800 per month ($18.25); to a salary perhaps double that plus permission to study, hold a part-time job, or keep a child on the job, in addition to receiving clothing and other gifts. Approaching the age of twenty-four, the servant has a seven-year career behind her and drops out of servitude to concentrate on her legal or common-law husband and her children.

FACTORS STIMULATING OR INHIBITING CHANGES

Looking at domestic service in Lima, we may isolate factors which are stimulating or inhibiting changes at three levels: at the individual level for servant and employer participants; at the level of the urban institution of servitude; and at a national level. Among these, eleven factors appear most prominent.

The Individual Level

The changes at the individual level are the most notable and, in the long run, probably will emerge as the most significant in determining what broader changes will be taking place and how fast these changes will be occurring. Three pertinent elements at this level include the servant as a migrant, the servant's attitudes toward her position and toward change, and the employer's attitudes toward her servants.

THE SERVANT AS MIGRANT   Most servant women are migrants from other parts of the nation who have come to Lima voluntarily. Whatever are their individual reasons for making the move, they have heard first-hand or via letter from friends and relatives who have visited in or moved to the capital city that life there is very different from that in the home town. They have been alerted, before migrating, to the idea that they will have to make changes in their life upon moving to the capital. Because migrants (soon to become servants) are for the most part self-selected; and because it takes "guts" to migrate, it might be suggested that only those individuals who are willing to make change a part of their lives will be willing to take the first big step of making the move to Lima. It is those people who are seeking change or at least are willing to accept it who will be the migrants.

HER ATTITUDE TOWARD HER POSITION AND CHANGE   There is no indication that new servants have difficulty adjusting to their occupational status. Long before, they have internalized their subordinate socioeconomic position and learned the appropriate deference-behavior patterns to be used with their employers and other social superiors. They remain easily exploited and intimidated. In most cases, this exploitation takes the form of making the servant work long hours;[6] not permitting a weekly day off (or restricting it to less than a full day); not providing sufficient food; withholding vacation pay or denying the annual vacation altogether; or deducting breakage from the servant's salary – practices which, with the exception of the last one, are prohibited by law but not infrequently encountered. Intimidation is not unknown. Servants may lodge complaints against their employers (in matters pertaining to salary, vacation, and indemnization) with the Division of Women, Children, and Domestics in the Labor Ministry, but there they submit themselves to the challenges of the bureaucrats working there, who automatically assume the servant is not telling the truth (Smith 1971: 300–301).

In addition, servants appear to be perpetuating the status quo by not taking more interest in social change. It is reported, for example, that servants are not caught up in the "revolutionary spirit of change" sought by the Velasco government[7] even though that government has been responsible for significant legislation benefiting the servant segment of the labor force.

However, a recent innovation is being made by servants on the job. Instead of accepting whatever the employer chooses to dole out, servants, particularly the more experienced ones, now ask for raises and fringe benefits, expecially permission to attend school. If the request is denied, or the servant has a complaint against her employer which is unresolved,

---

[6]   For example, one study indicates that 70 percent of the servants work in excess of eight hours daily ("Encuasta de la Parroquia" 1976: 67). Supreme Decree #002–70 TR of March 10, 1970, makes mandatory eight hours of rest daily, a recognition of the fact that servants had not been receiving that much time.

[7]   Personal communication, Joan de Riviero de Carvalho.

it is not uncommon for the servant simply to quit and seek employment elsewhere.

Servants are not enthusiastic about their occupation. Four different recent studies of Lima servants (Pascual 1968; "Encuesta de la Parroquia" 1967; Baldárrogo 1970; Stillinger 1966) indicate that, if given their choice of occupation, a maximum of 17 percent would select work as servants (Baldárrago 1970). Instead, they indicated preference, in decreasing order of frequency for jobs as seamstress, hairdresser, cosmetologist, self-employed (which, for women, usually is taken to mean street or market vending), secretary or office worker, nurse, school teacher, and commercial employee. Although this appears to reflect servants' definite interest in changing their individual situations, these expectations, with the possible exception of self-employment, are unlikely to be realized at the present.

Finally, servants are able to express their interests publicly, but they usually don't do so. Two demonstrations by servants in Lima are known, and both of these occurred during the first half of 1970. In the first, 200 servants rallied in the small plaza in the affluent San Isidro neighborhood dedicated to Marshall Ramón Castilla (who is remembered for having freed the slaves in Peru). The parading servants carried placards calling for unionization of servants, an eight-hour work day, and a thirty-day annual paid vacation. These servants utilized methods popular with other lower class groups to court governmental approval of their cause: they all were dressed impeccably, waved Peruvian flags, shouted their support of the government and President Velasco, and elicited sympathetic news coverage in the tabloid *Ojo*. However, two weeks later, a governmental proclamation warned servants against partisan proselytism for social action. Although this demonstration had been organized by Túpac Armando Yupanqui, a radical leftist student group from the National Engineering University, rather than by the servants themselves, the other demonstration was a spontaneous servant effort. On the occasion of the television wedding of María Ramos, the heroine of the rags-to-riches television soap opera *Simplemente Maria*, 10,000 servants turned out for the ceremony in the church located at the border joining a commercial area and a middle class residential neighborhood. Lima servants are fanatical fans of María, a peasant girl from the provinces who migrates to the capital city, is exploited and eventually befriended in her jobs as a domestic, attends school to become literate and to learn sewing,[8] eventually rises to world fame as a high

---

[8]   This is responsible in no small measure for the servants' enthusiasm for education

fashion Paris designer, and marries her former school teacher.

What happened to María could, or so some servants believe, happen to others too. This is unlikely however, because the acquisition of a sewing machine alone is clearly beyond the economic means of most servants. Can future servant activism be anticipated, then, when they realize, as a few already have, that they lack the vocational training, financial resources, and luck of María? So far, María Ramos has left her mark only on a small group of self-identified radical servants called Las Marías which has emerged since 1970.

THE EMPLOYER'S ATTITUDE TOWARD THE SERVANT   There appears to be some awareness on the part of a minority of employers that the employment situation of their servants should be changed. For example, increasing numbers of employers are permitting, and in some cases insisting, that their servants attend school. In addition, in 1969, a sociologist from the Catholic social science agency (CAP) and a parochial school for servants sponsored a round-table conference for about twenty-five affluent employers on the improvement of living and working conditions of their servants. A "typical" employer, who considered herself enlightened on the subject of "good treatment" for servants, insisted that she treated her servant "just like a member of her own family." Yet, upon questioning, the same woman consistently referred to her servant as a *muchacha*, acknowledged that her servant wore a uniform (the badge of her status), ate by herself in the kitchen off of dishes especially set aside for her after the rest of the family had finished eating, and received hand-me-down clothing as gifts. Other employers would not allow time during the day for their servant-students to study or do other homework. Few are the employers who want to see changes in the servitude complex and support their talk of change with action.

Some employers do tend to acknowledge that changes ARE taking place in the Lima servant world. But these are heralded as detrimental changes marked by a "new servant" who is less obedient and more independent than those of a decade or two ago. Foreigners residing in Lima are also held accountable for this noticeable change because they are said to pay their servants above-average wages and "do not know how to treat servants."

There remain numerous employers who speak of servants as half-savage, who consider them invisible objects generally to be ignored (except

---

in general, vocational training in sewing (now often included in academic school curriculum as a lure), and their expressed preference for work as a seamstress.

when needed to do something), or who do not see any need for changes to occur. Education is largely opposed (there is too much work in the household to allow that much time off); classes meet at inconvenient times; servants should not be allowed out of the house without direct supervision; there is no need for servants to be educated (certainly not beyond the basics of reading, writing, and arithmetic); education only would "give the servants ideas" (about changing the status quo); and so on.

At the Institutional Level

An additional five factors can be noted on the institutional level: formal education programs, the government, unionization, employment agencies, and the servant labor market.

FORMAL EDUCATIONAL PROGRAMS   Numerous programs of formal education are available to the Lima servant. The Ministry of Education has established special programs which, although they do not cater exclusively to servants, do list servants in the enrollment records: primary-level night school (*vespertinas*); capacitation (literacy, vocational, and social education) programs; Feminine Industrial Institutes (a primarily vocational curriculum); and the comprehensive Institute of Special Education (day care for the children of working mothers, adult primary education, and training in household skills).

The Catholic church also sponsors various educational programs directed specifically at the servants in particular parishes. The St. Andrews School and the Sevilla Institute for Domestic Service provide elementary education and vocational training (household skills, sewing, and typing) for migrant girls, who later are placed as domestic servants in "approved" households. Twenty Lima parishes also offer other programs including literacy, primary school, vocational training, medical and dental care, and social (recreation and personal development) clubs for those already working as servants.

In addition, the government of the San Isidro (suburban Lima) district sponsored a short-lived program to teach servants literacy, arithmetic, and the skills requisite to become a competent servant. But servants don't want to go to school to learn to become better servants, so the school folded when it was unsuccessful in recruiting a student body. Small private vocational schools abound, and servant-students are particularly attracted to those offering sewing, hairdressing, and cosmetology.

In spite of the plethora of opportunities to enroll in some kind of vocational program, these programs do not provide the servant-student with the skills necessary to get a new job related to her training. Sewing courses, for example, prepare a servant to do sewing for herself, but do not prepare her to the level where she could work as a seamstress.

Some of these institutions have a social worker or a teacher assigned to look after the "best interests" of the servant-students in terms of correcting abuses (nonpayment of salary, not allowing the servants sufficient nightly sleep, and sexual exploitation, among others), leading them toward "proper moral standards and attitudes" according to middle class Peruvian standards, and often acting as informal placement channels by helping servants to find new jobs with "approved" families. Servants are not urged by their teacher or social worker counselors to aspire to any occupation beyond domestic service, nor are they urged to attempt to change the status quo. The goal appears to be to prepare the young women to be good wives and mothers. Any changes to be made should be made by them as individual servants. Any changes in the "system" are the prerogative of the government or of individual employers.

The Young Catholic Working Women, known as the JOC (Juvented de Obreras Católicas), is a program of personal education and consciousness raising, sometimes affiliated with another academic or vocational program. First opened to servants in 1962, it had twenty-one local branches in operation by 1969 in addition to a large house available for members' use. Inasmuch as the purpose of the organization is to "broaden horizons and stimulate thought processes" (Stillinger 1966:9) of servants via peer group discussion, this organization has been like a bolt of lightning hitting the servant complex. Many employers consider this to be an inflammatory organization because they do not wish their servants "to have their eyes opened" or "to get ideas." They fear the JOC will foment ideas of socioeconomic self-improvement and discontent with the status quo.

So far, according to JOC members, it provides a setting in which servants can feel free to talk to one another about their problems, in which they can have a feeling of self-respect and personal dignity, and in which they can talk about orienting their lives according to their conception of the Christian doctrine. JOC discussions, with perhaps eight to twelve servant-participants plus a servant-moderator, revolve around topics theoretically relevant to young servant women, including: appropriate behavior in a variety of situations, Christian virtues, a work ethic, preparation for motherhood, and the development of friendship. Although this does provide a context in which servant-leaders might emerge, the impact of the JOC on the entire servant community has been small indeed so far; the organization had recruited only 200 members by 1968.

THE GOVERNMENT   Governmental action has the potential for providing significant changes in urban servitude. Legislation providing social benefits for the servant was not forthcoming until two major laws pertaining strictly to domestics came out in 1957. A supplement was effected in 1970, which for the first time included servants as mandatory participants in the national social security program. Servants with complaints against their employers may lodge them with the Labor Ministry's Division of Women and Children and Domestics, or with the police. However, few complaints are lodged: the Labor Ministry office recorded a monthly average of eighty-eight in 1968 and 1969; and less than 1 percent of the police cases involve servants in any capacity. Servants seeking jobs may, and, with a record 1,879 placements in 1969, increasingly do take advantage of the labor Ministry's employment service, the largest employment agency for servants in the city. The Ministry of Education provides educational programs enumerated above.

However, domestic servants never have occupied a high priority with the government; neither have they had any power or influence to exert leverage to gain additional legal rights, or even to enforce the ones they have. Servant legislation has managed to keep only one step ahead of demands, and has tended to represent final legal recognition of the status quo: benevolent paternalism, employment of minors, and minimal obligations on the part of employers. And to the extent that the laws are observed, it is due solely to the voluntary compliance of the servants and their employers. Legal rights are ignored, abuses of them go unreported, and compensation for reported abuses cannot be enforced.

UNIONIZATION   Domestistic servants have not yet been unionized. Personnel in the Labor Ministry maintain that they recall the registry of a union for servants "many years ago," but they are unable to find documentation of this union. In any event, if such a union did exist at one time, it was ineffectual in bringing charges to the urban servitude complex, and at the present has faded into obscurity.

During 1969, a representative of the Túpac Armando Yupanqui campaigned to organize servants by approaching those who lodged complaints against their employers with the Labor Ministry. This was short-lived because, after a few weeks, the national police, Policía de Investigaciones de Peru (PIP), expelled the organizer from the Ministry offices for making "offensive advances" toward the female servants. Túpac also is responsible for the graffiti demanding social legislation for the benefit of servants, which adorn walls in several locations in the central city and the two middle class residential suburban districts of Miraflores and San Isidro:

Domestic Social Security.
Social Benefits for Nursemaids, Cooks.
Indemnization for Domestic Employees. We want justice.
We Household Workers demand social benefits. TUPAC.
We Nursemaids, Cooks, Etc., demand social benefits.

There are a substantial number of servants in Lima from which to form a union membership. In addition, there is a feeling of camaraderie among servants, and most servants have many social ties with other servants: former or present servant neighbors or co-workers, fellow students, and friends from the same home town. Servants also are considered to be a social necessity by their urban employers, who cannot imagine how they possibly could survive without their *muchachas.*

Counterbalancing these factors, which might be evaluated as those encouraging unionization and its effective operation, are other factors which effectively are inhibiting the organization of Lima servants. Servants tend to be highly suspicious of outside supervision, such as that directed by the government or employers. So far, leadership has not emerged from among the servant ranks, out of employment agencies, or the schools run for servants. Servants in multiple-servant households often find themselves in an atmosphere of hostility and competition with their co-workers. Servants are transient and difficult to keep track of; they change jobs frequently, and employers have been known to deny that particular servants are, in fact, working for them. Servants are dispersed in tens of thousands of households throughout the city. Some servants also feel that they are "better off" working as domestics in Lima than they were in the provinces. Finally, servants consider their tenure as domestics to be a brief transition in their lives, and they lack a long-term commitment to their occupation.

EMPLOYMENT AGENCIES. Employment agencies have personal contact with more servants and employers than any other urban institution. But their primary concern is placement rather than fomenting social change among servants. In individual cases, the agencies will try to talk an employer into offering a higher salary: "For that salary, we cannot get you what you are looking for. Good cooks are earning S/—." They also might try to convince the employer to hire a servant-student who will work for a lower salary. Or they might tell a servant that her salary expections are too high or that she lacks the experience and/or recommendations to get a better job. One chain of agencies has a servant's creed hanging prominently on the wall which advises servants to obey, to seek the love and respect of their employers, to be truthful, not to talk back, etc. — certainly in no way a challenge to the status quo.

THE SERVANT LABOR MARKET   The servant market in Lima is a sellers' market. There is no shortage of available jobs.Organized servants could utilize this to get increased salaries and other work benefits. However, there is a constant supply of potential new servants invading the capital. These new migrants have very few occupational opportunities available to them: domestic service, street or market vending, prostitution, and a few factory or workshop jobs. Those who enter domestic service, as the largest number of migrants do, are not attuned to the prevailing conditions in Lima and are less aware of what they could demand from their employers.

At the National Level

Changes which might take place in the broader context of Peruvian society in relation to servants in the capital city can be seen in three areas: stimulation of young provincial girls to migrate to the capital; the introduction of new ideas and material goods to their relatives and friends in the provinces or in the other lower-class neighborhoods of Lima; and the providing of a channel of upward mobility for lower class provincial girls.

URGE TO MIGRATE   Servants tend to retain very close ties with their relatives in the provinces. This is maintained via letter, news reports sent with friends from the home town, and, for many, by at least one annual visit to the home town for a vacation. This visit is an opportunity to tell sisters, cousins, and friends what life is like in the capital, usually in very glowing terms. The young women do not miss noticing the servant-visitor's transistor radio, beauty parlor coiffure, make-up, and miniskirt. They hear about having an income and about opportunities to attend school. It is not an unexpected finding that many servants have been prompted to migrate to Lima because an older sister, cousin, or friend was already there. There is no indication that Lima servants will stop encouraging a steady stream of migrants.

INTRODUCTION OF NEW IDEAS AND MATERIAL GOODS   Because of their intimate participation in the households of their middle and upper class employers, servants working in the capital are acculturated much more rapidly to the cosmopolitan urban arena, both in terms of new ways of doing things and new material items, than are their migrant sisters who remain in the lower class residential neighborhoods, such as the squatter settlements ringing the city. Although one might suspect that this would provide the servants with an excellent opportunity for introducing new ideas and new artifacts to their families remaining in the provinces, it appears that the servants' impact is minimal. On the job servants are exposed to new foods, telephones, all kinds of household appliances, new ways of educating and raising children, and new behavior patterns. But on vacations, servants find it easy to slip back into provincial ways. For example, in the house with her family, Navidad M. prefers to wear the midi-length woolen skirts belonging to her mother and sister instead of the miniskirts she wears in public. Most of the servants enjoy living according to provincial patterns for the short vacation period which usually ranges from a week to one month.

At the same time, domestics acknowledge that they would not return to the provinces to live permanently because they feel they could not easily readjust to provincial life; *ya no me acostumbro* is a frequently heard evaluation. There is no evidence to suggest that servants are introducing new items into the provincial material culture or suggesting new ways of doing things. There is no talk of "why don't you do it this way instead, the way we do it in Lima." And it is impossible superficially to identify the relatively few provincial women who have worked as servants in the capital but who have returned to the provinces to live.

Even in Lima, servants generally do not adopt the artifacts and behavior of their employers beyond a superficial mimicking of fashion or hair style. The households of former servants do not appear modified versions of the houses they once worked, nor are the servant's children raised according to patterns used in dealing with their former employers' children.

From the opposite perspective, it can be noted that the "ruralization" of the city, i.e. the introduction of provincial material culture and behavior patterns, has not been passed from servant to employer, even though it is a prominent feature of contemporary Lima. Employers have not adopted provincial music, dance, or food. Neither do servants appear to utilize provincial child-rearing techniques on the offspring of their employers.

PROVIDING A CHANNEL OF UPWARD MOBILITY   Servitude is most significant in the context of broad social change by providing a channel of
upward mobility for the provincial girl (Smith 1973). Migrating to
Lima and working as a servant is one of the few opportunities such a
girl has. With luck, she will, during her tenure as a servant, meet in
Lima a young man (who is more than likely a migrant to the capital
as well) who will marry her and permit her to drop out of the servant
world to become an upper lower-class housewife.

When balancing these eleven factors influencing servants and social
change in Lima, one can see that the potential for change is greater than
what is being realized. By taking greater advantage of the educational
opportunities available, servants would gain self-confidence and the
background knowledge (literacy and arithmetic) which are necessary
before effectively competing with the better-educated Lima-born women
for jobs outside of the servant sphere. Competent vocational training,
currently unavailable, could prepare servants for new jobs. Unionization
and more active government support of servants could bring improvements to those who remain employed as domestics. Servants do continue to stimulate the migration of other young girls to Lima, thus perpetuating part of the wave of rural-urban migration toward the capital
and assuring a fresh supply of potential servants for the Lima market,
a market which continues to take advantage of their inexperience and
urban naïveté. Domestics also have the opportunity of serving as a
channel to convey ideas and material from the city to the provinces, but
they do not seem to be doing so effectively. At the present time, the most
important contribution servitude is making to the area of social change
in Peru is in providing a means of upward mobility for this lowest-
ranking urban group. The potential for change is present; the actual
changes taking place are small steps, though increasing in frequency.
The servant has yet to emerge as the standard bearer for social change in
Peru.

REFERENCES

ANONYMOUS
   n.d.   "Encuesta de la Parroquía, 'Santísimo Nombre de Jesús.'" Type-
          written manuscript of data gathered in 1967. Lima.
BALDÁRRAGO, MARIETTA
   1970   "CIC noticias" (January 8). Mimeographed manuscript. Lima: Centro
          de Información Católica.

BONILLA, F.
1968   *Manual y leyes del obrero.* Lima: Editorial Mercurio.
CARETAS
1970   Un mito de la vida doméstica. *Caretas* (February 17–28, 1970):30–44.
CARRIO DE LA VANDERA
1966   *Reforma del Perú.* Lima: Universidad Nacional Mayor de San Marcos.
CENTRO ARGUIDEOCESANO DE PASTORAL
1967   Unpublished census cards, coded and reduced to various tables.
DE LA FLOR CUNEO, MIGUEL
1966   *Beneficios sociales de los trabajadores domesticos.* Lima: Escuela Sindical autónoma de Lima.
DELGADO, CARLOS
1968   Hacia un nuevo esquema de composición de la sociedad en el Perú. *América Latina* 2:3.
DONOSO, JOSÉ
1965   *Coronation.* New York: Alfred A. Knopf.
1967   *This Sunday*, Translated by Lorraine O'Grady Freeman. New York: Alfred A. Knopf.
DOUGHTY, PAUL L.
1970   "Behind the back of the city: 'provincial' life in Lima, Peru," in *Peasants in cities.* Edited by William Mangin, Boston: Houghton Mifflin.
ESCUELA MUNICIPAL DE SERVICIO DOMÉSTICO PAPA JUAN XXIII.
1965–1966   Unpublished data in the Registro de Matrícula (school enrollment records), originally recorded by the school director.
FLORES GUERRERO, TERESA
1961   *"Reglamentación y problemas que conforte el servicio domestico en el Perú."* Unpublished thesis, Escuela de Servico Social del Perú, Lima.
HELFER, RUTH, M. S. C.
1966   *El problema social de la empleada doméstica.* Lima: Escuela Normal Superior de Mujeres. San Pedro, Monterrico (Thesis in secondary education).
La Prensa
1970   "Incorporan a domésticos al seguro social." *La Prensa* (March 12): 1, 9. Lima.
LEWIS, OSCAR
1959   *Five families.* New York: Random House.
LOCKHART, JAMES
1968   *Spanish Peru 1532–1560.* Madison: University of Wisconsin.
MINISTERIO DE HACIENDA Y COMERCIO
1940   *Quinto censo nacional de población 1940*, volume one: *Resúmenes generales.* Lima.
1961   *Sexto censo nacional de población 1961*, volume four: *Características económicas.* Lima.
1965   Unpublished data from computer printout sheets. Lima: Dirección Nacional de Estadística y Censos.
1966   *Encuesta de immigración Lima metropolitana*, volume one (October). Lima: Dirección Nacional de Estadística y Censos.

MORALES ARNAO, ELENA
1969   *Informe anual Agencia Abancay*. Lima: Servicio de Empleos y Recursos Humanos, Ministerio de Trabajo.

NETT, EMILY
1966   The servant class in a developing country: Ecuador. *The Journal of Inter-American Studies* 8:(3) 437–452.

Ojo
1970a   "El mitan de las Mariás." *Ojo*. (April 27):1. Lima.
1970b   "Domésticos se quejan por la jornada de 16 Horas." *Ojo*. (April 27): 6. Lima.

PASCUAL BADIOLA, MARÍA PILAR
1968   "*Diagnosis ético-social de las empleadas domésticas.*" Unpublished thesis in family education. Pontífica Universidad La Católica, Lima.

PLAN REGIONAL
1959   "La organización social en el Departamento de Puno" and "La cultura: factores institucionales" in *Plan regional para el desarrollo del Sur del Perú 22*. Lima.

PRADO, JAVIER
1941   *Estado social del Perú durante la dominación española*, volume one. Lima: Gil.

SMITH, MARGO L.
1971   "Institutionalized servitude: the female domestic servant in Lima, Peru." Unpublished thesis, Indiana University, Bloomington.
1973   "Domestic service as a channel of upward mobility for the lower-class woman: the Lima case," in *Female and male in Latin America*. Edited by Ann Pescatello. Pittsburgh: University of Pittsburgh.

STILLINGER, MARTHA
1966   "Domestic service in Lima, Peru." Photocopied manuscript.

VÁSQUEZ, JESÚS MARÍA, O. P.
1969   "Estudio sobre la situación del servicio doméstico en Lima." Mimeographed manuscript. Lima: Misión Conciliar.

VISIÓN
1970   El gran éxito de "Simplemente María." *Visión*. (September 11):87.

VON TSCHUDI, J. J.
1966   *Testimonio del Perú 1838–1842*. Lima: Universidad Nacional Mayor de San Marcos.

Sociocultural Factors Mitigating Role Conflict of Buenos Aires Professional Women

NORA SCOTT KINZER

Latin American society is popularly viewed as constricting to female ambition. Recently there have appeared a series of essays and articles which refute this commonsense stereotype (Chaney 1973; Kinzer 1973a, 1973b; Pescatello 1973).

This study examines the general theoretical concepts and definition of role conflict and attempts to show that, for the Buenos Aires professional woman, there is a series of role relationships that mitigate her potential or actual role conflict. Indeed in many respects the *portena* female professional is more fortunate than her North American sister.

The data are based on a random stratified sample of 125 full-time employed professional women, resident in Buenos Aires, from the fields of law, medicine, pharmacy, biochemistry, architecture, engineering, and agronomy. Data on each woman were obtained in 1967 through a face-to-face interview, using a questionnaire consisting of open-ended and forced-choice questions. Statistical analysis revealed no differences among professions.

Occupations were ranked high, medium, or low, using rankings devised by Germani and revised by Sautú (1967). Data were analyzed using percentages and gamma. (For a more detailed description of the sample and methodology see Kinzer 1973a.)

While much has been written about the concept of role, there is a great deal of discrepancy in regard to the definitions of role, often because the definers tend to reflect the biases of their particular academic disciplines (Gross, et al. 1958:16; Biddle and Thomas 1966:29). Although the concept of role may denote either behavior or expectations, Biddle and Thomas (1966:29) and Gross, et al. (1958:29), having thoroughly reviewed the literature, agree that "expectations" are a common element to the definition of role.

We choose, for the sake of convenience and simplicity, to use the definition of Gross, et al. (1958:67) for role: "a set of expectations applied to an incumbent of a particular position." As in Gross' definition, we separate role "behavior" from "role." However, we choose to use the term STATUS as synonymous with position simply because of a personal preference for this term.

Merton attempted to show that role and status were related. He introduced the concept of ROLE-SET, which is "that complement of role relationships which persons have by virtue of occupying a particular status" (Merton 1963:369). MULTIPLE ROLES are those various roles which "refer to the complex of roles associated, not with a SINGLE social status, but with the VARIOUS STATUSES (often in differing institutional spheres) in which individuals find themselves..." (Merton 1963:367–370).

While status and role are related, they are not exact equivalents. The proscriptions and prescriptions of a status allow for a wide range of behavior. However, ascriptive statuses are limiting factors on the individual's behavior, especially if his status is low. For example, the difficulties of a Negro doctor arise from the fact that behavior in his achieved status of "doctor" may not be considered by others as appropriate behavior for a person who has the ascribed status of "Negro."

Yet, who or what determines the "appropriateness" of a person's behavior? Who or what forms the expectations of role? In order to know the rules of the game for living in society so that people know how to behave, there must be some form of consensus regarding particular roles and their performance. This consensus, then, is the basis for the rules or the norms. For example, the status of mother implies that feeding her child adequately is part of her role as mother; however, the value of the adequacy of the diet is quite wide, ranging from hot dogs to caviar. There may be a narrow range of acceptable behavior; for example, a mother is expected to discipline her child, but, while mild spankings are tolerated, severe beatings are prohibited by law. Consensus — whether allowing a wide range of activities or a narrow one — is seen as "the degree of agreement of individuals on a given topic" (Biddle and Thomas 1966:33).

When there is consensus as to the appropriate behavior of a person and he (or she) violates this norm, what are the conseuqences? The result is defined as role conflict. Sarbin (1954) defines role conflict as occurring "when a person occupies two or more positions simultaneously and when the role expectations of one are incompatible with the role expectations of the other." Gross, et al. (1958) find Sarbin's definition somewhat restrictive and they define role conflict as "any situation in which the incumbent of a focal position perceives that he is confronted with incompatible expectations...." They further make the two following distinctions: (1) intra-role conflict is associated with different expectations that others hold for a person as the incumbent of a focal position (i.e. role-set) and (2) inter-role conflict is associated with the different expectations that are associated with a person as the incumbent of two or more positions, i.e. multiple roles (Gross, et al. 1958:248–249). Thus, inter-role conflicts occur when a woman (low ascribed status) violates the norms surrounding her role as woman and acts according to the norms of her achieved status of doctor. We are concerned here with women professionals in occupations with varying proportions of females and will focus on inter-role conflict. In other words, the multiple statuses of "woman," "wife," and "mother" with their correspondingly multiple roles are each (and in combination) potential sources of conflict with the role associated with the status of professional.

Although many role theorists, including Sarbin (1954), view role conflict as abnormal and a barrier to the smooth functioning of a society or an individual's life, Gross, et al. (1958), focusing primarily on inter-role conflict, show that this type of role conflict is an everyday occurrence for the school superintendent. Goode, in two companion articles (1960a, 1960b), attempts to illustrate that in modern secular societies role strain is normal and consensus on roles is often vague. Goode's positions in these articles are that role strain (what we call role conflict) is inherent in all relationships, Commitment to norms varies according to the variables of class strata, age, occupation, geographic region, and religion; commitment does not imply conformity or vice versa; as social positions of individuals change, so do behavior and value orientations.

Goode develops the idea that individuals "shop around" for "role bargains" in order to reduce their role strain. For example a lazy person seeks a job that will not demand too much effort. A married woman with children finds a job and develops a work schedule or hires household help in order to allow her to fulfill her roles of wife, mother, and employee. Goode feels that an individual's total role obligations are impossible to fulfill and there must exist various means to mitigate the role strain. If not, the individual could not withstand the constant tugging at his emotions, time, and abilities.

Ascriptive status, or at least, low ascriptive statuses, (such as female or Negro) produce role conflict situations of high intensity, for the female cannot change her sex nor the Negro his skin color. Still, norms and conformity to these norms change over time, so that what was once considered

184 NORA SCOTT KINZER

to be unacceptable behavior becomes acceptable. If this were not so, modern society would be as rigid as a caste-ridden culture. A woman doctor, a hundred years ago, was unthinkable; today in the United States she may be a rarity but is seldom refused admission to a hospital just because she is a woman.

Role conflict is inherent in all role relationships; sanctions vary in their intensity and ego's conformity to alter's (or third party's) sanction varies. Role conflict is a situation in which an individual must make a choice between or among roles and their corresponding sanctions. There exist mechanisms by which the individual seeks to reduce or eliminate the role strain (or role conflict). Goode lists ways in which ego is able to make decisions which reduce role strain (Goode 1960a:486–487). Also, there are structural limits and determinants of strain-reducing mechanisms (1960a:490–492).

We are concerned with the female professional involved in a situation of inter-role conflict. In the best of all possible worlds for a social scientist, choices are clearcut, either-or, black-and-white decisions. If we had studied a woman professional fifty years ago, we would have termed her a "deviant," for she would clearly have been flouting the norms of a society which deemed that woman's place was in the home.

However, as 40 percent of the working force of the United States is composed of women and nearly 70 percent of the physicians in Russia are women, we can no longer term the working woman a deviant. There is neither black nor white in a world where there is no consensus on whether or not a woman should work, or on appropriate behavior for those who do. The consensual relationship is seen as one of nonpolarized dissensus.

Although being female or a member of a low ascriptive status is a limiting factor on the bargaining power of the woman, this factor may not be quite as important as we assume. Goode noted that an individual's value commitment varies according to characteristics of "class strata,... social position, age, occupation, geographic region and religion" (1960a:484). Thus, while we assume that a female professional is faced with the conflicting roles of the ascribed status and the achieved status professional and that her inter-role conflict is compounded with the roles associated with the statuses of "wife" and "mother," these are only ASSUMPTIONS. It is better to state that a female professional is faced with POTENTIAL role conflict.

The woman professional is faced with many potential sources of conflict which are derived from the fact that she may occupy the statuses of female, professional, wife, and mother. (Depending on her marital status and if she has children, her courses of conflict range from two to four).

If she works with the approval of her husband, makes provision for the care of her children, associates with people who share her views, and is happy in her job, then no role conflict may occur. Even though all the foregoing conditions exist, the woman herself may feel so inadequate and inept as a wife and mother that she is indeed in a situation of acute role conflict. If her husband complains, the children demand more of her attention, and her friends critizice her working, she may also be caught in a role conflict situation. At the same time, all the criticism and carping of her family and friends may not matter a whit to the woman, for she finds her joy and solace in her work. Role conflict then is a muddy situation where an individual's behavior and the expectations held by her or others does at times, and does not at other times, produce strain and tension.

Role conflict in regard to the working woman is felt to be due to the fact that women are of "low "ascribed status. It seems to be true that women are held in lower esteem than men. Hacker (1951) and Goldberg (1968) illustrate that women display the characteristic of self-hatred associated with members of minority groups. Yet it seems reasonable to assume that a low status may be balanced by another which is higher. In other words, a woman has a low ascribed status, but if she is from a high status family perhaps her high status family background lessens (or even obviates) the stigma of being female.

We choose here to concentrate on the mechanisms that are available to a woman in order to mitigate the traditional view of woman's role as solely wife and mother. We shall follow Goode's analysis (1960a) but shall focus primarily on those structural aspects of strain-reducing mechanisms. We call these structural aspects "supportive role relationships."

We advocate that general cultural norms may be mitigated by specific role relationships and specific cultural norms. These mitigating factors are: (1) specific cultural norms (or legislation such as laws protecting the woman worker, access to the educational system, etc.); (2) spouse approval of his wife's working; (3) means by which the mother is relieved of continuous supervision of her children; and (4) norms (more often implicitly than explicitly) relating to the role of a professional WOMAN.

Factors which mitigate the sources of inter-role conflict with which the Argentine professional woman has to contend are presented in terms of supportive role relationships. These supportive role relationships are, in turn, divided according to the following: (1) specific societal norms or legislation, (2) family background characteristics, (3) peer or job role relationships, (4) marital status and attitude of spouse, and (5) children. This division is for the sake of clarity and convenience, although many of the factors are interrelated.

1. EXTERNAL ROLE RELATIONSHIPS: LEGISLATION AND HISTORY OF EDUCATING WOMEN IN ARGENTINA

The political rights of women in Argentina date from 1921 when women in the Province of Santa Fé were granted the right to vote in municipal elections. Only women of majority age who were free to administer their own estate or had a degree entitling them to exercise a liberal profession could vote in the Santa Fé election. The right to vote in provincial elections was first granted to women in the Province of San Juan in 1927. Eva Perón was responsible for the women of Argentina receiving the right to vote in all elections (federal, provincial, and municipal) in 1947. After the fall of Perón, the Women's Peronist Party lost its influence in national affairs and the number of women deputies and senators decreased noticeably. In the Parliament of 1966, before the declaration of the military junta, there were four women deputies and no women senators in the Argentine Federal Parliament. As of 1967, there was one woman Supreme Court judge, one judge in the Federal Court of Appeals, and several municipal judges in the Province of Buenos Aires. Judges are appointed, not elected, in the Argentine legal system.

The civil and social rights of Argentine women and all workers, male and female, are protected by the Conventions of the International Labour Organization of the Conventions of the United Nations, all of which Argentina has signed. In many instances, probably due to the influence of Eva Perón, the woman worker is protected in Argentina more than her counterpart in the United States. Because Perón's strength was drawn from the working classes, much of the social legislation that exists in Argentina was instigated by the Perón regime.

Workers receive a multitude of guaranteed holidays, days off, Saint's Days, and annual vacations. Maids are guaranteed vacations, decent meals, lodging, and sick leave. Female workers are prohibited from working in dangerous or unhealthy industries such as explosives factories or dockyards.

Maternity legislation dates from 1924, with additional provisos added in 1934 and 1961. All women workers ages fourteen to forty-five are covered under the Maternity Protection Section of the Social Security Administration. Generally, women are given maternity leave six weeks prior to and six weeks after the birth of the baby. Free pre- and postnatal care, a free layette, and free hospitalization were added bonuses, courtesy of Evita Perón. Since 1924 employers have had to provide a baby nursery where more than fifty women are employed. Also, there is a state-run and a private system of baby and child nurseries located throughout the cities, servicing working mothers.

The contractual capacity of women is determined primarily by marital status. Single women have the same rights and privileges as a male, but married women cannot take part in judicial proceedings without the consent of the husband, nor may married women administer their properties. To protect right of dower and property a prenuptial contract is often drawn up which specifically outlines those goods, monies, and properties which belong to the wife. Married women may engage in employment, be guardian, executrix, and witness without the consent of the husband. However, a husband is assumed to have power of attorney over his wife and can dispose of her or their properties without her consent.

There is no divorce in Argentina, meaning dissolution of a marriage, but divorce indicating separation of goods and residence does exist. There was a divorce law promulgated by Perón in 1954, but it has been suspended (not revoked) since 1956. Because the husband has the legal right to determine the residence of his family, his wife, in order to live apart from him, must secure a court order. This permission is granted on presentation of proof of adultery, gross drunkenness, sexual perversion, or severe physical cruelty. (The proof of adultery must be through the husband's sworn testimony or that of two witnesses. However, in the case of a woman accused of adultery, the act of being alone with a man for more than half an hour is sufficient evidence of adultery.)

In order to counteract the absence of any provision for the dissolution of a marriage, many Argentines obtain Mexican, Bolivian, or Uruguayan divorces. These are not legal in Argentina but at least give a semblance of propriety to a couple who are living in what is otherwise considered to be an adulterous (and illegal) union, if either one or both of the parties has been previously married and the spouse(s) is (are) living. Civil marriage is the only marriage which has any legality according to the civil code.

The Argentine civil code recognized a Napoleonic convention called the *Patria Protestas*, which means that legitimate children are considered to be the property of the father. Children cannot be taken from Argentina without the father's written consent.

The education of women in Argentina, until a hundred years ago, was the province of private tutors and nuns who educated the daughters of the middle classes. Sarmiento, in the 1860's and 1870's, was impressed by the educational system of the United States which he had observed while traveling as a journalist, and later, when he was Argentine Ambassador to the United States. A close friendship with Mr. and Mrs. Horace Mann of Massachusetts, who were leaders in the founding of the United States normal school system, convinced Sarmiento that the normal school system was the starting point for improving the primary and secondary school system of Argentina. Sixty-five American women teachers, chosen by Mrs. Mann, were brought to Argentina between 1869 to 1883 to found the kindergarten, primary, secondary, and normal school system of Argentina. This system has almost completely eradicated illiteracy in the Argentine Republic (Luiggi 1965). Women who graduated from the normal schools were eager for higher education.

Slowly women began to graduate from the University of Buenos Aires in those fields that were considered to be the exclusive domain of men. The first woman university graduate was Cecilia Grierson who received a degree in medicine in 1889. The first woman graduated in law, 1911; pharmacy, 1914; dentistry, 1915; engineering, 1918; architecture, 1929; agronomy, 1929, and veterinary science, 1939.

Nevertheless, women are still concentrated in the field of teaching, much like their Protestant lady teachers of the past. Yet, the higher the level of education the less the number of women. Ninety-nine percent of nursery school teachers are women; 89 percent of primary school teachers, 59 percent of junior high teachers, 41 percent of high school, and only 9 percent of university professors are women. (These figures are from the Women's Bureau, Ministry of Labor and Social Security, Buenos Aires, Argentina). Traditional female occupations still attract the majority of women students: all graduates in library science and midwifery from the University of Buenos Aires are women, 95 percent of social workers, 85 percent of graduates from the School of Education, and 66 percent of physical therapists are women.

However, as shown in Table 1, women comprise a sizeable minority in fields traditionally considered to be "masculine" professions. Indeed,

Table 1.   Graduates of the University of Buenos Aires in predominantly masculine fields in 1965

Field	Men	Women	Total	Percent Feminine
Law[a]	379	106	485	21.85
Medicine[b]	1,156	311	1,467	21.19
Pharmacy	63	85	148	59.44
Biochemistry	21	20	41	48.78
Dentistry	240	240	480	50.00
Architecture	151	65	216	29.68
Agronomy	55	7	62	11.29
English (total of all specialties)	368	8	376	2.17
Exact and natural sciences (total of all specialties)	106	56	162	34.56
Veterinary science	37	9	46	19.56

[a]   Degree of Lawyer only — excluding notaries, solicitors and advanced degrees.
[b]   Degree of Doctor of Medicine excluding graduate degrees.

compared to the United States, Argentine women comprise a greater percentage of these fields without exception. It was a surprise to find that dentistry is a "neuter" occupation in Argentina. Fifty percent of Argentine dental graduates are women, while scarcely 2 percent of United States dentists are women. Pharmacy and biochemistry are also considered "neuter" fields in Argentina, but not in the United States.

Although we are using figures for the University of Buenos Aires, rather than for all Argentine universities, UBA grants approximately 80 percent of all degrees in Argentina. Nevertheless, it is astounding to note that in absolute numbers, UBA graduates nearly as many women in law and medicine as the United States, while in dentistry it graduates more than ten times as many women as the United States (Kinzer 1973a). Argentina has a population of twenty million and the United States is ten times as large.

2. SUPPORTIVE FAMILY ROLE RELATIONSHIPS

a. *Parental Attitudes Towards Higher Education for Women*

A woman is helped, if she has the encouragement of her family, to continue her education beyond secondary school. Parental support of higher education is a factor highly related to socioeconomic status of the family, for usually upper and upper-middle class families encourage female children to attend university.

But the socioeconomic status of the family is not the only characteristic that determines the family's attitude towards higher education. Ginzberg (1966:31–32) reports that many women in his sample of Colombian university graduates had immigrant parents who realized that education was an escape route from the alien past into the new society; they "set high educational goals for their children and push their daughters as well as their sons to go to college."

Argentina has experienced massive waves of immigration. Germani (1966) writes that in 1961, in metropolitan Buenos Aires, of the population of eighteen years of age and over, 33.1 percent were Argentine-born of foreign parents (one or both parents born outside the Argentine) and 27.6 percent were foreign-born.

Ninety percent of the sample were Argentine-born and 60 percent had one or both parents foreign-born. Rossi (1965) writes that women who enter male occupations undergo different childhood socialization than do women who enter the traditional female occupations or who opt for the homemaker role. This is the case for this sample of Argentine professional women. Data indicate that immigrant parents inculcate their daughters with achievement motivation (see also Kinzer 1973a).

b. *Religion of the Family*

Although Roman Catholic women are generally considered not to be achievement-oriented, we must treat North American data with caution. Although 90 percent of the population of Argentina is estimated to be Roman Catholic, only 10 percent attend Mass regularly. Argentine Roman Catholicism is about the lackadaisical equivalent of the average North American Episcopalianism. Only seven termed themselves "militant" Roman Catholics and two-thirds considered themselves to be nominal Roman Catholics.

While there was only one Protestant in the sample, nearly one-quarter were Jews. Actually the number of Jewish women rises to nearly 30 percent if we include eight of the women who called themselves "atheists" but who indicated that their parents were Jewish.

This finding is entirely consistent with Horowitz (1962), who found that while Jews comprise only 7.7 percent of the population of Argentina, they are overrepresented in the universities. Jewish students comprise 22.5 percent of the enrolled students. Argentina has the highest proportion of Jews of any country in the Western Hemisphere. Jewish respect for education is extended to the daughters as well as the sons (see also Kinzer 1973a).

Roman Catholic or Jewish, the weakness of organized religion is a specific societal characteristic which changes the traditional view of woman's role and allows women to work outside the home.

c. *Role Models of Career-Oriented Women*

Argentine history is replete with vibrant, exciting women, ranging from the fierce women of Independence to Eva Perón. The reader is referred to an excellent summary of the role of women in Argentine history by Nancy Caro Hollander (1973). Even though Evita Perón was not mentioned by the sample as a role model, her influence upon Argentine history and upon the feminist movement can scarcely be denied.

Support from both parents, their lack of piety, and their child-rearing practices all mold the personality of the career-oriented woman. United States research (Rossi 1965) indicates that the professional woman chooses her father as an important role model. Data for this sample indicate that 46.4 percent ($n = 58$) chose their father as their role model; 28.0 percent ($n = 35$) the mother; 17.6 percent ($n = 22$) both mother and father; 4.8 percent ($n = 6$) neither; and 3.2 percent ($n = 4$) refused to answer. These percentages are considerably lower than those reported by Rossi (1965) and perhaps indicate that the role of mother is also salient for the immigrant daughter.

d. *Socioeconomic Status*

United States data (Rossɪ 1965; Kinzer 1973a) indicate that the higher the social status of the father the more likely it is that the daughter will attend college.

Also, high-status females are drawn to male fields regardless of the ranking of the field. High-status females enter high-status male occupations (e.g. law and medicine) just as high-status males do. But high-status females enter low-status male professions (such as engineering or veterinary science). This may be due to the fact that high-status females have the support of their families both to enter these fields and to withstand the male-female competition.

While not statistically significant, there is a slight tendency for women of upper and middle class status to enter male fields of law, engineering, architecture, and agronomy (Kinzer 1973a). This difference between United States and Argentine research is probably due to Argentina's massive immigration.

3. SUPPORTIVE PEER (OR JOB) ROLE RELATIONSHIPS

a. *Socioeconomic Status of a Woman Professional*

The ranking of the field, the socioeconomic status of the woman graduate, and the percentage of women graduates from that field are linked together as supportive peer role relationships. In terms of supportive peer relationships, we feel that the high-status woman is secure enough not to heed the ratio of men and women in particular professions. The low-status woman enters "neuter" professions because she needs the support of other women. Therefore low-status women who enter "male" fields would experience more role conflict than high-status women in the same field. The higher the percentage of female graduates the less the role conflict for the woman graduate, regardless of her status. Argentine sociologists have found that the three high-ranking professional schools at the University of Buenos Aires were law, medicine, and agronomy (Miguens 1964; Izaguirre 1965).

When we asked women in male occupations for their perceptions of sex-based discrimination we found a difference, as predicted. The high-status women reported few if any problems based on sex, whereas the medium- or low-status woman recounted horror stories (gamma:.72318, prob. ≤.01).

b. *Norms of Adequacy*

Goode (1960a:493) writes that members of low ascriptive statuses tend to underperform. Although women have lower salaries, lower rate of promotion, and are less likely to have supervisory positions compared with men of equal education and experience, they are, on the whole, satisfied with their jobs (Ginzberg 1966:182).

In Argentina, Miguens (1964) found that women are more likely than men to express satisfaction with their jobs. The female professional, according to Miguens, by virtue of being female and of low ascriptive status, is satisfied with her lowly position because she recognizes her inferior status.

While Miguens may be right in his assumption, we prefer to see the underperformance of the woman professional in terms of "norms of adequacy." The woman professional, in particular the married woman and/or mother, has limited time and energy. These are factors which she (ego) and her employer (alter) both recognize. Norms of adequacy of performance, while perhaps not explicitly stated, are nevertheless implicitly extant. The woman biologist does not offer (nor is she asked) to work evenings in order to complete an experiment; the woman lawyer does not undertake cases involving travel to other parts of the country, and the woman doctor avoids a heavy surgery schedule. Low salaries and low rates of promotion may be seen as part of the norms of adequacy, since the woman professional does not work at peak performance. Alter cannot reward ego if she under-performs. Also ego recognizes and accepts the justice of alter's action. Although we refer mainly to the married woman and/or mother, there does not seem to be any clearcut evidence as to whether or not single women underperform. Most women work for "self-realization and interpersonal relations" more than for "income and prestige" (Ginzberg 1966:88).

As a feminist I should point out that women's liberation, affirmative action, and a host of law suits pending in the United States courts challenge the assumption that women work only for intrinsic rewards. Yet there are no data to indicate that women, AS A WHOLE, do work for extrinsic rewards, and, until such research is forthcoming, we are left with the sexist implications of the Ginzberg (1966) and Miguens (1964) studies.

Results of this sample indicate that women professionals in Buenos Aires do work for intrinsic rewards, such as service to others, helping people, serving humanity, and the like: 62.8 percent ($n = 71$) report that they work for intrinsic rewards; 18.6 percent ($n = 21$) for external rewards, such as salary, awards, and promotions; and another 18.6 percent ($n = 21$) for both self-satisfaction and external rewards. (Twelve women refused to answer the question, stating that they were job failures and worked only to fill time or support themselves.)

4. MARITAL STATUS AND SUPPORTIVE ROLE RELATIONSHIP OF SPOUSE

Marriage is of prime importance to the lives of most women. Of course not all women marry, regardless of their desire to do so. But, for married women, the husband's attitude towards a wife's working is very important (Ginzberg 1966; Rossi 1965).

The marital status of the Buenos Aires sample was as follows: 24.7 percent ($n = 31$) were single; 66.4 percent ($n = 83$) married; 4.0 percent ($n = 5$) widowed and 4.8 percent ($n = 6$) divorced or separated. (The anomalous situation of the divorce law and the *Patria Potestas* in Argentina account for a low percentage of divorced and separated women.) These women married men of similar or comparable education. Seventy-one percent married men with university education. Twenty-five (26.9 percent) of the ninety-three women who had ever been married, married "down," that is, married men with lesser education or social status.

There were few differences between women with high-status husbands and women with low-status husbands. While not statistically significant, more high-status husbands ($n = 50$ or 73.5 percent) were perceived by their wives as being in favor of the wife's working than were low- and medium-status husbands ($n = 15$ or 60.0 percent).

Women with high-status husbands and women with low-status husbands are quite homogeneous in their life styles. These husbands are probably giving their wives the support that they need in order to work. Harmonious relations with the husband, regardless of his socioeconomic status, may be a further extension of United States findings that the opinion of the husband regarding his wife's working is a factor which often determines whether or not she DOES work. We have a chicken-versus-egg problem here. The women in the sample are full-time employed professionals. The married women probably work with the approval (tacit or not) of their husbands. Those who were unable to cajole their husbands into allowing them to work simply were not included in the definition of the universe. There was a tendency for younger women to indicate that their husbands felt it an absolute necessity for the wife to work, given Argentina's chaotic economy.

Nearly every wife made statements on how unique and special her husband was. She would point out that, *machismo* and masculinity complexes aside, her husband was well enough adjusted not to feel threatened by a wife with a profession. Cant or not, rhetoric or not, married women in this sample seemed convinced that their husbands were more emancipated and liberal than the "average" Argentine male who might prefer a traditional housewife for a marriage partner (Kinzer 1973a).

Single women are relieved from a situation of potential role conflict and are less likely to experience the intense role conflict of the married woman. On the basis that the single woman (i.e. spinster, widow, or divorcee) does not have to contend with the whims and vagaries of her spouse, she has one less source of potential role conflict.

While there were not enough divorced, widowed or separated women to use for a comparison group, we did ask single women a series of questions regarding their sense of personal and job fulfillment. Not too surprisingly, the single women (76.7 percent of $n = 21$) were more career-oriented than the married women (7.4 percent of $n = 6$). However, nearly two-thirds of the single women (58.1 percent of $n = 18$) regretted not having married. Marriage is still paramount for these women. Whether the country be Argentina or the United States, "spinster" is still a pejorative term.

5.   SUPPORTIVE ROLE RELATIONSHIPS MITIGATING ROLE CONFLICT OF A MOTHER

Children add one more role, mother, to those of professional and wife. The exigencies of child-care detract from job performance. Children are an extra emotional outlet for a woman and detract from a woman's job being her only source of satisfaction.

Even though the Roman Catholic Church is blamed for high birthrates, literacy levels rather than Church control are more accurate predictors of a high or low birthrate (Kinzer 1973b). The Roman Catholic Church in Argentina is weak, literacy levels are high, contraceptives are readily available, and, excluding Uruguay, the birthrate is the lowest in Latin America. Also, it is estimated that 25 percent of Argentine women have at least one abortion (Kinzer 1973b).

While 80 percent of the sample of married women were mothers, very few women had more than three children. All but two women in the sample report a favorable attitude toward birth control methods (i.e. 98 percent). Given the far-reaching Argentine system of maternity benefits and baby and child nurseries, the working mother is well protected. Most mothers worked until the last few days of their pregnancies and over 80 percent returned to work within six months after the birth of the baby.

Household tasks are multiplied by the arrival of children, and all women had domestic servants to care for their children. While the use of full-time, live-in servants is nearly exclusively an upper-class phenomenon in the United States, most Argentine families have domestic servants. This is due to internal migration from the provinces and migration from poorer neighboring countries, such as Bolivia and Paraguay.

The writer has observed that the general pattern of upper and upper-middle class families' child-rearing patterns is to leave children in the care of servants. For families of high socioeconomic status, a pattern of attenuated motherhood is established, freeing a mother of the obligation of constantly caring for her children. Women of high-status Argentine families are not obligated by the norms of their references group to fulfill the role of mother, as it is smotheringly viewed in the United States. Thus the Argentine woman of middle or upper class may spend her time at the beauty parlor, engage in volunteer activities, or work outside the home.

Attenuated motherhood and availability of domestic help and/or nurseries are factors viewed as external supportive role relationships which mitigate the potential role conflict of the roles "mother" and "working professional."

We can further elaborate on the "typical" respondent from this sample of Buenos Aires professional women: She is likely to be from a high-status family which does not adhere closely to the precepts of any organized religion. She was socialized to be independent and non-nurturant. Familial support was given to her pursuit of higher education as a preparation for a carreer. The adult role model chosen by this woman was her father. If her father's social status was medium or low, she was more likely to enter a field in which male graduates do not predominate. Women from families with high-status fathers entered predominantly masculine fields.

She is more likely to be married than single. She married a man of her own social status and education who approves of her working. She has one or two children and has domestic servants to care for them.

She works in a subordinate position for low pay and yet is satsified with her job because of the personal satisfaction it gives her.

The respondents in this study were in many ways much less neurotic and much less harried by role conflict than their United States sisters. By and large, the Argentine environment is more amenable to professional women than the ambiance of the United States. However, in view of recent Argentine turmoil, galloping inflation, kidnappings, murders, riots, strikes, and general civil unrest, Argentina is itself an unhappy place for serious professionals, male or female.

Actually, at this date (July, 1973), it is worthwhile speculating that perhaps this research may be tabled as a classic historical piece in view of Argentina's bleak future.

REFERENCES

BIDDLE, B. J., E. J. THOMAS
  1966 *Role theory: concepts and research.* New York: John Wiley and Sons.
CHANEY, ELSA
  1973 "Women in Latin American politics: the case of Peru and Chile," in *Female and male in Latin America.* Edited by Ann Pescatello. Pittsburgh: University of Pittsburgh Press.
GERMANI, GINO
  1966 *Mass immigration and modernization in Argentina.* Social Science Institute, Washington University 2(11). St. Louis.
GINZBERG, ELI
  1966 *Life styles of educated women.* New York: Columbia University Press.
GOLDBERG, PHILIP
  1968 Are women prejudiced against women? *Trans-Action* 5(5):28–30.
GOODE, WILLIAM J.
  1960a A theory of role-strain. *American Sociological Review* 25:483–496.
  1960b Norm commitment and conformity to role-status obligations. *American Journal of Sociology,* 246–258.
GROSS, N., W. MASON, A. MCEACHERN
  1958 *Explorations in role analysis: studies of the school superintendency role.* New York: John Wiley and Sons.
HACKER, HELEN M.
  1951 Women as a minority group. *Social Forces* 30:60–69.
HOLLANDER, NANCY CARO
  1973 *"Women: the forgotten half of Argentine history,"* in *Female and male in Latin America.* Edited by Ann Pescatello. Pittsburgh: University of Pittsburgh Press.

HORWITZ, IRVING LOUIS
1962   The Jewish community of Buenos Aires. *Jewish Social Studies* 24: 195–222.

IZAGUIRRE, INÉS DE CAIROLI
1965   Estratificación y orientación profesional en la Universidad de Buenos Aires. *Revista Latinoamericana de Sociología* 3:333–362.

KINZER, NORA SCOTT
1973a   "Women professionals in Buenos Aires," in *Female and male in Latin America.* Edited by Ann Pescatello. Pittsburgh: University of Pittsburgh Press.

1973b   Priests, machos and babies: or Latin American women and the Manichaean heresy. *Journal of Marriage and the Family* 35 (2).

LUIGGI, ALICE H.
1965   *65 Valiants.* Gainesville: University of Florida Press.

MERTON, ROBERT
1963   *Social theory and social structure.* Glencoe, Illinois: Free Press of Glencoe.

MIGUENS, J. E.
1964   *Capacidades profesionales y su aprovechimiento en la Argentina,* Buenos Aires: Fundación Bolsa de Comercio. Volumes one, two, and three.

PESCATELLO, ANN, *editor*
1973   *Female and male in Latin America.* Pittsburgh: University of Pittsburgh Press.

ROSSI, ALICE S.
1965   "Barriers to the career choice of engineering, medicine or science among American women," in *Women and the scientific professions.* Edited by J. Mattfield and C. van Acken. Cambridge: MIT Press.

SARBIN, THEODORE
1954   "Role theory," in *Handbook of social psychology.* Edited by G. Lindzey, volume one. Reading, Mass; Addison-Wesley.

SAUTÚ, RUTH
1967   "Economic development and social stratification in Argentina." Buenos Aires: Instituto Torcuato di Tella. (Unpublished mimeo.)

STABILE, BLANCA
1961   *Report on the status of woman in Argentina.* Report submitted to President Kennedy's Advisory Committee concerning Latin American problems.

ZIMMERMAN, MARY H.
1954   The contractual capacity of married women in the Americas. *Michigan State Bar Journal* 33:27–36.

Life and Labor of the Woman
Textile Worker in Mexico City

VIRVE PIHO

This study deals with the life of the Mexican woman worker in general, and with the life of the textile worker in particular. It is concerned with her working conditions, her income, her relationships with other workers in the factory, and with her living conditions in the home, her main problems, and her role in the family, all in the context of the situation of the family as a whole — housing conditions and the total family income. I was able to gather this information only by gaining the confidence and friendship of the women in the study, spending long hours with them, talking to them on the job or in their modest homes. Only by listening to each one separately and by discussing her problems from all viewpoints did I obtain gradually a compact image of her life and thoughts.

The investigation was carried out in one of the oldest textile factories in Mexico City, established in the early 1890's. Some of the machines still in use dated from that decade and provided a low-range income to female pieceworkers. Seventy out of a total of ninety women were interviewed over a period of about six months. By the end of this time, the remaining twenty women, all elderly, had been instructed by their priest to avoid the interview.

It might be assumed that the best place for a personal interview would be in the subject's home, but the results showed that information was best obtained in the factory, except from those operators paid at a piecework rate. In the factory, the monotonous noise of the machinery provided a degree of privacy and a feeling of security and confidence not possible in the subjects' congested homes. Even so, only a short questionnaire was used in order that the workers not be inhibited by this academic, formal approach. Moreover, the questionnaire was folded into three parts in order to provide the smallest possible view of the paper. To the semi- or totally illiterate lower-class Mexican the printed page is still an object of mistrust. This applies especially to older women. Therefore, only numerical data were recorded immediately — all other personal information had to be remembered and noted down after the interview. Use of a tape recorder would have interfered with the one-to-one relationship; the information was obtained through a personal conversation between the subject and interviewer, and any official flavor had to be avoided.

On the other hand, a considerable amount of information was derived from observations made in the subjects' homes; short questions were occasionally asked to bring the picture into focus.

Because of the confidential nature of the interviews, no names, addresses, or detailed physical description will be given. However, in order to explain better their reactions and ways of thinking, the ages of the workers are included in the study.

It was immediately apparent that the female worker received an income barely sufficient to cover her minimal necessities. Was that due only to a low salary, or were other factors influencing her living standard? The answer to the problem seemed to be contained in the worker's home situation. How many persons did she support? What were her responsibilities inside the family group?

HISTORICAL REVIEW

Historical records of female labor date from Aztec times. Although in many ways their position was inferior to that of men, Aztec women had the right to inherit property from either parent and to own it. They could enter into contractual relationships and could claim justice in the court (Vaillant 1955:100). Their importance, both within the family and in society in general, was considerable. They produced such items as foodstuffs and clothing for home consumption. Outside the home, women were occupied professionally as midwives and medicine women and in religious service. The common woman was especially active in the market as a retail vendor, but she also functioned at times as a wholesale merchant. Women excelled in the fields of weaving and featherworking for home and market consumption.

In colonial times, women as well as men were obliged to render personal services to the estates granted by the Spanish kings to the lords of the estates. In the cities the situation of working women was apparently similar to that of the workers in the Spanish guilds, as can be seen by the protective laws for females in Book VIII, Title XXIII, of the *Laws of Spain*, edited during the last quarter of the eighteenth century (Carrera Stampa 1954:74; Moreno 1958:22).

During the second half of the nineteenth century, exploitation of female and child labor was even more severe than was exploitation of male labor because of the lack of protective laws. Women were primarily occupied as seamstresses and in the tobacco industry (Cosio Villegas 1957:295). In 1876 the first labor congress in Mexico was held, and in the early 1880's, several labor strikes took place. During the Mexican Revolution, women fought along with men and won the legal protection under Article 123 of the Mexican Constitution (Morales Jimenez 1951:63–64).

Nevertheless, in spite of the protective provisions of the Federal Labor Law, the conditions of working women during 1962, when my research was undertaken, showed not only a very difficult economic situation, but also an exposure to a continual double stress derived from their activities in both home and factory. Since then, although both wages and prices have changed, the status of women in the home and the factory remains unchanged.

LABOR ENVIRONMENT

General Factors (Figure 1)

The present factory was started by a German dry-goods vendor in 1890. Wanting to manufacture some of the products himself, he imported from England a circular knitting machine and other machines, some of which are still in use. During the first part of the twentieth century, the factory grew considerably, but as no money was invested in later years, by 1962 both the machines and the productive processes were outmoded.

Most of the women workers had spent their lives within the high walls (with only two entrances) that surrounded the factory buildings and gave the impression of a big jail. Together with their machines, they had grown old and had become a problem to the management.

Hiring Procedure

Most of the women got their jobs through personal recommendation from friends and relatives. Table 1 shows the percentages.

Table 1.

Acquisition of the job	Number of persons	Percentage
Asking personally	6	9
Recommendation of a friend working in the factory	27	39
Recommendation of a family member working in the factory	37	53
	70	101

The bonds of friendship or kinship were so strong that in later years if somebody from the street asked the gatekeeper about job possibilities in the factory, he would answer: "Don't even try it. You can't get on there unless you're related to somebody." In some cases four or more members of one family worked in this factory.

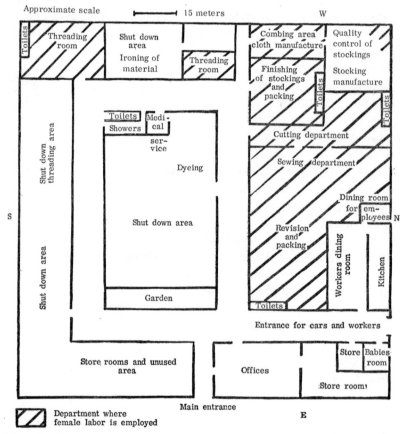

Figure 1.   Factory outline

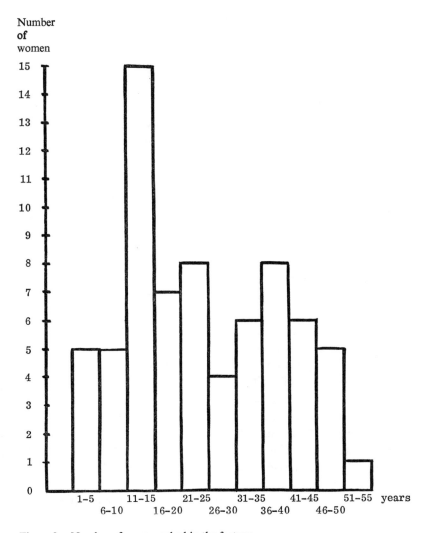

Figure 2. Number of years worked in the factory

Number of Years Worked in the Factory

Figure 2 shows the distribution of length of service in the factory. Only five women had worked there for fewer than five years, and five had worked from five to ten years. The largest group was that of fifteen women who had been working in the plant from eleven to fifteen years. These three categories contained mostly younger girls and older women who had not married. After marriage, most of them retired from the factory while the children were small, but they went back to work after a few years. Thus twenty-five women, or 28 percent of the total, had worked up to fifteen years. The remainder, or 72 percent of the women, had been working in this factory from fifteen to fifty-five years. The five women with forty-six to fifty years of service were thinking about getting their pensions. One woman had worked for fifty-four years and refused to accept her pension, strongly fearing an unsatisfactory arrangement from the Social Security because she had no documentation certifying her date of birth or baptism.

Age of Women

The mean age of the seventy women interviewed, who represented appproximately 80 percent of the female labor force of the factory, was 42 years. The women ranged in age from twenty to seventy years. The variability was apparent in the standard deviation (s $=$ 14).

Lives of hard labor made these women often appear older than they actually were. In some cases, no reliable record of their age existed; only the date when they started at the factory could be firmly established. Also, the subjects generally tended to claim to be younger than they really were, not for reasons of vanity, but for fear that their age might cost them their jobs. One woman actually did become a victim of this practice. She had no personal documentation, and when she was asked her age by the Social Security officials, she said that she was fifty. Soon after that (and while this study was being conducted) members of her family calculated her age at between sixty-four and sixty-eight. But as the Social Security files listed her as fifty years old, she would have to work for some ten to fifteen years more in order to receive her old-age pension at the official age of sixty-five.

Origin

Table 2 shows that the majority of the women interviewed were born in Mexico City. The highest percentage of women working in the factory were from Mexico City. Those from the state of Guanajuato left largely because its arid soil is unsuitable for agriculture and Guanajuato is mainly a mining district, where jobs are available primarily to men. The states of Mexico, Querétaro, Michoacán, Hidalgo, and Jalisco are situated in the center of the country, and their residents are therefore attracted

Table 2

Place of origin	Number of persons	Percentage
Mexico City	48	69
Guanajuato	6	9
Querétaro, Michoacan, and Jalisco (Two women from each state)	6	9
Oaxaca, Veracruz, Hidalgo, Zacatecas, Tamaulipas, and Yucatán (One woman from each state)	6	9
State of Mexico	4	6
	70	101

to the capital. The remainder came from states situated farther away. Some of the women still remembered their birthplaces, as well as some details of childhood, with a mixture of warmth and sadness.

Years of Schooling

Table 3 shows that the highest percentage of women, or 27 percent, finished six years of primary school. These were mostly young women, because by 1962 a primary school education was a legal requisite for factory employment and other jobs. Among older women, the majority had had three or four years of schooling. There were no cases of complete illiteracy; even those who never had gone to school managed somehow to learn to read, although several could not write. Their reading was mostly confined to comic books.

Table 3

Years of schooling	Number of of persons	Percentage
0	8	11
1	4	6
2	8	11
3	11	16
4	10	14
5	4	6
6	19	27
7	5	7
8	0	0
9	1	1
	70	99

A case of exceptional personal intiative was that of a girl who came from a family of twenty living in only two rooms and a kitchen. On her own she learned reading, writing, and arithmetic. Because of these abilities, she became assistant to the woman who supervised the sewing department.

Working Hours

Work began at seven-thirty and ended at four. The threading department started at six-thirty and ended at three. At seven-thirty there was a whistle, followed by a five-minute grace period, after which no one entered; those who were late lost the day. Between nine and nine-thirty there was half an hour for breakfast. From then on work continued until four o'clock (with the exception of the threading department). At the noon whistle the pieceworkers stopped working, although some would have liked to go on in order to complete the dozen by which the merchandise was counted. On Saturdays, work stopped at twelve, and between twelve and one o'clock the machines had to be cleaned. After that the workers received their weekly pay. These working hours were regulated by Chapter III, Article 69, of the Federal Labor Law, which called for eight hours of work, plus half an hour for lunch.

CONDITIONS OF WORKERS

The worker has only the services of his hands and his health to offer. Both are unstable factors, so the workers tend to suffer from marked insecurity. Poverty begins with the breakdown of health and mind (Zweig 1949:19). The factory's ability to fire workers has instilled in them a deep sense of responsibility toward their jobs and their machines. In spite of all the difficulties they experienced, they nonetheless felt that their real field of activity was the factory rather than the home, and not only from the point of view of income. They identified themselves so strongly as factory workers that domestic work never appealed to them in the same way. In some sense, they had assumed the male roles in their family circles. They were the ones who brought the money home, and they were accustomed to the kind of special attention that in other families was given to the man as head of the household. They certainly spent more time in the factory than at home.

Relationships between management and labor

There are two kinds of management-labor relationships. One is characterized by confrontation, where the workers fight in every possible way to obtain their rights and benefits. The other involves a policy of accommodation, in which management considers peaceful agreement as more advantageous. The situation in this factory seemed to be one of accommodation, although tensions and intrigues existing below the apparently peaceful surface later became evident. Contact with the owner of the plant was impossible, but workers could present their grievances personally to the manager, who was disliked.

Another link of communication between the two groups was the labor union, but the women had considerable reservations about the secretary of the union. He never entered the departments where most of the tensions existed and only rarely visited the stockings and packing departments — the most peaceful areas. Even there the women did not pay any attention to him. The women had to pay a relatively high contribution each week to the union regardless of the amount of their wages. The salary of the secretary was paid from this money. In special cases a worker could ask the union for a loan. Three times a year the union held an assembly in the rooms of another factory. The women believed that this union was "white" (paid off by the management), and that they could not expect any kind of help from it in matters involving the management.

A younger woman represented the workers in the downtown offices of Social Security. For this work she received about 60 percent more than the wages earned during a normal working day. Her male assistant received twice the amount of the daily earnings of the seamstresses. These extra salaries were also paid from the union funds. The women argued that it was unnecessary to send two people each time to the Social Security; instead they preferred the female delegate.

The factory had recently adopted the policy of dismissing people who had worked there for fifteen to fifty years, paying them an indemnification equivalent to a few hundred dollars. This was basically illegal, but because the factory had declared bankruptcy, the workers had no legal recourse. Persons who reached sixty years of age and could show dues paid to the Social Security for 500 weeks would receive a reduced pension. Those who had reached sixty-five and the minimum of 500 weeks of dues would receive a full pension.

At the time of the research, new tensions arose in the factory, and again elderly workers were threatened with losing their jobs. The women workers exhibited every emotional reaction from extreme militancy to complete resignation. One extreme militant was a woman of fifty-eight who had worked in the factory for forty-six years. She was not willing to leave her position unless she was paid the legal indemnification according to the number of years she had worked. She had the moral support of her sons, who had received university educations (one of them was a lawyer). She maintained that she had been widowed at an early age, although it was more probable that her children were illegitimate and their education was paid for by their father.

On the other hand, an example of resignation was a woman of about sixty-four who seemed to be deeply preoccupied. Four years earlier, she had been hit by a car and lost her memory; even during our conversation her mind wandered. All her life had been dedicated to others; she had raised and supported six nephews and nieces. They were now adult and independent, leaving her with a feeling of uselessness. Finally she said: "I am not good for anything any more. I am only waiting to be dismissed. But my intestines, my innards, do not understand. They balk, scream and shriek with hunger, and I have to give them something to eat. I have still to wait for God to call me."

The older women especially were strongly attached to their machines. This was the reason they often refused to teach a younger worker how to run them so that he might be able to operate them on another shift. On the one hand, they expressed misgivings that "their" machines might be mishandled by an inexperienced worker. On the other hand, they were afraid of competition. At the same time, they themselves were not willing to work a second shift a day. Many of them, especially the older women, would have been physically incapable of standing for more hours. Most of them suffered severe pain from varicose veins. One of them lifted her skirt and showed her legs to be totally disfigured by black, protruding veins. She had to stay in bed all the time at home in order to be able to stand the following day of work. The medical service of Social Security did not consider varicose veins sufficient reason for an early pension.

Categories of Women Workers

According to Mexican law, workers fell into three distinct legal categories: those with job tenure, those with temporary and specific contractual relationships, and those described as employees.

The relationship between the management and the workers in each department depended on the particular legal position the women occupied.

Table 4

Categories	Number of persons	Percentage
Women laborers with job tenure	50	71
Women hired for a special period	13	19
Employees	7	10
	70	100

The majority of the women had steady positions acquired many years earlier when the whole situation of the factory was different. During 1962 the factory followed the policy of dismissing the old workers and replacing them with younger ones who were employed under temporary contracts.

WORKERS WITH JOB TENURE   Women laborers with job tenure had worked from seven to fifty-five years in the factory. They worked in various departments where female labor was used: spinning, threading, weaving on circular looms, stocking and packing, cutting material and sewing, quality revision, and packing sweatshirts. They were paid by the day or by the piece. These women were paid each week and had two weeks of vacation each year — one during Easter week and the other between Christmas and the New Year.

Another advantage for the tenured workers was the savings fund. With the last salary payment before vacation they received their savings, consisting of 8 percent for cotton workers and 7 percent for sewing department workers of each weekly payment. The company paid the workers an amount equivalent to that which they had saved. In case of illness they received support from Social Security from the fourth day on, but they received nothing for the first three days.

WORKERS ON CONTRACT   The management could have a contract with a whole department of workers or with an individual. All long-term contracts were renegotiated every two years. Salary increases were usually incorporated into the new contract. At the end of the contract, if no renewal took place, the management was free of all obligations toward the workers. Thus the women had to demonstrate their efficiency constantly in the hope that their contracts would be renewed. Since about 1955, workers were taken only on a contract basis. With union connivance, the management was able to persuade the whole threading department to renounce their status as workers with job tenure and accept a labor contract. For this change, each woman received approximately four hundred dollars, the exact amount depending on the number of years worked.They were then given a contract for two months, which was extended for another two. At the time of this research, the contract was about to expire and the situation of these women was desperate.

Among them was one thirty-nine-year-old woman who had twelve children. Although both she and her husband worked, they could barely survive. Another woman, twenty-nine years old, supported a daughter who was an outstanding student at school, and a sister who was unable to find a job. The worker's mother was a cleaning woman who earned a minimal salary, hardly enough for herself. Another of these women was thirty-seven years old, an unmarried mother with three children, all under ten. Another unmarried mother had four children from fourteen to twenty-two years old. Only the oldest son had a job. The fourteen- and sixteen-year-old daughters could not find work because they were too young, nor could the fifteen-year-old son, because while working as a cutter, he had cut off one of his fingers, a decided handicap for a manual laborer. Another single woman of forty-six supported her mother and a sister. A sixty-four-year-old woman lived with a daughter who supported her; the mother gave her entire salary for the maintenance of her son's eight children because the son could not support his family. Only one woman, who worked as though threatened by invisible forces, said that she was sure her contract would be renewed because she was a very fast worker and the management knew it. Another woman of thirty-nine had tried to find a job in another factory, but she was considered too old and the job was given to a young man of twenty.

THE EMPLOYEES   These women were doing the same kind of labor as the other workers but were termed employees. The majority of them were older, but there were some younger employees working in various departments. These employees received their salaries every two weeks, the amount being comparable to that of the laborers. They did not benefit from the saving system, but on the other hand, in case of illness and absence of less than three days, they were not affected by loss of wages.

Nearly all the women who worked in supervisory capacities were called employees. A supervisory position could be held only by an employee. It was difficult for a woman who was a simple worker to occupy such a position, although during the early decades of this factory this had been possible. All employees had direct access to the management and did not belong to the labor union. Although these employees constantly associated with the other women workers, they seemed to feel superior to them. One of the supervisors did not go to breakfast with the other women; some voluntarily came to work each morning half an hour earlier than the others.

This was done also to prevent small-scale theft of stockings or panties.

Nevertheless, in at least one department, employees and ordinary workers did the same kind of labor. The management was free to send the employees to any department where urgent help was needed. Therefore, with the exception of the department masters, the employees constituted a kind of floating labor force not bound to any department. Their vacations were the same as those of the workers — Easter week and the days between Christmas and the New Year. Only seven women, or 10 percent of the total seventy, were employees.

PIECEWORK LABORERS   Twenty-six women, or 37 percent of the total seventy, were pieceworkers. Forty-four women, or 63 percent, were dayworkers.

At one time, when a woman started at the factory she could choose between being paid by the day or on a piecework basis. In later years she had to accept whatever was offered. In the beginning, piecework offered the possibility of higher earnings through harder work. But the piecework payments had been lowered to the point where the pieceworkers had to rush in order to reach the same salary as the dayworkers. Generally, it might be thought that daywork was less exhausting than piecework, but that depended on a woman's place in the productive process. Dayworkers were visited about three times each day — at any time — and were not supposed to sit down at work, although in the department where material was woven on circular looms, the production process of the machines (some of which dated from the nineteenth century) allowed for short intervals of rest.

A woman of seventy, who had worked with these machines for fifty-four years, walked restlessly from one to the other. She was on piecework. She changed the needles, put new thread in, and constantly knotted broken threads. Her fingers were curved like eagle's claws; it seemed that she never could straighten them. She also had diabetes. When asked how she could stand that kind of work until four o'clock in the afternoon, she answered: "At four I am dead." She did not ask for a pension because, totally lacking any personal documentation, she suspected that she would not be given one. When asked why she was still working at her age, she answered: "Hunger." She supported a sister of eighty who kept house and an eleven-year-old girl who also lived with her. In the slum compound where the old woman lived, she had picked up this child, whose family was so large that there was not enough food for all of them.

These two persons at home, her sister and the little girl, were her motivation for continuing to work. She held on to her position like an old soldier who knows that he has to die, but holds on to the end. There was another motivation: she was so accustomed to work that she did not feel comfortable at home. Her place was behind the machine, so that despite the absolutely exhausing work, she said: "The housework is harder than the factory because at home it never ends, especially when there are children. That's why many women prefer to work in the factory."

SERVICES

The service facilities provided by the factory were the dining room, the shop where the workers could buy articles produced by the factory at reduced prices, the shower rooms, and a medical dispensary attended by Social Security personnel. According to law, there should have been a child-care facility for babies and young children, with a nurse in charge, but this was nonexistent.

The Dining Room

Near the time clock at the north entrance of the factory was the entrance to the workers' dining room. This room originally formed a part of the packing and sewing department, and was separated from that room only by thin wooden walls about six feet high. Here everything was the same color: the walls, the tables, and the wooden chairs were painted green. On the wall, near the entrance, hung a lithograph of the Holy Virgin of Guadalupe. Each morning men and women crossed themselves in front of the Virgin before they started working. Sewn to the picture of the Virgin was a real pink silk dress decorated with white flowers. This had been made some years earlier by a woman who had asked permission to take the Virgin home in order to dress her. The Virgin had a fine metal crown on her head, lace curtains, an ever-burning candle, and two vases with artificial flowers. A glass-covered table contained silver- and gold-plated replicas of various anatomical parts which had allegedly been cured through the miraculous intervention of the Virgin.

The majority of the women brought food from home for breakfast because they liked it better, and it was even less expensive than the very low-priced food prepared by a couple in the kitchen. Officially it was prohibited to use the dining room during the working shift, but occasionally some of the workers rushed in to wolf down a *taco* [rolled tortilla with beans in it] or a "jello."

The dining room was the only place where some sort of social communication took place. If somebody had a birthday, it was here they celebrated and sang the traditional birthday song "*Las Mananitas.*" After work, problems were sometimes discussed here, both work-connected and private ones. There were small lockers in the dining room where belongings were kept during working hours. Off to one side was another small dining room, painted cream color and with Swiss landscape photographs on the walls. This room was for the use of the employees.

The Checkroom for Babies

To the northeast of the block, there was a tall, high room without windows, where the sun never entered. In order to obey the law, the room was officially designated for babies and small children, and although it was almost never used, there were small beds, children's chairs, and a small table. The women believed that if the factory hired a woman to supervise the children, the Social Security would provide milk and bottles for the babies. At one time the women had tried to leave their babies in the small beds there so that they could give them their bottles during the officially established half-hour allotted to nursing mothers. Either a family member would pick up the baby some hours later and take it home, or else the baby had to stay there until the mother herself could take it home. But this turned out to be very complicated, particularly because there was no one in charge of the babies. This procedure was abandoned, and the women left their children at home or in a government-operated kindergarten. These kindergartens were overcrowded, and it was difficult to find a place there. Also, although the monthly payments were very low, the low-paid working mother could hardly afford them.

The factory itself paid a certain amount to the union each week for the maintenance of the children's room and for sports activities, but it did not care whether or not they actually functioned. It considered that this was the union's business, and that the factory had fulfilled its obligations.

The Shop

The factory shop was open twice a week — on Wednesdays and on Saturdays. The prices charged for its own products were lower than those charged outside the factory. If the workers could not pay for their purchases at once, they were able to buy on credit, signing debit slips. The debts were then deducted from their weekly salaries.

The Bathrooms

Several departments had their own bathrooms, and several others were located at the south end of the establishment. All were of white tile, and in those at the south end, thought to be used more frequently, the water ran constantly. There was a sign reading: "Please use the services in a correct and decent way." To one side, there were sixteen white-tile showers without doors. There was hot water all day long. The women could shower daily, but most of them preferred Saturday. Some of the older women, however, did not like to undress in front of the others and preferred to pay for a room in a public bath.

Medical Service of the Social Security

One room was equipped for medical services and had a doctor and a nurse in attendance. They worked in two shifts, mornings and afternoons. The medical service consisted chiefly of distributing some basic products: vitamins B1 and B12, aspirin, liver extract, and especially penicillin. After the doctor left at eleven o'clock, the medicines could be dispensed by the nurse. When some worker showed up, the nurse asked: "What do you want?" Sore throats, common colds, and backaches were treated with penicillin. Most of the workers would have preferred to go to the regular Social Security clinic, but they would have lost too much time from the workday. Opinions about the medical service of the Social Security varied with the age of the respondent. Some women who had children in the clinics of the Social Security were content with their service, whereas some older women were strongly prejudiced against it.

Thirty women out of seventy used only the medical service of the Social Security. Thirty-six women used both the official medical service and private doctors. One woman used only a private doctor. Three women did not use any kind of medical service.

All these women had the right to use the official medical service of the Social Security for other members of their families as well, yet of the thirty women who used only the medical service for themselves, ten employed private doctors for their children or parents. According to the women they could not afford private doctors for themselves but nevertheless preferred them for their relatives. This attitude showed their self-abnegation and deep devotion to their families. Furthermore, three fourths of these women were the heads of families, and on their health depended the well-being of the others. Often the charge for a visit to a private doctor, especially those who work among poor people, is relatively low, but the cost for the prescription medicines is high, whereas at the official medical service the medicines are free. In general, Social Security medical service was used for light illnesses, while a private doctor was preferred for more severe cases. Social Security does not grant early pensions for cases of varicosis, which is considered a result of multiple births, nor for cases of diabetes, from which several of these women suffered.

PRODUCTION

In this factory women worked in the departments of threading, cones, circular looms, material cutting, sewing, packing, and stocking. Thread for the production of sweatshirts was purchased, because to produce it in the factory would have been more expensive. These skeins of thread went first to the threading department, where women threaded them on spools. Each time the thread broke, the machine stopped automatically, and the woman in charge had to knot the thread and start the machine moving again. From there the spools went to the cone department.

There the air was full of cotton lint, which clung to everything like snow in display windows at Christmas. Nevertheless, the women said that masks impaired their breathing and they did not use them. As most of these women had worked in the same department for twenty-three to thirty-six years, they probably suffered from considerable lung congestion.

It was here that tension was highest. All these women had lost their job tenure, and by their contract, they would have to leave the factory in two months. The ages of these women ranged from thirty-nine to sixty-four. As they were paid on a piecework basis, each of them worked to maximum capacity in order to earn as much as possible before losing the work permanently. The atmosphere of resentment toward the present and fear of the future restrained talk or gossip. In addition, each woman attended long files of cones and had to walk fast from one to the other. The thread, which ran from the spool through a disc of paraffin to the cone, broke frequently. Each time the machine stopped, a woman had to knot the thread and get the machine moving again.

From there, the thread went to the department of circular looms, some of which dated back to 1896. These machines also stopped each time the thread broke and had to be started again when the needle was re-threaded.

The knit material produced went into the department of velveting and ironing, where only men worked, and from there to the cutting department. Here the material was prepared for cutting by six women. In former years everything had been cut by hand, but now there were two cutting machines, one managed by a man and the other by a woman. In the cutting deparment the workers had formerly been paid by the piece, but at the time of the research they worked by the day. The atmosphere was thus relatively peaceful.

The cut material was distributed among the women of the sewing department, who worked in groups doing the same kind of work. Products were counted by the dozen and varied according to the model. The average output of a woman who sewed sweatshirts ranged from three to five dozen shirts without a collar. This was the only department where the younger women generally worked. It was accepted that sewing was the hardest work of the whole process. Here tension was high because each lost minute meant lost money. All these women suffered from aching backs and what they called "aching kidneys." They said that the pain was tolerable in the morning, but in the afternoon it was continuous. One of them, who was unmarried and had two boys, said that in the evenings at home she sewed dresses to earn some extra money.

To save time in the sewing department, two groups of four women employed on their own account two girls of seventeen and eighteen as assistants, one for each group. These girls brought to the women at the sewing machines the cut material and the necessary additional accessories, which were distributed from a central point. They took the sewn shirts to the quality control department. During the sewing process they aligned the parts and prepared each kind of work as far as possible. For this job they earned just enough for their food, but they had the opportunity to fill a vacancy in case one occurred.

In one corner sat a pregnant woman who did delicate sewing on a small machine. Her table vibrated from the powerful machine next to hers, spoiling much of her work. Often she had to redo her sewing, which meant lost time on her piecework. The baby to be born would be her eighth child.

In the next department, all the seams were inspected by old women, all of whom belonged to the category of employees. Each defective piece was given back to the worker, who had to sew it again. From there the sewn articles went to the ironing and the packing department. The

cheaper goods were packed by the dozen, and the better ones by the piece.
In the stocking department there were about twenty-five women, all
paid by the day. This peaceful department, with mostly elderly women,
was protected by the figure of Christ dressed in white lace and a red
velvet cloak. Twenty-five years before this study, the women of this
department had taken up a collection and bought the figure. Each year
expensive material was bought for a new robe, which was sewn by one of
the women. After the Christ had been dressed in his new outfit, a private
festival was given in his honor. In this department, the women felt as if
they belonged to one family. When one of them had a birthday, the others
gave her a little present; it did not matter how modest it was. They tried
to console each other in the event of grief, and tried to help even if only
with words.

SALARIES

Employees' Salaries

Although workers and employees did the same kind of work in many cases,
the workers received their wages on a weekly basis and the employees
fortnightly. But even among the employees doing the same kind of work,
the amount of payment depended on the number of years worked, age,
and enthusiasm for work, as well as the relationship with the management.
The monthly salary of an employee was calculated by deducting the
amount payable as taxes and adding to the rest one-twelfth of the annual
bonus paid at Christmas. This sum was divided by thirty, and in that
way the daily salary with the quota payable to Social Security was
determined.

Wages of the Workers

Here, too, tax and Social Security payments were deducted from the
gross income. The calculation of the tax paid to Social Security took into
account that the wages varied from week to week and from month to
month. To obtain the average monthly wage, the annual earnings were
divided by twelve; that result was divided by thirty, giving the average
daily wage. This served as a basis for the Social Security payment. Twice
a year, before each vacation, the workers received a sum of money which
consisted of their savings and an equal amount provided by the factory.

In some departments it became necessary to stop the payments by piecework and to pay the women by the day. In some cases two women who did the same kind of work received different payments for it. This was due to a law that prohibited the lowering of a worker's wage. The daily income was therefore based on the average of the worker's piecework earning.

Maximum and Minimum Salaries

Of the six women who earned the highest wages, only one woman was as young as twenty-nine years; the others ranged from thirty-nine to forty-seven years old. All of them were on piecework. This kind of work required long experience. One of these women had worked in the factory for fifteen years, four of them for twenty-three to twenty-seven years, and one for thirty-four years.

The woman who had the highest income of the group had a very aggressive personality. She criticized everything and everybody, and probably used the same amount of energy in her work. Her husband worked also, and she was one of the few women in the study who practiced birth control. Her thirteen-year-old daughter was in school and intended to go on studying.

The woman with the second highest earnings supported her mother and a niece. She was lucky to be able to work on a relatively modern machine, one that produced a bit more than the older ones.

The woman with the third highest income was thirty-nine years old. She lived with a man five years her junior and had a total of twelve children: seven from one man and five from another. The next woman, also thirty-nine, was separated from the father of her three children and had to support all of them alone. These last two women seemed to have gentler natures and attitudes, but the responsibilities of their children made them work very hard.

The woman in fifth place said that she was "the man and the woman" in her home. She supported a daughter and a sister. She was full of nervous energy and concentrated fully on her work. The last one in this group was a married woman of forty-seven who had two children and was very active in her private life, as well as in her work.

This sample seems to indicate that the most productive ages for women were from the late thirties to the late forties. This was contrary to the hiring policies of most factories, which gave preference to women of twenty.

The working capacities of these six women derived from personal character as well as experience and still undiminished physical abilities. However, there were women over fifty working on a piecework basis who tried in every way to maintain their average general income. Their "free" time was used for relaxing and preparing themselves physically for the next day. Zweig (1949:15) maintains that workers reach their peak earning capacity during their forties.

The women who drew the lowest salaries were above or below the age of forty. Five of them were between twenty and thirty years old, and one was fifty-five. One of them earned a steady monthly salary, and the others did piecework. The one who earned the least had been working for less than a year in the factory, and her low salary was probably due to a lack of experience. Two of these women had worked for four years, one for ten years, and one for fifteen years. Only one of them was married. They were all quiet and introverted. It appeared that in this factory this type of person was not suited for piecework.

Rates on which Wages were Based

The rates for each piece of production on which the workers' weekly wages were based created constant tensions and discussions. In the cone department, the rate was based on each kilogram of thread; the thickness of the thread had to be taken into account. In the circular loom department, the salaries were based on each kilogram of material produced; this also varied with the thickness of the material. In the sewing department, each kind of work was based on a different piece rate by which the sets of a dozen were calculated. Each Wednesday all the seamstresses tried to finish whatever they could, because on Thursday the accounting for the weekly wage began. One woman mentioned that soon after they reached a higher rate for some kind of work, that article was dropped from production.

Commerce and Loans

Some years previously it had been possible to buy everything on credit in the factory and to borrow money as well, but at interest rates ranging from 5 to 20 percent per week. The new management prohibited all such activities, but one of the women workers sold all kinds of articles in the factory and lent money. She had never been to school, but she managed to keep a little book with the names of the persons who owed her money and the amounts owed. Workers who were dismissed tried to disappear without repaying their loans; besides, the high interest payments had usually already covered the principal. Other women also lent money, but in a more modest fashion. The biggest loans could be obtained from a woman who no longer worked in the factory but knew all the workers. Each Saturday she was at their entrance with an account book in her hands. Still, the relationship between debtor and lender was marked by the utmost courtesy on both sides. Even a misunderstanding regarding payments was cleared up politely.

A certain feeling of liberation prevaled on Saturdays; it took shape in a desire to buy something. Some workers did enter the factory shop, but most of this transient euphoria had to be suppressed by thoughts of the children and other helpless family members at home. However, one woman, in talking about the Saturday paydays, said that she preferred working herself instead of waiting outside the gate for her husband, who, according to her, could escape through the other door of the factory.

FAMILY LIFE

To complete the picture of the life of the women workers it was necessary to know about the conditions of their homes and the role they played in their families.

Income and Expenses

The basic income of the worker is usually taken as the main factor in calculating such expenses as food, rent, utilities, and clothing (Zweig 1949:8). This might be true for a male worker, the head of a family, in an industrialized country. But in our study, where the female worker was the principal support of the family, the situation was different. In Mexico the family is often larger than the nuclear family, and it was necessary to see to what extent each member contributed to the common welfare. The women of the factory in Mexico answered questions about the family income with: "It is not enough. Sometimes we have to borrow." Nevertheless, the difficulties of a family member could worry the women even more than a lack of money. Therefore, the savings that they obtained twice a year were used mostly for covering the debts incurred between these periods.

To calculate the gross income of these women, additional savings from income had to be taken into account. Some women who owned pieces of land on the outskirts of the city rented one or two rooms; others earned something by washing, ironing, or cleaning for other people. One woman sold candy. Some of the younger women asked about what kind of work they could do in the afternoon after leaving the factory. The lack of a better education was always the reason for not being able to obtain better-paying jobs.

To calculate the average income for each family member, the total income of the family was divided by the number of family members. Excluding the working woman herself, the families were made up of 44 percent adults and 56 percent children, which naturally contributed to the very low per capita income. Only four of the seventy women, or 6 percent, could use their salaries entirely for themselves. All the others provided full or partial support for other family members: mothers, children, sisters, grandchildren, nieces and nephews, and so on. In rare cases, a male satellite could be observed.

Of the expenses, only the rent and electricity were stable items. Expenses for food varied according to the situation of each family. A single person sometimes spent three times as much for food as the per capita amount in a family with children. After paying for rent, electricity, and food, 22 percent of the women had nothing left for such items as transportation, school necessities for the children, clothing, etc. It must therefore be assumed that they either borrowed money, had some additional income, or covered these expenses by holding back even more on food.

Among those who could use their full salaries for themselves was a woman of fifty-eight who had worked for forty-five years in the factory and whose two sons had received higher educations. She worked nearly all that time on piecework. At the time of this research she lived in a house owned by her sons. The married son lived with his family on the lower floor; the mother and the other son lived on the upper floor. Each morning at seven-thirty one son took his mother by car to the factory entrance. Because of her bad eyesight, the woman had once been hit by a bus. Although she was not dependent on her income, she insisted on continuing to work in the factory in order to be eligible for her pension.

Another woman who used all her salary for herself was a spinster of fifty-nine. She had built a one-room house on a piece of land which did not belong to her and on which the toilet and washing facilities were used communally by all the others living on that land.

Another woman, thirty-three years old, who lived with other family members in a privately owned house, could also use her total income for herself. Her brothers were working, and the mother cooked for all of them. This young woman gave her mother the amount necessary for the food and kept the rest.

The last of the four who did not have others to support was a woman of twenty-two who had left her large family behind in the state of Zacatecas and had come to Mexico City, where she had some cousins. Working as an assistant she earned only enough for food, but her cousins helped her with her other needs.

Food

Apart from the question of food costs was the matter of home economics and the kind of food consumed by the women. Many of them got up at five o'clock in the morning to buy low-priced milk from the CEIMSA, a government-controlled chain of stores for poor people. The women agreed that this milk did not taste good, but taking it with coffee or oatmeal made this less noticeable. At least once a week they went to the big wholesale market, *La Merced*, where prices were often relatively low, and bought vegetables, fruit, and dry food for several days. They all said that it was impossible for them to pay the prices asked in the small shops in their neighborhoods. Some of the women had relatives who were better off, so they visited them once or twice a week and took home leftovers and other food.

One woman went often to see her sister because her sister's mother-in-law had a small fruit store, and all the unsold fruit was kept for the poor relatives. Another woman, sixty-six, had a sick brother at home who could not work. The food they ate was prepared by a sister who lived elsewhere and who was paid to cook for them. The brother went daily to see this sister and bring the food home. The worker said that at night she took only a glass of milk and a banana and cooked only on Sundays.

Another woman, fifty-eight, lived on the outskirts of the city. She owned a little piece of land on which she had begun to build a small one-story house. It remained unfinished because her money had given out. She was most eager to repay a loan she had received; otherwise the house would be taken away by the bank. In this family the mother and one daughter worked, while another daughter remained at home in charge of the household. The family included the elderly, sickly brother of the mother as well as three nieces and nephews of another brother who had died. The mother of the children was an alcoholic and could not take care of them. There was still another girl of fourteen who was said to be a niece. A staple of their diet was a soupy mixture of meat and herbs called *xocoyol*. This was eaten by spooning it up with tortillas.

One family with eleven children went to the government soup kitchen, where a full meal could be bought for only a token payment. But after some months they stopped going there because they did not like to stand in line with street beggars and other outcasts. Nevertheless, there was never enough food at home, and often they were hungry after eating.

Rent

A high percentage of the women lived in slum tenements. These dwellings, rented many years previously, came under the government's rent-freeze. Nearly all the tenants had difficulties with the landlords. One woman of thirty had lived with her aunt and grandmother in such a compound for a number of years. Their living quarters consisted of two rooms without windows, kitchen, or corridor. She was so afraid of the landlady that on the day the rent was due, she kept the door closed all day; when the land-lady knocked at the door, she opened it just long enough to stretch out her hand with the money. She had seen another family evicted from this compound because they were unable to pay the full amount of the rent at the moment it came due.

Electricity

Electricity was used not only at night for lighting the rooms, but often during the day as well, because in the tenements the rooms often lacked windows. Electricity also satisfied the cultural needs of the working class for radio and television, and sometimes it was used to operate a sewing machine for some poorly-paid home sewing. Only 7 percent of the women did not have electricity in their homes.

Entertainment and recreation

Zweig (1949:43–47) has proposed that the need for entertainment is greater in the working class than in the middle class. Persons of higher economic and social levels who are fortunate enough to do work that satisfies their interests, who have nice homes, cultural interests, and opportunities to travel, have less need for entertainment outside the home than a worker who is continuously subjected to a monotonous and tiring job. To deprive the latter of a change would produce emotional imbalance and serious psychological problems. Therefore, better social conditions for the working classes mean not only sufficient income for the basic necessities, but also opportunities for entertainment and recreation (Zweig 1949).

The worker is a slave of the machine, and after finishing his shift, especially on Saturday, he needs to fulfill himself and do something to underline his momentary sense of freedom. Not only is his body tired, but also his spirit is depressed by monotonous work. In many cases labor accidents have been caused by monotony and the fatigue of the worker. Some kind of satisfying entertainment or recreation is essential as a means of maintaining mental equilibrium. A member of a low-income group often cannot entertain his friends at home, so he goes out to a public place. The necessity for recreation is inversely related to the amount of satisfaction a person obtains in his work and home (Zweig 1949).

However, in the case of the female Mexican workers, entertainment played only a small part in their lives. The working woman who wants to forget about the daily difficulties goes to the movies, especially in Mexico, where there are many inexpensive second- or third-class movie houses in low-income areas. But even here, television has largely taken over the role of the movie house because it is even less expensive. At night and on Sundays neighbors gather at the home of someone who has a television set, watch the programs, and make a small contribution for the favor.

In this study, 55 percent of the women went to see a movie once a month; 40 percent went between one and four times in a month; and 6 percent (mostly young girls) went more than four times a month. Those who went rarely wanted to save the money because they had other family members to support. Many of the older women were so tired after coming home from the factory that they rested for a while and then did housework.

The woman has to take care of the home and therefore has much less free time than a man does. But at the same time she is also much less subject to boredom than is the sort of man who does not know how to find satisfaction in his free time. In general, Mexican workers are not accustomed to reading, except for sensationalist newspapers or comic books. A larger number of public libraries all over Mexico City would be a great advantage. On the other hand workers also often lack a hobby, which pyschologists consider important in maintaining emotional balance.

Women used their "free moments," after their kitchen chores were completed and after the children were cared for, for washing and ironing. This was their activity after more urgent tasks were done. Because washing machines are relatively expensive in Mexico, they are still used mostly by the middle and upper classes; and public laundries with self-service washing machines are being installed in middle-class living areas only. Therefore, in the lower-income areas, washing is still done by hand. Only one working woman possessed a washing machine, and this was primarily because her husband was also working.

Sunday was when relatives were visited or invited for lunch. Many of the women complained that they worked even harder on Sundays than during the week because they had to prepare everything in advance for the whole week. One woman of forty-six went with her nephews and nieces to the public park on Sunday afternoons. While the children played, she sat on a bench crocheting. This kind of handicraft is deeply rooted among Mexican women, much more so than knitting. But it seems strange that they produce mostly doilies, not garments.

The women read mainly illustrated romantic novels with short accompanying texts. Thirty-two percent of the women bought them or some other kind of family or women's magazine. More than a third of the women borrowed rather than bought them and sometimes paid a small contribution as a kind of rent for the material. Price was established by the thickness of the volume. Nevertheless, some girls had finished primary school and read books and *Readers Digest* in Spanish. Thirty percent of the women did not read at all because they said that it tired their eyes and gave them headaches. These were mostly older women who had learned to read only a little and, in addition, had damaged their eyes in the factory through repairing machine knitwork for many years.

Centers for education and cultural diffusion have been established by the Social Security Institute for employees and workers. But the study showed that only one woman out of the seventy had taken and finished some of the courses offered. Another one had tried, but she soon felt lost among the women who were employees and whom she considered to be "upper class" and to have different manners. It was also a considerable sacrifice to spend the money for bus fare and use the time normally set aside for ironing. She was made uncomfortable by the better-dressed women and by the elegance of the building. Once, when a free concert was given, she and her girl friend took courage and entered the hall. It was the first time she had heard and seen a real concert. She liked it profoundly, but never went back again.

HOUSING

Figure 3 shows that nearly half of the women (49 percent) lived relatively near one another, south and southeast of the factory within a radius of 1.3 kilometers (1 kilometer = 0.625 miles). This was a residential area with slum tenements. There were no women living in the north or northwest part of Zone I because this area was part of the downtown section of the city. All the women of Zone I had been living there for a long time, sometimes for several decades, as had the 29 percent of women of Zone II (beyond Zone I but within a radius of 5.3 kilometers), where the buildings were subject to rent-freeze. With the growth of the city, the price of land in these areas has risen. If the workers had to abandon their old living

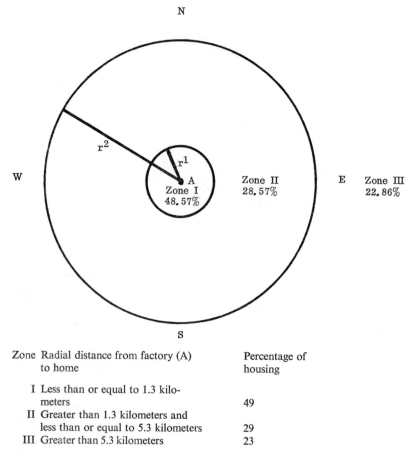

Zone	Radial distance from factory (A) to home	Percentage of housing
I	Less than or equal to 1.3 kilometers	49
II	Greater than 1.3 kilometers and less than or equal to 5.3 kilometers	29
III	Greater than 5.3 kilometers	23

Figure 3. Location of housing of the seventy interviewed women in relationship to the factory

Plate 1.   Slum tenements I

Plate 2.   Slum tenements I

Plate 3.
Slum tenements II

Plate 4.
Slum
tenements II

quarters, they would have to seek a new place on the outskirts of the city (Zone III).

One of the women lived so far away that she had to get up each morning at five in order to be at the factory at seven-thirty. Even at those distances, low-rent housing could be found only north and east of the city because the better residential areas were located south and west. The questionnaire showed that 72 percent of all women lived in rented apartments; only 27 percent lived in small houses rented by themselves or by relatives. These were always located in the outskirts.

Table 5

Rented	Percentage	
Slum tenements	37	
Apartments	14	55
Room in an apartment rented by somebody else	3	
Room on a flat roof	1	
Privately owned		
House owned by the informant	6	23
House owned by relatives	17	
Mixed		
Rooms with collective services on a piece of land	21	
	99	

Slum Tenements

The highest percentage (37 percent) lived in the slum compounds. These were generally a series of single rooms around a central patio. Toilets and washing facilities were located in the patio for public use. These compounds usually consisted of only one floor, but sometimes there were two or even three floors. The number of people living in them increased constantly because of migration from the countryside. Most of the migrants had some relatives living in the city, often in such a compound.

Sometimes an old building filled with people was called a slum compound because the toilets and washing facilities were used by several families. Often whole families slept in one room. It is understandable that this way of living could easily result in promiscuity and criminality. Adolescents in these environments often join gangs which may later develop criminal tendencies. Statistics show that a high percentage of juvenile delinquents grew up in this sort of environment. (Carrancá y Trujillo 1955).

The area where most of the women in this factory lived was characterized by such living conditions. In one such compound, where a twenty-
eight-year-old woman worker lived, there were 141 "apartments," the
majority of them consisting of only one room. Although most of these
apartments were of equal size, the rent varied according to the number
of years the tenant had lived there. Each tenant paid the amount of rent
agreed on at the time he moved into the room. Each time a room was
vacated, the new price was fixed according to the demand and the in-
increased cost of living at that time. Some rooms were occupied by only
one person, but in others, several persons slept; often more than one
family lived in a single apartment. There might have been a thousand
persons sleeping in the compound at night. At ten o'clock at night the
gate was closed and a janitor placed his bed inside the patio at one side
of the door near the altar of the Holy Virgin of Guadalupe. Everybody
who wanted to get in or out had to pay him a small fee. At six in the
morning, passage through the gate was again free.

Many of the buildings where the workers lived were old and in very
bad condition. Because of the rent-freeze, the landlords were not willing
to maintain them, and no repair work was done. The landlords would have
liked to get rid of the renters, but federal law prohibited putting them out
without paying them an indemnification based on the number of years
lived in the building. In one old building occupied by several women
workers of the factory and many others, no rent was paid because the
building was to be torn down, but the people refused to leave. No service
at all was given. In the upper floor water could be obtained only between
four and seven in the mornings, so the tenants would fill all kinds of
containers with enough water for twenty-four hours. Each night big rats
had lively battles in the central patio. The best place in this building was
still the big flat roof because of sun and light. Up there were three separate
rooms built of wooden boards. In each of these rooms a family lived and
cooked food.

The Apartment

An apartment can be defined as living rooms in a building with a common
entrance, its own toilet, and washing facilities. Some of the women lived
in small, poor apartments of one-story construction which sometimes
had central openings in the roof where the kitchen smoke escaped. Some
of the workers had applied to the government housing offices for better
apartments or small houses on the outskirts of the city, but they stated

bitterly that only the employees were helped and that the workers were forgotten and neglected.

The Private House

A building with an independent entrance, standing a certain distance from neighboring constructions, was considered a private house. In cases where women workers lived in privately owned houses, the buildings either belonged to some relative or were owned by the entire family. The piece of land was bought on credit and paid for monthly by all economically active family members. Sometimes they built one room at a time, adding more rooms later as economic conditions permitted. Only 6 percent of the seventy women interviewed lived in private homes. In one case, a twelve-year-old orphan had built a room for his stepmother, and she said proudly that this room was better built than two other rooms that were added later. The women who lived in some kind of private house did not care how modest it was. They felt more secure and calm than did those who had to live in rented rooms. A woman who lived in a half-finished house that belonged to her mother and consisted of only unfinished walls and a roof said that she could not imagine life with all the children if she still had to pay rent. Another woman had, in her youth, worked a few years in Chicago and had saved some money. With her savings she bought a piece of land and built a room on it. She said that in the rainy season the mud was so high that she had to take off her shoes and walk home barefoot.

The average number living in a room was 3.8 persons. In two extreme cases, twenty persons lived in two rooms and twenty-three persons shared three rooms.

The Inventory

Most workers used oil stoves, which cost much less than gas stoves. The kinds of cooking facilities found, in percentages, were as follows: oil stove, 44; gas stove, 41; carbon brazier, 13; electric hot plate, 1.

Old women preferred the carbon brazier, saying that food cooked that way was more flavorful. Those who used an oil stove usually wished to exchange it as soon as possible for a gas stove, because the smell of oil affected the taste of the food.

Seventy-three percent of the women had radios in their homes, although sometimes the sets belonged to another member of the family. A television usually belonged to the whole family. As media for education among a low-income population, television and radio certainly could be better exploited than they have been so far.

Some 57 percent of the women owned sewing machines. In the past, the sewing equipment, like the kitchen utensils, belonged solely to the woman. Even in modern society, where the clothing industry is characterized by mass production, young women workers exhibited a great interest in sewing.

The total number of persons living in the seventy homes was 385. There were more than five chairs and three beds per family. About 83 percent of the workers had one table which was used principally for eating, but also for the children's schoolwork, for sewing, and for other purposes. Some large families (9 percent of the group) had two tables. A number of families (9 percent) had no table at all, in which case the family might sit on the bed while eating.

Over half of the women had a cabinet for clothes or a closet in the home. Closets exist only in private houses. The cabinet with a mirror and drawers is a basic piece of furniture of poor people because it serves several purposes at once. About 16 percent of the women had no cabinets or closets.

Nearly all the woman had some kind of cupboard for keeping kitchenware; 4 percent of the women had two such pieces. In cases where such furniture did not exist (3 percent of the women), the kitchenware was kept in a wooden box.

About 61 percent of the respondents did not possess a glass-cabinet. The glass-cabinet is a furniture item of the middle class in which cups, plates, glassware and, porcelain are kept. Nevertheless, 31 percent—quite a high percentage—had a glass-cabinet perhaps showing aspirations toward a higher social status.

This motivation seemed also to characterize the women who had a dresser with a big mirror. This is furniture typical of the middle and upper class, where it automatically comprises part of the bedroom furniture bought at the time of the wedding. The dressers usually belonged to married working women or to young women who were about to be married.

MARITAL STATUS

Of the seventy women 61 percent were single. For a woman with little

Table 6

Civil status	Number of women	Percentage
Single	43	61
Married	14	20
Widows	6	9
Married and separated	4	6
Free union	3	4
	70	100

education, the only possible source of income was in domestic service or in factory work. Women who lived without men — widows, women who were separated (officially counted as married), and single women — comprised 76 percent of the workers. There was not one case of divorce, which occurs more frequently among the middle and upper classes but is still rare within the working class. Married women and those who lived in free union represented 24 percent, or nearly one-quarter of the total.

In accordance with the Catholic Church (which prevails in Mexico) and governmental requirements, civil and religious marriages predominated. Free unions — men and women living together — were frequent among the lower-income groups; separations occurred without formalities and gave both men and women freedom to form new unions. The man extended economic help to the mother and children while the union existed; once they separated, the man generally forgot any paternal obligations. Children were linked to their mother and her relatives. Thus in the lower-income classes, the family was less stable. The maternal lineage was the predominant one, and the mother had the reponsibility of supporting the children.

In research done among women in Mexico City, José Gómez Robleda found that emotional disturbance was highest among widows; in second place were married women; in third place were single women; and the least emotional disturbance could be found among divorced women. At the same time, it was shown that marital status accounted for little emotional disturbance among men, which meant that in their social life marital status was of little importance (Gómez Robleda 1962).

Marriage

An unmarried woman of sixty-six stated that it was better for a woman to be married. But the majority of the single women felt that marriage caused many problems and that they were better off alone. The verbal accounts of matrimonial relations reflected a wide variety of value systems and emotions. The question of marriage elicited some reactions that are common to all social classes, but some typically working-class responses were also found.

PREMARITAL RELATIONS AND FREE UNION   Some authorities on Mexican psychology describe one type of woman as introverted, passive, and self-abnegating. (Paz 1959:34–35). Once she has "opened" herself, she starts waiting for marriage to the man. When she asks for something, it is for her child and not for herself. In contrast to the self-abnegating woman would be the so-called "bad woman," who is active, screams, and causes scandals. The male partner does not take anything seriously; he is deeply dependent on his mother yet wants to be independent, especially in front of women.

Similar types were found in the factory. One woman had known a man for several years, since the time she studied commerce in secondary school. Later they both worked in the factory, she in the threading department and he attending the machines. They hardly spoke to each other. The woman was at that time going with another man, but her co-worker, Ricardo, also had another girl friend, whom he was to marry. One day the woman worker was invited to a dance, which Ricardo and his girl friend also attended. As he tended to be a tease, Ricardo started talking and flirting with the woman from the factory until his betrothed became angry and began breaking glasses and porcelain. That was the end of the engagement and Ricardo started dating the factory woman. "Everything happened the way it had to," the woman said. At the time of the interview the son she had borne Ricardo was a year old. He gave her only a little money to buy milk for the child; the rest of his salary was turned over to his mother. The woman had to buy everything else for the baby. Sometimes they had disputes about money and on these occasions she told him: "I don't want that money for me, it is for your child." She also knew and sometimes told him that he would never marry her. On these occasions he used to answer: "If I did not like you, I would not always come over here." But the woman knew well that as long as his mother lived, there was no hope of his marrying her.

THE RECENTLY MARRIED GIRL   One recently married girl of twenty-eight had been engaged for four years. She always gave the money she earned to her family because one of her sisters did not work, and a young brother was still studying. The young man she finally married, who was a specialized worker in another textile factory, several times had saved enough money for the marriage. He had requested her to stop working, but she did not want to give up her job because her brother and sister needed her money. When she refused to stop working, he spent his savings. Finally, they agreed that she would go on working after the marriage.

Formerly, a woman who got married would stop working at the factory for a few years, but when the children grew older, she often tried to return because the husband's income was not enough for the whole family. During the time of this research, jobs in the factories were very hard to obtain, so this woman decided not to give up her place as long as her brother was still studying; moreover, she thought that she might need her income later, after she had children. Her husband really did not like her to work. "It makes you tired," he used to say. But she answered: "I can't give it up just for your pride." They got up at five in the morning so that he could get to his factory on time. After he left, she did some cooking before she had to leave, so that food would be ready when he came home. In the afternoon, she sat with him and tried not to be busy, so that he could not insist that the double work was too much for her.

THE MARRIED WOMAN   One of the older married woman had to cope with the problems of her family and to take care of her grown children and grandchildren as well. She did not lose her courage because of her husband's drunkenness. Although this situation was not typical, it reflected the atmosphere of continual family quarreling so common in the living compounds.

There was the husband who irritated everybody in the family, even his little granddaughter. When his wife tried to put him out on the street, he would not go until she gave him some money. He was also a worker, and she preferred him to work the shift from three to eleven at night, because that kept him from hanging around at home and drinking in the afternoon. Although she had to get up very early in the morning, she waited for him at night in order to give him his food.

Of the twenty-four women who were married, widowed, or separated from their husbands, fifteen (62 percent) had been married by the Church. They felt that the union would be more stable that way. One woman of forty-four stated that those married by the Church should not separate. Even with all the difficulties she had with her husband, she did not think of leaving him. Her young son had had a civil wedding, and the parents were waiting to see how the young couple got along before having a religious ceremony.

THE SEPARATED WOMAN   Fewer moral obstacles existed in dissolving a free union or a civil marriage. A woman of thirty-nine had been separated from her husband for a year, but when he was drunk he still came back to her home and started fights. Sometimes the oldest son defended his mother, and at other times the mother defended her children.

Another criticism of cohabitation stemmed from a husband's having relations with another woman. In these cases, the middle-class woman, who does not have her own income, is willing to tolerate much more to avoid losing her social prestige and to continue being the recognized wife. A major concern is that her husband continue to give her the necessary household money. The working woman, who has her own income, is much more forthright if her husband commits adultery. Her reactions are like those of the upper-class woman, who also has an income at her disposal. The working woman refuses to play a passive role in this situation. As she neither requires money from her consort nor suffers social prejudice, she often demands a resolution of the problem, even if that jeopardizes the relationship.

This was the case of a woman of fifty-eight who had lived with her husband for over twenty years. She discovered the identity of his mistress, who had had three children by her husband, and went to see her. The second woman suggested that the man should decide which woman he preferred. But the wife replied that he had to fulfill his obligations to his legal family, because he had been married according to both civil law and the church. They went on fighting for seven years, but as the husband gave the wife money only for his own food, the wife got tired of the situation and one day she made a definite break with him.

Occupations of the Husbands

The respondents' husbands (seventeen in all), legal or common-law, had the following occupations: three textile workers, one shoeshine boy, one hairdresser, two furniture painters, one taco seller, one metal worker, one lottery ticket seller, one employee, one wine salesman, one tile layer, one typesetter, and one unemployed worker; two other husbands were unemployed because of chronic illness.

About half of these men worked in industry and the other half in commerce. The rest consisted of economically unproductive members and those not catalogued in the two main divisions. Although it is generally assumed that the man is the head of the family, among the women in the study this was true in only eleven cases out of the seventeen. As the working woman is economically independent, she sometimes maintains her husband if he is sick or has lost his job. In one case, a man gave nearly all his earnings to his mother and therefore could not be considered the head of his own family. In general, a man ceases to be the head of the family if he is economically inactive and if he does not have the respect of his family.

Related Family Members

A domestic group does not always consist of consanguineal members. These "adopted relatives" and economically inactive relatives are a real burden to the female worker who takes on the responsibility of supporting them.

One working woman who lived with the family of her nephew helped to maintain her brother's widow. "We cannot leave her on the street," she said, "she had her own home before." A woman worker of forty-six and her daughter, who worked as a secretary, supported the following family members: the old mother of the worker herself, her sick husband, and six nephews and nieces who were the children of a sister who abandoned them. They all lived in a small unfinished house. After the working woman got home, she did washing and ironing for other people.

Another woman of twenty-eight with a small boy lived with an older couple and their old grandmother. The worker paid the older woman for taking care of her child and regarded the couple as adopted parents.

Another woman, who lived in a common-law marriage, had seven children from her first husband and five from her second. In addition, she had taken care of two boys whose mother had gone off with another man. Years later, she sent the younger boy back to his father. The older child was run down by a bus while he was working as a porter, and it took years for him to recover. Finally, he began to work as a shoeshine boy. The woman and her husband worked in the same factory. Her daughter of sixteen, from her first husband, gave the family financial help. This girl worked on an illegal and grossly underpaid enterprise, making cheap handkerchiefs from morning till night. Her long day's work was just enough to pay for breakfast for the big family. But they were still deeply thankful to the man who exploited her and who each week brought the bulk material which had to be cut according to a printed pattern, sewn on the still unpaid-for electric sewing machine, and finally ironed. The working woman received an additional small income by preparing and selling tamales to the neighbors each Saturday. Her own children, who stood in line, each got only two for supper. The woman was very much afraid of losing her job in the factory, not only because of the income, but even more because of the badly needed free medical service available through Social Security.

The Children

The study revealed that forty-one women out of seventy (59 percent) had had 147 children, including those born dead. There were thirty-three deaths (22 percent of the total number of children). During the time of this research, thirty-nine women (56 percent) had 114 living children. The average number of living children for the seventy women was 1.63 which is low because the majority of the women were single.

Table 7.

Fertility index:	$\frac{114}{39} = 2.92$		
Productivity index:	$\frac{114}{70} = 1.63$		
Fertility (number of children):	Number of women	Percentage of women	Percentage of children
Low (1 to 3)	29	74	50
Medium (4 to 6)	8	21	32
High (7 or more)	2	5	18
	39	100	100
Productivity:			
No children	31	44	
Low (1 to 3)	41	41	
Medium (4 to 6)	8	11	
High (7 or more)	2	3	
	70	99	

As seen above, 61 percent of the women were single and only 39 percent had ever married. To this last group belong the married women, the common-law wives, the widows, and the separated women. Forty-one women out of seventy had had children; therefore 20 percent of the total of the seventy female workers were unmarried mothers. During the time of the research, only fourteen women (20 percent) were married. Of the forty-one women who had had children, twenty-seven (66 percent) could be classified as single mothers who had to bring up their children without male help. But although the situation of the married woman might have appeared easier, in reality the married woman often had to take the financial responsibility for her children.

Most of the female workers left their children with other family members. Generally, the grandmother took care of the grandchildren, but sometimes they had to play alone on the street until the mother came back. There were government-supported nurseries where the mothers could leave their children during working hours for a small fee. Other nurseries were supported by the Public Health Department, and there the children were also given food. The procedure for getting children into these nurseries was somewhat complicated, however; it included considerable paperwork and even a blood test of mother and child, which was greatly resented by the women. Only the younger and more energetic mothers tried to find places for their children there.

When the children got older, they also had to help in the household, as was the case in the home of a woman of thirty-eight. The father, who worked as a varnisher, took the eight-year-old daughter in the morning to school and picked her up after school. The mother took the two youngest children to her sister before she went to the factory. There they met at lunchtime with their two older brothers and their sister. They stayed there until their mother picked them up after work. At home the children had to do their homework and help with all the household work. On Sundays the bigger ones had to take care of the smaller ones, so that their mother could rest longer.

The unwed mothers were very careful of their daughters. One mother even took her daughter out of the fourth year of primary school because she feared that the girl might get into trouble with some boy. Others refused to send the girls to work for the same reason, although they badly needed some extra money. They felt a special lack of confidence toward office bosses. But when one mother finally decided to send her sixteen-year-old daughter to look for work, the girl could not find any because she was unskilled. Finally, she found employment selling plastic bags from house to house, but the sales were so low that she decided to give it up. Even for jobs as office employee or salesgirl a secondary school certificate was needed, and the daughter of this factory worker did not have one. Sometimes these mothers even had to take care of their grown-up children, as in the case of a working woman whose daughter was going to have a baby. Her mother had to arrange all hospital matters.

The Grandchildren

It might be assumed that when the children grew up, became independent, and married, the life of the woman worker would grow easier. However, financial worries, which formerly were related to children, were now concerned with grandchildren. One woman of fifty-six gave as much as she could to the nine children of her son, who hardly earned enough for himself. Another woman of sixty-four gave everything she could to the eight children of a son who had lost his job, but even that was not enough. Another woman of forty-four gave all her money to a daughter who was waiting for her fourth child to be born. The son-in-law worked intermittently.

One day a woman worker of fifty-three was crying in the patio. She had a daughter of thirty who was paralyzed. The daughter had been abandoned by the father of her three children. A girl, who was four years old at this time, had been born paralyzed. The grandmother had to take care of the whole family. The grandchildren were not covered by the medical service of Social Security because they were not the worker's own children. Now the little paralyzed girl was sick, and the grandmother did not know what to do. Although the medical service in the General Hospital was free, she was not willing to hospitalize the child because of the separation involved.

The same attitude was found in another woman who had a single daughter with six children. The children's mother sometimes worked cleaning homes, but mostly they lived on the grandmother's income. Being illiterate, they were afraid of any kind of official form and did not want to leave any of the children in an orphanage or children's home, although one boy had been hit by a car. "I love them so much," said the grandmother. Besides, they were afraid that the father of the children might return and take revenge if some of the children were institutionalized.

The Aged

It was not always the children or grandchildren who constituted a moral and economic burden for the worker; in some cases, the greatest burdens were the elderly who had become senile.

This was the case for a woman of thirty who lived with her aunt of sixty-four and her grandmother of about a hundred. The young woman was the daughter of a man reputed to have women and children everywhere. She had worked in the factory since she was fifteen years old. At twenty-five she was engaged to a young Mexican-American who wanted to marry her and take her across the border. But the girl refused because there was nobody to take care of her aunt and her old grandmother. A memento of that engagement was a dresser with an oval mirror in the bedroom. The aunt, who was also working in the factory, was losing her eyesight because she had repaired fine knitwork all her life. On her way home from the factory to their two rooms, the aunt did the marketing, but always forgot something, and it took her an hour to do the errand because she was so slow. In the meantime, the girl took care of the old grandmother, who, at the time of this research, was unable to carry on a normal conversation. She could only express lament and she sometimes screamed. About five years before, one of her legs had been amputated. The whole family had gathered at the hospital to wait for the grandmother to die, but she recovered. As there was no crematory in the hospital, the young woman was asked to take the amputated leg home, but she refused, preferring to pay an agency to bury the leg.

Later, the grandmother was given a wheelchair by the Rotary Club, but she could never use it because the two women, aunt and niece, were not able to carry her down the two staircases, and in the two upstairs rooms there was no space to wheel around. While the two worked in the factory, the grandmother stayed home alone. As she was already blind, she could not distinguish day from night, and slept all day. However during the night she felt stimulated by the company of the two other women and did not let them sleep at all. Both of them said that because of the grandmother they had not had a real night's sleep for years.

Religion

Gómez Robleda states that during their religious education children repeat texts which they do not understand. Religious cults develop social theatrics rather than authentic religious feelings. Especially among the uneducated classes, life is mysterious, and consequently waiting for a miracle to be realized becomes a way of life (Gómez Robleda 1962:67). This was the type of religious feeling that could be observed among the women in the study.

Of the women workers, 84 percent practiced their religion and 16 percent did not. The practitioners were Catholics (the only exception was an Adventist). Most of the workers had in their homes a small altar for the Virgin of Guadalupe. They also usually had framed pictures of

Chirst, praying, teaching, and at the Last Supper. There was a special predilection for San Antonio, the patron of lost objects, of poor people, and of those who want to marry. There seemed to be a strong link between religion and poverty, as if one could not exist without the other. The women's great insecurity manifested itself in the cult of the saints, each one a protector against a particular misfortune.

Formerly, when the earnings at the factory were better, the workers made more frequent pilgrimages to famous holy places like Chalma and San Juan de los Lagos. Later, they did not leave the city and, in cases of great grief, went to the Villa de Guadalupe in Mexico City. One woman of thirty-nine had gone once a year to Cuauhtla, because the Christ of that place had performed a miracle for her. Years ago her two-year-old daughter was very sick and had a high fever. She took the child to the Cristo de Cuauhtla. Putting the child near the foot of the image, she asked him: "Señor, save my child. Perform a miracle." Half an hour later the little girl was well and could stand on her feet. The woman promised to go each year to the Cristo de Cuauhtla and thank him. Her brother, however, went to Amecameca, because the Christ of that place had performed a miracle for him.

In Mexico City most of the women workers went each Monday night to the Mass of the Divine Providence in an old colonial church near the factory. The whole mass could be characterized as an act of spectacular sociability. The people filled not only the entire church, but also the lawn in the park outside. The priest stood in the door and spoke through a loudspeaker, so that he could be heard both inside and outside the church. Some three thousand people listened in absolute silence. The priest knew well the problems of his people. He almost demanded that the Divine Providence help his people to obtain permanent work and improve relations in their homes and communities. He paused three times for examinations of conscience, and two minutes for intensive thought about three intimate wishes, which, he said, would be fulfilled according to the will of the Divine Providence. After mass he read applications for work written on small pieces of paper. Those who could offer jobs raised their hands and the deals were concluded.

Of the female workers, 16 percent did not go to church and preferred to stay in their homes and work. They said that they disliked the Church's money-grabbing.

Conclusions

This study was done to investigate the real economic and social situation of women textile workers in Mexico City. It was also done to test the hypothesis that the working woman, although she did specialized work that gave her an income adequate to support a lower-class life style, could not enjoy its benefits because of her poor education and the family obligations for which she felt a strong sense of responsibility. The findings show that the use of the working woman's income was directly related to the number of family members depending on her, although some of them helped to pay the common costs of living for the whole family group. Only 33 percent of the dependents of the workers were their own children. The others included grandchildren, nephews, nieces, mother, and other family members. Only four of the seventy women did not have to give some kind of economic help to other family members. Some families in the group lived in an absolute state of misery, because of their many economically inactive members (e.g. children, the aged, the sick).

The woman worker might extend her help in the hope of some reciprocal benefits in the future or the recompense promised by the Christian religion, but these hypothetical motivations do not exclude the presence of compassion and generosity. The woman textile worker is exposed to a double exploitation: first as a worker and second as a woman who has to fulfill family obligations. Her reactions to her situation are deep passivity and resignation. If she lost her job, only domestic service would be left. But the working woman is used to a certain personal freedom and therefore is willing to maintain her working status as long as possible. Also, staying home would not solve the problems of the other family members to whom she gives her time and economic support and in whom she sees the meaning of her life.

This same kind of passivity was demonstrated within the family group, where the woman worker never protested the demands of the persons she loved, but saw helping them as a sacred duty even if she had to do additional work that taxed her to the limits of her physical and psychological endurance. Sometimes this additional work produced some secondary income. At other times it was household work, which was economically unproductive, but necessary for the proper functioning of the home.

APPENDIX: SAMPLE OF A QUESTIONNAIRE

I.   Census data   Date:
1. Name:
2. Address:
3. Age:
4. Civil status: single, married, free union, separated, divorced, widow
5. Place of birth or childhood home:
6. Number and age of living children:
7. Number and age of deceased children:
8. Number of years of schooling:

II.   Labor and social environment   Date:
9. Number of years in the factory: in others
10. Category of labor executed in the factory:
11. Income per week: $ per fortnight: $ per month: $
12. Secondary income $ per fortnight: $ per month: $
13. Cost of food: $ per fortnight: $ per month: $
14. Rent: Electricity: Others:
15. How many persons maintained (apart from worker):
16. Amount of maintenance for others: Who else contributes?
17. Social Security: Permission for   Medical service:
                leave of absence:
   Private doctor: Costs for private medicines
                per year:

III.   Home and family environment   Date:
18. Head of the family:
19. Number of family members: 20. Number of beds:
21. Furniture: Kind of stove:
    radio: television: sewing machine:
    books: which: comic books:
22. Other furniture:
23. Occupation of husband:
24. Difference between age of wife and age of husband:
25. Age of the woman at time of marriage:
26. Number of years of marriage or free union:
27. Former marriage or union of the woman:
28. Number of children by husband with other women:
29. Time dedicated to household labor, hours per day:
30. Friends:
31. Visits to relatives:
32. Movies per month:
33. Vacations:
34. Affiliation to associations: Labor union: Religious:
35. Religion: Degree of religious enthusiasm:
                fervor: medium: indifferent:
   Observations:

REFERENCES

BECKER, HOWARD
1958 "Anthropology and sociology," in *For a science of social man.* Edited by John Gillin. New York: Macmillan.
BELL, W. NORMAN, EZRA F. VOGEL
1960 *The family.* Glencoe, Illinois: Free Press of Glencoe.
BENNET, W. JOHN, GURT H. WOLFF
1956 Toward communication between sociology and anthropology. *Current Anthropology.*
CARRANCA Y TRUJILLO, PAUL
1955 *Principios de sociología criminal y de derecho penal.* Mexico City: Imprenta Universitaria.
CARRERA STAMPA
1954 *Los gremios mexicanos.* Mexico City.
CAVIEDES VIVANCO, ORIANA
1961 *Participación de la mujer obrera en la industria de rayón.* Mexico City: Trabajo de Campo.
Constitución Federal de los Estados Unidos Mexicanos
1957 [1857] Facsimile edition. Mexico City: Fondo de cultura Económica.
Constituctión Política de los Estados Unidos Mexicanos
1961 [1917] Texto vigente (fifteenth edition). Mexico City: Editorial Porrúa, S.Q.
COSIO VILLEGAS, DANIEL
1957 *Historia moderna de México: la república restaurada — el Porfiriato.* Mexico City.
DOLCI, DANILO
1959 *To feed the hungry: enquiry in Palermo.* London: Macgibbon and Kee.
ECHANOVE T., CARLOS
1957 *Diccionario de sociología.* Mexico City and Buenos Aires: Editorial José M. Cajica, Jr. S.A.
EL SAATY, HASSAN
1959 *Industrialization in Alexandria.* Cario: American University of Cairo, Social Research Center.
El seguro social en Suecia
1959 Stockholm.
FAIRSCHILD, HENRY PRATT, *editor*
1960 *Diccionario de sociologia.* Mexico City: Fondo de Cultura Económica.
GÓMEZ ROBLEDA, JOSÉ
1962 Psicología del mexicano. Mexico City: UNAM, Instituto de Investigaciones Sociales.
GÓMEZ ROBLEDA, JOSÉ, ADA D'ALOJA
1958 *La familia y la casa.* Mexico City: UNAM, Instituto de Investigaciones Sociales.
HERSKOVITS, J. MELVILLE
1957 *Antropología económica.* Mexico City: Fondo de Cultura Económica.

INSTITUTO MEXICANO DEL SEGURO SOCIAL
1960a *Centros de seguridad social para el bienestar familiar.* Mexico City: Instituto Mexicano del Seguro Social.
1960b *Declaración de México.* Mexico City: Instituto Mexicano del Seguro Social.
1960c *Ley del seguro social.* Mexico City: Instituto Mexicano del Seguro Social.
1960d *Unidad independencia.* Mexico City: Instituto Mexicano del Seguro Social.

KAHL, A. JOSEPH
n.d.   Some social concomitants of industrialization and urbanization. *Human Organization* 18 (2).

KAHN, ROBERT L., CHARLES F. CANNELL
1957   *The dynamics of interviewing.* New York: John Wiley and Sons.

KAHN, ROBERT L., CHARLES F. CANNELL
1957   *The dynamics of interviewing.* New York: John Wiley and Sons.

LEWIS, OSCAR
1959   *Five families.* New York: Basic Books.

LEY FEDERAL DE TRABAJO REFORMADA
1950   Con bibliografía, comentarios y jurisprudencia. Mexico City: Editorial Porrua, S.A.

LUNDBERG, GEORGE A.
1949   *Técnica de la investigación social.* Mexico City and Buenos Aires: Fondo de Cultura Económica.

México: 50 años de revolución
1961   Volume two: *La vida social.* Mexico City: Fondo de Cultura Económica.

Meyers Lexikon
1924   Volume one: *Arbeiter.* Leipzig: Bibliographisches Institut.

MONZÓN ESTRADA, ARTURO
1960   "Diferencias y traslapos entre la sociología y la antropología social," in *Congreso Internaciología.* Mexico City.

MORALES JIMÉNEZ, ALBERTO
1951   *Historia de la revolución mexicana.* Mexico City: Instituto de Investigaciones Políticas, Económicas y Sociales del PRI.

MORENO CONTRERAS, CARMEN
1958   "Mano de obra femenina en México." Unpublished thesis, Escuela Nacional de Ciencias Políticas y Sociales, UNAM, Mexico City.

MURDOCK, GEORGE PETER
1954   *Guía para la clasificación de los datos culturales.* Washington, D.C.: Unión Panamericana.
1958   *Sociology and anthropology for a science of social man.* New York: Macmillan.

Nomenclatura Nacional de Ocupaciones 1940
1941   Mexico City: Secretaría de la Economía Nacional, Dirección General de Estadística.

PAZ, OCTAVIO
1959   *El laberinto de la soledad.* Mexico City: Fondo de Cultura Económica.

POVIÑA, ALFREDO
1958   *Balance de la sociología contemporanea.* Rome: Sociedad Italiana de Sociología.

POZAS ARCINIEGA, RICARDO
1961   *El desarrollo de la comunidad.* Mexico City: UNAM, Escuela Nacional de Ciencias Políticas y Sociales.

RADVANYI, LAZSLO
1951   Lectura de historietas entre la población adulta de la Ciudad de México. *Revista de la Facultad de Ciencias Políticas y Sociales.* Mexico City: UNAM.

SOUSTELLE, JACQUES
1956   *La vida cotidiana de los aztecas.* Mexico City: Fondo de Cultura Económica.

VAILLANT, GEORGE CO.
1955   *La civilización azteca.* Mexico City: Fondo de Cultura Económica.

ZWEIG, F.
1949   *Labour, life and poverty.* London: Victor Gollancz.

YOUNG V., PAULINE.
1953   *Métodos científicos de investigación social.* Mexico City: UNAM, Instituto de Investigaciones Sociales.

Women as Workers: The Experience of the Puerto Rican Woman in the 1930's

BLANCA SILVESTRINI-PACHECO

Recently, there has been a surge of interest in the application of the social history approach to Caribbean historiography, However, the study of Puerto Rican history from the social history point of view has been virtually non-existent. Social scientists have directed their attention primarily to the study of institutions and organizations, and the central role of their leaders, rather than to the people who belonged to those organizations and their relationships within the group (García 1970; Quintero 1971). One of the most neglected areas of research has been the study of the roles that women have played in Puerto Rican society. There is an absence of titles from a historical, anthropological, or even psychological perspective which focus on women as their major concern. Only a few studies, mainly in anthropology, mention indirectly the status of women; however, the scope of these studies has been restricted to portraying women predominantly within the family setting and usually only as enacting the mother-housewife role.

The present study was begun within the context of the limitations of the available studies, which generalize about women without studying their actual status in society or the particular cultural understandings within which they have to act. The purpose of this paper is to analyze the role that women played in the socioeconomic transformation undergone by Puerto Rican society as reflected particularly in the events of the decade of the 1930's. The emphasis of the study is on the participa-

The research for this paper was partially funded by the Social Science Research Center of the University of Puerto Rico and is part of a broader project on changing roles of women in Puerto Rico.

tion of women as workers, including women's role in politics, since by then politics was one of the main concerns of the workers.

The decade of the 1930's in Latin America and in the United States has been described as a time of distress and of constant unrest for labor, which saw the emergence of new groups and labor alignments (Rama 1962; Ginzberg and Berman 1963; Bernstein 1960, 1970). Puerto Rico was not an exception. During those years Puerto Rican workers suffered from prolonged unemployment, extremely low wages, and deteriorating working conditions (Governor of Puerto Rico 1933: 6). These problems were not simply a product of the world economic depression; they had existed in Puerto Rico from the beginning of the century, although certainly they were aggravated by the grim economic conditions of the decade. In this panorama of economic distress, what was the status of the Puerto Rican woman?

The 1935 Census of Puerto Rico showed that 16.1 percent of all women in Puerto Rico were "gainfully occupied," and that 26.3 percent (134,371) of all women fifteen years old and over were employed (Puerto Rico Reconstruction Administration [PRRA] 1938: 57,60). The gradual increase in the number of women who entered the labor force was a significant factor in altering the position of women in Puerto Rican society, since it also gave women access to other fields of social action, such as party politics and social protest movements in which they later made significant contributions. However, the above-mentioned figures were not equally divided among the various occupations and industries in Puerto Rico, but were clustered in three fields: (1) the needlework industry; (2) the tobacco industry; and (3) domestic services.[1] In view of the economic importance of the needlework and tobacco industries in the economy of Puerto Rico during the 1930's, women's participation in these two occupations is given particular consideration in this paper.

A broad spectrum of problems converged on the island at the onset of 1930, creating unemployment and a sense of hopelessness for Puerto Rican workers. Many of these problems had their roots in the socioeconomic structures established during the Spanish regime. More difficulties ensued with changes introduced into the island's living patterns by the American occupation in 1898. With the American occupation the island's economy veered toward intensive commercial agriculture, thus

---

[1] In the 1935 Census (PRRA 1938) the following percentages of women per occupation are given: agriculture 7.3 percent (10,451 persons); cigar and tobacco factories 7.8 percent (10,770); clothing and embroidering shops 13.8 percent (17,986); home needlework and embroidering 35.8 percent (49,714); domestic and personal services 22.7 percent (31,462).

weakening the prevailing subsistence agricultural structure and making the people more dependent upon imported foods and goods. Four major economic changes took place in Puerto Rico during this period: unprecedented growth of the sugar industry, development of the tobacco-growing industry, rise of needlework as an industry of economic value, and the decline of the coffee industry from its previously privileged position (Steward 1956:63).

Two of these changes — the development of the tobacco-growing industry and the rise of the needlework industry — had a considerable effect on the status of women in the island, because they helped to incorporate large numbers of women as workers. Previously women had participated indirectly in agricultural activities, such as sugar and coffee production, but since they did not participate directly in the actual production or elaboration of the products, their role was less important than that of the male workers. For example, women in the sugar cane fields kept small stores, took care of animals and were responsible for the preparation of foodstuffs for sale on payday (Mintz 1956:371), but usually they did not work in the sugar cane fields as cane cutters or directly in the sugar factories.[2] In coffee cultivation many times women had to help in the management of the operation or sometimes complemented the family income with their work elsewhere; however, the major responsibility for the farm often lay on the husband's shoulders. By contrast, in both the tobacco processing and the needlework industries women constituted a significant portion of the labor force and were directly responsible for the elaboration of the end products. Thus they had the opportunity to participate actively, together with male workers, in the labor struggles of the time.

The transformation of the Puerto Rican economy during the first decades of the twentieth century generally altered the living and working patterns of the workers and encouraged the organization of a labor movement. A major change in the Puerto Rican labor scene during the twentieth century was the emergence and development of a strong trade union movement. Groups of workers throughout the island, organized either in formal unions or in *sociedades de estudio* [study groups], had emerged in the second half of the nineteenth century and eventually joined to establish a national federation in 1899, Federación Libre de Trabajadores de Puerto Rico (FLT). Since its beginning the Puerto Rican movement demanded government's recognition of labor organizations and of the

---

[2] The *Annual report* of the Puerto Rico Department of Labor in 1940–1941 shows that in 36 sugar factories inspected the labor force was 12, 687 males and 22 women.

collective bargaining principle, the adoption of a shorter workday, higher wages, and universal suffrage (Pagán 1959: 59–60). In addition, convinced of the need for swift political action to redress the prevailing social inequalities, this same group of workers founded the Socialist Party. Although the Federation and the Party were separate organizations, their local and national leaderships often coincided, and the ideals of one group complemented those of the other. Both organizations supported the woman worker's right to work and at least on paper advocated equality. In a book published by the Federación Libre de Trabajadores for the purpose of instructing the workers in trade unionism, Santiago Iglesisas, the FLT's president, summarized the policies of the organization regarding women workers:

...that the labor leaders should make every possible effort to organize all the workers of both sexes, of all trades and professions, and especially farm workers.

We should organize the women in all the areas of industry in which they are employed. We should organize the office employees as well as the women working in the telegraph, the typists, the clerks, the seamstresses as well as the cooks and maids (Iglesias 1914:6).

Even more interesting than the official views on women's participation in the labor movement were the ideas expressed by a rank-and-file member of that movement. Juan S. Marcano, a shoemaker (*zapatero*) succinctly expressed the Socialist Party's cry in its initial days for better conditions for the woman worker:

Women in Puerto Rico and in the rest of the world have yet to occupy the place they deserve as equal human beings. It is sad to see women walking to the workshops and factories — to those traps of exploitation and misery — in which they leave the best of their lives, their youth, ... in which they suffer from being constantly at the working tables until gradually tuberculosis takes a hold of their lives. The conditions at the workshops are intolerable... places without ventilation in which our fellow women workers have to spend from 8 to 9 hours in daily imprisonment... and all of this for the wealth of a few rich owners.

But this has to be stopped. The woman worker is our fellow companion in misery and deprivation — it is impossible that she continues to be shamefully exploited... The Socialist Party will end this situation... (Marcano 1919: 66–67).

Regardless of this support for women's rights, few women ever occupied top leadership positions in either the FLT or the Socialist Party. Nevertheless, given the precarious state of affairs, the Socialist Party and the labor federation became useful channels through which women, as rank and file, fought for their causes. Consequently, although women workers did not have the same access as men to the high policy-making positions of the labor federation, they participated actively in its initial stages of organization. Tomasa Yupart, for example, a representative of the Union of Tobacco Strippers of Juncos, was among the delegates to the Sixth Congress of the FLT in 1910 which drafted the federation's constitution. Juana Colón, a *planchadora y lavandera* [a woman who washed and pressed clothes for a small fee] who later became a tobacco worker, organized protests and strikes against the American tobacco corporations in Comerio, a town in the tobacco producing area of Puerto Rico.

At the beginning of the twentieth century Luisa Capetillo also became a national figure among Puerto Rican workers. She participated prominently in the labor campaigns of the Federación Libre de Trabajadores throughout the island, demanding both improvement of the workers' living conditions and recognition of women's rights. In her book *Mi opinión sobre las libertades, derechos y deberes de la mujer* (1911), she described a campaign trip around the island in which she exhorted the workers to join efforts against capitalism:

Fellow workers, you are in a state of slavery worse than the one of ancient times. Aren't you eager to abandon it? Don't forget that in your hands you have the redemption you need so badly. Peasants... your slavery is far from gone. Before, your master owned you and deprived you of your will — today he frees you but leaves you without means to exercise your will (Capetillo 1911:23).

With impassioned oratory she described the abuses against the workers in general, and demanded a new role for the woman worker.

Luisa Capetillo developed the idea that a woman who had to work outside the home and at the same time take care of the house chores could continue to develop fully as a human being. In her writings she deplored the inequalities of an economic system which favored the rich people. "The home of the rich woman is never touched by these problems," explained Luisa Capetillo (1911:24), because the rich woman either did not have to work outside her home or if she used some of her spare time in work or social activities she had another woman to take care of the house, to such an extent that even the children were reared by others. Perhaps Capetillo's most important contribution is that she went beyond the feminist point of view of defending women's rights; she also criticized some of the abuses that other women, frequently because of their social class, committed against women workers. During those years the woman worker had to deal not only with a multitude of inequalities, but also with the day-to-day confrontation with employers, at times female, who exploited her.

The living and working conditions described by Luisa Capetillo in

1911 did not improve very much during the following decades. Unemployment and underemployment, seasonal work, and low wages increased during the 1920's, and by 1930 the workers were rapidly losing their faith in the Socialist Party and the FLT. A series of alliances with the conservative and bourgeois political parties gradually made the Socialist Party and FLT leadership an instrument of the large industrial and economic interests, leaving the workers without genuine representation.

By 1933 Puerto Rico was in the midst of economic chaos. Sixty-five percent of the population was reported unemployed. The Socialist Party, which had gained access to the government of Puerto Rico through its participation in a coalition which won the 1932 elections, tried to keep a balance between the demands of the workers and the wishes of its conservative partner in the coalition, the Union Republican Party. Paradoxically, the Union Republican was a party directed by rich people who owned much of the industrial and business capital of the island. The workers had hoped that with the Socialist Party and FLT leadership now in government, as well as with the implementation of the United States New Deal measures, rapid changes would come. But neither the Socialist Party's performance in government nor the application of the New Deal programs and controls brought changes in the life of the workers. On the contrary, unemployment increased from 20 percent in 1932 to 29 percent in 1934, wages decreased, and the cost of living almost doubled. Thus strikes proliferated and tensions mounted. In August 1933 the situation in Puerto Rico became explosive. Strikes began in various tobacco factories and in the needlework industry, and, in both, women played a major role.

Until the mid-1920's the tobacco workers, especially in the cigar factories, constituted the core of the Puerto Rican labor movement.[3] In the late 1920's, with the decreasing importance of the tobacco industry, workers from other economic segments partially replaced the *tabaqueros* [tobacco workers] as the leaders of the organized labor movement in Puerto Rico. Nevertheless, the tobacco-processing workers continued to constitute a militant labor group. During 1932 the workers of La Colec-

---

[3]   During the first decades of the United States regime in Puerto Rico, the production of tobacco experienced a noticeable boost. Free entrance into the American market, in addition to large investments of American capital, especially in the purchase of the processed product, and the development of new techniques of cultivation and manufacturing, increased the production of tobacco. Until 1927 the rate of increase in the production of tobacco was greater than that of sugar. Increases in the United States tariff, the mechanization and increased popularity of cigarettes, and the deleterious effects of hurricanes made the tobacco industry decline rapidly after 1927.

tiva, the factory of the Puerto Rican American Tobacco Company, constantly strove for improvements in their working standards. They protested against the tobacco company that brought American workers who did not speak Spanish and required the Puerto Rican workers to use that language. By 1933 unrest in the tobacco industry had intensified. Tobacco production was declining rapidly. Several factories had closed, and unemployment in the tobacco industry mounted as the manufacturers forced the remaining workers to work longer hours to compensate for the losses. Then came the strikes of August 1933. The tobacco strippers led the strike movement in the tobacco-producing area located in the the center of island.

In Caguas four thousand workers, mostly women, went on strike to protest against malpractices in the weighing of tobacco for stripping. Irregularities in weighing methods became an extremely important issue for the tobacco workers, since even when the employers argued that they paid the workers by the hour, wages really depended on daily work loads. These women had to work in "factories" that were small rooms without ventilation or any sanitary conditions, which frequently bred tuberculosis and other diseases. Prudencio Rivera Martínez, the Labor Commissioner, who was also a leader of the Socialist Party and the FLT, explained that the strike had not come as a surprise to the government, because working conditions in the tobacco industry had been steadily deteriorating. Rivera Martínez particularly deplored the working conditions of the women employed in this industry.

The exploitation of these poor women has become inconceivable. They have to strip more tobacco for twenty-five cents than what they stripped before for the same amount of money. During these weeks we have seen long caravans of these women who walk daily long distances... from other towns... to come to earn a quarter.... For sometime now we have been suggesting to the employers that some temporary measure must be adopted to improve these conditions, while a final agreement is negotiated regarding the codes of the Industrial Recovery Act (*Unión Obrera*, 3 August 1933).

Seasonal work was another problem for the working woman. Different from the plants in San Juan, in which the machines were operated throughout most of the year, the factories in the center of the island employed women as tobacco stemmers for only three or four months at most. While for an average week of 36.9 hours in a cigar factory the average earnings were $7.57, in the tobacco stemmeries the earnings averaged $2.29 for a 44-hour week (Manning 1934:26). Despite the intensity of the tobacco workers' protest, the strike ended without gaining much for the workers. They were forced to settle the strike for a nominal increase in wages, an increase which ironically they did not receive because the employers violated the collective agreements.

Strikes also erupted during 1933 in the needlework industry, which had gained importance after the First World War. Contractors and operators in the New York area began sending material to the island to be embroidered by Puerto Rican women, the finished pieces being then returned to the United States to be sold in retail stores. Puerto Rican women working in this industry were grievously exploited. During the 1930's the industry operated in Puerto Rico through a series of agents and subagents who contracted workers, mainly women. The principal corporation remained in the United States and very seldom had direct contact with the workers. Instead it developed a series of *talleres* [factories] that received the materials and acted as intermediaries between the corporation and the workers. Many times the *talleristas* [factory owners] were Puerto Ricans, some of whom were women with enough money to establish and manage a factory. A limited number of persons worked in these factories since most of the work was done in the home.

In order to distribute the loads to the homeworkers, the *talleristas* contracted agents and subagents who had direct contact with the workers at their homes and who checked that the work was done. The agents and subagents not only earned a commission from the contractors, but they also kept a part of the already low wages of the workers. Caroline Manning, in her report on *The Employment of women in Puerto Rico* said that sometimes the agent kept "very little of the amount paid per dozen for the outside work, sometimes as little as 10 percent, but on the other hand a few retained as much as 40 or 50 percent" (1934:8). Manning found that the average amount that the agents retained was approximately 22 percent. If the profits of the subagents are added to the profits of the agents the conclusion is that the homeworkers ended up earning just a few cents a day.

Wages in the needlework trades varied considerably. Workers were not paid by the hour but by bundles of work, and these bundles differed greatly in the number of pieces, types of work, and total amount of work required on the various garments. In 1933 an investigation conducted by the Department of Labor found that 19 percent of the women earned less than 25 cents per bundle, 23 percent earned between 25 cents to 50 cents per bundle, and 27 percent earned between 50 cents and a dollar. Two other factors have to be considered regarding wages. Frequently it took from two to five days, and sometimes a week, to complete the work in these bundles, thus making the above-mentioned wages the entire week's pay. The critical economic situation of the needleworkers was also based on the fact that although more than one member of the family usually worked to complete the load, employers paid only to the workers whom they had contracted directly; therefore, they actually paid only one worker when in fact the work was done by two or three persons. These working conditions were aggravated by unfair practices that included payment in groceries instead of cash, delays in supplying work, delays in payment, and retention by the agent of wage increases.

Confronted with low wages and soaring costs of living, the workers' position became untenable. Only one avenue was left: the strike. In Mayaguez, the largest city in the western part of the island and the center of the needlework industry, the strikes turned into violent riots at the end of August 1933, as the strikers, mostly women, clashed with strikebreakers and police. On August 30, 1933, the needleworkers declared a strike in Mayaguez to demand higher wages for the woman worker: "[the workers]... have not accepted the wages paid by those that have become rich at the expense of the unfortunate proletariat who spent his life working day and night ... to earn two dollars a week" (*Unión Obrera*, 31 August 1933). The employers' response was to summon the police to protect their property. The toll from the confrontation was two dead (a woman and a three-year-old girl) and at least seventy wounded, mostly women. The chief of the police argued that the use of guns was necessary due to the "violent and disorderly attitude of the strikers, who stoned both property and the police and also stoned Representative Arcelay's workshop.... We have had to use rifles and with great efforts have somewhat controlled the situation" (*El Mundo*, 30 August 1933).

The labor newspaper *Unión Obrera* reported the strike as a "*Masacre a indefensas mujeres* [massacre of defenseless women]." The newspaper explained that the only crime the workers committed was to demand higher wages to avoid starvation since by their work they enrich others. Based on the 31 August events, *Unión Obrera* predicted even more violent labor struggles in which men and women would join efforts in an attempt to improve their day-to-day living conditions: "Mayaguez's proletariat struggles have been baptized with blood and this is a sign of future actions.... Comrades of Mayaguez, fight on within the laws ... but if those in charge of executing the law are the first to act unlawfully then each of you should take your own guarantees" (*Unión Obrera*, 31 August 1933).

Mobilization for the strike provided a favorable climate for the organization of the workers in the needlework trade centers. The FLT reported that in 1933 more than 75 percent of the factory and shop workers had been organized and that a campaign to organize homeworkers was in progress.

By 1934 the FLT had already organized nine unions comprised exclusively of homeworkers, with approximately three thousand members. In its annual report to the American Federation of Labor (1934) the Puerto Rican federation stated that the strikes stirred great unrest among Puerto Rican workers and that the courage of the striking women facilitated the unionization of many others.

The workers in Mayaguez, mostly women... made a most courageous protest against unbearable conditions through a general strike. This gradually affected the entire industry. Through the cooperation and mediation of the Commissioner of Labor, who took charge of the situation at the request of Governor Gore, an agreement was secured by which the workers received an increase in wages ranging from 15 to 25 cents... As a result of the strike, unions have been organized in the greater number of the needle trade centers (A.F. of L. 1934: 170–171).

Women's participation in the needlework strikes of August 1933 raised their level of awareness and increased their collaboration with other social movements. The strikes provided an opportunity for organization. After these initial days women realized that they needed labor unions responsive to their social problems and thus began organizing their own labor groups. They also participated actively in consumer protests and protests of unemployed workers. Unemployment had been one of the major problems in Puerto Rico from the beginning of the century; however, during the 1930's it grew in geometric proportions. Tired of unfulfilled promises from the Puerto Rican government, from the United States government, and even from the organized labor movement, the unemployed workers around the island began a campaign to demand more job opportunities; and in these movements women again played an active role. Women's participation in the unemployed workers' movements is significant because in part it contradicts the commonly-held notion that Puerto Ricans, and especially Puerto Rican women, like to live on welfare and to depend on state assistance. In these protests the workers' cry was unequivocal: "we don't want relief, we want work" (*El Mundo*, 24 November 1934). Ironically, for the government it was easier to provide relief than a decent way to earn a living. The workers' protests fell once again on deaf ears.

One of the most important outbursts of discontent from the unemployed workers took place in Mayaguez in November 1934. Approximately six thousand persons participated in the protests, one third of whom were unemployed women who had lost their jobs in the needlework industry after the NIRA codes were approved. Protesting against the government's failure to keep its promises, the workers rejected the state's relief aid and demanded work (*El Mundo*, 17 july 1934). In a letter to the mayor of Mayaguez the workers described the city's state of poverty and pointed to the thousands of workers who needed work in order to escape starvation. The president of the Unemployed Women Workers Association also explained to Governor Blanton Winship the conditions of the needleworkers who were being evicted from their houses because they could not pay the rents. Again the government chose to disregard the women workers' pleas.

Women's militancy kept growing at a steady pace, in spite of the fact that many of their protests ended in defeat. One of the controversies in which women participated most actively during the 1930's was the debate over the Fair Labor Standards Act (FLSA). The act, passed by the United States Congress on 25 June 1938, primarily affected the needlework industry in Puerto Rico. Puerto Rican industrialists and commercial interests vigorously opposed the inclusion of Puerto Rico in the act, particularly objecting to its minimum wage provisions. The Puerto Rican government readily supported them and soon the then Governor of the island, Blanton Winship, went to Washington in an attempt to persuade federal public officials of the disadvantages of a strict application of the law in Puerto Rico. In contrast to the government's position, the workers demanded immediate enforcement of the FLSA on the island. On 23 October 1938, the Unión de Trabajadores de la Aguja [Union of Needleworkers] held a meeting in San Juan, in which delegations of needleworkers from all over the island supported the application of the minimum wage to the needlework industry. By January 1939, there was a rapid increase in the protests of the workers, mostly women, against the industrialists' maneuvers which were backed by Puerto Rican government officials.

The needleworkers were alone in their struggle. Neither the Federación Libre de Trabajadores nor the Socialist Party backed their demands. Although seemingly paradoxical, the position of the official labor organization was to be expected in view of their desire to please their partner, the Union Republican Party, in the government coalition. The Union Republicans, representing the big economic interests, supported the industrialists' position. The Socialist Party, out of its concern to retain control of government, failed to challenge its partner's policy and sided with the industrialists. For example, instead of presenting a strong case for the enforcement of the law in Puerto Rico, Labor Commissioner Prudencio Rivera Martínez, an active leader of both the FLT and Socialist Party, went on record expressing his reservations about the act. His position was closer to that of the industrialists than to the workers when he claimed that "industry has a right to operate normally without delays ... and organized labor has the duty to respond to the industrialists on the same basis" (*El Mundo*, 18 June 1938). At a conference with United Press, Rivera Martínez explained that the needle-work employers could not pay the minimum wages, mainly for three reasons: (1) the unfair competition of Chinese and Belgian cheap labor; (2) the excessive earnings of the intermediaries who contracted with the operators and the workers; and (3) the high costs of packing and transportation. However, Rivera Martínez ironically failed to describe the oppressive living conditions of the needleworkers, such as their average wage of 2 to 5 cents an hour.

Tired of depending on Governor Winship's and the FLT's "defense" of the workers, various labor groups sought help from United States Congressman Vito Marcantonio, who had been defending in the United State House of Representatives a viewpoint contrary to that supported by Puerto Rican officials. Consequently, when Representative Mary T. Norton presented a bill to amend the FLSA, thus making special provisions for Puerto Rico and the Virgin Islands, Congressman Marcantonio was the only one who supported the workers' point of view in Congress. Even Puerto Rico's official representative to Congress, Santiago Iglesias, himself a labor leader and founder of the Socialist Party, remained silent and did not oppose the conspiracy against the Puerto Rican workers.

Congressman Marcantonio began his defense of the Puerto Rican workers by disclosing Governor Winship's personal involvement with industry. Subsequently he exposed the abuses to which homeworkers were subjected.

These chisellers from New York ... brought their work to Puerto Rico. Then they gave the work to a contractor. Then the contractor gave it to a subcontractor, ... and it goes all the way down the line ... each of them receiving a profit from the toil of poor women and children. The poor woman at home receives the following pay: She gets as low as 3 to 5 cents a dozen for hand-rolled handkerchiefs of the best types. They retail for $3 a dozen in Macy's in New York. This means they are paid from 8 to 15 cents a day, and no more ... (*Congressional Record* 1939: 5466).

As in the case of previous strikes and protests, the workers were the losers. An amendment was passed in the United States Congress excluding Puerto Rico from the minimum wage provision of the FLSA. The women workers of Puerto Rico would remain in misery, earning a few cents for a day's work. Meanwhile the industrialists, government, and the "party of the workers" had their day. By this time the workers had learned a bitter lesson: they could not rely on labor leaders and government officials to help them in their struggles. The road was paved for increased rank-and-file militancy and for the indictment of those leaders who had betrayed the workers by joining in a conspiracy of silence.

During the 1930's the participation of Puerto Rican women workers in labor struggles was instrumental in exposing the weaknesses of the leaders of organized labor. By their efforts the Puerto Rican women workers had begun a new chapter in the social history of Puerto Rico. They succeeded in showing that the workers could challenge the leaders of their own movements, hence disproving the myth that the workers were only what their leaders were. In spite of defeats, they repeatedly fought the alliance of industry and government, and they struggled to teach government a lesson — they wanted work, not welfare. These years were a time of growing awareness for Puerto Rican women; their participation in the labor force was a major stride in the road towards their *conscientizaçao para la libertad*.

Women's work and their participation in the economy of Puerto Rico certainly facilitated their engagement in political and social struggles on the island. Gradually, women also became active in the pro-independence movement and in other political activities. Nevertheless, in few cases did they become the actual major leaders of either the political movements or the labor organizations. Unfortunately, in the late 1940's and 1950's, with the takeover of the Puerto Rican unions by American labor organizations, women had a smaller chance to become the leaders and organizers of the workers in Puerto Rico; by then even the Puerto Rican man had to yield to the power of international labor organizations. Discrimination against women in the new industrial structure established in Puerto Rico after the 1940's has continued to increase; recently, however, a new awareness of the inferior position of women in today's industries is slowly developing. Women's struggles in the 1930's are being rediscovered and increasingly seen as the ideological backbone for today's action movements.

REFERENCES

AMERICAN FEDERATION OF LABOR
 1934   *Report of Proceedings of the Fifty-Fourth Annual Convention.*
BERNSTEIN, IRVING
 1960   *The lean years: a history of the American worker, 1920–1933.* Cambridge, Massachusetts: Houghton Mifflin.
 1970   *Turbulent years: a history of the American worker, 1933–1941.* Cambridge, Massachusetts: Houghton Mifflin.

CAPETILLO, LUISA
1911   *Mi opinión sobre las libertades, derechos y deberes de la mujer*. San Juan: The Times.

Congressional Record
1939   Seventy-sixth Congress, First Session, 84.

El Mundo
1933–1938   30 August 1933; 24 November 1934; 17 July 1934; 18 June 1938.

GARCÍA, GERVASIO
1970   Apuntes sobre una interpretación de la realidad puertorriqueña. *La Escalera* 4: 23–31.

GINZBERG, E., H. BERMAN
1963   *The American worker in the twentieth century*. New York: Free Press.

GOVERNOR OF PUERTO RICO
1933   *Thirty-third annual report of the Governor of Puerto Rico*. Washington: Government Printing Office.

IGLESIAS, SANTIAGO
1914   *¿Quienes somos?* (*Organizaciones obreras*). San Juan: Tipografía de N. Burillo.

MANNING, CAROLINE
1934   *The employment of women in Puerto Rico*. Washington: U.S. Department of Labor.

MARCANO, J.
1919   "Páginas rojas," in *Lucha Obrera*. Edited by A. G. Quintero, 66–67. Río Piedras, Puerto Rico: CEREP.

MINTZ, S.
1956   "Cañamelar: the subculture of rural sugar plantation proletariat," in *The people of Puerto Rico*. Edited by J. H. Steward, 314–417. Urbana, Illinois: University of Illinois Press.

PAGÁN, BOLÍVAR
1959   *Historia de los partidos políticos puertorriqueños, 1898–1956*. San Juan: Librería Campos.

PUERTO RICO DEPARTMENT OF LABOR
1940–1941   *Annual report*.

PUERTO RICO RECONSTRUCTION ADMINISTRATION
1938   *Census of Puerto Rico: 1935. Population and Agriculture*. Washington: Government Printing Office.

QUINTERO, ANGEL
1971   *Lucha obrera*. Río Piedras, Puerto Rico: CEREP.

RAMA, CARLOS M.
1962   *Revolución social y facismo en el siglo XX*. Buenos Aires: Palestra.

STEWARD, JULIAN H.
1956   *The people of Puerto Rico: a study in social anthropology*. Urbana, Illniois: University of Illinois Press.

Unión Obrera
1933   3 August 1933; 31 August 1933.

Resistance as Protest:
Women in the Struggle of Bolivian
Tin-Mining Communities

JUNE NASH

Resistance is opposition to an authority that has lost its basis for legitimacy in some sector of the population. It requires a strong conviction of the morality of one's position and self-respect combined with a sense of when that has been violated. It usually takes nonviolent forms because it is the action of people who have limited access to the technology and techniques of warfare and who have only informal channels with which to realize their collective action. Resistance is a peculiarly feminine form of protest because in the very act of self-definition, women must resist a culturally imposed role that denies their sense of being.

The special role of women in resistance derives from the circumstances in which they enter into and carry out collective action. They usually do not undertake active roles until the possibilities of sustaining life are threatened. Recognition of a genocidal threat or awareness that they no longer can rely on male protectors triggers women's resistance movements. The character of resistance changes with their entry into it. Symbolic acts generated in all resistance action become more meaningful to women as they become active in their creation. Although women may curb actions of their male comrades that could unleash a violent reaction against the total population, they have frequently demonstrated willingness to sacrifice themselves. Lacking political power, their major show of resistance is to withdraw their labor power, their bodies, and ultimately to threaten or commit suicide. There is a heightened affect in demonstrations by women because their very presence reveals the breakdown of normal channels of protest. Women, as the protected sector of the society (along with children and pets), threaten the male image by their entry into the arena of public protest.[1]

Acts of resistance, by rejecting a given model of how the society should operate, force the attention of the public on to the need for alternative models and thus become the first step toward innovation. Resistance begins with withdrawal of labor power, or noncompliance with the institutional framework within which the authority acts. This may take covert form in unwillingness to comply fully with work requirements or bureaucratic obligations, or it may take overt form in a strike or demonstration. It is the overt forms of resistance that are necessary if innovative responses are to follow since only they can publicize the grievance, raise the consciousness of others, and secure their support, thus paving the way for change. It is at this stage that resistance moves from the individual moral reaction to collective action.

Systems that have lost the flexibility to respond to the needs of a wider polity meet acts of resistance by an increase in repressive forces. They do this at the risk of making further inroads on the legitimacy of an incumbent group such that resistance movements may turn into a revolutionary force as the people seize the arms and turn them against their oppressors. Revolutionary vanguards with deep roots in resistance movements that have mobilized the people far in advance of the armed takeover are better prepared for the tasks of reorganizing the society.

In the mining communities of Bolivia, women have played an active role in the labor force and in the resistance movement against inhuman standards imposed upon workers. Women enjoyed the respect of their male comrades and had considerable decision-making power in the family, especially until the 1960's, before mass layoffs from the concentration pits reduced their numbers in the total labor force.

Bolivia has deep cultural and historical roots in the preconquest and colonial period that cultivate a sense of the importance of women in the society. Belief in the *Pachamama*, the time/space concept reduced in the primitive Spanish translation to Earth Goddess, is expressed in all contemporary rituals and cultivates a sense of the feminine generative force which nurtures and sustains life on earth. While this mythic image of the female principle as positive may not directly influence the historical role of women, it provides a favorable climate for them to participate in the significant events that affect their lives.

Bartolina Sicas, the wife of Tupac Katari, shared the perils as well as

---

[1]   A classic revelation of the threat posed to men by women's entry into political life is contained in Turner's quotation (1967) of colonel Velarde, who, after the Mexican revolution, stated his fear that "the Latin character would be ended if women lost their femininity and their charms as they mixed in the tumult of political life."

victories of her husband in the civil uprisings of the late eighteenth century.[2] Mother's Day is celebrated on the day the women of Cochabamba seized the guns of their dead men in the Civil War for Independence. Maria Barzola became the prototype of the twentieth century heroine when she seized the Bolivian flag as the miners of Siglo XX faltered in their march to demand higher wages and was the first to be shot in the massacre of 21 December, 1942.[3] From this historic past, there is a selection and cultivation of those themes that enhance the characteristics essential to resistance: self-respect, courage, and a culturally rooted sense of identity as human beings.

The Bolivian mining woman's sense of self is underwritten by an independence greater than that enjoyed by the majority of women in the world, although it is based on the extreme exploitation and disruption of the labor force. The substandard wages given to men and early deaths in the mines mean that women are forced to work. The 1950 census, the last one taken in Bolivia, shows that 43 percent of women were actively employed in the labor force, 3 percent of which were in mining and ex-

Table 1. Bolivian women in economically active population, ten years old and over (per 1,000 population), 1950.[a]

| | Total | Economically active | | | Economically inactive | | | Other | Percent active |
		Total	Occu-pied	Unoccu-pied	Total	Stu-dents	House-wives		
Women	983	582	580	2	396	51	322	23	59
Men	917	780	771	9	131	88	—	43	85
Total	1,900	1,362	1,351	10	527	139	322	66	72

[a] From *America en Cifras* (1970). Bolivia has not had a census taken since 1950.

[2] Posters advertising the recent mobilization of *campesinos* prior to the Hugo Banzer coup of August 19, 1971, used the images of both Tupac Katari and Bartolina Sicas in recognition of their historic roles in the fight for independence.
[3] Miners' versions of this struggle have always emphasized the character of Maria Barzola as a full-time *pallire* [concentrator of minerals] who represented the other women in the union. They say that she took the front position in the march, seizing the Bolivian flag from the men who had fallen back when they saw the army massed above them on the hills surrounding the administrative buildings to which they advanced. She is quoted as saying, "We women are the ones who have to face our children and tell them there is no food; we will go on even if they kill us."
Nestor Taboada, a leftist intellectual admired in the Soviet Union and elsewhere, presents a perverted picture of Maria Barzola in his novel, supposedly based on authentic data, *El Precio de Estaña*, in which she appears as a prostitute who, seeing the workers advance on the administrative buildings, staggers from the arms of her lover, an employee of the company, and in a drunken stupor seizes the flag from the workers and is shot. I have spoken to a lifetime resident and hotel owner in Llallagua, the town adjoining the mining camp of Siglo XX, who knew her pesronally and supports the miners' version. I never heard the Taboada caricature suggested by any worker.

traction industries.

Although the numbers employed in the regular industrial work force may have gone down with the "white massacres" or mass layoffs of the sixties, women's involvement in marketing and domestic services probably maintains the same proportionate level. Zondag (1966) estimated that 40 percent of women were employed in the estimated 2.3 million actively employed population. Most workers were recruited from Indian communities over two generations ago. In the process of becoming integrated in the work force, they acquired the characteristics — Spanish language and style of dress — that identify them as *cholas*, or acculturated members of the urban industrial sector.

The special nature of the mining community cultivates a total participation of all those who live and work in it, in part because of the isolation and in part because everyone is directly or indirectly dependent on the same enterprise. The rate of pay directly affects men, women, and children. When there is a massacre, all are killed without discrimination. As a result of the solidarity that grows in such communities, women have formed a housewive's association that has been active in demanding better food supplies and in defending the civil rights of men imprisoned for political (i.e. trade union) activities.[4] Men and women have joined together in economic and political action to demand improvement.

Consciousness of the need for change and the demand for a better way of life followed the debacle of the Chaco War against Paraguay. In the 1930's women formed the militant *Sindicato Feminino de Oficios Varios* [Women's Union of Various Occupations], which "fought memorable battles against authorities and exploiters. Soon this union became the most combative of the *Federación Obrera de Trabajadores* [Labor Federation of Workers]" (Lora 1971:88). In this union, composed primarily of vendors (who are, for the most part, women), women had a stronger role to play than they did in other sectors of the economy, where their voices were lost in the male-dominated labor force.

---

[4]   The social isolation of women in the domestic nest means that in most societies they are deprived of social knowledge and social education (Dalla Costa and James 1972: 27). Mining women are not isolated from each other or from the scene of industrial struggle because the encampment is an extension of the industrial complex itself, often crowded up against the slag pile, in intimate contact with the noise and in view of the workers. As active participants in the work process. the women have developed their own organizations to defend their rights as workers.

The social deprivation that comes of the usual social isolation may also be overcome in revolutionary situations. As Turner (1967:604) points out, the Mexican revolution released the women from the isolation of the house, where they had been cut off from social participation in the colonial period.

The brief period of populist rule when the National Revolutionary Movement (MNR) held power — from 1943 until the assassination of President Villarroel in July, 1946 — gave workers an opportunity to organize openly and to bring their top leader, Juan Lechin Oquenda, to national prominence as minister of labor. Women in the mining sector had their own representative, but their role was limited. In the six years of repression following the assassination of Villarroel, labor organizations were again outlawed and the social reforms of the Villarroel period were scuttled. In 1947 miners were killed in Potosi, and in a "white massacre" more than 10,000 workers were fired in Catavi. The army was sent to the Catavi-Siglo XX mines in 1948, 1949, and 1950 by the "Butcher," President Mamerto Urriolagoitia.[5] Women were among those who were victimized and who resisted the oppression. Their most publicized act of defiance as a group took place in 1951, when twenty-seven women entered the *Palacio Justicial* to demand the freedom of political prisoners and began a public hunger strike. *Los Tiempos* (April 29, 1951) attributed to the women success not only in obtaining the release of relatives and comrades, but also in revealing a plan by the government, dominated by the tin oligarchy, to exile candidates of the MNR as subversives — a disclosure that influenced the elections, which the MNR won.

Despite the victory at the polls, the candidates of the MNR were not seated. It required the revolution in the streets in April, 1952, to bring the party to power. Lydia Gueiler, one of the women who had organized the hunger strike and served in the underground *Comando Obrero Feminino*, proceeded to organize the Committee of Women within the victorious party, but she later admitted (1959:154–155) that the women failed to achieve equality and full political and economic rights. After working in the election of Siles in 1956, the women were not given any important positions in the government and returned "to their positions as *Rumy Canastas* and the poor to their drab and monotonous lives" (Gueiler 1959:157), She attributed the failure to gain independent recognition for their contribution to a lack of support from national party leaders and to a lack of maturity on the part of women who acquired positions in the party.

---

[5]   Lora (1971:268) summarizes the violence of the 1946–1952 period and the reaction of the workers. In 1947 miners were killed, in Potosi and afterward there was a *massacre blanco* [white massacre], mass layoff, of 10,000 workers in Catavi. In 1948, 1949, and 1950 there were general strikes. When in 1951 the oligarchy of tin barons refused to recognize the democratically elected MNR party leader, Paz Estenssoro, the workers rose up. Lora comments: "This process made mature the popular discontent, and the other working sectors of the country gravitated toward the spirit of resistance of the miners."

Another movement of women, known as Barzolas after the martyred Maria Barzola, disrupted labor union meetings in which rank-and-file discontent was beginning to be expressed against the MNR government in the late fifties. Organized by opportunistic male party leaders for their own ends, the women were manipulated as a brigade of prostitutes. As Gueiler pointed out, this taught women the importance of working together in their own groups to carry out political activities.

Working-class women in the mining camps were not as exploited by the kind of party tactics used in La Paz to divert the tide of discontent. Ten years after the first hunger strike undertaken by women, the wives of labor union leaders and other women of the encampment Cancañiri in Siglo XX mine began a hunger strike to protest the lockout of workers in a plan to "rationalize" the working force. One woman spoke to me of the movement in which she took part:

The housewives organized themselves because they [the mine administration] did not pay the salaries on time. The army came and imprisoned the union leaders. Then all the workers declared a strike. Those women whose husbands were in jail, the wives of Escobar and Pimentel, went to get their husband's liberty, but failed. They decided to unify and make a solid front to ask for their liberty. The mine administration had cut off bread, pay, water, everything. The committee went to La Paz and declared a hunger strike. Radio Pio XII censured the act because it was immoral — a person could not declare a hunger strike because it was against God's Law.

But the hunger strike was successful because they brought in the food and pay and also their husbands. At first there were only seventeen women in the strike, but it grew.

When the miners took European technicians as hostages in order to back their demands, we women organized a twenty-four hour watch to protect them because the men had threatened to kill them if the company did not respond to our petition. We thought that that would give an excuse to the government to send in the army for a massacre, and we wanted to prevent that.

The following excerpts from an interview I had with one of the prisoners give some of the quality of interaction between men and women in the mining community, the strength of the women's resistance, and the respect they commanded from the men:

In Catavi they put us in a room on the second floor. There were nineteen managers in with us. We didn't know what was going on. The *amas de casa* ['lovers of the house'] — that was a helluva name for them! — were our guards. (One of them told me that they went in to prevent the hostages from being killed by the men.) That's like getting protection from Madame La Farge! We got along well with the men, but the women wouldn't even let us out to go to the bathroom.

During the eleven days we were there, there were mass meetings going on below, but we weren't afraid. Juan Lechín and a state senator — a short, swarthy guy with dark glasses and a leather jacket — came to see us. He said, "They are my guests. Let them go." The women told them to drop dead. Then he said to the guards, "If you shoot them, shoot me first'." The women said, "Drop dead!"

The only trouble I had was with the women. I was suffering from ulcers and I called for milk and got it...

The army started to advance. My brother went to the prison where Pimental and Escobar were held and he prevailed on them to release us since the U.S. was not involved. Escobar issued a statement in *El Diario* and then scheduled an announcement to be made at the mass meeting. The radio announced that Escobar would speak at 7:30. We all gathered around at the appointed time. Escobar was on. He urged that the captors release us. There were 5,000 men there who agreed, and there were happy embraces. But the women said "No." One of them said, "I've known Escobar all my life, and it's not him talking." Another added, "They are beating him and forcing him to say it."

So they wouldn't let us go. It was a hopeless gambit. The women guards made our life impossible after that. They would come in and say, "No one goes to the toilet this morning." In a million ways they bothered us. We gave them money for cigarettes and they said, "You'll wait for it'."

They would say to the men guards, "I want the floors swept. Put down your guns and sweep."

The women used to pack dynamite in boxes. When the newsmen came in, they put on a big show of it.

The engineer, who was basically sympathetic with the miners, told me how it was with them. The average child lives in a family with one man after another passing through, and the women have the power in the family.

A housewife spoke of the breakdown of the women's organization:

However, the women's organization faltered after the strike. The women hadn't yet arrived at a level to behave with assurance; there was a lack of understanding between them and the organization declined in 1963 or 1964. They imprisoned or deported the husbands, and sometimes these men turned against the women. They told the women not to get mixed up in things. We organized the committee again in 1965 and it included both the women of the parish as well as of the encampment. We used to have our meetings at the door of the *pulperia*. There were 300 or 400 women that made demands, and we would elect a representative.

The repression of labor unions which began in the mines in the early sixties broke out into open battle during the Barrientos regime. In May, 1960, Barrientos announced a new wave of layoffs and the need to cut wages by a third. When workers resisted, he sent in troops, who were always quartered close to the major mines. One man spoke of the resistance movement:

In Itos we resisted with dynamite and arms that we had taken from the barracks in 1952. The Rangers were in San José as well as the Chicha regiment, and they had modern weapons — M-1's. We made a line of defense and stayed awake all night. At dawn a miner fell prisoner and we went to recapture him, but the army had moved up on the hill watching us. And so we had to give up our arms and from that day on we became slaves.

A woman in the encampment of Itos mine spoke with pride of the miners' resistance against the army:

I hope some day you will see one of these confrontations of miners. What does the miner defend himself with? With a piece of dynamite. And however Herculean he may be, he can't throw it more than five meters. And the armaments the regiment carries now are so powerful they destroy anything. It is an unequal battle.

The army has enough fear of worker resistance to prohibit the sale of rubber bands, which the miners use as slingshots to fire "arrows" fashioned of dynamite, before making their raids.

When the miners began to reorganize their forces in June, 1967, the worst massacre in the history of the mine occurred, taking the lives of eighty-seven men, women, and children.

We were dancing and drinking in the warming of the earth ceremony on the night of San Juan, when at 3:30 in the morning we heard what we thought were firecrackers. Then the regiment entered the encampment with machine guns. They killed men, women, and children; they fired into the houses where some people had gone to sleep in order to get up for the early morning shift. Since that year, the people of Cancañiri light more fires because it is in memory of this history... Our forefathers lit fires to make the flocks of llamas increase, and we light fires so that the veins of mineral will be richer and we can live on this earth.

The assertion of the right to live, to work, to pursue a daily routine, becomes an act of resistance when the ruling group rejects demands for a living wage and relies on force to maintain itself in power. Recognizing a threat to their very right to live, the housewives revived their organization. When Dorotea, the leader of this group, spoke against the slaughter, she was imprisoned and her husband was fired and blacklisted by all the mines. She spoke to me of these times:

I have a deep rancor in my heart for all the outrages we have suffered... Repression is very strong and the family suffers a great deal. It is precisely for this that I believe that I ought not to be quiet since we have suffered so much. I lost a child when they imprisoned me — I was pregnant at the time — from the abuses I received in jail. So for all these reasons there is this deep hatred in my heart. I cannot keep quiet. I do not want my children to live the same life I have lived. We feel it when our children cry because of their decayed teeth when we can't give them proper food. They must have a better life!

Look at this room: in this room we have to prepare two beds right on the floor. There are from twelve to fifteen people sleeping here, children kicking off the blankets so we are never properly covered. We eat on short rations.

I believe that the fundamental thing is to speak out for everyone. I don't like to be selfish. I do not want only the happiness for my children. I have seen the rest of the children suffering and I want all to be happy.

When the Federation of Mine Workers Unions of Bolivia (FSTMB) tried to reorganize its ranks in 1970 after the repression, killing, and exiling of leaders in the Barrientos period, the housewives' committee sent Dorotea as their representative to speak at the inauguration. She was one of the very few women in the crowded union hall. As she spoke, the murmur of voices rose from the audience as the men lost interest in the proceedings until she said:

I echo all the widows in the massacres, those of September and of San Juan, when hundreds of children were orphaned. I ask that all the goods of General Barrientos be confiscated in order that the proceeds be used for the feeding of these children and the education of these children.

All the delegates who have preceded me have referred to the problems of the working class; we also echo these because we are participants in the exploitation of our workers, of our husbands. We want this congress to take certain means, always working in unity with all of the working class, to take the responsibility of the vanguard. And all of us are disposed to support the means which are developed in the congress.

Also, I want to echo the inhuman exploitation of the wives, mothers, and children of workers of the slag pile, and I want to invite all of the delegates to visit such places of work and see with their own eyes the inhuman exploitation of these women.

In closing I only want to say, "Glory to Federico Escobar; glory to all the victims of all the massacres."

The tragic irony is that miners rarely recognize the support that women give in times of struggle; when they do notice it, they do not permit access to decision-making positions in the union. Not only did the union leaders fail to support the cooperative organization that the women formed to bring supplies into the community — an organization that might have helped to break the workers' dependency on the company store — but they were the first to order their wives back to the kitchen. This reaction expresses the fear that the wage slave has of losing his own slave in the house.[6] When the women were fired *en masse* from the con-

---

[6]   Dalla Costa and James (1972:25) disclose the hidden nature of the exploitation of women who, while not receiving wages, nonetheless provide services for men and make them available as an exploitable work force. While the women seem only to be the victims of male chauvinism, as slaves of wage slaves, they are also exploited in the wage system.

centration pits in 1967, the men said nothing, It was through their own efforts that the women won the right to work on the slag pile.

In the recent wave of repression instituted by Colonel Hugo Banzer, who seized power in the *coup* of August 19, 1971, women have again used the strategy of the hunger strike to force the government to release labor leaders and to back the demands of the textile workers who have barricaded themselves in the factory (*New York Times*, November 25, 1972). Their public display of resistance reveals both the intensity of repression under this regime and the persistence of their own traditions of resistance.

Resistance movements epitomize the striving toward consciousness which is the essence of humanity. Huizer (1970) has shown that the "resistance to change" often noted among Latin American Indians is a reaction to a culture of repression, in which traditional institutions become a defense against the complete loss of identity. When we recognize the violence and oppression that give birth to it, we can recognize in resistance a positive force. Resistance as a basic step toward self-determination is the genesis of liberation movements. As Camus (1966:96) noted for the Algerian resistance movement:

The rule of our action, the secret of our resistance can be easily stated: everything that humiliates labor also humiliates the intelligence and vice versa. And the revolutionary struggle, the centuries-old straining toward liberation can be defined first of all as a double and constant rejection of humiliation.

But we know the disillusionment that came to Algerian women after the liberation struggle was over and they were told by its ideologues to go back to the veil.[7]

Why is it that women, even after their participation in resistance and rebellion, have no share in the new power structures that emerge with the success of such movements? Women's entry into the resistance movements signals the breakdown not only of a normal social structure, but also of the personal relationships that underlie it. Because women are the dependent, subordinated sector of most societies, their acts of resistance threaten men's public role as protector. Thus the same acts of resistance that men may perform have a different significance when performed by women. Women's resistence heightens the sense of social breakdown and shakes the very foundation of the dominant-subordinate hierarchy which has its roots in the home and family network.

---

[7]   Equating women's liberation from the confines of purdah society with "aiding and sheltering the occupier," Fanon (1965:39) called for the return to the veil and all that this implied after Algerian independence.

Women's acts of resistance in liberation forces in the French underground during World War II, in Algeria, and elsewhere, have thus far been contained within the parameters set by men. In the immediate postrevolutionary euphoria, women may enjoy some of the rewards of the victory, but except where basic structural changes have taken place, they are typically restricted from public positions and are forced to return to the domestic scene. In Bolivia, where there has been no victorious outcome to the struggles of the past decade, women have consistently lost power in political and economic arenas. Their experience demonstrates the need for separate organizations of women within liberation movements so that their rebellious acts will not be perverted by political opportunists and their demands for change will include their own liberation.

REFERENCES

America en cifras
    1970   Statistics in *America en cifras.*
CAMUS, ALBERT
    1966   *Resistance, rebellion and death.* New York: Alfred Knopf.
DALLA COSTA, MARIAROSA, SELMA JAMES
    1972   "Women and the subversion of the community," in *The power of women and the subversion of community.* Bristol: Falling Wall Press.
FANON, FRANTZ
    1965   *A dying colonialism.* New York: Monthly Review Press.
GUEILER, LYDIA
    1959   *La mujer y la revolución.* La Paz.
HUIZER, GERRITT
    1970   "Resistance to change" and radical peasant mobilization: Foster and Erasmus reconsidered. *Human Organization* 29.
JACQUETTE, JANE
    n.d.   "Women in revolutionary movements in Latin America."
LORA, GUILLERMO
    1971   *Historia del movimiento obrero boliviano,* volume three. Cochabamba: Los Amigos del Libro.
Los Tiempos
    1951   Article appearing April 29.
New York Times
    1972   Article appearing November 25.
TURNER, FREDERICK
    1967   Los efectos de la participación feminina en la revolución de 1910. *Historia Mexicana* 16: 602–620.
ZONDAG, CORNELIUS H.
    1966   *The Bolivian economy, 1952–65; the revolution and its aftermath.* New York: Frederick A. Praeger.

SECTION THREE

Women in the United States

Introduction

The papers in this section deal with the following areas: an analysis of the patriarchal family as the principal means by which women in class-stratified societies such as the United States are subordinated and exploited; the negative reactions of the male social scientists to the women's movement in the late nineteenth century; the continuing disadvantaged position of women in the twentieth century; the laws finally passed in the last few years to deal with these inequities; a case study of a woman academic, demonstrating the inefficacy of these laws; a critique of the contemporary women's movement; and a reply to left-wing male criticism of this movement.

In "The economic basis of the status of women," Larguia shows how the patriarchal family system is perpetuated by a specific ideological coercion of women which she considers is probably the most powerful coercive instrument ever invented. In order to persuade the female sex to provide "a huge mass" of unpaid labor for men and for the ruling classes, to tolerate the laws that convert women into private property and the culture that disciplines them into passivity from birth, women's economic functions are confused with their biological functions and psychological identity. The socialization of individuals according to gender allows all men, even those in the lower classes, a degree of freedom. But on women in all classes, says Larguia, "a cultural lobotomy" is performed which undermines their physical and intellectual capacities and guarantees, under the most exploitative conditions, the reproduction of human labor power.

"The women were made domestic slaves," writes Larguia, "cramped into the job of wife and mother," persuaded that only through child-rearing and housework, without remuneration, could they demonstrate their love for husband and children. "No exploited sector has been deceived through greater mystification," she concludes. "Never has human nature been more cruelly confounded."

Although an increasing number of married women work outside the home because their salaries are urgently needed, the myth that they are economically supported by men results in their being paid a lower wage than men, even when they have identical qualifications. The capitalist "makes a double profit per worker's family," says Larguia, but he "makes greater profits from women workers." Moreover, the lower wages for women reduce the average wages for all workers, and male workers resist the entrance of women into the work force.

In addition, the work that women do in the household limits the work they do outside to jobs that are projections of domestic tasks, perpetuating the social image of women as reproducers of labor power and nurturers of humanity. Since the married woman who works outside the home is usually not relieved of her household work, her working day is much longer than that of the man. But she can do the two jobs only when the outside work is neither complex nor demanding. Thus, as Larguia points out, the male monopoly of economically skilled jobs and political power is due to the great mass of labor appropriated from women through the family structure.

In "Evolutionism and the place of women in the United States, 1885–1900," Ehrlich discusses the several social phenomena that conjoined in the late nineteenth century to arouse great apprehension in the United States about the changing roles of women. A basic factor was the increasing number of women entering the labor market in response to the demand for cheap labor by a rapidly expanding industrialization. At the same time women's organizations were stepping up their drive for women's suffrage, greater educational and economic opportunity, more equitable property laws, easier divorce, and control over their own earnings. Men felt themselves threatened in the economic arena, where women were competing for jobs, and in the family, where women were struggling for a degree of autonomy against male domination.

Other sources of economic competition were the newly-freed slaves and the millions of immigrants, particularly from southern and eastern Europe and the Orient, who were also responding to the demand for cheap labor in the United States. To decrease the competition from women, blacks, and immigrants, the principal weapons were sexism and racism, both with a history in the New World as old as the European settlement. And under the guise of science, particularly the new evolutionary theories, many social scientists in this period contributed to the dissemination of both racist and sexist propaganda, according to Ehrlich, frequently combining them.

For example, the relatively greater fertility of the immigrants, which was said to be "mongrelizing" the American nation and "smothering" the Nordics, was linked to the declining birthrate of the native Americans and this was attributed to the increased educational opportunities and greater economic independence of women. Another popular "scientific" argument was that the less "civilized" the race, the fewer were the physical differences between the sexes. In the West, hailed as the pinnacle of civilization where women, it was said, had reached their highest status, the differences between men and women were greatest.

Women were compared with men in much the same terms as the poor with the rich, blacks with whites, the colonialized peoples with their colonizers, and the "inferior" races with those that were "civilized." The absence of great women scientists, inventors, artists, and writers was proof that women were not creative and could not reason logically or on an abstract level. Since they were innately unfit for higher intellectual training, said the scientists, twisting their own logic, it was a waste of time and money to provide them with access to the culturally-valued forms of knowledge. Indeed, the smaller female brain "was a blessing, for if woman was equal to man intellectually, it would introduce new and violent competition into the social struggle." This, of course was the crux of the argument for keeping women within the nuclear family.

Only a small minority of social scientists, including Thorstein Veblen and those who were themselves women, championed the cause of women's emancipation, a situation not unlike the present. The great majority, as Ehrlich points out, used the language of evolutionism, which presumes change, to prevent change and to preserve the traditional status of women, expressing the misogynistic and androcentric views typical of patriarchal civilization, whether Eastern or Western, religious or scientific, ancient or modern.

But as a class the social scientists were merely the mouthpiece of the establishment. The crucial economic and political decisions were made by the leaders of commerce and industry, and by their representatives in government, law and medicine, the universities, and the trade unions. As Heath points out in "Legislation: an aid in eliminating sex bias in education in the United States," these men had no difficulty in circumventing the laws that were finally passed during the last decade to eliminate discrimination against women.

The proportion of women in the labor force rose steadily from 14 percent in 1901 to 44 percent in 1973, with an occasional drop, as at the

end of World War II when they were forced to make way for the returning service men. According to Saffioti, in "Female labor and capitalism
in the United States and Brazil" (Section 2), the increased number of
women workers in the United States was due primarily to three factors:
(a) the growth of the war industries, especially since 1940, which absorbed
large numbers of women; (b) the drive for upward mobility, stimulated
by the media and expressed in increased consumption of both material
and non-material goods (especially education), so that the man's salary
was no longer sufficient to support a family; and (c) the inflationary
increases in prices, which cut the real salaries of men and required wives
to work outside the home.

While in 1920 the majority of women in the work force were unmarried
and in their twenties, in 1970 two-thirds were married, with an average
age of 39. These women generally entered the labor market when their
children were of school age. The fact is, as Saffioti points out, about
70 percent of the women who are economically active in the United
States are forced to earn money because of dire need: they are the women
who are single, widowed, divorced, separated, or married to men who
cannot earn enough money to support a family.

But the working woman who is married is generally much less well off
economically than the woman who has never married and who has spent
her productive life in carving out a career and building up her pension or
savings. Married women who work outside, as well as inside, the home,
do not usually work long enough or earn enough to build up a substantial pension and they are unable to accumulate much in the way of
savings because their income goes to meet family needs. Only 3 percent
of women workers earn $10,000 a year or more, compared with 28
percent of men, and 60 percent of those who earn less than $500 a year
are women, compared with the 20 percent who are men.

As Saffioti notes, U.S. women are also low earners because they suffer
widespread discrimination in the well-paid professions, especially as
compared with women in the U.S.S.R.: women constitute 7 percent of
doctors in the U.S. and 75 percent in the U.S.S.R.; 3 percent of lawyers
in the U.S. and 36 percent in the U.S.S.R.; 2 percent of pharmacists in
the U.S. and 95 percent in the U.S.S.R. Moreover, U.S. women are
losing ground in the professions, as Babey-Brooke demonstrates in
"Discrimination against women in the United States." The proportion
of women college teachers was 33 percent in the 1920's and 18 percent
in the 1960's. Women are virtually absent as administrators even in
fields where they constitute the vast majority of the workers: libraries,
social services, elementary schools, and government. Of the 10,000 judges

in the United States, only 200 are women, and almost all are in the lower courts. In New York City, only 24 of the 300 highest positions in the municipal government are held by women.

In addition, the gap between men's and women's salaries is continuously widening. In 1956, women earned about 62 percent of men's salaries for the same work; now women earn about 59 percent of men's salaries. In 1970, one-third of all families living in poverty were headed by women, compared with 7 percent of such families headed by men. In that year, according to Saffioti, about 80 percent of those who subsisted only on the meager income provided by social security were women.

When discrimination on the basis of sex and age is compounded by racism, women are in triple jeopardy. About 57 percent of poor black families are headed by women, as compared with about 30 percent of poor white families. Using salaries as a marker, racism has softened but sexism has increased. In 1939 and in 1969, white men earned the highest salaries and black women the lowest. In 1939, white women earned more than black men, but in 1969 black men earned more than white women. The white woman is relatively more disadvantaged than she was 35 years ago. For the black woman the lessening of economic racism has been offset by the increase of economic sexism.

This discrimination against women occurs in the richest industrialized country in the world, where a Women's Bureau was established as part of the Labor Department in 1920, more than half a century ago, to formulate policies to promote the welfare of wage-earning women. Although, as Heath points out, the Women's Bureau studies clearly demonstrated the disadvantaged position of women in the United States, in the 1960's various commissions were instituted to examine and report on women's status and to make recommendations to rectify it. Laws were finally passed in the late 1960's and implementing agencies were set up to eliminate sex discrimination. But the case of Babey-Brooke demonstrates the inefficacy of these agencies.

Thus, out of the anger and frustration of women who, as an increasingly larger segment of the labor force, were paying taxes to bring about higher wages and fringe benefits for men, in 1966 the first new feminist organization in almost fifty years, the National Organization for Women, was founded. NOW, along with other groups of mainly professional women, constitutes the branch of the women's movement dedicated to the goals of eliminating legal and economic discrimination against women. The other branch consists mainly of women who in the late 1960's left the civil rights movement, the dissident student groups, and the New Left, where they had been shunted into traditional helping roles and kept out of important policy-making. Unlike NOW, these groups reject establishment structures and leadership roles, and are concerned primarily with changing women's perceptions of themselves and of society. This they are doing through "consciousness-raising" in rap groups and speakouts (on areas such as rape and prostitution) which develop an understanding of the institutional forces that relegate women to an inferior status, create new positive percpetions of women, and explode the myth of the individual solution. Men are excluded from these groups, and male members of the New Left are particularly hostile to a women's movement that is autonomous and independent of radical organizations, as Schoepf and Mariotti point out in "Politics of theory."

According to Freeman, in "The Women's Liberation movement in the United States," two basic ideas have emerged from the women's movement: the egalitarian ethic and the liberation ethic. The first strives for the elimination of institutionally structured sex differences and sex roles; the second is based on the belief that the social institutions that oppress women as women oppress people as people. If the two ethics work together, says Freeman, the abolition of sex roles will continually be incorporated into the restructuring of society, and both ethics will lead to the liberation of women and men. But this will require a feminist critique of society, since, as Freeman points out, no male ideologist has ever "comprehensively challenged the sex role structure."

The Economic Basis of the Status of Women

ISABEL LARGUIA

Discrimination against women is the result of a hidden economic structure inherent in class society, a structure which has essentially been defined in relation to the way in which surplus labor is extracted from the producing classes. Only recently has historical materialism made clear that the appropriation of surplus by the ruling hierarchies was possible to a great extent because of a huge mass of unpaid women's labor, which is extracted through the family, the economic unit of class society. Class societies then, are ruled by two structural principles: the division in classes which is the fundamental characteristic, and the family economic unit, which remains relatively constant throughout the evolution of class societies. Class division is the motor of history, but it cannot develop without the existence of the second hidden structure that nourishes it and that exists only to the extent that huge masses of unpaid labor may be extracted from it. The two economic structures are interdependent and the changes that take place in the social or visible structure, where class antagonisms predominate, cannot be separated from the second, more conservative structure. The two are today coming into conflict with the highly developed productive forces which are at an advantage.

In order to analyze the status of an exploited group, this paper will deal with the main factor affecting the status of women in the working classes. The economic and legal structure through which the ruling classes confiscate a huge mass of unskilled labor from women is the family as an economic unit — the household — in which an important labor activity takes place, the counterpart of social production. This economic unit appears at the beginning of the division of society into classes. The patriarchal household is one of the oldest roots of private property, one of its sturdiest supports; and it is destined to disappear as an economic structure in the transition to a classless society. The patriarchal family has thus constituted an economic structure underlying the class division and has nurtured the development of various modes of production.

The sources of discrimination against women may be found in the appropriation of surplus labor. Forms of discrimination vary considerably in different cultures and periods, under the influence of developmental and ethnic factors, natural conditions, and outside influences. But the economic basis that determines discrimination is generally the same.

The authoritarian character of the family comes from this extraction of women's labor. The positive aspects of the family are distorted by the economic activities occurring within it. The purpose of this paper is not to question the positive social and psychological aspects of the family, but rather the hidden economic activity that absorbs half of human labor. I believe it is this unrecognized extraction of unskilled labor and the necessity of prolonging it which lays the basis for discrimination against women (Larguia and Dumoulin 1971).

The key concept for the definition of woman's role in the division of labor, and thus for the mode of appropriation that determines her status, is LABOR POWER and its reproduction or replacement. Labor power is the working person's physical and spiritual energy taken as a whole, his or her capacity for work. In any productive process, labor power plays the fundamental role. Each day as men and women do their jobs, they use up their energies; they must have food, clothing, and shelter in order to continue producing the next day; a large part of the replacement of labor power is carried out through daily individual consumption of products. As each generation grows old, it definitively consumes its labor power and must be replaced in production by young people who have been cared for, brought up, and given the necessary socialization.

It is of fundamental importance in this connection to distinguish economic reproduction from biological reproduction. Economic reproduction is a clearly non-biological sphere of life, carried out exclusively through work. It involves the replacement of all the factors of the economy that are consumed, at varying rates, during its operation. A common example of economic reproduction is the continual replacement of goods, whether consumer or producer, that are used up in the economic process. However, human labor power is an equally important economic factor that is also consumed and is reproduced by women's largely unpaid labor.

For final consumption to take place, a specific kind of labor must mediate between social production and the consumer. This labor is appropriated through the economic unit that provides the corresponding goods and services: preparation of food, maintenance of clothing in good condition, cleaning of the dwelling, and education of children according to the norms required of the next generation of working people. These tasks, specific to the replacement of labor power, which we know today as "housework" in the broadest sense, have been assigned to women with increasing specialization and separation from the rest of the economy throughout the development of class society.

PRECAPITALIST DEVELOPMENT

In the preclass community, these tasks had a different significance. The replacement of labor power was not differentiated from the general flow of production. The different tasks were carried out within the same group without intermediate exchange, and the technology employed was at the same low level. The growing division of labor between the sexes tended to specialize women in industries that kept them close to the common center of production; these industries were, under certain conditions, the ones that allowed the group to achieve a level of stable, simple reproduction. There was no discontinuity in production between these tasks and those of the men. Correspondingly, women enjoyed a social status that was equal or superior to that of men.

The simple replacement of labor power is the fundamental goal of economies with low levels and rates of development. The group's aspiration is to assure the prolongation of its life (to guarantee biological, economic, and cultural reproduction), which manifests itself in the succession of new generations that have all the force of their ancestors.

With the breakup of the preclass community, the common production and residential unit gave way to private families, which constitute the basic economic unit of the various class sytems. In the transition to the nuclear family, the single flow of production characteristic of the preclass community underwent a split. Social production began to be differentiated from the direct reproduction of labor power. In social production, besides exchange between the producers, the production of a surplus appropriated by a ruling class stands out as the most important aspect, a function that ties the family into the class structure of society.

Thus, in a closed economy, the family was a productive unity in which various activitites took place in a state of apparent indivisibility:

1. strictly biological reproduction (which does not concern us in this paper);
2. the reproduction of labor power (which includes the care and socialization of the new generation of working people);
3. social production (which consists of two aspects: surplus appropriated by the ruling classes and production for exchange among the producers).

In the precapitalist closed economies, the family was both a unit of reproduction of labor power and a unit of social production for consumption and exchange. Throughout the development of such economies, women participated in both social and subsistence production. The means of production were attached to the household and women could alternate their labor in the two functions.

The extraction of surplus by the ruling classes in precapitalist societies presupposed an indissoluble union between the domestic industries and agriculture. In European feudalism, for example, "in the countryside it was taken for granted that men and women worked together. One got married and had children in order to create the very prerequisite of labor on the farm" (Kuczynski 1960). But in such economic formations, the two aspects of women's work, i.e. social production and the direct replacement of labor power, enter into conflict.

At first, the domestic handicraft industries were mainly women's responsibility. But the development of exchange and the appropriation of surplus by the ruling hierarchies stimulated improvement and specialization in some branches of handicraft production. The need to develop improved tools and more complex products came into conflict with the need to reproduce the labor power of all the members of the family, an activity that was considered from very early times a specifically feminine task, an extension of gestation and lactation. At the same time, the work involved in replacing labor power also acquired a certain amount of specialization. A refinement of domestic subsistence technology absorbed an ever greater amount of women's labor.

The heavy obligations of the reproduction of labor power forced women to retire from most of the specialized crafts, while men found themselves free to develop greater skills in these tasks or in agriculture. Gradually men monopolized the work that produced visible, exchangeable products. Through this process, in the development of class society, the family took shape as a legal and productive unit by means of which, through the men, the ruling classes appropriated the surplus labor of the women.

The total mass of labor was progressively split into two great sectors.

Women's labor became identified with housework and with the sphere of the private family, while "productive" labor and its products in the public sphere were identified with male labor. Men's work thus crystallized in products that were socially and economically VISIBLE in the form of taxes, rent, or commodities. The division of labor between men and women is the oldest historical association between biological differences and labor.

WOMEN UNDER CAPITALISM

The economic system in class society has a specific mode of coercion which allows the ruling classes to extract the surplus from the producing classes. In schematic terms, it may be said that classical slavery used open physical coercion, feudalism used ideological coercion and economic coercion through the peasant's interest in increasing his means of production; while capitalism uses predominantly economic coercion through wages and other market incentives.

The family economic structure underlying all class systems is accompanied by a specific ideological coercion of women as reproducers of labor power, an ideological coercion that is perhaps the most powerful in history.

In order that half of humanity be channeled from birth into a reduced set of social functions to provide free labor to the male sex and the ruling classes, women were coerced into confusing their economic function with their biological and psychological identity, to justify or at least tolerate the legal structure that turned them into private property and the culture that disciplined them into passivity. This ideological coercion arose over several millennia, aided by the fact that the reproduction of both children and labor power went on in a place where only women were confined. Both end products — but especially children — took shape in the persons of women, and both were the property of the husband as head of the household and owner of all its goods and persons.

Thus the strictly biological function of reproducing the human species was superimposed on the work that produced values of usefulness for consumption. Economic and social laws were translated into biological terms and were thereby made invisible. Worse still, women's habits of work were slowly inserted into their very sexual condition, which came to constitute a sort of identity from which work aptitudes seemed "naturally" to emanate. Aptitudes for physical labor and for intellectual creation were closely tied to the "natural division of labor," and society as a whole proceeded to "socialize" individuals according to their sex, developing certain aptitudes in one group and "complementary" ones in the other.

But while the so-called masculine or virile aptitudes gave their possessors a certain freedom (though subject to class limitations), a cultural lobotomy was practiced on the whole female sex, undermining women's physical and intellectual capacities from the cradle. They were made domestic slaves, cramped into the job of wife and mother, obliged to reproduce labor power without remuneration, through the family economic structure. Women's work and women's temperament were established as a biological category, under the common denominator of sexuality. Under these circumstances, women's work was represented socially in only one way: as maternal abnegation and conjugal love. Patriarchy, class society's main antecedent and ally, was able to cloud the social consciousness of the exploited and the exploiters, confusing love and work. No exploited sector has been deceived through greater mystification. Never has human nature been more cruelly confounded. But it must not be forgotten that the confusion between love and work had a precise economic function: to convince women that their true human identity could be realized only through housework in its broadest sense. The necessary reproduction of humanity's labor power was thus guaranteed under the most exploitative conditions for women.

In more recent times, under class society, women's economic activity in simply reproducing labor power gave rise to a negative mythology that acted as a form of ideological coercion on all women, whether members of the producing classes or not.

Sexism, socialization according to sex, and the feminine mystique are aspects of the ideological coercion to which women have been subjected. As a sociopolitical structure, this ideological coercion has the function of conditioning new generations of women to the reproduction of labor power and to the maintenance and reproduction of the nuclear family, the economic cell of class society.

This coercion disguises the frontier between economic and sexual activity. The new generation of reproducers of labor power is educated under this coercion, its members destined from birth, by virtue of their sex, to a particular kind of servile labor in the household. Thus this coercive ideology arises from the economic situation of women, and its function is to perpetuate the kind of familial formation through which surplus labor is appropriated.

The development of the capitalist money economy deepens the division between reproduction of labor power and social production, until it finally splits the latter away from the family. It begins by breaking up the closed economy. It destroys the autarchy of the peasant family, with its necessary combination of agriculture and domestic handicrafts which served all its needs.

With the industrial revolution, the latent contradiction between women's functions in social production and their work in the replacement of labor power came into open conflict. Women entered the labor market and left the home before large-scale industry had significantly reduced housework. The industrial workday of twelve hours and more was incompatible with a second day's work in the home. Because the industrial economy was not yet capable of absorbing enough of the subsistence functions, the basic economic unit of class society underwent a premature crisis. And once the primitive accumulation necessary for capitalist developement had been accomplished, many working women became unemployed, because it was a vital necessity for class society that they continue with the private replacement of labor power. In order for women to gain a secure foothold in the labor market, the industrial economy would first have to absorb an important part of the replacement of labor power, emptying the family of half of its economic content and reducing it to a consumption unit.

Social production is concentrated in large capitalist units; the small-scale producers succumb to their far more productive competition. The mass of working people no longer control their own means of production: they become salaried workers.

This process makes the worker's family doubly dependent on the market: for the commodities it consumes and for the sale of the only commodity it produces — the salaried worker's labor power. The change in production relations thus effects an important change in the economic structure of the family. The destiny of the whole mass of women's labor suffers a change. It is expressed, not in exchangeable products or a directly appropriable surplus, but only in the production of labor power as a commodity. The concept of feminity comes ever closer to that of servitude.

The ideal of women's isolation in the household had first been established in the ruling classes, where it was associated fundamentally with the inheritance of property from father to son for which the wife's fidelity to her husband was especially important. Isolation of women in the home is directly associated with private property and the division of society in classes. Industrial capitalism makes it possible to spread this isolation among the producing classes and push it to its final consequences for the deterioration of women's status.

First, the husband no longer possesses the means of production — land and equipment — which had formerly been attached to the household, which therefore has lost its function in social production. The women and children no longer contribute to the production of visible articles. The small-scale commodity production formerly done by women on their own account is eliminated in the same way.

Second, when the wage labor regime takes the place of small-scale family production, social labor is physically separated from the family, the place of work from the household. Social labor is, of course, by its very nature not destined for the family's consumption, and the most outstanding part of the labor power reproduced in the household is exercised, not within it, but rather in a capitalist production center.

Third, in the vast majority of cases, the man with his wages becomes the "provider" for the whole family, that is, its sole source of goods from the social sector. The woman's invisible work is no longer considered labor; it becomes merely housework necessary but having no economic content. It is dogma that housewives do not work; they are "economically inactive," The economy has been defined as the production and distribution of commodities, and women apparently have been excluded from it.

This exclusion is only partial, however, for women also go out to work. The development of the urban economy absorbs the domestic handicrafts formerly made by women in the household, thus freeing part of women's total labor fund. In order to purchase the products that were previously made in the home, the worker's family needs more money, which can only be obtained by marketing women's extra labor power. In any case, the norm of seclusion was not applicable to those women who had to support a family, a situation that is ever more frequent now. Capitalism thus pushes women into the labor market, where they must compete with men, many of whom are unemployed.

Because the norm defines a woman's job as housework and states that there must be a man responsible for the family, the working woman is not thought to need a wage equal to that of the working man. Capitalists pay her a lower wage for the same work; added to the wage of the man, it covers the family's expenses, for which the man's wage is no longer sufficient. Where the capitalist formerly made a simple profit from the work of the head of the family, the increased incorporation of women into social production gives him a double profit for each worker's family. The capitalist makes greater profits from women workers.

Women in the labor market have the status of pariahs (Kuczynski 1960), similar to that of ethnic groups that suffer discrimination. The pariahs as a whole make up a second stratum of the working class and fulfill an important function for the system. Because they are badly paid, they reduce the average wage, and their status is a menace to the other workers, who could be replaced by them or could themselves fall to the lower wage level. The discrimination against women contributes in this way to the general depreciation of wages.

Another manifestation of discrimination in the labor market is the division of labor between the sexes within the working class. The limitation of women to certain kinds of jobs depends on the existence of the family economic unit. Both historically and economically, women's work in the household has limited them to certain occupational sectors. Historically, women have been admitted to those jobs that are the social projections of the tasks that they traditionally perform in the home. It is no accident that they have been admitted preferably to the textile and clothing industries, the food and drug industries, and the services. (nurses, manicurists, elementary school teachers, secretaries, waitresses, and the archetypal role of maid-of-all-work). The social labor of women must not conflict with the female image, conditioned historically by women's function as reproducers of labor power.

There are also economic limitations. When her social day's work is done, the working woman must be prepared to cope with another day's work, equally long, in the household. In order for millions of tiny household workshops to continue to exist, they must be fed by a huge mass of labor. It is vitally important for the survival of class society that women not exhaust all their labor power in social production, that they reserve enough energies to maintain the private economic unit.

It is evident that the hourly productivity of labor is in inverse proportion to the number of working hours. Insofar as the workday is prolonged, its intensity must diminish; and as its intensity rises, the workday must be shorter. As a result, there is a contradiction between women's two workdays, determined by the limits of human working capacity. The intensity and/or complexity of the job that a women can do is reduced by the extension of her domestic workday. Women are therefore forced to accept low-intensity jobs that allow them to keep a fund of energy for housework. Women require light work that does not exhaust their muscular or nervous energies, because when they return home, they must continue working to replace their own labor power and that of their husbands, and to bring up the new generation of workers.

Similarly, men's complex and/or intensive work is done at the expense of women's simple labor in the household, which saves men from the extra hours necessary to replace their labor power. Men's high skill in and monopoly of political power typical of class society are due to a great mass of invisible labor appropriated through the family economic unit.

While capitalism sharpens the discrimination against women, on the one hand, it prepares the conditions for the leap to socialism on the other. In the social sector of the productive process, capitalism developed large-scale industry, in which human labor reached a productivity level many times greater than in handicraft labor. The workers are grouped into large collectives to perform their tasks; this facilitates a more articulated division of labor, as well as the application of more advanced technology. But the replacement of labor power continues to be organized on the domestic handicraft model. As a result, the productivity of housework cannot surpass its traditional level. The hours of housework do not diminish appreciably, and the production of one household goes no further than the satisfaction of the needs of one family.

The social sector, which began as an outgrowth of subsistence production, progressively absorbs the latter's economic content. For example, a sequence can be traced from the subsistence production of grain and its grinding and preparation in the home, to the pervasiveness of commercial bread and pasta. The same process is now occurring with precooked foods.

The absorption of the main body of production by the social sector makes room for the expansion of capital and the development of the productive forces. But it does not lead, at least under capitalism, to the elimination of the family economic unit.

Recent studies indicate that today the family's unpaid labor in the United States still takes up approximately half the country's total work time (Sirageldin 1969). Thus, instead of reducing the importance of the household in the labor balance, the absorption of economic content by the social sector leads rather to a relative loss of productivity, to the worsening of the disparity between the two sectors. It follows that there is some justification for considering housewives to be economically unproductive.

The present tendency to fill the household with equipment designed to facilitate housework does not eliminate the backward character of the family as a productive unit; on the contrary, it makes its weight more onerous for the economy as a whole. The productivity of equipment has grave limitations in any one-man enterprise, especially when many different tasks are performed, something which does not occur in large-scale production. However much is invested in household equipment (and one can spend a considerable sum), the necessary hours do not diminish beyond a certain point and production does not exceed the family's consumption. By contrast, investments in the social sector yield high productivity. Household applicances are a caricature of technological advance precisely because they cannot provide what is demanded of such progress: an increase in labor productivity. Although they alleviate the intensity of housework, they do not make it significantly briefer.

The harm done by the organization of the reproduction of labor power in tiny household workshops is more serious in a highly developed economy. The largest block of labor power, that of housewives, is wasted on the lowest level of productivity. The services are in general limited to small-scale operations. A significant part of the total industrial product is wasted on unproductive equipment: much of consumer-durable industry exists only for the production of equipment for the tiniest possible enterprise, when cheaper and more efficient equipment would do the same job on a larger scale. An extraordinarily complex and costly system of transportation, storage, and individual retailing is required for numerous items that could be consumed collectively. As time passes, this situation can only grow worse.

Discrimination against women then, is, by no means limited to the sociocultural surface; it masks a backward economic structure that is now hindering the development of the human species as a whole.

WOMEN UNDER SOCIALISM

A solution to this problem emerges in the historical development of socialism. But the transition to a classless society should not be analyzed from a utopian point of view, in the hope of a quick end to the problems of women and the family.

The conditions created by capitalism determine the immediate possibilities of change. Capitalism concentrated the means of production and the workers into large units, making them interdependent through a highly developed division of labor. It created the technological level and the forms of organization, and built the installations. These conditions make possible the socialization of property in the fundamental means of production.

In the domestic sphere, on the other hand, capitalism progressively eliminated the survival of the closed economy in the family economic unit. It abolished the uninterrupted flow of subsistence production from the making of raw materials to final consumption. It transferred the whole process of making and processing raw materials to the social sector, leaving to the basic economic unit only the finishing process and maintenance, the aspects closest to final consumption. In this way it stripped the household of all productive activity not linked directly to the replace-ment of labor power. Capitalism eliminated the autarchy of the family and made the family, both as a consumption unit and as a seller of labor power, totally dependent on social production and on the market. But far from concentrating the reproduction of labor power in large units, capitalism reinforced the household's character as a private enterprise. This atomization of the replacement of labor power is one of the condi-tions necessary to fortify the market and particularly the development of a consumer-durable industry which caters to the individual domestic enterprise.

Under these conditions, capitalism can neither technologize the repro-duction of labor power nor develop a division of labor that makes house-wives interdependent as producers. This explains the considerable ideological backwardness of housewives, who constitute the most re-tarded sector of society, especially in underdeveloped countries where women's technical level is very low. It also guarantees the atomization of the working class after the workday is over.

This is the economic situation inherited by socialism. The conditions created under capitalism make it relatively easy to socialize the means of production and distribution. For its own survival, on emerging in little-developed countries surrounded by hostile powers, socialism has had to concentrate on developing social production, building plants, and estab-lishing a more advanced technology and organizational structure.

Capitalism does NOT hand down favorable conditions for socializing the replacement of labor power. Whereas the public sphere exhibits concen-tration of production, the replacement of labor power under capitalism is discharged in millions of tiny individual enterprises – unconnected, anarchic, and unproductive.

On the economic level, the first task that socialism faces with respect to women is to incorporate them into social production, whatever their cutural conditions may be. This incorporation takes place in much more favorable conditions in a socialist economy because of the lack of private ownership of the means of production and the consequent elimination of unemployment. As a result, the pariah status eventually disappears for both women and men, and with it wage discrimination; women receive equal pay for equal work.

Engels (1972) foresaw that a social revolution in the capitalist economy would bring the speedy incorporation of all women into the industrial economy and that the rapid disappearance of the family as the economic unit of society would follow or accompany this process. What is generally passed over in Engels' insight is his belief that this would be made possible through a very quick socialization of domestic labor. However, for reasons which we have discussed such a swift rate of development has not been possible; Engels has been proved right in his thesis, but the pace of events has been slow with respect to the family.

Socialism tends to diminish and then eliminate the economic features of the family which are those of a private enterprise, not to fortify or "modernize" them. The household workshop fulfills no function of reinforcing private property or of atomizing the working class. As the household's economic functions are transferred into the public sphere, women's labor power is progressively liberated for more skilled and/or more intensive jobs — jobs that require greater continuity and concentration.

With unemployment eliminated, as household working hours diminish, the division of jobs between the sexes gradually loses its basis: no large mass of labor is needed for after-hours reproduction of labor power. The disappearance of the barrier that had impeded women's access to traditionally "male" jobs and to the power structure is directly related to investment in the service industries that alleviate housework, as well as to the improvement of household implements as a transitional measure. It is no longer necessary for women to do relatively unintensive and uninteresting work in order to save their energies for the household, although the corresponding transformations are prolonged, laborious, and only partly conscious processes. There is a notable diversification and elevation of women's skills in the socialist countries, especially with their massive invasion of all the professions. There is a tendency, as in Vietnam, for example, to establish a new morality whereby men and women share equally in the household chores that social production cannot yet absorb.

What are the tendencies in the development of socialism? In order to socialize the reproduction of labor power it is necessary to retrieve it from the backward handicraft organizational model imposed upon it by the family. It is also necessary to relieve the services and the production of certain kinds of equipment from the deforming and stunting influence of millions of tiny workshops. It is not a question of abolishing the family, as some utopians would have it (although a lessening of the dependence of young people on their parents may be expected if present trends continue): rather, the family must cease to be a place of work and exploitation. Through socialism the role of the family is simplified with the decrease in housework. The regenerative side of family life, both spiritual and sexual, is enhanced.

The full socialization of the replacement of labor power will require the construction of large-scale complexes of services, analogous to factory complexes, covering all the services necessary to replace housework with much greater efficiency and improved quality, employing the technology of mass production. All this implies a prolonged process that includes organizational and technological redesigning of production and dwellings, and the very costly construction of the corresponding installations.

The future collectivization of the replacement of labor power through the development of service-oriented production complexes (Moll 1973) will be associated with the growth of automation. Such complexes cannot be subordinated to the traditional domestic sweatshop. Their creation is intimately tied to the disappearance of the basic economic unit of class society and the full development of the human personality. The collectivization of what is now housework implies both a technological revolution and profound changes in social consciousness.

The reproduction of labor power will cease to exist as a separate and opposed self-subsistence sector of the economy and will become incorporated as a full-fledged part of social production. The economy will cease to function in two disparate sectors as it does under private property; it will regain the fully social character it had in the preclass community but on a far higher level of productivity and division of labor. The notion of private property will lose its grip by this change, and with it the hidden relation through which women's labor has been exploited in the family. Only with the final elimination of the regressive economic aspects of the family can the last traces of discrimination against women disappear.

This process has another important implication. Housework, as we have defined it, is the most common of all full-time jobs. In the dichotomy between manual and intellectual labor, it falls very evidently on the manual side. Therefore only when housework is socialized can the manual-intellectual dichotomy be overcome. And only then can labor cease to be an alienating and alienated activity.

Capitalism created the preconditions for the full socialization of production in the public sphere, but it did not do so for housework, that is, for the direct reproduction of labor power. Socialism tends to create these conditions, emptying the household of its economic content and freeing women for the full development of their human personalities.

The contemporary family is the result of a long and complex process. Its history and present structure can be understood, not simply through its biological function, but rather through its production relations, which have undergone many changes and will continue to do so. As the basic economic unit of class society, the family has been a tiny private enterprise, a place of exploitation. On the other hand, it includes human relations that are of great value. These two aspects must be clearly distinguished; the family's authoritarian and repressive features, the distorted psychological situation that often exists within it, are derived from its economic content and not from the positive sexual and emotional relations that it contains. The persistence of housework is now an impediment to the full liberation of the human potential of women and of all the family members. The concept of labor power and its reproduction is of fundamental importance for understanding this process.

REFERENCES

ENGELS, FRIEDRICH
  1972 *The origin of the family private property and the state.* New York: International Publishers.
KUCZYNSKI, JURGEN
  1960 *Die Geschichte der arbeitenden Frau* in *Die Geschichte der Lage der Arbeiter unter dem Kapitalismus,* volume eighteen. Berlin. Dietz Verlag.
LARGUIA, ISABEL, JOHN DUMOULIN
  1971 Hacia una ciencia de la liberación de la mujer. *Casa de las Américas* 65–66: 37–55.
MOLL, MARCELO
  1973 "La igualdad social real de la mujer y el hombre, requisito para la liberación total de la mujer." Unpublished paper.
SIRAGELDIN, ISMAIL H.
  1969 *Non-market components of national income.* Ann Arbor: University of Michigan Survey Research Center.

Evolutionism and the Place of Women in the United States, 1885-1900

CAROL EHRLICH

In the history of social science in the United States, the late nineteenth century marked the rise of professionalism, of a search for a scientific method that would shift the study of man from speculation to empiricism, and of an effort to define man in his natural state without the aid of traditional moral judgments or value-laden preconceptions. Until 1885, remarked Albion W. Small (1916:726), "benevolent amateurishness" characterized American attempts to deal scientifically with human experience.[1] But the appearance of the first generation of professionally trained social scientists marked "a revolution in the analysis of social problems" (O'Neill 1966:291).

The attempt to ground the study of human experience in a scientific method led the practitioners of the new sciences to examine other disciplines for materials that might be applicable to the study of man and his institutions. One major source for many scientists was the cluster of ideas that comprised evolutionary theory. As used by the students of human experience, evolutionism was applied not only to that biological phenomenon, the species *Homo sapiens*, but also to human social institutions, such as government and the family.

[1] From the vantage point of 1970, with its relatively clearly defined sciences of the human species, it is hard to know exactly what to call their less sharply delineated forebears. I have settled upon a synonymous use of "social science" and "the sciences of human experience." A look at the late nineteenth century periodicals for sociology, psychology, anthropology, and so on — as well as such general meeting places as the *Popular Science Monthly* — shows a constant flow of the same scientists (either directly or by reference) back and forth. The searchers for a rigorous scientific method still had far more in common than they would have fifty years hence, when different methodologies and scientific languages would act as barriers between disciplines. Today, Veblen would have to settle for either economics or sociology, not both.

This paper will not trace the complex of evolutionist ideas to their origins, nor will it discuss specific schools of evolutionary thought, for evolutionism was often used in a very non-specific fashion. Frequently the word EVOLUTION itself was employed only in the loosest sense, to indicate a series of changes in a given object that were governed by some sort of lawful process. Key terms such as MODIFICATION, VARIATION, ADAPTATION, and NATURAL SELECTION were part of the intellectual superstructure and were often used without regard to precise meaning or consistency; further, they were often mingled with ideas of progress or decline along the yardstick of contemporary values. Evidence of the pervasiveness of the concept of evolution is the frequency with which it appeared in the scientific periodicals of the late nineteenth century. Titles such as "Evolution of the bicycle," "Evolution of patent medicines," and "Evolution of the storage battery" were extremely common.

The growth and professionalization of the sciences of human experience were reflected in the explosive proliferation of scientific journals. It was here that the scholars of sociology, anthropology, psychology, political science, and the other young empirical disciplines defined the current issues in their professions. Important social problems of course received considerable attention.

This paper will survey the literature of twenty American scientific periodicals[2] between 1885 and 1900 for the application of evolutionist thought to a social problem that was of great concern in the rapidly changing society of late nineteenth century America: the place of the

[2]   The periodicals are:
American Anthropologist
American Antiquarian and Oriental Journal
American Historical Review
American Journal of Archaeology
American Journal of Philology
American Journal of Sociology
Annals of the American Academy of Political and Social Science
Johns Hopkins University Studies in History and Political Science
Journal of American Folklore
Journal of Morphology
Journal of Political Economy
Journal of Social Science
New Science Review
Pedagogical Seminary
Political Science Quarterly
Popular Science Monthly
Psychological Review
Quarterly Journal of Economics
Science
Zoological Bulletin

woman. It will consider, first, the bioevolutionary sources of social science attitudes toward the woman; second, the application of bioevolutionary ideas to one particular dispute — education and the woman; and, finally, biocultural evolutionist theories of the family as they pertained to the woman.

Although the primary emphasis here is on the impact of one set of ideas upon another, certain social phenonema of the time were unquestionably influential in shaping social scientific perspectives on the American woman. The growth of industrial capitalism and its demands for a large labor force meant at best that a woman did not need to marry unless she so chose, at worst that many whose husbands had inadequate incomes had to work in order to survive. In either case, there were increasingly large numbers of women whose lives were no longer confined to the home. In the words of Falkner (1897:112–113): "As women's labors are eliminated from the household, the greater the proportion of women workers whose labor is removed from the quasi-patriarchal form of the family and made to harmonize with the conditions of modern industry."

The great changes wrought by geographic mobility and rapid urbanization also exacerbated the fears of many traditionalists that the American family was being destroyed. Further, many believed that a declining birthrate among native Americans (which was caused, according to two rival notions of the day, either by the increasing independence of women or by their decreasing health), combined with the influx of immigrants from strange and un-American lands in southern and eastern Europe and the Orient, would result in a mongrel race. In 1889, British scholar Grant Allen stated in an article considered pertinent enough to Americans to be reprinted in *Popular Science Monthly* (1889:173) "To the end of all time, it is mathematically demonstrable that most women must become the mothers of at least four children, or else the race must cease to exist." Eighteen years later, this belief still retained its potency: in 1907, Theodore Roosevelt was exhorting American women to marry and produce their share of four for the good of America (Hofstadter 1955:189).

Further, the feminist push for the vote, for an adequate education, for justice in the areas of property laws, divorce, the right to a job and to control over their own earnings, all sent great shock waves through the value systems of many Americans. American scientists, of course, were no exception. Many of their arguments about these issues, both pro and con, were phrased in the language of what the laws of evolution "proved" about the natural capacities of the woman. These capacities usually were less than (or at least different from) those of the man. One gentleman, writing in the *American Journal of Sociology*, granted that the category "human beings" must include "women, children, slaves, foreigners" (Crafts 1896:507); while he was somewhat more revealing in his assumption of feminine inferiority than were many others, his attitude was not atypical. In any case, whether she was considered man's inferior, his equal, or his superior, "the new woman" (a common catchphrase of the 1890's) was the object of much concern — and not a little moralizing — by the scientists of human experience.

In 1895, psychologist G. T. W. Patrick evaluated the evidence from "modern anthropological studies" that bore upon the four leading theories of women's "peculiarities." Patrick's paper deserves some attention, because it included essentially all the major bioevolutionist speculations about human sex differences as they were understood by late nineteenth century American scientists. The four theories as listed by Patrick (1895:210) were:

1.   Woman is a "stunted or inferior man and represents arrested development."

2.   Woman is a grown-up child, belonging to "the child type."

3.   Woman is indeed a "child type," but this is "in truth the race type and represents greater perfection" than man, "whose natural characteristic is senility."

4.   Throughout the animal world, the female is physically superior in size and vitality, "and more truly represents the essential qualities of the species."

Patrick examined the physical and psychological evidence for each of these theories in some detail. The data bearing upon psychological differences between male and female are particularly interesting, because remnants of yesterday's science can still be found in today's folk wisdom. Briefly: the female's perception is "decidedly quicker," although "less accurate"; she is more subjective (thus a poorer critic and rarely an impartial judge); her mind is better adapted to the "concrete and individual" than to the formation of abstract concepts; her memory is superior; she is better at "quick associative reasoning," but lacks "logical feeling" and is "less disturbed by inconsistency.... Analysis is relatively distasteful to them [women], and they less readily comprehend the relation of the part to the whole." Their thought is "less methodical and less deep."

The woman is more patient and more intuitive; she excels in tact, reaches her mental maturity earlier, and is very good at routine work but cannot endure protracted overwork. She is less original ("woman's thought pursues old rather than new lines"), more conservative (she "acts as society's balance-wheel"), more emotional, but less prone to strong passions and "appetites," more religious, and more moral. She is fearful and timid. Her greatest virtue is altruism; her greatest vice, untruthfulness (Patrick 1895:215–218).

Patrick concluded that all four theories were in part confirmed, except in their implications of feminine inferiority. Yet the female is truly different from the male and ought to be treated accordingly. May not woman be "too sacred to be jostled roughly in the struggle for existence"? Does she therefore not deserve from man "a reverent exemption from some of the duties for which his restless and active nature adapts him"? (Patrick 1895:225). Patrick thought so, as did British student of mental evolution George J. Romanes.

Romanes' list of feminine virtues and defects overlapped considerably with Patrick's. He presented the female as inferior to the male except in the more altruistic emotions (she is "mentally and physically the weaker vessel" [1887:385]), while denying that she is inferior (her "type of human nature" is at least equal to the male's), and made a rather patronizing bow to her (she is "the sweetest efflorescence of evolution" [1887:397]). However, as we shall see later, she is uniquely suited to bloom in the home and will quickly wither outside its walls.

Despite Patrick's and Romane's peculiar disclaimer of feminine inferiority, the argument about which sex was higher on the phylogenetic scale consumed much scientific energy and was spread across many pages in late nineteenth century scientific periodicals. To answer the question, debaters from the sciences of human experience borrowed heavily from biological sources. We shall look at five such biological concepts and some uses to which they were put in determining the relative evolutionary positions of male and female. They are: (1) environmental determination of sex, (2) variation, (3) physical sturdiness and vitality, (4) the evolution of the maternal instinct, and (5) inheritance through the male.

Among the plethora of theories attempting to solve the riddle of what caused an organism to be male or female, there were those stating that environmental stimuli such as temperature and nutrition were the causative factors. When such a theory of external determination of sex was cast in an evolutionist mold, it could be used to contrast the female unfavorably with the male. For example, W. K. Brooks (1885:325) stated that a "favorable environment" (defined as one conducive to a high birthrate) causes "an excess of female births, and an unfavorable environment an excess of male births." Brooks' materials indicate how primitive the early collection of demographic data must have been: wild animals, Hottentots, and residents of rural areas, barren regions, and cold climates have a high rate of male births, while their more fortunate counterparts — domesticated animals, Boers, and residents of towns, fertile regions, and warm climates — have a high rate of female births.

Why does this law of nature hold? Because

the female is the conservative factor in reproduction, and new variations are caused by the influence of the male. While the environment remains favorable, no change is needed, but as the conditions of life become unfavorable, variation becomes necessary to restore the adjustment (Brooks 1885:328).

The implications of an evolutionist theory of environmental determination of sex for defining the human female's place in society are sharply apparent in a series of articles by sociologist W. I. Thomas (1897, 1898, 1899a, 1899b, 1899c).[3] In these articles, Thomas set out to extend the theory of Geddes and Thomson (1889) of sex differentiation from "the lower forms of life" to humans. The theory distinguishes the sexes on a metabolic dimension: anabolism and catabolism.

The plant is anabolic: it stores energy, stays in one place, "converts lifeless into living matter, expending little energy and living at a profit." The animal, however, is catabolic: it roams, consumes energy, can "prey upon the plant world and upon other animal forms," and "lives at a loss of energy." Thomas (1897:31) believed that human males tend to be catabolic; females, anabolic.[4] Or, put another way, "femaleness is an expression of the tendency to store nutriment" (1897:34).

Not only are there basic metabolic differences between male and female, but metabolic factors also determine which sex an organism will be. The female is the result of a surplus of nutrition or of outbreeding: both factors increase metabolism, and increased metabolism produces females. Thomas used demographic techniques to prove his point. Two of many interesting examples are data from furriers ("furriers testify that rich regions yield more furs from females and poor regions more from males" [1897:32]) and statistics about Jews ("among the Jews, who

---

[3]   By the time thse articles were collected a few years later in *Sex and Society* (1907), Thomas' perspective had shifted somewhat from the biochemical to the cultural. A comparison of the journal articles with the book shows that they were in part rewritten; in 1907, Thomas acknowledged the existence of some cultural as well as biochemical causes of the female's apparent inferiority.

[4]   This same belief in the male nature as aggressively footloose and fancy-free, and in the female nature as quietly, peacefully stationary, is implicit in a biologist's description (Watasé 1892) of the difference between "male" and "female" cells in the Mollusca: the male cell leads a "free and a more or less migratory existence," while the female cell is "sessile and non-migratory."

frequently marry cousins, the per cent of male births is very high" [1897:37]).

Thomas drew heavily upon these biochemical differences between the sexes in discussing the evolution of human society and the female's place. By placing her nearer to the plant, and thus lower on the evolutionary scale, Thomas limited her roles in human society to "natural" expressions of her anabolic nature, as all social structure and function stem from this "fundamental contrast in the metabolism of the sexes" (1897:59). The human female's roles all focus on maintaining the human community, and the chief means of so doing is through reproduction and care of the young.

While it would be going too far to say that theories of environmental determination of sex had to lead to a conclusion that the male is higher than the female on the phylogenetic scale, it is clear that Brooks' and Thomas' theories did exactly that. Similarly, both Brooks and Thomas spoke of variation in a manner that was weighted in favor of the male. This orientation was not peculiar to these men: assumptions of the superiority of variation *per se*, and the superior variation of the male were common to late nineteenth century discussions of male-female differences. Variation was considered important because it was presumably the mechanism of adaptation to the environment (Thomas 1897:37–39; Brooks 1885:328; Patrick 1895:216, 224).[5]

However, what VARIATION meant was not always clear; like many other catchwords from evolutionist thought, it was used in more than one sense. Thomas himself used at least three meanings of the term, the first of which was Darwin's law of the more complex development of "secondary sexual characters" in the male (Thomas 1897:38).[6]

Thomas' second use of the term can be traced to Haeckel's evolutionary interpretation of von Baer's biogenetic law.[7] Its application to

---

[5] Often, such "scientific" discussions were shot through with value-laden terms. Thus, one biologist (Montgomery 1896:293, note) speculated that the female may be more conservative and less progressive than the male, and passing a more (physiologically) monotonous existence than the latter, is less influenced by the struggle for existence, and accordingly is less variable structurally.

[6] Watasé (1892:492) carried this law even further back: the sperm cell is more varied than is the ovum.

[7] "The individual organism reproduces in the rapid and short course of its own evolution the most important of the changes in form through which its ancestors, according to laws of Heredity and Adaptation [the latter defined as reproduction and nutrition], have passed in the slow and long course of their paleontological evolution" (Haeckel 1896, 1:2). This was first stated by Haeckel in *Generelle Morphologie* (1866). The catchphrase that usually summarizes the preceding is "ontogeny recapitulates phylogeny."

male-female differences, by Thomas and others, hinged on the idea that the female is closer to the child in evolutionary development. As Thomas put it, the woman is "intermediate in development between the child and the man" (1897:40). The woman has "infantile somatic characters" (i.e. a greater proportion of fat to muscle) and, as befits one not advanced to the developmental plane of the male, "a greater tendency to atavism" 1897:34, 40).

Thomas' third use of the term is closely tied to the second; it is that males vary more from each other, or from some norm. If this has mixed blessings for the male in one sense (there are more males than females at the extremes of genius and idiocy), its implications for the superiority of the white civilized male are nonetheless very clear: "Morphological differences are less in low than in high races, and the less civilized the race the less is the physical difference of the sexes" (1897:43, 41). As we shall see later, in the discussions of the maternal instinct and of education, the more alike the sexes are deemed to be, the more gloomy are the prognoses for Western civilization.

All three meanings of VARIATION implied that progress comes through the male. Because an evolutionist by definition valued change, in the sense of adaptation to the environment, the sex that varied more, in whatever sense of the word, was the progressive sex.

However, there were dissenters from these perspectives on variability. Patrick noted that WHICH sex one thought to be superior depended upon one's evaluation of the importance of variation (1895:224). Anthropologist Daniel G. Brinton (1894) pointed out that Havelock Ellis believed that the female's lesser variability makes her the source of evolutionary development. Ellis' reasoning was that the female is closer to the child, and that this is to her advantage. Man, on the other hand, quickly deteriorates from age three onward; to an extent, his growth is a plunge downward to degeneration and senility. "Hence, the true tendency of the progressive evolution of the race is to become child-like — to become feminine."

Eliza Burt Gamble agreed with the common view that the male shows greater variability in secondary sexual characters but disagreed that this advances the species (Patrick 1894a). On the contrary, "ornaments" such as "colors, wattles, beard" are produced at the cost of deterioration. It is the female who is at the highest stage of development in all orders of life.

Ellis and Gamble, then, accepted the notion that the female is the less variable sex but found this to be to her advantage in the evolutionary process. Two other scientists presented an unusual argument: Karl

Pearson and Alice Lee (1897) found that the civilized female is MORE variable than the male, and that this greater variability is caused by the decrease in the struggle for existence. Because the lessened struggle affects woman more than it does man, she therefore has the greater tendency toward variation.

Several writers commented on the greater physical sturdiness of the female but drew opposing conclusions about its meaning for her place on the evolutionary scale. Thomas felt that her hardiness was yet further evidence of her backwardness. He noted that "lower forms" can regenerate a lost organ. While the human female is not capable of such a feat, nonetheless "the lower human races, the lower classes of society, women and children" all have a better tolerance for surgery than does the physiologically more sensitive male of the higher races and classes (Thomas 1897: 50).

However, Gamble and physiologist A. Mosso (1892), both of whom believed the female is higher up the scale than is the male (Mosso cited as evidence the female's pelvic structure and her absence of body hair), stated that her greater physical hardiness (males die earlier and are more prone to disease) combined with the "fact" that more favorable conditions are needed to produce the female are proof of her superiority. (This last "fact," as we saw earlier, could be used to demonstrate exactly the opposite.)

The evolution of the maternal instinct was a subject of great interest to late nineteenth century scientists. As might be expected, W. I. Thomas had a great deal to say about it. First of all, natural selection provided the human female with the "altruistic sentiments" that make her wish to care for her newborn. Among the "lower animal forms," the "physiological waste" involved in spawning a thousand eggs is nature's way of ensuring the survival of one, in the absence of any natural feeling of mother love.

But a higher type of development involves a closer association between the parent and offspring, and this is secured through natural selection by a modified structure in the female, culminating among the mammals in the intra-uterine development of the young and the disposition in the female to care for the young after bringing them forth. The expansion of the abdominal zone in the female in connection with this modification of her reproductive system is the physical basis of the altruistic sentiments. Feeling is a physiological change, and its seat is not the encephalon, but the viscera.... The superior physiological irritability of woman, whether we call it sensibility, feeling, emotionality or affectability, is due to the fact of the larger development of her abdominal zone, and the activity of the physiological changes located there in connection with the process of reproduction (Thomas 1897: 60–61).

The first social unit in human society was thus the mother-child bond. However, the maternal instinct was not limited to this dyad, but expanded to all society. "Both social feeling and social organization are thus primarily feminine in origin — functions of the anabolism of woman" (Thomas 1897:60).

Psychologist G. Stanley Hall's discussions of motherhood (1891) focused, not upon its evolutionary origins, but upon its importance in ensuring that the child would pass through the proper stages of mental development.[8] Thus, motherhood is the woman's most important function. The mother "soon comes to stand in the very place of God" to the infant. At this stage of development, the less the child's rudimentary religious sentiments are cultivated toward the mother, "the more feebly they will be later felt toward God. This, too, adds greatly to the sacredness and the responsibilities of motherhood" (1891:199). Further, "the mother must not lose her influence over the child before adolescence,[9] when the maternal influences and home-ties should be at their strongest and best" (1891:200). A sacred trust indeed — and with only a passing mention of the importance of the father at this stage, Hall's psychology implicitly supported the conventional division of labor between the sexes: the mother in the home with the children, the father out in the world, earning their living.[10]

The evolution of the maternal instinct as an argument for a sex-based division of labor had a central place in the thinking of George J. Romanes and Edward D. Cope. Romanes believed that the maternal instincts are "perhaps the strongest of all influences in the determination of [her] character." They are inherited and cumulative, and derive from the long infancy and childhood of human children (Romanes 1887:392). For Cope (1888), the existence of the maternal instinct was terribly important, because it was an effective weapon to be wielded against advocates of woman suffrage (which was, of course, a major issue in 1888). Within the family, he argued, the sexes have different functions based upon their

[8] The von Baer/Haeckel biogenetic law was central to Hall's thinking; he believed that just as the embryo passes through all the stages of human biological history, so does the child's mental development recapitulate the stages of man's cultural history.
[9] Adolescence "does not normally end before the age of twenty-four or five" Hall 1891:205).
[10] Often, those who debated whether woman's sphere could include anything outside the home simply ignored the whole class of working women, spinsters, widows, etc., who had no choice about whether or not they would work. The dispute over working women was thus essentially a middle class and marriage-oriented argument. In general, those articles that did detail the miserable working conditions of the female proletariat were concerned with reform and did not bother with questions of sphere and duty. (For a representative article, see Anna S. Daniel [1892].)

"best emotions." These exalted feelings are the maternal instinct of the female and the masterful behavior of the male.

According to Cope (1888:721–722), these emotions and their correlative, the sex-based division of labor, evolved as follows: When the mode of reproduction changed from non-sexual to sexual, the male was freed from the "disabilities" of maternity to take a more active part in the struggle for existence. However, the female has continued to inherit the maternal "disability" (a curiously pejorative description of her "best" emotion) that keeps her from being active in the world. Thus, the biological imperative has decreed that the home is woman's proper sphere, while political activity must be the prerogative of the man.

In support of this belief, Cope drew upon two common arguments based upon woman's innate limitations: woman is neither rational (therefore, she cannot be just) nor physically capable of enforcing any law she might enact. In addition, he added a more singular argument against the subversion of "the natural evolution of humanity" that would result from granting women the vote — one based upon use inheritance. In effect, the vote would make woman's "feminine virtues" disappear altogether after a few generations, because "as in all evolution, disuse ultimately ends in atrophy" (1888:728). Gazing bleakly into the future, Cope predicted that the home would disappear, for women "would produce a race of moral barbarians, which would perish ultimately through intestine strife" (1888:728).[11]

The Darwinian principle of inheritance through the male could be used as another "proof" of woman's inferiority. This theory stated that inheritable characters were transmitted more fully to the male offspring; hence, over time, man gradually became superior to woman.

Sometimes, however, elements of the Anglo-Saxon racism which was so prominent in the late nineteenth century complicated scientific

---

[11] Late nineteenth century scientists were quite interested in Cesare Lombroso's theories of the female criminal, which were couched in an evolutionist framework in *La donna delinquente* [The criminal woman]. As the subject of female criminality is peripheral to this discussion, I refer the reader to Helen Zimmern (1893) and to G. T. W. Patrick (1894) for an explication (and, seemingly, an acceptance) of Lombroso's views, and to Daniel G. Brinton (1898) for a rejection of them. One point, however, is particularly pertinent: according to Zimmern (1893:222), Lombroso said that the few women who are born criminals have "a total want of maternal affection, pity, and love; they are excessively erotic and revengeful." As Lombroso accepted the prevalent idea that maternity and chastity are the strongest feminine sentiments, his conception of the female criminal is, obviously, a reversal of these. But more than that, this set of traits is usually thought of as part of "masculine" human nature. They are, in moderation, useful for warriors and pioneers, and are thus not in themselves defined as "criminal" in the male.

discourse on the subject, so that some females proved to be biologically superior to some males. For example, Cope believed that the female of a "higher race" is superior to the male of a "lower race" because she has inherited (from her father, of course) "the general progress of the race" (1888:722). Because Cope believed that inherited characters are much more influential than are acquired ones, the male of the species, particularly the male of the penultimate races, not only must be the source of race progress, but also is the parent through which such progress is transmitted.

The idea of the male's role in inheritance received a wild twist in a pair of articles appearing in *Science* ("The persistency of family traits": Williams 1892). The first article stated that the first male to impregnate a female indelibly stamps the characteristics of all future offspring. ("Every breeder of cattle knows that a pure-bred heifer that is first coupled with a mongrel bull is ruined for breeding purposes" ("The persistency of family traits" [1892:156]). Moreover, "the influence of the male as determining the character of the offspring increases with each successive pregnancy of the female by the same male."

The second article applauded the first and expanded upon it with two further notions: (1) Family members come to resemble one another on the paternal side because when the mother's blood circulates through the fetus and returns to her, "the strain of blood derived from the father is shared by the young with the mother." Thus, with each succeeding child, the proportion of paternal blood increases, and each child inincreasingly resembles the father. (2) In a "love match, the face of the father is reproduced," because the mother dwells on the father's features and this "marks" the child (Williams 1892:221).

Both social and biological scientists, as we have seen, applied evolutionist thought to "the woman question" in a manner that, instead of casting new light upon old prejudices, all too often perpetuated them with the aid of scientific "proofs." There were those, however, who disputed the validity of such judgments. In the words of one dissident, "the real tendencies of women can not be known until they are free to choose, any more than those of a tied-up dog can be" (Tanner 1896).

One factor that would help women to become "free to choose" was education. The question of educating women was hotly debated in the late nineteenth century, and those on either side of the issue turned to biological and social science for definitive answers.

For those scientists who worked within an evolutionist framework, science had to answer two questions: first, what kind of education did woman's natural capacities permit her to receive; and second, aside from the question of capacity, would the continued development of the race be served by educating her for anything outside her family duties? All too frequently the answers to these questions reinforced each other, as science and conventional social values became hopelessly entangled.

Bioevolutionist theory unquestionably provided important support for those who wished to maintain the traditional American practice of educating the female (if at all) in subjects that would be useful to her in her role as wife and mother. To take the principle of variation as an example, it was only a short step from the "fact" that the female is underrepresented among geniuses (Thomas 1897:43; Patrick 1895:216) to a belief that if she attempts to compete intellectually with men, she is wasting her time and fighting nature's dictates. It was also easy to move from the belief that "the female is the conservative factor in reproduction" (Brooks 1885:328) to the idea that she is of conservative and unoriginal mind. ("Her tendency is toward reproduction, while man's is toward production" [Patrick 1895:216].) There were, of course, opponents of such beliefs. One observer commented that "the prevalent theory of the essentially conservative nature of woman's intelligence seems to me a fiction of the male intelligence, maintained in order to keep this inconvenient radicalism of woman in check" (J.D. 1894).[12]

Many social scientists believed that evidence from biological science showed the female's chief abilities to be reproduction and child care (the latter because of her natural "altruism," developed over eons by the long infancy of human children); showed her to be less variable, less logical and rational, more emotional and instinctual, and more prone to break down physically from mental overwork than was the more highly developed male. These beliefs, of course, had great implications for the question of what subjects she could be expected to learn. And behind all the debate over her "natural" capacities loomed the twin specters of the decline of the traditional family (with its traditional helpmeet and mother) and of "race suicide," caused by the apparently declining birthrate in the educated classes.

If it could be demonstrated that the female brain was anatomically inferior to that of the male, this would be powerful evidence to be used against those women who demanded the right to an equal education. There would be actual proof of British physician Withers-Moore's dictum (transplanted to a leading American periodical) that "Bacon's mother (intellectual as she was) could not have produced the *Novum Organum,*

---

[12] This was probably John Dewey, who was at that time a "cooperating editor" of the *Psychological Review.*

but she, perhaps she alone, could and did produce Bacon" (Linton 1886).[13]

In 1887, a debate between physician William A. Hammond (1887a, 1887b) and anthropologist Helen H. Gardener (1887) over sex-linked differences in the human brain erupted in the pages of the *Popular Science Monthly*. After six months, the editors called an end to the battle on the grounds of space limitation, after giving Hammond the last, as well as the first, word.

In his initial article, Hammond claimed that with "nations low in the scale of progress" (1887a:731), male and female brain size is very similar. However, the evolution of higher civilization brings with it an increasing difference in favor of the male brain, with the crucial factor being the relative amount of gray matter. Therefore, "the larger the brain the greater the mental power of the individual" (1887a:730–731).[14]

Gardener promptly supplied evidence from "twenty leading brain anatomists, microscopists, and physicians of New York" (1887:266) to refute Hammond's statements. Hammond immediately counterattacked with HIS set of authorities, and threw a sneak punch against the presumptuous lady anthropologist and her "defective logical power, which appears, for the present at least, to be a characteristic of most female minds" (1887b:555).

Often scientists refused to say that women's minds were inferior to men's—merely that they were DIFFERENT. This was a variant of the "separate but equal" doctrine that in this same period in American history was being applied by whites to Negroes. As this "difference" was applied to the education of women, however, it condemned them to be kept ignorant of many subjects that were suited only to the masculine mentality. And the lack of such study (principally in science and mathematics), in addition to the disparagement of women's attempts to educate themselves sufficiently to broaden the narrow confines of their socially defined role, worked as a self-fulfilling prophecy to perpetuate the ideas of the female's limited "natural" mental capacity. Hammond, for example, believed that it was "the height of absurdity" to let girls study boys' subjects:

[13] Dr. Withers-Moore's comment was made in an address to the British Medica Association, August 10, 1886.
[14] Patrick ascribed the superiority of the male brain, not to gray matter, but to the size of the parietal region, which houses intelligence. Another common index of intelligence was brain weight: the female's brain supposedly averaged five ounces less than the male's. Further, brains of notable males (Georges Cuvier, 64.5 ounces; Daniel Webster, 53.5 ounces) were cited by Thomas, Hammond, Romanes, and others as evidence of male superiority.

"The effort to cram mathematics, for example, into the female mind almost always results in failure." He had "seen many cases of girls whose nervous systems have been woefully disturbed in the endeavor to master algebra, geometry, spherical trigonometry, and other mathematical branches of knowledge that could not by any possibility be of use to them" (1887a:722). And even if they knew their studies well, it "would not enhace their loveliness or render them any happier" (1887a:722). (It seems a virtual certainty that no scientist ever evaluated the appropriateness of a course of study for males on the grounds of whether or not it would make them handsomer or happier.)

Romanes, as noted above, denied the inferiority of the "feminine type of human nature." At the same time, however, he insisted upon her "marked inferiority of intellectual power," particularly her lack of originality (1887: 383). He believed that this handicap would never be overcome, for one could not suppose that "any exception to the general laws of evolution can have been made in her favor" (1887: 394). Romanes did not oppose the education of woman, provided that the curriculum neither trained her for "any professional or otherwise foolish rivalry with men" nor encouraged "intellectual specialization" (1887:400). Its purpose was solely to enhance her natural skills as wife and mother.

The idea that the better-educated woman would be a better mother motivated much of the effort devoted to female education throughout the nineteenth century in America. It was within this context that Cope urged that a woman be given as much education as a man (consistent with maintaining her health), because women are "the mothers of the human race" (1888:724). Cope sought to quiet the fears of those who worried about the pernicious effects of education upon the home: "For the normal woman, the home-life is both the easiest and the happiest" (1888:725). In short, no true woman would want to leave her sphere. To force her to do so (as a victory for the pro-suffrage forces would presumably do) would "check the development of woman as such" (1888:725).

Patrick's survey of the scientific evidence bearing upon sex-linked differences in intellectual capacity indicates what the woman seeking an education in 1895 must have been up against. She was believed to be "particularly adapted" to vocal music, the stage, learning languages, writing novels, and teaching. She was, however, "less adapted" to science, discovery, and invention; she could not compare to men in logic (she lacks "logical feeling" and is "less disturbed by inconsistency"), nor in arts, sciences, and philosophy (her thought is "less methodical and less deep"). She might well outperform man in college, because she would reach her mental maturity earlier, but he would excel afterward, when it really mattered (1895:215–216).

Within the bioevolutionist perspective, then, scientific opinion about the natural capacities of woman shaped the concepts of these same scientists about what nature had decreed woman could (and should) learn. By and large, most opinion severely limited her options. However, enough differences of opinion existed to occasionally touch off spirited debates. Two Italian scholars had opposing ideas on the subject that were sufficiently interesting to the psychologist-editors of the *Pedagogical Review* to warrant their summary and transmission to the American scientific community (Chamberlain 1892). "Professor Sergi of Rome" announced that woman's smaller brain and inferior intellect ("Where is the female Titian, Wagner, Goethe, Shakespeare? Where the lady Darwin or Edison?")[15] were a "blessing to humanity," for "'if woman were equal to man in intellectual power, it would introduce into the social struggle a new and violent competition'" (Chamberlain 1892:478). Sergi believed that woman should be educated to develop her twin abilities of "equilibirum and practicality," and not to compete with men. ("Useful to her would be knowledge of social facts and happenings, the constitution of the family, regulation of the state and the like," and "such facts of scientific character as might be of use in the household.")

A. Mosso, who felt the female was phylogenetically superior to the male, emphatically denied Sergi's conclusions. If the female is inferior to the male, stated Mosso, the reasons are social, for man has enslaved her, and male supremacy has created and maintained the division of labor. She is entirely able to compete intellectually with men (Mosso 1892:232).

If the question of woman's natural capacity for education aroused much debate among evolutionists, so too did the issue of whether such education might be harmful to the development of the race. In the late nineteenth century, when America was being (as it seemed to some) overrun by immigrants, "the good of the race" required American women to bear children in numbers sufficient to keep the superior native stock from being eliminated. Would educating the female reduce the number of children she would otherwise have? Would it make those offspring she DID manage to produce sickly and feeble? Many Americans were obsessed by such fears; for scientific authority they had the famous Herbert Spencer.

Spencer postulated that because the "cost of reproduction" is much

---

[15]   This was a common proof of female inferiority. Other frequently cited giants were Newton, Michelangelo, and Mozart.

greater for the female than for the male, she must maintain good health in order to be able to reproduce. Education has a pernicious effect upon her reproductive capacity, because "absolute or relative infertility is generally produced in women by mental labour carried to excess." Thus, "the deficiency of reproductive power" among upper-class girls

may be reasonably attributed to the overtaxing of their brains — an overtaxing which produces a serious reaction on the physique. This diminution of repro-ductive power is not shown only by the greater frequency of absolute sterility; nor is it shown only in the earlier cessation of childbearing; but it is also shown in the very frequent inability of such women to suckle their infants. In its full sense, the reproductive power means the power to bear a well-developed infant, and to supply that infant with the natural food for the natural period. Most of the flat-chested girls who survive their high-pressure education are incompe-tent to do this (Spencer 1896:II, 485–486).

American scientific periodicals provided space for those who considered the issue of whether or not the female's reproductive capacities were drained by mental work and the implications this had for her education. The *Popular Science Monthly* in particular devoted a relatively large amount of space to the matter.

The same Withers-Moore who extolled Mrs. Bacon's reproductive capacties warned that the woman who overstudies draws upon her "capital stock of vital force and energy" and is left "quite inadequate for maternity." Because of her selfishness, "the human race will have lost those who should have been her sons" (Linton 1886:173). Those who should have been her daughters are left unmentioned.

Lucy M. Hall, a physician at Vassar, undertook to correct Withers-Moore. While Dr. Hall agreed that "in America the small and rapidly diminishing numbers in the family is a matter of grave national import" (1887:612), one of her studies showed that "the largest families of the present generation belong to the most highly educated of the women" (1887:614). The two major reasons why women have small families are, first, physical disability (stemming from a multiplicity of causes, which range from the obviously physical, such as tight corsets and lack of exercise, to more nearly psychogenic factors, such as "pampered idle-ness" and a turning in upon themselves because they have nothing else to do); second, a disinclination to bear children. In either case, higher education has no pernicious effect upon reproduction — indeed, just the opposite is true. Mosso agreed with Hall. If a woman goes to college, she will not become unfeminine: 562 women who received degrees from Cambridge and Oxford had more children than did other women who were not so educated.

Among those with ideas on the subject was John Dewey, and his views were decidedly not in sympathy with those of Hall and Mosso. Dewey (1886) examined a study by the Massachusetts Labor Bureau of the health college alumnae. The general conclusion of the study had been that "the pursuit of collegiate education is not in itself harmful" (Dewey 1886:609). Dewey, however, disagreed. He noted (1886:610) that

the most important fact regarding the higher education of woman is, that we are educating wives and mothers. Few probably will regret this, but those few must still admit the fact in a society constituted like ours.

Given this undeniable truth, Dewey pointed to the implications of certain data: (1) of female graduates, 74 percent were single and only 26 percent were married, although the average years since graduation numbered more than six; (2) of married graduates, 37 percent had no children, although the average length of marriage was 6.2 years; (3) the 109 graduates who had borne children had produced only 205, of these, 12 percent had died; (4) among all married couples, there were 1.2 children per five years of marriage.

Dewey left these figures "to speak for themselves." Given his emphasis upon educating women for the wife-mother role, the message seems clear indeed.

Grant Allen, who calculated that the survival of the race depended upon each woman producing a minimum of four offspring, cited "Darwinian principles" (the community must increase to ensure "national health and vigor" [1889:170]) and Francis Galton ("a certain amount of overpopulation is necessary for survival of the fittest" [1889:172, note]) to demonstrate that women must not "shirk their natural duties" (1889:171). If woman was to be little more than a brooder hen, this necessity shaped the nature of the education she should receive. Clearly, she was not to be trained to leave the home, for each defection would mean that "a heavier task must be laid upon the remainder" of her sex (1889: 171). But the problem was not simply that the educated woman might choose not to become a breeder; if she were given "false education" (i.e. admitted to the curricula formerly reserved for men), she would become "unsexed." She would become "a dulled and spiritless epicene automaton.... Both in England and America, the women of the cultivated classes are becoming unfit to be wives or mothers." Even if she married, she would be "ill adapted to bear the strain of maternity." If there were children, these could only be "feeble and futile descendants" (1889: 179).

There was, then, considerable argument about whether education did or did not drain the "vital force" of women. ⸜oth supporters and opponents of this theory, in citing contrary sets oɪ data concerning the number of children produced by educated women, accepted (at least implicitly) the idea that woman's major function was to produce large numbers of healthy children for the good of the race, and that education was helpful to the extent that it did not interfere with this function.

Evolutionism, however, was broad enough to produce arguments that questioned the Spencerians' assumptions. In a reply to Grant Allen, Alice B. Tweedy (1890) remained within the ground rules of the discussion, but she shifted its focus. Although she denied that college education affects the health of female students or the production of healthy children, she said that the decline in the number of marriages was, in one sense, fortunate, because educated women were no longer forced to marry, "in defiance of natural selection" (1890:752). If the right to choose a husband (even on bioevolutionist grounds) were important, then some women need not marry. The "natural selection" argument had been shifted from Allen's emphasis on overproduction of offspring so that the fittest of these might survive and advance the race, to Tweedy's emphasis on a kind of natural selection that was based, paradoxically, upon the female's freedom of choice. If the good of the race was important, so too was the good of the individual.

Still another evolutionist perspective appeared in an unsigned "Review of: *The family*, by Charles F. and Carrie Thwing" (1887). The reviewer's feeling was that the growing social and legal independence of women was helping to curb the growth of population, which was reaching its limits. If some women could achieve self-support, the reviewer went on, then they would not need to marry. Remaining single, they would not contribute to the birthrate. And so,

evolution seems to be creating motives and an environment that will modify the effects of the most powerful of human instincts, and just at a time that will prevent the pressure from being too abruptly imposed upon civilization.

Although the question of education was not raised explicitly here, it was nevertheless present. Economic independence was not likely to come to the uneducated woman, and both those who would let her achieve autonomy and those who would tie her to her traditional sex roles were well aware of that.

Virutally all of the evolutionists examined thus far focused upon the female's "natural" physical and mental traits in a manner that reflected their belief that her most important functions must take place within the family unit, subordinate to the husband. Or as Romanes put it, quoting an unnamed authority on the subject: "'The position of man is to stand, of woman to lean'" (1887:392).

Many social scientists believed that just as the evolutionary process had led woman upward to her place within the walls of the patriarchal Victorian home, so had the family institution itself evolved from its prehistoric origins to its status as the keystone of Western civilization. Thus, theories of the origin and evolution of the family had great import for "the woman question." This final section of the paper will examine some of the elements of evolutionist family theory that had implications for the place of the woman in society.

Most late nineteenth century students of the family accepted a set of common assumptions: first, that all races, societies, and institutions go through the same stages of cultural evolution, although the "higher" races attain heights of civilization never reached by less gifted peoples; second, that the study of animal societies and primitive tribes gives valid evidence of civilized man's social institutitions as they were at "lower" stages; third, that the study of cultural artifacts, such as myths, ancient ruins, and "survivals," provides further knowledge of the origins of human institutions; and fourth, that the family in some form was the original social institution from which all other human institutions followed. As one social scientist proclaimed, "Here was the first social tie on earth, the beginning of the state" (Mason 1889:10).

Although it was commonly accepted that the family was the first social unit, there was wide disagreement about its original form. Was it patriarchal or matriarchal? Promiscuous or monogamous? Social scientists argued the issues in their periodicals. Those who believed that the family was originally patriarchal cited the theories of Aristotle and Maine; those who felt that it was promiscuous and matriarchal (the two forms were often linked by theorists) drew upon the work of Morgan and McLennan; and those who insisted that it was monogamous had the considerable authority of Westermarck behind them.

The majority of social scientists who commented upon the matriarchal-patriarchal dispute in the periodicals sampled agreed that the family had originally been matriarchal in structure. One who disagreed was Adolpho Posada, who surveyed the late nineteenth century "researches, opinions, and speculations" concerning the prehistoric family and then came out in favor of the theory of patriarchal origin. Three bits of linguistic evidence were offered in support: (1) the radicals "pa" and "ma" appear in many languages to denote father and mother; (2) "pa" is easier to pronounce, and therefore it is an older sound than "ma";

and (3) "pa" is a harsher sound than "ma," and therefore it must be associated with male authority. (One reviewer [Lindsay 1897] observed that he did not believe that this "interesting" suggestion would hold up.)

E. B. Tylor (1896) believed that the original unit had been patriarchal, that it had shifted to an exogamous maternal system at a later stage of development when tribes decided to bring in more men in order to strengthen themselves, and that still later it had "reverted" back to the lower paternal form. This occurred for two reasons dictated by nature: (1) because reversion itself is natural, and (2) because the man's superior strength makes him the natural head of the family.

One who opted for matrilineality and female dominance ("mother-right") in the original form of marriage was O. T. Mason (1889). However, although this form obviously did not persist, Mason did not deal directly with the implications of a sex-based shift in power. Instead, he merely noted that evolutionary theory tells us that the human species could not have survived, much less have been the "most favored" (because it has made the most progress), if one half had persecuted the other.

W. J. McGee (1896) developed a theory that three "culture grades" of "marital regulations and observances" preceded the era of Old Testament history, with its patriarchal and polygynous marital customs. In the first stage, marriage is "a collective institution for the benefit of the group" (1896:379), a "single great family of women" with "warlike spouses." Marriage is monogamous at this most primitive level, partly because it is the wish of the "reigning" women, partly because man's desire for marriage is "feeble." In this stage the man is a suitor "not so much from personal inclination as from tribal incentive" (1896:338). Monogamy itself at this early stage is "perhaps a heritage from bestial ancestry," which hardly gives it the high valuation it had when it emerged as the model of Christian marriage.

W. I. Thomas accepted a matriarchal theory of early social organization, not because paternity was uncertain (as McLennan and Morgan had said), but because the mother-child bond was "the closest in nature.' This closeness derived from the maternal instinct and from constant contact. Thus, physiology and propinquity made the mother-child dyad the first social unit, to be followed later by a maternal system of organization. "The primitive respect shown mothers" is a "survival" from the maternal stage.

However, Thomas disagreed with those (such as Bachofen) who equated the maternal system of descent with political power. Thus, he took up the question that Mason had ignored:

While it is natural that the children and the group should grow up about the mother, it is not conceivable that woman should definitely or long control the activities of society, especially on their motor side. In view of his superior power of making movements and applying force, the male must inevitably assume control.... There has never been a moment in the history of society when the law of might, tempered by sexual affinity, did not prevail.

Even in the lower prematernal and maternal stages of social organization, the male was "the carrier of the social will" (Thomas 1898:761–763).

Solotaroff (1898) stated that "social sentiment" was the original social tie that preceded any form of family organization, although he agreed with Thomas that the first family unit may well have been mother and child. He did not, however, invoke the "closeness" of this bond, citing instead the temporary nature of sexual unions, which was caused by the earliest humans having a definite mating season and by the sexual fickleness of the male. Fortunately, the evolutionary mechanism proved immensely helpful, as "natural selection worked in favor of those offspring only which were nourished by the secretions of the mother, and thus Nature herself dispensed with paternal care" (1898:234, note).

Thorstein Veblen (1899), alone among the social scientists sampled, spoke of the original family as "the household of the unattached woman." This form was characterized by "an absence of coercion or control in the relation between the sexes" and by a fairly enduring monogamous relationship terminable by the choice of either partner. As we shall see, this stage of family organization disappeared with the evolution of society from savagery to barbarism.

The preceding perspectives on the original form of the family are instructive not only as relics from early social science, but also for their assumptions about the place of the primitive female. In the absence of fact, these scientists drew conclusions that were based in large measure upon their own culture-specific values. Thus, it is hardly surprising to learn that the original male had "natural" authority; that he was the natural head of the family; that the female had a greater sense of social responsibility and a weaker sex impulse; and that motherhood conferred upon woman an exalted status that placed her somewhere near the angels. Although the long and arduous process of evolution had supposedly culminated in a male and female that were very different from the original savage pair, the prehistoric couple who sprang from the pens of these scientists would have fit without too much difficulty into late nineteenth century civilized society.

Regardless of the position taken on the question of the original family, it was generally agreed that at some "stage of development" the male became dominant, by reason of his greater strength, his stronger sex drive, his insistence upon exogamous marriage, or some similar reason relating to his greater sexuality or aggressiveness. Tylor opted for the male's superior strength; John R. Commons, Veblen, Thomas, and Solotaroff agreed that strength was a key factor, combined with the male's greater sexual aggressiveness and desire for variety, which led to a restless search for wives from outside the tribe. W. J. McGee stressed the sexual factors. Whatever reasons were given for man's takeover, it was agreed that the evolutionary process had so determined the outcome that there had been no alternative.

Solotaroff, for example, drew upon the work of Thomas, Mason, Ploss, and Havelock Ellis to detail the primary "bio-psychic" characteristics of the early male and female, and concluded that these traits, which were part of humanity's animal inheritance, dictated the shift in power from female to male. The female expressed her "bio-psychic individuality" through reproduction; she was relatively passive, reticent, and uninterested in sex. The male, on the other hand, desired strange women and sexual variety; he preferred to roam, to care for himself, and to exert "very powerful muscular effort." Given these differences, it was inevitable that the female was led into marital bondage: she was forcibly taken by the more powerful male, and once burdened with children, she needed his help and protection (Solotaroff 1898:241–242).

John R. Commons also commented on the female's essential helplessness, so that the need for food, clothing, and shelter "bind wife and children to the fate and service of the bread-winner" (1899:8). He believed that self-consciousness, man's distinctive psychic characteristic, had emerged in the evolutionary process at the exogamous stage of family development — that is, at the time when men began to desire more than one wife.

Commons' reasoning on this point is rather interesting. Following McLennan, he stated that exogamous mating arose because the custom of female infanticide produced a shortage of women. Murder would seem to have been a direct way of expressing the feeling of one sex that the other was undesirable. But then, following Westermarck, Commons listed among reasons for the desire for plural wives some that would indicate that the female was highly desirable, in a limited sort of way: "freedom from periodical continence, attraction for female youth and beauty, taste for variety, desire for offspring, wealth, and authority" (1899:12). At any rate, with the rise of the institutions of polygyny and slavery, the patriarchate came into existence.

As noted earlier, Thomas equated the male's authority with his superior physical strength and motor skills, which came from his anabolic qualities. As man's motor skills and "militaristic" nature led him to expand his tribe's territory, women and slaves (some of the slaves obviously must have been male, but none had the good fortune to belong to "the progressive races" who "managed the space problem best") became unfree because "neither class showed a superior fitness on the motor side." At the end of the nineteenth century, however, women were once again becoming free because violence, according to Thomas's hopeful reading of the trend in civilized society, was no longer the major means of dominance (1898:776).

In McGee's three-stage theory of the beginnings of marriage, the shift from a matrilineal to a patrilineal system came in the third stage, although there were warning signs in stage two: at this point monogamy persisted chiefly through "inertia," and upper-status males had already begun to take female captives. In the third stage, the male became the suitor, polygyny and wife capture became the norm, and the power of divorce (and punishment for adultery) passed from the female to the male. The motivation for mating shifted from the collective good to individual initiative. "At least in the higher stages, complete subordination or even partial enslavement of women" existed. And the whole process was guided by nature's own hand, for "the course of development was shaped at each stage by the survival of the fittest among the groups" (McGee 1996: 383).

Veblen marked the transition from an egalitarian marital relationship to male dominance at the barbarian stage of culture, when the formerly peaceable male became predatory and began seizing women as trophies. Might became right, for "men who are trained in predatory ways of life and modes of thinking come by habituation to apprehend this form of the relationship between the sexes as good and beautiful" (Veblen 1899:507).

In most of these speculations upon the origin of male dominance, it was explicitly stated that the female was not only the subordinate partner, but also the male's personal property. Remember, for example, Commons' statement that the emergence of self-consciousness — that characteristic which marks man off from the mere animals — made possible the development of polygyny and slavery. At that point, when the male began his "individual appropriation" of women, the right to own private property that had been taken by force was commonly acknowledged for the first time. At that historic point Commons (1899:12–14) marked "the true beginning of the human family."[16]

[16] In very different ways, both Veblen and Havelock Ellis attached importance to clothing as a symbol of the female's status as an owned object. Ellis (1899) felt that the

Veblen's description of "ownership-marriage" (1899:508) based upon actual (and later, ceremonial) wife capture and Thomas' discussion of women and slaves as "unfree classes" were further indicators that social scientists saw early marriage as a coercive property relationship. Further, both men felt that the owner-owned relationship still survived in the marriage institution of their own day. Thomas (1898:770–771) attributed the woman's "socially constrained position in history" and her "hindrances" to the barbarous custom of wife purchase, which treated her as property to be bought and sold. And Veblen called the male-headed household a predatory institution which, for the female, is a condition of servitude. However, both Veblen and Thomas saw indications that the late nineteenth century woman might be regaining some measure of equality within the family. Thomas thought that the devaluation of violence would emancipate her, while Veblen saw the rise of the modern peaceful industrial society, which was incompatible with the old customs of status and ownership, as the liberating factor.

Thomas (1899b) viewed the status of women as property from a slightly different angle in "Sex in Primitive Morality." Here he spelled out the implications of moral codes, which he believed were originally developed by the dominant male sex, imposed upon women, and maintained by physical force. With the rise of the patriarchal family system, men dictated child marriage for females, insisted on suicide for widows, assumed the right of killing or mutilating an adulterous wife and her lover, hired out their wives as prostitutes, and developed other similar practices which assumed the owned status of the female. Woman accepted this male-imposed morality and has been a "faithful follower" ever since. However, Thomas expressed the hope that eventually the relatively more "feminine" behaviors (such as the Sermon on the Mount, non-resistance, asceticism, and chivalry) would become more prevalent as women became more independent and developed "forms of activity appropriate to their nature" (1899b:784–787). Although Thomas did not mention the fact, all these "feminine" behaviors are usually associated with males.

It is not far from an assumption that there are distinctive masculine and feminine behaviors to the belief in a sex-linked division of labor based upon these behaviors. In addition to the bioevolutionist arguments

---

habit of excessively clothing the female had its origins in the barbarian stage of culture when the jealous male wished to hide his women from the prying eyes of other males. Veblen (1899:200), on the other hand, stated that the "progress of specialization of functions in the social organism" had assigned to the female the duty of exhibiting the pecuniary strength of the household through such indicators as expensive, elaborate dress.

for such a division (essentially, that the woman's peculiar psychic capacities and instincts dictate her presence in the home), there were certain biocultural arguments predicated upon the evolution of the family and its functions.

Edward T. Devine (1894) remarked that woman's economic function (consumption) had been unjustly ignored by those who concentrated on man's economic function (production). Chivalrously he set out to rectify this neglect. First, Devine stated that "harmonious groups" advance "the social progress of the race" by being victorious over "the older and cruder groups." And they win because they "yield greater pleasure."

Although it may not be immediately apparent, the thesis is based entirely upon the traditional divison of labor, for the home is a harmonious blending of many parts, and the "mother's love for the family and the home she has made them" is "the very keystone in this arch of enjoyment that we call home." Devine insisted that this pretty picture was "not a sentimental but a purely economic view of woman's work," for "the power to confer pleasure is an economic concept" (1894:327–48).

Just as Devine glorified the Victorian woman's role, so too did Mason and Thomas insist upon the unique beauty of primitive woman's domestic functions. Devine's domesticated female consumed what her man produced; similarly, the "share" of Mason's modern AND prehistoric woman was to "gather up and conserve the spoils" that her mate had won in his strenuous "war on nature and on his fellow-man" (1889:4).

Mason's early woman was extremely busy and creative: she was the first cutler, butcher, currier, pack animal, gardener, farmer, tanner, tailor, etc. As the first "toy-maker, milliner, modiste, hatter, upholsterer, and wall-decker," she created "at a single pass half a dozen modern industries"; it was "her role of industrialism" that was to "transform the face of the earth" (1889:6). If she no longer controls these industries, it is because man has "co-operated" with woman's arts to develop them into modern industry, now that "militancy no longer demands all man's waking moments" (1889:8). Fortunately, she still has her role as mother, because human offspring are so slow to mature, and "if there should ever come a time when this office may be delegated to irresponsible and paid assistants, the best that woman ever did for this world will be canceled" (1889:9).

Thomas' list of the jobs of primitive woman was very similar to Mason's, but it was couched in his animal-vegetable theory of sex differences. Hence, the labors of animal-like man required "strength, violence, speed," and "craft and foresight" (1899a:474). In short, he hunted and fished. The natural labors of plantlike woman required "slow, unspasmodic, routine, stationary" skills. She (1) was interested in shelter for herself and her children; (2) cultivated plants (being plantlike, this was only natural); (3) prepared food; (4) wove baskets and made pottery to hold the food; and (5) developed spinning, weaving, and dyeing, which was "to be expected" of one so close to the vegetable (1899a: 480–484).

Thomas, too, had the male eventually taking over the female's industries with his superior organizing capacities and the inventive and technological skills developed in making weapons. At that point a surplus of food was at least possible, thanks to the male, and the conditions for culture came into existence at last. Eventually the men withdrew their ladies from labor, because of their "desire to preserve the beauty of women, and their desire to withdraw them from association with other men" (1899a:476).

Veblen, as usual, looked on the darker side. At the barbarian stage, when men became predatory and enslaved women, the division of labor also was changed to reflect the seizure of power. Men assigned themselves the "honorific employments" (particularly associated with hunting and fighting); women were assigned the "humiliating employments" (those associated with peacekeeping). This has carried over to the present, he noted — for women's work is still considered inferior to men's (1899:507). However, he expected the situation to change, as Western civilization evolved into peaceable industrialism and the patriarchal household disappeared.

Although Veblen welcomed the changing social structure that he hoped would liberate the female, many other social scientists of his time decidedly did not. It is ironic that a number of the arguments used to keep the female in her traditional place were phrased in the language of evolutionism, for evolution presupposed change.

Yet an increasing number of American women of the latter nineteenth century were not intimidated by the flood of "scientific" arguments against their greater participation in American life. And they had their supporters — such as the contributor of this item in the *Popular Science Monthly* 1891):[17]

As a general thing, when the importance of individuality has been insisted on, the individuality in view is that of man. It is he who has been exhorted to assert himself, to be true to his opinions, to live his own life; the exhortation has not been to any great extent addressed to his wife or his sisters. Enough for them if they can be so fortunate as to minister not unworthily to some grand male individuality. Women, however, though not particularly invited to the lecture, have been listening to it, and — what people do not always do with lectures or sermons — are applying it to themselves.

[17]   The editor of the *Popular Science Monthly* was William Jay Youmans.

REFERENCES

ALLEN, GRANT
  1889   Plain words on the woman question. *Popular Science Monthly* 36:170–181.
BRINTON, DANIEL G.
  1894   Review of: *Man and woman: a study of human secondary sexual characters*, by Havelock Ellis (1894). *Psychological Review* 1:532–34.
  1898   Current notes on anthropology. *Science* n.s. 8:787.
BROOKS, W. K.
  1885   Influences determining sex. *Popular Science Monthly* 26:323–330.
CHAMBERLAIN, A. F.
  1892   Review of: *Per l'educazione e la colture della donna*, by Professor Sergi (1892). *Pedagogical Seminary* 2:477–79.
COMMONS, JOHN R.
  1899   A sociological view of sovereignty. *American Journal of Sociology* 5:1–15.
COPE, EDWARD D.
  1888   The relationship of the sexes to government. *Popular Science Monthly* 33:721–30.
CRAFTS, WILBUR F.
  1896   Note to editor. *American Journal of Sociology* 1:507.
D., J.
  1894   Review of: *The psychic factors of civilization*, by Lester F. Ward (1893). *Psychological Review* 1:400–411.
DANIEL, ANNA S.
  1892   Conditions of the labor of women and children. *Journal of Social Science* 30:73–85.
DEVINE, EDWARD T.
  1894   The economic function of woman. *Annals of the American Academy of Political and Social Science* 5:361–76.
DEWEY, JOHN
  1886   Health and sex in higher education. *Popular Science Monthly* 28 606–14.
ELLIS, HAVELOCK
  1899   The evolution of modesty. *Psychological Review* 6:134–45.
FALKNER, ROLAND
  1897   Review of: *Domestic service*, by Lucy Maynard Salmon (1897). *Annals of the American Academy of Political and Social Science* 10:112–13.
GARDENER, HELEN H.
  1887   Sex and brain weight. *Popular Science Monthly* 31 266–69.
GEDDES, PATRICK, J. ARTHUR THOMSON
  1889   *The evolution of sex.* New York: Scribner.
HAECKEL, ERNST
  1896   *The evolution of man*, volume one. New York: D. Appleton.
HALL, G. STANLEY
  1891   The moral and religious training of children and adolescents. *Pedagogical Seminary* 1:196–210.

HALL, LUCY M.
1887   Higher education of women and the family. *Popular Science Monthly* 30:612–18.
HAMMOND, WILLIAM H.
1887a Brain-forcing in childhood. *Popular Science Monthly* 30:721–32.
1887b Reply to Gardener. *Popular Science Monthly* 31:554–58.
HOFSTADTER, RICHARD
1955   *Social Darwinism in American thought*. Boston: Beacon Press.

1891   Individuality for woman. Contribution to "Editor's Table." *Popular Science Monthly* 39:696–97.
LINDSAY, SAMUEL MC CUNE
1897   Review of: *Theories modernes sur les origines de la famille, de la société et de l'etat*, by Adolpho Posada (1892). *Annals of the American Academy of Political and Social Science* 10:109–10.
LINTON, E. LYNN
1886   The higher education of woman. *Popular Science Monthly* 30:168–80.
LOMBROSO, CESARE
1893   *La donna delinquente*. Turin.
MASON, OTIS T.
1889   Woman's share in primitive culture. *American Antiquarian* 11:3–13.
MC GEE, W. J.
1896   The beginning of marriage. *American Anthropologist* 9:371–83.
MONTGOMERY, TOHMAS H. JR.
1896   Organic variation as a criterion of development. *Journal of Morphology* 12:251–308.
MOSSO, A.
1892   The physical education of woman. *Pedagogical Seminary* 2:226–35.
O'NEILL, WILLIAM L.
1966   Divorce and the professionalization of the social scientist. *Journal of the History of the Behavioral Sciences* 2:291–302.
PATRICK, G. T. W.
1894a Abstract of: *The evolution of woman*, by Eliza Burt Gamble (G. P. Putnam's Sons, 1894). *Pedagogical Seminary* 3:174–75.
1894b Review of: *La donna delinquente*, by Cesare Lombroso (Turin, 1893). *Pedagogical Seminary* 3:176–78.
1895   The psychology of woman. *Popular Science Monthly* 47:209–25.
PEARSON, KARL, ALICE LEE
1897   On the relative variation and correlation in civilized and uncivilized races. *Science* n.d. 6:49–50.

1892   The persistency of family traits. *Science* 19:155–57.

1887   Review of: *The family*, by Charles F. and Carrie Thwing (Boston: Lee and Shepard, 1887). *Science* 10:283–84.
ROMANES, GEORGE J.
1887   Mental differences of men and women. *Popular Science Monthly* 31:383–401.

326 CAROL EHRLICH

SMALL, ALBION W.
1916 Fifty years of sociology in the United States, 1865–1915. *American Journal of Sociology* 21:711–864.

SOLOTAROFF, H.
1898 On the origin of the family. *American Anthropologist* 11:229–42.

SPENCER, HERBERT
1896 [1867] *The principles of biology*, volume two. New York: D. Appleton.

TANNER, AMY
1896 The community of ideas of men and women. *Psychological Review* 3:548–50.

THOMAS, W. I.
1897 On a difference in the metabolism of the sexes. *American Journal of Sociology* 3:31–63.
1898 The relation of sex to primitive social control. *American Journal of Sociology* 3:754–776.
1899a Sex in primitive industry. *American Journal of Sociology* 4:474–488.
1899b Sex in primitive morality. *American Journal of Sociology* 4:774–787.
1899c The psychology of modesty and clothing. *American Journal of Sociology* 5:246–262.
1907 *Sex and society: studies in the social psychology of sex.* Chicago: University of Chicago Press.

TWEEDY, ALICE B.
1890 Is education opposed to motherhood? *Popular Science Monthly* 36:751–760.

TYLOR, E. B.
1896 Abstract of: The matriarchal family system. *American Journal of Sociology* 1:330.

VEBLEN, THORSTEIN
1899 The barbarian status of women. *American Journal of Sociology* 4:503–514.

WATASÉ, S.
1892 On the phenomena of sex differentiation. *Journal of Morphology* 6:481–493.

WILLIAMS, EDWARD H. JR.
1892 The persistency of family traits. *Science* 19:221–22.

ZIMMERN, HELEN
1893 Review of: *La donna delinquente*, by Cesare Lombroso (Turin, 1893). *Popular Science Monthly* 44:218–322.

Legislation: An Aid in Eliminating
Sex Bias in Education in the United States

KATHRYN G. HEATH

Encouraging today is the growing realization in many parts of the world that discrimination against girls and women, like discrimination on the grounds of race, color, religion, or national origin, works to the disadvantage of society as a whole. Those discriminated against bear unnecessary burdens and scars, while the discriminators, in turn, end up with some unnecessary burdens and scars of their own. In addition, the Nation is deprived of the skills and talents of many people.

Encouraging, too, is the abundant historical evidence that a day of reckoning eventually comes. For education, that day is at hand across the length and breadth of the United States of America. *American Education*, an official popular voice in its field and the official journal of the Nation's Office of Education, puts it this way:

...change in customary ways of doing things, change of revolutionary proportions, is now enveloping education at every level.

At its core is the issue of women's rights — and more paricularly three pieces of Federal legislation that have made 1972 a climactic historical date in the drive by women for treatment in education equal to that afforded men (Dorr 1972:5).

Looking back over the years for perspective reveals certain early events that determined the location of education power within the Nation and that have had continuing influence on related Federal legislative action. Various later events played their parts in the gradual development in education as well as in other fields of a climate that is more favorable to remedial and constructive action on behalf of girls and women and is beneficial to all.

EDUCATION POWER

Puritan colonizers arriving in the New World in the seventeenth century believed that the people should determine for themselves how their children were to be instructed and reared. Shortly after the Declaration of Independence declared the united colonies to be "Free and Independent States" on July 4, 1776, these thirteen sovereign states adopted the Articles of Confederation, under which they loosely bound themselves together for the common good.[1]

Two of the ordinances enacted by the Continental Congress under this fundamental law have special pertinence in education. One, dated May 20, 1785, excepted and reserved lot number 16 of each township on lands in the Western Territory "for the maintenance of public schools." The other, dated July 13, 1787, includes a provision that "Religion, morality and knowledge being necessary for good government and the happiness of mankind, schools and the means of education shall forever be encouraged."[2]

Needs of the states for a stronger union resulted in the drafting of a new fundamental law, ratification of this instrument, and, by 1789, formation of the Nation under the Constitution of the United States of America.[3] A few months after the new Congress became operative, a law dated August 7, 1789, continued in effect under the Federal system the provisions of the 1787 ordinance.[4]

Neither the original version of the Constitution nor any addition or change through the ensuing years specifies an education power for the Nation. Such an omission is characteristic of national instruments of the eighteenth century. Unlike the United States Constitution, however, most eighteenth century national instruments have long since been abrogated or otherwise set aside.

With few exceptions, currently operative basic laws of nations were adopted since the cessation of hostilities of World War II. Most of these recently drafted instruments contain provisions on education. In general, they call either for centralized or for partially centralized and partially decentralized educational power. The United States is one of the very few nations of the world constituting an exception to this generalization (Heath, et al. 1962:75–78).

[1] *United States Code* 1: xxix-xxxi and xxxiii-xxxvii.
[2] An ordinance for ascertaining the mode of disposing of lands in the Western Territory and an ordinance for the government of the territory of the United States north west of the river Ohio. *Journals of the Continental Congress: 1774–1789* 28:378; 32:340.
[3] *United States Code* 1: xliii-liii.
[4] *United States Statutes at Large* 1: 50–53; *United States Code* 1: xxxix-xli.

Buttressing the seventeenth century philosophy of the people on the education of their children is Article Ten in the Bill of Rights, added to the Constitution on December 15, 1791. This article specifies: "The powers not delegated to the United States by the Constitution, nor prohibited by it to the States, are reserved to the States respectively, or to the people."[5]

In other words, the Constitution vests NO specific education power at the Federal level. Indeed, Article Ten initially served to nullify the many Federal efforts to pass legislation of any kind involving education in the various states of the union (Miller 1961). Though the outbreak of civil war in 1861 marked the beginning of many far-reaching changes, the impact of Article Ten continued to be pervasive.

SOME NINETEENTH CENTURY ACTION

WOMEN'S SUFFRAGE   Lucretia Mott and Elizabeth Cady Stanton called the first women's rights conference in the country. They were among the five women who used the Declaration of Independence as their model in drafting their Declaration of Sentiments and Resolutions to present at the Seneca Falls Convention of July 19–20, 1848. There some 300 women and men met to "discuss the social, civil and religious conditions and rights of women" (in Schneir 1972:76–82).

The ninth of twelve resolutions "Resolved that it is the duty of women in this country to secure to themselves their sacred right to the franchise." This resolution is the only one not adopted unanimously. It finally passed by a narrow margin after vigorous support by Frederick Douglass, a self-educated Negro leader who worked for abolition of slavery and became an adviser to Presidents.

In general, men in the eastern part of the country derided the idea of women voting. It was pioneer men in the West who first cast favorable votes recognizing that their pioneer womenfolk were just as deserving of the franchise as themselves. The Wyoming Territorial Legislature granted women the franchise in 1869 and insisted on retaining that right for women when the Territory became a State of the Federal Union in 1890.

The flamboyant feminist, Victoria Claflin Woodhull, who was to run for President of the United States in 1872, was invited to address the Committee on the Judiciary of the United States House of Representa-

---

[5]   *United States Code* 1: xlix.

tives in 1871. She suggested that women's suffrage is an implied right because of the XIVth and XVth Amendments to the Constitution, added in 1869 and 1870. They respectively define all "persons born or naturalized in the United States as citizens entitled to equal protection of the law and specify the right of "citizens" to vote.[6]

Women were arrested for voting in Rochester, New York, in 1872. Defense in the trial of the ringleader, Susan B. Anthony, on June 17–18, 1873, held that women are entitled to vote because of the Fourteenth Amendment. The court ruled otherwise (See Case No. 14, 459 in *The federal cases*; Schneir 1972:132–136).

That same year, the National Women's Suffrage Association (founded in 1869 by such women as Elizabeth Cady Stanton and Susan B. Anthony) addressed a petition "To the Honorable Senate and House of Representatives in Congress Assembled" to enact appropriate legislation "to protect women citizens in the several States of this Union, in their right to vote (letter from Anthony, et al. 1873). Half a century was to elapse before success came.

CONSTITUTION REEXAMINED Among the far-reaching effects of the Civil War in the 1860's was a fresh examination of the powers delegated to the Congress of the United States by the Constitution. Attention centered on the power of the Congress to "provide for the common Defence and general Welfare of the United States."[7] The result was a new interpretation of the scope of power retained at the Federal level which transcends that held at lower levels.

OFFICE OF EDUCATION CREATED The new interpretation of the Constitution helped to open the way for a Federal law enacted on March 2, 1867, which established what is now known as the Office of Education of the United States Department of Health, Education, and Welfare.[8] The purpose of this entity at the Federal level was not to change the pattern of decentralized control and regulation of education but rather to collect and disseminate information to aid the people in the establishment and maintenance of efficient school systems and in otherwise promoting the cause of education.

INFORMATION ON FEMALE EDUCATION. Establishment of the office in turn led to the first Federal action relating to the education of women. Less

[6] *United States Code* 1: xlix–l.
[7] *United States Code* 1: xlv, section 8.
[8] *United States Statutes at Large* 14: 434.

than three months after Henry Barnard assumed his post in March, 1867, as the first United States Commissioner of Education, he developed a "Plan of Publication" calling for a series of educational documents and tracts. One in the thirty-two-part series is entitled "Female Education, with an account of different seminaries for females in this country, and in Europe" (Barnard 1868:XXIV).

That same year, the Commissioner addressed a *Circular respecting female education* to education leaders at home and abroad (Barnard 1868:369–371). Its request for information inaugurated the Federal practice of collecting and analyzing educational information and then distributing the findings in the interests of those concerned. Returns caused John Eaton, the second United States Commissioner of Education, to make some comments in 1873 which have validity a century later:

Educators, like all other workers in the field of modern civilization, must make use of facts for their guidance. Mere speculative theories have been too much followed heretofore in all subjects connected with education, and in none more than in that having reference to the position of woman as scholar, teacher, and worker. A gross conservatism on one side has naturally given rise to immoderate theory on the other. It is only by a philosophical study of accumulated facts and human experience that society can arrive at any judicious modification of woman's education and occupation or correct what is false in any of the numerous theories and plans for her benefit. Should the fact of sex make any difference in the relation of individuals to education either as trainer or trained? In the education of the young has one sex any work to do which the other cannot equally well perform, and are the children in our schools trained actually so different, on account of the difference of sex, as to render modifications in their respective training necessary? Are the essential duties of life different for each sex; and, if so, what correspondences and differences must be made in their respective physical and moral training? These questions at the very threshold of this inquiry point to vast fields of thought. Nothing can be more useful for the progress of human society than their judicious discussion; nothing more harmful than vague declamation and passionate rhapsody. Every community after learning the general facts must take into consideration its own special circumstances. Of these the preponderance in number of one sex over another is the most powerful in effect (Eaton 1874:cxxxiv).

AUTHORIZATION OF EQUAL PAY FOR EQUAL WORK. The United States Senate took a legislative step in 1870 to help ensure that women "shall no longer be held in a subordinate position and treated as inferiors." It passed a bill containing a mandate for equal pay for equal work in the Federal Service regardless of sex of the employee.[9]

Objection by some members of the House of Representatives on the

[9] *The Congressional Globe* 92, Part 5: 4353–55.

grounds that it would cost too much to pay women as much as men for equal work resulted in compromise language in the form of an authorization rather than a mandate for women to be appointed "upon the same requisites and conditions and with the same compensations, as are prescribed for men."[10] Until 1962, the law actually worked to the disadvantage of women because of the way heads of departments and agencies traditionally interpreted their appointing power.

FIRST SIXTY YEARS OF THE TWENTIETH CENTURY

CHILDREN'S BUREAU CREATED Shortly after the turn of the century, President Theodore Roosevelt took some action at the instigation of leaders especially interested in orphaned and other needy children. He issued a call to two hundred concerned people to participate in a Conference on the Care of Dependent Children on January 25–26, 1909.[11] This was the first of the White House Conferences on Children and Youth which are held at approximately ten-year intervals.

One outgrowth of the 1909 Conference was legislation on April 9, 1912, establishing the Children's Bureau in the United States Department of Labor to investigate and report "upon all matters pertaining to the welfare of children and child life among all classes of people."[12] Work of the Office of Education soon was supplemented by that of the Children's Bureau. Both had an impact on school attendance in the country.

Each state that had previously lacked a compulsory school attendance law enacted one (Steinhilber and Sokolowski 1966:3 [Tables 1, 2]). State laws also were enacted on foster care and the elimination of child labor in factories and commercial establishments.[13]

FEDERAL SUPPORT FOR NONGOVERNMENTAL ACTION Despite progress, the education of girls still was considered less important than the education of boys. Then something helped to spark a change. The Secretary

[10]   July 12, 1870. Revised statutes section 165. *United States Statutes at Large* 18:26.
[11]   1909. "Call for the conference, December 25, 1908," in *Proceedings of the conference on the care of dependent children held at Washington, D. C., January 25–26, 1909.* 60th Congress, Second Session. Senate document 721, 15. Washington: U.S. Government Printing Office.
[12]   Public Law 62–116, April 9, 1912. *United States Statutes at Large* 37:79.
[13]   U.S. Department of Health, Education, and Welfare Social and Rehabilitation Service, Children's Bureau. 1967. *The story of the White House Conferences on children and youth.* Washington: U.S. Government Printing Office.

of War was impressed with the contribution made by local women's groups to the war effort in 1917–1918. He responded favorably to a plan some of their leaders advanced for a nation-wide nongovernmental structure that could mobilize women in future national emergencies and be useful in peacetime as well.

He authorized the earmarking of some funds to permit women leaders to cross the country in early 1919 to interest women in coming to a conference in the summer. There the National Federation of Business and Professional Women's Clubs was founded in July, 1919. Of special interest here is that the new federation first launched its research program in response to need for "broad and accurate information as to the existing conditions obtaining among women engaged in gainful occupations"[14]

Reports of the Federation's Education Committee in the pioneer years led to the organization's broadly conceived education and training programs in the interest of maximum general education for girls and women, specialized education and training appropriate to their occupational choices, and training for leadership and personal development. An early action program was a campaign carried out through state and local clubs, with the cooperation of leaders in education, to encourage girls to stay in school beyond the eighth grade (Heath 1963a:5 [Appendix C]).

Today the federation and many other women's organizations are helping young women to go on to college and beyond. Among the many such nationwide organizations are the American Association of University Women, the General Federation of Women's Clubs, and the P.E.O. Sisterhood. Each is deeply involved in education programs and in assistance to girls and women through scholarships, fellowships, and loans.

WOMEN'S BUREAU CREATED The successor to a temporary structure known as the Women-In-Industry Service, established to help meet manpower needs on the home front with womanpower during the First World War, is the Women's Bureau, established in the United States Department of Labor on June 5, 1920. Enabling legislation specifies the duty of the bureau is "to formulate standards and policies which shall promote the welfare of wage-earning women, improve their working conditions, increase their efficiency, and advance their opportunities for profitable employment."[15]

[14] Resolution 7, 1919, "Verbatim minutes." Founding convention, St. Louis, Missouri. Washington: The National Federation of Business and Professional Women's Clubs (Unpublished).
[15] Public Law 66–259, June 5, 1920. *United States Statutes at Large* 41:987.

Many studies made by the bureau reflect the disadvantaged position of the female sex. One consequence was the evolution of a mass of state labor legislation specifically for the protection of women. Some of these state laws logically could have been expected to produce more than they did in the way of higher standards for conditions under which wage-earning men are employed. Instead, men, already in leadership roles in commerce, industry, and the trade unions, took administrative actions and negotiated contracts that worked to the disadvantage of employed women in rates of pay, on-the-job training, opportunities for advancement, leave, lay-off procedures, pensions, and the like.[16]

WOMEN'S SUFFRAGE NATIONWIDE Seventy-two years after the Seneca Falls Convention, the Nineteenth Amendment was added to the Constitution on August 26, 1920. The substantive provision specifies: "The right of citizens of the United States to vote shall not be denied or abridged by the United States or by any State on account of sex."[17]

Since that time, women have exercised their franchise on behalf of many worthy causes. Despite the franchise, nearly another fifty years elapsed before women became sufficiently irate to organize themselves into activist groups on behalf of THEMSELVES as a worthy cause.

POLICY ON EQUAL PAY FOR EQUAL WORK A little over half a century after the abortive Senate effort to require equal pay for equal work, the Classification Act of 1923 was signed into law on March 4, 1923.[18] It provided for the classification of positions with rates of pay varying according to difficulty, responsibility, and qualification requirements for the work. It established the policy, at least, of equal pay for equal work in the Federal Service. Full implementation of the policy was circumvented by such means as not employing women for higher paying positions in the first place or affording women few opportunities for non-clerical on-the-job training and few opportunities for promotion.

DISILLUSION OVER THE STATUS OF WOMEN Women had demonstrated their competence in the First World War. When war clouds broke over the horizon in 1939, the Nation already had a lion's share of the best-educated women in the world. One of them, Frances Perkins, was in the

---

[16] See, for example, Bowe, et al. v. Colgate Palmolive Company, September 29, 1969. *Federal Reporter Second Series* 416:711 (United States Court of Appeals, 7th Circuit, 1969). For brief discussion of the decision, see below.

[17] *United States Code* 1:li.

[18] Public Law 67–516, March 4, 1923. *United States Statutes at Large* 42:1488.

President's Cabinet as Secretary of Labor. During World War II women again demonstrated their competence, whether as "Rosie the Riveter" or as entrepreneur.

Not long after hostilities ceased in 1945, more and more women began to recognize that their capacity to cope and compete was not enough. Opportunity was also needed. What opportunities women had began ebbing away in the late 1940's when the soldiers came marching home. By mid-century, the role of women already was being redefined in the prewar sexist terms of *Kinder, Küche, und Kirche*.

DECADE OF THE 1960's

In the early 1960's, informed women pointed out that the very same barriers on the grounds of sex that had been prevalent forty years earlier when women gained the right to vote still existed. Soon after a new President took office in 1961, the smoldering anger of women ignited. President Kennedy practically ignored women when it came to his appointments to high political office. Women's groups found their champion in a former United States Representative to the United Nations Commission on Human Rights. So it was that the world-renowned Eleanor Roosevelt went to call on the President at 1600 Pennsylvania Avenue.

PRESIDENT'S COMMISSION CREATED One result of her visit to the White House was Executive Order 10980 "Establishing the President's Commission on the Status of Women" on December 14, 1961, as a temporary body with a mandate to report and make recommendations to the President by October, 1963.[19] Some actions of significance occurred in rapid succession before the Commission reported.

APPOINTING POWER The first action was a challenge of practice under the 1870 authorization of equal pay for equal work in the Federal Service. Appointing officers in the Federal Government are Cabinet Officers and heads of agencies. Traditionally, with few exceptions, they have been men. These men construed the 1870 law to give them unrestricted right to specify sex of candidates among qualifications for employment. The result was that their requests to the Civil Service Commission for registers

[19]   December 14, 1961. *Federal Register* 26:12059, codified at *Code of Federal Regulations* 3: 500–501, 1959–63 Compilation.

of eligible candidates specified "male only" for practically all positions other than those at low grades in the clerical and nursing fields. The Attorney General had sustained their right to do so on September 17, 1934.[20]

Mrs. Roosevelt — in those days called the "Chairman" of the President's Commission — asked the new Attorney General (who also was a member of the Commission) to review the earlier Attorney General's Opinion. The new Opinion, handed down on July 14, 1962, reversed the earlier stand.[21] Consequential changes in Federal Personnel Regulations then were ordered into effect not later than August 31, 1962.[22]

Changes in recruiting practices were dramatic.[23] Changes in appointment practices were anything but dramatic. Appointing officers rarely specified sex qualification in requests for registers after August, 1962. In most cases, however, they continued to appoint men to the high-level posts. From less than $1^1/_2$ percent of high level posts held by women, the figure rose to less than 2 percent.[24]

Disenchanted by such microscopic progress and by the lack of sensitivity to the interests of women in opportunities for advancement, women began to exert pressure to get the 1870 law off the statute books so that it could never again be interpreted to the disadvantage of women. Success came with repeal of the law on October 15, 1965.[25]

OTHER COMMISSIONS CREATED While deliberations were going on in the President's Commission on the Status of Women the second action was spearheaded by the National Federation of Business and Professional Women's Clubs with the cooperation of other women's groups. It resulted in establishment of structure in the states to study the status of women to help implement their recommendations and those of the President's Commission.

[20]   1934. *Opinions of the Attorney General* 38: 77.
[21]   1962. *Opinions of the Attorney General* 429:9.
[22]   United States Civil Service Commission. July 31, 1962 revision. "FPM letter No. 330–1 — elimination of sex discrimination," in *Federal personnel manual*. Washington.
[23]   Interdepartmental Committee on the Status of Women. 1968. *Amercan women 1963–1968: report to the President*, page 14. Wahington: U.S. Government Printing Office. Of 34 thousand requests for new appointments from examination lists, 40 specified sex of candidate.
[24]   Committee on Federal Employment. 1963. *Report to the President's Commission on the Status of Women*, page 3. Washington: U.S. Government Printing Office. U.S. Civil Service Commission Statistics Section. 1968. *Study of Employment of Women in the Federal Government, 1967*, pages 2–3. Washington: U.S. Government Printing Office.
[25]   Public Law 82–261, October 15, 1965. *United States Statutes at Large* 79: 987.

The first such organization was the Michigan Women's Commission (established by the Governor of that state) which first met on September 25, 1962.[26] Today there are also various county and municipal commissions, and in June, 1970, the Interstate Association of Commissions on the Status of Women was founded.[27]

WOMEN'S LIBERATION MOVEMENT While the President's Commission was deliberating, the third action also occurred in the private sector. A sleeper from the publishing world began rolling off the press in March, 1963. It turned out to be a best-seller. Betty Friedan's *The feminine mystique* (1963) in effect launched the Women's Liberation Movement in the Nation.

EQUAL PAY ACT OF 1963 The fourth action, encouraged by members of the Commission, was a long-sought addition to the amended Fair Labor Standards Act of 1938, whereby the Congress had exercised its power to regulate commerce by passing legislation setting certain standards, particularly for minimum wages and maximum hours of work.[28] The addition was signed into law on June 10, 1963, as the Equal Pay Act of 1963 "To prohibit discrimination on account of sex in the payment of wages by employers engaged in commerce or in the production of goods for commerce."[29] Nearly another decade elapsed before the education community was jolted by a few words added to the equal pay provisions.

PRESIDENT'S COMMISSION REPORTS The work of the President's Commission on the Status of Women represents the first concerted effort to produce a composite picture of the status of women in the Nation and the very first high-level examination of that status in terms of civil and political rights, education, Federal employment, home and community, private employment, protective labor legislation, and social insurance. A committee in each of these fields submitted a report to the Commission.

In addition, findings were summarized and presented on "Four Consultations" held to elicit the "wisdom and creative advice" of specialists and others interested in or informed about private employment opportunities,

[26] Michigan inaugurates Governor's commission on status of women. *National Business Women* 42: 11.
[27] Interstate association of women's commissions formed. *Washington Newsletter for Women* 1: 4.
[28] Public Law 75–718, June 25, 1938. *United States Statutes at Large* 52: 1060, codified at *United States Code* 29: 201–219.
[29] Public Law 88–38, June 10, 1963. *United States Statutes at Large* 77: 56, codified at *United States Code* 29: 206.

new patterns in volunteer work, portrayal of women by the mass media, and problems of Negro women. The Commission, in turn, compiled its findings and recommendations and reported to the President on October 11, 1963. Resulting influence of the Commission is both broadly based and specialized.

COMMITTEE AND COUNCIL ON THE STATUS OF WOMEN Less than a month after the Commission reported to the President, he signed Executive Order 11126.[30] This November 1, 1963, instrument has the force of law. It provides for an Interdepartmental Committee on the Status of Women and a Citizens' Advisory Council on the Status of Women. Members of the Committee are Federal Officers, namely, high-level political appointees in the Executive Branch of Government. Members of the Council are leaders from outside the Federal Government. An annual report is prepared for the President.

The Council is identified as a "primary means" for suggesting and stimulating action with private bodies and individuals working for improvement of conditions of special concern to women. It reviews and evaluates progress and recommends action to accelerate it. The Council also considers the effect of new developments on methods of advancing the status of women and recommends action. Sex discrimination in education, as well as in other fields, has been one of its concerns throughout its history, as evidenced by its special papers, its testimony at Congressional hearings, and the annual reports to the President.

ADULT AND CONTINUING EDUCATION The President's Commission on the Status of Women, acting on recommendations by its Committee on Education, reported to the President that "Means of acquiring or continuing education must be available to every adult at whatever point he or she broke off traditional schooling." Structure of adult education "must be drastically revised." It must provide "practicable and accessible opportunities, developed with regard to the needs of women."[31]

Even before similar ideas were included in the report of President Lyndon B. Johnson's Task Force on Education, submitted in 1964,[32] provisions on adult basic education programs were included in the

[30] November 1, 1963. *Federal Register* 28: 11717, codified at *Code of Federal Regulations* 3: 791–92, 1959–1963 Compilation.
[31] President's Commission on the Status of Women. 1963. *American Women: 1963*. Report to the President, page 13. Washington: U.S. Government Printing Office.
[32] November 14, 1965. "Report of the President's Task Force on Education." John W. Gardner, chairman. (Unpublished — on file Lyndon Baines Johnson Library, Austin, Texas.)

Economic Opportunity Act of 1964.[33] The next year, a title on "Community Service and Continuing Education Programs" was included in the Higher Education Act of 1965.[34]

A Women's Bureau publication on continuing education programs for women was completed in September, 1966.[35] A revision was issued in 1971. Both respond to needs evidenced by burgeoning requests (1) from women for information on special programs available in their areas; and (2) from educators seeking background information on women's interests in and their need for special programs, and for descriptions of what other educators are doing to aid women.

The 1966 report identified fewer than 250 programs offered at times and in ways appropriate to the mature woman's needs. The 1971 report lists some 450. Estimates indicate this number may have doubled by 1973 (see Robinson n.d.).

CIVIL RIGHTS ACT OF 1964 On February 28, 1963, President Kennedy sent a favorably received message to the Congress announcing his intention to recommend legislation to eliminate racial discrimination and to assure civil rights for Negroes.[36] By contrast, his June 19, 1963, follow-up message and draft bill infuriated many women — though not because of his proposal to prohibit discrimination on the grounds of "race." They were antagonized because he also added prohibition of discrimination on the grounds of "color, creed, or national origin" but left out "sex."[37]

During the legislative process, some women's groups felt that insult was added to injury. The chairman of the powerful House Rules Committee, a Democrat from Virginia, used a diversionary tactic. He attempted to defeat the bill's Title VII, Equal Employment Opportunity, and preferably the entire bill by introducing an amendment to Title

[33] Public Law 88–452, August 20, 1964, Title II, part B. *United States Statutes at Large* 78: 520 — later superseded by broadened below-college-level program under Public Law 89–750, November 3, 1966, Title III cited as "Adult Education Act of 1966," in *United States Statutes at Large* 80: 1216.
[34] Public Law 89-329, November 8, 1965, Title I. *United States Statutes at Large* 79: 1219.
[35] U.S. Department of Labor Women's Bureau. 1967. *Continuing education programs for women.* Pamphlet 10. Washington: U.S. Government Printing Office.
[36] House of Representatives. February 28, 1963. *Civil rights message from the President of the United States.* 88th Congress, First Session. House document 75. Washington: U.S. Government Printing Office.
[37] House of Representatives. June 19, 1963. *Civil rights message with a draft of a bill from the President of the United States.* 88th Congress, First Session. House document 124. Washington: U.S. Government Printing Office.

VII specifying "sex" as an additional prohibited basis of discrimination.[38]

The proposed amendment initially was looked upon as a joke. In fact, the debate on February 8, 1964, came to be dubbed "Ladies' Afternoon in the House." In the end, the Virginia Congressman's tactical maneuver backfired and laid the groundwork for some far-reaching successes for women.

Congresswoman Martha Griffiths, Democrat of Michigan, recognized that black women would be protected under the bill and raised the question of lack of protection of white women. The clincher came when she said "a vote against this amendment today by a white man is a vote against his wife, or his widow, or his daughter, or his sister. If we are trying to establish equality in jobs, I am for it, but I am for making white women equal also."[39]

Katharine Price Collier St. George, a Republican Congresswoman from New York, said: "We are entitled to this little crumb of equality. The addition of that little, terrifying word 's-e-x' will not hurt this legislation in any way. In fact, it will improve it."[40]

The amendment, even expanded somewhat, was adopted, though without overwhelming support. The reluctance of mankind to provide equality for all is revealing. Some nay-sayers preferred to sacrifice equality for more than half the population to assure passage of the bill. The record of the debate on February 8 and February 10, 1964, not only reveals the views of others but mirrors attitudes on the status of women at that time in history.[41]

Difficulty in getting a bill passed by the Congress in an area so fraught with conflicting attitudes is revealing, too (See Heath 1970a: 315–319). An amendment in the nature of a substitute for the Kennedy bill was reported by a subcommittee of the House Committee on the Judiciary. The parent Committee did not accept the Subcommittee proposal. Instead, it reported its own substitute. The House passed this substitute but only after action on many amendments.

The Senate circumvented its Committee on the Judiciary because of the latter's known antagonism toward the bill. More than 500 amendments were proposed in the Senate. Before there were so many, a bipartisan rump group of four Senators tried to bring order out of the chaos. This group produced a still different amendment in the nature of a sub-

[38] *Congressional Record* 110: Part 2, 2577.
[39] *Congressional Record* 110: Part 2, 2580.
[40] *Congressional Record* 110: Part 2, 2581.
[41] *Congressional Record* 110: Part 2, 2577–84 and 2718–21.

stitute bill. After more amendments were proposed, the group withdrew
that one in favor of another it proposed as a substitute bill. This one passed.

To prevent a reopening of the whole subject in a Conference to
resolve the differences between the House and Senate bills, a resolution
was pushed through the House on July 2, 1964, calling for acceptance
of the bill as passed by the Senate.[42] The bill was signed into law that
day — one fast action in the entire process.[43]

Every advance toward equality for one who is discriminated against
tends to mean that someone else considers his ox may be gored. And
indeed, it may be if he is privileged not on the basis of merit but solely
on the basis of something beyond his control such as his sex or his color.
And rare is the man — or the woman, for that matter — who willingly
cedes or shares a privilege that another has usurped as though it were
a just due.

The new civil rights legislation, like other laws in emotionally-charged
areas, evolved as a compromise, and compromise inevitably lacks universal appeal. Certainly the law was unsatisfactory as far as the needs of
girls and women were concerned.

Titles II, III, and V relate to relief against discrimination in places of
public accommodation, relief from deprivation of the right to equal
protection of laws in public facilities, and expanded jurisdiction of the
Civil Rights Commission. Coverage in every case is limited to discrimination on the grounds of race, color, religion, or national origin. Sex
discrimination is ignored.

Titles IV and VI, "Desegregation of Public Education" and "Nondiscrimination in Federally Assisted Programs" (the Federal assistance and
enforcement titles for education), followed the same pattern. Neither
contained a prohibition of discrimination on the grounds of sex. Thus,
discrimination on the grounds of sex in such areas as admission to
educational institutions, admission to particular curriculums, admission
to particular courses, and opportunities for scholarships and fellowships
was not covered.

Title VII created the Equal Employment Opportunity Commission
to help in carrying out the provisions in that part of the act. The title
is named "Equal Employment Opportunity," yet it originally included
an exemption in Section 70 that was devastating for women in academe.
Specifically, it stated in part: "This title shall not apply... to an educational institution with respect to the employment of individuals to per-

[42] *House Resolution* 789, July 2, 1964. *Congressional Record* 110: Part 12, 15869.
[43] Public Law 88–352, July 2, 1964. *United States Statutes at Large* 78: 246 and 252.

form work connected with the educational activities of such institution."[44]

Women employed in the larger industrial establishments are covered. Even so, implementation of Title VII initially centered on racial discrimination, despite the fact that more than a third of the cases received by the Equal Employment Opportunity Commission came from women in industry who charged discrimination on the grounds of sex.[45] Some of these women, though already at a disadvantage financially, decided to go to court when other efforts failed to bring relief. Two of these cases turned out to have significance for education.

One involves refusal of a company to consider a woman for a position classified as "switchman."[46] The decision in her favor opened the way for a Federal regulation requiring a narrow interpretation under the law as to what constitutes a "bona fide occupational qualification" for employment. According to the decision, women — like men — are to be considered on an individual basis rather than denied opportunity as a class, except in such cases as modeling of men's clothing.[47]

The other case involves a range of discriminatory practices against several women.[48] The decision of the United States Court of Appeals upset the company's practice of classifying jobs so that there was a cut-off level for women. It upset the company's lay-off procedure which permitted a man with short tenure to displace a woman with long service at a lower level. It put the skids under so-called protective labor law prohibiting women from certain weight-lifting unless the same restrictions apply to men as a class. It criticized the union for negotiating against the interests of women while accepting their dues. And it provided for financial relief to the women appealing and to women as a class in the company.

Additionally, the Court inserted into its judical decision the interpretation of a bona fide occupational qualification, which was first issued in the Federal regulation as a result of the earlier case. This regulation already had the force of law; now it is established in case law, too.

44   Public Law 88–352, July 2, 1964. *United States Statutes at Large* 78: 255.
45   U.S. Equal Employment Opportunity Commission. 1968. "Analysis of charges by basis of discrimination," in *Second annual report*, page 6. Washington: U.S. Government Printing Office.
46   Weeks v. Southern Bell Telephone and Telegraph Company, March 4, 1969. *Federal Reporter Second Series* 408 (United States Court of Appeals, 5th Circuit).
47   Guidelines on discrimination because of sex: sex as a bona fide occupational qualification, August 19, 1969. *Federal Register* 34: 11367 — codified at *Code of Federal Regulations* 29: 1604.
48   Bowe, et al. v. Colgate-Palmolive Company, September 29, 1969. *Federal Reporter Second Series* 416: 711 (United States Court of Appeals, 7th Circuit).

Though not generally recognized at the time, this interpretation was applicable under certain circumstances in the field of education even before Title VII of the 1964 Act was amended with reference to education.

Despite some gains, the correction of discriminatory practices against girls and women was not a priority concern at the Federal level in the 1960's. Callousness toward the interests of women by labor, management, and the media caused many a meeting to be held by women's organizations and contributed in no small measure both to the proliferation of activist women's organizations and to the solidifying of an underlying unity of purpose which the male-oriented media failed to sense (as evidenced by their emphasis of views that favored the status quo and denied the existence of discrimination against women).

It took more than five years to convince the United States Attorney General to have the United States Department of Justice file with the Supreme Court the first *amicus curiae* brief on behalf of a woman charging discrimination on the grounds of sex under the 1964 Act. A corporation, in this case, claimed its refusal to consider a woman's application for employment was based not on the fact that she was a woman but on the fact that she was a woman with preschool-aged children. The Supreme Court ruled early in 1971 that employers cannot refuse to hire women solely because they have small children unless fathers of small children also are denied jobs.[49]

The case sets a precedent in one respect. It is the first in which the Nation's highest court ever considered an individual woman as a "person" under the Fourteenth Amendment to the Constitution and, therefore, entitled in her own right to due process of law.

TASK FORCES RELATED TO EDUCATION Soon after Lyndon Baines Johnson became President on November 22, 1963, he began naming task forces on or partly related to education. He chose men as chairmen and other men as members. There are many evidences of the sensitivity of these men to the need for nondiscrimination on the grounds of race, color, religion, or national origin. There is little if any evidence that they paid attention to nondiscrimination on the basis of sex.[50]

[49] Phillips v. Martin-Marietta Corp., January 25, 1971. *Federal Reporter Second Series* 411: 1; 416: 1257 (United States Court of Appeals, 5th Circuit); and *United States Supreme Court* 400: 542.
[50] These unpublished task force reports are on file in the Lydon Baines Johnson Library, Austin, Texas. They were reviewed briefly when the Education Collection was opened at a January 23–25, 1972 Education Seminar at the Library. See Wilbur J. Cohen 1972. "Address," in *Congressional Record* 118 (12): H 615–18. For more detail on higher education in these reports, see *The Chronicle of Higher Education* 18).

Even so, their recommendations culminated in certain laws that have some significance in counteracting sex-role stereotyping and other forms of sex bias. One such law is the Elementary and Secondary Education Act of 1965, which also included amendments to expand assistance under a law enacted in 1954, the Cooperative Research Act.[51] Another is the Higher Education Act of 1965.[52]

Under these and other laws, the United States Commissioner of Education is authorized to make grants or contracts for appropriate purposes, including the stimulation of needed action. Thus, for example, Federal support was made available to the National Education Association of the United States for a Conference on Sex Role Stereotypes in November 1972 as a prototype for other conferences in the country which are aimed primarily at elimination of sex discrimination in education at elementary and secondary levels.

Similar examples are aimed primarily at postsecondary education. Illustrative is a series of Institutes on Women in Higher Education.

EXECUTIVE ORDER 11246 A draft executive order within the framework of Title VII of the Civil Rights Act of 1964, was prepared and sent to department and agency heads for comment prior to Presidential action. The draft was narrower in coverage than the act under which it was written. It left out nondiscrimination in employment on the grounds of sex despite such nondiscrimination policy enunciation in the act relating to Federal employment and provisions on employment in larger commercial and industrial establishments.

Some of the reviewers made recommendations to rectify the omission. Their suggested changes were ignored. The proposal was signed by President Johnson on September 24, 1965, as Executive Order 11246 entitled "Equal Employment Opportunity."[53] It called for nondiscrimination in employment in the Federal Government, under government contracts, and under contracts for federally assisted construction, but only on the grounds of race, creed, color, or national origin.

THE NATIONAL ORGANIZATION FOR WOMEN [NOW] IS CREATED Resistance to the long tradition of ignoring discrimination against girls and women began in earnest the next year. The National Organization for Women, popularly known as NOW, was the first of what soon was a steady stream

[51]   Public Law 89–10, April 11, 1965. Public Law 83–531, July 26, 1954. *United States Statutes at Large* 79: 39; 68: 533; 79: 44.
[52]   Public Law 89–329, November 8, 1965. *United States Statutes at Large* 79: 1254.
[53]   September 24, 1965. *Federal Register* 30: 12319 — codified at *Code of Federal Regulations* 3: 339–47, 1964–1965 Compilation.

of newly-founded activist groups working on behalf of girls and women. NOW was born on October 29, 1966, out of the anger and frustration of twenty-eight women leaders attending the Second Conference of Governor's Commissions on the Status of Women the previous June.[54]

The new organization aimed to work for reform through the "establishment." Though ridiculed at first, it rapidly became an organization that could not be ignored. Local chapters sprang up around the country, and the number registering at its national conventions grew from a tiny band to more than two thousand in 1973. NOW quickly chalked up some successes, while the total membership grew to some 35,000 in its first seven years.

EXECUTIVE ORDER 11246 IS AMENDED To NOW belongs the credit for the recommendation by the Citizens' Advisory Council on the Status of Women, the Interdepartmental Committee on the Status of Women, and the Federal Women Awardees for revision of Executive Order 11246 by adding the prohibition of discrimination on the grounds of sex to the prohibitions already identified. President Johnson signed the amendatory instrument — Executive Order 11375 — on October 13, 1967.[55]

This amendment transformed the basic order into the FIRST and the ONLY Federal enforcement support women educators had for the redress of grievances in the area of sex discrimination. The new provision became effective in thirty days in the Federal Service and on October 13, 1968, with respect to government contracts and federally assisted contracts.

TASK FORCE ON WOMEN'S RIGHTS AND RESPONSIBILITIES On March 17, 1969, shortly after President Richard Nixon was inaugurated, Congresswoman Florence Dwyer, Republican of New Jersey, released a letter to her former congressional colleague in which she suggested alternative arrangements to "expand women's opportunities and responsibilities, protect women's rights, and eliminate all forms of discrimination based on sex."

She and other Republican Congresswomen called on the President on July 8 to discuss and leave with him a memorandum on "positive steps" the Administration could take (Dwyer 1969). One of the continuing results is his appointment of women to high-level posts never before held by women. Examples are the positions of "Chairman" of the Federal

---

[54] National Organization for Women. 1966. *Statement of purpose adopted at the organizing conference, October 29, 1966.* Washington: the Organization.
[55] October 13, 1967. *Federal Register* 32: 14303 — codified at *Code of Federal Regulations* 3: 684–86, 1966–1970 Compilation.

Maritime Commission, "Chairman" of the United States Tariff Commission, and Member of the President's Council of Economic Advisers, filled by Helen Delich Bentley, Catherine Bedell, and Marina von N. Whitman.

Among other results of the visit was the President's appointment on October 1, 1969, of his Task Force on Women's Rights and Responsibilities.[56] Its blunt and to-the-point report — *A matter of simple justice* — was completed on December 15, 1969, and released to the public on June 9, 1970, when the Women's Bureau was celebrating its 50th Anniversary.[57]

Within three years, action had been consummated on more than half of the Task Force recommendations. Part of that action is in the form of legislation, including, without being limited to, legislation contributing to what the December 1972 issue of *American Education* calls the "change of revolutionary proportions" that is "enveloping education at every level." Legislative action includes Congressional passage of the Joint Resolution on the *Equal Rights Amendment*, amendments to equal day provisions in Fair Labor Standards law, and amendments to Civil Rights legislation of 1957 and 1964. Other actions include issuance of guidelines on prohibition of discrimination, initiation of action on behalf of a woman by the U.S. Attorney General before the U.S. Supreme Court, and establishment of a Women's Action Program in the Office of Education. Certain fringe benefits also have been equalized for women and men.

WOMEN'S CAUCUSES IN PROFESSIONAL ASSOCIATIONS Around the time the President's Task Force was appointed, women began to organize within professional associations and societies to make their dissatisfactions heard. They objected to paying the same dues as men while the male power structure perpetuated traditional practices of filling policy boards and conference program spots with men.

Women's caucuses began springing up at annual conferences to demand reform.[58] By the spring of 1973, more than seventy caucuses were

[56] October 1, 1969. Task force on women's rights and responsibilities: announcement of establishment and membership, *Weekly Compilation of of Presidential Documents* 5(40): 1352–53.
[57] President's Task Force on Women's Rights and Responsibilities. 1970. *A matter of simple justice: report, December 15, 1969*. Washington: U.S. Government Printing Office.
[58] See, for example: Official Proceedings of the American Sociological Association. *The American Sociologist* 5 (1): 59, 63–65. Malcolm G. Scully. Radical tactics eased at scholarly meetings. *The Chronicle of Higher Education* 5 (1): 1. Resolution and amendments on the status of women in the profession. *American Political Science Association business meeting, September 4, 1969*. Women's caucus meets in Denver; presents resolutions to ASPA Council. *News and Views* 11(5):1.

making themselves heard within their organizations and forcing a re-vamping of organizational practices and practices of the professions themselves (Oltman 1973).

THE WOMEN'S EQUITY ACTION LEAGUE [WEAL] IS CREATED Though little heralded at the time, the Women's Equity Action League, known as WEAL, was founded in Cleveland, Ohio, in November, 1968. During the next year, the new organization quietly plotted its course, using the talents of women in law, education, and other fields. It was ready to act when the decade of the 1960's ended.

BEGINNING OF THE 1970's

MOUNTING PRESSURE FOR REFORM WEAL zeroed in with its bombshell on January 31, 1970. That was the day WEAL, citing government contract provisions in amended Executive Order 11246, filed charges specifically against the University of Maryland and as a class action against all universities receiving federal contracts (letter from Dowding 1970). It soon was abundantly clear that WEAL's charges were solidly based. On March 9, Congresswoman Griffiths publicly accused the Federal Government of violating national policy and the President's Executive Orders by "providing billions of dollars of Federal contracts to universities and colleges which discriminate against women both as teachers and as students."[59]

On March 25, 1970, NOW filed charges against Harvard University and requested Federal withholding of millions of dollars from that institution on the grounds of discrimination against women.[60] Though it had taken more than two and a half years of pressure from women's groups, "Sex discrimination guidelines" were published on June 9, 1970,[61] under amended Executive Order 11246.

Women were making it clear that they were fed up with what amounted to a 100-year-old excuse that it cost too much to treat them equitably. More than a third of the work force was female, and the proportion was rising.[62] Many women, already disadvantaged in rates of pay and other

[59] *Congressional Record* 116 (35): H 1588–90.
[60] Women's Equity Action League. 1970. *Universities and colleges charged on sex discrimination under Executive Order 11246 as amended by 11375.* Washington: WEAL. List identifies institutions so charged either by WEAL or other organizations.
[61] June 9, 1970. Sex discrimination guidelines. *Federal Register* 35: 8888.
[62] United States Department of Labor Office of Information, Publication, and Reports. April 1973. *Women and work.* Inside back cover. Washington.

348   KATHRYN G. HEATH

work benefits, were paying taxes that helped to finance higher rates of pay and better fringe benefits accorded to men.

Acting under Executive Order 11246, the Secretary of Labor delegated to the Secretary of Health, Education, and Welfare certain portions of his contract compliance responsibilities, namely, those relating to fields within the latter's areas of competence. On June 15, 1970 — more than a year and a half after the provisions barring sex discrimination became effective in government contracts — the Department of Health, Education, and Welfare notified its Regional Civil Rights Directors that "investigations of sex discrimination must be a part of all compliance reviews and ... all affirmative action plans in the future must address themselves to overcoming patterns of sex discrimination" (Muirhead 1970).

On July 1, 1970, at Congressional hearings on discrimination against women, a representative of the Department testified: "With limited resources and staff, priority to date has been placed on overcoming the effects of racial and ethnic discrimination." He also said, "We intend to move as fast as possible on investigating allegations of sex discrimination in colleges and universities."[63]

On October 5, 1970, WEAL filed sex discrimination charges against all medical schools receiving federal contracts.[64] Similar charges against all law schools receiving federal contracts were filed on March 26, 1971, by the Professional Women's Caucus, founded on April 11 the previous year as an organization cutting across the professions and able to bring any needed competence to bear on discrimination cases (letter from Sassower 1971; Heath 1970b).

By this time, most of the more than 2,500 accredited institutions of higher learning in the country were included in class action charges. Many of them also had specific charges pending against them. Besides, compliance reviews were making it evident that Federal funds would be withheld pending acceptable plans for affirmative action by institutions. What seemed like a little tremor in the fault-land of a campus in the State of Maryland in January, 1970, was rumbling toward earthquake proportions for academe across the land.

WOMEN'S POLITICAL CAUCUSES CREATED Since 1923, women had succeeded

---

[63] House of Representatives Committee on Education and Labor Special Subcommittee on Education. 1971. *Discrimination against women: hearings July 1 and 31, 1970.* 91st Congress, Second Session, part 2, pages 658–59. Washington: U.S. Government Printing Office. The *Statement* identified in footnote 92 appears at pages 657–61.
[64] Women's Equity Action League. October 5, 1970. Letter (to Secretary of Health, Education, and Welfare Elliot L. Richardson).

in getting members of each Congress to introduce joint resolutions proposing an Equal Rights Amendment to the Constitution. None bore
fruit. Finally, Congresswoman Griffiths succeeded with a discharge
petition forcing a bill out of the House Committee on the Judiciary.[65]
The House of Representatives approved this bill on August 10, 1970,
by an overwhelming vote, despite the bitter opposition of the Judiciary
Committee Chairman, who had been successful in keeping such proposals
bottled up in the Committee for many years.[66]

More than two-thirds of the Senators in the same Congress had introduced similar bills calling for an Equal Rights Amendment. When the
House bill reached the Senate for action, it soon was clear that many
Senators had not expected the favorable vote in the House. Finally, by
request of organized women's groups, the proposal was allowed to die
without vote in the Senate after that body added riders to the proposal
that destroyed its usefulness.[67]

Disillusionment over actions in the overwhelmingly male Senate aroused
women to the importance of political clout. More and more of them
were beginning to see that long-range and enduring progress starts with
the political, broadens to include the economic, and then extends to the
social field — not the other way around. There is good reason for this
pattern. Political development leads to a climate of stability for economic
development. And economic development provides the wherewithal
to finance the social to the extent that it cannot be or is not yet self-
supporting. In these terms, education, for example, is a surcharge on an
expanding economy while children are in school and before they are old
enough to make their own contributions to the gross national product.

After social development has advanced sufficiently, then comes the
difficult task of coordinating and integrating the political, the economic,
and the social to make necessary frontal attacks on barriers to progress.
Enduring progress is not likely to come in any other way, as histories
of nations and the United Nations well demonstrate.

Indeed, disenchantment over what happened in the Senate in 1970
contributed in no small measure to the organization of women for
political action. Women representing political views ranging from those
of conservative establishment types to those of the *avant garde* of women's

---

[65]   July 20, 1970. *Congressional Record* 116 (122): H 6962–63.
[66]   August 10, 1970. *Congressional Record* 116 (137): 7984.
[67]   October 13–14, and November 16, 1970. Equal rights for men and women. *Congressional Record* 116 (180): S 17923–50; (181): part I, S 18075–78, 18043, 18088;
(182): S 18192–93. November 19, 1970. Feminists choose to wait. *The Washington
Post.*

liberation called for the organizing conference that was held in Washington, D.C., on July 10–11, 1971. The conference resulted in the founding of the National Women's Political Caucus. This multipartisan organization to "awaken, organize, and assert the vast political power represented by women" encouraged the creation of state women's political caucuses, which soon were springing up across the country.[68]

The mass media reported the initial successes. These successes presage the future of these organizations of womanpower for political purposes. What happened in the Democratic Primary in New York in 1972 illustrates a success. Elizabeth Holtzman running against Emanuel Celler, Chairman of the House Judiciary Committee, won the nomination for Congress on the Democratic ticket. She then won the election that November, and thus went down to defeat a man who had been in the House of Representatives since 1923 and who had steadily opposed the Equal Rights Amendment that women so clearly want.

EXERCISE OF FEDERAL POWER Legislative actions of far-reaching sinificance for women began in 1971. Each came about because pressure on the nationwide problem of sex discrimination had mounted sufficiently to cause the Federal Government to act. Some — not all — reflect the use of the Nation's Constitutional power "to provide for the ... general welfare of the United States."

Beginning particulary with the trauma of civil war in 1861, history shows that this power is invoked when the need and the pressure for reform are large enough and when such factors as inertia, vested interest, tradition, and failure of the states to act make it clear that urgently needed reform is not likely to occur otherwise. Thus, for example, civil rights legislation was enacted in 1964 and due process of law imposed against arbitrary practices at lower levels of government.

TRAINING FOR THE HEALTH PROFESSIONS The first of the Federal laws in the 1970's to contain a provision prohibiting sex discrimination is the Comprehensive Health Manpower Training Act of 1971.[69] This law, inserting the provision in the Public Health Service Act,[70] is forcing the

---

[68] *Congressional Record* 117 (106): S 10761–68. Isabelle Shelton. July 13, 1971. A single purpose. *The Evening Star*, Washington. 1971. *National Women's Political Caucus.* Washington.
[69] Public Law 92–157, November 18, 1971, Title I, section 110. *United States Statutes at Large* 85: 461.
[70] Public Law 78–410, July 1, 1944. *United States Statues at Large* 58: 682 — codified at *United States Code* 42: 201–300a-6 with specific provision at Supplement I to the 1970 edition at 295 h–9.

schools and training centers in the medical and other health fields to throw open their doors as widely to women as to men.

Some 1,400 colleges, universities, and hospitals are affected by the requirement that these schools and training centers not discriminate on the basis of sex in admission to their programs if they want Federal financial assistance. These institutions now know that they must take these provisions seriously, as more than $600 million in Federal funds went to them in the fiscal year beginning July 1 before the new provision became law on November 18, 1971.

Less than two weeks after the law was enacted, Alan Pifer, President of the Carnegie Corporation of New York recognized the need to use Federal power in this way in an address entitled "Women in Higher Education" delivered on November 29, 1971, at a meeting of the Southern Association of Colleges and Schools. He noted that higher education clearly is on the defensive on the issue of women's rights: "without the threat of coercion it seems unlikely higher education would have budged an inch on this issue. Certainly it had every chance to do so and failed" (Pifer 1972:2,13).

CHILD CARE COSTS The Revenue Act of 1971, signed into law on December 10, 1971, contains an addition to income tax laws of interest to families with a total income in the lower brackets. It authorizes an income tax deduction (up to specified amounts) for child care costs.[71]

EQUAL RIGHTS AMENDMENT When the Ninety-second Congress began in January, 1971, women's groups already had closed ranks. They had formed Women United (Laurence n.d.) specifically to plan joint strategy to get favorable action on the proposed Equal Rights Amendment, which had been before every Congress starting with the Sixty-eighth in 1923. The result was a lobbying blitzkrieg to get the Congress to agree that "Equality of rights under the law shall not be denied or abridged by the United States or by any State on account of sex."[72]

On October 12, 1971, the House of Representatives again acted favorably.[73] The Senate, with a third of its members coming up for elec-

---

[71]   Public Law 92–178, December 10, 1971, Title II, section 210. *United States Statutes at Large* 85: 518 — codified at *United States* Code 26: Supplement I to 1970 edition at 214.
[72]   United States Senate Committee on the Judiciary. March 14, 1972. *Equal rights for men and women.* Report 92–689, page 2. Washington: U.S. Government Printing Office.
[73]   October 12, 1971. *Congressional Record* 117 (115): H 9392.

tion the following November, concurred on March 22, 1972, with more than the required two-thirds vote.[74]

The state of Hawaii, in a time zone five hours earlier than Washington, D.C., ratified the proposal the same day. Delaware — the first state to ratify the Nation's Constitution — wanted to be the first to ratify the Equal Rights Amendment. It is in the same time zone as Washington, D.C., and its legislature had recessed. Its ratification action came the next day. By the end of 1973, thirty states had ratified the proposal. Three-fourths, or thirty-eight of the fifty states, must ratify the proposal for it to be added as an amendment to the fundamental law of the land.[75]

EQUAL EMPLOYMENT OPPORTUNITY IN EDUCATION Next, the Congress exercised transcendent power by passing the Equal Employment Opportunity Act of 1972, which the President signed into law on March 24, 1972.[76] It amends the Civil Rights Act of 1964 by extending the coverage of Title VII. Those employed in educational activities in public and private educational institutions now come within the purview of the equal employment opportunity provisions of the 1964 Act. In addition, the Equal Employment Opportunity Commission at the Federal level is given greatly strengthened powers to ensure compliance.

PROHIBITION OF SEX DISCRIMINATION IN EDUCATION The next pertinent law was signed on June 23, 1972, as the Education Amendments of 1972. Title IX of this law is "Prohibition of Discrimination."[77] Again, with implications that are far-reaching for education in the several states of the Union, the Congress has exercised its power of the purse.

With exceptions pertaining to admissions to such specified types of educational institutions as traditionally single-sex schools and those in transition to coeducational status, Title IX says: "No person in the United States shall, on the basis of sex, be excluded from participating in, be denied the benefits of, or be subjected to discrimination under any education program or activity receiving Federal financial assistance." Then, after setting forth procedure for Federal Administrative Enforcement and Judicial Review, Title IX amends other laws.

First, it amends the Civil Rights Act of 1964 by including sex as a

[74]   March 22, 1972. *Congressional Record* 118 (44): S 4612.
[75]   *United States Code* 1: xlvii, Article V. The thirtieth ratification was by the state of Washington on March 22, 1973.
[76]   Public Law 92–261, March 24, 1972. *United States Statutes at Large* 86: 103 — codified at *United States Code* 42: Supplement II to 1970 edition at 2000 et seq.
[77]   Public Law 92–318, June 23, 1972, Title IX. *United States Statutes at Large* 86: 373.

prohibited area of discrimination under its Title IV, "Desegregation of Public Education," and its Title IX, which pertains to certain judicial procedures. Then Title IX of the 1972 amendments further expands the coverage of the equal pay provisions in the amended Fair Labor Standards Act of 1938. Executive, administrative, and professional employees, including teachers, now come within the purview of the equal pay provisions of the basic act.

As far as education is concerned, the Congress again has exercised its transcendent power "to provide for the ... general welfare of the United States." And it has done so within a law initially enacted under its specifically enumerated Constitutional power to regulate commerce.

The earlier amendments under the Equal Pay Act of 1963 became operative in commerce and industry on June 10, 1964. As of May 20, 1973, the Department of Labor reports a total of nearly $64 million to be due to a total of nearly 139,000 employees — almost all of them women discriminated against in pay.[78]

These figures do not include some $7.7 million due approximately three thousand women under this legislation as a result of a negotiated Agreement recently confirmed by the United States District Court in Philadelphia in a case involving one of the largest companies in the Nation (AT&T and its 24 Bell System Companies).[79] In addition, the figures do not yet reflect action relating to education under the 1972 amendments.

JURISDICTION OF THE CIVIL RIGHTS COMMISSION Finally, another law, enacted on October 14, 1972, extends the life of the Civil Rights Commission for another five years. Of special interest to women is the fact that the Commission's jurisdiction is widened to include sex discrimination.[80]

FEDERATION OF ORGANIZATIONS FOR PROFESSIONAL WOMEN CREATED Women know the advantage of working together in individual organizations. They know the advantage of having representatives of their organizations join hands for specific purposes, as in the case of Women

---

[78]   United States Department of Labor. June 1, 1973. *Equal Pay Act findings.* Washington. Unrounded figures as of May 20, 1973 are $63,926,217 due 138, 737 employees, mostly women.

[79]   Equal Employment Opportunity Agreement between American Telephone and Telegraph Company and Equal Employment Opportunity Commission and U.S. Department of Labor. January 18, 1973. *Labor Law Reports: Employment Practices* 25. Washington: Commerce Clearing House. The total agreement involves $15 million to settle.

[80]   Public Law 92–496, October 14, 1972. *United States Statutes at Large* 86: 813.

United. In 1972 some of these representatives came to the conclusion that a federation of diverse organizations for women should be formed to function on a continuing basis. Planning was spearheaded by the Association of Women in Science and the American Association of University Women in three meetings between April and November, 1972.

Then the two associations cosponsored a conference held at Marymount College, Arlington, Virginia, on November 17-18, 1972. Representatives of some forty organizations came together to discuss the plan and to decide on action. The Federation of Organizations for Professional Women was founded on the second day of the conference.[81]

The purpose of the Federation is to provide member organizations with a means for combining their efforts in the interests of equality of opportunity for women in education and other careers. The Federation operates on the principle of not duplicating any activity one or more of its member organizations can more effectively carry out. It has already embarked on its clearing house functions to keep member organizations informed of pertinent activities in which each is engaged.

PENDING ACTION Many discriminatory state laws will be superseded when the Equal Rights Amendment has been ratified by eight more states and the Amendment becomes an operative part of the Nation's Constitution. Meanwhile, the Ninety-third Congress has before it a range of bills aimed at eradication of discrimination against girls and women, including proposals to amend Title VI of the Civil Rights Act of 1964, which does not yet specify discrimination on the grounds of sex. Bills relate to such areas as brokerage, credit housing for purchase or rent, marital status, and name status as well as to grants for financing state commissions on the status of women to conduct studies.

A CONCLUDING WORD

Perhaps a good way to close this historical sketch of legislation that is helping to eliminate sex bias in education in the United States of America is to quote from hearings held by the Ad Hoc Subcommittee on Discri-

[81] Program. November 17–18, 1972. *Federation of Professional Women's Organizations organizational conference*. Washington: Association of Women in Science. Fann Harding. December 27, 1972. *Address at 139th meeting*, American Association for the Advancement of Science Section on education, Graduate Women in Science. Washington: Dr. Harding. By decision of the conference in November, the name was changed to Federation of Organizations for Professional Women.

mination Against Women of the House Committee on Education and Labor. A Cabinet Officer had just introduced the staff he brought with him to the hearings. Congressman John M. Ashbrook, Republican of Ohio, asked: "Is there any significance in the fact that all the women are in the back row?" The Cabinet Officer replied in the negative.

Then Congresswoman Edith Green, Democrat of Oregon, made an oblique reference to Mrs. Rosa Parks, who refused to follow the mandate in existence in 1956 in the State of Alabama requiring black people to sit in the back of the bus. Her challenge triggered actions leading to the Civil Rights Act of 1957, which established the Civil Rights Commission,[82] the Civil Rights Act of 1960, primarily related to voting,[83] and the Civil Rights Act of 1964. Congresswoman Green said: "If it is symbolic, I might say to my colleague, the women have not yet waged a major battle on the back-of-the-bus argument, but it is coming."[84]

REFERENCES

BARNARD, HENRY
    1868   *Report of the Commissioner of Education with circulars and documents accompanying the same.* Washington: United States Government Printing Office.
CLEVELAND TASK FORCE ORGANIZING COMMITTEE
    1968   "Women's Equity Action League. Cleveland. (Mimeographed.)
COMMITTEE ON CIVIL AND POLITICAL RIGHTS
    1964   *Report to the President's Commission on the Status of Women.* Washington: United States Government Printing Office.
COMMITTEE ON EDUCATION
    1964   *Report to the President's Commission on the Status of Women.* Washington: United States Government Printing Office.
COMMITTEE ON FEDERAL EMPLOYMENT
    1963   *Report to the President's Commission on the Status of Women.* Washington: United States Government Printing Office.
COMMITTEE ON HOME AND COMMUNITY
    1963   *Report to the President's Commission on the Status of Women.* Washington: United States Government Printing Office.
COMMITTEE ON PRIVATE EMPLOYMENT
    1964   *Report to the President's Commission on the Status of Women.* Washington: United States Government Printing Office.

[82] Public Law 85–115, September 9, 1957. *United States Statutes at Large* 71: 634.
[83] Public Law 86–449, May 6, 1960. *United States Statutes at Large* 74: 86.
[84] House of Representatives Committee on Education and Labor Ad Hoc Subcommittee on Discrimination Against Women. 1973. *Oversight hearings on discrimination against women, April 26, 27, May 5 and 10, 1972,* page 66. Washington: U.S. Government Printing Office.

COMMITTEE ON PROTECTIVE LABOR LEGISLATION

1963   *Report to the President's Commission on the Status of Women.* Washington: United States Government Printing Office.

COMMITTEE ON SOCIAL INSURANCE AND TAXES

1963   *Report to the President's Commission on the Status of Women.* Washington: United States Government Printing Office.

CONFERENCE ON SEX ROLE STEREOTYPES

1972   *Airlie House, Warrenton, Virginia.* Grant USOE 0–72–2507. Washington: National Education Assocation of the United States.

DORR, ROBIN

1972   Education and women's rights: what the law now says. *American Education* 8:5.

DWYER, FLORENCE P.

1969   *Administration action re women.* Washington: Memorandum to the President.

EATON, JOHN

1874   *Report of the Commissioner of Education: 1873.* Washington: United States Government Printing Office.

Equal employment opportunity agreement

1973   *Between American Telephone and Telegraph Company and Equal Employment Opportunity Commission and U.S. Department of Labor: January 18, 1973.* Labor Law Reports: Employment Practices 25. Washington: Commerce Clearing House.

Four consultations

1963   *Report to the President's Commission on the Status of Women.* Washington: United States Government Printing Office.

FRIEDAN, BETTY

1963   *The feminine mystique.* New York: W.W. Norton.

HARDING, FANN

1972   "Address on December 27." 139th meeting, American Association for the Advancement of Science Section on Education. Washington. (Mimeographed.)

HEATH, KATHRYN G.

1963a   *Long-range program of the Business and Professional Women's Foundation.* Washington: the Foundation. (Processed.)

1970a   "A legislative history of equal employment opportunity provisions relating to education or training under Public Law 88–352," in *Discrimination against women: Hearings.* House of Representatives, Committee on Education and Labor, Special Subcommittee on Education. 91st Congress, second session. Washington: United States Government Printing Office.

1970b   *Report of Professional Women's Caucus, New York University, Saturday, April 11, 1970.* Washington: U.S. Department of Health, Education, and Welfare Office of Education. (Processed.)

HEATH, KATHRYN G., WITH THE COOPERATION OF SIXTY-NINE GOVERNMENTS

1962   *Ministries of education: their functions and organization.* Number OE-14064. Washington: United States Government Printing Office.

HOUSE OF REPRESENTATIVES

1963a *Civil rights message from the President of the United States: February 28.* 88th Congress, First Session. House document 75. Washington: United States Government Printing Office.

1963b *Civil rights message with a draft of a bill from the President of the United States: June 19.* 88th Congress, First Session. House document 124. Washington: United States Government Printing Office.

1971 *Discrimination against women: hearings July 1 and 31, 1970.* Special Subcommittee on Education. 91st Congress, Second Session. Washington: United States Government Printing Office.

1973 *Oversight hearings on discrimination against women, April 26, 27, May 5 and 10, 1972.* Committee on Education and Labor. Ad Hoc Subcommittee on Discrimination Against Women. Washington: United States Government Printing Office.

INTERDEPARTMENTAL COMMITTEE ON THE STATUS OF WOMEN

1968 *American women 1963–1968: report to the President.* Washington: United States Government Printing Office.

INTERDEPARTMENTAL COMMITTEE ON THE STATUS OF WOMEN

n.d. *Washington Newsletter for Women* 1:4.

LAURENCE, MARGARET

n.d. *Lets go all the way in the 92nd congress.* Washington: Women United. (16 April 1971. Women to fight for ERA. *Women Today* 1, 6:14)

MICHIGAN INAUGURATES GOVERNOR'S COMMISSION ON STATUS OF WOMEN

n.d. *National Business Woman* 42:11.

MILLER, HELEN A.

1961 *Federal aid for education: a history of proposals which have received consideration by the Congress of the United States (1789–1960).* Committee print of the House of Representatives Committee on Education and Labor. Washington: United States Government Printing Office.

MUIRHEAD, PETER H.

1970 *Statement* (before the Special Subcommittee on Education of the Committee on Education and Labor, House of Representatives, 8–9). July 1. Washington: United States Department of Heath, Education, and Welfare.

OLTMAN, RUTH M., *compiler*

1973 *Women's caucuses and commissions in professional associations.* Washington: American Association of University Women.

PIFER, ALAN

1972 *Women in higher education.* New York: Carnegie Corporation of New York.

PRESIDENT'S COMMISSION ON THE STATUS OF WOMEN

1963 *American Women: 1963.* Report to the President. Washington: United States Government Printing Office.

PRESIDENT'S TASK FORCE ON WOMEN'S RIGHTS AND RESPONSIBILITIES

1970 *A matter of simple justice: report, December 15, 1969.* Washington: United States Government Printing Office.

Proceedings of the conference on the care of dependent children

1909 *Held at Washington, D. C., January 25–26, 1909.* 60th Congress,

Second Session. Senate document 721. Washington: United States Government Printing Office.

Report of the President's Task Force on Education
1964   November 14. John W. Gardner, chairman. Austin, Texas (Unpublished; on file in Lyndon Baines Johnson Library.)

ROBINSON, LORA H.
n.d.   The emergence of women's courses in higher education. *ERIC Higher Education Research Currents.*

SCHNIER, MIRIAM, *editor*
1972   *Feminism: the essential historical writings.* New York: Random House Vintage Books.

STEINHILBER, AUGUST W., CARL J. SOKOLOWSKI
1966   *State law on compulsory education attendance.* Washington: United States Government Printing Office.

TASK FORCE ON WOMEN'S RIGHTS AND RESPONSIBILITIES
n.d.   Announcement of establishment and membership. *Weekly Compilation of Presidential Documents* 5: 1352–53.

UNITED STATES CIVIL SERVICE COMMISSION
1968   *Study of employment of women in the Federal Government, 1967.* United States Civil Service Commission, Statistics Section. Washington: United States Government Printing Office.

UNITED STATES DEPARTMENT OF HEALTH, EDUCATION, AND WELFARE
1967   *The story of the Rehabilitation Service. Children and youth.* Social and Rehabilitation Service. Children's Bureau. Washington: United States Government Printing Office.

UNITED STATES DEPARTMENT OF LABOR
1967   *Continuing education programs for women.* Women's Bureau. Pamphlet 10. Washington: United States Government Printing Office.
1971   *Continuing education programs and services for women.* Women's Bureau. Pamphlet 10, revised. Washington: United States Government Printing Office.
1973a   *Equal Pay Act findings: June 1, 1973.* Washington: United States Government Printing Office.
1973b   *Women and work: April 1973.* Office of Information, Publications, and Reports. Washington: United States Government Printing Office.

UNITED STATES EQUAL EMPLOYMENT OPPORTUNITY COMMISSION
1968   "Analysis of charges by basis of discrimination," in *Second annual report*, page 6. Washington: United States Government Printing *Office.*

UNITED STATES SENATE
1972   *Equal rights for men and women.* March 14. Committee on the Judiciary. Report 92–689. Washington: United States Government Printing Office.

Washington Post, The
1970   "Feminists choose to wait." *The Washington Post.* November 19, 1970.

WHITE HOUSE, THE
1973   *Women currently serving in non-career positions GS-16 and above.* Washington.

WOMEN'S EQUITY ACTION LEAGUE
1970   *Universities and colleges charged on sex discrimination under Executive Order 11246 as amended by 11375.* Washington.
WOMEN UNITED TO FIGHT FOR ERA
n.d.   *Women Today* 1:14.

Judicial References

"Case No. 14,459: United States v. Anthony, June 18, 1873," in *The Federal cases* 24. Comprising cases argued and determined in the circuit and district courts of the United States.

Federal reporter, second series. Cases argued and determined in the United States Courts of Appeals, United States Court of Claims, and United States Court of Customs and Patent Appeals. Saint Paul, Minnesota: West Publishing Company.

United States Reports. Cases at judge in the Supreme Court. Washington: United States Government Printing Office.

Legislative and Regulatory References

"Articles of confederation — 1777," in *United States code.* 1970 edition, title I, pages xxxiii-xxxvii. Washington: United States Government Printing Office.

Congressional globe, The. Containing proceedings and debates of the United States Congress from 1833–1873. Washington: Blair and Rives succeeded by F. J. Rives and George A. Bailey.

Congressional record. Containing proceedings and debates of the United States Congress beginning in 1873, with "No." indicating the daily edition and "Part" the bound edition. Washington: United States Government Printing Office.

"Constitution of the United States of America," in *United States code.* 1970 edition, title I, pages xliii-liii. Washington: United States Government Printing Office.

"Declaration of Independence, The — 1776," in *United States code.* 1970 edition, title I, pages xxix-xxxi. Washington: United States Government Printing Office.

"Executive orders," in *Federal Register* by date and in *Code of Federal regulations* by title and part. Washington: United States Government Printing Office.

FITZPATRICK, JOHN C. 1933. "An ordinance for ascertaining the mode of disposing of lands in the Western Territory," in *Journals of the Continental Congress: 1774–1789.* Edited from originals in the Library of Congress, XXVIII, 1785, page 378. Washington: United States Government Printing Office.

HILL, ROSCOE R. 1936 "An ordinance for the government of the territory of the United States north west of the river Ohio," in *Journals of the Continental*

Congress: 1774–1789. Edited from originals in the Library of Congress, XXXII, 1787, 340. Washington: United States Government Printing Office.

Opinions of the Attorney General. Washington: United States Government Printing Office.

"Public laws," in *United States statutes* at large by date and in *United States code* by code title and section. 1970 edition with annual supplements (except for July 12, 1870 law which appears in any earlier edition of the code with repeal in the 1965 supplement). Washington: United States Government Printing Office.

"Resolution 7, 1919," in "Verbatim Minutes of the Founding Convention, St Louis, Missouri." Washington: The National Federation of Business and Professional Women's Clubs. (Typed).

Letters

ANTHONY, SUSAN B., MATILDA JOSLYN GAGE, ELIZABETH CADY STANTON
   1873   "To the Honorable Senate and House of Representatives in Congress assembled," in handwriting in *National Archives.*
DOWDING, NANCY E., *President, Women's Equity Action League*
   1970   "To Secretary of Labor George P. Schultz," in *Congressional Record* 116 (Part 5): 6400.
DWYER, FLORENCE P., *Republican Congresswoman from New Jersey*
   1969   "To the President," in *Press release: March 17, 1969.*
"FPM letter"
   1962   Number 330-1 — Elimination of sex discrimination: July 21, 1962 revision," in *Federal Personnel Manual.* Washington: United States Civil Service Commission.
SASSOWER, DORIS L., *Chairman, National Legal Task Force, Professional Women's Caucus*
   1971   "To Secretary of Health, Education, and Welfare Elliot L. Richardson." New York. (Unpublished.)
WOMEN'S EQUITY ACTION LEAGUE
   1970   "To Secretary of Health, Education, and Welfare Elliot L. Richardson." Washington. (Unpublished.)

Discrimination Against Women in the United States: Higher Education, Government Enforcement Agencies, and Unions

ANNA M. BABEY-BROOKE

DISCRIMINATION IN HIGHER EDUCATION

Despite the reports that affirmative action programs in universities are upgrading the position of women in higher education; despite the numerous articles on how the Department of Health, Education and Welfare (HEW) and the Equal Employment Opportunity Commission (EEOC) are remedying the plight of women; despite the statistics published by the city commissioners and state commissioners of human rights throughout the nation that they are successfully helping women in their struggle for full social and economic rights — women are being frustrated at every stage in their battle against sex discrimination.

Present university employment, tenure, and promotion practices in relation to women must be changed. How? By more publicity about the injustices they perpetuate. By more pressure and action to force governmental agencies, subsidized by public taxation, to do the job for which they were created: i.e. to use more effectively and rapidly the processes established to eliminate discrimination against women. Because CUNY (City University of New York) pays a higher than average salary to its faculty, it is touted as a "progressive" university. Yet my own case may be cited to indicate that change in other respects is proceeding at a tortoise-like pace, if at all. In fact, the entrenched powers at CUNY are waging a strenuous battle to flout the laws that were promulgated to improve the position of women; and the agencies set up to enforce these laws seem to be powerless or reluctant to do so. Are they unable to cut through the red tape and speed the procedures available to them? Are they indifferent to the plight of women who eventually run out of the superhuman resources, strength, and courage that are required to continue this struggle? What happens to women when their unions fail to support them and when class-action suits prove ineffective? Many of the women involved in these battles not only suffer injustice based on sex discrimination, but also are depleted economically, physically, and psychologically. If this is what happens to academic women when they fight discrimination, how much more severely affected must be the women in lower economic statuses? How much more quickly must they give up in their struggles?

I started my action charging discrimination in October 1964, and proceeded through all the remedial steps: appealing to the Board of Higher Education; the State Commissioner of Education; to the City and State Commissions of Human Rights; to the Department of Health, Education and Welfare; the Department of Labor, and the Equal Employment Opportunity Commission. HEW found discrimination by reason of sex. Yet from 1964 to 1975, my position has remained unchanged. The government bureaucracy and the school administration proceed independently of judicial processes and exercise unlimited sovereignty in their respective areas. Women are employed in large numbers only at the lowest ranks. Affirmative action proves to be no action, and no action preserves and reenforces the status quo. And when women bring charges, despite the statistics of affirmative action reports, those without tenure never get tenure and those with tenure are not promoted.

Statistics on the status of women at Brooklyn College, a unit of CUNY, reveal the nature of discrimination against women in academia and show fully the failures of the various governmental and administrative agencies and unions in remedying the economic status and ameliorating the psychological strains on women.

From 1930, when Brooklyn College was founded, to 1964, when I started my action charging discrimination by reason of sex (a period of thirty-four years), 151 men and 16 women were promoted to full professor; 194 men and 48 women were promoted to associates.

As of 1964, the average number of years it took men to go from their initial appointment to the rank of full professor in the college was 11.5, but the average for women was 18.6; to go to the rank of associate — for men 8.5 years, for women 13 years; to go to the rank of assistant professor — for men 4.4 years for women 8.6 years.

In eight departments, including anthropology, art, geology, psychology, and sociology, no woman had been appointed to the rank of full professor up to 1970. In five of these departments no women had ever been promoted to associate professor. Yet in 1967 the Registrar at Brooklyn College reported a total enrollment of 12,330 women students as against

9,965 men students, the matriculated students in the day session being 5,246 women and 4,487 men (Congressional Record 1970).

What was the national situation at that time? The percentage of doctorates earned by women in 1967–1968 was: 25 percent in psychology; 34 percent in fine arts; 24 percent in anthropology; and 19 percent in sociology (Hooper and Chandler n.d.). Was there an improvement in the economic position of academic women by 1972–1973? The Department of Health, Education and Welfare, Office of Education, reports that the proportion of women faculty members has changed little in the past ten years: there is a sharp rise in the proportion of women with the rank of instructor. About 43.5 percent of all faculty with the rank of instructor were women in 1972–1973, compared with 30.9 percent in 1962–1963 However the increased percentage of women in all ranks was "little or nothing."

Women professors rose less than 1 percent, from 8.7 percent in 1962–1963 to 9.4 percent in 1972–1973; about 15.8 percent of all associate professors were women in 1972–1973 compared with 16.1 percent ten years earlier, a decrease of 0.3 percent; while some 22.5 percent of assistant professors were women as against 23.1 percent in 1962–1963, another decrease.

Health, Education and Welfare also reports that in 1972–1973 women employed as full-time faculty received an annual average salary of $11,862, which is $2,500 less than the $14,352 average for their male counterparts. Some 22.5 percent, or 57,297 of the 254,930 full-time faculty members employed in the United States, are women (Hooper 1973).

Why this continuing picture of discrimination against women in academia? The answer is that the various agencies — city, state, federal — and the collective bargaining bodies remain ensconced in their strength and do not move to remedy the situation, as illustrated by my case.

In 1964, after having taught at the college for twenty-six years, with a Ph.D. from Columbia received in 1938, I started a grievance procedure against Brooklyn College for failing to promote me to the rank of full professor, my reason: sex discrimination. I went through the customary channels spelled out in the bylaws: an appeal to the college president, to the local borough chapter of the Board of Higher Education, and to the Board itself. For attending these meetings, I was docked in pay, an illegal procedure. I lost at every step of the way, as was to be expected, as the New York City Board of Higher Education in all its history has NEVER UPHELD AN APPELLANT OR A GRIEVANT.

I then appealed, in the spring of 1965, to the State Commissioner of Education, Dr. James Allen, on the advice of Arthur Kahn, counsel for

364 ANNA M. BABEY-BROOKE

the Board of Higher Education. But this advice turned out to be detrimental to the interests of the grievant on two grounds: (1) it was a delaying tactic which served only the interests of the Board; and (2) the Commission of Education has always upheld the decisions of the Board of Higher Education, just as this Board has always upheld the decisions of the college presidents.

The meeting with Dr. Allen was postponed three times over a period of twelve months, at the request of the Board of Higher Education, which pleaded for more time to prepare the case. During this period I received a letter from the legal section of the State Department of Education which stated that by appealing to the Commissioner, I waived my right to bring my case to the courts. However, in my written response, I refused to waive my rights to go to court.

The meeting was finally held on April 21, 1966, in Albany, and not in the New York State downtown Manhattan office, as requested by the appellant. The Board submitted the minutes of its hearing, but DELETED TWO IMPORTANT EXHIBITS pertaining to the supreme power of the college president in appointments and promotions. My protests at the delays and the omission of vital material were of no avail. The twenty-minute session with the Commission was also futile, for the relevant materials were not even touched upon. Further, no minutes were taken; thus there was no record of the discussion, a fact which the Commissioner himself, in a letter to the grievant, admitted was the common practice. A typical Kangaroo Court! As grievant, I had not been told that a written brief should be submitted or that oral testimony was unacceptable. The reverse of this procedure is practiced in the New York State Commission of Human Rights: only oral testimony is admitted, and written testimony is excluded, as will be explained later. I was never informed of these procedures, and found out about them only when I was in the middle of them — to my great disadvantage.

On September 12, 1966, Acting Commissioner of Education Ewald B. Nyquist decided against me on two counts: (1) that he would not substitute his judgment for that of the Board (then why was the grievant advised to appeal to the Commissioner in the first place?); (2) that other candidates for promotion MAY HAVE HAD BETTER RECORDS (although he did not investigate to determine whether they did indeed have better records; the Commissioner's "may have" decision is like a Supreme Court decree ending with the statement, "This law may be constitutional.")

The Commissioner stated incorrectly that I was not familiar with the records of the members of the English Department (where I taught) who were candidates for promotion. But all teachers' *vitae* are circulated to the voting members of the department for ranking, and as I had been a voting member since 1941, I was thoroughly familiar with the records of candidates for promotion. Although I was consistently ranked first or second in the department from 1954 to 1969, 212 people at Brooklyn College, predominantly men, were promoted ahead of me. This can hardly be regarded a statistical accident.

In December, 1966, I filed a complaint with the New York City Commissioner of Human Rights (Mr. Booth), charging discrimination by reason of sex. Four years and three commissioners later,[1] the verdict was pronounced. It took five years, less two days, for the City Commission on Human Rights to rule against me (the grievant) on the technical ground that I had appealed to the State Commissioner of Education(on the advice, it will be remembered, of the lawyer for the Board of Higher Education). On December 30, 1970, Commissioner Eleanor Holmes Norton ruled as follows:

It is unfortunate that the Commission is compelled to make a determination in this matter on technical grounds [because she had appealed to the State Commissioner of Education]. The issues in the case deeply affect the welfare of our city, and the evidence uncovered by the assiduous and exhaustive investigation by Commission personnel tend to support the allegation that Brooklyn College discriminated on the basis of sex in its promotional practices. It is to be deplored, therefore, that the respondent, as a responsible public institution, has not welcomed an impartial public hearing as a forum within which to assist the Commission in reaching a just and fair result (Commission of Human Rights 1970).

With the inclusion of the sex discrimination clause in Executive Order 11246, Part II, as amended effective October, 1968, I filed in the spring of 1970 with the Departments of Labor, and of Health, Education and Welfare charging Brooklyn College with discrimination by reason of sex. I submitted statistics pinpointing the patterns of continuing discrimination against women in promotion from 1930 to 1970 in all the departments of the college. Materials were gathered exclusively from college catalogues because these were the only sources available to me.

After a thorough investigation, the Department of Health, Education and Welfare, in a letter to President John W. Kneller, dated April 30, 1971, found Brooklyn College guilty on thirteen counts of discrimination

---

[1] Delays are customary in the City Commissioner's office. Dr. Valentine Rossilli Winsey filed her complaint against Pace College with the City Commisison of Human Rights on July 30, 1970; had three fact-finding conferences; had fifteen cancellations; was advised to get her own attorney; won her case and received no job and no financial settlement — nothing. In short, a victory with no back pay, no job, and no money and now is not readily employable by any other university because she is regarded as "trouble."

by reason of sex and gave the college fifteen days (May 15, 1971) to correct the injustice and thirty days (May 30, 1971) to report to the government.

In this letter to Kneller, Mr. Joseph Leahy, Chief of Contract Compliance, indicated that the findings were derived exclusively from college records: Promotion Forms D, faculty folders, Personnel and Budget Committee Minutes, etc. The words "pattern" and "practice" summed up the government's method for detecting discrimination in the Department of English at Brooklyn College:

Comparing the Complainant's employment history with that of the College's criteria for promotion, we find that the Complainant meets your established criteria for promotion.

Since the investigation showed a pattern and practice of slower promotions for women in the English Department, since the Complainant fits this pattern and since we were unable to find any reason for the Complainant's slow promotional progress, other than her sex, we find that the Complainant is a victim of the general pattern of sex discrimination. The slow promotional progress of the Complainant and her delayed promotions have in effect constituted a "denial" of promotion to full professor because of her sex.

In accordance with the authority delegated to us by Executive Order 11246, as amended, we are recommending that the Complainant be immediately promoted to the rank of full professor. This promotion will serve to erase in part the discrimination on the basis of sex which has delayed or denied her promotion before this time.

With regard to the Complainant's second allegation, "that she has incured financial losses" because of this discriminatory denial of promotion, we also find that the evidence supports this allegation.

The data already presented support the conclusion that the Complainant would have been a full professor before 1968 had she not been discriminated against because of her sex.

All full professors who received that rank in 1968 or before are at the top of the salary schedule. These full professors are earning, and for the past three years have earned, between $9,000 and $10,000 more per year than the Complainant.

In accordance with the authority delegated to us by Executive Order 11246, as amended, we are recommending that the Complainant's salary be immediately raised to the top level of the salary schedule for full professors and that she be granted back salary to compensate for the salary lost as a result of discrimination. The Complainant's salary for 1971 should be brought to a level equivalent to the maximum of the salary schedule for full professors. The recommended back salary obligates your institution to compensate the Complainant for losses in pay since October 13, 1968 and the maximum salary a full professor could have received since October 13, 1968. The new salary, in addition to the recompense, will serve to erase the discrimination on the basis of sex which has resulted in a salary loss to the Complainant.

What was the significance to CUNY of HEW's findings at Brooklyn College? Executive Order 11246, signed by President Lyndon Johnson in

1965, forbids discrimination by all federal contractors because of race, color, religion, or national origin. Executive Order 11375, effective October 1968, amended this to include discrimination based on sex. The Executive Order was a series of rules and regulations which contractors were to follow if they wanted government monies. Because of the ruling that Brooklyn College discriminated against women, the Executive Order applied in 1971 to the entire twenty colleges in the CUNY complex, not to Brooklyn College alone. A city or state educational institution did not have to submit a report of affirmative action at that time UNLESS IT WAS FOUND GUILTY OF DISCRIMINATION. For this reason, the finding that Brooklyn College discriminated against me was, as some organizations have phrased it, a "landmark case in higher education."

President Kneller of Brooklyn College was ordered to remedy the situation by June 1, 1971, but he appealed to Congressman Emanuel Celler (dean of the New York Congressional District delegation and head of the Judiciary Committee, had who consistently voted against women's rights throughout his very long tenure in office) for a postponement and reconsideration of issues. At the Washington meeting, Kneller was supported by presidents from other colleges — Columbia, New York University, Rochester — and even by the Commissioner of Education. President Kneller argued that Health, Education and Welfare was interfering with the academic freedom of Brooklyn College; that the decision to promote me should not be enforced; and that any additional complaints against the University be abandoned.

Other Congressional representatives at the meeting, including Bella Abzug, Shirley Chisholm, and Edward Koch, urged that the investigation of CUNY continue for the purpose of ending discrimination. Koch reported the finding of this meeting in the *Congressional Record*, July 1, 1971.

As of January 1975, I am still not a full professor, and HEW's ruling remains unenforced. Why? The CUNY administration, supported by presidents of other colleges who are equally reluctant to equalize the position of their women faculty, appealed to the politicians and members of Congress to exert pressure on HEW. These university representatives claimed that the equalization of the status of women would violate "academic freedom," and withheld or distorted the data on their employment and promotion practices.

In the spring of 1972, more than a year after Leahy's directive to Kneller to rectify my status and that of other women at Brooklyn College, David Newton, Vice Chancellor, and President Kneller denied that Leahy's letter was issued as a directive. On June 14, 1972, I learned from Mr.

Barnett, the New York investigator at HEW, that the Leahy letter was still in force as a directive and had not been rescinded. But he did not send a written statement to this effect to me, as grievant.

The only other part that HEW played in this case was to have their representative, Kathy Fraser, approach me on January 12, 1973 and again on February 5, 1973 to suggest that the case could possibly be settled if I would accept a full professorship as of January 1, 1973 with the lowest salary on this level. I regarded this suggestion as a denial of HEW's ruling and refused, asking Mrs. Fraser to postpone any further discussion of my case because the State Commissioner of Human Rights was moving into action with my complaint.

On July 9, 1971 I had filed a complaint with the New York State Commission of Human Rights and with EEOC. Sixty days later, in accordance with regulations, I informed the Office of Equal Employment Opportunity that the State Commission had now started on my case. A year later, the summer of 1972, EEOC orally informed me that it would take them four years to process my complaint because of the huge backlog of cases. In the spring of 1973 EEOC further informed me that thereafter they would take only class-action complaints.

The New York State Human Rights Commission found probable cause in my complaint against Brooklyn College[2] and scheduled hearings for December 1973 and January 1974, about two and a half years after the grievance was filed. This delay is short when compared with the thirteen years it took for the State to find in favor of Dr. J. V. Lombardo of Queens College, CUNY, who had charged discrimination by reason of religion and national origin.

The processing of complaints with the New York State Commission of Human Rights reveals how cumbersome is the bureaucratic machinery when it comes to rectifying discrimination, although the money paying the salaries of the Commission officials comes from the taxes of the citizenry:
1.   Any event that occurred one year before the filing of the complaint is admissible as evidence; thus, any event that is more than one year old is inadmissible. This ruling may eliminate vital facts in the case.
2.   Any finding published in letter form is inadmissible: for example, Mr. Leahy's letter from HEW directing Brooklyn College to remedy sex

---

[2]   Case Cs 24641-71, State of New York, State Division of Human Rights on the Complaint of Anna M. Babey-Brooke, Complainant, against The Board of Higher Education of the City of New York and John W. Kneller, President of Brooklyn College, Respondent.

When the State Commission concludes this case, the procedures, statistics, and transactions will be published by Santa Barbara Press.

discrimination is inadmissible to the State Commission's examiner. Only if Mr. Leahy or his investigating agents testify personally before the examiner is the evidence of discrimination considered.

3.   Any statistical studies covering the period prior to one year before filing are inadmissible unless the examiner accepts the statement that there is a pattern and practice of discrimination.

4.   Although the law places the responsibility of investigating squarely on the agency, it often does absolutely no investigating on its own. Instead, the officials merely hold a "conference," where the complainant is not advised that he or she carries the burden of proof and must produce evidence and witnesses to support the complaint. The complainant is not advised of his or her rights or of the procedures of the Division.

5.   The complainant is not made aware of the fact that a finding of "no probable cause" completely severs one's rights under the Human Rights Law. The complainant cannot get another opportunity to present evidence in his or her own behalf because by appealing to the State Commission, one relinquishes one's right to appeal to the Courts.

6.   The decision of the Commission may be appealed to the State Human Rights Appeal Board, but this Board considers only the evidence that is already in the record, and no other evidence may be offered, almost guaranteeing that the Appeal Board will confirm the decision of the Commission.

7.   The State Commission and the respondent negotiate and both sign a conciliation agreement which is then submitted to the complainant who had been barred from the negotiations. If the complainant rejects the agreement, the State has the power to dismiss the complaint, and the only remedy is to start all over again in the courts. This procedure has been severely criticized by representatives of the National Organization for Women and by Women's Equity Action League.

THE UNION AND COLLECTIVE BARGAINING

In 1964, there were two unions at CUNY: the United Federation of College Teachers and the Legislative Conference. I belonged to both, but I went to the Legislative Conference, which had jurisdiction over professors, to process my request for promotion from assistant professor to full professor. The Legislative Conference at this time was somnolent; it did not even have a grievance machinery nor a place to meet with grievants. I asked the president, Belle Zeller, to present my grievance, but Zeller replied that the union representative could go "only in an auditory capacity." The union representative made her "auditory" and useless position clear to the Brooklyn Committee of the Board of Higher Education in January of 1965.

In 1965 no union representative even accompanied me when I presented my case independently to the complete Board of Higher Education, which consisted of twenty-two members and all the college presidents. I went in alone, knowing full well that the New York City Board of Higher Education had never, in all its history, upheld an appellant or a grievant. I had to prepare my own case at a time when I was totally unfamiliar with the procedures in the University bylaws. The Legislative Conference did nothing.

In 1970, the staff of CUNY could engage in collective bargaining because of the Taylor law, and it voted for two unions: the Legislative Conference representing the professorial ranks and the United Federation of College Teachers representing the other members of the college. The two unions drew up collective bargaining contracts with CUNY with procedures for processing grievances. I then filed another complaint, but this time the Legislative Conference said I had no grievance. This was the usual tactic to discourage grievances, for the Legislative Conference claimed it had no money and, further, it did not wish to process grievances. I, however, insisted so that mine became the first Legislative Conference case to come before the Brooklyn College president at step one and before Vice Chancellor Bernard Mintz and his labor advisor Manson at step two for the professorial rank.

At this stage, Manson stated, on January 22, 1970, that my promotion to associate professor in 1968 was "a form of restitution," "a delayed promotion," and that there had been gross error. He added that if I were not promoted to full professor in the next year or two (by 1971–1972), that would be malice. "He stated that her best argument would be discrimination by reason of sex."

No minutes were taken at step two, the meeting with the vice-chancellor and no one was allowed to testify other than the union representative and the grievant. On the following day I, as grievant, submitted a memorandum of the discussions at the meeting and requested a correction of facts within five days. (If there is no written record, the purpose of the meeting is destroyed and the confrontation valueless. Grievants are advised always to submit memoranda of the proceedings at any meeting for which records are necessary.)

The Board of Higher Education refused to accept my memorandum, and the union representative, Philip Sheinwald orally supported the Board's ruling. Within a year, this man, without a Ph.D., received a promotion to full professorship in 1971.

The vice-chancellor denied my complaint, and the next step in labor bargaining procedure was to submit the matter to arbitration. I requested the Legislative Conference to proceed, but it refused to go to arbitration. The UFCT agreed to go to arbitration if I paid all expenses. I refused.

Early in 1971 the Legislative Conference appointed me chairperson of the Committee on Discrimination against Women for three reasons:

1. HEW's directive, spelled out in Leahy's letter, ordering President Kneller of Brooklyn College to promote me to full professor as of October 13, 1968;

2. the temper of the times on affirmative action; and

3. the fact that I was a member of the prestigious Ad Hoc Committee of CUNY, consisting of more than thirty outside organizations, as well as chairperson of the Education Committee of the New York City Chapter, American Association of University Women.

The members of the Committee on Discrimination against Women met bimonthly with the Chancellor's representatives on women's grievances and women's needs at CUNY, but they got nowhere. Therefore on December, 1971, women faculty set up an independent organization, CUNY Women's Coalition, which could be more militant than the Committee on Discrimination against Women operating within the terms of the Union contract. So the battleground shifted to the CUNY Women's Coalition, the members of which were both within and outside both unions.

In September 1971, the members of the New York City Council met with the chancellor of CUNY to establish a committee of women drawn from all twenty of the CUNY colleges. Instead, however, the chancellor formed his own advisory committee on the status of women. This was, as a CUNY Women's Coalition Newsletter reported, "a clever ploy to divide women, to serve as as a buffer between the women faculty of CUNY and the Administration, and to prevent women from organizing themselves" (CUNY Women's Coalition 1972, 1975:55). In June 1972, the CUNY Women's Coalition prepared a study of discrimination against women in CUNY. What was true in my case was found to be true of other women throughout CUNY. But the administration, determined not to correct past discrimination, give affirmative action committees no power to rectify or to make recommendations.

The Chancellor's Advisory Committee on the Status of Women had no powers to implement recommendations or to protect from harassment those women faculty members who testified before it. (In fact, one woman was indicted for "unprofessional behavior" as a result of her testimony.) I testified both on my own behalf and as a representative of the Legislative

Conference Committee on Discrimination. But a perfectly closed system was established to prevent action to rectify sex discrimination and yet to give the appearance of action. It is noteworthy that the project director for the Chancellor's Advisory Committee was made an assistant to the chancellor in the summer of 1973, upon the completion of a report on "The status of women at the City University of New York," which documented the discrimination against women in CUNY, since the fall, 1971, thereby presenting a less dire picture. But no action has as yet been taken to remedy the basic situation on all levels.

Rectification of discrimination is a mockery at CUNY. Both the administration and the union manipulate grievances, distort facts, engage in dilatory tactics, and flout federal rulings. They are expert at dodging legal directives and at dangling promises of reward to those whom they can co-opt.

Odell Shepard — writer, poet, university professor, and Pulitzer Prize winner in 1957 for his biography of Bronson Alcott — made an observation when he was Lieutenant-Governor of Connecticut in 1940 that supports one conclusion to be drawn from this study on the discrimination against women at Brooklyn College and throughout CUNY:

I've never lived in an ivory tower and I never want to.
Ivory tower, indeed! On a college faculty political activity
is just about twice as poisonous as any I'll ever see
in the State House.

Despite the fact that in 1971 HEW found Brooklyn College guilty of discriminating against women and ruled in my favor, no federal monies have been withheld from Brooklyn College and the City University of New York up to this time.

CONCLUSION

Under the regulation of Title Seven, the principal weapon from 1970 to 1972 was the Affirmative Action plan required under the Executive Order; this applied as much to a college president as to a contractor. Colleges and universities with Federal contracts in excess of $ 15,000 were required to file an Affirmative Action plan ostensibly barring discrimination on the basis of sex or race. The government's only legal action for noncompliance was to suspend the federal contracts.

But there were three weaknesses obstructing the path of women seeking redress of grievances for discrimination by reason of sex: (1) the legal action had to be taken by the Department of Health, Education, and Welfare, not by the individual herself; (2) the Affirmative Action course was likened to a nuclear weapon by some of the feminists — the suspension of contracts involving millions of dollars was too big a cudgel to use for enlisting the cooperation of the university administration; (3) the numerical goals stipulated by Affirmative Action were interpreted by some critics as constituting employment quotas.

Thus, late in 1973, a shift in tactics occurred, away from reliance on the Federal government and toward the use of the local courts in the fight against alleged sex discrimination. The class action suit filed by CUNY Women's Coalition followed this pattern of filing a complaint with EEOC and after the stipulated 250-day period, filing a court suit. Twenty-one women signed the Coalition complaint. Will this maneuver chart a new pathway for women? Or will the twenty-one be martyrs? The battle continues, and the women must prove endlessly energetic, resourceful, and relentless in pursuit of their goals.

REFERENCES

Congressional record, the
    1970   E 5103–5104. June 3.
    1971   July 1.
COMMISSION OF HUMAN RIGHTS
    1970   Commission of Human Rights on the complaint of Anna M. Babey-Brooke, Complainant, against Brooklyn College, Respondent, Complaint 2709-CE.
CUNY WOMEN'S COALITION
    1972   "Discrimination against women: a study of the City University of New York." June. New York. (Unpublished mimeo.)
HOOPER, MARY EVANS, MARJORIE O. CHANDLER
    n.d.   *Earned degrees conferred: 1967–1968.* Part A, Summary data, OE 54013-68. Department of Health, Education and Welfare.
HOOPER, MARY EVANS
    1973   *Earned degrees conferred: 1970–1971.* OE 73-11412. Department of Health, Education and Welfare, Office of Education. September.

The Women's Liberation Movement
in the United States

JO FREEMAN

Sometime during the 1920's, feminism died in the United States. It was a premature death — feminists had just obtained that long-sought tool, the vote, with which they had hoped to make an equal place for women in this society — but it seemed an irreversible one. By the time the suffragists' granddaughters were old enough to vote, social mythology had firmly ensconsed women in the home, and the very term FEMINIST had become an insult.

Social mythology, however, did not always coincide with social fact. Even during the era of the "feminine mystique," the 1940's and the 1950's, when the relative number of academic degrees given to women was dropping, the absolute number of such degrees was rising astronomically. Women's participation in the labor force was also rising, even while women's position within it was declining. Opportunities aside, the trend toward smaller families plus a change in preferred status symbols from a leisured wife at home to a second car and a color television set, helped to transform the female labor force from one primarily of single women under twenty-five as it was in 1940, to one of married women and mothers over forty, as it was in 1950. Simultaneously, the job market became even more rigidly segregated; traditional female jobs such as teaching and social work were flooded by men; and women's share of professional and technical jobs declined by a third, with a commensurate decline in women's relative income. The result of all this was the creation of a class of highly educated, underemployed and underpaid women.

In the early 1960's, feminism was still an unmentionable, but it was slowly awakening from the dead. The first sign of new life was President Kennedy's establishment of the National Commission on the Status of

Women in 1961. Created at the urging of Esther Peterson of the Women's Bureau, the short-lived Commission produced several radical reports which thoroughly documented women's second-class status. It was followed by the formation of a citizen's advisory council and fifty state commissions. Many of the people involved in these commissions, dissatisfied with the lack of progress made on their recommendations, joined with Betty Friedan in 1966 to found the National Organization for Women (NOW).

NOW was the first new feminist organization in almost fifty years, but it was not the only beginning of the organized expression of the movement. The movement actually has two origins, in two separate strata of society with different styles, orientation, values, and forms of organization. Although the composition of both branches tends to be predominantly white, middle-class, and college-educated, in many ways the two movements have remained separate. Initially the median age of the activists of what I call the older branch of the movement was higher. This branch also began earlier. In addition to NOW, it contains such organizations as the Women's Equity Action League, Federally Employed Women (FEW), and some fifty other organizations and caucuses of professional women. Their style of organization has tended to be traditionally formal, with numerous elected officers, boards of directors, bylaws, and the other trappings of democratic procedure. All started as top-down organizations lacking a mass base. Some have subsequently developed a mass base, some have not yet done so, and others do not want to do so.

In 1967 and 1968, unaware of and unknown to NOW or to the state commissions, the other branch of the movement was taking shape. Contrary to popular myth, it did not begin on the campuses; nor was it started by Students for a Democratic Society (SDS). However, its activators were on the younger side of the generation gap. Although few were students, all were under thirty and had received political educations as participants in or concerned observers of the social action projects of the preceding decade. Many came direct from New Left and civil rights organizations, where they had been shunted into traditional roles and faced with the contradiction of working in a freedom movement but not being very free. Others had attended various courses on women in the multitude of free universities springing up around the country during those years.

In 1967 at least five groups formed spontaneously and independently of one another in five cities — Chicago, Toronto, Detroit, Seattle, and Gainsville (Florida). They arose at a very auspicious moment. The blacks had just ejected the whites from the civil rights movement, student power had been discredited by SDS, and the disorganized New Left was on the wane. Only draft resistance activities were on the rise, and this movement, more than any other, exemplified the social inequalities of the sexes. Men could resist the draft. Women could only counsel resistance.

There had been individual temporary caucuses and conferences of women as early as 1964, when Stokely Carmichael of the Student Non-violent Coordinating Committee (SNCC) made his infamous remark that "the only position for women in SNCC is prone." But it was not until 1967 that the groups developed a determined, if cautious, continuity and began consciously to expand. In 1968 they held their first, and so far only, national conference, attended by more than 200 women from the United States and Canada on less than a month's notice. For several years they continued to expand exponentially.

This expansion was more amoebic than organized, because the younger branch of this movement prides itself on its lack of organization. Eschewing structure and damning leadership, it has carried the concept of "everyone doing her own thing" almost to its logical extreme. The thousands of sister chapters around the country are virtually independent of one another, linked only by journals, newsletters, and cross-country travellers. Some cities have coordinating committees that try to maintain communication among local groups and to channel newcomers into appropriate ones, but none of these committees has any power over the activities, let alone the ideas, of any of the groups it serves. One result of this style is a very broadly based, creative movement, to which individuals can relate as they desire, with no concern for orthodoxy or doctrine. Another result is political impotence. It would be virtually impossible for this branch of the movement to join together in a nationwide action, even if its component units agree on issues. Fortunately, the older branch of the movement does have the structure necessary to coordinate such actions and is usually the one to initiate them, as NOW did for the August 26, 1970 national strike.

It is a common mistake to try to place the various feminist organizations on the traditional Left/Right spectrum. The terms REFORMIST and RADICAL are convenient and fit into our preconceived notions about the nature of political organization, but they are irrelevant here. Feminism cuts across normal categories and demands new perspectives in order to be understood. Some so-called REFORMIST groups propose changes that would make our society unrecognizable. Other so-called RADICAL groups concentrate on the traditional female concerns, of love, sex, children, and interpersonal relationships (although their views are untraditional). The activities of the organizations are similarly incongruous. The most typical division of labor, ironically, is that those groups labeled RADICAL engage primarily in educational work, while the REFORMIST ones are the activits. Structure and style, more acurately than ideology, differentiate the various groups and even here there has been much borrowing on both sides. In general, the older branch has used the traditional forms, often with great skill, while the younger branch has been experimental. The most prevalent innovation developed by the younger branch has been the "rap group." Essentially an educational technique, it has spread far beyond its origins and has become a major organizational unit of the whole movement, most frequently used by suburban housewives. From a sociological perspective, the rap group is probably the most valuable contribution by the Women's Liberation Movement to the tools for social change. Because of its importance, I shall disgress briefly to discuss it.

The rap group serves two main purposes. One is traditional; the other is unique. The traditional role is simply to bring women together in structured interactions. It has long been known that people can be kept down as long as they are kept divided, so that they relate more closely to their social superiors than to their social equals. When social development creates natural structures in which people can interact with one another and compare their common concerns, social movements occur. This is the function that the factory served for the workers, the Church for the Southern civil rights movement, the campus for the students, and the ghetto for the urban blacks.

Women have been largely deprived of a means of structured interaction. They have been kept isolated in their individual homes, relating more closely to men than to other women. Natural structures for women's interactions are still scarce, though they have begun to develop. But the rap group has provided an artificial structure that serves this purpose. These groups themselves have mechanisms for social change for they have been created specifically to alter the participants' perceptions and conceptions of themselves and of society at large.

Rap groups accomplish their purpose by "consciousness raising." The process is very simple. Women come together in groups of five to fifteen and talk about their personal problems, personal experiences, personal feelings, and personal concerns. From this public sharing comes the realization that what were thought to be personal problems have social causes and probably political solutions. Women learn to see how social structures and attitudes have molded them from birth and limited their opportunities. They ascertain the extent to which women have been denigrated in this society and how they have developed prejudices against themselves and other women.

It is in this process of deeply personal attitude change that the rap group has such a powerful tool. A movement's need to develop "correct consciousness" has long been known, but this consciousness is usually not developed by means intrinsic to the structures of the movement and does not require such a profound resocialization of one's concept of self. This experience is both irreversible and contagious. Once one has gone through such a "resocialization," one's view of oneself and the world is never the same again, even if there is no further active participation in the movement. Those who do drop out rarely do so without first spreading feminist ideas among their own friends and colleagues. All who undergo "consciousness raising" feel compelled to seek out other women with whom to share the experience.

There are several personal results from this process. The initial one is a decrease of self-depreciation and group depreciation. Women come to see themselves and other women as essentially worthwhile and interesting. With this comes the explosion of the myth of an individual solution. If women are the way they are because of society, they can only change their lives significantly by changing society. These feelings in turn create the consciousness of themselves as members of a group and the feeling of solidarity so necessary to any social movement. From this comes the concept of "sisterhood."

This need for group solidarity partly explains why men have usually been excluded from the rap groups. This was not the initial reason, but it has been one of the more beneficial by-products. Originally, the idea was borrowed from the Black Power movement, which was much in the public consciousness when the women's liberation movement began. It was reinforced by the unremitting hostility of most men of the New Left at the prospect of an independent women's movement not tied to radical ideology. Even when this hostility was not present, women in virtually every group in the United States, Canada, and Europe soon discovered that the traditional sex roles reasserted themselves in mixed groups regardless of the good intentions of the participants. Men inevitably dominated discussions and usually spoke only about how women's liberation related to men or how men were oppressed by the sex roles. In segregated groups women found the discussions to be more open, honest, and extensive. They could learn how to relate to other women, not just to men.

To return to my earlier discussion: while the two branches of the movement do not have significantly differing ideologies, their different structures and styles have resulted in significantly different activities. The women and men who formed NOW and its subsequent sister organizations created a national structure prepared to use legal, political, and media institutions. This it has done. The Equal Employment Opportunity Comission has changed many of its prejudicial attitudes toward women in its rulings of the last few years. Numerous lawsuits have been filed under the sex provision of title VII of the 1964 Civil Rights Act. The Equal Rights Ammendment has passed Congress. The Supreme Court has legalized some abortions. Complaints charging sex discrimination have been filed against more than 400 colleges and universities, as well as many businesses. Articles on feminism have appeared in virtually every news medium, and a whole host of new laws has been passed prohibiting sex discrimination in a variety of areas.

These groups have functioned and continue to function primarily as pressure groups within the limits of traditional political activity. Consequently, their actual membership remains small. Diversification of the older branch of the movement has been largely along occupational lines and primarily within the professions. Activity has stressed the use of the tools for change provided by the system, however limited these may be. Short-range goals are emphasized, and no attempt has been made to place them within a broader ideological framework.

Initially, this structure hampered the development of older branch organizations. NOW suffered three splits between 1967 and 1968. As the only action organization concerned with women's rights, it had attracted many kinds of people with many different views. With only a national structure and, at that point, no local base, it was difficult for individuals to pursue their particular concerns on a local level; they had to persuade the whole organization to support them. Given NOW's top-down structure and limited resources, this placed severe restrictions on diversity and, in turn, severe strains on the organization. Additional difficulties were created for local chapters by the lack of organizers to develop new chapters the lack of a program into which they could fit.

Eventually these initial difficulties were overcome, NOW and the other older branch organizations are thriving because they are able to use effectively the institutional tools that our society provides for social and political change. Yet these groups are also limited to the rather narrow arenas wherein these tools are designed to operate. The nature of the arenas and the particular skills they require for participation already limit both the kind of women who can effectively work in older branch groups and the activities they can undertake. When their scope is exhausted, it remains to be seen whether organizations such as NOW will wither, will institutionalize themselves as traditional pressure groups, or will show the imagination to develop new lines for action.

The younger branch has had an entirely different history and faces different prospects. It was able to expand rapidly in the beginning because it could capitalize on the infrastructure of organizations and media of the New Left and because its initiators were skilled in local community organizing. Because the prime unit was the small group and because no need for national cooperation was perceived, multitudinous splits increased its strength rather than drained its resources. Such fission was often "friendly" in nature, and even when it was not, it served to bring ever-increasing numbers of women under the movement's umbrella.

Unfortunately, these new masses of women lacked the organizing skills of the initiators, and because the ideas of "leadership" and "organization" were in disrepute, they made no attempt to acquire them. They did not want to deal with traditional political institutions and abjured all traditional political skills. Consequently, the movement institutions did not grow beyond the local level, and they were often inadequate to handle the accelerating influx of people into the movement. Although these small groups were diverse in kind and reponsible to no one for their focus, their nature determined both the structure and the strategy of the movement. To date, the major, though hardly exclusive, activities of the younger branch have been to organize rap groups, to arrange conferences, to put out educational literature, and to run service projects such as bookstores and health centers. Its contribution has been more the impact of its new ideas than its activities. It has developed several ideological perspectives, much of the terminology of the movement, an amazing number of publications and "counter-institutions," numerous new issues, and even new techniques for social change.

Nonetheless, this loose structure is flexible only within certain limits, and the movement has not yet shown a propensity to trancend them. While the rap groups have been excellent techniques for changing individual attitudes, they have not been very successful in dealing with social institutions. Their loose, informal structure encourages participation in discussion, and their supportive atmosphere elicits personal insights; but neither is very efficient in handling specific tasks. Thus, while they have been of fundamental value to the development of the movement, the more structured groups are politically more effective.

Individual rap groups tend to flounder when their members exhaust the virtues of consciousness raising and decide they want to do something more concrete. The problem is that most groups are unwilling to change their structures when they change their tasks. They have accepted the ideology of "structurelessness" without realizing the limitations of its uses.

This is currently causing an organizational crisis within the movement because the formation of rap groups has become obsolete as a major movement function. In the last few years, Women's Liberation has become a household phrase. Its issues are discussed and informal rap groups are formed by people who have no explicit connection with any movement groups. Ironically, this subtle, silent, and subversive spread of feminist consciousness is causing political unemployment. With educational work no longer such an overwhelming need, Women's Liberation groups have to develop new forms of organization to deal with new tasks in a new stage of development. While the resurgence of feminism tapped a major source of female energy, the younger branch has not yet been able to channel it. New groups form and dissolve at an accelerating rate, creating a good deal of consciousness and very little action. Most of the women who go through these groups do not stay within the younger branch. They are either recruited into NOW and the other national organizations or they drop out. The result is that most of the movement is proliferating underground. It often seems mired in introspection, but it is in fact creating a vast reservoir of conscious feminist sentiments which awaits only an appropriate opportunity for action.

The widely differing backgrounds and perspectives of the women in the movement have resulted in widely differing interpretations of women's status. Some are more sophisticated and some are better publicized. Yet there is no comprehensive set of beliefs that can accurately be labeled Women's Liberationist, feminist, neofeminist, or radical feminist ideology. At best one can say there is general agreement on two theoretical concerns. The first is the feminist critique of society, and the second is the idea of oppression.

The feminist critique starts from premises that differ completely from those of the traditional view of society, and therefore neither can really refute the other. The latter assumes that men and women are essentially different and should serve different social functions. Their diverse roles and statuses simply reflect these essential differences. The feminist perspective starts from the premise that women and men are constitutionally equal and share the same human capabilities. Observed differences therefore demand a critical analysis of the social institutions that cause them.

The term OPPRESSION was long avoided as too rhetorical, but there was no convenient euphemism, and DISCRIMINATION was inadequate to describe what happens to women and what they have in common with other groups. As long as the word remained illegitimate, so did the idea. But the idea was too valuable to ignore. Although it is still largely an undeveloped concept whose details have not been sketched, oppression appears to have two aspects which, like two sides of a coin, are distinct, yet inseparable. The social structural manifestations are easily visible in the legal, economic, social, and political institutions. The social psychological manifestations are often intangible — hard to grasp and hard to alter. Group self-hate and distortion of perceptions to justify a preconceived interpretation of reality are just some of the factors being teased out.

For women, sexism describes the specificity of female oppression. Starting from the traditional belief in the difference between the sexes, sexism embodies two core concepts. The first is that men are more important than women: not necessarily superior — we are far too sophisticated these days to use that tainted term — but more important, more significant, more valuable, more worthwhile. This value justifies the idea that it is more important for a man (the "breadwinner") than for a woman to have a job or a promotion, to be paid well, to have an education, and in general to receive preferential treatment. It is the basis of men's feeling that if women enter a particular occupation, they will degrade it, and that men will have to leave it or themselves be degraded; and of women's feeling that they can raise the prestige of their professions by recruiting men, which they can only do by giving men the better jobs. From this value comes the attitude that a husband must earn more than his wife or suffer a loss of personal status and that a wife must subsume her interest to those of her husband or be socially castigated. From this value come the practices of rewarding men for serving in the armed forces and of punishing women for having children. The first core concept of sexist thought is that men do the important work in the world and that the work done by men is what is important.

The second core concept is that women exist to please and assist men. This is what is meant when women are told that their role is complementary to that of men; that they should fulfill their natural "feminine" functions; that they are "different" from men and should not compete with them. From this concept comes the attitude that women are and should be dependent on men for everything, but especially for their identities, the social definition of who they are. The concept defines the few roles for which women are socially rewarded — wife, mother, and mistress — all of which are pleasing or beneficial to men. It leads directly to the Pedestal theory, which extols women who stay in their places as good helpmates to men.

It is this attitude that stigmatizes women who do not marry or who do not devote their primary energies to the care of men and their children. Association with a man is the basic criterion for a woman's participation in this society, and a woman who does not seek her identity through a man is a threat to the social values. This attitude also causes Women's Liberation activists to be labeled as "man-haters" for exposing the nature of sexism. People feel that a woman who is not devoted to looking after a man must be motivated by hatred or inability to "catch" one. The second core concept of sexist thought is that a woman's identity is defined by her relationship to a man and her social value by that of the man to whom she is related.

The sexism of our society is so pervasive that we are not even aware of all its manifestations. Unless one has developed a sensitivity to its workings by a self-consciously contrary view, its activities are accepted as "normal" and justified with little question. People are said to "choose" something about which they have never actually thought. For example, the sudden onslaught of World War II radically changed both the whole structure of social relationships and the economy. Men were drafted into the army and women into the labor force. When women were thus desperately needed, their wants, like those of the boys on the front, were met. The Lanham Act, providing federal financing of day-care centers, passed Congress in a record two weeks. Special crash training programs were provided for the new women workers to give them skills they were not previously thought capable of mastering. Women instantly assumed positions of authority and responsibility that were unavailable only the year before.

But what happened when the war ended? Both men and women had heeded their country's call to duty to bring the war to a successful conclusion. Yet men were rewarded for their efforts and women punished for theirs. The returning soldiers were given the G.I. Bill and other benefits, as well as their old jobs and a disproportionate share of the new ones created by the war economy. Women, on the other hand, saw their child-care centers dismantled and their training programs ended. They were fired or demoted in droves and often found it difficult to enter colleges flooded with former GIs matriculating on government money. Is it any wonder that they heard the message that their place was in the home? Where else could they go?

The eradication of sexism and the practices it supports is obviously one of the major goals of the Women's Liberation Movement. But it is not enough to destroy a set of values and leave a normative vacuum. The old values have to be replaced by something. A movement can only begin by declaring its opposition to the STATUS QUO. If it is to succeed, eventually it has to propose an alternative.

I cannot pretend to be definitive about the possible alternatives contemplated by the numerous participants in the Women's Liberation Movement. Yet from the plethora of ideas and visions that feminists have thought, discussed, and written about, I find two basic ideas emerging which express the bulk of their concerns. I call these the "egalitarian ethic" and the "liberation ethic." They are closely related and mesh into what only can be described as a feminist humanism.

The egalitarian ethic means that the sexes are equal; therefore, sex roles must go. Our history has proved that institutionalized difference inevitably means inequity, and sex-role stereotypes have long been anachronistic. Strongly differentiated sex roles were rooted in the ancient division of labor; their basis has been torn apart by modern technology. Their justification was rooted in the subjection of women to the reproductive cycle; that has been destroyed by modern pharmacology. The cramped little boxes of personality and social function to which we assign people from birth must be broken open, so that all people can develop independently, as individuals. This means that there will be an integration of male and female social functions and life styles until, ideally, a person's sex will say nothing significant about his or her social role. But this increased similarity of men and women will also mean increased options for individuals and increased diversity in the human race. No longer will there be men's work and women's work. No longer will humanity suffer a schizophrenic personality desperately trying to reconcile its "masculine" and "feminine" parts. No longer will marriage be the institution where two half-people come together in hopes of making a whole.

The liberation ethic says that this is not enough. Changes must be made not only in the limits of the roles, but also in their content. The liberation ethic looks at the current kinds of life led by both men and women and concludes that they are deplorable and unnecessary. The social institutions that oppress women as women also oppress people as people, and they can be altered to make a more humane existence for all. So much of our society is hung upon the framework of sex-role stereotypes and their reciprocal functions that the dismantling of this structure will provide the opportunity to make a more viable life for everyone.

It is important to stress that these two ethics must work in tandem. If the first is emphasized over the second, then we have a movement for women's rights, not women's liberation. To seek only equality, given the current male supremacy in social values, is to assume that women want to be like men or that men are worth emulating. It is to demand that women be allowed to participate in society as we know it, to get their piece of the pie, without questioning the extent to which that society is worth their participation. This view is held by some, but most feminists today find it inadequate. Those women who find what is considered the male role to be compatible with their personalities must realize that this role is made possible only by the existence of the female sex role — in other words, only by the subjection of women. Therefore women cannot become equal to men without the destruction of the interdependent, mutually parasitic male and female roles. To fail to realize that the integration of the sex roles and the equality of the sexes will inevitably lead to basic structural change is to fail to seize the opportunity to decide the direction of those changes.

It is equally dangerous to fall into the trap of seeking liberation without due concern for equality. This is the mistake made by many leftist radicals. They find the general human conditions to be so wretched that they feel that all efforts should be devoted to the millennial revolution in the belief that the liberation of women will follow naturally the liberation of people.

However, women have yet to be defined as people, even among the radicals, and it is erroneous to assume that their interests are identical to those of men. For women to subsume their concerns once again is to ensure that the promise of liberation will be a spurious one. There has yet to be created or conceived by any political or social theorist a revolutionary society in which women were equal to men and their needs were duly considered. The sex-role structure has never been comprehensively challenged by any male philosopher, and the systems they have proposed have all presumed the existence of a sex-role structure to some degree.

Undue emphasis on the liberation ethic has often led to a sort of radical paradox. Women of the New Left frequently found themselves in such situations during the early days of the movement. They found repugnant the pursuit of "reformist" goals which might be achieved without altering the basic nature of the system and would thus, they felt, only strengthen the system. However, their search for a sufficiently radical action and/or issue came to naught. They thus found themselves able to do nothing, for fear that anything they did might be counterrevolutionary. Inactive revolutionaries are a good deal more innocuous than are active "reformists."

But even among those who are not rendered impotent, the unilateral pursuit of liberation can take its toll. Some radical women have been so appalled at the condition of most men and at the possibility of becoming even somewhat like them that they cling to the security of their familiar role and wait complacently for the revolution to liberate everyone. Some men, fearing that role reversal is a goal of the Women's Liberation Movement, have taken a similar position. Both have failed to realize that the abolition of sex roles must be continually incorporated into any radical restructuring of society; both have failed to explore the possible consequences of role integration. The goal that they advocate may be one of liberation, but it does not involve women's liberation.

Separated from each other, the egalitarian ethic and the liberation ethic can be crippling; together, they can be a very powerful force. Separated, they speak to limited interests; together, they speak to all humanity. Separated they are but superficial solutions; together, they recognize that while sexism oppresses women, it also limits the potentiality of men. Separated, neither will be achieved because their scope does not range far enough; together, they provide a vision worthy of our devotion. Separated, these two ethics do not lead to the liberation of women; together, they lead to the liberation of women and men.

Politics of Theory: Participant Observation in the United States

BROOKE GRUNDFEST SCHOEPF and AMELIA M. MARIOTTI

Women's Liberation is a new household phrase in the United States. The ideas of feminism have spread and their impact is felt by vast numbers of women who, even five years ago, shied away from images of bra-burning, bar-storming feminists projected by the media. Once a scorned and despised group, the women's movement has become an important social force which must be dealt with by political candidates, government agencies, educational institutions, employers, trade unions, and organizations which are pressing for radical social change. Many who once dismissed it as a collection of personal problems are now beginning to understand that the women's movement is a justifiable revolt against systematic exploitation and oppression. We are witnessing the rise of a new ideology, a new practice which for some reaches to the deep well-springs of identity and world view (Newton and Walton 1971). Thus the contemporary women's movement offers a fertile field for analysts of social change.

Literature and analysis coming out of the movement document the variety of processes and institutions that contemporary United States society uses to press half of the population into submission by masking

This paper is the outcome of months of discussion of our past and current experiences in the Women's Liberation Movement, which both of us entered in 1969. The data on which we base our analysis are culled from notes developed from participant-observation in a variety of women's groups, workshops, and conferences. We have also interviewed key informants and read extensively in feminist and Marxist literature. In addition Schoepf has carried out fieldwork in two predominantly working class communities, a village in southern France (1957–58) and a suburb of New York City (1971–72). Both studies contain data on women's domestic roles and their non-domestic roles in production and politics.

the true essence of women's oppression. By sharing experiences and using one another as informants women are beginning to lay bare the structures masked by the conscious models or ideology that maintain our exploitation. Injustices and human needs become political issues only when they are crystallized by a social movement with the power to bring them forcefully to public attention. In order for people to enter the political arena they must not only become conscious of their needs; they must also feel that their activity can result in change. In their efforts to change the circumstances of their lives, women develop strength. Our numbers and our energies are reflected in the diversity of the movement which encompasses a range of political theories about the origins of women's oppression and strategies for social transformation.

Other writers are exploring the history of the women's movement. In this paper we will address some problems of theory and perspective related to social change. Like the Marxist movement, the women's movement is a teaching as well as an action movement. We learn from studying ourselves in action in the real world. Our present helps us to understand the past; the past to imagine and to build the future. At the same time theory must reflect the learning derived from our shared experience. This challenge to build a scientific and useful analysis is being taken up by feminists with and without academic credentials. Professionals and non-professionals help each other; checking each other out, we increase the breadth and validity of our perception.

Our stance is that of native anthropologists analyzing our own culture (Jones 1970). As participants we are insiders, as anthropologists we are outsiders drawing upon a body of data and theory wider than our immediate experience. We bring our experience as participants to our work as students of society and social change. We apply our professional training to give our sisters what we can from the study of social processes and other cultures. For us as for many other theorists in the Women's Liberation Movement (WLM), our work is both political and personal. In stating our biases we also underscore our need for rigorously objective analysis of historical and contemporary events. We need it to win. The stakes are our survival and growth as human beings with dignity. We believe that WLM is a positive force in the struggle to transform a capitalist society in a socialist and humanist direction. The perspective offered here is one of Marxist feminism, a frankly partisan stance. Many women now see a need to alter the sex roles that doom all but a few to extreme exploitation. They are asking how this can be done and some see the need for a far-reaching social transformation. Growing numbers are turning toward Marxist analysis and yet, as one Latina who is open to the ideas of socialism, said: "I agree that the Movement should be all one social movement. But I can't trust a male-dominated movement, so my basic PRIORITY now is WOMEN!" Like many other feminists she will not become part of an organization which demands that she continue to accept a subordinate position or be told that her oppression as a woman is insignificant to the struggle for socialism.

In the summer of 1973 in a workshop on "Women and Marxism," participants were repeatedly pressed to choose between Marxism and feminism. Some rejected this attempt to pose a dichotomy, saying, "There is no contradiction, no need to choose." This paper is an attempt to convey our understanding of the relationship between the two which we believe is one of dialectical interpenetration. That is, the two apparently opposed tendencies are essentially an integral part of the same process of social change, each activating or retarding the progress of the whole. In the view of present-day feminist-Marxists, those who would force women to choose do the entire worldwide liberation struggle a disservice, for they divide natural allies. They split the movement and retard the coming social transformation.

The first section of this paper outlines the Marxist theory of women's oppression. We apply this theory to what we believe to be the present conditions in the United States. Then we take up the criticisms directed at the Women's Liberation Movement by some sections of the Left and explain why we believe the women's movement has revolutionary potential. We offer some suggestions about what Marxists and other radicals can learn from the women's movement, and conclude with some reflections on the relationship between theory and practice.

MARXIST FEMINIST THEORY

The importance of the position of women in human history and of their role in social change are stressed in the writings of Marx, Engels, and Lenin (see Marx and Engels 1948; Marx 1947; Engels 1972; Lenin 1938; Zetkin 1934.) Central to their theory of the evolution of class society is an analysis of women's role in social production and the relationship between the development of the family and private property. According to Engels the patriarchal nuclear family is not a biological unit of human existence. On the contrary it is a set of social relations which developed with class society and shattered the wider kinship structures that formed the basis of social relations in earlier societies.

Following Morgan (1963) and other early evolutionary anthropological theorists, Marx and Engels shared the view that the status of women in preclass societies was much higher than in the class societies which later developed. Their historical materialist interpretation related the origin of the state and the subjugation of women to the development of the forces of production (technology), differential access to the means of production (strategic property used to produce wealth), and the production of commodities for sale in the market. Both the state and the family were seen as structures used to maintain and extend the class domination of property owners in order to control those who worked but did not own. They argued that the position of women in early human history had been qualitatively different and would again be different — equal to that of men — in the communist society of the future. They viewed women as the first proletariats.

Peeling off the layers of male-biased and class-serving ethnography, which makes no distinctions between the instititutions and forms of relations in class and classless societies, we indeed find that in many small-scale, "primitive" societies women were not subordinate to men until their cultures were shattered by the impact of colonialism (Boserup 1970; Leacock 1972). In many other non-Western societies as in the West, however, the patriarchal family appears to have come into being during struggles to exclude some people from access to strategic resources in order to capture their energy in the production and reproduction of the means of human existence, for the benefit of the controlling group. Ethnographies of transitional societies in Africa, Latin America, and Melanesia show very clearly the process of the struggle between the sexes. This process is considered crucial by Lévi-Strauss (1969) who writes:

I would go so far as to say that even before slavery or class domination existed, men fashioned an approach to women that would one day serve to introduce differences among us all.

For a number of anthropolgists, as well as Marxists, the state historically represents a freezing of stratified social relations into class rule (cf. Fried 1967). The state, which Marx and Engels conceived of as "the executive committee of the ruling class," consolidated class power by shattering the power of the kin group. The corporate kin group was transformed into family units without social and economic power. The subordination of women was central to this process. In broad outline their conception of human social evolution is supported by the ethnographic evidence, although the process must be seen as stretching out over centuries and taking different forms according to variations in specific natural and social conditions. For example, while the state was generally subversive of the kin principle, in some instances the wider kin organization was manipulated by the ruling class. The state societies of Ashanti, Aztec Mexico, and China are examples of the transformation of preexisting kin structures into instruments of class control. In the Chinese countryside at the present time the class struggle involves shattering the clan myth. Expressed in the phrase, "We Changs are all one family," the clan ideology masked the exploitation of the poor by landowners of the same surname.

The form taken by the family and the nature of women's oppression within it depends upon the particular type of class society in which it exists. The nuclear family as we know it came into being with the rise of capitalism in the West. In their discussion of the nature and workings of capitalism Marx, Engels, and Lenin investigated the condition of women both in family and in wage labor. The Marxist analysis of the family under capitalism is twofold. One aspect is the role of the family in regulating property relations among the owners of the means of production. The other aspect deals with the part the family plays in the reproduction — both physical and social — and maintenance of wage laborers, the producers of wealth. The contradictory nature of capitalism lies in the fact that while industrial production is social (and becomes increasingly concentrated in large workplaces as the productive forces develop), the ownership and control of property is increasingly concentrated in private hands. Among the owners of property, the "monogamous" nuclear family facilitates orderly transferal of ownership across generations through inheritance, and its control within generations by marriage. Yet there is another contradictory aspect of capitalist society: while production is social, the reproduction and daily maintenance of the work force is the private responsibility of each nuclear family. From these structural features the basic condition of the majority of women under capitalism is derived.

In a society in which labor power is a commodity to be bought in the form of wages, women work to maintain the members of a family without being paid directly. The husband's wage is supposed to be sufficient to sustain the whole family. Yet in reality the employer buys the labor power of two individuals for the price of one (cf. Benston 1969). Not only are women rendered economically dependent but their exploitation is masked by the fact that their domestic work remains outside of commodity production.[1] Moreover, domestic work becomes stultifying as the household shrinks in size and its creative and productive aspects are supplanted by mass production. In the process, domestic labor is reduced

[1] This concept, which Schoepf learned from her mother, Rose Danzig Grundfest, is explored in depth by Larguia and Dumoulin (1972) and Larguia (in this volume).

to a low level of skills while the general level of skills in the society rises. The majority of women do not benefit from the industrialization of domestic tasks which is done only when and in such a way that it is profitable. Rather, this process brings the alienation of the assembly line into the home, but in domestic work women are deprived of the companionship and stimulation of co-workers.

Labor-saving devices do not generally free women's time for creative activity. As Friedan (1963) citing Ogburn, points out, the trivialization of housework, by fetishizing cleanliness and order, results in the expansion of housework to fill the time. The fetishism is an ideological manipulation that fosters low self-esteem. This low self-esteem in turn helps render women susceptible to consumerism and credit-buying which commit the family's future wages, and thus ties workers, both women and men, to their jobs.

Yet, while "women's work" is confined to the household, women also labor outside the home. When women work for wages they must perform two jobs: one unpaid, the other systematically underpaid (see Tables 1 and 2). Discriminatory wages, for women as well as minorities, not

Table 1.　Wage or salary income of full-time year-round workers[a], by sex 1955-69

Year	Median wage or salary income		Women's median wage or salary income as percent of men's
	Women	Men	
1955	$2,719	$4,252	63.9
1956	2,827	4,466	63.3
1957	3,008	4,713	63.8
1958	3,102	4,927	63.0
1959	3,193	5,209	61.3
1960	3,293	5,417	60.8
1961	3,351	5,644	59.4
1962	3,446	5,794	59.5
1963	3,561	5,978	59.6
1964	3,690	6,195	59.6
1965	3,823	6,375	60.0
1966	3,973	6,848	58.0
1967[b]	4,150	7,182	57.8
1968[b]	4,457	7,664	58.2
1969[b]	4,977	8,227	60.5

[a] Worked 35 hours or more a week for 50 to 52 weeks.
[b] Data are not strictly comparable with prior years, since they include earnings of self-employed persons.

Source: United States Department of Commerce, Bureau of the Census: Current Populations Reports, P-60.

Table 2.   Median wage or salary income of full-time year-round workers, by sex and selected major occupation group, 1969

Major occupation group	Median wage or salary income Women	Men	Women's median wage or salary income as percent of men's
Professional and technical workers	$7,309	$11,266	64.9
Nonfarm managers, officials, and proprietors	6,091	11,467	53.1
Clerical workers	5,187	7,966	65.1
Sales workers	3,704	9,135	40.5
Operatives	4,317	7,307	59.1
Service workers (except private household	3,755	6,373	58.9

Source: United States Department of Commerce, Bureau of the Census: Current Population Reports, P-60, number 75.

only yield a greater rate of profit for employers, but become a source of divisiveness among workers. Women are further set apart by the myth that they are temporary or intermittent workers for whom homemaking and family are the primary responsibility. This myth masks the reality that regular wage labor is a necessity for almost half of the women in the United States between the ages of 18 and 65. Women's participation in trade unions is also hampered by this double-bind. Women and men do not participate in labor unions to the same extent. In 1966 only about one in seven women in the female labor force were union members, as compared to the more than one in four men in the male labor force who belonged to unions (1969 Handbook on Women Workers, United States Department of Labor, Women's Bureau, Bulletin 294). More than four out of five union members are men; however, the proportion of women union members is increasing slightly.

Table 3.   Women as members of national and international unions, 1958–1966

Year	Number	Percent of all members
1958	3,274,000	18.2
1960	3,304,000	18.3
1962	3,272,000	18.6
1964	3,413,000	19.0
1966	3,689,000	19.3

Source: Lisa Vogel (1969).

A cafeteria worker who became an active unionist after her children had grown up and left home explains this:

The men say that we women are not active in the union. How can we be? A woman I work with was dissatisfied with the proposed contract because it did not extend benefits to her job classification. I told her that she should go the next union meeting and complain. She said she couldn't because her husband wouldn't take care of the children and told her she could not get a babysitter for this. I was talking to another women about running for election to the union's arbitration committee. She said she wouldn't be able to go to the arbitration meetings after work because her husband expects her to have supper on the table when he gets home from work.

When men refuse to share domestic tasks, they limit the women's participation in labor struggles and their sexism helps to keep both men and women down. When working class women insist on their rights at home they clarify the class struggle.

The burden of women's two jobs takes still other forms. For example, hard-won protective legislation is used by employers against women and men, as well as by conservative union bureaucrats who maintain their positions by gaining concessions for one part of their constituency (i.e. men) at the expense of another (i.e. women). An example of the first situation is related by a Black Marxist-feminist:

In one New York factory, under the guise of equal employment, women were hired to perform a job that had been filled by men who were paid $2.90 per hour. The job was reclassified and the women were paid $2.15 per hour. The men were Black and Puerto Rican, the women, predominantly white. The men, quite understandably, saw women as a threat to their jobs.

The union did not fight to retain the job classification that would have ensured equal pay for equal work, nor did it struggle to prevent the company from laying off the men. In a system such as ours, where unemployment is endemic, sex and ethnic divisions are used to create competition among workers.

The situation in which union officials discriminate against women is reflected in the cafeteria worker's complaint that her job classification which was filled largely by women was not included in the new benefits that were being negotiated. Moreover, many women are not involved in unions at all because union officials have not considered certain occupations in which women predominate important enough to organize, as well as because of the low percentage of unionized workers in general.

The total number of union members (women and men) has remained about constant since the mid-fifties; because the labor force is increasing, this means that the proportion of workers who are unionized is falling. Thus, 33.2% of employees in non-agricultural establishments were members of unions in 1955, 31.4% in 1960, and only 28% in 1966. Blue collar unionists comprise 85% of all union members; white collar workers make up the other 15%; service workers remain largely unorganized (in Vogel 1969).

The family and women's role in it also make women a labor reserve. They are hired or laid off depending upon the needs of the economy. Not only does this labor reserve give industry flexibility for rapid expansion to make profits when the conditions are favorable and to contract during an unfavorable period, but it helps keep the wages of all workers depressed by pitting workers against each other for an artificially limited number of jobs. Women are thus brought into wage labor to meet the needs of an expanding economy or to undermine the militancy of organized labor, only to be sent home to their other job when no longer needed in industry.

The notion that the nuclear family is universal in the contemporary United States is belied by statistics which show that only about a third of the population live in nuclear family households. Yet there are few structural alternatives for women, since their wages are low and social services rudimentary. The family is a refuge as well as a trap.

In a group of women workers and housewives, a divorced nurse's aid in her thirties said, "I'd prefer to be dependent on a man. My lousy job doesn't pay enough to feed my kids! I'm trying to stay off welfare, but I don't know how long I can hold out."

The position of working class women is characteristic of relations between the sexes throughout the society. This is what middle class women come to realize as they strip away the veils of the feminine mystique which mask their oppression. This is what is meant by the Marxist-conception of the dominant mode of production imposing its character upon all the institutions of the society. The relations of women and men become cast in the capitalist mode. Even in the middle class family, the women is the proletarian and the man is the boss.

Let us now return to the question posed in the introduction regarding the revolutionary potential of the women's movement. What inferences can we make about the future from past and present conditions, from theory and data? When Engels wrote that for women to achieve full equality they must work in paid employment, he was stating a necessary but not sufficient part of the process. This condition did not obtain in Europe a century ago when capitalist development had still left large sectors of preindustrial rural und urban activity. Not only were large numbers of women yet to enter capitalist production, but so were the majority of men. This is a major problem of the societies that have abolished capitalism to date. In all these nations the shape of the work force is quite different from that of an advanced industrial society.

In the United States, however, productive capacity, technology, skills and knowledge are already highly developed. Fifty percent of women now work for wages and nine out of ten will do so at some time in their lives. As a result of the new consciousness generated by the Women's Liberation Movement we can expect that increasing numbers of women will seek work outside the home. As they discover what so many already know — that our present society cannot provide creative, fulfilling work and human services — their demands will further strain the legitimacy and stability of a faltering social system. Consciousness and material conditions interpenetrate.

From this brief summary we can see that the exploitation of women in capitalist society flows from the class relations. At the same time Marxism recognizes the special oppression of women, its institutional and ideological supports, Marxism also offers a theory about the functions of sexist institutions, ideology and behavior in supporting and maintaining the total social system. Sexual antagonism is one of the major social conflicts that helps to hold the society together. Marxists argue that in order to eliminate male chauvinism and male supremacy throughout the society it is necessary to transform the system of class relations. In this transformation women have a crucial role — it cannot be done without them. The next section further explores sex, ethnic, and class divisions in relation to the dynamics of social change.

THE DIALECTICS OF SOCIAL CHANGE

In the preceeding section we outlined Marxist theory related to women. We noted that the status of women, their domestic and non-domestic roles, and the nature of the family are central to the materialist theory of human social evolution. Not only anthropological theory has been distorted by the male bias of class society but some contemporary Marxist thought as well. Now we apply Marxist epistemology to criticism directed at the Women's Liberation Movement by some sections of the left and assess their relevance to the theory. We have chosen a number of areas of contention to illustrate what we believe to be a fruitful method of assessing the strategy and tactics of the Women's Liberation Movement. We take up the criticisms one by one and then explore briefly how they are interrelated.

Feminism is bourgeois and middle class. The Women's Liberation Movement is not revolutionary.

There are many white middle class women highly visible in the movement, particularly the popular writers and the members of the larger organizations. Many movement women have come to accept this stereotype and those who are not white and middle class are hardly even noticed. When issues of class origins are confronted in women's groups, the qualitative differences in exploitation and oppression can be used to deepen the consciousness of all women. However, there are many groups in which the atmosphere of middle class homogeneity makes passing less onerous for working-class women than self-disclosure. Thus the group cannot learn from its own heterogeneous composition and stereotypes are perpetuated.

At the second meeting of a women's group in 1970, most of the professional women assumed that their backgrounds were relatively homogeneous. Yet one woman said, "I feel very strange hearing about your privileged upbringing. The choices you had — even though sex-typed — are so much wider. My family was very poor and I always knew I'd HAVE to work. My mother pushed me to stay in school so I wouldn't have to work in a factory or clean other people's houses."

Although we have both been in groups where working class and Marxist women could make an explicitly accepted contribution of their experience, not all women realize the potential for honest and open exchange which characterizes the most highly conscious and active groups. Here is an example of this process at work:

We were going around the room identifying ourselves and telling a little about our background to break the ice. A women spoke of her childhood experiences on picket lines with her mother and living in a 6-story walk-up tenement. Another women said "It makes me feel so terrible to have just an ordinary middle class background." There was envy in her voice. Nobody in the group said anything about it but others got the message that they'd better not expose themselves and their "deviance." So other persons who came from working class and really poor families and who had all kinds of interesting things to contribute just shut up about their personal experiences. Discussion stayed abstract until power struggles destroyed the group.

This was not a representative women's group, but a group of women and men. The high-status participants are among those who discount the lessons of Women's Liberation and claim to criticize it "from a 'Marxist' perspective." Unable to open themselves to group criticism and self-criticism, they would not commit themselves to building a collective. Their sexism is only one variant of elitism. Left critics of the women's movement condemn its future on the basis of present composition without recognizing that the objective conditions of society are what determines the potential to grow and develop into a revolutionary force. It would be incorrect to dismiss the Left or the Marxist movement within it in this way, for criticism should focus not merely on present composition but on directions and possibilities for change. Many non-Marxist women's groups are involved in fighting for the rights of working class women, and we expect that working class women will become decisive in the leadership of the women's movement in the years ahead.

The Women's Liberation Movement is white. Black and Latin women know how to place the main struggle ahead of their selfish demands.

A black feminist active in civil rights struggles since the fifties replies:

That's a crude joke! We've been oppressed for centuries by men, both white and black, who were doing the system's business. I have a lot more hope for movement women overcoming their racism than I do for men who try to split us for their own reasons... No more of this nonsense about walking behind our men and producing babies for the revolution.

A black woman Health Center worker reports:

When jobs were opening up here the men said they should get first choice because they needed to regain their self-respect. So I'm supposed to go on carrying a paper bag? (The emblem of 1,300,000 domestic workers who are among the most severely exploited in the United States.) We have to fight for decent jobs for ALL workers. We women are the poorest and what about OUR dignity?

The organizing of the women's movement for equal pay and equal work, for free abortion and an end to forced sterilization, for free child care are supremely relevant to the lives of women oppressed by both racism and sexism. In struggles on these issues, white women in WLM can learn and very concretely the consequences of super-exploitation and divide-and-rule from the lives of Third World women.

When a dichotomy is posed between the two liberation struggles, or when a hierarchy is established, women who sense that they belong in both experience great conflict. The way out of this dilemma lies in political analysis. After a session exploring the divide-and-rule process from a class perspective, a black anthropologist expressed her relief:

I have felt so torn by the people pressing me to choose: Am I black? Am I a woman? Which comes first! Now I know: I'm BOTH and that's fine. Today was a very good day!

Asked which status she find MOST oppressive, an American Indian sister replied:

How do you rank oppressions? I'm oppressed both as a woman and as an Indian. It's a weird question that shows a real lack of political understanding.

Although racism and sexism are both useful as a means of dividing people with common interests in social change, and are both bolstered by arguments of inherent biological inferiority, they are not identical. There are structural differences in the situation of women and oppressed minorities. Women comprise half the population of all classes and ethnic groups, whereas the ethnic groups are a relatively small percentage of the wider popluation.

While violence is perpetrated against women in the form of rape and physical attack, the violence of racist attacks against oppressed ethnic minorities has often taken on the nature of extermination campaigns against the entire group. Minority women are doubly oppressed and most are exploited as workers as well. Their life chances are quite different from those of white women. In the women's movement we have the opportunity to explore these similarities and differences in everyday situations. Women who are conscious of sexual politics can understand that not only middle class whites but also white working class men who get the jobs denied to minorities and women benefit from racism and sexism in the short run. In the end we all lose because the divisions perpetuate the entire system of exploitation. But to propose, as some Leftists do, that white workers hold these favored positions solely as a result of their own efforts in the early days of union organizing is to ignore the past and present struggles of black, Latin, and women workers.

This perspective also suggests that white workers are racist out of some strange psychological process, when in fact divide-and-rule and kick-the-cat, (that is, stomp on those below when you do not have the confidence that you can eliminate the oppression that comes down on you from above) are two well-documented aspects of the social psychology of capitalism. On the level of psychodynamics racism may appear irrational; from a cross-cultural perspective it is a rational system-maintaining process.

In the women's movement one discovers that people are capable of developing a sophisticated understanding of the complex process of divide-and-rule without resorting to either/or dichotomies. We do not oppose Black Liberation to Women's Liberation. We are not saying that blacks have made it now and women are still oppressed. Nor do we view all women as more oppressed than all members of minority groups. Blacks and other minorities have won token gains that serve to obscure further the true situation of racist discrimination in all phases of life, from employment to health care. Within the minority groups, women are the most exploited. Women who work in garment sweatshops, textile mills, canning factories, fields, launderies, restaurants, and hospitals; who clean office buildings and the homes of the well-to-do, are among the lowest paid workers, and a high percentage are women from minority groups. Their struggles must be strongly supported (by the Women's Liberation Movement.

Some middle-class white women in the Movement exploit the labor of black women domestic workers. Should we demand that they fire their maids? A black sister whose mother is a domestic worker laughed at this:

Another guilty white conscience salved perhaps, but there's the black woman on the street, out of work! No, white women can pay decent wages and stop acting patronizing. But beyond this INDIVIDUAL solution, there's the struggle of almost two million women to unionize that has to be supported. And the fight for full employment... Black women take these jobs because they can't get better-paid work — they can't afford to wait for the revolution.

Raising consciousness against racism in the women's movement takes many forms. Much is done by minority women speaking, writing, and sharing their experiences with others, as well as by their exemplary struggles, past and present. Some white women in the Movement see racism as a crucial barrier to the power of sisterhood. In the groups with which we have worked there are white women who have opposed the sterotyped view of working class and Latin men as MORE sexist than white professional men. In the context of the movement, women can understand how sexism takes different forms in the different subcultures of a complex society. They can see how all these forms are part of the wider structure.

The feminist perspective demythologizes many accepted truths. For example, the unemployment and underemployment of black men in our society has resulted in a higher percentage of female-headed black households. Black women have gone to work (at the lowest paid jobs) because they had to, and their central role in the family has developed from this. In recent years many social scientists and male activitsts have presented a distorted analysis of the social and psychological situation of black working class women. By not specifying the sources of oppression and exploitation they have laid the blame for poverty on the most oppressed rather than on the social system. Criticizing one such analysis, Jones (1974) writes that the authors:

observed that "In almost every female-centered household, the woman began to shift from support to varying degrees of opposition to the man's new role" [as an industrial worker]. What I wondered from reading this chapter was whether the woman was not so much in opposition to the man's new role as she was *resisting the implicit attempt to relegate her to a traditional female position.* [For example] to one man it meant his wife "getting up to fix breakfast, making him lunch, and attending to the house and children" — *the standard desires of most middle class men* (our emphasis).

Understanding can be strengthened by Marxist feminists working within the Women's Liberation Movement. It will not be aided by throwing brickbats from the sidelines. We are confident that white women can understand how racism holds back our liberation; and our struggles will grow out of sisterhood rather than from charity or guilt. The fight against male chauvinism need not weaken either the class struggle or the struggle for the liberation of oppressed nations and minority groups in the United States. Rather, it can sharpen the struggle by clarifying who it is that really fights for equality and human liberation.

The Women's Liberation Movement is a subjective, ego-tripping quest for self-identity and selfish personal emancipation.

The awareness of one's real self interests when one is not a member of the ruling class is distorted by what Althusser calls the "ideological state apparatus." "State-maintaining" would probably be a better term for institutions such as the schools, the church, the media, the family, and so forth. In this, the Marxist critique of capitalist society has found an echo in the writings of Max Weber and other social scientists.

Consciousness-raising can be a vehicle for breaking the ideological control of false consciousness. Used as a tactic, consciousness-raising brings women together to explore their experiences as women (as daughters, girl-friends, school girls, wives, mistresses, working women, students, mothers, grandmothers). Going around the room, sharing autobiographies, and venturing to trust each other, women learn the varieties of meaning encompassed in "I am woman." Isolation and feelings of powerlessness recede. With the support of the group, women try out new, active roles. Solidarity is further built when women decide to engage in cooperative political activities such as writing and speaking to other women, organizing conferences and demonstrations, studying and analyzing history and contemporary social events. Used in this way, consciousness raising politicizes personal experiences and brings a conscious awareness of the ideological control mechanisms of contemporary United States social institutions. Problems that our society has taught women to regard as invididual failings, the group redefines by studying the political and economic sources of their oppression as women. Instead of blaming the victim, women indict the system. Finally, honest with self and others, each sees that in real life, every woman — even the most envied — is demeaned by the oppression of her sex. Women determine to work for fundamental change; they call for revolution, for they understand that no minor reforms will really change their situation.

Yet women struggle around many issues to gain reforms. Even though a particular reform can be accommodated by the system, it does not end the struggle. Women are not thereby co-opted, for small gains on principled issues free women to struggle further. Winning minor gains is very important. First it shows that organized struggle pays off; small gains won in a broader context sustain the struggle. Second, it shows that since the system is still as corrupt and oppressive as ever, the entire system must be changed. How to do this and what to put in its place are now subjects of heated debate in the Women's Liberation Movement.

In the fullest development of its original purpose consciousness-raising is a means, not an end in itself (Kathie Sarachild, personal communication). When the consciousness-raising group is isolated from political activity and used as an end in itself, however, women are not committed to changing their society, but are simply trying to make their situation more tolerable. The group turns inward and becomes a refuge rather than a springboard. This has occurred in groups that have mistaken the tactic for a strategy. However, this error is not intrinsic to the consciousness-raising process nor is it an inevitable consequence of feminism. Similar confusion of tactics for strategy have also occurred in the Marxist movement from time to time. Yet, as Robin Morgan (1970) points out, some Left critics have consigned the Women's Liberation Movement to political damnation out-of-hand for adopting consciousness-raising.

The Women's Liberation Movement elevates spontaneity and leaderlessness to the level of a strategy. The movement is anarchist and without serious revolutionary potential.

The women's movement in the United States both offers and constitutes a critique of the forms of leadership that exist in this society, including Left movements. The structure and dynamics of the Left organizations reflect the human relations of the society which they are trying to change. Feminists reject leadership that is authoritarian, undemocratic, and irresponsible, resting on illusions and oftentimes functioning by means of manipulation and coercion. These defects come to characterize even organizations without formal structure. Lack of organization in the New Left did not eliminate undemocratic leaders. Instead, it fostered elitist, self-assertive and self-glorifying leadership who would not take responsibility for their actions and could not be controlled by those for whom they presumably spoke and acted. These groups mirrored the distortions of the larger society instead of developing forms of organization and leadership for transforming it.

The radical women's movement that sprang up in the mid-1960's was initiated by women who had abandoned the anti-war and New Left movements (cf. Burris 1971) out of their anger and frustration at being relegated to the position of second-class political activists, providing necessary services while being excluded from public leadership. Sex role-typing in these movements went hand-in-hand with sexist attitudes and treatment. Outspoken women who refused to capitulate were verbally abused and excluded. Many who were not excluded left anyway, realizing that this was a political and not individual conflict. Sisterhood grew under duress.

In this early stage of the women's movement the only form of organization that existed was the small group. In these small groups, women discussed their problems, feelings, and concerns in a self-organized, self-determining manner. Through such consciousness-raising many women have seen the need to develop organizational forms that can accomplish the task of their liberation. Feminist publications contain serious discussions of the political and organizational development of the women's movement. Those who criticized the women's movement for its leaderlessness and spontaneity not only are ignorant of these efforts but also ignore the accomplishments of feminists in turning to mass action. Numerous demonstrations, conferences, and public meetings have been organized by women for women around issues such as defense of political prisoners, child care, health care, equal pay, defense of welfare mothers against cutbacks and women workers against lay-offs. We are apparently witnessing a convergence of civil rights and Women's Liberation forces in the southern textile mills where the lowest paid workers, black and white, are struggling for the right to organize and bargain collectively.

Women are searching for new ways to develop their potential for political action. Many reject the "star system" of charismatic, publicly-acclaimed leaders untested in struggle. Through participating in political analysis, planning, and organization, women learn to overcome their feelings of personal inadequacy and dependency. In some groups spokes-women are chosen on a rotating basis and often go out in teams of three or four until the least experienced develop the confidence that grows from success. They in turn work with less experienced women. Responsibility for particular tasks is undertaken out of commitment rather than in order to rise in rank. There are more than enough leadership roles to be filled without competing for positions, because organization-building requires active reaching out. The groups provide a format for expansion.

One of the most valuable lessons that the women's movement offers people who recognize the necessity for fundamental transformation of capitalist society is that the process of social change requires developing the political understanding, effectiveness, and leadership potential of every person. This does not obviate the need for specific forms of leadership. It does, however, demand that leadership be rooted in the strengths of the participants, strengths that are further developed by their participation in the movement, rather than by exploiting people's weaknesses.

While it would be utopian to try to create in a social movement a microcosm of a future society, a movement must be adequate to its task of social transformation. The failure of the Marxist movements in many countries to become the nucleus of a mass movement for social change is in large measure a failure of leadership. While a number of individuals on the Left and in the Marxist movement have resigned themselves to this situation, and others are resorting to old, authoritarian forms in new guise, the women's movement is consciously trying to create new forms of leadership that are neither opportunist nor sectarian. Feminists are determined to construct forms of organization through which liberation can be won, forms adapted to the needs of specific situations. In our experience this can best be accomplished with the participation of Marxist feminists who are part of the women's movement as well as the Marxist movement and not by an infusion of leadership from an aloof and at times hostile Marxist movement in which the problem of leadership remains unresolved. Leadership will be shared according to the requirements of the developing movement and not captured by those whose narrow perspective blinds them to the revolutionary potential of an independent women's movement.

Oftentimes criticism of lack of leadership is simply another veiled attack on the women's movement, particularly for its independence. Yet the independence of the women's movement is one of its greatest strengths. The struggle of the women's movement to remain independent and not be transformed into a wing of one or another capitalist political party or a caucus within the Left movement reflects the determination of a large number of feminists — both non-Marxist and Marxist — not to rely on the good intentions of men but to become a political force in their own right.

The demand for full equality is utopian. Men's heads cannot change that fast. The liberation of women will be accomplished when women are brought into social production in a socialist society. A socialist society cannot afford egalitarianism because it needs certain kinds of workers more than others. Wait until the emergence of the new communist man (sic).

Not only women but workers of all strata suspect self-serving motives in those who espouse this line, suspect them of seeking to step into leadership roles which can bring them special rewards and privileges. Privations and responsibilities must be shared rather than imposed from above. Without clear evidence of this commitment and dedication, few people will join in what is necessarily a long and difficult struggle.

In the United States education and expertise are widely distributed (though not equally so) among the population. Workers have shown proof of their capacity for innovation from which even the initial stages of a socialist transformation will be able to draw. The creative energy unleashed by egalitarian social relationships, when added to the already highly developed industrial and scientific capacity, will set off rapid and far-reaching changes. No longer needing to police the world, the United States will be able to redirect its resources to harnessing nature and society in the service of human development. There is nothing utopian about this analysis.

However, none of this will happen automatically, and bringing women into production is no guarantee of equality for women or for men. The end of economic exploitation does not in and of itself end the alienation of the formerly powerless. Only the power of self-determination can do that. But a little power, a little edge over others is a dangerous and corrupting situation before a new human nature has emerged. Men whose "heads cannot change" have avoided coming to grips with their role in perpetuating the oppression of others and thus in prolonging their own alienation. When they criticize women for egalitarianism such men show that they lack both serious social purpose and scientific imagination.

Many women feel that men raise these criticisms out of short-sighted self-interest. As one expressed it:

The Movement is a power trip for a lot of guys and not a people's liberation. But working people won't substitute new tyrannies for old. Okay, so change is scary. But men can change, if they're serious. Resocialization comes out of confronting the issues day-by-day. So many guys avoid them and invoke bad theory as a defense.

Feminism is counterproductive. By attacking male chauvinism, women make men angry and resistant to change.

Is this a criticism of women or of men? Blaming the victims and advising them not to struggle is a conservative, system-maintaining tactic. Feminists' anger at men will be removed when they see clear demonstrations that men can change. To say that we are all the products of a racist, sexist, class-structured society is no excuse for acting as the system directs. Feminists do not demand perfection, but evidence of steps in the right direction. If women can change, then why not men who profess to share our goals? The notion that change is somehow easier for women (or for working class men) than for upper middle-class men patronizes oppressed people by denying the intensity of their struggles to overcome the psychological burdens of our social system.

Women in the Women's Liberation Movement are obsessed with sex. Sex is not a political issue; sexual freedom is trivial, bourgeois, and decadent. It will all be taken care of after the revolution, when sex will be a private affair. Those women are either ball-busters or dykes.

Sour Grapes? Seriously, though, this criticism ignores cultural dynamics and the psychology of individuals and groups. Humans have the potential for a wide variety of behavior in sexual expression, as in other areas of life. Yet every society has rules and norms of sexual conduct. Some behaviors are encouraged, some tolerated, some disapproved and others punished. As feminist writers have documented in some detail (cf.

Engels 1972, Firestone 1970, Mitchell 1971, Millet 1970), sexual relations are related to the forms taken by the power relations that characterize society in general. In a society in which women are subordinate to men, a double standard of sexual relations pervades all institutions and behavior.

The process of coercing human beings into accepting their status as exploited and alienated workers includes repressing and channeling sexuality. Notions of what is right and proper for each sex in sexual expression, love, courtship, and marriage reflect the dominant patterns of social relations under capitalism. By means of the family, school, and mass media, sexuality is infused with guilt and its full expression perverted. Only with the most active resistance and reeducation can relationships between men and women in our society take the form of equally shared, joyous, guilt-free, and energizing sensuality.

There is much more to sex role stereotyping than pay scales, education, and occupation. There is much more to sexual politics than sex. Those who claim that women's desires for sexual fulfillment are draining energy from the revolution may be avoiding the full recognition of their own alienation; avoiding, too, the depth of their need to control other people. In the view of many feminists, they are threatened by the challenge posed by politically experienced women who demand equality in all aspects of life. In any event, criticism on this point is frequently a cover used to avoid dealing with the sexual exploitation of women NOW! Nowhere in the world today has the full liberation of women been achieved. Thus the conditions for sexual equality and sexual privacy do not exist. To demand that women accept their suffering privately is to pervert Marxism by transforming it into an ahistorical dogma.

Sexism is not merely an epiphenomenom that will vanish with the demise of capitalism. Sexual politics will endure so long as patriarchal attitudes and behavior are allowed to run their course. They will infect men and diminsh the creative energies of women who try to relate to them unless new institutional forms and group supports are used to eliminate them. The active challenge of politically conscious women is necessary to bring about the allocation of social resources to effect these changes. This is why an independent women's movement is crucial to social transformation.

The feminist view of the family as a key institution in the oppression of women is anarchistic, anti-working class, extreme, and unrealistic.

These critics are themselves guilty of being unrealistic in their view of the family in the working class. It is true that there are qualitative differences between the working class family and the family among capitalists. While the function of the bourgeois family is the control of property for the exploiting class, the function of the proletarian family is to control labor and its reproduction for the exploiting class.

In view of this fundamental assymetry of the family in the two main classes of capitalist society, it is all the more striking to discover that both oppress women. Duplicity, endemic dissatisfaction, and insecurity more often than love, warmth, and comfort characterize the family in both working and ruling classes under capitalism. It is unrealistic to say that the working class family is spared from this distortion. Although oppressed in different ways and degrees, women of both classes are controlled as a means of controlling and maintaining property relations and labor. Personal relationships are inevitably damaged and distorted by this coercion.

Feminist insist that the liberation of women requires that the political, economic, and social functions of the family as an institution be destroyed. Marxist feminists agree. Engels wrote that the liberation of women requires the socialization of the functions of the family, which in effect would dismantle the family as an institution. According to Engels, the future communist society will transform the relations between the sexes into a purely private matter which concerns only the persons involved and into which society has no occasion to intervene. However, he warned that until the economic and social functions of the family become public responsibilties, and until women earn equally with men, economic and psychological dependence will be foisted upon women and children. What, then would remain? The possibility of personal relationships based on and sustained by choice and not coercion.

The Women's Liberation Movement is diversionary because it does not address the main enemy, imperialism.

Objectively the Women's Liberation Movement is an anti-imperialist struggle, for it attacks significant aspects of the maintenance structure of capitalism, of which imperialism is the most developed form (Lenin 1939). It develops the political consciousness of large numbers of women. An individual need not be immediately conscious of all the results of her or his actions in order to be counted as an ally; the same is true of a social movement. In rejecting the Women's Liberation Movement for demands that most of the groups do not raise at the present moment, instead of assessing its objective role, this criticism is idealist, sectarian and undialectical. Moreover, attempts to divert women's energies from concrete struggles against their oppression undermine the basis for eventual unity.

It is not evidence of national chauvinism to propose that events within the United States are crucial to the world-wide emergence of a new social epoch, for when our government is turned from its imperialist course, dictators and compradors around the world will crumble from internal pressure. At the same time the economic stability and political credibility of capitalism have been shaken by nationalist forces in the Third World. The dialectical processes of history are international, and the women's movement is one of these worldwide forces.

The Women's Liberation Movement ignores the principal contradiction of capitalism.

This is an attempt to deny the legitimacy of the movement by contending either that sexism is "trival" or that only the working class can wage a fight against sexism. The sexist double standard of these critics becomes evident when they support other struggles which they recognize, but do not denigrate, as secondary to the contradiction between labor and capital, such as revolutions against colonialism and imperialist domination. Some of these critics ignore or deny the material basis of women's special oppression, contending that sexism is simply an ideology. This formulation allows them to avoid specifying how women's oppression will end and what role women will play in social change.

Lacking a strategy for social transformation grounded in Marxist theory and its application to concrete historical conditions, these critics are blind to the radicalizing effect on the working class of the struggles of oppressed sectors of the population. One dramatic example of the catalytic effect of such struggles is the role of the women's protests in sparking the February Revolution of 1917 in Czarist Russia. Yet the current Women's Liberation Movement in the United States provides the same lesson no less valid although not as dramatic thus far. In the past two years the women's movement has grown to mass proprotions and in so doing has begun to spread to the work place and the union hall. Women are beginning to organize against the sex discrimination of employers, to challenge the conservatism and class collaboration of entrenched union bureaucrats and to confront the sexism of their male co-workers and fellow unionists. In doing so, women politicize issues previously conceived of in narrow economic terms. They pose the political question of worker solidarity against the employer by demanding that men make a choice: are they going to ally with women who are workers like themselves; or go against the women to gain special privileges as men? This is the essence of the demand expressed by a woman unionist to her husband who is a member of the same union:

You men had better fight as hard for us as you fight for yourselves [in negotiating benefits in a labor contract]. After all, we pay the same dues that you do.

In dealing directly with a fundamental division in the working class, women are defining the class struggle more clearly.

Many critics on the left overlook the simple fact that women, including women workers, are currently in motion on a mass political level. These critics reveal their lack of political understanding, for they fail to recognize that the Marxist theory of capitalism itself demands that the liberation of women be an integral part of any socialist revolution. They reveal their lack of political seriousness in their refusal to support the struggle of women against their oppression both as a legitimate struggle in its own right and as an aspect of the overthrow of capitalism. Serious revolutionaries do not stand at the periphery of a movement to attack it, but involve themselves as supporters of and fighters for women's liberation. They commit themselves to helping the women's movement realize its revolutionary potential as a catalyst and an aspect of the class struggle.

Several feminists we spoke with expressed the view that sexism on the Left holds back social change more than do attacks on the Women's Liberation Movement from the Right. Said one college student:

So many women know we need a revolution. But we can't trust the spokesmen of the parties and left groups. Their attacks on the women's movement discredit their strategy for the future. Their everyday sexism makes women so furious that they can't believe the future will be any different. When they pile on theory, to boot, it's just too much!

By selfishly ignoring the fight against sexism on personal and political levels and by downplaying its importance, many Left groups have transformed a tactical weakness into a strategic error. They have found it necessary to justify their practice by distorting theory. This outcome is predictable from the Marxist theory of social change in which theory and practice interpenetrate in dialectical fashion. Here we have an example of the process whereby conflicts between opposing elements are synthesized in theoretical formulations that distort the original. Recognizing that this regressive process has taken place is the first step in moving forward once again.

CONCLUSIONS

The Marxist perspective on social change illuminates how social movements develop out of objective conditions in all their contradictory aspects. Not only the forces of production but the ideas that people translate into action shape the conditions that will determine the future.
Productive forces and social relations interpenetrate. Otherwise why
would Marxists bother to organize and to write down their ideas? The
women's movement is growing and reaching out for theory. More women
from the Marxist and non-Marxist Left are resisting demands to renounce
feminism as decadent, petty bourgeois, self-indulgent ego-tripping that
divides the struggle to end exploitation. They question the sincerity and
judgement of those who maintain that there is nothing revolutionary in
feminism. Still feminists who are not Marxists are supicious of Marxist
women as well as men. We have presented evidence of the feminist consciousness of the founders of Marxism and analyzed how some sections of
the Left have distorted the Marxist theory of society and social change.
Over the past several months we have seen a group of women grapple with
the ideas of feminist Marxism and begin to move away from their Left
sectarian ideology. We are confident that others will do the same when
they open themselves to the feminist critique. When this ideology is
translated into consistent praxis we know many non-Marxist feminists
who will move rapidly to the Left.

As with the evolution of new forms of organic life, so the development
of new social forms proceeds by slow, almost imperceptible steps until
converging processes culminate in the qualitative transformation we term
a revolution. Sometimes the steps themselves are readily recognizable
but their apparent discreteness and temporarily contradictory directions
mask their essential unity. Hence we are left in doubt about their ultimate direction. This seems to be the case with many people's perception
of the liberation movements that are growing throughout the world
today: national liberation struggles in colonial and neocolonial areas;
women's liberation movements in developed and developing nations;
the struggles of workers in many industrial countries for self-manage-
ment and control of the workplace; the struggles of intellectuals and
students to liberate their work from the dead hand of received ideas and
the structures of political control.

The Marxist movement has not yet solved the problems of social transformation in an industrially developed nation with a large middle sector
of people who neither own their means of production nor live in dire
poverty. In a letter of 7 October 1858, to Marx (cited in Lenin 1939),

Engels drew the connection between this embourgeoisement and imperialism which brought "the fruits of the British world market and colonial monopoly" to both workers and owners, albeit in unequal proportion and with unequal consequences. For the owners, imperialism saved their system from the effects of a declining rate of profit and internal collapse. The workers got the crumbs from the table in cheap consumer goods, but in their complicity delayed their own emancipation. As Lenin commented upon citing this passage, "the imperialist permeating ideology is also the working class. There is no Chinese wall between it and the other classes." Thus, did the founders of Marxism view the socioeconomic and cultural framework of the divide-and-rule tactic of racism, which they termed "social chauvinism." When Engels wrote somewhat facetiously of the embourgeoisment of English workers he was referring to a small labor aristocracy of skilled workers, for most of the English proletariat lived in misery, and Engels (1958) himself had helped to document and publicize their conditions in 1845. As a result of labor militancy and the profits of imperialist expansion this is no longer the case for the majority of workers in the United States and Europe. Here the socioeconomic structure and cultural conditions pose quite different problems for planners of social change.

This paper has focused on women in the United States today. By exploring what a feminist Marxist perspective offers both anthropology and the Left, we have attempted to draw attention to some of the connections between these contemporary movements for social change. Already we are witnessing new labor militancy arising from the convergence of influences from the civil rights struggles and women's liberation, as, for example, in several textile mills and garment factories in the South. As this trend grows in scope and force we expect that the women's movement will develop a clearer class perspective and deeper roots as a mass movement.

For Marxists the struggle between opposing classes arises inevitably from the mode of production in class societies, the dominant class fighting to maintain and extend its wealth and control, others trying to get more of what is rightfully theirs. While this opposition is the key to social change, the form taken by the class struggle is specific to each historical period. Under capitalism the decisive struggle is between those who own and control industrial production and those who through their labor create new wealth.

To state this general theory, however, does not create a program for social transformation. This requires examining the details of specific conditions. The various forms of oppression nurtured by capitalism and necessary to its maintenance need not appear to be related to the exploitation of workers in order for the connection to exist. As the women's movement demonstrates in its concrete experience and theory, the dominant mode of production penetrates all contemporary social life: institutions, interpersonal relations, the psychology of social groups. In class society ethnic and sex conflicts take on the appearance of antagonistic contradictions and in so doing mask the conflict of classes so that only by the most intensive effort in concrete situation can the unity necessary for social revolution in the present epoch be won, or the future transformation be accomplished.

There are several contradictory tendencies within the women's movement, a few of which we have explored here. These arise out of objective conditions and the ideology that has developed as a part of the maintenance structure of our society. Some feminists appear to be unaware of the evidence for qualitative differences in women's oppression and the historical processes through which they came about. They accept the assertion that women are everywhere and have always been subordinate while at the same time they argue that what has always been need not forever be (cf. Firestone 1970; de Beauvoir 1972; Gough 1971; Millet 1970; Ortner 1973). Thus the contemporary processes through which oppression is maintained have been projected back into history and forward into the future. Lacking a theory of social evolution this kind of critique employs psychobiological explanations and views the conflict between women and men as the basic contradiction of all societies, past and present. The anthropological work that will make the evolutionary perspective known is only now becoming a major intellectual trend (cf. Leacock 1975; Leavitt 1975; Liebowitz and Schoepf n.d.; Mariotti 1973; Oakley 1972; Sacks 1970; Schoepf 1971, 1974). We are confident that as more anthropologists and others free themselves of the biases that have distorted attempts to develop a scientific perspective on societies past and present, new work will document the basic truth of Marxist-feminist theory, and feminist analysis will be both more accurate and more optimistic.

Our experience in the women's movement confirms the theory that the type of struggle that must be waged to bring about the future envisaged by Marx and Engels is a profoundly humanist and humanizing process. The material and intellectual conditions of our present stage of sociocultural development require the active participation of huge numbers of people on a worldwide scale to bring about change. The rulers of the old societies have perfected control systems with coercive and ideological power reaching into every corner. No small band of revolutionary heroes, no small army can topple the fully developed bourgeois state despite its economic difficulties and moral chaos. Those who must be won as leaders and allies in a protracted struggle to transfer power to the people will not submit to elitist, bureaucratic domination. Nor will they be persuaded by slogans which conflict with what they observe to be the day-to-day practice of would-be revolutionaries. When Left critics tell feminists that the principal contradiction is class, not sex, feminist Marxists point out that the move is theirs to make. Just as the primary responsibility to turn ethnic conflict into class conflict rests with whites, so Marxist men must begin the struggle to turn sexual antagonism into class struggle. A feminist who is also a socialist writes:

This is not the time or place to plead with women to enter into "comradely struggle" with working-class men around their sexism. It is the time for men to enter into revolutionary struggle with their sexism so that more and more women can also "become the real leaders of the united front against imperialism and the struggle for socialism." And to hold these men responsible if with their backward ideology, they alienate their potential allies.

For if the movement turns its back on women now, be sure that it will be the movement, not the "myth of sisterhood" or "retreat into self" or its alleged decadence, that will be responsible for the lack of unity. The retreat from the fight against sexism will exact its own heavy price (Morales 1973).

We would extend the criticism to include academics on the Left. Marxism is not merely a methodology for the social sciences, but "an interconnected whole grounded in the concrete experience of millions of people" (Lichtheim 1966:1). We have attempted to show that in the development and application of Marxist theory there can be no separation of structural analysis and critical humanism. A mature Marxist perspective necessarily joins the two because in real life the two are intimately related. Since the task of Marxist philosophers is to understand the world while attempting to change it, a Marxist theoretician by definition is one who combines theory and practice. Those who do not cannot legitimately lay claim to the title. In the struggle to transform society, those who would be Marxists must also allow themselves to be transformed and actively seek this transformation despite the pain involved. The nature of this struggle will in part determine the character of the post-revolutionary transition.

We have explored here as best we can what the Marxist theory of social change offers women. We wish to thank all our beautiful mothers and sisters for teaching us by sharing their experiences of pain and struggle, as well as all those who have shared their criticisms of this paper. As anthropologists we are engaged in the difficult task of liberating ourselves from some of the political and personal damage of our professional socialization. Striving with others in recent years to develop collective forms of work we recognize how much our growth as anthropologists has been fostered by involvement in the Women's Liberation Movement. We hope that this beginning will be useful to others in our common struggle.

REFERENCES

BENSTON, MARGARET
    1969   The political economy of women's liberation. *Monthly Review* 21(4).
BOSERUP, ESTHER
    1970   *Women's role in economic development.* London: St. Martin's Press.
BURRIS, BARABARA
    1971   *Fourth world manifesto: an angry response to an imperialist venture against the women's liberation movement.* New Haven: Advocate Press.
DE BEAUVOIR, SIMONE
    1972   *The second sex.* New York: Bantam.
ENGELS, FRIEDRICH
    1958   *The condition of the working class in England.* Stanford: Stanford University Press.
    1972   *The origin of the family, private property and the state.* Edited by Eleanor B. Leacock. New York: International Publishers.
FIRESTONE, SHULAMITH
    1970   *The dialectic of sex: the case for feminist revolution.* New York: William Morrow and Company.
FRIED, MORTON
    1967   *The evolution of political society.* New York: Random House.
FRIEDAN, BETTY
    1963   *The feminine mystique.* New York: W. W. Norton.
GOUGH, KATHLEEN
    1971   The origin of the family. *Journal of Marriage and the Family* 33(4).
JONES, DELMOS J.
    1970   Toward a native anthropology. *Human Organization* 29(4):251–259.
    1974   Review of "Stay where you were: a study of unemployables in industry," by Harlem Padfield and Roy Williams. *Reviews in Anthropology* I(2).
LARGUIA, ISABEL, JOHN DUMOULIN
    1972   Toward a science of women's liberation. *Political Affairs* 51(6).
LEACOCK, ELEANOR BURKE, *editor*
    1972   "Introduction," in *The origin of the family, private property and the state.* By Friedrich Engels. New York: International Publishers.
    1975   "Class, commodity and the status of women," in *Women Cross-culturally: change and challenge.* Edited by Ruby Rohrlich-Leavitt. The Hague: Mouton.

LEAVITT, RUBY ROHRLICH
1975   *Anthropological perspectives on women's studies.* New York: Harper and Row.
LENIN, V. I.
1938   *Women and society.* New York: International Publishers.
1939   *Imperialism: the last stage of capitalism.* New York: International Publishers.
LÉVI-STRAUSS, CLAUDE
1969   *Elementary structures of kinship.* Boston: Beacon Press.
LICHTHEIM, GEORGE
1966   *Marxism in modern France.* New York: Columbia University Press.
LIEBOWITZ, LILA, BROOKE G. SCHOEPF
n.d.   "The biological background of sex role differentiation." Unpublished manuscript.
MARIOTTI, AMELIA
1973   "The division of labor in anthropological theory: a critical survey of selected works." Masters thesis, University of Connecticut.
MARX, KARL
1947   *Capital.* New York: International Publishers.
MARX, KARL, FRIEDRICH ENGELS
1948   *The communist manifesto.* New York: International Publishers.
MILLETT, KATE
1970   *Sexual politics.* New York: Doubleday.
MITCHELL, JULIET
1971   *Women's estate.* New York: Pantheon Books.
MORALES, ROSARIO
1973   *A feminist replies to revolutionary union. Guardian.* August 15.
MORGAN, LEWIS HENRY
1963   *Ancient society.* Edited by Eleanor B. Leacock. New York: World Publishing Co.
MORGAN, ROBIN, *editor*
1970   "Introduction: The women's revolution," in *Sisterhood is powerful.* New York: Random House.
NEWTON, ESTHER, SHIRLEY WALTON
1971   "The personal is political: consciousness raising and personal change in the women's liberation movement." Paper presented at the 70th Annual meeting of the American Anthropological Association. November. New York.
OAKLEY, ANN
1972   *Sex, gender and society.* New York: Harper and Row.
ORTNER, SHERRY
1973   Is culture to nature as man is to woman? *Feminist Studies.*
RAINWATER, LEE, RICHARD P. COLEMAN, GERALD HANDEL
1962   *Working-man's wife.* New York: MacFadden-Bartell.
SACKS, KAREN
1970   "Social bases for sexual equality: a comparative view," in *Sisterhood is powerful.* Edited by Robin Morgan. New York: Random House.

SCHOEPF, BROOKE GRUNDFEST
  1971   "Raging hormones or raging females: a biocultural review." Paper presented at the 70th Annual meeting of the American Anthropological Association. November, New York.
  1974   Sex differences: genuine and spurious. *Reviews in anthropology.* 1(1).
VOGEL, LISA
  1969   *Women workers, some basic facts.* Boston: New England Free Press.
ZETKIN, CLARA
  1934   *Lenin on the woman question.* New York: International Publishers.

SECTION FOUR

Women in the Planned Societies

Introduction

The papers in this section deal with the roles of women in the socialist and other planned societies: the U.S.S.R., China, Vietnam, Cuba, Chile, Israel, and Sweden. In differing degrees, the ideology of these societies derives from the principles of the founding fathers of socialism and their adherents or critics. Their official view on women is summed up by Engels (1972a:612): "In any given society the degree of women's emancipation is the natural measure of the general emancipation." According to this tenet, the papers in this section also reveal the degree to which the societies discussed have achieved the goals of socialism—i.e. "general emancipation"—which depend on "the degree of women's emancipation."

Despite historical differences and cultural variations, the patterns common to the pre-revolutionary status of women in the socialist societies are quite clear. Women lived in a condition of legal slavery to fathers and husbands, with little redress against total tyranny, exploitation, and brutality. In the belief that only through socialism could they liberate themselves and gain human status, very many women risked their lives in the revolutionary movements, expecially the terrorist groups, in the U.S.S.R. and China. But though they played important political roles on local levels, the women constituted a very small proportion of the top leadership that directed the revolution and established and ran the new societies, despite the frequent reiterations in the socialist literature that "there can be no socialist revolution, unless a vast section of the toiling women takes an important part in it."

With little power to ensure that egalitarian sex roles were integrated into the new structures, women found that their role as followers in the revolution had prolonged male hegemony in societies which the patriarchal elites defined as socialist. True, the new societies were established under the most adverse and bitter circumstances, characterized by internal and external attempts to destroy them before they could gain a firm foothold. However, from the beginning, according to the articles in this section, the Communist Party leaders viewed the condition of women as only one—and at that, not the most important—of the many problems confronting them. This condition was separated out as the "woman question" by men who, operating within a hierarchy of pragmatic priorities, came to political decisions that resulted in the manipulation and exploitation of women. If, as Lenin wrote (1934:69), "the building of socialism will begin when we have achieved the complete equality of women," then the socialist countries have not yet begun to build socialism.

A primary factor is the fact that women participate only minimally in the top political decision-making and administration of the state, although Engels, as well as the other socialist ideologues, recognized that this was the *sine qua non* of both democracy and socialism:

Unless women are brought to take an independent part not only in political life generally, but also in daily and universal public service, it is no use talking about full and stable democracy, let alone socialism (Marx and Engels 1958: 233).

The vast majority of women are kept out of top-level policy making by techniques traditional to the patriarchy, according to the papers in this section.

First, the male elites gain control over women's reproductive functions for two purposes: (a) to regulate the supply of human labor, the most crucial of natural resources; (b) to achieve the most basic form of male domination over women. When women are subjected to this fundamental entrapment, they are prevented, no matter what the society, from participating freely and equally in the important institutions. When their bodies are controlled by decisions in which they have little input, they are treated as dehumanized commodities.

At the same time that women in the socialist societies are expected to participate fully in "socially productive" labor, they are also expected to assume full responsibility for child-rearing and domestic labor. Although these functions are said to be social roles which should be given the highest priority, they are in reality low on the list, and women are expected to take up the slack by the performance of two jobs, one unpaid, as in the capitalist countries. To the extent that child-rearing and domestic tasks are privatized, women's ability to participate equally in economic and political life is reduced. What Lenin pointed out more than fifty years ago in the U.S.S.R. (1951:56) seems still to be largely true today:

> Notwithstanding all the liberating laws that have been passed, woman continues to be a DOMESTIC SLAVE, because PETTY HOUSEWORK crushes, strangles, stultifies and degrades her,...and wastes her labor on barbarously unproductive, ...nerve-racking...drudgery. The real EMANCIPATION OF WOMEN, real communism, will begin only when a mass struggle...is started against this petty domestic economy, or rather when it is TRANSFORMED ON A MASS SCALE into large-scale socialist economy.

Moreover, as in the capitalist countries, these tasks are unpaid when they are performed by individual women in the home, being defined as "socially unproductive" and not deserving of economic remuneration. Done by women, these are the only tasks that are unpaid, although child-rearing and the preparation of food, etc., ensure human reproduction and survival whatever the circumstances under which they are performed and whether done by women or men.

As in the capitalist countries, women work mainly in the "feminine" fields that are projections of their family roles. These roles also limit their time and energy for advancement in the economy and participation in politics. No matter what the field, women do not occupy the positions that bring the greatest prestige and economic rewards, and their mobility in the economy is further restricted by the fact that they are pushed into and out of various activities according to such variables as a shortage of male labor.

Most important, to the extent that child-rearing and domestic work are the domain of women and are privatized, monogamous marriage, the nuclear family, and male supremacy are perpetuated. Or, putting the horse before the cart, both socialist and capitalist countries hail the nuclear family as the basic social cell because, as Larguia points out, it is the principal patriarchal vehicle whereby male hegemony is maintained and a huge mass of unpaid labor is expropriated from women. Engels' analysis of this family system (1972b:137) almost a century ago, still applies in the socialist as well as the capital nations:

> The modern individual family is founded on the open or concealed domestic slavery of the wife.... Within the family [the husband]... is the bourgeois, and the wife represents the proletariat.

The socialist theoreticians proposed only vague alternatives to monogamy and the nuclear family. But the nineteenth-century Swedish writer Almqvist, discussed by Westman Berg, proposed the elimination of this family system in favor of a matrilineal, matrilocal system, based on that of the Nayar on the Malabar coast of India who practiced both polyandry and polygyny. Almqvist regarded this system as more advanced and democratic than any system espoused by the European socialists: "Men are not treated as subordinate beings and do not acquire minority complexes. Their status is not dependent upon the status of their 'wife' but upon themselves. There are no double standards as regards sexual morality.... The 'husband' is not expected to work in his 'wife's' house as the wife has to work in her husband's home in patriliny." Engels (1972b:125) also reported favorably on this system as "a specialized form of group marriage."

How do the women in the socialist and planned societies react to their inferior status? In the U.S.S.R., women seem to be determined to control their reproductive functions.

Despite the lack of contraceptives and the varying policy on abortions, despite the economic and social rewards given to mothers of many children, despite the official harangues about "sexual individualism" and the joys of motherhood, and despite the official reprimands against women who treat child-bearing "as if it were a personal matter," the one-child family is the norm in European Russia, according to Rosenthal. And despite the varying policy on divorce and the diatribes on the need for family stability, whenever the divorce laws are liberalized the divorce rate rises rapidly in the U.S.S.R. The fact that women are taking the initiative in instituting divorce proceedings seems to indicate their dissatisfaction with the individual nuclear family and its built-in male supremacy.

As for China, the following quotation from Davin's paper appears to sum up the contradictions facing the women's movement there:

Women revolutionaries during the Chinese revolution, like other women in history, were confronted with the contradictions that arose between the interests of women and the interests of the revolution, both nationalist and socialist .... Women, though feminists, as revolutionaries had to make a united front with forces that represented male chauvinism in the interests of another cause which, by implication at least, took priority.... But in socialist construction, the problem of priorities arose again. ... Some women party leaders repressed feminist impulses and accepted the sacrifices of the years of stagnation or retreat.... All this raises the problem of how to judge the real interests of the revolution and those of women, and how to reconcile them with each other.

The primary problem, however, might be the correctness of decisions made by "male chauvinists" about the real "interests of the revolution." The primary error would appear to be the creation of a dichotomy by the same "male chauvinists" between "the real interests of the revolution and those of women."

As Chaney observes in her paper on women in Vietnam, Cuba, and Chile, "the whole process of development, whether capitalist or socialist, is viewed as a male project in which women are given only token participation," so their "men continue to mediate the relationships of women to society and the polity."

In Vietnam, as well as in much of the rest of southeast Asia, the family, especially in the agricultural areas, was co-terminous with the community, and women played roles that were roughly equal with those of men. The indigenous status of Vietnamese women was higher than that of women in the Indian, Chinese, and European patriarchies, surviving to a considerable extent the imperialisms of the Chinese, the French, and the Americans. During the American occupation, women feminists as well as male leaders urged Vietnamese women in both the north and the south to struggle more actively for their rights, including the assumption of important political positions, and they also criticized the Communist Party leaders for not placing competent activist women in such positions.

Comparing women's status in Vietnam, Cuba, and Chile, Chaney reports that the Vietnamese women were more thoroughly integrated into the labor force and many more served in high government positions than the women in socialist Chile and Cuba. Although Allende often pointed out that the revolution in Chile would not succeed unless women were incorporated into all levels of the economic and political system, later in his regime he articultated women's social roles primarily in terms of their family roles, in spite of the "pool of outstanding Communist and Socialist women militants in Chile." Moverover, Chaney points out that even these women enthusiastically accepted the "feminine" projects assigned to them because they, too, saw their functions as an extension of the *supermadre*. Judging from reports about the present regime in Chile, these women appear to have achieved equality with men in the number imprisoned, tortured, and killed.

In Cuba, Chaney notes that the impressive gains made by women are "a modernization of women imposed from above, in the face of serious resistance on the part of the Cuban male." And despite the establishment of a number of day-care centers and communal dining rooms, Cuban communism has not solved the problem of the "double burden of the working woman." Moreover, since the "initiative for and control of the modernization of sex roles is in the hands of the [male] political elite," it may be sacrificed "when it competes with higher priority goals for limited political and economic resources," says Chaney.

In Israel, the establishment of the kibbutz at the beginning of the century projected an image of female-male equality in every aspect of life in the Jewish community. But, according to Padan-Eisenstark, this image is simplistic "and does not promote the aim of establishing real sex equality in Israel or other countries." Sex roles in the kibbutz were to be the model for bringing about equality between the sexes throughout Israel, but even in the kibbutz these roles are segregated, women participating far more in educational and cultural activities, with economics and politics mainly in the hands of the men.

However, the socialization of child-care, the mechanization of housework, and the professionalization of both have transformed them into occupations which are among the most respected and desirable in kibbutz life. The complete economic independence of the kibbutz woman is also in marked contrast with the dependence of women in the cities, the vast majority of women in Israel, who suffer a drastic economic decline when they are widowed or divorced.

In Sweden, most of the changes recommended by Almqvist have by now been incorporated into the laws but, according to Westman Berg, although sexual equality is the accepted ideology, patriarchal practices are still in effect, and the "sexual exploitation of women is still common."

REFERENCES

ENGELS, FRIEDRICH
   1972a "Socialism: utopian and scientific," in *The Marx-Engels reader*. Edited by Robert C. Tucker. New York: W. W. Norton.
   1972b *The origin of the family, private property and the state* Edited and with and introduction by Eleanor Burke Leacock. New York: International Publishers.
LENIN, V. I.
   1934 *The emancipation of women: from the writings of V.I. Lenin.* New York: International Publishers.
   1951 "Women and society," in *The woman question.* New York: International Publishers.
MARX, KARL, FRIEDRICH ENGELS
   1958 *Selected works*, volume two. Moscow: Foreign Language Publishing House.

The Role and Status of Women in the Soviet Union: 1917 to the Present

BERNICE GLATZER ROSENTHAL

> ...in any given society the degree of wo-
> man's emancipation is the natural measure
> of the general emancipation.
>
> FRIEDRICH ENGELS[1]

Equality of the sexes was an announced goal of the Russian revolutionary movement which culminated in the Bolshevik Revolution of 1917. Upon assuming power, the new Bolshevik regime reaffirmed its commitment to the equality of all citizens regardless of sex, religion, or nationality, and quickly moved to eliminate the legal barriers to woman's equality. Intending to move beyond legal forms, the Bolsheviks aimed to make women the economic, social, intellectual, and cultural equals of men by removing the bases of women's traditional subservience. Transforming women's role from housewife to worker was an essential element in Bolshevik plans for the revolutionary transformation of the entire society.

Since then, half a century has elapsed. Women work as a matter of course and in all segments of the economy. Holding jobs formerly considered unsuitable for women, they are construction workers, engineers, doctors, and ditch-diggers. But they are still expected to keep house and the primary responsibility for raising children is theirs. The "dual burden" of home and work poses a formidable barrier to equality which is yet to be surmounted.

It both its successes and its failures, the Soviet attempt to revolutionize

---

[1] In: *Origin of the family, private property, and the state.*

the role and status of women is pertinent to women today. My aim here is to place the Soviet attempt in historical perspective by studying the evolution of Soviet policy toward women and the effect of that policy on women themselves. It will be seen that Soviet policy falls into three distinct periods (1917–1928, 1928–1953, and 1953 to the present), each corresponding to a distinct stage in the evolution of Russian society as a whole. At each period, the role and status of women conforms to a general pattern of expectations for all citizens. The constant, the crucial, factor in role definition was social need as perceived and defined by the ruling Communist party.

Before the revolution, most Russians were peasants. Both men and women did hard physical labor. Drunkenness was common and wife-beating was taken for granted. Women were, in effect, slaves — first of their fathers and then of their husbands. Their unquestioning obedience was prescribed by law. Neither law nor custom provided redress against a tyrannical husband and divorce was almost unobtainable. But it hardly mattered; an unhappy wife had no place to go. As late as 1897 most women who worked were domestic servants. On the eve of World War I, women industrial workers earned less than half the wages earned by men, and their illiteracy rate was three times as high. Wives of aristocrats or rich merchants were more comfortable, but they were no freer. All women were expected to sacrifice their own needs for the sake of husband and children.[2]

Women were clearly among the oppressed; liberating them was a stated goal of both the Populist and Marxist parties. Women themselves (chiefly from the privileged classes) were numerous in both groups and were particularly prominent among the terrorist wing of the Populists. Most women revolutionaries believed that only under socialism could they attain equality. Sacrificing personal happiness, risking their lives for the sake of the revolution, women placed the needs of the revolution before their own. Adopting an extremely ascetic lifestyle, they considered any thought of personal happiness or comfort as "bourgeois." For most revolutionaries, women's equality was an outline with the details to be filled in afterward. Revolutionary women did not form their own groups; they worked together with men. But they were not the leaders.[3]

[2]   See A. Kharchev (1964). For a summary of the rights and duties of women and children in Russian Law see *Pervyi Zhenskii Kalendar* 3, 1901: 107–177.
[3]   For women in the revolutionary parties see Franco Venturi (1966); Robert McNeal (1972a, 1972b); Nadja Strasser (1915); and V. A. Amfitreatov (1897).

An explicitly feminist movement began to develop after 1905. Liberal rather than socialist, it stressed legal guarantees such as equal rights to education and employment and divorce reform, and it concentrated on the right to vote. Women workers were also beginning to organize and were becoming aware of their special problems as women. Except for Alexandra Kollontai, however, few Marxists recognized the need to develop a specific woman's program. Kollontai herself was a Menshevik until 1914.

The Bolshevik program for women developed out of the struggle with feminism and reformism and stressed equality through economic independence. The cause of women's subservience, Bolsheviks argued, is economic. Women must support themselves and socialism will provide the conditions enabling them to do so. Society will be reorganized so that it takes up the economic and educational functions now performed by the family. Communal facilities (dining rooms, child-care centers, laundries, dormitories) will be established which will free women from domestic bondage and enable them to work on equal terms with men. Bolsheviks also insisted that household work was, by definition, unproductive and that the "bourgeois family," based on male supremacy, had to be destroyed. Marriage would then be based solely on love and would last only as long as both partners desired. Given all these conditions, Bolsheviks concluded, complete equality between the sexes would be only a matter of time (Lenin 1972; Engels 1972; Zetkin 1933).

1917–1928

Almost immediately after assuming power, the Bolsheviks took steps to implement their ideal of equality. But by June 1918, the country was torn by civil war and by 1921 the economy was at a standstill. From 1921–1928 economic reconstruction took first priority. Resources were not made available to women in amounts large enough to be effective. Women did have equal rights, but illiteracy, lack of skills, male prejudice, and their own attitudes barred economic equality. Social equality was even more elusive; the "sexual revolution" of the twenties turned out to be favorable to men. By 1928, new problems were evident and old ones had not been solved.

Legal equality was quickly achieved. In December 1917, all the Tsarist marriage and divorce laws were repealed and the clergy lost its power to perform marriages. After that date, only civil marriages would be valid; a network of offices was established to register them. This was part of a campaign to weaken the power of the Orthodox Church. Other legislation mandated equal pay for equal work, forbade the dismissal of pregnant women, and instituted paid maternity leave and nursing breaks. Elaborate labor codes aimed to protect women's health by prohibiting hot, heavy, or hazardous work, night work, and overtime (Schlesinger 1949). But these were all preliminary measures. The Bolsheviks' ultimate goal was to abolish the "bourgeois family" by removing the legal props of male supremacy and by reconstructing society to enable women to work.

The Family Code of 1918 eliminated the bourgeois family as a legal institution. The "socialist family" would be based on blood relations, not legal ties. All distinctions between children born in or out of wedlock were abolished. Within the household, man and woman were equal. A wife not only could retain her own name and establish her own residence; she had a separate passport and identity card. Conjugal rights and community property were abolished. Each had equal authority over the children and controlled his or her own earnings. Divorce was obtainable upon written application of either party and alimony (considered by Bolsheviks degrading to the woman) was eliminated except in cases of physical disability. The Code specifically stated that women were expected to work (Schlesinger 1949; Geiger 1968).

Alexandra Kollontai was named People's Commissar of Social Welfare and devoted special attention to establishing model nurseries. But she resigned in March 1918. Economic disaster precluded the expenditure of funds for communal facilities.

Civil war began in June 1918 and lasted over two years. Women took jobs because their men were at the front and because food rations were allotted on the basis of job category, with housewives receiving the least. Communal agencies did develop but they were emergency measures of almost uniformly poor quality. Communal restaurants were soup kitchens, communal hostels were requisitioned homes where workers slept on the floor, and homeless children occupied all the places in the children's shelters. In 1920, because of the desperate situation, abortion was legalized. (Lenin had originally viewed both birth control and abortion as "bourgeois defeatism.") The decree explicitly stated that abortion was a necessary evil and looked to improved conditions to obviate the need for it. In the interim, the populace was urged to use contraceptives, but they were unknown and unavailable (Schlesinger 1949:44, 172–187; Lenin 1972:28–30).

The civil war was bitter and bloody. Cities emptied out and the entire nation reverted to a primitive mode of life. *De facto* anarchy was particularly harmful to women; brute force prevailed. Soldiers raped the enemy's women and even their own. Half-educated Communists took Marx's "community of women" quite literally and in at least two cities — Saratov, in agrarian Southern Russia, and Vladimir, an industrial city not far from Moscow — local Soviets proceeded to "nationalize" women. In Saratov, it was a crime for a woman to "refuse a Communist." In Vladimir, all single men and women had to register at a central marriage bureau in order to select partners (Kharchev 1964:139, Geiger 1968:65–70).

Comparatively few women were active combatants. Sixty-three women were decorated for heroism and two thousand women were killed or wounded. But these were stalwart party activists. Most women were engaged in a harsh struggle for survival. Protective legislation was a dead letter; the prohibitions against night work and mining were formally repealed in 1919. Women were drafted for the labor armies organized by Trotsky to do hard manual labor and they were expected to work on the "Communist Sabbath" (*subbotnik*). Recognizing that illiteracy doomed women to menial jobs, in 1919 the Bolsheviks decreed compulsory education through the primary grades for both sexes. But there was no money to implement it.

The civil war was over by 1921. But five million died in the famine of that year and seven million homeless children roamed the countryside. Factories closed for lack of supplies. A "workers' opposition" developed within the Communist party and revolutionary sailors of the Kronstadt garrison demanded "Soviets without Communists." In 1921, in a startling about-face, Lenin instituted a New Economic Policy (NEP) of limited private trade in order to provide incentives for production. Economic development absorbed all resources.

This meant that the social support women needed in order to be truly equal was not available. Most children's shelters were disbanded; those that remained were of such poor quality that only women with no other choice used them. Resources were not used to upgrade female labor. Still illiterate and unskilled, most women qualified only for menial jobs. Furthermore, protective legislation backfired. Cost-conscious managers were reluctant to hire women because paid maternity leave and nursing breaks made them more expensive to employ. Women were last hired and first fired. Those who had to support themselves and could not find jobs sometimes turned to prostitution which, though illegal, was widespread in the cities. Given these conditions, most women opted for marriage and stayed home.

Recognizing that traditional domesticity was the enemy of the new order, that unliberated women inculcated the old mores, particularly religion, in their children, Bolshevik policy urged women to change their way of life by their own efforts. Lenin urged women to become politically active and to run for election to the local soviets. He also exhorted men to practice at home the equality they preached outside. A true Communist stays home and "rocks the cradle" so that his wife can go to night school or attend a party meeting. A host of studies demonstrated the economic irrationality of individual households in terms of labor time. One study decried the millions of labor hours wasted on cooking. The idea was to inspire women to form communes on their own initiative.

Literature of the NEP period features the woman activist as heroine and new role model. Completely dedicated to her work, she is independent, unafraid of life, quite able to take care of herself. Taking the lead in establishing communal facilities, particularly child-care centers, she educates women in Marxism at the same time. Explicitly described as "not beautiful," she scorns cosmetics and is indifferent to fashion. Husband, boyfriend, and children all take second place to her work in building socialism (Luke 1953; Gasiorowska 1968).

Convinced that women must be politicized or the new order would flounder, in 1919 the party established a special division *Zhenotdel'* (Women's Delegation) in order to reach them. Elected by women in each factory and village, *Zhenotdel'* representatives helped women with their problems, attacked their grievances, and thus hoped to gain their confidence.

In the factories, the *delegatka* functioned as a combination shop steward, grievance committee, and big sister. *Zhenotdel'* took women's side against male management, set up factory arbitration committees, and combatted the tendency to freeze women out when job cuts were made. The single most common grievance was against male managers who used their plants as a harem. *Zhenotdel'* also selected some women for advanced training, sponsored outstanding women for election to local soviets, set up child-care facilities, and, after the revised Family Code of 1926, helped women file applications for divorce and support (Halle 1933; Rowbotham 1972).

Zhenotdel' was less effective in the countryside. In the village of Viriatino (selected as typical by a team of Soviet anthropologists) only five or six women could be persuaded to become activists and these were either widowed or divorced. Younger women feared to flout their husband's or father's authority or to alienate potential suitors (Benet 1970).

The Party itself did not always take *Zhenotdel'* seriously. Never sufficiently funded, its existence within the Party remained precarious. Without the authority to make arrests or impose fines, *Zhenotdel's* effectiveness depended on mobilizing public opinion by shaming or ridiculing the offender. It was dissolved by Stalin in 1929 as "no longer necessary." Relations between men and women were in a state of flux. Many women were widowed by the war, others simply abandoned. Husbands were hard to find and easy divorce laws enabled a man to "walk off, happily whistling."[4] The problem was that men suffered no financial penalty and women were not yet equal economically, socially, or psychologically. Trying to get, or to keep, husbands, they still deferred to the man.

Among urban youth, a crude form of Kollontai's theory that the sexual act means no more than "a glass of water" prevailed. Promiscuity became *de rigueur*; a girl who resisted was accused of "bourgeois prudence." Many unions were not registered; usually it was the man who objected to legal marriage. Both the number of abortions and the birthrate rose markedly.

By 1925 the bourgeois family was clearly disintegrating. But the socialist family in which all loved one another still had not appeared and the number of destitute women and children was rising rapidly. Letters to the press decried the sexual exploitation of the weakest members of society as unsocialist. One cited the phenomenon of "spongers" living off the earnings of working girls (Susnovski 1926). Lenin himself had spoken out against the "glass of water" theory before his death and urged that communists apply their energies to building socialism instead of dissipating (Zetkin 1933).

In 1926, the Family Code was revised to protect the women and children of broken unions. Common law marriage, defined as "a mutual intention to live together, recognized as such by both parties," was recognized and made legally binding. Whether or not the union was registered, women were entitled to alimony for one year and to support for their children. All property acquired during the union was divided in half. All women were entitled to file paternity suits. If they did not know who the father was they could name the possibilities; each would then be partially responsible for the child's support (Schlesinger 1949).

Only fragmentary figures are available, but it is clear that after the new

---

[4] Louise Luke cites one character who says, "Everyone is divorcing their old wives now." She adds, "Apart from the wives themselves, no one seemed to object" (1953:77). Kent Geiger argues (in Brown: 1968) that "a large number of Soviet women were subject to extreme hardship by the policy of easy divorce... its *de facto* effect was often one of exploitation and an increased number of exposed and helpless women forced to raise their children by themselves."

law the divorce rate rose rapidly — 450 percent in Petrograd and 300 percent in Moscow alone. Most actions were initiated by women hoping to get support from men who had abandoned them. Though divorce was rarer in the countryside there are cases of peasants taking "a wife for a season" and divorcing her when the harvest was in. Because few peasants had personal property of any significance, support payments were fixed in terms of food, but these were difficult to collect. And in the cities men simply disappeared (Schlesinger, 1949; Luke 1953; Madison 1968: Chapter 3).

The courts tended to allot one third of a man's earnings for support. But as the incidence of multiple divorce also rose, meaningful support for two or more former wives became impossible. The terms "husband" and "wife" tended to be used quite loosely as the concepts themselves blurred (Winter: 1933).

Kollontai's "glass of water" theory, expressed in her novels *Red love* and *Love of three generations*, must be understood in the context of the situation in which women found themselves in the twenties. Arguing that men were not yet ready to recognize women as an equal "spiritual-physical force" she insisted that women must learn to seek fulfillment in creative work. Romance is a delusion, Kollontai claimed; it is the means men use to enslave women. Until a new generation of men arises which will accept women as persons, women must avoid emotional involvement; they must treat sex as a purely physical need. The double standard must be ended. Monogamy must be recognized as "bourgeois possessiveness." No one belongs to anyone. The maternal instinct can be fulfilled outside of marriage. But most important, women must dedicate themselves to socially productive work (Kollontai 1971).

Though the focus of this study is in European Russia, the campaign to liberate the Moslem women of Central Asia from their truly subhuman status merits attention.[5] In 1923, the Party decided that women were the "structural weak point" of Moslem society. Liberate women, the Party reasoned, and the entire edifice will collapse, the authority of the *cadis* (priests) will cease, and the poor will fight the rich because the latter have access to more women. A series of laws prohibited bridal purchase, raised the marriage age to sixteen, discouraged polygamy, and gave women equal rights in marriage, divorce, inheritance, education, property, and positions in public service. Cadres of dedicated women activists

[5]   The following is based on Gregory J. Massell's study (1968). An extended version is soon to be published. Massell also describes at length the conditions of Moslem women before the campaign.

were sent to enforce the law and to raise the consciousness of women. Party functionaries were to take the lead by removing their wives' veils and bringing them to public meetings. Women were encouraged to divorce husbands who mistreated them.

But the campaign backfired. The Party had not allocated resources sufficient to enable women to make the transition from seclusion to independence. Completely unskilled, many became prostitutes in order to survive. Men used the laws against polygamy to cast out their older wives and the wives' own families would not take them in. More important, the Party had underestimated the ferocity of male resistance. Men killed their wives for removing the veil and local courts did not punish them. Party functionaries dragged their feet on implementing the laws. By 1927 a real reign of terror against independent women began; two hundred were kidnapped, raped, and even murdered in Uzbekistan alone. Local officials failed to protect them. By 1928, a counterrevolutionary movement led by the *cadis* and including men of all social classes emerged. Party control of the area itself was threatened. In 1929, Stalin personally called a halt to the campaign.

1928–1953

Early Bolshevism considered industrialization the answer to all problems. Lenin's quip "communism equals soviets plus electricity" typifies the attitude which made equality dependent on the economic level of society. Massive industrialization began in 1928 as Stalin introduced and directed the first five-year plan. It stressed heavy industry and skimped on consumer goods. Subsequent five-year plans followed a similar pattern. Between 1928 and 1940 real wages dropped between 22 and 43 percent. World War II caused a further decline. Only in 1952 was the 1928 level of real wages regained. (Geiger 1968:152). By the time Stalin died, in 1953, almost all women worked; but they had not been liberated from traditional tasks.

The first five-year plan created an acute need for labor. Capital was scarce; "hands" took the place of machines. Each year the number and percentage of women in the labor force increased: 24 percent in 1928, 26.7 percent in 1930, 31.7 percent in 1934, 35.4 percent in 1937. Protective legislation restricted women's employment in heavy or hazardous work and lists of occupations deemed especially suitable for women (i.e. assembly line work in factories) were drawn up (Dodge 1966: Chapters 3 and 6).

In four years, over 1,500 complexes of heavy industry were built by untrained young workers, most of them girls. Many were simply drafted and sent to work in virgin wildernesses. Conditions were extreme. They worked "without proper tools or shelters and often went hungry" (St. George 1973:48). The first five-year plan had the aura of a military campaign; through sacrifice and struggle, they were building a dream of universal prosperity. In this atmosphere, protective legislation was simply ignored. Women filled the hardest jobs; illiterate and unskilled, they were unqualified for anything else.

After 1931 efforts were made to upgrade the entire labor force, including women. Wage differentials were introduced for skilled workers. (Before that all workers received the same pay). Pro-female quotas were established in the factory training (*rabfak*) schools. In 1929, 25 percent of new enrollees had to be women; by 1934 it was 50 percent. On the plant level, efforts were made to identify and promote hard-working women; they became foremen, supervisors, and, after 1934, *Stakhanovites* (workers who markedly exceed their production norm and are held up as models of emulation). On the new collective farms, model statutes decreed equal pay for equal work and ordered that women be paid in their own names, not their husbands'. By 1934, there were 6,000 women collective-farm chairmen, 7,000 women tractor drivers, 9,000 women section managers, 28,000 brigade leaders and 100,000 team organizers. In the universities, 25 percent of new admissions in each department were reserved for women and the number was raised each year. Particularly benefitting women in engineering, science, mathematics, and agricultural technology, these norms aimed to utilize women brainpower. (By 1928, women were already half the medical students [Dodge 1966; Dewitt 1961: 346–348; Franklin 1972:267–269; Serebrennikov 1937].)

Sustained efforts were made to recruit women into the Party and to place them in prominent positions on local soviets, People's Courts, and factory committees. The percentage of women in the Party rose from 8.2 in 1925 to 15.9 in 1932. A drive to eradicate illiteracy increased opportunities for both sexes; by 1934 a network of primary schools covered the countryside and the number of secondary schools was increasing rapidly. All this was part of a campaign to revolutionize society, to shake up traditional mores.

Literature of the first five-year plan period lauded the "new Soviet women," muscular, hard-working, and enthusiastically toiling. She can dig ditches, haul heavy loads, drive a tractor, or solve a mathematical problem as well as a man. She is not flighty, or flirtatious, but very serious. At night she "develops her qualifications" by further study. Almost sexless, when she meets a man it is on the job and if she marries, the attraction is mutual interest and a common dedication to building socialism. When married couples go to bed, they discuss the plan. Children are neither seen nor heard (Luke 1953; Gasiorowska 1968).

The first five-year plan had provided for extensive child-care facilities. From 62,000 places in 1928, the number rose to 600,000 in 1932. The increase after that was slower: 718,200 in 1937, 824,000 in 1940. But this accounted for only a small percentage of pre-school children. (Soviet children start school at seven). As late as 1936 most married women with young children stayed home (DeWitt 1961: 74–76, Dodge 1966: Chapter 5).

Building and maintaining child-care facilities were the responsibility of the enterprise (factory or collective farm), not the government. Managers of the enterprise shunted responsibility to women workers and party activists who made the necessary arrangements on their own time. As shortages developed, due to defective planning, plant managers tended to shift funds from child-care facilities to direct investment in production. Originally, child-care facilities were to be open twenty-four hours a day in order to give women time for housework and self-development. By 1935, the hours were reduced to cover working time only. Combining work and motherhood was increasingly difficult; the birthrate declined.

Overcrowding and primitive housing conditions also account for women's reluctance to bear children. The plan did not provide for housing the millions of workers flooding into the cities. Entire families lived in one room. Few houses had running water and electricity; central heating and hot water were almost unknown. Carrying water in buckets, hauling fuel for the stove, were daily tasks. Laundry was a full day's work but working women did it on their day off or after work. Labor-saving appliances simply were not manufactured. And men refused to help at home; that was "women's work" (Geiger 1968: Chapter 7; Dodge 1966:97).

In the newer industrial areas, conditions were even worse. At Magnitogorsk, a steel city in the Ural Mountains, tents and dugouts provided the only shelter against the bitter winter winds. Sanitary facilities were poor; visitors report waitresses in the workers' restaurant picking lice out of each other's hair. At the Dnepestroi Dam site, single women slept on plank beds, seventy-one to the barrack, surrounded by their wailing infants. Circular letters had restricted abortion since 1931. At Kuznetsk, in Eastern Siberia, abortions could be performed only if the mother's life was in danger (Luke 1953:77–80).

The nuclear family continued to disintegrate. More and more, inflationary pressures created a need for the wife's salary. Marriage brought women neither security nor a higher standard of living. Industrial plants operated around the clock and on a continuous five or six day work week with no common day off. A working couple, on different shifts, rarely saw one another. By 1934, unsupervised, or poorly supervised children were creating a serious juvenile delinquency problem.

Young people often saw no need to marry. Ella Winter, in her sympathetic study *Red virtue*, reports that many young women chose not to marry, but still had a child and placed it in a child-care center. (Unmarried women had priority.) She does not indicate, however, whether these women preferred independence, or whether they could not find suitable husbands because men's attitudes had not changed. (Alcoholism was still prevalent.)

In 1936, new legislation enforced a return to the nuclear family. The precipitous decline in the birthrate was one reason, but official dismay at permissiveness and anti-authoritian attitudes was another. Sexual individualism and personal hedonism were out of line with the collectivist attitudes desired by the regime. As early as 1928, Riasanov, the leading party theorist, had attacked "libertinism" and warned that a casual attitude toward family obligations engenders social irresponsibility. Government publications began to stress the exemplary family lives led by Marx and Lenin, and couples in registered marriages received preference in the allocation of scarce housing. The campaign to restore the family accelerated in 1934. That year Stalin visited his old mother in the Caucasus, accompanied by great publicity. That same year, parents were made legally liable for the vandalism of their children and the entire family was held collectively responsible for the treason or defection of any one of its members. Homosexuality became a criminal offense punishable by hard labor; sexual preference was no longer a personal matter. The 1936 decrees restricting divorce and abolishing legal abortion were the culmination of this trend.

Stalin announced that the "foul and poisonous idea" of the liquidation of the family is a "false rumor... spread by enemies of the people." Fees, high in comparsion with average Soviet wages were introduced for divorce, and they went up with each divorce. The plaintiff had to appear personally in court, thus losing the day's earnings, and the fact of divorce was stamped on the labor books of both partners. Criminal penalties were introduced for non-support of children (Schlesinger 1949: 251–362).

The decree abolishing legal abortion stated that the conditions necessitating the original decree of 1920 had been overcome. "Mass abortions for egoistic reasons cannot be tolerated." Women protested in letters to *Izvestia* and *Pravda*, but the editors scolded them for treating child-bearing "as if it were a personal matter." Unprepared for the vehemence of their protest, Stalin increased maternity leave, promised more and better child-care centers, adequate housing, and instituted a program of assistance to large families (Schlesinger 1949). Literature began to laud the joys of motherhood and posters of happy families appeared all over the Soviet Union. Makarenko's *A book for parents* (1937) lauded the large family as the place where personal discipline and collective attitudes are first learned. Contraceptives were not included in the plan. In one year the birthrate rose 37 percent; 100 percent in Moscow alone. In 1938, due to the need for military preparedness, maternity leave was again reduced.

Women were still expected to work. Literature featured a new ideal Soviet woman, a kind of superwoman who made a "serene home" for her husband, was a devoted mother, and still equalled her husband's performance on the job (Luke 1953:88–99). But the new emphasis on motherhood checked women's ability to advance at work. Expecting frequent pregnancy, managers hesitated to invest in training women. Domestic responsiblities deflected women's time and energy away from activities leading to promotion. At the same time, Stalin eliminated pro-female quotas in the *rabfak* schools and *technikums*. Since women are now equal, he said, special measures are no longer necessary. From 1936–1937 the number of women in these institutes plummeted; after 1937 Stalin ordered that publication of figures on women's advance cease. When State Labor Reserves for job training were established in 1940, at first women were barred (Luke 1953:90–101; Geiger 1968 Chapter 4; DeWitt 1961).

Restricted opportunities to learn skills and primary responsibility for the home combined to relegate the vast majority of working women to the lowest skilled, most easily replaceable job categories. Only at the university level was no serious effort made to discourage women; the number of women medical, engineering, and science students continued to rise.

In 1936, the Stalin Constitution was promulgated. Article 122 guaranteed equal rights for women. It reads:

Women in the USSR are accorded all equal rights on an equal footing with men in all spheres of economic, government, political, and other social and cultural activity.

The possibility of exercising these rights is ensured by women being accorded the same rights with men to work, payment for work, rest and leisure, social insurance, and education and also by state protection of the interests of mother and child, state aid to mothers of large families and to unmarried mothers, maternity leave with full pay, and the provision of a wide network of maternity homes, nurseries, and kindergartens.

But it was as hollow as the guarantees of civil liberty to the millions in the forced labor camps. Women's low profile, however, was a kind of protection. In the "Great Terror" which lasted from 1934 to 1953 women made up only one tenth of those arrested. Wives of arrestees, however, were persecuted as wives of "enemies of the people," fired from their jobs, and evicted from their lodgings (Conquest 1966: 289–290; Mandelstam 1970).

World War II created a manpower vacuum which women filled. By 1941 women were half the labor force of the Soviet Union. George St. George credits the Soviet victory to its use of womanpower (1973:55–61). They worked fourteen to eighteen hours a day under severe conditions, in factories hastily evacuated to Siberia with roofs but no walls. By 1944 women were a third to a half of the laborers at the Baku oil fields and a majority of the miners. Doing back-breaking physical labor, they were the road maintanence crews and the ditch-diggers. Pre-war restrictions were eliminated and women were urged to learn skills. By 1942, women constituted 31 percent of the welders, 44 percent of compressing-machine operators, 27 percent of the stokers (formerly prohibited by law) and were electricians, locomotive operators (the latter also formerly prohibited) and other highly skilled workers in large numbers. "Baba" (grandma) kept house and watched the children (Dodge 1966; DeWitt 1961).

Women fought in the Red Army, particularly in guerrilla units. "There were several air regiments 'manned' entirely by women flyers. There were thousands of women snipers and machine gunners; and there was no unit in the Red Army without some women in it, mostly in medical and signals service, but also fighting side by side with men.... There was a woman—Major Anna Nikulina—in the unit which stormed and captured Hitler's Chancellery" (St. George 1973:55–61).

The war upset the demographic balance of Russian society. Twenty million men died. In 1944 the Family Code was revised to maintain family stability and to encourage a high birthrate. Returning soldiers sought younger women. To discourage wholesale abandonment, fees for divorce were raised steeply and proceedings deliberately complicated. The father had sole responsibility for child support and the amount, fixed by law, was automatically deducted from his salary. A tax on single persons was also introduced.

The same law stigmatized illegitimate children and denied unmarried women their right to file paternity suits. The latter was explicitly designed to protect returning soldiers from their "field brides." To discourage the "brides" from illegal abortion and to achieve a high birthrate, the state assumed direct responsibility for the support of illegitimate children at fixed rates. (These rates were halved in 1947.)[6]

Special honors, including cash subsidies, were introduced for women who bore many children. Ten children made a woman a "Mother Heroine" and seven to nine entitled her to a lesser award. Family allowances were introduced for three or more children and fees for crèches, nursery schools, and kindergartens were halved.

After the war, all resources were directed to reconstruction. The industrial heartland of European Russia lay in ruins and huge tracts of formerly fertile farmland had become "scorched earth." There was no money for communal facilities and consumer goods. Housing was in critically short supply and the standard of living remained low. But the official pro-natalist policy continued. The fact that women were expected to be both workers and mothers meant that while a talented minority became doctors, engineers, and scientists, the majority of women were confined to the lower echelons of the economic ladder (Dodge 1966:175). And the shortage of men militated against equality in personal relations.

1953–1973

Stalin's heirs have improved living conditions and released the average citizen from the terrors of the Stalin era. Women have beneffited from the general improvement. But their role and status have fallen short of the Soviet ideals of 1917. Women work but have not reached the top levels of Soviet society and instead of disappearing, the family is officially considered the basic social cell of society. Communal facilities have not released women from domestic chores and the weight of the "dual burden" of home and job is openly recognized as a major barrier to equality by the Soviet press.

Women are half the Soviet labor force. They are found on all levels of the economy, in all types of jobs from manual labor to exacting scientific work. The high number of Soviet women professionals is particu-

---

[6] St. George appears to believe that the intention of the law was a humane one — to allow women who would never marry to at least have a child. He ignores the halving or the allowances in 1947. He does mention, however, that the bonus given to unmarried women depended on the sex of the child — 100 rubles for a girl and 150 for a boy! (1973:66–70). See also Y. Mirenonko (1966).

larly striking. Women are 72 percent of the doctors, 35.4 percent of the lawyers, 47 percent of the judges and associate judges, 90 percent of the dentists, *feldshers* (medics), and nurses, 58 percent of the agricultural specialists with advanced degrees, and 76 percent of the accountants, statisticians, and planners; 38 percent of all scientists are women (half the chemists and four-fifths of the biologists) and a third of the engineers. Of associate and full professors, 20 percent are women. Women have become architects, geologists, and economists. Women pilots are not unusual and there has been a woman astronaut. Women are half the certified specialists and 38 percent of the technicians. Their percentage of the skilled labor force is high compared with other parts of the world; 37 percent of machine-building and metal workers, for example, are women. On construction sites, women can be seen in all types of jobs, from plasterers and painters to laborers (Brown 1968:25–40; *Zhensh-china i deti V SSSR* 1970; DeWitt 1961:490–500; Dodge 1966: Chapter 11; Mickiewicz 1971:59–62).

Set against the almost universal female illiteracy of Tsarist days, this is a stupendous achievement. But these impressive figures are somewhat misleading. The position of a Soviet doctor cannot be compared to an American one. Medicine is notoriously ill-paid, possibly BECAUSE it has become a woman's field. Within the medical profession, men head the hospitals and departments; they are the surgeons, the highest paid specialty, and women are the general practitioners, midwives, nurses, and ward attendants (Dodge 1966 128; Mandel 1971:286–310; Lennon 1971:47–58). Law is not a particularly lucrative profession either and within it the "advocats" (the best paid specialty) are usually men. Women judges and associate judges (the official figures lump the two together) are concentrated in the lower courts.

Women engineers, scientists, and mathematicians have indeed invalidated an old stereotype, that women cannot think logically or handle abstract concepts, but engineers and scientists do not give orders. They work on assignments given by executives and these are usually men. Moreover, official statistics do not reveal the type of work women engineers and scientists actually do, or who does the routine work and who gets the more interesting assignments. A breakdown of engineering, by specialties, reveals that far more women are engaged in food production and consumer goods engineering than in geological or construction engineering (DeWitt 1961:348). (The latter two require frequent relocation, often to severe climates. Whether women themselves avoid these specialties or whether they are discriminated against is thus difficult to ascertain). Recent observers report quotas against women in heavy industry and aviation caused by the fact that women leave earlier or transfer to less difficult jobs (*Soviet Studies* 1966:65).

Within the research hierarchy, only 2 percent of the Full Members of the prestigious Soviet Academy of Science are women and only 2.5 percent of the Corresponding Members. No woman has ever been President, Vice-President, Chief Scientific Secretary, or member of the Presidium of the Soviet Academy of Science (Dodge 1966). The paucity of women at the top reflects the educational handicaps under which Soviet women labored until the thirties.

But the large number of women doctors, engineers, and scientists also reflects the impetus to woman's careers given by the labor shortage of the first five-year plan and of World War II. In the fifties, war veterans and experienced skilled workers received preference in university admissions, thereby resulting in an anti-female bias (DeWitt 1961:348, 421). Men are admitted to medical school on the basis of lower scores. Women now comprise only 25 percent of students at the higher schools of industry, construction, transportation, and communication, and only 27 percent at the higher schools of agriculture (Lennon 1971). Again, it cannot be ascertained whether women themselves are opting out of these fields or whether there is discrimination. But it is clear that within the professions, definite women's fields and women's specialties are emerging: medicine, teaching, and social-cultural work.

In Soviet society, power, money and prestige go to top executives in factories and collective farms. Women are extremely rare in positions of authority where they have to give orders to men. In factories, women are 6 percent of the directors, 16 percent of the chief engineers, and 12 percent of the department heads. Recent visitors report that factory welcoming committees, composed of junior executive types, are almost uniformly male. Women executives are most prominent in routine jobs; they do not set policy. Secondary level positions such as bookkeepers, "rate-setters," and technicians are predominantly female. The number of women collective farm chairmen has remained constant since the thirties, even though the percentage of women farmers has risen because of the war. Lennon argues that differential training is increasing and that many qualified women end up in dull tedious jobs. Jancar (1972:4–9) claims that increasing discrimination is forcing women to moderate their ambitions in both education and employment.

On the top levels of government, until Khrushchev appointed Ekaterina Furtseva as Minister of Culture, no woman sat on the Presidium of Ministers (Cabinet) of the Soviet Union. Furtseva was on the Politburo of the Party only four years. Though women are approximately a third of the members of the Supreme Soviet and the Council of Nationalities, according to Jancar the high degree of turnover indicates tokenism. Women are 45 percent of local soviets, which do most of the work. All these bodies, however, either rubber-stamp or implement decisions already made at the top levels of the Communist party.

A steady effort has been made to attract women to the Party. But although women now comprise 21 percent of Party members, few have reached the top levels. At the 1966 Party Congress, women were 23.3 percent of the delegates, but only 2.5 percent of the women (5 members) had voting rights in the Central Committee, the most important body. Only two women have ever been on the Party Politburo, Orgburo, or Secretariat; most have gone only so far as the Auditing or Control Commissions. Taking the top committees of the Party together, women are only 4 percent of the members. In 1971, half of the full Central Committee members and three of the seven women candidate members were new; of the others, only Furtseva and Lykova go back to the Stalin era. Yagda Nasriddinova (who is also Chairman of the Republic of Uzbekistan) and N.V. Popova were elected in 1956, Kolchina in 1961, the rest in 1966. Of the three women on the Presidium of the Supreme Soviet, none is a member of the Central Committee of the Party. In the entire history of the Party as a ruling entity, only 84 women have risen high enough to fill any of the approximately 4,600 possible positions in leading organs and most of these were first-generation Bolsheviks (Jancar 1972:11–12, 29–38).

Not only are the top levels of Soviet society less accessible to women than to men, but women are overly represented at the lowest levels of the Soviet economic spectrum. Though women constitute half the labor force, their total wages are only one quarter of all wages earned (*Narodnoe khoziastvo SSSR* 1969:654; St. George 1973: 114). Well over half of Soviet women earn less than the average Soviet wage of 103 rubles/ month. Furthermore, many women are paid at piece rates; their wages often fall below the official Soviet minimum wage of 60 rubles/month (Dodge 1966:180–181; Lennon 1971:54; *Zhenshchina i deti* 1970: 72–73, 102, and *passim*).

For much of the Soviet period, women did the hard physical labor. Increasingly, however, routine, but not physically-arduous jobs, are specifically perceived as "woman's work." Most of the workers in the low-paying textile industry are women: 98 percent of the sewing machine operators. Women are employed in the food trades, as streetcar conductors, subway and bus drivers, postal workers, oilers and sweepers in factories, elevator operators, waitresses, secretaries, and routine clerical

workers. But street cleaners, snow shovelers, road and railroad maintenance crews are still almost exclusively female. Done by hand, these are
arduous jobs.

Though many women are skilled laborers — 17 percent of milling
machine operators, 11 percent of electricians, 10 percent of automatic
machine-tool adjusters, 15 percent of metalworkers — these figures are
a decline from their World War II high and within the general job categories women hold the lesser jobs. Of the metalworkers, 73 percent of the
women in that category were actually drillers and simple machine operators
(DeWitt 1961:159; Jancar 1972:7).

In the countryside, 83 percent of women are classified as unskilled
laborers as compared with 66 percent of the men. Women are the seasonal farm hands and tend the cows and chickens. Except for a brief spurt
during the war, the number of women tractor drivers is the same as in
1937 (Lennon 1971:51–58). The norm is that "men administer and women do the work." These are Khrushchev's words and he urged that
women be trained and promoted. Men have let tractors stand idle rather
than train women to use them. In 1969 a decree ordered that agricultural
machinery be modified for easier use by women. But the belief that women
cannot learn to use machinery and that mental work is too hard for
women, but physical work is not, lingers on.

Articles in the Soviet press recognize women's unequal achievement and
openly discuss means to remedy the situation. One article, "Irina's Career" by (Dr. I. M. Pavlova: *Literaturnaia Gazeta* 39, September 22,
1971), asked, "Why do so few women enter the door marked 'Upstairs'?"
Male prejudice — in particular, the reluctance to take orders from
women — was given as one reason. But the author also pointed out that
women themselves consistently choose the easier jobs and generally
evidence little desire to advance. In one factory, for example, only
19 percent of students in evening courses considered prerequisites for
advancement were women. Pavlova argues that conflicting pressure of
home and job force women to opt for positions in the middle of the job
hierarchy. Women's "second shift" at home is both tiring and time-
consuming.

Despite constant exhortations from the press, men do not help at
home. Apartments are small and facilities are poor. Even now, 25 percent of city dwellers share kitchen and bath; fifteen years ago, the figure
was 70 percent. As late as 1961, 61 percent of urban families had no running water and only 2.2 percent had hot water. Appliances are still
rare. In 1970, in the highly industrialized Moscow-Penza-Leningrad

triangle, only 38 percent of apartments had refrigerators and these were small. Poor storage facilities necessitate frequent shopping. Only 13 percent of apartments had washing machines — the wash is done in the bathtub. Cooking is on a one-burner primus stove. Many women rise early in order to prepare dinner before going to work. They shop on the way home. The distribution system is inefficient; several lines are required to make one purchase. Lines are long and shortages are common. Each category of purchase (i.e. milk, meat) requires a different line. Shopping is thus tiring and nerve-wracking (Jacoby 1972; Geiger 1968:297; Dodge 1966:97; Mandel 1971:309).

A recent study done in Tula revealed that women get one hour less sleep each night and have far less leisure time than men. Women spend evenings and weekends on household chores while men are free. An article in *Komsomolskaya Pravda* (May 27, 1966:2) was entitled, "We ask our men" (to help in the kitchen.) Zoya Yankova also found that women spend more time on household chores than they did forty years ago because men have abdicated (*Nedelia* 18, April 24–30, 1970: 20). Both occupational choice and the ability to advance within the occupation are thus limited. The six-hour day is one of the reasons women opt for teaching and medicine, despite the comparatively low pay. Women teachers often choose not to become principals because the additional compensation does not make up for the extra time the higher position requires. Women do produce less and managers consider them poor "ruble-risks" for training and promotion. Norton Dodge considers discrimination against women economically justifiable (1966:97). Women's lower productivity is also discussed in Brown (1968:50–56). A self-perpetuating cycle is thus created. In research, for example, on all levels, women publish less. Though women are 27 percent of the Ph.D. Candidates, only one of seven actually finishes her degree. There is a time limit and women do not get extensions for pregnancy. Women have been nominated to high party posts and declined because they cannot spare the time. Neither can they do the unpaid volunteer work expected of Party officials.

Easing the housework aspect of the "double burden" is comparatively simple; it is a matter of money — more consumer goods, more appliances, more efficient distribution systems, better housing, and the like. The problem of motherhood is far more difficult and will become even more acute in the future as the next generation of grandmothers is also working. Since the sixties, child-care facilities have been expanding rapidly but are still in short supply. In Moscow, the most heavily supplied with child-care centers, only 50 percent of children under seven are accomodated and there is a long waiting list. In the entire Soviet Union, 10 percent of children under three are in crèches and 20 percent of children between the ages of three and seven (1970 figures). Schools with extended hours are also increasing. But all these facilities are closed for the summer and only children above the age of seven are eligible for camp. The quality, moreover, often leaves much to be desired (Madison 1972: 833–834).

Motherhood is still woman's role. It is she who takes time off from work when the children are sick and it is she who consults with the teacher when problems arise in school. The most popular Soviet child care manual mentions the father's role almost as an afterthought (Bronfenbrenner 1970:76; see also N. Baranskaia 1969, translated into English by St. George 1973:233–256).

In European Russia the one-child family is the norm. Salaries are low and the woman's salary is needed. Moreover, three room apartments are considered too small for more than one child. The European population is not reproducing itself; concern with the "demographic crisis" is a common theme in the Soviet press. Abortion was legalized in 1955; since then the regime has stressed inducements for childbirth. Women now get 56 days of paid maternity leave both before and after childbirth; their job is held open for one year and they do not lose seniority or pension rights. But most women return to work immediately after their paid leave expires because they need the money. Caring for more than one child is just too difficult. Access to contraception is still a problem; *coitus interruptis* is the most common form of birth control with frequent abortion as a back-up measure.

Since the sixties,[7] suggestions made in the Soviet press to raise the birthrate have included paying the mother (not the father) to stay home until the child is three, shorter hours for women workers with a proportionate decrease in pay, and increased family allowances to cover the actual cost of child rearing. But these concessions would place women at a competitive disadvantage in their careers, possibly freezing them out of top positions.

"What kind of work should women do?" is another frequent topic of the Soviet press. A consensus, though by no means unanimous, that women should not do heavy physical labor, seems to be emerging. One

---

[7]   In the late fifties and early sixties there was talk of placing all children in huge children's cities immediately after birth to free the woman and to develop a true communist consciousness. But the scheme provoked such an outcry that Khrushchev personally disavowed it. A. L. Weeks summarizes the Strumilin proposal to place all children in boarding schools in "The boarding school," survey 5–6 (July, 1965, 83–94).

author spoke of a "special equality of socialist humanism," another called for a return to chivalry and insisted that women must cease being treated like beasts of burden. Attention to training women, he pointed out, has been relaxed. Women have been passed over for promotion. (*Pravda* August 24, 1965:1, July 11, 1966:3; see also Brown 1968: 21–22; St. George 1973: 106–108).

The 1969 Labor Code includes many protective provisions (though Lennon argues that they are not enforced) and excludes women from hot, heavy, or hazardous work such as mining, tunnel-building, steel-making, and chemical plant operations. These are highly paid occupations. Women are barred from night work, and pregnant women from overtime and out-of-town assignments. These carry bonuses and are sought after by men.

A recent survey in Kostroma indicated that many men would prefer to have their wives stay home (*Literaturnaya gazeta* 39, September 22 1971). Women themselves, however, consistantly choose working over having another child. A higher standard of living, and the bargaining power within the household of an independent income prevails over the supposed joys of motherhood. For professional women, job satisfaction is another reason to opt for work (St. George 1973: Chapter 6).

The official *Principles of marriage and the family* considers the family the "basic social cell" (*Izvestia* 28, September 1968, an English summary can be found in *Current digest of the Soviet press* 1968: 27). Family stability is considered necessary for social stability and psychic health. Equality within the marriage and sharing of household chores is now the stated ideal. But the three-generation household is still common; grandma's help is still needed. According to Vera Dunham (1970) responsibility for a happy marriage is said to be the woman's; she is expected to be the strong one (cf. Brown 1968:98–104, 125–129, 130–136).

Since the divorce law was liberalized in 1968 divorce has been rising rapidly. In Moscow, two out of three marriages now end in divorce. Most divorces are initiated by women; alcoholism is the most common ground.

Sexual mores are quite conservative and the double standard survives. A study of Leningrad men indicated a surprising number who hoped to marry a virgin. Conventional images of "femininity" and "masculinity" have returned. Soviet girls still wish to marry and they pursue the "good catch" (Brown 1968: 57–59). The press urges women to look pretty, to dress well, to fix their hair. "Female beauty is no bourgeois prejudice" one article in *Literaturnaya Gazeta* said. Beauty parlors are proliferating and the consumption of cosmetics has doubled in the past ten years. All these are government enterprises.

While there is resentment of the "double burden" carried by women, there is no real woman's movement in the Soviet Union today; there is only reformism. The absence of civil liberties is not the only reason. Soviet women are exhausted; both sexes have experienced fifty years of upheaval, suffering, and sacrifice. Both yearn for "the good life," for "normalcy." Already, wives of executives and high officials do not work and 10 percent of Soviet women are classified as housewives. If economic conditions improve to the point where one salary is sufficient to support a family, an idle wife may well become a status symbol.

CONCLUSION

Soviet women exemplify the transference of a traditional role to a new situation. Despite surface changes, the inner core — sacrifice — is the same. Russian women have always worked hard. Never were they on a pedestal; women of all classes placed their own needs last; husband and then children came first (the nobility did not raise their own children). Under the soviets women continued to sacrifice; it was merely the object and purpose of sacrifice that changed. Women were "liberated" to release their labor power for social production. Perceived as a means to revolutionize society, their own needs were forgotten.

In the twenties, women were urged to place society's needs above personal needs, to value work more than family. But even Kollontai considered motherhood a social duty. In the thirties, women became workers, but their lives became harder. Full equality was deferred to the elusive communist future. Even their right to abortion was denied. When budgets were tight, it was woman's needs that were cut first. Economic priorities were political choices, conscious decisions. A more balanced and humane scheme of industrialization, which included consumer goods and communal facilities, was also possible.

The areas where woman's advance was most conspicuous — medicine, science, engineering — were areas of critical social need and the advance was greatest during periods of labor shortage, the early thirties, World War II, and after. At such times, antifemale prejudice was a luxury the Soviet Union could not afford. Much of the current Soviet effort to ease the weight of the "dual burden" may well be due to the dearth of men in the leadership age 35–59 and to the "demographic crisis."

Recognizing the hardships experienced by Soviet women, current writers are beginning to erect a new feminine image, a secular version of the Virgin Mary, whose moral superiority consists of the fact that she demands nothing for herself. Solzhenitsyn lauds Matriona, a woman "so comical, so foolish that she worked for others with no rewards. This woman, who had buried six children, had stored up no earthly goods.... was that one righteous person, without whom, as the saying goes, 'no city can stand,'" (Matriona's House" 1972: 41–42). A young poet, Nicholas Starshinov, considers his poem to his mother his best. He speaks of her as a saint and extols her selfless sacrifice (Brown 1968: 66). A revulsion from the Stalin era has made materialism and "careerism" unfashionable; some writers laud women because they did not "sell their souls" for money. But this literary trend does not necessarily bide well for women. It can be but a small step from recognizing sacrifice, to expecting, and then demanding it.

Soviet women today are demanding their share of "earthly goods"; they are insisting on an easier life and on real equality as distinct from tokenism. But the ability of the state to act independent of popular demands makes predicting their future hazardous. The low birthrate is the greatest reason for uncertainty; it is difficult to predict what the state will do. But in Poland and other Eastern bloc nations, women are being paid to stay home and raise the children. Another enigmatic factor is the effect of the end of the male deficit on women's career opportunities. When the sex ratio evens up, as it already has for the under thirty-five age group, when women's labor is no longer crucial to economic development, the pressures now tending to push women back to more traditional roles may well become stronger.

If present trends continue, most women will probably continue to work, but in occupations which enable them to combine work and personal life most easily. In other words, few will aim for the top. Employers and educational officials, however, judge by averages; those few women will be under great pressure to justify themselves, to prove their seriousness and dedication. They will have to be better in order to be equal. And the cost, in personal terms, of such pressure, may well dissuade capable women from exercising the equality promised by the Constitution.

The high divorce rate, however, may pose a countertrend. Finding happiness in personal life elusive, women may follow Kollontai's advice and seek fulfillment in careers; thus they may become more ambitious than they have been in the past. Only time will tell.

REFERENCES

AMFITREATOV, V. A.
  1897   *Zhenskoe nestroenie.* Petersburg.

BARANSKAYA, N.
  1969   Nedel' kak nedel'ia. *Novyi mir* (December): 23–55.

BENET, SHULA, *editor*
  1970   *The village of Viriatino: an ethnographic study of a Russian village from before the revolution to the present.* New York.

BRONFENBRENNER, URIE
  1970   *Two worlds of childhood: US and USSR.* New York.

BROWN, DONALD, *editor*
  1968   *Women in the Soviet Union.* New York.

CONQUEST, ROBERT
  1966   *The great terror.* New York.

CURRENT DIGEST OF THE SOVIET PRESS
  1968   Volume twenty. And other volumes from 1965 to the present.

DE WITT, NICHOLAS
  1961   *Educational and professional employment in the USSR.* Washington, D.C.

DODGE, NORTON
  1966   *Women in the Soviet economy.* Baltimore.

DUNHAM, VERA
  1970   "The strong woman motif in Russian fiction," in *The transformation of Russian society.* Edited by C. E. Black. Cambridge.

ENGELS, FRIEDRICH
  1972   *Origin of the family, private property, and the state.* New York.

FRANKLIN, BRUCE
  1972   *The essential Stalin.* New York.

GASIOROWSKA, XENIA
  1968   *Women in Soviet fiction: 1917–1964.* Madison.

GEIGER, KENT
  1968   *The family in the Soviet Union.* Cambridge.

HALLE, FANINA
  1933   *Women in Soviet Russia.* London.

Izvestia
  1968   September 28.

JACOBY, SUSAN
  1972   *Moscow conversations.* New York.

JANCAR, BARBARA
  1972   "Women and Soviet politics." Unpublished paper written for workshop "Politics and Social Change in the USSR" at the American Political Science Association meeting, Washington D.C.

KHARCHEV, A.
  1964   *Brak i semia v SSSR.* Moscow.

KOLLONTAI, ALEXANDRA
  1971   *Autobiography of a sexually emancipated communist woman.* New York.

Komsomolskaya Pravda
1966   May 27. And other issues.
LENIN, V. I.
1972   *On the emancipation of women.* Moscow.
LENNON, LOTTA
1971   "Women in the USSR." *Problems of Communism* (July-August):
47–58. Washington D.C.
Literaturnaia Gazeta
1971   Number 39. September 22. And other issues.
LUKE, LOUISE
1953   "Marxian woman: Soviet variants," in *Through the looking glass of Soviet literature.* Edited by E. Simmons, 27–109. New York.
MADISON, BERNICE
1968   *Social welfare in the Soviet Union.* Stanford.
1972   Social services for families and children in the Soviet Union since 1967. *Slavic Review* (December): 831–852.
MAKARENKO
1937   *A book for parents.*
MANDEL, WILLIAM
1971   Soviet women and their self-image. *Science and Society* 35:286–310.
MANDELSTAM, NADEZHDA
1970   *Hope against hope.* New York: Atheneum.
MASSELL, GREGORY, J.
1968   Law as an instrument of social change in a traditional milieu: the case of Soviet Central Asia. *Law and Society Review* 2 (February): 179–228.
i.p.   *The surrogate proletariat: Moslem women and revolutionary strategies in Soviet Central Asia 1919–1929.* Princeton: Princeton University Press.
MC NEAL, ROBERT
1972a Women in the Russian revolutionary movement. *Journal of Social History* 143–163.
1972b *Krupskaya: bride of revolution.* Ann Arbor.
MICKIEWICZ, ELLEN
1971   The status of Soviet women. *Problems of Communism,* (September-October): 59–62.
MIRONENKO, Y.
1966   The evolution of Soviet family law. *Bulletin: Institute for Study of the USSR* 13(5): 33–41.
Narodnoe khoziastvo SSR
1969   Moscow.
Nedelia
1970   Number 18. April 24–30.
PAVLOVA, IRINA
1971   Irina's Career. *Literaturnaya Gazeta* 39 (September 22).
Pervyi Zhenskii Kalendar
1901   Number 3.
Pravda
1965   August 24.

1966   July 11. And other issues.

ROWBOTHAM, SHEILA
1972   *Women, resistance and revolution.* New York.

SCHLESINGER, RUDOLF
1949   *The family in the USSR: documents and readings.* London.

SEREBRENNIKOV
1937   *The position of women in the USSR.* London.

SOLZHENITSYN, ALEXANDER
1972   "Matriona's house," in *Stories and prose poems.* New York.

ST. GEORGE, GEORGE
1973   *Our Soviet sister.* Washington, D.C.

STRASSER, NADJA
1915   Die russische Frau in der Revolution. *Suddeutsches Monatsheft 12,* 615–752.

SUSNOVSKI, LEV
1926   *Bol'nye voprosy.* Leningrad.

Soviet Studies
1966   Education and social mobility in the USSR. Soviet Studies 18: 57–65. Oxford.

VENTURI, FRANCO
1966   *Road to revolution.* New York.

WEEKS, A. L.
1965   The boarding school. *Survey* 5–6, 83–94.

WINTER, ELLA
1933   *Red virtue.* New York.

YANKOVA, ZOYA
1972   *Nedelia* 18 (April 24–39):20. (An English summary can be found in the *New York Times,* January 18, 1971.)

ZETKIN, CLARA
1933   *Lenin on the woman question.* New York.

Zhenshchina i deti V SSSR
1970   Moscow.

The Women's Movement in the People's Republic of China: A Survey

DELIA DAVIN

The patriarchal family system of traditional China restricted and oppressed women of all classes. Nor were women its only victims. Power was conferred not only by sex but also by age, and the family power structure subjected young men as well to the decisions of their seniors until a comparatively late age. Confucian family ideology was at its strongest among the elite who had the wealth, time, and education to practice it, and it was in this class that the dependence of young people in general and women in particular was greatest.

The first women's movements in China, strongly influenced by foreign thought, drew their support mostly from women of the elite classes who claimed the rights of education and free-choice marriage that they heard were enjoyed by women in other countries. They were able to draw on considerable male support, at least in the earlier stages of their personal struggles, because their brothers and sweethearts could see in the struggle for women's emancipation an idealistic justification for their own rejection of arranged marriages and their demands to be allowed romantic matches. In time the struggle was perceived as a political one, and in rather mechanistic emulation of the West, suffragists stormed the almost powerless parliament at Nanking in 1912.

As men took part in the women's struggle, so too did women take part in general political struggles. Women were active in the early nationalist and republican movements, and women's armies fought in the 1911 revolution. In 1924–1925, during the Nationalists' northern expedition against the reactionary northern warlords, a fusion of women's military, revolutionary, and feminist work among ordinary people took place for the first time. Women soldiers marched in the expedition and women propagandists from the political department of the army set up women's leagues among peasant women to fight for women's rights in each community through which they passed. These, like the peasant leagues set up at the same time, were later crushed in the reaction of 1927–1928. However, these inland southern areas were soon to be the scene of the Chinese Soviet areas and of the short-lived Central Soviet Republic (1931–1934), so that some of the former members of these women's leagues must later have become members of the Communist women's movement.

In the following description of the Communist women's movement, I shall telescope the Soviet, anti-Japanese war, and Civil War periods. But it must be remembered that the Communists were administrating quite large areas even in the late 1920's; that they set up the Chinese Soviet Republic in 1931; and that after the collapse of this stronghold and their long trek north, they built up new power bases during the anti-Japanese war. They controlled a territory with a population of nearly twenty million by 1945 before they swept on to control the whole Chinese mainland by 1949. Thus they had, even before the establishment of the People's Republic, a very long period in which to develop and try out social policies, among them policies to alter the position of women.

Women played an important part in the revolution and in the revolutionary base areas. At times they fought on the front lines as regulars or irregulars. Far more often they played vital roles in their own villages because the majority retained their family responsibilities, which made them less mobile than men. But in guerrilla warfare there is no true front line and no true rear. Combatants and noncombatants are complementary, and the former are aware of their absolute dependence on the latter. Both therefore, have status, and the division between them is less sharp than is sometimes imagined. Women laid mines, dug tunnels and organized tunnel warfare, and acted as stretcher-bearers, nurses, scouts, messengers, and food collectors. Food collecting was no mere routine job; the problem presented by the sudden arrival of a hundred hungry men in a village that practiced subsistence agriculture would have been considerable. It could only have been solved by local people of tact who would know who might have the surplus food required and how they could be persuaded to part with it. Later, during the Civil War (1946–1949), many men left the base areas as the Communist armies swept their way southward, and women tended to take a greater part than before in the political and administrative work of the villages.

Land reform was carried out in 1946 in the old Communist base areas and by 1952 was complete over most of the country. Land reform regulations stated specifically that women should receive their share of land and that either their names should be included as co-owners on family title deeds or title deeds should be issued to them as individuals. Women were not slow to realize the implications of this, and indeed their reactions show an interestingly clear perception of the relation between their oppression and their economic dependence. For example, William Hinton (1967:397) recounts that women in Yellow Hill village, Hopei Province, when they heard that they were to receive land, said, "After we get our share we will be masters of our own fate." There is evidence that women sometimes used the threat of withdrawing themselves with their shares of land from their husbands' families to force a capitulation, or at least a compromise, when they felt themselves to be oppressed.

Women were urged everywhere to work outside the house as a means to achieve liberation, but land reform gave them more stake in doing so. At the same time it was a big political campaign in which they were expected to take part. For many it was the first occasion on which they appeared in public and spoke out in front of men. Often it was difficult for them to find the courage to do so. The Women's Federation, a mass organization for women, led by the Communist party, provided a closed forum for women, with meetings attended only by women, which was recognized as a necessary preliminary to speaking at mixed meetings. Often in the land reform team that came to each village to guide the course of land reform, there was a woman cadre who showed the peasant women that a woman could be an active and independent person, demanding and getting respect from her male colleagues as a true equal.

Local village activists were also of great importance in championing women's causes. Given an official capacity as the women's representative or as an officeholder in the Women's Federation, they had a power base from which to protect women's interests and launch attacks on those who mistreated women. In the early years we find accounts of such women organizing struggle meetings against men whose wives complained of being beaten, and reports of these women even beating up brutal husbands (Belden 1949:297). Such incidents did not receive Party support—contradictions in the ranks of the people were supposed to be solved by reason and persuasion rather than by violence — but they were probably rather effective where they occurred. Chinese women had always used their menfolk's fear of loss of face as a weapon; in the new society they were able to do so to great effect.[1]

However, village women were not a united force in their struggle to change

[1] For a very interesting description of the manipulative power developed by women, see Wolf (1972:40).

their place in society. One of the tragedies of the old family system was that it set woman against woman and made one woman the means of another's suffering. A bride entered her husband's home as a lonely figure, friendless and without allies in her new household. She took on the toughest domestic work, endured the resentment of her new family if the bride-price had been high, and became a convenient scapegoat when one was needed. She would normally have no affectionate ties with her husband at the start, and many factors militated against their development, at least in the early years. The couple saw little of each other, did not speak together in public, and in quarrels between bride and mother-in-law, the husband was as likely to intervene for his mother as for his wife.

Only by giving birth to children, preferably a son who would stay in the family, could a young woman ease her position and in time build up a circle of allies and thus a power base.[2] When her son was approaching adulthood, a new young woman was introduced into the household as his wife. The mother's jealousy and concern that the newcomer should not disrupt her relationship with her son is understandable only when viewed against the investment she had made in her son and her dependence on him. Hence the notorious tension of the relationship between mother-in-law and daughter-in-law in China.

The marriage law of the People's Republic of China promulgated in 1950 (like the marriage laws of the liberated areas and the Soviet Republic before it) laid down a system of monogamous marriage, with free choice of marriage partners, the right of widows to remarry, the prohibition of bride-price and child-betrothal, and the right to divorce by consent. The law was presented as being fundamental to the liberation of women, and the local branches of the Women's Federation were relied on heavily for its implementation. Yet there is much evidence that older women were among its most active opponents.

Older women "rationalized" their opposition to the new law by saying that it was immoral for young unmarried men and women of different families to meet and become friendly, a necessary precondition to a system of free-love marriage; that young people "were not good at" choosing their partners; and that it was not fair that the younger generation should have life so much easier. However, clearly a strong factor in their opposition to the new law was the fear that the security they had gained over many years, by raising sons whose primary loyalty was to their mothers, might be shattered if love marriages took place.

[2]   Wolf has observed and described with great insight (1972:32–41) the particularly important, but neglected, family grouping whose focus is "mother" as the "uterine family."

Because this division could sometimes split women's organizations down the middle, the issue had to be handled very carefully. Much of the advice on marital problems given in newspapers and in women's magazines is on how to get along with the mother-in-law rather than her son. Furthermore, in spite of the great marriage law enforcement campaigns of 1950, 1951, and 1953, occasional reports in the press show that old customs die hard, that marriages are still sometimes arranged in the old manner, and (more rarely) that bride-prices are sometimes paid. In the countryside today, a compromise form of marriage is probably the most common. By the time of the ceremony, the young couple and their families all know each other. The young couple may indeed have been "introduced" at the initiative of their parents or some other outsider, but they have had few chances to meet and make up their minds about each other. Certainly many books about marriage, from the late 1950's onward, advise young people to consult their parents about marriage, without, of course obeying them blindly.

These "semifree marriages," as the Chinese term them, are probably realistic institutional adjustments in cases where good relations between the mother-in-law and daughter-in-law are very important to both. For as much as the face of peasant agriculture has changed, mother-in-law and daughter-in-law are still often workmates and, in those areas where work is still strongly sex-typed, are likely to see more of each other than of their menfolk. Where work is less segregated between the sexes, it is likely to be the younger woman who joins the man in heavy outdoor work, and if she has children, she may at times entrust them to her mother-in-law, which necessitates a reasonably amicable relationship. Where relations are not good, this arrangement could also raise the mother-in-law's ire. When the young women formed a textile cooperative in Chehu village, Hopei Province, and their mothers-in-law not only lost their assistance in the kitchen but even had to prepare their meals, the older women complained, "Everything's turned upside-down since the Communist party came. Mothers-in-law have become daughters-in-law" (Liu 1949: 17). But this problem was usually solved as the mother-in-law realized the material benefit to the whole family when the daughter-in-law took part in productive labor.

Other difficulties arose when women began to work in the fields. They lacked the necessary skills in all but their traditional tasks, which, in fact, varied enormously from one region to another and, if they included farm work at all, tended to be the least skilled jobs. They almost never included such prestige-bearing tasks as plowing. Indeed, judging from reports of the fierce opposition to plowing by women and the space that the press devoted to stories showing that they could do so successfully, I am inclined to believe that there may have been a superstitious taboo against it. The Women's Federation overcame these problems by holding classes to teach agricultural skills and by organizing women's pilot plots on which bumper crops were grown.

Collectivization of agriculture, which took place in stages in China in the 1950's, gradually shifted the basis for income division from the ownership of land to the amount of labor contributed. Land was henceforth owned and earned collectively and jobs were valued in the form of work-points. When the crops were brought in, they were divided according to the number of work-points earned during the year. Furthermore, because the work points, theoretically at least, were recorded in the names of individuals, the system increased general awareness of each individual's contribution to household income.

If women were to take full advantage of this, they had to solve various problems. The first, of course, was the demand on their time and energy made by housework, meal preparation, and child care, all of which tend to be particularly laborious in a backward rural economy. The canteens, nurseries, and sewing stations set up on a large scale under the communes have been much discussed in the West, the grain-husking and flour-milling centers less so, perhaps because, to those of us who are not accustomed to undertake these tasks for ourselves, they seem less of a new departure. Economically, however, they all represent the same process: the transfer of work from the household sector, where it is unmeasured and unpaid, to the public sector, where it is recorded and given an economic value. Once it has entered the market, it also begins to confer a social prestige on the person who does it, which it did not do as household work. This work can also be performed by fewer people if it is efficiently organized and done on a large scale, thus freeing women to do other types of work.

Of course, all this presupposes that worthwhile alternative occupations exist in the economy. This has been the second great difficulty hampering women who wished to enter the labor force. China in the 1950's was still a very poor country, desperately short of capital and with an unfavorable ratio of people to land. Job opportunities in the towns increased very slowly, and there was a danger that if the labor force increased too fast, rapidly decreasing returns to labor would result. In concrete terms, in collective agriculture this would mean that the number of work-points earned would increase more rapidly than the amount of grain produced, and that the remuneration of each work point in grain would fall. Such a fall obviously would be unpopular, and if it were associated with the entry of women into the work force, it would hardly bring them enhanced status.

Health has been another constraining factor on the contributions of Chinese women to the work force. The countryside had almost no modern health facilities in 1949, and Chinese traditional medicine, useful though some of its practices have proved to be, was certainly not adequate to maintain all women in good health. The high value attached to big families meant frequent childbearing. Low nutritional levels, poor living conditions, and complete ignorance of the nature of infections (traditional midwives did not sterilize their instruments) meant high infant and maternal mortality rates and many chronic postnatal complications. Poor menstrual hygiene and ignorance caused vaginal infections. The large number of articles in the women's press that deal with menstrual pain and the many articles on agricultural management that advise cadres to give women workers two or three free days during their periods suggest that this is also quite a problem for Chinese women. During the 1950's and 1960's, the Chinese did achieve a huge expansion of their health service. This, however, was largely urban-oriented until the Cultural Revolution. In the countryside maternal and infant mortality were greatly reduced long before this by a huge program of midwife training, but minor gynecologic ailments seem to have remained rife.

Until very recently, Chinese women continued to bear many children and thus spent a large proportion of their lives pregnant or nursing. The birth control campaign has been pressed with a proper degree of seriousness only in recent years (in fact, the health and freedom of the mother are presented as the prime rationale for family planning), and at the same time public attitudes are becoming more receptive. People accustomed to a high infant mortality rate have many children to ensure the survival of two or three, and even when infant mortality has fallen, there is a credibility lag before the old practice is perceived as unnecessary. Yet a reduction in the birthrate, as it is presented in China, is certainly a prerequisite if women are ever to achieve equality with men in the economy and society.

Common regulations decreed that men and women should receive equal pay for equal work. When men and women do the same type of work at piecework rates, this is simple to apply. In other cases, where the value of an hour of picking cotton has to be calculated against the value of an hour of carting fertilizer, for example, it becomes complicated. Work evaluation, always a problem of collective agriculture, can be used to conceal pay discrimination against women, and women have waged many struggles against this practice.

In rural China most able-bodied women work in the fields and in handicraft or minor manufacturing enterprises, at least at busy times of the year.

Women's contribution to the work performed outside the house certainly comprises less than one-half—it probably equals about one-third. Nor do women always in fact receive equal pay for equal work. Furthermore, crèches (which may be either permanent or temporary, and open only for peak work periods), though sometimes partly subsidized, are not free, and people in China, as elsewhere, tend to discount the cost of child care against women's earnings when evaluating their contribution to the household. Nevertheless, as participants in the work force, women have at least the potential for the independence necessary to gain any degree of self-determination and authority within the home. Their work also gives them a place and a voice in commune and village affairs, where before they were largely confined to the women's community. And because women now have a productive economic value, the birth of a girl need not be the crushing economic blow that it once was to a poor family. Furthermore, the campaign to encourage later marriage, which is partly to give girls more chance to train and develop independence before marriage, has been given a far greater chance of success by the fact that young unmarried women are no longer a burden but are an asset to their families.

The women's movement is much further advanced toward its goals in the towns than in the countryside in China. Problems are fewer and more easily overcome. The problem of disbelief in women's capabilities has been largely overcome by the use of shock teams. The first women pilots were trained in 1950; a few years later the first all-woman train crew began to run one of the Peking-Tientsin expresses, and women engineers and steelworkers were employed at the great Anshan metalworks. In 1970 an all-woman oil-drilling team started work on the famous Taching oil field, and the first March 8th bridge-building team came into being. Perhaps all this smacks of tokenism, but it has a truly great psychological impact. Such women are given tremendous publicity in all the media, and no girl growing up in China today can believe herself disqualified by sex alone from scientific or technical jobs. Even the incredulity of men has been shaken.

Work opportunities in the towns, like the towns themselves, have expanded enormously. In fact, urban expansion has been so rapid as to cause difficulties. Many towns have a severe housing shortage, and facilities such as schools and hospitals are also under strain. The expense of such facilities, as well as that of roads, shops, and food supplies (social overhead costs, to use the economist's jargon) can be held down by large-scale introduction of women into the work force. By lowering the ratio of dependents to total population, this makes it possible to expand the labor force without a proportionate increase in the town's population.

This should provide a long-run economic incentive to the state to get women into urban employment.

Because work is by nature more permanent in the towns than in the countryside, canteens, crèches, and other collective facilities are more economical to develop there. Enterprises are still sometimes accused of discrimination in their employment policies, and they clearly have some incentive to practice it, because if they employ women they have to bear at least part of the cost of child-care facilities and all of the cost of maternity leave. The impact of such dis-incentives to nondiscrimination is presumably declining with the birthrate in urban areas, where young couples, under heavy political pressure reinforced by the housing shortage and other practical factors, increasingly limit the number of children to two or three.

Women in 1949 had a far lower literacy rate than men. Though the problem has been tackled by literacy classes, often run by the Women's Federation, and though primary school in the cities is universal for the younger generation, older women are certainly educationally disadvantaged. Many women, then, are unable to take factory jobs, for which there is great competition, and men remain in the majority among factory workers, who are themselves an elite minority among city dwellers.

Women are certainly more strongly represented in health and education, and probably also in service and distribution trades. Women are clearly a majority in the neighborhood factories. These usually begin as ad hoc groups of housewives making clothes or simple items for daily use, though the most successful now produce components for China's electronics industry. Like small workshops in Japan and Hong Kong that produce components for large enterprises, they give China's industry a valuable flexibility. Their equipment is simple and versatile, and because they depend on housewives' labor, they can increase or decrease production and employment without too much social disturbance. They usually work on a largely self-financing, cooperative basis and do not offer medical insurance. They therefore involve no financial risk to the state and have low overheads and therefore low unit costs.

The implications of such enterprises for women are mixed. Their workers earn less and enjoy fewer welfare benefits than true industrial workers. On the other hand, neighborhood factories demand low levels of skill and literacy, offer work close to the home, often with flexible hours, and expand the demand for labor. Thus, housewives who would otherwise be unemployed gain employment and with it an individuality independent of family identification, an independent source of money, and a new self-respect. Psychological factors are probably especially important in neighborhood factories, because the ventures are small and tend to be run by the most enterprising of their workers. They can therefore provide a feeling of real participation in management more easily than can big factories.

Street committees, which are in effect basic-level organs of government, and welfare agencies have also given women a real vehicle for achievement. At street level they depend on volunteers, and these are most often housewives. The day-to-day tasks of such women include mediation in family disputes; hygiene inspections to check that privies are covered, courtyards swept, and breeding grounds for flies eliminated; distribution of ration tickets to the unemployed; registering new arrivals in the area; and reading newspapers to the illiterate. Street committees also have close contacts with neighborhood factories and often run nurseries for women who travel to work but prefer to leave their children near home. Obviously these women have power — petty power perhaps, but power as it impinges on the lives of ordinary people. And, importantly, at least in the early years, this was a power that women could exert directly over men if, for example, they violated the hygiene rules.

The Marxist proposition that women's liberation can come only through their participation in socially productive labor has always formed the theoretical basis of the Chinese Communist party's policy on women, but the effort expended on this goal and the comparative emphasis on it and on other strategies for women's liberation have in fact varied considerably over the years.

In 1942, in Yenan, the revolutionary capital, during the rectification movement certain women intellectuals were attacked for "narrow, divisive feminism" which attempted to solve women's problems by attacking their family situations without reference to economic factors. A Central Committee resolution claimed that "we have not given enough attention to economic work among women" and presented productive work for women almost as a panacea (Chinese Communist Party 1942). The greatest effort was at first devoted to getting women to work in textile handicraft production; later, coinciding with the departure of many men in the army, came the campaign to get women to work in the fields. At this time, however, a Central Committee resolution admitted that productive labor was not in fact the only and ultimate solution to the woman problem, that remnants of feudal ideas about women would remain for some time, and that a prolonged period of education would be necessary to overcome them.

The campaign to get women to take part in productive work gathered momentum and was applied on a national basis in the 1950's, but it suffered a strange lull in 1954 and again in 1957. It revived briefly in 1955–1956 with the cooperative movement and again in 1958 during the Great Leap Forward, only to suffer another, though apparently slighter, eclipse in the early 1960's. During the Cultural Revolution, involvement in productive work was again presented as the major goal for women and this line has been maintained since then. In 1973 the *People's Daily* editorial for Women's Day, entitled "Working women, a great revolutionary force," quotes Lenin (1938:26–27) on the importance of getting women to "take part in socially productive labour, to liberate them from 'domestic slavery,' to free them from their stupefying and humiliating subjugation to the eternal drudgery of the kitchen and the nursery."

Lenin's words contrast strangely with the mood of 1955, when, under the slogans "Housework is glorious too" and "Let's be pretty," a positive cult of the housewife was fostered, women were urged to seek fulfillment through raising a socialist family, and the pages of women's magazines were filled with recipes and dress patterns (*Chinese Woman*, all issues 1955). The reaction of the 1960's, perhaps to avoid arousing the indignation of women cadres again, was less overtly against career women but still laid great stress on the joys of marriage and motherhood.

The Chinese explanation of fluctuations of policy toward women is that they reflect the struggle between the two lines. During the Cultural Revolution, the editor of *Chinese Woman*, the organ of the Women's Federation, was attacked for having followed the Liu Shao-ch'i line, and the Women's Federation itself was dissolved, though it seems that it will now be reorganized on a new basis. The cynical economist would fit policy fluctuations to changing economic policies and conditions and would relate the volume of encouragement for women to work at a given time to the current demand for labor. These explanations are not, of course, incompatible because the Chinese define the lulls in the recruitment of women as a period when the Liuist line controlled the economy and prevented more radical expansionist policies.

Whether we accept either or both of these explanations, the Chinese experience raises some problems of international relevance for women. What is the relation between women's participation in the work force and the status of women? Clearly it is not a simple one, for we know of many societies where women slave and are despised. The existence of the work ethic is crucial, but where work is considered a mug's game, hard workers are mugs. What other factors count?

How can we make cross-cultural judgments about the aims and achievements of women's movements? If the family reforms advocated by the Chinese women's movement seem limited and its sexual morality repressive to women in Western movements, do we conclude that they have been duped or that such differences are a natural and desirable consequence of culture and history?

Women revolutionaries during the Chinese revolution, like other women in history, were confronted with the contradictions that arose between the interests of women and the interests of the revolution, both nationalist and socialist. Marriage reforms, for example, though proclaimed by law in the liberated areas, were certainly not pressed with great energy, for social disruption was too dangerous in a war situation. Women, though feminists, as revolutionaries had to make a united front with forces that represented male chauvinism in the interests of another cause which, by implication at least, took priority. As Marxists, these women were able to do so because they regarded the victory of the revolution as a prerequisite to the liberation of women. To them the contradiction was a temporary and nonantagonistic one, which in the long term must disappear.

But in the socialist construction, the problem of priorities arose again. It is difficult to liberate women in a poor country; difficult to supply the necessary welfare, education, employment, and health facilites when the overwhelming problem is to feed the people; difficult to allocate scarce resources to social reform in a developing country where economic growth is so vitally needed. Yet too passive an acceptance of other economic priorities may also be an error, may lead to an underachievement of potential. Some women party leaders repressed feminist impulses and accepted the sacrifices of the years of stagnation or retreat, when women's traditional roles were glorified, because they believed that these sacrifices furthered the interests of the revolution as a whole. Since the Cultural Revolution, this line has been condemned as a Liu Shao-ch'i policy contrary to the true interests of women. All this raises the problem of how to judge the real interests of the revolution and those of women, and how to reconcile them with each other. If temporary contradictions arise, priorities must be chosen, but by what criteria are they to be selected?

Women in other countries face a problem of evaluation when they examine the Chinese women's movement. Should its achievements be praised or its compromises and shortcomings criticized? Dispassionate study seems impossible, but cross-cultural criticism is dangerous. Surely the context is vital here. Chinese women fought an oppression blacker and more absolute than that faced by women of the West. The official institutions of traditional China were male dominated to a degree unsurpassed in the world. Chinese women once dealt with this situation with a combination of passivity and covert sabotage. In a few decades they changed their strategy to one of open struggle, and, in alliance with the forces of national and socialist revolution, they have demolished much of the social framework of their oppression.

These developments have taken place under a state that officially guarantees full sexual equality but still lacks the resources to provide all the necessary material conditions for it. Nor is the idea of the equality of men and women entirely accepted by the people. Old ideas die hard. Such limitations are inevitable. Mao Tse-tung himself has acknowledged that women's liberation is not yet complete (Malraux 1970:463–465), and as long as the Chinese women's movement itself does not accept the status quo as satisfying its ultimate aspirations, we can surely salute its achievements without ignoring its problems.

REFERENCES

BELDEN, JACK
1949   *China shakes the world.* New York: Harper Brothers.
CHINESE COMMUNIST PARTY
1942   "Resolutions of the Central Committee of the Chinese Communist Party on the present direction of work amongst women in the anti-Japanese base areas," in *Documents of the women's movement of the liberated areas* (in Chinese). Edited by the Women's Federation of China. New China Publishing House.
HINTON, WILLIAM
1966   *Fanshen.* New York: Monthly Review Press.
LENIN, V. I.
1938   "International Women's Day," in *Women and society.* By V. I. Lenin. New York: International Publishers. (Reprinted from *Pravda*, March, 1920.)
LIU, HENG
1949   "Chehu, the village where cloth is produced in every home," in *The production campaign of village women in the liberated areas of China.* New China Publishing House.
MALRAUX, ANDRÉ
1970   *Anti-memoirs*, English edition. New York: Bantam Books.
PEOPLE'S DAILY
1973   "Working women, a great revolutionary force" (in Chinese). March 8.
WOLF, MARGERY
1972   *Women and the family in rural Taiwan.* Stanford: Stanford University Press.
WOMEN'S FEDERATION OF CHINA, *editor*
1955   *Chinese women* (Chinese-language monthly). Peking.

The Mobilization of Women: Three Societies

ELSA M. CHANEY

Today mankind — and here the first syllable of the word is deliberately emphasized, MANkind — is attempting to control and direct, and in some cases merely to understand and survive, change so rapid and profound that the process defies any experience the human species ever before has undergone. Some doubt whether the human person's fragile psychological equipment and weak physical frame can endure. Others see the technological revolution as the only hope to feed, shelter, educate, and employ the millions who now inhabit the earth and the millions more who will swell the world's population by the turn of the century. They say we simply must endure the upheavals which technological progress brings because there is no other way for the human race to survive.

But why emphasize MANkind in speaking of change? Because of one particular feature of this world in flux that is beginning to be noted: the absence of women's contribution. Of course, this is not a literal absence: women have always performed essential tasks even when society (and scholars) did not recognize them as such. Certainly, they have always borne the children. As gatherers they supplied the staple foods and later invented plant cultivation, a primary factor in the emergence of civilization. They were the "hands" in the first phases of the industrial revolution; later in manufacturing, and especially in service occupations. Erik Erikson (1964:44) rightly deplores academic minds that "blithely go on writing whole world histories [whole anthropological accounts] without a trace of women...." and James Lockhart (1968:150) remarks on the tradition among Latin American historians to ignore women, commenting that the practice makes it very difficult to know anything exact about them.

Yet at the leadership level, few women have ever collaborated in policy-making. Whether we look to the councils of statesmen and planners who strive to induce and direct change, or to the world of academics, philosophers, and theologians who attempt to understand and interpret the meaning of change, or to the professionals and technicians most closely linked to the technology of change, we see the woman only here and there, an isolated and often token presence. Whether the enterprise is called "development," "liberation from dependency," or "class struggle" makes no difference. Women play an insignificant role in any government, party, movement, or private agency working for structural change or reform.

Writing of Asia and Africa (his remarks apply equally to Latin America), sociologist Chester L. Hunt (1959:20) notes that in most areas of the world the process of development is viewed as a male project in which women are given only token participation. "Development represents an effort to bring the male part of the world into the twentieth century," he writes, "leaving most of the women in the restricted culture of a previous era."

In some places, it is true, increasing numbers of women are taking advantage of new educational and professional opportunities, particularly in "feminine" fields. Yet this does not appear to give them access to leadership. Recently the United Nations Commission on the Status of Women (1970:3-4) asked government and private organizations for their views on the role women might play in social and economic development. Replies from seventy-seven countries and thirty-six nongovernmental agencies showed that even where women are active professionally, their level of responsibility is low except in certain sectors of the social field traditionally considered suitable for women. Their participation in higher planning bodies related to innovation and social change is "practically nonexistent." According to the survey, there is growing awareness all over the world that women's role is changing and should change, yet "only a few countries have come fully to grips with the problem or are ready to embark upon new avenues."

Summing up the findings of another detailed assessment of women's participation in political life around the world, Mrs. Lakshmi Menon (1968:39), who herself served as Indian Secretary of External Affairs, points out that "a prime minister here or a judge there or a few ambassadors in relatively minor stations" do not indicate that women have been successful in politics. Even in socialist countries where special efforts have been made to involve women, she says, "the results, strangely enough, have been identical."

The status of women is raising many questions today in almost every country of the world. Studies on women's professional and economic activities, and their participation in political and social life, particularly their changing role in the family, give increasing evidence that the evolution of social structures is closely linked to the evolution of women's role in society.

Until now, emphasis has been focused in both analysis and action upon the dependent, secondary status of women in most societies — and upon the necessity and justice of securing wider options for women in education, work, and professions, as well as in politics and government. If we define emancipation to mean equal access for women — in law and in fact — to responsible roles in political, economic, and social life, then it is obvious that women are not emancipated even in developed societies, whatever the type of regime or the nature of its guiding ideology.

We need to continue such investigations where the position of woman is the dependent variable — that is, where the historical and contemporary structures of society are examined in order to explain how and why the male continues to play the instrumental role in most institutions, mediating the relationship of women to the society and the polity. In Third World countries, in particular, we know only the gross trends of male/female participation, but very little about the exact characteristics of women's involvement in work, professions, and politics.

The questions I am exploring, however, approach the status of woman from another direction, closely related to the central problem engaging researchers, analysts, and policy makers all over the world: social and economic change. How will women's increased involvement in work, education, and politics affect society's structures? (This does not mean that we lose sight of the fact that the influence runs in both directions, and that the structures continue to affect women's outlook and behavior.)

In most countries today, women are beginning to participate, if not at the command echelons, then at least at the lower levels of economic and political life. Yet scholars and policy makers alike have been slow to question the implications of women's increased involvement, or to ask whether women's behavior and attitudes might be crucial variables in accelerating, delaying, or modifying change. The image of woman and her style of participation might turn out to be important factors in the complex value/attitude/behavior patterns related to the modernization process. Yet many modernization studies ignore sex as a possible independent or explanatory variable in accounting for the persistence of traditional values and attitudes (for example, those of Lerner [1958], Kahl [1966], Inkeles [1969], and Whyte [1965]). Do we not need at least to ASK to what degree the sex status "female" influences women's economic, social, and political behavior? Sex might be more strongly associated with behavior than class, ethnic origins, urban or rural residence, age, education, religion, and the like. To mix a metaphor, Pandora is out of her box, and her behavior and attitudes are bound to have profound consequences for society. Once women begin to close the gap in the electorate, educational institutions, and professions and become available for social and political mobilization, they cannot continue to be ignored.

The price of NOT facing these questions may be that most women, as Hunt suggests, will remain locked in cultural attitudes and conservative behavior appropriate to another era; will continue to define their professional options in terms of the traditional "womanly" professions; will pull, as voting behavior studies amply document, electorates towards the right even when there is a choice of candidates advocating ordered change; will play a large role in socializing the next generation in conservative values.

Moreover, if women are not involved, the development process will continue to be deprived of those important, often intangible values, attitudes, and qualities centering around what might be called the "feminine pole" of existence in modern societies — the concern for persons and for human happiness and fulfillment; the life of culture and the life of the spirit — all those things we lately have come to call "quality of life" and that we try to measure as "social indicators." Without entering into the intriguing question of whether or not woman has a special nature (and whether it is biology or culture which exerts the strongest influence in shaping human beings) the FACT is that women do stand for some important values often denigrated in the achievement-oriented, competitive, masculine quest for mastery over the environment, the economy, and the polity. In our concern for technical progress, for higher rates of growth, for political domination, the qualities associated with the feminine mode of existence (there is no suggestion here that some men do not also possess what have come to be identified as "feminine" values and no assertion that ALL women do so!) are needed to temper the harshness of the modernization process, and they will be needed even more in the post-industrial world.

What do we know, so far, about how women's outlook, attitudes and activities might affect political and social institutions? We may be able to learn most about how women's participation affects modernization by looking, however briefly, at three societies which have made some progress in the integration of women in public roles. These three societies have not been entirely successful, yet on many indices of participation — higher education, professions, work force, political activity — the women would register high in relation to the women of other cultures: Cuba, Chile, and North Vietnam.

From my own work — and drawing upon the few systematic studies we have of women in the Third World — it appears that three problems must be solved before women can be incorporated, at responsible levels, into public tasks and make positive contributions to structural change and reform. All these problems are related; they are separated here only for purposes of analysis. The first problem is the TENTATIVENESS of women's own commitment to public affairs. The second is the tendency of women (and their societies) to define their public role narrowly in terms of their TRADITIONAL TASKS of nurture and mothering. The third is the evident fact — whether in a socialist or capitalist economy — that women's incorporation into the workforce, so far mainly in low level, unchallenging tasks, neither liberates them nor paves the way for creative, innovative contributions to their societies. This latter problem is one of degree: in the Soviet Union, for example, women's professional options are rather broad. Yet not even there do women have equal access to the decision-making hierarchies — economic, professional, or political.

What do I mean by women's tentativeness of commitment to public tasks outside the home? Women's public intervention in any numbers always has occurred at the crisis points of history. Women tend to become active only in times of extreme challenge, then sink or are pushed into apathy when the emergency is over. The typical pattern of feminine involvement is one of entry followed by retirement. In a crisis, behavior outruns belief; when the crisis is over, the image of woman's proper role has not changed sufficiently to allow them to remain active at a responsible level.

Elizabeth Mann Borgese (1963:65–66) contends that the emergence of a more participant type of woman may be associated with a shift from a transitional growth to an incipient decline society, and points to three periods in history when it appears that women not only were numerically superior, but gained a certain measure of power and influence "in the wake of expansion and urbanization at the time of the crusades; in the wake of the intellectual conquest and commercial expansion of the Renaissance; and, obviously, in our own day...." She cautions that population statistics are scarce and thus the contention would be hard to prove or disprove. She also cautions against regarding these as periods of more than potential power shifts; in the Middle Ages, she says, a small number of chatelaines were affected, but not the common woman. The difficulty is that after these extraordinary times, there has been no possibility for women to organize and consolidate their gains. Ludovici (1965:128) makes the same comment about women of the Renaissance.

The Conquest and Independence movements in Latin America, the winning of the West and the abolition movement in the United States, the two World Wars, and the peace movements in 1918 and in the 1960's were some of the events which called forth women to share the risks and tasks of society side by side with men. But in each case, women's participation was provisional and tentative, often indirect and anonymous, and almost always justified in terms of the feminine image, i.e. women were called to activity because the very life of the nation was threatened or the institution of the family was endangered. Society calls for women's help in an emergency, but has not yet legitimated or institutionalized her permanent collaboration on an equalitarian basis.

Thus, the self-sufficient pioneer woman of the North American West was succeeded (in image, at least) not by the woman entrepreneur, senator, or professional, as might have been expected, but by the fainting sheltered Victorian lady. In Brazil, as Freyre (1963: 74) records, the capable and energetic "early plantation or ranch mistress" on the colonial frontier became in the succeeding patriarchal period an artificial, morbid being, [a] sickly person deformed by her role of servant to her men and doll of flesh and blood to her husband."

More recently, we have seen women in Latin America take to the streets when they perceived "the life of the nation in danger" as the women of Poder Femenino, a rightist alliance of women in Chile put it: in Brazil in 1964 and in Chile in December 1971, when thousands of women marched to be beat of their empty *cacerolas* or cooking pots. Morris J. Blachman (1973), who is completing an extensive investigation of women's organizations in Brazil, thinks that women see their role in Brazilian politics in much the same way that the Brazilian military view theirs: as a kind of guardianship of the nation's basic institutions. Neither group may legitimately take a public role when the nation is doing well; if they step in at a time of crisis their intervention is accepted and even lauded.

The intervention of women in the life of the nation in North Vietnam and in Cuba may fit this crisis pattern: the crucial question is whether the current involvement of women can be successfully institutionalized. In pre-revolutionary Cuba, only 9.8 percent of the labor force was female; by 1968, the number had increased to 23 percent. At the same time, women in the university population increased to about 40 percent, and many were enrolled in scientific and technical disciplines; women formed one-half of all science students in 1970 and one-half of medical students. In the same year, some 600,000 Cuban women were in the workforce (Ramos 1972:6). Cuba has made an impressive commitment to daycare centers and to other material incentives to make it easier for women to work (for example, because of the long lines at grocery stores induced by scarcities, women who work are permitted to go to the head of the line or to shop at *bodegas* installed in their workplaces).

The fact that the political elite has been committed to equality for women has meant that the gains women have made in Cuba have been impressive. Yet, as Susan Kaufman Purcell (1973:259), has pointed out, as this is a modernization of women imposed from above, in the face of serious resistance on the part of the Cuban male, there are several serious drawbacks. For one thing, the revolution has not been able to solve the problem of what Fidel Castro has called the "double burden" of the working woman who faces all her housework when she returns from the factory or workplace; the male permits his wife to work outside the home in order not to appear anti-revolutionary, but his *machismo* does not allow him, in turn, to share the housework.

More serious, in Purcell's view, is the fact that because the initiative for and control of the modernization of sex roles is in the hands of the male political elite, unless such modernization has the highest priority goal, "it will be sacrificed when it competes with higher priority goals for limited political and economic resources" (Purcell 1973:259). In the early years of the revolution, when emphasis was on an expanded and more productive labor force, traditional attitudes which stressed that woman's place was in the home were dysfunctional to the revolutionary goals, and women had to be mobilized and re-socialized into attitudes compatible to their becoming productive members of the labor force (1973:262). The regime's effort met with resistance, but as both equalitarian goals for women and developmental goals could be attained through the commitment of the same resources, the commitment to the modernization of the Cuban woman was made. If women no longer are needed for production — for example, if industry becomes more capital-intensive and competes for scarce resources — she predicts the resources then will go to the higher priority, production. When this occurs, the stage will be set for women's withdrawal or dismissal from the labor force.

North Vietnam's women have made some formidable advances since 1954 when there were only 500 women in the workforce (Bunch-Weeks 1970:6). Today women form about half of the labor force, and they took a very active part in the war effort. Women of the North can be members of the militia, and under certain conditions of emergency they fought, even though they were not allowed to go to the front. In South Vietnam, women of the National Liberation Front engaged in front-line fighting, and a woman is deputy commander-in-chief of the armed forces (Chaney 1973a:24). A much larger group of women serves in high government positions than in Cuba or Chile. There are 125 women deputies (of a 420-member assembly) in North Vietnam, and women hold the vice-ministries of labor, light industry, and commerce (Chaney 1973a:24). Women also hold the important portfolios of Minister of Defense and of Foreign Affairs in the Provisional Revolutionary Government (PRG) of the South (the so-called Vietcong); Madame Nguyen Thi Binh, who holds the latter portfolio, also was the PRG representative to the Paris Peace Talks. Women constitute from 40 to 50 percent of the leadership at the provincial and district levels in the liberated zones of the South (Teitelbaum 1973:38).

Here again, however, it is difficult to separate out what part of women's participation is war-induced and what part will remain as "the men come back." If the 125 women elected to the North Vietnamese National Assembly in April 1971 are seriously committed to remaining in political office, then a formidable barrier will have been overcome. In analagous situations, this has not occurred. After World War II, for example, Europeans entered upon a period of ferment and idealistic fervor as they rebuilt their nations. There were 40 women in the assembly that drafted the 1946 constitution in France, and 23 in the senate. By 1970, the numbers had dwindled to 8 and 5. Italy today has only 5 women senators and 25 deputies (of houses with 249 and 596 members respectively), but immediately after the war there were 43 Italian women in parliament. Nowhere is the trend more striking than in Japan, where 39 women were elected to the first postwar diet (of 410 positions); by 1970 their number had declined to 8 of 467 (figures from Gruberg 1968: 76–77; United Nations, Secretary General 1970:10, 1971:21).

Even in the Soviet Union, a recent study of all the top Soviet decision-making bodies since 1917 reveals an extremely high rate of turnover of female officials — and their scarcity. The study shows that of 4,600 top positions available since the revolution in the Soviet political hierarchy, women have filled only 84 (Jancar 1972:37). Moreover, few of the SAME women remain from one party congress to the next; only five women who presently are in the top hierarchy go back before 1961. "Those women who have held really important party positions have been truly exceptional," the author concludes (Jancar 1972:33). (Jancar excludes purely ceremonial bodies such as the Council of the Union and the Council of Nationalities in her calculations.) The two facts probably are related: in general, women either are not willing to serve (or are prevented by responsibilities to household and children from serving) the long apprenticeship in party and government that appointment to high office requires. The Soviet State has not, as Rosenthal points out in her article in this volume, made nearly so large a commitment to daycare as we sometimes imagine, and Soviet women undertake careers in politics and professions at great personal sacrifice.

My own research (Chaney 1971) showed a similar disinclination of women to continue in office. Of the 167 women interviewees in elective or administrative posts in Peru and Chile in 1967, 104 disclaimed any interest in continuing beyond their current term or appointment. Fully 67 percent of these — or 41 percent of the entire sample — were in their first position; these figures show the high number of women disillusioned after only one experience in political office.

Let us now move to the second question posed at the beginning of this analysis: the style of women's participation as a factor affecting the social and political institutions where the woman has begun to appear in the lower echelons.

Several studies, my own among them and also that of Armand and Michèlè Mattelart (1968), have shown that the traditional images of women's proper activity still are so strong in Latin America that when women do enter professions or government, they (and the men) almost invariably define their intervention as an extension of their family role to the arena of public affairs. I think it is fair to say that enough studies now have been done to indicate that this may be a worldwide phenomenon. Jancar also finds in her recent study of women in the Soviet Union (1972:1) that official sanction has supported the survival of the traditional concept of the feminine role, as well as traditional male attitudes to women's tasks in the home and at work. Most women who study — and this also is a worldwide trend, not confined to Third World countries — prepare for professions in fields of traditional feminine concern: education, health, welfare of women and children. (For an interesting discussion of this trend in the United States, see Gross 1968.) And many women envision women's political offices (to use descriptions originated by Talcott Parsons [1956:47] to characterize current female/male role images) in terms of the nurturant and affectional tasks society assigns to women, rather than in terms of the instrumental male role which is more aggressive, active, and achievement-oriented. The mass media reflect and reenforce these images in a circular manner very difficult to break.

My own study showed that a woman official in Latin America often sees herself as a kind of *supermadre* [supermother] tending the needs of her big family in the larger *casa* of the municipality or even the nation. In the survey I did of Peruvian and Chilean women *politicas*, this approach to public tasks was associated with a conservative outlook and an ambivalent attitude towards change. Women in my survey often were preoccupied with what Chileans call *mejoras* — little improvements to relieve the most pressing problems of food, clothing, and shelter — and with little understanding of the the economic and social structures which cause such conditions. (For a more detailed discussion, see Chaney 1973b.) Women in the survey revealed a lack of ability to conceptualize on a macro-social level and a fear of radical economic and social change because they also fear the disruptions to home and family which such change sometimes brings.

But even where women are in the vanguard of movements advocating sweeping change, the feminine stereotype prevents their access to policy-making areas outside the traditional feminine fields. In Chile, the regime of Salvador Allende moved very slowly to mobilize women or to involve them in the mainstream of the Unidad Popular program. Nowhere else in the world have events conspired to make women's political participation so vital an issue as in Chile. Because women's votes are tallied and reported separately from men's votes there, no government can have any illusions as to where it stands with either sex. On many occasions, Allende reminded the men of Popular Unity, the governing coalition, of "All the elections we lose because of the women's vote." He always told the men that it is "our fault because we haven't found out how to reach the consciousness and the heart of the woman" (1972a:178). There is "still prejudice among the men of Unidad Popular," he said, "a Political *machismo* which denies to women the equal rights she has" (1972a:105).

During his first years in office, Allende frequently asserted that his revolution would not succeed unless it incorporated women at all levels of responsibility. His statements showed that he was quite aware of Chilean women's well-documented conservative tendencies within EACH social class (although such tendencies were less marked by the March 1973 congressional elections). He often tried to quiet the fears of women by asserting that his revolution would be "creative and not identified with violence"; that it signified "moral achievement, generosity, a spirit of sacrifice and dedication to achieve a new life for all Chileans within the framework of the nation's free institutions" (1972b:196–197).

In spite of many allusions to women's importance, Allende moved slowly to increase their role in his government. Only after two years in office did he appoint a woman to a cabinet-level position. Mireya Baltra, a Communist and official of the Centro Unico de Trabajadores, Chile's largest trade union organization, assumed the post of minister of labor and social welfare, but she lasted only a few months. From the pool of outstanding Communist and Socialist women militants in Chile, only one other high appointive post went to a woman. Carmen Gloria Aguayo, a member of the Movimiento de Acción Popular (MAPU), headed Desarollo Social, [Social Development], the agency which links together the neighborhood councils and mother's centers; created in the previous administration, the Popular Unity government attempted to make them more dynamic and less paternalistic organizations (Bussi de Allende 1972:3).

The President rightly complained that men did not properly esteem the talents and capabilities of women, yet he often revealed his own narrow vision of what women could contribute, always articulated in terms of their role as mothers or potential mothers. He was fond of using an image which he said came from his own experience as a medical doctor: "*el binomio madre-nino*," literally "the mother-child in one being." Often he returned to this theme:

When I say "woman", I always think of the woman-mother.... When I talk of the woman, I refer to her in her function in the nuclear family... the child is the prolongation of the woman who in essence is born to be a mother (1972a:204).

Projects to mobilize women invariably were cast in a "feminine" mold, and none had materialized after three years of Allende's administration. A ministry of the family was the scheme Allende most often talked about in his speeches to women. In mid-1973 the bill for its creation still languished in a parliamentary committee with no political pressure applied to bring it to a vote after two years. Even if the new ministry had been inaugurated, however, the plan appeared to be an attempt to create a number of "appropriate" but marginal posts for women so that important ministerial slots would not be wasted on them.

Another of Allende's favorite ideas — to recruit women between the ages of sixteen and twenty-one for three months' obligatory "*Servicio Femenino*" — would not have assigned them to projects according to their talents and training, but would have used them in hospitals, social welfare centers, and as the 120,000 auxiliaries needed to set up day nurseries and kindergartens. These tasks were to have been distributed on a strict feminine-masculine basis; the single young woman would learn fundamental things for her own future, the President said, and she would be "linked to babies and children... learn to prepare bottles, change diapers, warm the food.... How fine it would be if these girls could help the children get off and on the buses, WHILE A TRAINED MAN DRIVES THE BUS" (1972a:204; emphasis added).

Allende's speeches were full of projects to include housewives in social security provisions, to allow women to retire at an earlier age "because of the biological inequality between the man and the woman" (1972a:180), to distribute more free schoolbooks, to equalize family allowances among workers, white-collar employees, and government functionaries. Yet he rarely talked about more equal professional opportunities for women or more collaboration in leadership responsibilities.

How did the women accept these programs? They were enthusiastic. Many were projects women of the Left had worked for energetically in the past. Hortensia Bussi de Allende (1972:7–8), Chile's first lady, outlined the major programs on which women should concentrate in the revolutionary process as: care for the aged, recreational areas and playgrounds for children, youth centers, vacation programs for working-class families, rent control, and legislation concerned with family planning and the status of the illegitimate child. Certainly all were worthy projects — but it is difficult to see why they should have been singled out as the special concerns of women.

It is important to note, as many observers have done, that women in Chile have made some remarkable advances. Under Allende, they formed nearly one-half the university population and 22 percent of the workforce, high proportions for Latin America. Yet when they become professionals Chilean women, too, tend to cluster in the less-prestigious, low-level feminine fields. My own study (Chaney 1971: 180–81) shows that 80 percent of the women university graduates in Chile over the past ten years have prepared for a traditional feminine profession (teaching, social work, paramedical fields); 11 percent studied for traditional "masculine" professions (law, medicine, and journalism); and only 9 percent went into fielps which touch more directly upon development (scientific professions, economics, social sciences, engineering, and the like).

Luis Hernandez Parker, one of Chile's leading political writers, has described the political style of Chile's women politicians, whether of the right or the left:

...the woman constitutes a "political world" apart from the male.... When the woman speaks in the *poblaciones* [marginal areas around the cities] or in the countryside, she does so in the language of the heart. In Parliament — and with the sole exception of Maria de la Cruz and Carmen Lazo, who are as spectacular and combative as the men — they fulfill their role in another style... they are the untiring ants, valiant and tender. The men will be preoccupied with problems as abstract as constitutional reforms. The women are fighting for kindergartens, for drinking water in the *poblaciones*, for daycare centers (1969:11).

In Cuba, too, there are indications that even though many women have been incorporated into the revolution, the division between men's and women's tasks persists, not only at the workforce level, but in the leadership. Most Cuban teachers still are female, and the teacher-training program of the Federación de Mujeres Cubanas has not been duplicated by a parallel program to train male teachers. Only women are considered as appropriate to staff the Circulos Infantiles [daycare centers] (Bergman 1970:13; Purcell 1973:268). Purcell notes that no attempt has been made to encourage more men to become workers in traditionally female industries, such as food processing, tobacco, and textiles; conversely, "only in those traditionally male occupations where sufficient male labor is unavailable has the regime made a special effort to recruit female workers." Statistics on women in industry bear this out. Only 20 percent of the industrial labor force is female (most women work in the service sector), while the textile industry is 77 percent female; *artesanía*, 90 percent; and education and culture, 68 percent. Purcell (1973:268–269) reports that almost all the highly-placed women in the Castro regime supervise other women. Vilma Espin, the highest-ranked political leader, heads the Women's Federation; Nina Fromenta, Minister of Light Industry, has under her jurisdiction the highly-feminized textile and plastics industries. Raquel Pérez is in change of social welfare, and Clementina Serra is National Director of the child care centers.

Even under the emergency conditions of life in North Vietnam there appears to be a strong tendency to define the female role in traditional terms. Madame Bui Thi Câm, member of the National Assembly in the North and a lawyer, told me in an interview (Chaney 1973a:22) that the women in her country had become active "in defence of their homes and families." In a moving address at a recent ecumenical meeting in Quebec, she stressed the suffering which the war and the American bombs had brought upon women and children, reporting on the number of schools, nurseries, kindergartens, and churches destroyed. I mention this not to play down the seriousness of what American bombs did to the civilian population, but to show the striking similarity in the range of concerns of this North Vietnamese congresswoman to the motherhood themes stressed by women officials in other countries. At no time did Madame Câm mention, for example, the damage bombs had done to factories, transportation, communications — leaving these facts to the males in her delegation.

There is evidence all over the world that whatever the nature of the regime, when the women begin to move out to the larger society, the boundaries and style of their participation are profoundly influenced by their classic role as mothers and preservers of the race. The ideal, in a world without prejudices, would certainly be that men and women would fill posts in government and elsewhere for which their talents and training prepared them, without any special note being taken of their sex. Men and women would dedicate themselves to primary and secondary institutions — would perform instrumental or affective tasks — as their own particular capacities and bents dictated. The ideal justly asks: Why should not both men and women, according to their own desires, concern themselves with improving the lot of the woman, the child, the old, the sick, the juvenile delinquent — and with planning industrialization, balance of payments, inflation, monetary reform, agricultural development, and outer space?

But the ideal world is not yet, and traditions have designated certain areas of life and concern as "feminine." So far, only a few women have shown any inclination to venture very far beyond these boundaries, either in their professional or political life. In my own view, it is the enduring image of the supermother which may best account for women's style of participation, not only in the three countries mentioned, but in many other cultures as well. We badly need to explore the consequences of such a definition of women's role, particularly its implications for the mobilization of women for social and political change. For one thing, women do not improve their inferior position very much by turning professional or taking on a government career. Feminine fields are neither prestigious nor powerful because they are associated with the hidden, unspectacular tasks of birth and nurture, tasks which males in patriarchal societies do not deem of prime importance.

Finally, let us look briefly at women's participation in the workforce, always regarded as a kind of index to measure women's emancipation. The crucial question is whether the liberation of women for meaningful and creative involvement in professions and public life necessarily follows from their incorporation into the workforce. If so, then perhaps we need not make any special effort on woman's behalf: women will be freed for leadership in social and political life when they can be drawn into productive work.

Evidence that women's liberation follows economic development and their incorporation into the workforce would seem to be almost universally negative. For one thing, we know that many women work in discontinuous fashion and from economic necessity, a motivation that has little to do with realizing individual potential or contributing at a responsible level to national development. Leaving the home MAY indeed be a first step for a woman toward widening her horizons and securing some economic independence, but there is no guarantee that paid employment will lead to emancipation, or automatically free her to enter a career on an equalitarian basis with men or to participate in the decisions affecting the economy and the polity.

Indeed, in certain industries numbers of women appear to decrease as industrialization advances and manufacturing becomes more capital intensive. There are fewer women today employed in industrial manufacturing in Peru and Chile, for example, than in the 1950's when these countries were at the height of their import-substitution manufacturing efforts. The decrease of women in industry in Latin America also is due to "premature" social legislation: it is more costly and bothersome to hire women who will have to be given three months' maternity leave with pay and for whom a full-time social worker at the factory must be provided. David Chaplin (1967), in a study of the Peruvian textile industry, found factories where no woman had been hired since the social legislation had gone into force. Thus there is evidence that women's relative position may WORSEN rather than improve as modernization proceeds; many of their productive tasks are removed from the household by industry, and at the same time, the centralized, bureaucratic state diminishes their part in the education, socialization, health care, and recreation of their families.

It is interesting to note that several prominent Marxist women theorists in Chile and elsewhere have begun to join their bourgeois sisters in pointing out that expanded opportunities in the labor force do not bring about an automatic expansion of women's liberty, even in socialist countries. Bambirra (1971), Benston (1969), and Mitchell (1966 and 1973) are three Marxist women analysts who no longer accept the thesis that drawing women into the battle of production will improve women's inferior position. They all agree that doing productive work outside the home is the precondition for changing women's status, but they insist that obstacles in the sociocultural superstructure must be DIRECTLY attacked if women are to be available for full political and intellectual participation in the revolution of their societies.

Paradoxically, however, women's lack of opportunity in industry and margination to feminine "service" fields has certain positive aspects. The division of labor into masculine and feminine spheres, accentuated as it is in some countries, gives some women an advantage North American women have largely lost: the opportunity to rise to the top in certain professions. In North America since World War II, men have moved into primary and secondary schoolteaching, social work, paramedical fields and library services; they also have moved quickly upward to take over the administration of these fields (cf. Wilensky 1968 for an interesting discussion of these trends). But the work of society designated as feminine in some countries is not unimportant, even if males do not value it. In another study (Chaney 1971; Chapter 10), the author has suggested that women in Latin America, more in control of certain fields than their North American sisters, might work to transform them, using them as a base towards acquiring more influence in social and political life. Because of the *macho* tradition, there may be less risk that Latin American men will take over these tasks as they are modernized and up-graded (and as wages improve).

Someone must undertake the nurturant, affectional tasks of society — and this may be another reason not to counsel women to denigrate such work, but rather to convince them that these tasks have value and should be shared with men. Although no one now seriously doubts their ability to excel in masculine-stereotyped fields, Latin American women in particular, as already noted, give little evidence that they wish to cross the traditional boundaries. The utopias which some sectors of the world's youth are striving to create ask, after all, for the very skills and values which society has designated "feminine"; thus what appears at first glance a retrogressive prescription — let women remain in feminine fields if they wish to do so — takes on, in another context, a revolutionary aspect.

This same idea is explored in a discussion on women's future edited several years ago by Robert Theobald (1967). In the developed world, we are rapidly moving out of an industrial age and into a cybernated era. The basis for this new society will not be a production-transportation net, but an "information net" — and its effective functioning will demand fundamental shifts in the attitudes of industrial society. In the light of the coming changes, the volume argues, goals presently valued — higher gross national product, more goods and services, greater control over the environment — will no longer be important. It is therefore absurd to abandon what society designates as "female" values at this point when the major areas of work in coming periods will be education, the human care of human beings, and the creation of the good community, activities which demand "empathy, intuition and cooperation which appear to be predominantly feminine characteristics" (Theobald 1967:14–15).

There is a view beginning to be expressed today that without the values for which women stand it may quite simply be impossible to preserve viable society. Women not only have a vitally necessary and complementary role to "humanize" and temper the modernization process; in the post-industrial era, woman may, at long last, come into her own.

REFERENCES

ALLENDE GOSSENS, SALVADOR A.
   1972a "La historia que estamos escribiendo: el presidente Allende en Anto-

fagasta." Santiago: Consejería de Difusión de la Presidencia de la República.

1972b "El pueblo debe organizarse... y actuar: el Presidente Allende en Concepción." Santiago: Concejería de Difusión de la Presidencia de la República.

BAMBIRRA, VANIA
1971   La mujer chilena en la transición al socialismo. *Punto Final,* Suplemento 133 (22 de junio).

BENSTON, MARGARET
1969   The political economy of women's liberation. *Monthly Review* 21 (September).

BERMAN, JOAN
1970   Women in Cuba. *Women: a Journal of Liberation* 1 (4): 10–14.

BLACHMAN, MORRIS J.
1973   "Eve in an Adamocracy: women and politics in Brazil." New York University Occasional Paper 5. New York.

BORGESE, ELISABETH MANN
1963   *Ascent of woman.* London: Macgibbon and Kee.

BUNCH-WEEKS, CHARLOTTE
1970   Asian women in revolution. *Women: a Journal of Liberation* 1(4): 2–9.

BUSSI DE ALLENDE, HORTENSIA
1972   *Women and the revolutionary process in Chile.* Translated by Jaime Fernández and Fernando Alegría. Washington: Cultural Department of the Embassy of Chile.

CHANEY, ELSA M.
1971   "Women in Latin American politics: the case of Peru and Chile." Unpublished doctoral dissertation. University of Wisconsin, Madison.
1973a Marie Cam: my friend from Hanoi. *The Church Woman* 39(4): 20–24.
1973b "Women in Latin American politics: the case of Peru and Chile," in *Female and male in Latin America.* Edited by Ann Pescatello, 130–139. Pittsburgh: University of Pittsburgh Press.

CHAPLIN, DAVID
1967   The Peruvian industrial labor force. Princeton: Princeton University Press.

CHOMBART DE LAUWE, PAUL H.
1962   Introduction to "Images of women in society." *International Social Science Journal (UNESCO)* 14(1): 7–25.

ERIKSON, ERIK H.
1964   *Insight and responsibility.* New York: W. W. Norton.

FREYRE, GILBERTO
1963   *The mansions and the shanties: the making of modern Brazil.* New York: Alfred A. Knopf.

GROSS, EDWARD
1968   "Plus ça change...? The sex structure of occupations over time" *Social Problems* 16(2): 198–208.

GRUBERG, MARTIN
1968   *Women in American politics: an assessment and sourcebook.* Oshkosh, Wisconsin: Academia Press.

HERNÁNDEZ PARKER, LUIS
1967   La mujer en política. *El Mercurio, Revista del Domingo* 11. March 26.

HUNT, CHESTER L.
1959   *Social aspects of economic development.* New York: McGraw-Hill.

INKELES, ALEX
1969   "Participant citizenship in six developing countries." *American Political Science Review* 63(4).

JANCAR, BARBARA W.
1972   "Women and Soviet politics." Paper presented at the American Political Science Association annual meeting, September.

KAHL, JOSEPH A.
1966   *The measurement of modernism: a study of values in Brazil and Mexico.* Latin American Monographs 12. Austin: University of Texas Press.

LERNER, DANIEL
1958   The passing of traditional society: modernizing the Middle East. Glencoe, Illinois: The Free Press.

LOCKHART, JAMES
1968   *Spanish Peru: 1532–1560, a colonial society.* Madison, Wisconsin: University of Wisconsin Press.

LUDOVICI, L. J.
1965   *The final inequality: a critical assessment of woman's sexual role in society.* New York: W. W. Norton.

MATTELART, ARMAND, MICHÉLÉ MATTELART
1968   "La mujer chilena en una nueva sociedad." Santiago: Editorial del Pacífico.

MENON, LAKSHMI
1968   From constitutional recognition to public office. *The Annals of the American Academy* 375 (January):34–43.

MITCHELL, JULIET
1966   Women: the longest revolution. *New Left Review* 40 (November-December):1–27.
1973   Marxism and women's liberation. *Social Praxis* 1(1):23–33.

PARSONS, TALCOTT, ROBERT A. BALES
1956   *Family, socialization and interaction process.* Glencoe, Illinois: The Free Press.

PURCELL, SUSAN KAUFMAN
1973   "Modernizing women for a modernizing society: the Cuban case," in *Female and male in Latin America.* Edited by Ann Pescatello, 257–271. Pittsburgh: University of Pittsburgh Press.

RAMOS, ANA
1972   La mujer y la revolución en Cuba. Translated from the Spanish and adapted by Janet Berkenfeld. *Cuba Resource Center Newsletter* 2(2) 3–11.

TEITELBAUM, M.
1973   Women against the system: Nguyen Thi Binh. *London Sunday Times Magazine* (April 28):37–38.

THEOBALD, ROBERT, *editor*
1967   "Introduction," in *Dialogue on women.* New York: Bobbs Merrill.

UNITED NATIONS COMMISSION ON THE STATUS OF WOMEN
  1970 "Women in the economic and social life of their countries." Doc.
       E/CN.6/513/rev.1. New York.
UNITED NATIONS, SECRETARY GENERAL
  1970 "Political rights of women." Doc. A/8132, November 30. New York.
  1971 "Political rights of women." Doc. A/8481, December 15. New York.
WHYTE, WILLIAM F.
  1965 "High-level manpower for Peru." in *Manpower and education.* Edited
       by Frederick H. Harbison and Charles A. Meyers. New York:
       McGraw-Hill.
WILENSKY, L.
  1968 Women's work. *Industrial Relations* 7 (May):235–258.

Image and Reality:
Women's Status in Israel

DORIT PADAN-EISENSTARK

Since the beginning of the century, when the first *kvuzot* and *kibbutzim*[1] were established in what was then called Palestine, the Jewish community in Israel became known as a society in which women had achieved full equality with men in all fields of life. Jewish National Fund posters distributed throughout the world depicted the Israeli woman as a tractor driver, construction worker, and road builder. Later, reports about the role of women in the underground military activities of the Haganah and Palmach[2] lent further support to the image of the Israeli woman as one to whom equal status was accorded. The political activity of a small number of significant women, of whom Golda Meier is a representative, and the conscription of women into the Israeli Defense Forces, added substance to the appearance of equality.

In my view, however, this image is a simplified and idealized one, and does not reflect the complexities of women's status in Israel. If Israeli experience is to serve as a "social experiment" from which realistic and operative conclusions may be drawn, the idealized image has to be abandoned in favor of a sober analysis based on facts, including successes and failures.

Adhering to an unwarranted, idealized image of Israel, as a society in which sex equality has already been achieved, does not promote the aim of establishing real sex equality either in Israel or in countries which want to learn from its experience. Idealizing Israel's achievements, on the one

---

[1] *Kvuzot* and *kibbutzim* are plurals, respectively, of *kvutza* and *kibbutz*, i.e. collective settlements.
[2] Haganah and Palmach were Jewish underground military defense organizations during the British Mandate.

hand, leads many people to the unrealistic belief that sex equality may be achieved rather easily by a mere ideological commitment and a few organizational devices. On the other hand, when confronted with the discrepancy between their idealized image and reality, many draw the false conclusion that Israeli women have voluntarily abandoned the equality they achieved, thus apparently proving that all recent attempts to promote sex equality are futile and doomed to failure.

Like any social change, the establishment of sex equality is a many-faceted process which cannot be attained overnight. Israel, like other countries, has achieved sex equality in certain legal, institutional, behavioral, and attitudinal aspects, but remnants of traditional discrimination remain. An integrated picture of the lessons to be drawn from the successes and failures of a large number of countries attempting to establish sex equality will enable us to draw more general conclusions regarding the factors which promote and those which hamper the full participation of women in all aspects of social activity. Israel's experience may serve as an important contribution to this aim.

This study is a factual survey of the extent of equality achieved by Israeli women in the areas of work and political activity, measured by the following criteria:

1. the extent to which Israeli women participate in the labor force compared to Israeli men and to women in selected industrial countries;
2. the extent to which the traditional division of labor into "masculine" and "feminine" occupations continues to prevail;
3. the proportion of Israeli women in top jobs, i.e. in professional, managerial, administrative, and political key positions, compared to that of men and of women in selected industrial countries; and
4. the extent to which the social prestige and economic benefits attached to occupations regarded as "feminine" are equal to those attached to comparable "masculine" ones.

Particular attention will be devoted to the status of women in the kibbutz, whose structural framework was designed to solve women's inequality in the context of solving general social inequality.

GENERAL PARTICIPATION OF WOMEN IN THE LABOR FORCE[3]

The *Israel statistical yearbook* (1972c: 308) reveals that women constituted

---

[3]   The data in this article refer to Jewish women and to the Jewish labor force alone.

32.4 percent of the Jewish labor force in Israel in 1971, and that 32.5 percent of all Jewish women in Israel are part of the labor force. What do these numbers acutally mean? Do they indicate high or low representation of women in the labor force? Compared to Israeli men, the representation of women in the Israeli labor force is relatively low: whereas two-thirds of Israeli men participate in the labor force, only one-third of women do so.

It might be justifiably argued that so long as women assume primary responsibility for the family, such comparison with men is invalid. We will therefore compare the participation of Israeli women in the labor force with that of women in selected industrial countries.

In the early 1960's women constituted 54 percent of the labor force in the Soviet Union, 38 percent in France, 35 percent in England, 34 percent in the United States, and only 28 percent in Israel (Golan 1966:6, 21). By the early 1970's Israeli women had increased their representation to 32.4 percent but this achievement is still less than the percentages noted in other industrially developed countries in the early 1960's. It is clear then that both in comparison to the Israeli male, and in comparison to women in other countries, the percentage of women in the labor force in Israel is relatively low.

Can this lower representation be attributed to social processes which were in evidence after the establishment of the State, such as the massive immigration of Jews from Islamic countries, etc.? If so, was women's representation in the labor force prior to the establishment of the State more consistent with the image of full and equal social participation of both sexes? The statistics indicate that the opposite was, in fact, the case. Women's representation in the labor force during the earlier period was even less, although it rose continually beginning in the 1930's. In 1930 women constituted only 20 percent of members of the Jewish Labor Federation, the Histadrut. During World War II, a period in which the numbers of working women reached new heights throughout the world, their numbers in Israel rose to only 29 percent of the working Histadrut members (Histadrut 1951:26).[4]

Representation in the labor force of non-Jewish women in Israel is extremely low, and totalled only 9 percent in 1971. However, there have been substantive changes in the status of the Arab woman in Israel since 1948 and in the occupied territories since 1967. The unique social situation of the Arab woman demands special and separate consideration. Moveover, the unequal position of the Arab woman in virtually all areas of life no doubt strengthened the egalitarian image of the Jewish woman in Israel.

[4] No statistical data on women in the general labor force are available for the pre-State period. Yet there is reason to suppose that women who were not members of the General Workers' Federation at that time had even lower representation in the labor force.

COUNTRY OF ORIGIN

Representation of Jewish women who immigrated to Israel from Asian and African countries is relatively low, although it is increasing. Whereas in 1955 only 19.9 percent of these women worked, this percentage rose to 27.7 percent in 1971. Comparable figures for Jewish women of European and American origin are 31 percent in 1955 and 34.2 percent in 1971 (Israel 1972a:309).

Differences between the characteristic work pattern of the two groups of various ages are of particular interest. A relatively high proportion of girls of Asian and African origin enter the labor market at the age of fourteen, with the completion of compulsory education. In contrast, most girls of European-American origin continue their studies and begin work only with the termination of their military service or on completion of higher education. Thus, we find 20.8 percent of girls of Asian-African origin in the fourteen-to-seventeen age group working, while only 8 percent of girls of European-American origin are employed.

The traditional view that the "place of the woman (and the married woman in particular) is in the home" still carries considerable weight among persons of Asian-African origin, and many husbands dislike the idea of their wives working outside the family framework. The larger number of children in families of Asian-African origin constitutes an added obstacle confronting the woman seeking employment. The low wages and minimal satisfaction associated with the unskilled jobs available to women with relatively little education make the effort involved in combining family and work roles simply not worthwhile.

For these reasons, we find that among women of Asian-African origin who are above the age of eighteen (i.e. of child-bearing age), the percentage of those employed is half that of comparable women of European-American origin. For example, only 35.6 percent of women of Asian-African origin between the ages eighteen and thirty-nine are employed, as against 50.2 percent of women of European-American origin of the same age who immigrated to Israel in the same period. Comparable statistics for ages thirty-five to fifty-four are 22.7 percent for women of Asian-African origin, and 42.5 percent for those of European-American origin.

It is of interest that the largest differences between the two groups are to be found among women over fifty-five years of age. Women of European-American origin tend to continue working until the age of sixty-five and in many instances return to work after having raised their children. In contrast, persons of Asian-African origin consider men and women in their fifties too old to be required to work or indeed to be capable of working. Furthermore, the women, who generally lack education and professional skills, find it most difficult to obtain work. Consequently, only 5.3 percent of women of Asian-African origin between fifty-five and sixty-four, as compared with 28.6 percent of women of European-American origin, who came to Israel in the same period, are represented in the labor force (Israel 1972a:309).

The pattern of employment and representation in the labor market of native-born Israeli women resembles that of women of European-American origin. Women born in Israel are, after all, the daughters of parents from both origins. The relatively high percentage of Israel-born women from families of Asian-African origin who are employed indicates that the cultural and educational barriers which limited their mothers' employment opportunities are gradually disappearing.

The percentages of employed women of various ages who were born in Europe and the Americas resemble those of women of comparable ages in Western countries, but are lower than those of women in the Soviet Union (Fogarty, Rapoport, and Rapoport 1971:514–519).

EDUCATION

The representation of women in the labor force seems to be directly related to educational level. Whereas only 10 percent of women lacking any education are employed, 25 percent of those with elementary school education, are employed, 36 percent of those with high school education, and 61.2 percent of those with higher education are employed. Moreover in the thirty-five to fifty-four age group, where the children of most mothers are of school age, 80.9 percent of women who possess some higher education are employed (Israel 1972a:310).

Educational level is a greater determining factor in women's patterns of employment than is ethnic origin. Thus, we find that in 1963, 36.4 percent of women of European-American origin with high school education were employed, a percentage almost matched by women of Asian-African origin with comparable education: 35.4 percent (Golan 1966:25). Furthermore, women with higher education tend to continue to work, regardless of the number of their children. We find that 70 percent of women who have high school education and three to four children are employed, whereas only 23 percent of mothers who have a similar number of children, but whose educational level is lower, are employed (Shamgar-Hendelman 1971:38, 36).

The implication of educational level for patterns of employment is similar in the United States, where 70 percent of women with master's degrees, 50 percent of those with bachelor degrees, 40 percent of those with high school education, and only 30 percent of those with elementary school education are employed (Ginzberg 1967:108–109). Yet even among women with higher education, one-third of those in the child-bearing age group, eighteen to forty-three, leave the workforce. The loss to the national economy and to the professional advancement of these women during their period of absence is obvious. When women do continue to work during the years when their children are still young, they generally seek part-time work or jobs which do not demand considerable or extensive investment of time. The implications of such work patterns become evident, for example, in the low percentage of women in senior positions.

PROFESSIONAL RANGE

Examination of the distribution of Israeli women among the various occupations reveals a "traditional" occupational division, with women constituting a majority in conventional "feminine" fields, such as education, welfare, auxiliary office work, care of food and clothing, etc., with a negligible minority in "masculine" fields, such as technology, politics, administration, economics, etc. Women constitute 85 percent of secretaries and typists, 80 percent of nurses, 68 percent of elementary school teachers, and 31 percent of doctors, but only 8 percent of political officeholders, 7 percent of lawyers, 5 percent of engineers, etc. (Israel 1972a:178, 191).

The representation of women in "masculine" occupations in Israel is low compared with that of women in Eastern Europe in these areas. For instance, in the Soviet Union women constitute 30 percent of engineers and geologists, 72 of doctors, 32 percent of lawyers, and 40 percent of agronomists and veterinarians. Similar figures may be cited for East Germany, Rumania, and Poland.

In the Soviet Union women constitute 25 percent of students of mechanical and motor vehicle engineering and 15 percent of skilled workers in the metal industry. As early as 1959, women constituted 78 percent of printing workers in the Soviet Union(Fogarty, Rapoport, and Rapoport 1971:60, 61). In contrast, the printing industry in Israel was totally closed to women until only last year. The newspaper *Ha'aretz* of February 2, 1973, reported that for the first time in the history of the country, twenty-one girls were accepted to study printing in a vocational school in Israel.

Printing is not the only profession to exclude women, as shown in the press and radio in recent months. On February 21, 1973, a representative of the bus company, Egged, stated in a radio interview that the company in principle does not grant bus drivers' licenses to women, and consequently does not accept women as members of the cooperative. On the same day, *Maariv* reported that women plasterers, recently arrived from the Soviet Union, decided to form a union in order to protect their right to work in their profession. The struggle of El-Al stewardesses to win the right to serve in the capacity of steward-economist continues. A year ago a woman won a lawsuit in the Supreme Court, allowing her to represent a bank on the Tel Aviv Stock Exchange, hitherto closed to women brokers. A systematic survey would undoubtedly reveal several areas of work from which women still are totally excluded.

In this context, the work assignments of civil servants reflect a clearly sexual division. Women constitute a majority of the typists, key-punch operators, coders, switchboard operators, laboratory workers, nurses and social workers, but almost no women are to be found among the journalists, spokesmen, telegraphists, managers, warehouse supervisors, tax and income tax supervisors, and technical workers of the civil service (Israel 1972b).

The occupational sex division in Israel may thus be regarded as "traditional" in comparison with East European countries. Compared to Western countries, though, Israeli women have achieved a relatively large occupational range, which is quite similar to that of Western Europe, and larger than that of women in the United States. In the early 1960's women in the United States constituted only 6 percent of doctors (compared to 31 percent in Israel), 4 percent of lawyers, and less than 1 percent of engineers.

In summary, Eastern European countries have expanded the professional opportunities available to women, both in educational institutions and in the job market. Israel's successes in this respect, similar to those of other Western countries, are not very impressive.

SENIOR POSITIONS

The figures reveal that occupational advancement of women throughout the world, including the communist countries, is rare beyond the middle levels of the occupational hierarchy in all fields. Even in characteristically feminine occupations, such as teaching and social work, men hold most of the supervisory and administrative positions with high wages, prestige, and significant decision-making power. The higher the job level, the smaller the percentage of women to be found at that level.

Israel is not exceptional in this respect. Women occupy less than 10 percent of all the senior professional and administrative positions, except in medicine, where women constitute almost a third. The situation is quite similar, even in the "feminine" professions. Women constitute only 7 percent of the administrators and supervisors of public education in Israel. In the humanities, women constitute only 2 percent of the professors.

The tendency for women to be found in the middle levels of professional status, in jobs which allow reasonably comfortable integration of the roles of mother and wife, is clearly evidenced by the position of women in the universities, both as students and as staff members.

THE HEBREW UNIVERSITY, JERUSALEM

About half the applicants and recipients of bachelor's degrees at the Hebrew University — the first and largest university in Israel — are women. Thus, women are fully represented among university students at this stage. Upon completion of the B.A., however, most women students enter the labor market as teachers, clerks, and research assistants. Relatively few continue their studies. Thus, women constitute only 27 percent of the recipients of master's degrees. The percentage of women declines to 13 percent for recipients of doctorates (Israel 1972c: 895).

The departure of women from institutes of higher learning upon receipt of the B.A. or B.S. degree effectively removes them from competition for a large portion of those senior positions for which possession of a higher degree is a necessary qualification. Examination of the academic staff reveals a characteristically pyramidal distribution of women over ranks. Whereas women constitute 21 percent of the staff of the Hebrew University, they comprise 25 percent of assistants and instructors, 18 percent of lecturers, 15 percent of senior lecturers and only 4 percent of professors.

In addition to being concentrated in the lower echelons of the staff hierarchy, women also characteristically tend to fill roles which are marginal to the central hierarchy. Thus, they hold 63 percent of the special university positions of "teacher." Although the role of teacher is similar to that of more senior staff members, teachers do not enjoy full material rewards, pension rights, and professional advancement (Padan-Eisenstark 1973). In other employment areas in Israel, as well as in other countries throughout the world, women occupy a majority of the marginal positions of this type (Fogarty, Rapoport, and Rapoport 1971; Bernard 1964).

GOVERNMENT WORKERS

Women occupy 28.4 percent of the lowest-ranking jobs in the civil service and 27 percent of the middle-level jobs, but only 9 percent of the highest positions. In addition, about half of the women holding senior positions in the civil service occupy jobs which are defined as "feminine," such as nursing and social work, and which are outside the range of senior administrative positions.

POLITICAL ELITE

Dr. Sehvah Weiss' recent investigation (1973) shows that for years there has been no woman member on the General Labor Federation (Histadrut) Central Committee, nor has any woman ever been considered as a candidate for the position of General Secretary of the Federation. In the foreign service there are only a few women, and only two ever held the position of consul or ambassador. The number of women in the Israeli Parliament (Knesset) has decreased from eleven in the First Knesset to eight in the present Seventh Knesset. As of the Sixth Knesset, no women held a seat in the Foreign Affairs and Security Committee. With the exception of the Fourth Knesset, no woman ever sat on the Finance Committee. These last two Committees command the major resource-distributing and decision-making positions in the country. Although many women have served as Deputy Speakers of the Knesset, no women has ever been suggested as candidate for the role of Speaker. No woman other than Golda Meier has ever served as a minister.

In many Eastern and Western countries, local government posts have been considered particularly suited to women, in keeping with their professional experience in the fields of sanitation, health, welfare, community, and social activities, etc. (Golan 1966: 11, 12). In this context, the absence of women in local government authorities in Israel is particularly notable. During the five terms of the one hundred local authorities to date, only four women have ever held the position of head of a local authority. That is to say, women's representation in local government is confined to 1 percent (Weiss 1973).

ISRAEL DEFENSE FORCE (IDF)

The conscription of women into the IDF has been mentioned as one of the factors contributing to the image of equal status for women in Israel. Without doubt military service has given Israeli women a feeling of participation and contribution to the country's defense and security, which is so vital to the existence of the State. Nonetheless, by its very nature, the IDF constitutes a framework which contributes to the patterns of inequality between the sexes.

The distinction between frontline combat roles, designated for men alone, on the one hand, and rear auxiliary roles, designated for women, on the other, establishes an unequal hierarchy, in which advancement and acquired experiences are not equal. As this distinction seems to a large extent inevitable, given the present conditions of combat, we will only relate to those aspects of inequality which go beyond this necessary division of roles. In the absence of (classified) statistics on the distribution of roles and professions in the IDF, we will give a few examples.

The fact that women's service is restricted to twenty months, compared to thirty-six months for men constitutes, in one way, an extra right, and in another, a source of inequality. As a result of the relatively short period of service for women, investment in their professional training becomes less worthwhile. Consequently women cannot be found in many rear-line positions which demand special skills. Women are not accepted in prestigious skilled positions, such as that of pilot, even of cargo planes and helicopters. The absence of women among military pilots also removes them from the field of civil aviation, which recruits most of its pilots from discharged military personnel.

Moreover, the increasing tendency in Israel to recruit high-ranking officers retiring from the IDF for senior civilian administrative positions, reduces the already small possibility that women might occupy these positions in the future. This is a result of the fact that the very structure of the army calls for a relatively small number of high-ranking women officers.

Thus with regard to the third criterion of equality, i.e. equal representation of women in high-ranking positions, Israeli women have not yet achieved fair representation.

WAGES

The last *Statistical yearbook* reveals that the average yearly income of

a male wage-earner was 9,300 Israeli pounds whereas for women it was only 5,100. In other words, the average wage for women in Israel constituted
only 55 percent of the average wage for men. The greatest difference between the wages of men and women is in the crafts and in industry, where
women earn only 45 percent of the wages received by men (Israel 1972c:
328). This wage differential is only partially explained by the fact that
many women work only part-time and that more men than women find it
possible to work overtime. The 1972 strike at the Elite Chocolate Factory
shows that the "equal wages for equal work" law is presumably being
violated in many factories.

Moreover, the distinction between "feminine" and "masculine" work,
which is quite common in Israel, renders the above slogan meaningless,
insofar as technically equal work is almost nonexistent. The low wages
paid to women in Israel show that the monetary reward for "female"
work is usually much lower than that for "men's" work. To the extent that
wages are determined by job analysis, this difference shows the lower value
set on the skills needed to perform "women's" work: for instance, manual
dexterity, as compared to "physical power," which defines "male" work.
Furthermore, even when men perform "light" tasks, such as assembling
delicate instruments, their work is said to demand "intelligence and experience," with correspondingly high rewards, but when women perform
the very same tasks, they are defined as "light work" and the monetary
reward is substantially lower.

PENSIONS, SOCIAL RIGHTS AND TAXES

Social and pension rights constitute an integral part of the financial
rewards of labor. Many of the laws determining the social and pension
rights of the Israeli citizen are most progressive as regards women's
equality and rights, although remnants of the traditional notion of the
woman as a dependent or an auxiliary earner continue to prevail in certain areas of the law. With regard to this last criterion of equality, i.e. the
prestige and economic rewards attached to "feminine" as compared to
"masculine" jobs and occupations, the status of Israeli women leaves
much to be desired.

THE KIBBUTZ

The kibbutz is a unique social framework, with a social, ideological, and political impact on Israeli society which far exceeds its numerical importance.[5] The kibbutz was intended, among other things, to bring about a crucial change in the status of women.

For more than fifty years, supporters and critics have been examining the progress of this social experiment. There are those who regard the kibbutz as an exemplary institution in which full equality and cooperation of the two sexes has indeed been achieved in all areas of life. There are others who claim that the fact that no substantive change has occured in the status of women in the kibbutz is a proof that the inequality between the sexes has a biological basis which cannot be altered by change in social conditions.

The two sexes in the kibbutz have achieved full equality with regard to the extent of their participation in the labor force. All men and women of working age and of good health work a full day.[6] Yet equality has not been achieved in the professional distribution of women in the kibbutz. There is a clear distinction between "female" and "male" occupations, with most women working in education and services and most men working in agriculture and industry.

In 1965, for example, 36 percent of women members of the Kibbutz Artzi (the largest kibbutz federation in the country) were employed in the care and education of children, and 36 percent in food and clothing services. In contrast, only 13 percent of women were employed in industry and in agriculture (Givat Haviva 1967). Moreover, the village character of the Kibbutz has not yet permitted full development of those occupational fields (clerical, welfare, sales, etc.) in which many urban women are involved. Therefore, the range of occupations open to women in the kibbutz is relatively restricted.

The proportion of women in central decision-making processes in the kibbutz, although higher than that of urban women in comparable political and managerial roles, is still relatively low compared to kibbutz men. The percentage of women chairing the various committees is rather low. As in the city, women are primarily active in committees which deal with "female" areas, such as education and culture, while their representation in the political and economic committees is much lower.

In the Kibbutz Artzi, only 20 percent of all women, as compared to 42 percent of all men, chaired committees, or served as branch coordinators. Eighty-four percent of these active women were in the "female" fields of education, services, and welfare committees (Rosner 1965:21; Givat Haviva 1967:19). Moreover, an investigation conducted in the Kibbutz

[5] Kibbutz members comprise only 4 percent of the Jewish population of Israel.
[6] In recent years a shortened workday for mothers of small children has been adopted

Artzi in 1965 (Rosner 1965), revealed that the basic attitudes towards the division of roles among the sexes had not changed. As a result, despite an egalitarian ideology, men do not take an equal part in the education of infants nor do they share equally in the food and clothing services. Within the small family apartment in the kibbutz, whose standard of living is steadily rising, the bulk of household responsibility is borne by the women (Talmon-Garber 1970:58–70).

An organizational expression of this fundamental traditional approach to sex role division may be found in the shortened workday instituted in several kibbutzim for mothers, NOT for fathers. As a result, women in the kibbutz have the main responsibility for services and child-care (albeit collective), and for their small private households. These facts also limit women's ability to engage in the public and political activities of the kibbutz, as they are less able to be absent from home for long periods of time. The relatively limited range of occupations and economic enterprises in which kibbutz women participate tends to limit their experience and involvement in decision making in these fields.

Nevertheless, significant accomplishments may be noted in the professionalization and prestige accorded to the "female" occupations in the kibbutz. Although the kibbutzim still preserve the distinction between productive and community occupations, with higher status accorded to the former, the increasing professionalization and mechanization of the collective services have transformed the housewife's role to one defined as professional and skilled. Occupational roles within the kibbutz communal educational system, including the infant-care nurses, kindergarten teachers, school teachers, youth instructors, etc. are among the most respected and sought-after occupations in the kibbutz. Most important, though, are the lessons to be learned from the kibbutz's collective education regarding the possibility of freeing working women from the "child-care part" of their "double role" for an eight-hour work day.

Many investigators have shown that the overall influence of collective education on the development of children is positive.[7] Kibbutz education is different from other institutional socialization in that it combines the advantages of continuous contact with parents and integration in a large and varied age group with the guidance of trained and professional educators. Kibbutz education demonstrates the possibility of freeing the mother

---

[7]   Parents, educators, and psychologists disagree about the influence on infants of sleeping in children's houses, apart from their parents. In a number of kibbutzim, the arrangement has been modified so that infants sleep in their parents' apartment. However, there is agreement about the positive effect of collective education during the daytime hours upon children's development in all age groups.

to participate fully in work without disturbing the emotional and intellectual development of her children.

The kibbutz framework has also brought about a fundamental change in the status of the women by freeing her from economic dependence on her husband's income, with all that this implies. This change is a by-product of the general structure of the kibbutz in which the standard of living of a member is not related to his/her individual earning power. Although the impact of this fundamental equality on family life and on the general status of the women has not been adequately studied, its meaning in time of crisis can be demonstrated. Whereas in the city, divorce or widowhood often brings about a drastic decline in the standard of living of a woman and her children, in the kibbutz such situations have no economic implications.

CONCLUSIONS

Establishment of sex equality is a goal or a guideline for a process of fundamental change in all aspects of life. Israel, like many other countries, had not achieved sex equality but has adopted it as an ideal and as part of its central value system. The salience of Israel's commitment to this ideal has varied in different periods of its short history. Most important, though, is the fact that the rate of approaching this goal in the different life areas is not equal. As a result we find that different countries, including Israel, reflect different profiles and mixtures of sex equality side by side with sex inequality and sex discrimination.

A detailed analysis of the implications of the different legal and institutional arrangements is beyond the scope of this study,[8] but some conclusions regarding the general conditions conducive to sex equality may be drawn.

1.   Full sex equality can be established only in a social setting in which men's superior physical strength is of minimal importance, i.e. in an economy based on developed technology and a political setting of peace. Israel's rather partial achievements in sex equality, in spite of its ideological commitments to this aim, are partly due to its relatively "pre-industrial" economy up to the last ten years, and the constant situation of "war" with its neighbors.

[8]   We have limited this study to the status of women in work and political activity. We have not discussed Israeli women's status in marital laws, leisure activities, cultural activities, etc., nor we have discussed child-care arrangements in Israel outside the kibbutz.

2.   Developed technology, a political setting of peace, ideological commitment to sex equality, and legal and institutional arrangements which
facilitate women's participation in occupational roles and political activity are necessary but insufficient conditions for full sex equality.

So long as there is no change in the basic images of both male and
female sex roles, i.e. as long as women are regarded as primarily responsible for child-care and household services, whether private or collective,
women will not be able to participate fully in society's nonfamily roles.

REFERENCES

BERNARD, JESSIE
   1964   *Academic women*. Philadelphia: Pennsylvania State University Press.
FOGARTY, M. P., ROHNA RAPOPORT, RALPH RAPOPORT
   1971   *Sex, career and family*. London: P.E.P. George Allen and Unwin.
GINZBERG, E.
   1967   Paycheck and apron revolution in women power. *Industrial Relations*
          7 (May).
GIVAT HAVIVA
   1967   *Data regarding the status of women of the Kibbutz Artzi*. Givat Haviva:
          Givat Haviva.
GOLAN, YONA
   1966   *The woman in modern society*. Tel Aviv: Sifriyat-Hapoalim.
HAHISTADRUT HAKLATIL SHEL HAOVDIM HAIVRIM BE ERETZ ISRAEL
   1951   *In the 30th year*. Tel Aviv: Havaad Hapoel.
ISRAEL
   1972a *Work force*, part one. Jerusalem: Central Bureau of Statistics.
   1972b *Comparative study of government workers in the years 1955–1967*.
          Jerusalem: Ministry of Finance.
   1972c *Israel statistical yearbook*. Jerusalem: Central Bureau of Statistics.
PADAN-EISENSTARK, DORIT
   1973   "Women on the academic staff." Unpublished. Jerusalem.
ROSNER, MENACHEM
   1965   *Summary of research on women in the kibbutz*. Givat Haviva: Givat
          Haviva.
SHAMGAR-HENDELMAN, LEAH
   1971   *Status self rating of Israeli civil servants and their wives' employment*.
          Jerusalem.
TALMON-GARBER, YONINA
   1970   *Individual and society in the kibbutz*. Jerusalem: Magnes.
WEISS, SEHVAH
   1973   Women in Israeli politics. *Social Research Review of the University of
          Haifa* 3: 5–14.

Sources of the Matrilineal Family System in the Works of Carl J. L. Almqvist

KARIN WESTMAN BERG

Carl Jonas Love Almqvist (1793–1866) was a Swedish Romantic author who, by the end of his productive literary career, had become a radical social critic, one of the pioneers of political radicalism in Sweden. A very advanced type of feminism was, however, the center of his radicalism, based on legal reforms of the marriage institution, for he felt that the most effective way of achieving a democratic society would be to change the existing patriarchal family system. He spent years inventing such a family system, which he first described in a novel, *Sara Videbeck* (1839) and then in a dissertation *Reasons for the dissatisfaction of Europe* (1850).[1]

My aim is to describe the utopian family system created by this Swedish author more than a hundred years ago; to point out that its central element is matriliny; to show where he got his ideas; and to demonstrate that the androcentric attitudes of scholars led them to false conclusions about this system.

Neither conservatives nor liberals appreciated the system. Almqvist was regarded as an immoral seducer of young people and had to leave his position as headmaster of a school. He became a journalist but was regarded as an outsider in society, and his only adherents were a small number of young socialists and feminists. He ended his days as a destitute refugee in the United States. But nowadays he is admired not only as the most advanced Romantic author in Swedish literature but also as one of the very radical forerunners of the Women's Liberation Movement in Sweden, and still a bit ahead of present-day developments.

---

[1]   Throughout the text, Almqvist' *Europeiska missnöjets grunder* (1850) and his other works will be referred to by their translated titles.

Although male literary historians have published a large amount of research on his life and letters, none of them was interested in studying the basis of his utopian family system after it was labelled "matriarchal" in 1908.

In my dissertation (1962) on Almqvist's views on women, I pointed out that he was extremely critical of legal discrimination against women and did not agree with the socialist utopian family systems discussed in his day; that he experimented with matrilineal ideas more than twenty years before Bachofen wrote *Das Mutterrecht* (the first scientific description of matriliny); and that evidence points to the Nayar caste on the Malabar coast of India as his main source. These points will be more fully developed below.

UTOPIAN MARRIAGE IN *SARA VIDEBECK* AND *REASONS FOR THE DISSATISFACTION OF EUROPE*

Because he was a very famous author, Almqvist decided to introduce his ideas in fiction before he published the facts about his marriage system in a dissertation. In 1839 he wrote a realistic travel story, closely related to the *voyage imaginaire*, the genre writers especially used during the nineteenth century to spread radical new ideas without being punished for criticizing the Establishement.

Almqvist called his novel *Det går an* [It can be done], translated in English as *Sara Videbeck*. It is one of the most inspired and genial of all his works, and it can very well be read today. The plot is very simple. Two young persons, Sara Videbeck, who is a glazier, and Albert, a sergeant, meet on a steamboat, fall in love, decide to travel together for a few days, and have sexual intercourse during the trip. Before reaching Sara's home in the small town of Lidköping, they have decided to live together, but not to marry in the traditional way.

When the novel was published in English (Almqvist 1972), the introduction summarized its contents as follows:

The story begins on the quay below Riddarholm Church in Stockholm, where Yngve Frey is about to depart on a trip across Lake Mälaren. It is certainly one of the first occasions on which a steamship is navigating through Swedish literature; the boat moreover is taken from real life, even down to the timetable. Also in continuation of the story the author brings forward plenty of realistic stuff: the contemporary reader received a good deal of topographical, economic and technical information, represented in the form of traveller's reports, while a late posterity has an incomparable opportunity to call to mind a part of Sweden and Swedish life during the 1830s. The detailed descriptions, e.g. the scenes from the inns along the route or the glimpses of Sara's work as a glazier, give the whole story an authenticity that had been extremely rare in Swedish literature before Almqvist's time.

Against this background of fresh colours the human problems are enacted. Sergeant Albert is — or becomes — a rather passive figure upon which Sara Videbeck's program of life is to be tried. She is the one who has the bright and unconventional mind and the courage to act accordingly. Warned by her parent's failure, Sara revolts against the old patriarchal order. She will not submit to her husband's domestic authority, not professionally, not economically, not sexually. She suggests a life together with Albert unbound and in complete equality.

With the ideas and the claims made in *Det går an* Almqvist was quite in keeping with and partly a great step ahead of the radical movement for reforming the women's role in society by giving them full rights upon reaching their majority, equal inheritance, general education and professional training, more generous opportunities in the labor market, etc. Marriage had not yet been attacked, however, and it was also on this point that *Det går an* aroused the greatest uproar. A great many polemical pamphlets appeared and Almqvist was designated a seducer of youth and destroyer of morality (Björck in Almqvist 1972:9–10).

This is a fairly good description of the book. Staffan Björck, Professor of Comparative Literature at the University of Lund, who wrote the introduction, mentions its feminist tendency. However, he gives more details about the reforms Almqvist supported, which were not his own inventions and which have long since been passed, but little information about the marriage system Almqvist invented, which is the central theme of the novel. Thus Björck follows the academic tradition of omitting controversial points. Because equality between the sexes is still an unsolved problem, Almqvist's most advanced ideas are generally passed over quickly. To understand Almqvist's objectives it is necessary to understand the oppression of Swedish women in his day. This background has usually been omitted by male scholars. They seem to have forgotten that if relevant data are left out reality is falsified. As a consequence of ignoring the condition of Swedish women, scholars could say that Almqvist wasted much of his time and energy on an insignificant project. They regarded his system as "subjective-individualistic" (mainly a result of his own unhappy marriage) and said he wanted to abolish marriage, not to reform it; they overlooked its matrilineal organization, and regarded it as totally devoid of legal form.

The status of Swedish women in the 1830's and 1840's differed drastically from that of men.[2] Higher education was designed entirely for men,

---

[2]   Westman Berg (1962): 20–41, gives detailed information about the social condition of Swedish women from 1800–1850.

as were professional training and university teaching.The only obligatory instruction that was given equally to both sexes was that provided by the Church for confirmation. This included the learning of the Lutheran *Haustafel*, which decreed that in marriage the husband was to lead and the wife to obey and serve, as Sarah obeyed Abraham. By law the wife was under the guardianship of her husband. She was completely subordinate to him; everything she owned was his to do with as he pleased. He decided where to live and she had to follow. He decided how she was to use her working power. He even had the right to decide everything in the household sphere, e.g. the upbringing of the children, which was normally her job, and when he wanted sexual intercourse she had no right to refuse. He generally maintained her, but was not legally obliged to do so. She had little possibility of working outside the home, but if she did earn money he had the legal right to take every penny.

The prevailing Lutheran marriage ideology contained the belief that love between husband and wife grew out of their sexual relations. Thus it was not necessary for the partners to know each other before marriage. Even if they did not eventually fall in love with one another, they had to remain married for the rest of their lives, divorce being almost impossible to obtain. Faithfulness was expected, but only from the wife. Unfaithfulness from the husband was common and looked upon as "natural." The wife was expected always to sacrifice her own wants and needs to those of her husband and children.

An unmarried woman could not decide for herself whom she wanted to marry, nor could she handle her own affairs, because she was under the guardianship of her father or nearest male relative. Only a widow could act on her own account regarding her person and property. Most girls inherited only half as much as their brothers. Economic legislation excluded women from all the more profitable forms of livelihood. To be married was almost the only way in which a woman could exist economically and have some status in society.

A woman had to remain virgin until marriage; if she was not her husband could divorce her the day after the wedding. Sexual intercourse between partners who were not married to one another was regarded as a crime, but only the woman was punished because men could swear that they were not guilty, while a woman who became pregnant was obviously guilty.

The most difficult social problem of those days was the unemployment of unmarried women. Owing to the rapid increase in population and the declining marriage rate this group was increasing enormously, and could not find sufficient employment in the permitted forms of livelihood that were available for women: household work, unskilled labor, and factory work for the lower classes; and governess jobs for the upper classes. Consequently, a great number of unemployed women in the lower classes became prostitutes. Worst of all was the lot of the unmarried mothers. Forty-five percent of the children born in Stockholm in the 1840's were illegitimate! The father was not obliged to support such a child; the mother had no support from society and her chances to get jobs were nil. The death rate among illegitimate children was high and suicide not unusual among their mothers.

What especially concerned Almqvist in *Sara Videbeck* and in *Reasons for the dissatisfaction of Europe* was the fact that women were not allowed to maintain themselves economically in a satisfactory way. He knew they were potentially capable of participating in all kinds of professions. Why should they be forced into marriage that exploited them in order to earn their livelihood? What sort of love could exist between completely unequal partners where the one was the master of the other? And where the other, out of hatred for her oppressor, could be tempted to ruin his life by making home life a hell for him? Why should the unmarried women be forced to live in celibacy or else become prostitutes, and why should unmarried mothers be treated as outcasts? Women were forced into a kind of slavery, deprived of all human rights, rights that were given men.

If women had the power, what kind of economic system would they institute? What would be their relation to men? To find the answers Almqvist studied the works and personalities of many pioneer feminist women. The personalities of Sara Videbeck and Albert are part of the answer. Almqvist understood that equality between the sexes would mean a fundamental change in the roles of the sexes. Sara Videbeck is allowed to break or criticize all the laws and customs limiting the lives of women. Yet she is both charming and attractive, and very moral. In spite of the fact that husbands, children, and housework were then considered to be the whole world of woman, Sara is permitted to love her job as a glazier (Westman Berg 1962:220–327). Like the women of Harriet Martineau (1832–34), she illustrates the right of women to work, and shows the pleasure in work that this freedom produces. She is also allowed to love Albert, without, at the same time, having the slightest intention of changing her job or giving up her economic independence, as French socialist women (e.g. Gatti de Gamond 1838) suggested. In her love of Albert she ignores all the traditional demands to preserve her chastity until marriage and thus exemplifies also the *emancipation passionelle*, as preached by George Sand (1832, 1833) for example.

Sara at first dreams that her lover will live with her and share her work and interests, but she later realizes that this is a selfish hope and rejects it. By changing the male and the female roles, Almqvist here cleverly criticizes the patriarchal ideology which destroys the high ideal of romantic love, as it is generally interpreted to mean that the woman is expected to share the interests and love of the man (Schlegel 1799[1907]: 129, 143). Albert, on the other hand, out of his love for Sara, represents the man who learns to do without the traditional privileges of the male and to respect the independence of the woman (Almqvist 1972: 115, 123).

In the novel Sara argues for new sex roles because they make true love possible. To Almqvist, who was a prophet of romantic love since his youth, true romantic love — implying a total commitment, body and soul, both partners equally engaged — was the only moral basis for sexual intercourse because it was the only way for both partners to achieve equal happiness. His criticism of the nineteenth century marriage system in Sweden was often motivated by the argument that because of its patriarchal structure it made equality in the love relationship between the partners impossible. In *Reason for the dissatisfaction of Europe* and in his journalism during the 1840's, his compassion for women was more openly expressed and their situation used as an argument for reform.

In the novel, Sara Videbeck is made to propose matrilocal marriage. She wants to live on in her childhood home, where she will continue to earn her own living as a glazier, as she has been doing for some time. As an only child she knows she will inherit the house when her parents die. Albert will rent two of the rooms on the first floor of her house. Having been trained in her father's workshop she has a professional career from which girls by law were excluded. And being clever enough to invent some new methods and models in her craft she knows she will be among the very few women who are legally allowed to earn a living in a handicraft. She hopes to receive visits from Albert, and she visits him now and then.

Neither is to entail any economic obligation for the other. Neither will have the right to decide about the belongings of the other. They will give each other gifts, but not of such a size that either is really supporting the other. Their relationship will not follow the marriage laws of the time and will not be initiated by any religious ceremony. No mention is made of any arrangements for children. Sara, however, is given a surname, which is omitted in Albert's case. This is one indication that Almqvist has the MATRILINEAL SYSTEM in mind. Also it is briefly hinted that their future children will belong to her more than to him; that he will be close to them emotionally and give them gifts,[1] but not support them, although he wants to call them his children.

All this is woven into seemingly innocent conversations between Sara and Albert, who hardly use any legal terms at all. The following discussion shows how Sara manages to avoid falling into the traditional role of a wife.

Sara   "I don't intend to give up my trade."
Albert: "But if I rent those rooms?"
Sara: "Then I'll attend to my affairs on the ground floor by myself."
Albert: "And then you'll never attend to anything up on my floor?"
Sara: "If you stay there for any length of time, Albert, you also will have a large number of matters to attend to for yourself and must keep things in order, according to your needs. There is a good inn nearby. You can get some one to care for your rooms very cheaply, and your washing and ironing can be done by good people who will thus make a trifle for their own support, Albert. But I want you to know that I hope to invite you down for an improvised meal when I have time.[3] Perhaps you will invite me up sometime too. I shall never, never take anything that belongs to you or interfere with your mode of living — I shall merely answer you if you ask my advice, which you can take or reject, just as you please — and least of all will I ever hamper you in your work."

These daring criticisms of the patriarchal order are often left out of abbreviated editions of the novel. They were also excluded from two dramatized versions of the novel, one given on Swedish television a few years ago and the other by the Royal Dramatic Theatre, Stockholm, in 1973. Almqvist's views are usually described as advocating the substitution for the entire marriage institution by a relation that was only legitimated by love, unrestricted by laws and regulations of both society and Church, and dissolvable when the legitimation lost its validity. This description, however, leaves out all the advantages freedom gives to women, liberating them into independent human beings, the equals of men, their former masters.

In his dissertation, however, Almqvist went further. He urged the passage of laws to establish his marriage system.

Eleven years after *Sara Videbeck* appeared, Almqvist presented his utopian family system in greater detail and in a slightly different version in his dissertation *Europeiska missnöjets grunder* [Reasons for the dissatisfaction of Europe], which was published in 1850. In this work Almqvist aimed at annihilating patriarchal marriage, proposing a society with an ideal balance between men and women. The book also contains strong criticism against class discrimination and the title indicates that the pro-

---

[3]   The Sweidsh word *risp* has been incorrectly translated in *Sara Videbeck* (Almqvist 1972), as breakfast. What the original text says is improvised meal. Because that is important in the context, I have taken the liberty to correct the English translation.

blem he regarded as central to all European countries was the general dissatisfaction with class and sex discrimination. However, no solutions are presented other than the new marriage system.

The book, far ahead of its time, proposes new laws giving women complete personal freedom, including majority at the age of eighteen; political rights, education, and economic independence through professional work; control over their own property; and the right to choose where they would live and with whom they would have sexual relations. The matrilocal aspect of the system since *Sara Videbeck* seems to have disappeared, but woman's status will not depend on man but on herself. The marriage system is called the *"samband"* [connection], or "union" or "It can be done" system. Love between the partners is to be its only basis. There will be no compulsory initial ceremony, neither religious nor secular. The "husband" will not maintain the "wife". The "wife" will not be subordinate to the "husband." The connection will be a completely voluntary relation between economically independent partners. They will not be expected to cohabit if they do not want to. The connection will last as long as the love between the partners. Divorce will be obtained without legal procedure. No law will prevent the formation of new connections and it will be legally possible to have more than one connection at the same time. Jealousy will not exist. (Polyandry is thus accepted beside the already existing polygyny.)

The only legal claims on the mother will be the obligation to have her children living with her and to bring them up until their majority. They will inherit from her, males and females getting equal shares. The father will not maintain the children. It will not even be necessary to know his name. Consequently the children will belong to their mother's family and take her name. The mother and the children will together make up the home and the father will visit them.

The only legal claim on the father will be that he retain one third of his estate, which, at his death, will be inherited by a "child insurance office." This office will pay annually to every mother "an income corresponding to the minimum costs of keeping and educating the children until they attain their majority" (somewhat similar to our child allowance, but larger), so that the children will be supported until they are well established in their professions.

The children will have the legal right and duty to live with their mother until their majority. They will have a duty to obey her, but not the father. Sexual education will be compulsory for every young man and woman, and will inculcate the principle that sexual intercourse without love is immoral.

Thus Almqvist managed to solve, at least in theory, some of the most difficult problems regarding equality between the sexes. The *"samband"* indicated a way of alleviating the terrible misery of the unmarried mothers, for whose problems no solution had so far been suggested.

His system would result in the following changes in the lives of women and children:

1. No woman would have to be subordinate to a man to get bread.

2. As no woman would be married in the ordinary sense, the difference in status between married and unmarried women would automatically disappear.

3. All women would be sexually independent. No unmarried woman would have to live in celibacy or earn her living by prostitution, or be an outcast because she had children without being married. No married woman would any longer have to agree to unwanted sexual intercourse or legal prostitution.

4. No illegitimate children would exist. All children would have a secure home and good care.

5. All women would be economically independent, would share the right to work. Mothers would also choose the work they preferred, either in a profession or in the home. Because the income they received from the child insurance office would include the cost of taking care of children, they could either do the work themselves or pay somebody else to do it.

Not all the results would be favorable to women, however. Nowadays we do not consider it an ideal situation for a child to be raised by one parent, either for the parent or the child. The mother in Almqvist's *"samband"* would not even have the support of a joint family. Almqvist himself seems to have been uncertain about the injustice done to the father in his system. It was already described as a problem to Albert in *Sara Videbeck*. Almqvist was fond of children and probably a rather modern father to his own two children.

In several ways his dramas during the 1840's show how he was working on other solutions: either a central kitchen in every block, or a sort of family hotel. Women who did not like to cook would have other alternatives, while those who wished to cook would have proper training, good pay, and as much mechanical help as possible.

In his personal life, Almqvist's wife and children mostly lived outside Stockholm and he himself visited them. Although his marriage was not a very happy one, he gave his wife and children all the money he could scrape together and all his property after *Sara Videbeck* was published. His family was not directly hurt by the economic debacle that he himself suffered.

THE SOURCE OF ALMQVIST'S MATRILINEAL IDEAS

Almqvist never stated clearly the sources of his ideas about his utopian family system. The knowledge that it was derived from a "heathen" culture would undoubtedly have had an adverse effect.

Matrilineal customs are not part of the Western Christian cultural pattern, and none of the female pioneers Almqvist studied had mentioned them. The first scientific description of matrilineal systems was published in 1861 by the Swiss lawyer, J. J. Bachofen, in *Das Mutterrecht*. But Almqvist did not limit his interests to Western civilization. Being a Romantic author, exotic customs appealed to him. The Orient fascinated him; he belonged to the so-called "Indian Renaissance," and he often secretly introduced into his fiction Hindu thoughts, motives, and even words from Sanscrit literature. His friends tried to secure his appointment as professor of Indian Philology at the University of Uppsala in 1837.

In 1839, the same year that *Sara Videbeck* was published, he also published the beginning of a gigantic work, *Menniskoslägtets Saga* [History of mankind], volume one, a historic and geographic description of the whole world, starting with oriental countries. Only the first volume was finished.

History of mankind shows us how Almqvist was searching in the Orient for knowledge about the position of women in different countries. In every country described he reports on the marriage customs and the work and life of women. It is clear to him that there is a connection, between the political systems and the laws and customs limiting the lives of women. He finds most countries patriarchal and authoritarian and the women subordinate. He idealizes the very few people where women were given some freedom — e.g. the Ainu in Japan and the people of Formosa — and describes them as belonging to the most ancient Oriental way of life. To him they have preserved a pure and altruistic community from the original state of humanity and they are the source of his ideas about how to create a happy society in his own country.

History of mankind being a textbook, not fiction, Almqvist gives footnotes indicating his sources, which include many travellers' descriptions and missionary reports, some of which contain accounts of matrilineal customs. These were also the type of sources Bachofen used. The best known matrilineal system in these books seems to be that of the Nayar caste on the Malabar coast of India.[4] However, Almqvist does not use this

---

[4]   Books mentioned among Almqvist's footnotes in *History of mankind*, containing

material in his text. Although he was an expert on India he never described India in his book. There are good reasons to believe that he would have mentioned the Nayars favorably if he had continued his gigantic work but instead he wrote *Sara Videbeck*. Facts about Nayar marriage customs might also have reached him from an English author, who suggested that these customs be introduced into the Western cultural patterns.

The few words Almqvist wrote about the origin of his family system show that he regarded it as more advanced than any of the socialist systems created in France, England, and Germany. It seemed more to resemble the most ancient Oriental marriage systems, and in some respect it might be compared to one of the old Indian conjugal forms, *Gandharva*, or to prehistoric Sweden. But neither *Gandharva* nor prehistoric Sweden had anything to do with matrilineal inheritance. *Gandharva* was a form of "love-marriage," entered into without any ceremonies. The Swedes belong to the same Indo-European race as the Hindus and Almqvist believed that the original state of mankind, with equality between the sexes, must have existed in Sweden too, and especially in the part of Sweden where Sara Videbeck lived. But Almqvist's family system most resembled that of the Nayars.

The Nayars (or Nayers, Nayrs, Nairs) have been living in Kerala on the Indian southwest coast, the Malabar coast, for several thousand years. They are an influential Dravidian noble caste and their marriage system is regarded even by modern scholars as a survival from pre-Aryan days (Ehrenfels 1959). It has been described several times by Europeans since the Portuguese discovered it in the fifteenth century. Ethnographers regard it as one of the most marked matrilineal and matrilocal forms of family organization in existence.

The Nayars call their marriage *sambandham*, a Sanscrit word with the same meaning as the Swedish word *samband*, which Almqvist often used instead of the word "marriage" in describing his utopian system. The similarity between the two words is no doubt an excellent example of the linguistic relationship between the different Indo- European languages, discovered during the "Indian Renaissance."

---

descriptions of the Nayar matrilineal system, include Buchanan (1807:411–412); de Camoëns, (1572 [quoted from the English translation of certain verses in Duncan, 1799: 8–30] Hamilton (1727 [quoted from Thurston 1909:309]); Sonnerat (1782:65); Ritter (1835: 939); and Rhode (1827: 195).

Other sources available in Almqvist's days were Kerr (1811:351–353) and Munro (1817). Later ethnographic descriptions include Bachofen (1861: 198), Thurston (1909: 302–412).

Briffault (1927: 302, 700–712), and Ehrenfels (1941: 50–112). See also Ehrenfels (1959: 11–33). A present-day travellers description is Höjer (1970)

In the sources Almqvist used for *History of Mankind,* the descriptions of *Sambandham* were often vague and contradictory. They seemed to be only partly understood, mainly because they were described from an androcentric point of view, which is not the most objective view of matrilineal customs. The independent Nayar women living in polyandry (as the men were living in polygyny) were often described as prostitutes (de Camoëns 1572:14). That a man did not have a family of his own in the same sense as in a patriarchal society but lived as a member of his mother's family even as an adult is expressed as follows: "A man's mother manages his family" (Buchanan 1807:412).

Nevertheless it was possible — although a bit difficult — to pick up from these sources the main elements constituting the system. *Sambandham* was entered into without any ceremony. As in the *Gandharva* marriage, mutual love and consent were the only conditions. It had no legal standing and could be dissolved without any legal formalities, but it did not lack organization.

According to Duncan (1799:13, 29) the Nayars

Do not marry according to the usually received sense of that term in other parts of the world, but form connections of a longer or shorter duration, according to the choice in the parties... they look upon the existence or non-existence of the matrimonial contract as equally indifferent.

The grownup woman lived in her mother's home (matrilocal system):

Die Weiber bleiben aber bei den Müttern wohnen [The women, however, live with their mothers] (Ritter 1835: 939). She lives in her mother's house... (Buchanan 1807:411)

The "husband" did not cohabit with his "wife" but visited her. He did not maintain her but gave her gifts (matrilocal system):

When a lover receives admission into a house, he commonly gives his mistress some ornaments, and her mother a piece of cloth; but these presents are never of such value as to give room for supposing that the women bestow their favours from mercenary motives (Buchanan 1807: 411).

These customs have survived into our century. Briffault interviewed a Nayar man in the 1920's and reported:

There was neither permanent cohabitation nor economic association of any kind between husbands and wives. The husband was a visitor and the woman never left her maternal home. ... There was no economic bond or association between a man and his sexual mate. There was no law of maintenance; "wife and children do not possess the legal privilege of claiming maintenance from the father" ... (Briffault, Vol. I, 1927:704).

There are two sides to a marriage ... a legal and a religious. Now in the case of our marriage both elements are wanting. They are not legal because they do not create any correlative rights and duties, and because in the majority of cases there is no agreement between the contracting parties. We have no law of divorce or maintenance.

There is in fact, no fixed rule or custom as to marriages in Malabar. They are terminable at the will of either party and the law takes no notice of them (Briffault, Vol. I, 1927:705).

Polyandry was accepted and common, as well as polygyny, but there was no jealousy:

Among the Nayrs it is custom for one Nayr woman to have attached to her two males, or four, or perhaps more ... and it but rarely happens that enmity and jealousy break out on this account.... They visit her in turns (Duncan 1799 13, 14).

It is no kind of reflection on a woman's character to say that she has formed the closest intimacy with many persons. ... love, jealousy, or disgust never can disturb the peace of a Nair family (Buchanan) 1807: 411–412).

Alone in lewdness, riotous and free, No spousal rights withhold ... they know Nor jealousy's suspense, nor burning woe;
The bitter drops which oft from dear affection flow (de Camoëns 1572: 14).

The father did not support the children and they inherited nothing from him; often they did not even know his name. Thus it may be concluded that they were supported by the mother, inherited from her, and took her name (matrilineal system).

...no Nair knows his father (Buchanan 1807:412).
...the children are never heirs to their father's estate (Hamilton 1810:309).

The children are only considered as the offspring of the mother ... all relationship being counted only by female consanguity and descent. (Kerr 1811:351).

It is possible to conclude that the women were economically independent, that the children of different fathers but the same mother lived together in her home as complete sisters and brothers, and that they had far closer relationships with their mother than their father.

On all these points Almqvist's system is strikingly similar to that of the Nayars. But there are also differences. Matrilocality was not explicitly mentioned in *Reasons for the dissatisfaction of Europe*, in which he advocates the support of children by a "child allowance" system. In the Almqvist system a father has nothing to do with the rearing of children if he does not wish to be involved.

Among the Nayars a man had certain duties to his sister's children living in the house in which he resided. The maternal uncle was almost a substitute for the father of our Western family system, in all the sources Almqvist mentioned, although he himself did not use this datum.

...every man looks upon his sister's children as his heirs. He, indeed, looks upon them with the same fondness that fathers in other parts of the world have for their own children. (Buchanan 1807: 412).

...les enfants, quoi qu'en dise M. de Voltaire, n'appartiennent point à celui qui les a faits, mais au frère de la mère (Sonnerat 1782: 65).

The extended family system, typical of the Nayar caste, was hardly mentioned in Almqvist's sources. Nothing was said of the old, revered mother or grandmother, the head of the joint family. The role of her brother or nearest male relative who was her adviser was often misunderstood in the sources as the head of the family. (Buchanan 1807: 412).

That some sort of communism existed inside the family was mentioned by Buchanan (1807:412) — "each individual has a right to a share of the income" — but he did not describe how the old mother was responsible for this sharing of property and for the peace and collaboration among all the members of the family. Nor did he mention that the Nayars were a landed gentry, that the land was mostly owned by the women, and that they derived their income from agriculture. Almqvist could probably not have known such details. Only modern reports describe how the men left their mother's homes, where they worked during the day, to go to their "wife" and children in the evenings and then return in the mornings. All the obvious advantages to the women of the existing system were generally left out of the reports, e.g. that the Nayar girls were clearly privileged by inheritance and education.

All travellers, ancient as well as modern, stress the fact that the Nayars seem to be a people with a very happy family life. Ehrenfels (1959), for example, states that the main reason was that the matrilineal family pattern was much more democratic than the patrilineal: (1) Men are not treated as subordinate beings, and do not acquire minority complexes. (2) Their status is not dependent upon the status of their "wife" but upon themselves. (3) There are no double standards regarding sexual morality. If the young woman is allowed premarital sexual relations, the young man is allowed the same. If the mature woman can have several sexual relations at the same time the men have the same right. (4) The "husband" is not expected to work in his "wife's" house as the wife has to work in her "husband's" home in patriliny. Instead, he continues to live and to work in his mother's home as he did before the relation to his "wife." (5) The authority among the Nayars never rests in one person only. The eldest female member who is the head of the family has to listen to her brother or other male advisers. The children have to obey their mother and their maternal uncle. But then they also have a very close and psychologically important relation to their father.

As a consequence, Nayars are known to be well trained in democratic collaboration. Both men and women are known, even internationally, as excellent politicians (Ehrenfels 1959:20–23).

As a complement to the picture of the Nayars I will add the points of view of two modern members of the caste whom I interviewed in the 1960's:

Lakshmi Menon, Minister of State for External Affairs in the Government of India, New Delhi, former Chairman of the Status of Women Comission of the United Nations, former professor of history, is an imposing and strong woman, She does not regret that matriliny is now disappearing among the Nayars as a result of the new inheritance law after "Independence":

All boys and girls now inherit equal shares everywhere in India. That means that Nayar girls are no longer privileged as regards inheritance. The matrilineal customs had started to degenerate anyhow, because they did not suit modern society with its industrialization, urbanization, greater population mobility, dissppearance of extended families, etc. Besides they meant a very heavy constraint on the eldest daughter of a family. She had to be trained to be the head of the joint family (which often consisted of a hundred persons) and could not leave the home, could not choose a profession or be a politician.

I asked whether Indian women did not need privileges, e.g. matriliny, to be able to reach equality between the sexes in society, just as the Harijans got certain privileges so that they could be raised out of their position as outcasts. Menon's answer was: "No. We will reach equality between the sexes without help from inheritance privileges. But we will have to fight hard to reach it, just as we have fought to get all our new laws improving the position of women after Independence."

Gundhappa Radjasekharan, with a doctorate in education at the University of Uppsala, has spent several years in Sweden. He made the following statement:

My mother belongs to the Nayar caste. You would probably not understand our family system, if I described it, because its main characteristic is that all women are economically independent, which you are not here in Sweden. Important things I can discuss only with women, not with men. We are used to that at home....

...I am more related to my mother than to my father, because of the influences I got from her during the nine months she was pregnant with me.... Your author Almqvist might well have known the basic facts about our marriage system. We have been known in Europe since the Portuguese started to write about us.

It is certain that Almqvist was influenced by the Nayar customs, as they were known in his day. There are too many similarities between their system and his: *Sambandham* and *samband*; visiting marriage; no cohabitation; polyandry without jealousy; father's name not necessarily known; man's gifts not meant to support woman; no initial ceremony; no fixed rules as regards forming and dissolving the connection; children of different fathers living togeher as complete sisters and brothers in their mother's home, etc. Thus he was twenty-two years ahead of Bachofen in his interest in matriliny. Two of the travellers' books Almqvist mentioned, those by Ritter and Buchanan, were used by Bachofen in his description of the Nayars (Bachofen 1861:198).

However, it is striking that Almqvist is much more conscious than were his sources of the advantages of the Nayar system to the women.

A proposal that the customs of the Nayar caste be introduced into Europe was put forward in 1793 by a young English writer, James Lawrence, who was influenced by Mary Wollstonecraft and combined her concern to improve the lot of women with his own desire for a happier way of life for everybody. He was not completely familiar with the Nayar customs; for example, he did not know about the joint family, and was unrealistic about the economic institution, apparently because he did not know that the Nayars were great landowners. But he did not hide the fact that his model was the Nayar society.

Lawrence's article, "*Über die Vorteile des Systems der Galanterie und Erfolge bei den Nayren*" [On the advantages of the courting and inheritance customs among the Nayers], was published anonymously in the German magazine *Der Neue Deutsche Mercur* [The New German Mercury] (1793), edited by the well known author, C. M. Wieland. Later it was published in his novel *Paradies der Liebe* [Paradise of Love] (1801), the second edition being called *Das Reich der Nairen* [The Province of the Nairs].

Lawrence propagandized openly for the liberation of women and wanted to make men conscious of their prejudices against women so that they would help their sisters and wives to get out of their subordinate status. He did not understand that in Europe women lacked the right to work but thought that liberation could be reached most quickly by introducing the Nayar marriage system. Consequently he described all the main aspects, including the role of the maternal uncle.

Being especially interested in love, Lawrence dwelt upon the need to improve sexual relations, so that no woman would be forced to marry against her will or have to experience sexual intercourse without love. The partners would be more careful about being agreeable to one another, since divorce was easy. The connection would last as long as the love of the partners and no laws would prevent the partners from forming new, happier connections. Some noble people would always practice fidelity but polyandry and polygyny would be available.

The following quotations from Lawrence (in my translation) demonstrate: the matrilineal customs of the Nayars; Lawrence's traditional attitude towards the tasks of women; his suggestions that society should intervene and give child allowances to poor mothers; and his summary of the patriarchal customs that would surely disappear:

Let the children belong to their mother and inherit only her property (1793:185).

After her death her property should be distributed among her children (1793:186).

The children can stay with their mother who will be responsible for bringing them up (1793:186).

The care and control of the children must be entirely handed over only to the mother (1793:250).

There is the same reason behind these two facts: (1) a child has no legal right to use its father's name and inherit his property; (2)...a father has no responsibility to bring up his child and to maintain it (1793:250).

The word "father" can even be erased from the code of laws (1793:185).

Every woman should be allowed to live completely without male control and enjoy independence without any sort of constraint...(1793:185).

Women should be allowed to live alone, dependent on themselves only, and run their own households (1793:249).

Women are meant for household duties (1793:249).

Lawrence never considered the problems of women in maintaining themselves if they were not supported by men while they worked in their own households, although he briefly suggested that the state could help them if necessary:

It should be arranged that every woman who lives in poverty receives a fixed sum of money from public taxes according to the number of her children (1793:119).

Almqvist was also deeply compassionate about subordinate wives who had to cohabit without love, about unmarried women forced to live in celibacy or prositution, unmarried mothers living as outcasts, and he created new sex roles in *Sara Videbeck*, for Sara did not obey her husband. But he never summarized the advantages of breaking down patriarchal marriage in the outspoken way that Lawrence did:

There is no more reason for women to obey men than for men to obey women (1793:172).

Would not every man of noble feelings prefer to be loved by an educated and stimulating Eloise[5] than to be obeyed in the way a weary Sara obeys the orders of her master Abraham (1793:256).

What a wonderful change this sytem would bring about in the manners of the female sex! Women would no longer be those insignificant creatures ... but they would develop a more determined and, if I may say so, a more male character 1793:250).

When no married women exist, there will be no wh**** either; when no child can be legitimate, it will not be possible to call any child a bastard (1793: 185).

Although Almqvist rejected Lawrence's traditional attitude towards woman and household work, as well as the role of the maternal uncle, and advocated that men and women share the right to work, there are striking similarities both in intention and detail between Lawrence and Almqvist. It seems almost as if Lawrence had inspired Almqvist to create a new woman.

In spite of this, Almqvist could not have learned about the Nayars only from Lawrence who does not mention several Nayar traits found in Almqvist's *samband*.

Lawrence's article stimulated other authors besides Almqvist. The following aphorism appeared in the magazine *Athenaeum* in 1794, published by Friedrich and Wilhelm Schlegel (1794): "The male sex cannot be improved by the female one, until the inheritance system of the Nayers from mother to child will be introduced."

---

[5] This is probably a reference to the heroine in Jean-Jacques Rousseau's famous novel, *La Nouvelle Héloise*, published in 1761.

CONCLUSIONS

Against the background of the social situation of women in his day, Almqvist's radical analyses, based on matriliny, sound shockingly modern: e.g. his clearsighted understanding of the mechanisms of the patriarchal marriage system and his insight into its function of depriving women — both married and unmarried — of fundamental human rights; his brave challenge of sexual exploitation of women, his compassion for the desperate need of the right to work even among married women; his abolition of the male privilege to use a wife as a private servant.

It has been proved here that he introduced matriliny in his works, at first in *Sara Videbeck* (1839) and then fully developed in *Reasons for the Dissatisfaction of Europe* (1850), and that he used the family system of the Indian Nayar caste as a model. That he managed to find a marriage system that was extremely democratic, compared to almost every other system, was itself remarkable. It is evident that he knew the Nayar customs both from travellers' descriptions in the same sources used by Bachofen and in an article by the English author, James Lawrence. There is no doubt that his goal was complete equality between the sexes.

Almqvists understanding of Nayar matriliny is also remarkable when compared to travellers and scholars in Western culture, who have difficulty in understanding marriage systems that are not planned mainly out of concern for masculine satisfaction. However, he was not the only European author who wanted to raise the position of women and improve society by introducing Nayar customs.

Several examples have been given of the androcentric attitudes among scholars towards Almqvist's utopian family system and the false conclusions they reached because of their bias.

Almqvist's marriage system was not "subjective-individualistic" but rather a heroic relief expedition, motivated not mainly by personal experiences but by a strong compassion for women. It was not aimed at abolishing marriage, but at abolishing the Christian marriage institution in Sweden in his day, where husbands were privileged, wives exploited, and divorce almost impossible. It was a system not without legal norms, with a matrilineal organization intended to raise the status of oppressed women, abolish patriarchal customs, and thus achieve a democratic society. Moreover, his work was advanced for his time and also for the present in its appreciation of the greater morality of "heathen" than of Christian customs.

APPENDIX

The impact of Almqvist's family system on Swedish society has not yet been studied in detail and only a tentative outline can be given.

Most of the changes he recommended, except matriliny, have now been incorporated into the laws of Sweden. This is due to the efforts of many pioneers, some of whom were inspired by Almqvist. His system could never be referred to openly in official reform discussions. The label "immoral" has continued to be fixed to it because one of its results would be that the common secret polygamy of men would be openly accepted and also available to women.

By law Swedish women now have political rights, education, professions, control over their own persons, property and working power, the right to decide about their own children and about themselves with regards to where to live and with whom to have sexual relations, etc. No children are regarded as illegitimate, they all have child allowances; unmarried mothers are not outcasts and can marry; divorce is possible; fathers have less authoritarian attitudes to their children; and the custom of the formal wedding is disappearing, even as a legal claim.

Nevertheless patriarchal ideology remains in practice, with men more highly valued than women. Equality between the sexes has not yet been realized, although it is the accepted ideology, both publicly and privately. Traditional sex roles are common: married women are more responsible for the household and children than their husbands and have less freedom to choose professional work (see above, where the omission on the stage of Sara's criticism of this custom is described). Child allowances are too small to give mothers the right to work, as Almqvist wanted. Most women have a lower income than most men. Although the rigid control of women's sexual life has disappeared, jealousy has not, nor has men's privilege to take the erotic initiative. Sexual exploitation of women is still common.

Sara Videbeck is still regarded as an advanced role model and greeted with enthusiasm on the stage. Women are still working to make this role model possible, e.g. the women's rights organization, the Fredrika Bremer Society, has recently demanded that married women should be legally regarded as maintainers in the same way as married men. A modern women's liberation movement organization, Group 8, is calling attention to the deplorable consequences of patriarchal ideology upon female sexuality, and demanding changes.

Much more work will have to be done to abolish the discrimination against women that Almqvist regarded as built into the institutions of patriarchal society, created without female collaboration, and therefore more favorable to men.

REFERENCES

ALMQVIST, CARL J. L.
1839 [1972]   *Det går an* [It can be done], translated as *Sara Videbeck*, introduction by Staffan Björck. New York: Twayne Publishers.

1850 [1923]   *Europeiska missnöjets grunder* [Reasons for the dissatisfaction of Europe] in *Samlade skrifter* 16 [Collected works 16]. Edited by F. Böök. Stockholm: Bonniers.
1839   *Menniskoslägtets saga* [History of mankind], volume one. Stockholm: Hörbergska Boktryckeriet.
BACHOFEN, J. J.
1861   *Das Mutterrecht* [Mother-right]. Stuttgart: Krais und Hoffmann.
BRIFFAULT, R.
1927   *The mothers*, volume one. London: G. Allen and Unwin.
BUCHANAN, F.
1807   *A journey from Madras through the countries of Mysore, Canara and Malabar.* London: Cadell. (Also 1810 in J. Pinkerton, *Voyages and travels, volume eight.* London: Longman).
DE CAMOENS, LUIS
1572 [1799]   Os Lusíadas. *Asiatic Researches* 5. Calcutta.
DE GAMOND, GATTI
1838   *Fourier et son système.* Paris: Librairie Social.
DUNCAN, J.
1799   Historical remarks on the coast of Malabar with some descriptions of the manners of its inhabitants. *Asiatic Researches* 5. Calcutta.
EHRENFELS, R.
1941   *Mother-right in India.* London: Osmanis University.
1959   "Kvinnor på väg" [Women on the march] in *Kvannovärld i vardande* [Women's world being created]. Edited by the Fredrika Bremer Society. Stockholm.
HAMILTON, A.
1727   *New account of the East Indies*, volume one. Edinburgh. (Also 1810 in J. Pinkerton *Voyages and travels*, volume eight. London: Longman.)
HOJER, SIGNE
1970   *Kvinnomakt — könsroller i tropikerna* [Woman power — sex-roles in the tropics]. Stockholm: Askild och Kärnekull.
KERR, R.
1811–1824   *A general history and collection of voyages and travels.* Edinburgh, London.
LAWRENCE, JAMES
1793   *"Über die Vorteile des Systems der Galanterie und Erfolge bei den Nayren"* [On the advantages of the courting and inheritance customs among the Nayers], *Der Neue Deutsche Mercur* 2. Edited by C. M. Wieland. Published anonymously
1801   *Paradies der Liebe* [Paradise of Love]. (Second edition entitled *Das Reich der Nairen* [The province of the Nairs].)
MARTINEAU, HARRIET
1832–1834   *Illustrations of political economy*, volumes one to nine. London; C. Fox.
1837   *Society in America*, two volumes. Paris: A. and W. Galignani.
MUNRO, T.
1817   *The judicial system of the Malabar coast.* Place and publisher unknown.
RITTER, C.
1835   *Die Erdkunde* [Geography], volume five. Berlin: Reimer.

RHODE, J. G.

1827   *Über Religiöse Bildung, Mythologie und Philosophie der Hindus...* [On the religious education, mythology and philosophy of the Hindus...], volume one. Leipzig: Blockhaus.

SAND, GEORGE [DUDEVANT, AURORE]

1832   *Indiana.* Paris: J.-P. Roret.

1833   *Lélia.* Paris: H. Dupuy, Tenré.

SCHLEGEL, FRIEDRICH

1799 [1907]   *Lucinde.* Edited by R. Frank. Leipzig: Insel-Verlag.

SCHLEGEL, FRIEDRICH, WILHELM SCHLEGEL

1794 [1882]   *Athenaeum* in *Friedrich Schlegels Prosaische Jugenschriften.* Edited J. Minor. Vienna.

SONNERAT, M.

1782   *Voyage aux Indes Orientales et a la Chine 1774 – 1781.* Paris: published by the author.

THURSTON, E.

1909   *Castes and tribes of Southern India,* volume five. Madras: Government Press.

TRISTAN, FLORA:

1838   *Pérégrinations d'une Paria.* Paris: A. Bertrand.

WESTMAN BERG, KARIN

1962   *Studier i Carl Jonas Love Almqvists kvinnouppfattning* [Studies in C.J.L. Almqvist's views on women]. Women's History Archives 3. Gothenburg: Scandinavian University Books. (Dissertation with English summary, Uppsala University).

SECTION FIVE

Women in Anthropology

Introduction

The papers in this section describe women's status in the discipline of anthropology in England and the United States and the new perspectives that women anthropologists are evolving as a spin-off from the women's liberation movement. The first three papers deal with the problems women encounter as students, teachers, and fieldworkers. Although the statistics I include about women in U.S. anthropology do not exactly parallel those about women in English anthropology, the similarities are striking. The last four papers are critical evaluations of the body of received knowledge and assumptions regarding sex roles; they raise new questions in theory, methodology, and fieldwork, which reveal that women anthropologists are developing independent approaches.

Caplan's survey of three schools of the University of London where anthropology is taught, over the six-year period from 1966 to 1972, shows that women are most numerous at the lecturer level and that their numbers decrease at each higher level, only one of the eight professors of anthropology at the University being a women. Comparing the ranks of women and men in anthropology departments of U.S. colleges and universities in two academic years, 1971–1972 and 1973–1974, the Committee on the Status of Women in Anthropology found a similar situation:

In comparison with men, women are generally under-represented in the higher tenured ranks and over-represented in the lower ranks. The discrepancy at the professorial rank is most unfavorable to women: only 12% of the women are professors, as compared to 28% of the men. In comparison to 1971–1972, the percentage of women professors actually declined by two points (1973:10–11).

According to the Committee's report, "the under-representation of women in the higher ranks was more severe at the prestigious institutions." The

Committee's data "suggest that this is not because of any deficiency in their training but simply because of their sex."

Caplan notes that over a five-year period women wrote 19 percent of the articles published in *Man*, the leading British anthropological journal. In the *American Athropologist*, the leading U.S. journal, women wrote 17 percent of the articles and 19 percent of the reviews during 1974.

Caplan also points out that women comprise 16 percent of those who obtained research money from the Social Science Research Council, the main source of research funds. However, a much larger number of women do the research without receiving much of the credit or economic rewards, according to Caplan:

...often the project is actually carried out by people other than the person who actually applies for the money. And in nearly all such cases of which we...know personally, the "frontman" is a male, while a larger number of the actual researchers are female. At SOAS [the School of Oriental and African Studies], for instance, the category of "research assistant" over the five-year period has been overwhelmingly filled by women (69 percent).

Caplan's survey also shows that the proportion of women who received the Ph.D. in anthropology at the three colleges of the University of London is 36 percent. In the United States, the proportion of women who received Ph.D's in anthropology from the top five universities jumped from 19 percent for the period 1963–1968 to 31 percent for the period 1969–1970 (United States Office of Education n.d.). Although this represents a considerable increase, the proportion is lower than the 36 percent of women Ph.D.'s in the three schools of the University of London surveyed by Caplan.

Analyzing the factors underlying the decreasing numbers of women in English anthropology from 60 percent at the Bachelor's level to 52 percent at the Master's, to 36 percent of the Ph.D.'s, to 23 percent of the staff, to 19 percent of those whose work is published in *Man*, and 16 percent of those who receive research money from the Social Science Research Council, Barker points out that "pre-selection in anthropology acts against any but extra well-qualified and...ambitious girls getting the chance to study the subject."

Supervisors treat male and female students differently. Since women students do not represent much of a future threat, some supervisors collect them as members of their "tribe," as "clients," the women maintaining dependent emotional and intellectual relationships with their male "gurus." Thus, only a woman student is accused, when she marries, of disloyalty to her teacher and of a lack of seriousness about her career. In fact, Barker notes, "marriage is the institution which produces many of the difficulties of women." Concerned about whether occupational goals are compatible with marriage, before graduation only 21 percent of the women, as against 41 percent of the men, consider an academic career.

The important break occurs between the Master's degree, usually based on library research, and the Ph.D., based on fieldwork, "the initiation by fire which allows entry to teaching jobs." After graduation, fewer women than men undertake fieldwork because the women believe that the period away from home base will reduce their chance of marriage.

Many male anthropologists go into the field with their wives, which reduces loneliness and provides personal services and support. But it is less usual for women to take their husbands into the field, says Barker, and even rarer for husbands to provide wives with the same services that wives provide for husbands. If a husband and wife do fieldwork together, on their return the man is selected for the desirable job in an anthropology department. Married women have little bargaining power because they feel they must take jobs in schools that are close to the home.

The greater social and domestic visibility of women is used to account for their "shortcomings," according to Barker. If they are unmarried, or married but childless, women are regarded as too young and unsettled to be considered for the good jobs but, since salaries are age-related, women who return to work when their children are grown are told that they are too old and expensive. Faced with a choice between hiring equally well-qualified women and men, the latter are chosen.

Thus, Barker concludes, the relatively small number of women academics in anthropology is due to the fact that the work situation is not "gender neutral"; even in academia women are defined and circumscribed by the general social expectations about marriage and sex roles.

The fieldwork situation is also often characterized by status ambiguity for women, according to Bujra, based on their self-evaluation in their own culture and on the status of women in the cultures they study. In the West, says Bujra, professional women feel that in order to succeed they must choose between two roles: "pseudo-man," and "feminine woman." The "pseudo-male" approach in anthropology means accepting the assumption that men are the principal actors in the important social spheres, and that women anthropologists who study women are second-rate researchers. Women often feel that they must assume a "pseudo-male" identity with male informants, although men never play a "pseudo-female" role in order to acquire information from women.

However, playing the "pseudo-male" role in communities where sex segregation is enforced and where women take no overt part in public affairs may compromise rapport with the women. This would distort the understanding of events, since women's influence in public affairs is often underestimated. Also, in societies where women do not participate directly in politics, they may be less articulate informants than men, but their information may be as valuable. Thus, different fieldwork techniques must be developed to gain information from the women, for a political system can be understood only when it is studied from the perspectives of both the ruled and the rulers, according to Bujra.

Bujra also compares the problems confronting single women with those who are married and bring husbands and/or children into the field. In sex-segregated societies, single women are constantly subjected to attempts to resocialize them into the local roles for women. As single women they may not be allowed to attend certain ceremonies, may not be fully admitted to the company of married women, and may be ridiculed if they are unable to do the hard physical labor expected of single women. When a husband and wife go into the field together, he often urges her to behave according to local expectations about a wife's role rather than as a fellow worker, in order to collect what he defines as accurate data. The best situation, Bujra concludes, is for a woman to go into the field with children, but not with a husband. Children are "generally an unmitigated help," aside from the problem of inadequate medical facilities in many areas.

Discussing the significance of women's studies, Ifeka points out that what is specific to such studies is the awareness of "the female factor." an awareness notable for its absence in traditional anthropology and one which raises a number of questions for exploration. To what extent does the female factor determine the political and cultural structures of a society? How do women actually adapt to a male-dominated system? To what extent is female status dependent on or independent of male status? Is the extent to which women control resources a primary basis for the distribution of power? How do women structure themselves into an organized collectivity? How do women's organizations function to produce and maintain women's solidarity, reduce individualism, and develop consciousness of themselves and their roles? Are women's value systems, their inner ethos, structured by or independent of the public, central value system? Do both women and men have a concealed view of the other sex?

The papers by the U.S. women anthropologists indicate the distortions that ensue in theory, methodology, and findings when the "male factor" is assumed to be central and the "female factor" is represented as subordinate or negligible. The paper on Australian aboriginal women illustrates the discrepancies that occur in ideology and data when, on the one hand, the male factor is paramount and, on the other hand, both female and male factors are given equal wight.

Generally depicted by male ethnographers as ill-treated drudges and pawns in a male exchange system, the Australian aboriginal women are shown by women anthropologists to play crucially important economic roles which are acknowledged and repsected in their own societies. They exercise full control over their reproductive functions and religious rituals and participate significantly in the marriage system, from which they accrue important benefits.

The authors conclude that the androcentrism of the male scholars, or the view of the male factor as central, is the primary aspect of their general ethnocentrism, and that androcentrism "blinds the men to the realities of aboriginal life, leading to a distorted representation of this life." The women scholars, on the other hand, reveal that despite the great inroads that European colonization has made on aboriginal culture, the women and men generally continue to strive to maintain the traditional egalitarianism between the sexes.

In "Women, knowledge, and power," the central theme is the crucial connection between women's status and their access to the valued knowledge of a society. In the West, where the male factor has long been primary, the kinds of knowledge that are culturally valued have long been determined by men. By preventing women and other subordinate groups from carrying into action their own definitions of valued knowledge and from gaining full access to the knowledge that the ruling elites define as valued, these men have perpetuated their own hegemony. Thus the male elites have assigned to the male sex the roles and traits that are pre-defined as positive, attributing to women and other oppressed groups those from the cultural repertoire that are negative.

Exploring this theme in relation to women's status in three societies — Moroccan, Tlingit Indian, and black Barbadian — the authors demonstrate that the egalitarian relationships between women and men among the Tlingit and Barbadians derives from their equal access to local economic and political activities, which in turn leads to equal access to the knowledge that is valued in their own subcultures, as well as that of the dominant society. Moroccan women, however, are subordinated to such an extent that their access to valued knowledge is very limited and it is difficult for them to organize against their oppression.

In "Class, commodity, and the status of women, " Leacock notes that women's status and various forms of the family are peripheral considerations in social analysis. This hides the reality of the family in a class-stratified society as a crucial institution for the exploitation of both women and men and impedes the search to understand the origins and perpetuation of class society. This way of dealing with women's status and family forms is analagous to the treatment of racial and national oppression as secondary issues by contemporary Marxists, according to Leacock. Although Marx analyzed exploitation as a principle that is colorless, raceless, and sexless, contemporary scholars and self-styled revolutionaries, white and male, are centrally concerned with the exploitation of white males. This accentuates the divisions between white, male industrial workers and those who are neither industrial workers, nor white and male.

Leacock also points out that a number of contemporary anthropologists, both male and female, insist that male dominance over women has always existed everywhere. In the sway of a resurgent biological determinism, these anthropologists generalize from data gathered in the twentieth century, ignoring the global changes over the last five hundred years brought about by European mercantilism, colonialism, and imperialism, and "transmuting the totality of tribal decision-making structures into the power terms of their own society."

Using ethnohistorical data, Leacock cites examples of pre-class societies in Africa and the New World where women and men shared authority through the collective functions and dispersed nature of decision-making. The Europeans sought to break up the collectivity, in which individual autonomy meshed with group interdependence, and supplant it by their own system of hierarchical controls, in which the individual family was the basic unit. With the separation of unitary social systems into public and private spheres, the "male supremacy" of ethnographic accounts began to take shape, "although doubtless often exaggerated as largely male ethnographers recorded the views and experiences of largely male informants."

In conclusion, Leacock urges cross-cultural ethnohistorical research to "redress the imbalance" and to cast new light on the nature and origins of the subordination of women.

REFERENCES

COMMITTEE ON THE STATUS OF WOMEN IN ANTHROPOLOGY
  1973   Statistical data on occupational status of women in anthropology departments. *Anthropology Newsletter* (November): 10–11.
UNITED STATES OFFICE OF EDUCATION
  n.d.   *Earned degrees conferred*, 72–2. Washington, D.C.: National Center for Educational Statistics.

Women in the Anthropology Profession – 1

DIANA BARKER

Tessa Blacksone (1973) in "The Scarce Academics" uses findings from the London School of Economics Higher Education Research Unit's survey of university teachers in Britain to show that the proportion of women declines as one moves from researchers (23 percent), to lecturers (12 percent), to senior lecturers and readers (6 percent), to professors (1 percent). She suggests that women are not discriminated against when appointments are made to academic posts — because equal proportions of women and men candidates are offered jobs, and the women who have managed enter the profession are slighly less qualified than their male colleagues. Rather, she suggests that the position of women in the wider society leads them to have role expectations which cause them to drop out of the serious pursuit of a profession, i.e., it is the women who discriminate themselves out of the job market — possibly aided and abetted by their teachers, since "they [may] not receive the same sponsorship and encouragement as their male peers." (This "evidence" for lack of discrimination could be disputed on the basis that men probably set their sights higher and also apply for more jobs in more parts of the country, so that they are candidates for more jobs. And the point about lower qualifications may be a feature of women being concentrated in the arts and social sciences.)

But beyond this suggestion of lack of encouragement, Blackstone felt able to proffer no evidence on the way (to use Goffman's phrase) "the mark is cooled out," on how women are taught to accept that they do not want or are not worthy or able to become academics, or that they should aim to be "low flyers" — in short-term research posts, part-time teaching, or journal sub-editing (see Hughes 1973).

It is therefore of interest to look closely at one particular area — the social sciences — where there is a high proportion of women students but not a particularly high proportion of women staff, and at one particular discipline, anthropology, as a possible way of sensitizing ourselves to the processes involved. This allows, of course, for the fact that in many cases these are just micro-academic examples. Of course, many of the academic examples are just microcosms of the general social pressures to which Blackstone refers.[1]

The London Women's Anthropology Group decided to try to get some measure of the extent and timing of women's withdrawal from anthropology by collecting information on the proportions of men and women who attained various qualifications in anthropology from the colleges within London University (the London School of Economics, University College, and the School of Oriental and African Studies) over a five-year period. The data follow the general trend that the higher the degree, the smaller the proportion of women: women comprised 60 percent of those getting first degrees in anthropology, 52 percent of those getting master's degrees, 36 percent of those getting doctorates, and 23 percent of staff during the period (for further details, see Caplan 1973). The important break is between those getting master's degrees and those getting doctorates: doctorates based on fieldwork (as opposed to library research) are the initiation by fire that allows entry to teaching jobs.

We also tried to collect information from the three departments about what happened to their graduates, or indeed what the FIRST jobs of their graduates were. This information was marked by its absence. (This is certainly not a peculiar feature of anthropology. Most university departments are prepared to spend enormous amounts of time and patience dealing with the problems — academic and emotional — of their students while enrolled, but once these young men and women have left the university, the staff wash their hands by writing references without ever discovering which job, if any, the young person achieves. It would add an extra dimension to discussions on changing the nature of courses — with what OUGHT a graduate in sociology or anthropology become acquainted: particular empirical studies? Marx? path analysis? linguistics? — if we had concrete evidence of the relevance of *any* particular nuggets to the future life interests of the majority of students.)

We were thus thrown back onto using the results of surveys done by other people — notably those by Kelsall, et al. (1970, 1972) and Abbott (1969). These, unfortunately, deal with "the social sciences" and "so-

[1] See the American Sociological Association i.p., American Historical Association 1971; American Political Science Association 1972.

ciology and social anthropology," not with anthropology as a separate discipline.

Abbott (1969: Table 9) shows that, compared with sociologists, anthropologists are very much the sons and daughters of the upper middle class (over 60 percent fall in this category). This is partly because the particular universities where anthropology has been taught have not contained a large lower middle-class or working-class intake; partly because anthropology is a "non-school" subject and "not useful"; partly because it is less known and only those who know and understand the difference between sociology and anthropology would be likely to apply to an anthropology department.

Kelsall and Abbott agree that equal proportions of men and women get first-class and upper second-class degrees in social studies/sociology and anthropology. More women get lower seconds while more men get thirds or pass degrees. But this homogeneity ceases after graduation, when the aspirations of men and women vary markedly. More men than women plan to undertake further study after graduation, though equal numbers actually do so — women drift in and men opt out. The majority of women take Diplomas in Education or social work training courses, regardless of the class of their degrees, while the men take doctorates, master's degrees, or other professional training.

Noteworthy is Abbott's finding that before graduation only half as many women as men (21 percent against 41 percent)THINK OF THE POSSIBILITY of an academic career. But she also noted:

Few of the female graduands [in sociology or anthropology] in fact plan to give up their career after graduation for marriage or children... Most are determined to use their degree... [But] many openly stated that they (have) to consider what occupational goals would be compatible with marriage rather than what they would do given a completely free choice. This makes social work and teaching desirable for other than purely vocational reasons.

A further loss to anthropology after graduation occurs when a substantial number of anthropologists move sideways — into sociology — for their postgraduate training (19 percent of Abbott's sample planned to do this, as opposed to 4 percent who planned to move the other way). It would not be surpising if a substantial proportion of these were women, given the problems of anthropological fieldwork.

Kelsall found that, six years after they graduated, women who undertook postgraduate degrees had a worse record of completion than men did, especially for doctorates. (The difference was less marked for master's degrees, and women had a rather better record for "other professional qualifications.")

Kelsall also found that, by six years after graduation, half of all women graduates had dropped out of gainful employment altogether. This held for all career patterns on graduation, except for women who had university teaching or research in mind before they graduated. Among the latter a fairly high proportion apparently succeeded in realizing their initial plans, and subsequent withdrawal was a good deal less marked. This confirms Blackstone's suggestion that an academic job allows freedom to organize the work as one thinks fit, and the vocation and interest of the work encourage one to continue. (Her finding that married women with children are in fact, the only group of university women whose publication rate is as high as that of their comparable male colleagues is interesting in this context.)

Our studies and those of Abbott and Kelsall suggest that much of the "cooling out" has occurred before graduation and more occurs before potsgraduate work is completed. The standard explanation is the following.

"Women are their own worst enemies. They themselves, not the profession as such, take a short-term view of their academic careers and put first priority on finding a husband and having children. Any job they may take must fit around this (hence overwhelming numbers of women become schoolteachers). More specifically women choose anthropology as a trendy liberal arts course — of great intrinsic interest and broadening to the consciousness — without any intention of making a career within the discipline. Men, by contrast, think much more seriously before they go to the university and choose their subjects instrumentally, with a view to using their university course as a basis for a job. Thus, one reason why so many more of the men entering the discipline finally make it into teaching jobs is because of PRESELECTION."

We would argue against this that such empirical evidence as exists suggests that both men AND women who study what may loosely be categorized as "humanities" have, at the start, very vague ideas about what they will do at the end of their time at the university. Both sexes appear to feel that the world is their oyster until some time during their final year.

Certainly there is need for research to discover the interactional processes between undergraduates, between staff and students, and between students and their parents that contribute to the observed discrepancies between men and women. It may be that the relations of academics with their students are more sexist than they recognize. (A few happy male chauvinists believe that nothing SHOULD be changed, because there is enough competition already.) We would certainly argue, with Blackstone, that the sexes SHOULD be treated differently, that for several generations a positive discrimination is needed to raise women's aspirations, and that this encouragement should continue all through their course and beyond. As matters stand, at the end of each year the faculty wrings its hands over the girl who gets a first but refuses to change from the "low-flying" job pattern on which she had settled before she took her examinations.

But the argument so far has blandly accepted that there is no prejudice against women in the academic world. We have often discussed whether we felt discrimination existed within the universities and specifically within the discipline of anthropology. This (honest) emphasis on "felt discrimination" may seem unfortunate politically, because it leaves us open to charges of false consciousness and persecution delusions. We can counter this, of course, by saying that whether or not the chauvinism or the structural disadvantages we experience are "objectively" there, our collective feeling that they exist is important and requires explanation. It is important if for no other reason than that we can all cite instances when we have consciously adapted our behavior because of our perceptions of the likely reactions of (supposed) sexism of our seniors and peers.

In any event, we argue that we feel discrimination because it IS there. In support of this, we can present a few instances, all of them first-hand experiences of members of our group. We have heard of many, many more, but we are (we hope) suitably skeptical. Our evidence is based mainly on our experiences as graduate students and job seekers, but because preselection has been mentioned, we should note that preselection in anthropology ensures that only unusually well qualified and (initially, at least) ambitious girls will get the chance to study the subject. Anthropology is largely taught at Oxford and Cambridge, where there are low proportions of women students; one of the London colleges that teaches anthropology exercises a quota system, not allowing more than 50 percent of women among its anthropology undergraduates, whatever the quality of the applicants of the two sexes. The husband of one member of our group, when working on an admissions committee charged with checking through Universities Central Council for Admissions forms and issuing provisional places at a provincial university that taught anthropology, was told by the chairman that it was the policy of the committee to exercise more stringent requirements for women than for men.

After graduation there occurs a problem specific to anthropology — fieldwork, supposedly the *sine qua non* of a teaching job. As mentioned above, fewer women than men undertake the prolonged, first-hand study of a distant society for a doctorate. Why? Are we not tough enough, not committed enough? Apart from those cases where governments are unwilling to let women go alone into distant areas, the problems faced by women are usually the same as the problems faced by men: loneliness and lack of personal support. But many men anthropologists have their wives with them in the field. How many men could take time from their careers to go with a wife or girl friend into the field for twelve to eighteen months? A woman, it seems, also needs a wife/servant.

Another important consideration for a woman is whether, if she goes away, she will get married or miss the boat. This is by no means a trivial problem for a woman in our society, scoff who will. Many of the women of the first generation of anthropologists who were pupils of Malinowski remained unmarried. Several of those who did marry and are currently in senior positions were able to do fieldwork because their husbands (including of course, those husbands who were anthropologists) went abroad.

This suggests that a possible solution is to marry an anthropologist — or at worst, an academic. But this has a Catch 22: if a female anthropologist marries a male anthropologist, she can satisfy herself through him, if she does not, she fades away. If the wife is difficult enough not to want to work through her husband, she may find it hard to get a job: (1) Certain types of job seem not to be offered to women because they are given to those who are thought to NEED them. For example, we noticed that when men come back from doing fieldwork, they are often offered research assistantships in anthropology while they write their theses. This gives them (and their families) a reasonable salary, and in many cases it leads to offers of tenured teaching jobs. This does not happen to women (cf. the role of sponsorship in Epstein [1970]). (2) If a woman and her husband do fieldwork together and have the same "special area" and interests, they will not (reasonably enough) both be able to get jobs in the same department. There may indeed be rules preventing, or strong social pressures against, employment of spouses together, even if their interests are different. (3) This combines with the general lack of mobility among married women — they cannot take a first job wherever one is offered, but must take what is available nearby, thus they have no bargaining power. Wives are often used as cheap labor for tutoring on a never-to-be-altered "temporary" basis. An extreme example appeared on an application form for a professorship (male specified) which requested information on the wife's professional qualifications and experience!

Why don't the women apply for jobs in their own right? Why does the husband's job always take precedence? This certainly involves a consideration of the position of women in the wider society, for many women who are anxious to have and to continue a career would prefer to stop full-time work when they have small children. A double bind is created because there is in fact no easy way to do anthropology part-time. Apart from problems of fieldwork — which could be put aside for a few years — to be an academic one must "be somewhere." This is necessary not only to establish and maintain your identity, to have access to libraries, secretarial help, the stimulation of seminars, etc., but because you meet people; in anthropology the "old boy" network is extraordinarily invidious.

Thus far much of the argument has been concerned with married women. This is not surprising, for marriage is the institution that produces many of the difficulties of women. Because most women marry, to discourage married women is to discourage almost all women. Single women are not immune from some of these disabilities, though academically they face fewer problems. Socially, however, theirs is a more difficult furrow to plow.

This leads to another point: relationships between supervisors and male students seem to be rather different from those between superviors and female students. Specifically, certain anthropological gurus seem to collect and support women students in a way that does not happen with men students. The relationship is very close — not sexual, but emotional and intellectual — and one-way dependent. We suggest that it is established in part because the supervisor feels that women will never be threats (as bright young men might be), that they will play the part of his (decorative) students, his tribe, his clients, his children. In part, certainly, having students of the opposite sex can transform a boringly familiar teaching situation into a more social one. But within this relationship, tensions arise either because the student may marry — this, and especially having children, is evidence of insufficient seriousness about one's career (and showing disloyalty to one's teacher?) — or because the "social," heterosexual element becomes too strong and leads the student to make demands on the instructor that he is unprepared to satisfy.

This ties in with another observation: the social/domestic lives of women are much more socially visible than those of men, and this is what is used to explain the shortcomings of individual women. For example, a male colleague who refuses to sit on any committees or one who is totally disorganized and does not turn up to give lectures or does not mark essays, is said to be lazy or concentrating on his research, no good at teaching though "he's brilliant", or ill, or just "having problems" (unspecified). Women's academic or administrative problems are said to arise because they are neurotic, frustrated, or have to get home to cook supper.

This leads to the, often quite openly expressed, view held by some men and established women academics that, faced with the choice between a man a woman who were equally qualified, they would unhesitatingly choose the man (*pace* the London School of Economics finding), because women cause trouble — they have emotional problems and/or babies and eventually drop out anyway. If they do not take time off, their children become maladjusted, what good, "white," liberal professor wants to be responsible for helping to produce a mixed-up child. Thus, what women are encouraged to reveal to their sympathizers in a semi-social situation is turned against them in a professional context.

Women in their twenties and early thirties therefore do feel that there is discrimination against them. Certainly, one hears reports from job interviews that women who are not married or who have no children are told that they are considered too young and unsettled. Women returning after having children know that people are reluctant to appoint them on low salaries because, as salaries are age-related, it is felt that in a few years these women will use their age as a bargaining tool; in other words, they are too old and expensive in the long term.

One obvious result of these combined disabilities is that many women think it not worth fighting and "vote with their feet" into teaching and social work. Others try but are discouraged. Many of the remaining, determined women become defensive and secretive about their personal lives (for example, they have very pronounced objections to questions in this area at interviews): wary or guarded if they are single; anxious to "square it" with their supervisors first if they are thinking of getting married, because they fear that they or or their work will not be treated seriously (Max Gluckman, after all, announced recently on television that, as far as he could see, a career and a family were alternatives for a woman); somewhat embarrassed if they are pregnant because they feel that people are saying "there you are, you see she wasn't serious about her research;" and challenged if a male colleague asks after their children.

A second and more serious result is that until recently women have struggled to avoid studying women — partly because they have felt compelled to tackle "really difficult" subjects to prove their own worth; partly because they knew that women were considered "second-rate subjects," low in academic esteem when compared with political institutions or male secret societies. (This, of course, also applies in sociology.)

In one particularly revealing meeting of our group, several people who had been at the School of Oriental and African Studies discussed the tremendous reaction there had been to a woman anthropologist who had joined her husband on his field trip and (it being a Muslim society) had learned a great deal about rituals that he had been unable to tap, so that their efforts had worked in well together. On her return, some men were encouraging, some were patronizing ("just right — the womens' place"); but it was the WOMEN who made the most damning remarks ("terribly unimportant," "intrinsically boring," "a waste of time," "letting the side down because now people would insist that that is all women are good for"). The fieldworker herself said that she had found all very demoralizing and that she still regards her work as having been "not proper fieldwork"; it was "easy" because she was with a "protector." Possibly we are now faced with an equal danger of becoming too trendy and encapsulated.

The general conclusion emerging from this look at why there are relatively few women academics in anthropology is that work situations are not gender neutral and that women remain defined and circumscribed by the general social expectations about marriage and their sex role even in academe. This can be demonstrated in a small ritual: university calendars and ballot forms insist on using initials for men and forenames (with their greater familiarity and implicit condenscension) for women, regardless of how the individuals wish to title themselves and regardless of the irrelevance of an individual's sex in these matters. There is also a frequent failure to use a woman's professional title in a professional situation: to refer and write to her as Miss or Mrs. Mary Smith (or worse, as Mrs. John Brown) when she is, and has been for some time, Dr. Mary Smith.

If you telephone a university and ask to speak to Dr. Brown, and there are two Dr. Browns, one male and one female, the call will unhesitatingly be put through to the man. As anthropologists, we accept that such symbols express, and by their expression reinforce, profound underlying values.

REFERENCES

ABBOTT, JOAN
    1969 "Employment of sociology and anthropology graduates, 1966–1967."
        British Sociological Association. Mimeographed.

AMERICAN HISTORICAL ASSOCIATION
  1971   *Final report of the Ad Hoc Committee on the Status of Women in the Profession*. Washington, D.C.
AMERICAN POLITICAL SCIENCE ASSOCIATION
  1972   *Women in political science 1967–1971*. Washington, D.C.
AMERICAN SOCIOLOGICAL ASSOCIATION
  n.d.   *The status of women in the profession*. Washington, D.C. In press.
BLACKSTONE, TESSA
  1973   The scarce academics. *THES*. March 16, 1973.
CAPLAN, PAT
  1973   Article in *Proceedings of the Women's Anthropology Workshop*. London Women's Anthropology Group. Mimeographed.
EPSTEIN, CYNTHIA FUCHS
  1970   *Women's place*. Berkeley: University of California Press.
HUGHES, HELEN MACGILL
  1973   Maid of all work or departmental sister-in-law: the faculty wife employed on campus. *American Journal of Sociology* (January).
KELSALL, R. KEITH, *et al.*
  1970   *Six years after*. Sheffield: Sheffield University Press.
  1972   *Graduates: the sociology of an elite*. London: Methuen.

Women in the Anthropology Profession – 2

PAT CAPLAN

1.   The orignal aim of the London Women's Anthropology Group was to compare the careers of male and female anthropology graduates over a period for fuller study by sending a questionnaire to a sample of graduates from a number of universities where anthropology is tauhgt. We soon rejected this project as too ambitious, although we still think it worthwhile. Instead we tried to examine the proportions of females to males at four levels — Bachelor of Arts or Bachelor of Science, Master, Doctor of Philosophy, and staff — in three London University departments (the School of Oriental and African Studies [SOAS] the London School Economics [LSE), and University College [UC]) over a five-year period. We had great difficulty in getting hold of satisfactory figures in the case of LSE and UC, where the departments concerned did not appear to keep records, and the published list at Senate House had a surprising number of gaps.

2.   Table 1 shows the available data.

Table 1.   Numbers of Men and Women in Anthropology at Four Levels

	Staff*	Doctor of Philosophy	Master of Arts	Bachelor of Arts/ Bachelor of Science
Men	123	21	22	67
Women	36	12	24	101
Total	159	33	46	168
Percent women	23	36	52	60

* in person-years

Table 1 represents an amalgamation of the figures for 1966–1971 (SOAS),

1967–1972 (LSE), and 1966–1972 (UC). In the last case a six-year period was used because the numbers were so small that the periods 1966–1971 and 1967–1972 gave quite different results. Furthermore, we had to use the UC undergraduate input figures (the number of people who registered to do degrees) because the output figures (the number of people who actually obtained degrees) were unavailable. These problems, coupled with the very short period that the figures cover, make our results very tentative, but we feel that they are worth noting because so clear a trend emerges.

At the undergraduate level, there is a marked preponderance of women: two departments had more women than men, and one had equal numbers. The figure of 60% of undergraduates being women can be further divided according to class of degree, for which figures for SOAS and LSE were available (Table 2).

Table 2.   Numbers of men and women anthropology undergraduates obtaining first-class, second-class, and third-class degrees

	first and upper second	Lower second and third	Total numbers obtaining degrees
Men	11	13	24
Women	11	24	35
Total	22	37	

Thus, only 31 percent of women succeeded in obtaining a "good" degree, as against 46% of men. However, in terms of absolute numbers, as many women as men did obtain a "good" degree.

This failure on the part of women to be as well represented in the numbers obtaining a degree adequate to allow for postgraduate work as they are in the total undergraduate body might well be discussed, particularly as I have heard university staff say that because the number of female applicants for undergraduate papers is so high, attempts are made to restrict their entry, and in some cases, men with slightly lower qualifications at "A"level are admitted in an attempt to balance the sex ratio.

As far as master's degrees are concerned, the proportion of women is more or less equal to that of men. This fits in with the fact that 50 percent of those getting a good first-class degree are women. It would also seem to indicate that of those students who do obtain a first or upper second, equal proportions of each sex carry on to the master's level.

By the doctoral level, the proportion of women has dropped to just over a third. However, quite a high proportion (perhaps 25 percent) of these people are from abroad, which means that they have already gone through a selection process elsewhere. If we ignore the "obviously foreign" students (using names as the sole criterion), we would find a somewhat higher proportion of women. This point might also have some validity at the bachelor's and master's levels too.

At the level of teaching staff, the proportion of women drops even further: 23 – 21 percent at SOAS, 25 percent at UC, and 22 percent at LSE. When the figures are broken down by seniority, we find that women are more highly represented at the lecturer level. At the moment, only one of the eight professors of anthropology in the university is a woman.
3. Let us look for a moment at those who have obtained a university post. How do they fare in other ways? Two fairly accessible sets of figures were the proportion of women who had articles in the leading British anthropological journal, *Man*, and the proportion of women who obtained research money from the Social Science Research Council, the main source of research.

Over a five-year period, there were 199 articles in *Man*; of these only 34 were written by women, while 8 others were written jointly by a man and a woman. This gives an overall figure of 19 percent which is somewhat lower than the percentage of women university teachers. Here, however, as with all the figures I have presented, we cannot know the full story without having the input as well as the output figures.

The proportion of women who obtained SSRC money was even lower – 16 percent (six of forty-six recipients, with three other cases of money awarded jointly to a man and woman). Here, of course, we come up against the problem of the "front man," for often the project is actually carried out by people other than the person who actually applies for the money. And in nearly all such cases of which we in the London Women's Anthropology Group know personally, the "frontman" is a male, while a large number of the actual researchers are female. At SOAS, for instance, the category of "research assistant" over the five-year period has been overwhelmingly filled by women (69 percent).

Thus, despite the brevity of the period that we covered, the lack of input figures, and the approximate nature of the figures themselves, a clear trend does seem to emerge (just as one might expect): the higher up the ladder one goes, the fewer women are to be found.

Women and Fieldwork

JANET BUJRA

This paper is based on the fieldwork experiences of the participants in the London Woman's Anthropology Group and therefore covers a variety and range of experiences. Fieldwork is a normal starting point for most careers in the social sciences. A few of us have worked within our own cultures, but the majority have worked in other cultures. Some have done fieldwork in more than one area. Some have worked alone, others with husbands. A few of us had children with us in the field. Most of us felt that the fact that we were women had a definite influence upon the character of our fieldwork, and this paper suggests the nature of that influence.

Two preliminary points must be made, however. The first is that inevitably we found ourselves discussing general problems of fieldwork, whether done by men or by women — problems that perhaps are not often brought into the open, concerning personal relationships, self-evaluation, role playing, and so on. The second point is that we do not wish to give the impression that only WOMEN have fieldwork problems, or that their problems are vastly more difficult to solve than are those faced by men. Actually, we know very little of the personal, sexual, or identity problems faced by men in the field.

We felt that both these points reflected the fact that fieldwork is often discussed in traditional competitive seminars, where each speaker is under pressure to prove the success and adequacy of his or her particular fieldwork techniques. In such an atmosphere, consideration of the kinds of problems raised above is severely inhibited.

As a framework for this discussion, I would suggest that we first look at the researcher's view of of herself, both as a woman and as a social scientist, within the context of her own society. If our own social milieu is THESIS, then the ANTITHESIS is the other culture in which we work. We know from our own experiences that communities differ widely in their attitudes toward and treatment of women. The SYNTHESIS is the fieldwork situation itself, which for women fieldworkers often seems to be characterized by a high degree of status ambiguity.

THESIS: RESEARCHER'S SELF-EVALUATION IN RELATION TO HER OWN SOCIETY

The professions have traditionally been a man's world, into which women have forced themselves by determination and toughness. Anthropology is no exception — to survive, women have had to learn to ignore the patronizing hostility of male anthropologists, including jokes about "bluestockings" or suggestions that women have succeeded in their profession only by seducing, or being seduced by, famous male anthropologists. The jokes, in fact, highlight the two roles generally open to women with careers — i.e. the role of "pseudo man" and the role of the woman who plays upon her feminity in order to get on.

Most of us, I suspect, adopt a "pseudo-male" approach, in that we consider ourselves not just equal to, but no different from, men in the profession. In the past this has led women anthropologists to accept, without question, unspoken male stereotypes about society, Several of us now recognize the extent to which our choice of fieldwork topic and location were influenced by our acceptance of such stereotypes. We assumed that studying a society did NOT mean studying women, because MEN were the only real actors in important spheres of social activity. We greeted with hostility the suggestion that we study WOMEN, for it carried the implication that we were second-rate researchers, not fit for anything else, not capable of dealing with men's worlds. Generally speaking, we chose topics that, as far as we could judge in advance, would not involve us with women. Some of us even chose particularly difficult topics or locations in order to make absolutely clear that we were equal to any male anthropologist. That many of us adopted from the start an asexual or more positively a pseudo-male role in the field can be seen as a logical corollary to our behavior in our own cultures as professional women.

More recently, it has become fashionable to carry out "women's studies," and undoubtedly this is a by-product of the women's liberation movement. (We must add, however, that the movement has sometimes treated anthropological evidence in a cavalier manner.) Despite this new interest in women, old attitudes persist. Those of us who have carried out research relating to women have noted the contempt with which male anthropologists greet our work and the condescension with which we are treated as researchers.

ANTITHESIS: OTHER CULTURES

Our success — or lack of it — in the field seemed to be directly related to the status held by women and the range of roles played by women in the communities that we studied. Thus, in any society where sexual segregation was deeply entrenched, we were constantly faced with difficult choices. For while WE might place ourselves in the asexual category of fieldworker the community saw us first and foremost as women. Often, when it was realized that we actually intended to LIVE in the community, an attempt was made to resocialize us into the local rules for the female category. To those of us who were single, this might be a particularly galling experience, since the status of "unmarried girl" is often the lowest one in such a society. In general these communities have prescribed rules for feminine behavior and spheres of activity, as well as conventions concerning dress, deportment, and other cultural minutiae. In all these matters, the woman fieldworker is often under pressure to conform.

Generally speaking, in communities characterized by strict sexual segregation, women play no overt part in public affairs (political meetings, dispute settlements, and the like). For those of us who were interested in precisely such public affairs, a pseudo-male fieldwork role seemed the only possible one, and its choice in some cases undoubtedly compromised a concomitant rapport with women. When we remember that the influence of women in public affairs has often been underestimated in the past, we have to admit that this fieldwork strategy may well distort our understanding of events.

The exclusion of women from political life also had its significance, however, for those of us who, whether by choice or by necessity, elected to work through women. We noticed that women were less effective informants than men, that they were less articulate, less straightforward, and less coherent. One of us found men more fortcoming even on women's topics, such as menstruation. Certainly in terms of just the time it took to get information on a particular topic, women were less satisfactory informants than were men. It was suggested that in most societies women were simply not trained to express themselves in speech or to concentrate on topics other than repetitive domestic ones. However, such women do not learn to be articulate because they are excluded from participation in the fields where effective communication is vital — that is, the sphere of politics, in the widest sense of the word. In my own experience, ANY category of people that is so excluded will be less articulate than those who take a full and equal part in political life. Thus a category of ex-slaves in a village that I studied were noticeably less articulate and coherent than freeborn men. The conclusion seems to be that we must develop different fieldwork techniques to gain information from such people, because we cannot fully understand any political system unless we see it from the angle of the ruled as well as that of the rulers.

It is not necessarily easier to come to terms with communities in which sexual differences are not so clear-cut. It might simply be that in these communities the rules are unspoken and concern less obvious marks of distinction, but that they are equally binding. Problems of socially enforced sexual differentiation affected even those of us who worked within our own cultures. For even in these cases, we were not working in our usual environments, hence we were not always sure of the rules or of the extent to which we could afford to break them. Within a university or research institute there is usually a degree of easy familiarity between the sexes, simply because men and women may be performing equivalent work. This does not apply to the same extent in rural Wales or in a suburban housing estate, where an equivalent rapport with both men and women may be far more difficult to create and maintain.

The degree to which a woman fieldworker can break the rules relating to gender in any particular community seems to depend on whether the members of that community view male-female relationships as exclusively sexual (or maternal) or whether they also allow scope for other kinds of relationships between men and women.

SYNTHESIS: "STATUS AMBIGUITY"

The range of problems that we faced as women in the field were almost as varied as the communities that we set out to study. But a few general points can be made.

The first is that role playing is in itself a traumatic business, easier for some personalities than for others. As women in what is largely a man's world, often we have already learned to play roles that in our own cultures are unconventional for women, but these may not be roles that are useful in the field. Once a woman has adopted a certain role in the field-work situation — and this may be forced on her by circumstances — it is often very difficult to switch to a different role. All attempts at role playing may in any case be overridden by her status as a "stranger." This status has certain advantages, of course — notably, it allows her to break rules — but I would suspect that in many cases these are outweighed by the disadvantages.

In speaking of role playing, I am referring here mainly to the choice of SEXUAL roles open to a woman fieldworker, although other identifications will also be made in the course of fieldwork. It is perhaps significant that women anthropologist are thought to have some CHOICE in the matter. I have never heard it suggested that a male anthropologist might adopt a pseudo-female role in the field in order to get information from women. Presumably, to adopt such a role would be thought to be too threatening to male egos. Moreover, there seems to be an implicit assumption that what the women in any culture have to say will be of little interest. Male anthropologists also argue that in most societies they could not be on friendly terms with women without incurring the wrath of their male informants and consequently ruining their fieldwork. It is less often considered that a woman playing a pseudo-male role will incur the jealousy and suspicion of local women concerning her motives, and that this hostility can also have a deleterious effect on her work.

In discussing our various fieldwork experiences, we were surprised at the degree to which communities varied in their ability to accept the woman fieldworker in an asexual role. But in some cases, our attempts to gain the status of honorary male were seem by local women as sexually provocative. They might then redouble their efforts to make us conform to local rules of behavior or even to persuade certain of their menfolk that we were not desirable persons to have in their communities. Some of us tried to get around this by playing the role of "respectable woman" and projecting an image of modesty and "decency" in dress and behavior. In this way we hoped that women would NOT think of us as competitors for their men, and that the most influential men in the society would treat us with respect. To a large extent this role paid off, although we were constantly throwing doubt on it by our continued use of male informants. It could also be overplayed, so that people felt uneasy in our presence, did not joke about matters considered unseemly by the respectable, and so on. Those in the community who were themselves not considered respectable would regard us with suspicion and would not speak openly about their activities and beliefs. This problem, of course, is merely an example of a more general problem faced by all fieldworkers, i.e. the utter impossibility of being all things to all men — or all women.

There are anthropologists, both male and female, who use their sex explicitly to get information — though there are undoubtedly a good many more rumors than actual cases of this. I do know of a male anthropologist who studied prostitutes at first hand, so to speak, and we have all heard stories of women anthropologists who sleep with male informants and of male anthropologists who take local mistresses. We ourselves would not expect that this strategy, simply as a fieldwork technique, would be particularly successful; but it is of some consequence that, as the recent case of Miss/Mrs. Wynn Sergeant showed, such a tactic is condemned far more violently when used by women than by men. (I realize that the whole incident of Miss Sergeant was misrepresented in the press.)

There seem to be inherent differences between doing fieldwork alone, as a single woman, and doing it in the company of a husband and/or children. Whereas the choice of roles that may be played by a single woman is potentially great, the status of unmarried woman in many societies is fairly low. In the village where I conducted my first fieldwork, for example, unmarried girls were secluded, did most of the hard work in the house, were not allowed to attend ceremonies (even weddings), and were referred to contemptuously as "oh, just an unmarried girl." Clearly, a fieldworker could not accept such a restricted status, unless her specific interest was in adolescent girls. Fortunately, she is usually able to play off against this her status as "stranger," her age, and her knowledge of the world. But this, too, puts her in an anomalous position — for how can we be so old and still be unmarried? We cannot be fully admitted to the company of married women for, in theory, we know nothing of sex and childbirth. We may not even be able to equal the capacity for hard physical work taken for granted by local women, and we may therefore be subjected to ridicule and scorn for our weakness. Thus the wide choice of role open to the unmarried woman fieldworker is often more apparent than real, and her position is generally highly ambiguous.

A married woman, on the other hand, is more restricted in her choice of fieldwork roles, though at the same time the status of "married woman" is generally given local value and respect. She is considered "normal" and acceptable by both men and women, and this impression is often heightened if she has children. On the other hand, the fact that her position is less ambiguous also generally means that she has less leeway to create a role for herself in the field. Friendly relations with other women would generally be automatic, but attempts to approach men could be considered as betrayal by female friends and could be misinterpreted by men.

The married woman who accompanies a husband who is also a fellow anthropologist does not always find things easy. Her relations with her husband may be complicated or even threatened by their doing fieldwork together — or perhaps it would be more accurate to say that the tensions of most marriages are aggravated by the isolation of the fieldwork experience. Often women suffer more in this process, because husbands tend to take advantage of the situation and suggest that rapport with local people could best be achieved if their wives behaved like wives rather than like fellow workers. On the whole, unless the husband is exceptional, a woman fieldworker who is married but not actually ACCOMPANIED by her husband seems to have the best situation of all, one that can be exploited very effectively in the field. Children, on the other hand, do not pose the problems that husbands do. Apart from the responsibilities of caring for them in places that might well have inadequate medical facilities, children are generally an unmitigated help in the field.

Those of us who have concentrated on working primarily through women have emphasized the danger of overstating the pivotal role of women in any sphere of activity. Anthropologists have in the past greatly underestimated women's roles and significance, but in correcting this bias, we must not swing too far in the other direction. The analysis of most social phenomena requires us to look at both male and female dimensions. For most of us, however, in most fieldwork situations, there are frustrating limitations on the degree to which we can look at both sides of the picture effectively.

The Female Factor in Anthropology

CAROLINE IFEKA

I intend in this short paper to explore some issues with which people involved in women's studies are grappling.

SPECIFIC problems of theory have been discussed at meetings of the London Women's Anthropology Group. We have agreed to differ on some theoretical questions. I think we all feel that divergent views on theoretical perspectives, when formulated in a friendly atmosphere among people who are trying to cooperate rather than compete, can facilitate insight into hitherto unsuspected defects in one's own analytical model. I think that so far we fall into two camps: the neo-Marxists, and a less doctrinally committed grouping influenced by the pragmatism of mainstream anthropology. A third camp, that of the cognitive structuralists, is not represented among us. But it is a theoretical approach which is currently stimulating a few male colleagues to take up women as a hitherto neglected, and therefore, little known category. They claim that research on women will demonstrate the validity of structural approaches to analyzing thought.

Other questions to do with more GENERAL issues in the study of women have not really been explored by us. Clearly, it is important that we try and make a start on resolving such issues as:

1. What is the intellectual framework of women's studies?
2. What are we looking for? Are we trying to prove the virtues of theories to which we are already committed? To use the study of women, an unknown quantity, to generate new theories of society? Or do we want to use women's studies to help bring about a new millennium?

This is a working paper and not, in any sense, a definitive essay on the topic.

3.   Do womens' studies exist in any acceptable disciplinary sense?
4.   What problems most call out for immediate research?
    Clearly we can not deal satisfactorily with the question of what kind of theoretical approach will eventually distinguish women's studies from other areas of sociological inquiry until we have decided if women's studies exists.

DO WOMEN'S STUDIES EXIST?

Evidently this is an issue which has academic (in the sense of an ideal norm that sees knowledge as pursuable for its own sake) and political and moral aspects.

THE POLITICAL DIMENSION   Since women's studies is a direct spinoff from the women's liberation movement, it is obvious what kind of political goals are most favored. Some people are attracted to the problem of rethinking the roles of women in society and others are concerned with direct action. For some people women's studies has a strong moral component. That is, it is a duty as educated women to pursue and further the study of women, but again this does not necessarily result in political action. Two separate stances are possible.
    Is it possible, then, and desirable to separate off an academic interest in the opening up of a hitherto neglected area of research, from a political view of women's studies which defines it as a means to a larger end — changing the contemporary power structure? While political commitment can channel research on the female factor in a few very specific directions, which give the illusion of clarity of vision, it also has the disadvantage of restricting the imagination, of checking one from seeing patterns and regularities which one might otherwise observe if less fettered by doctrine. In the long run it seems that women's studies will not be contained in the vessel of radical politics, which will constitute but one of many orientations.
    For myself, I can envisage doing research without a doctrinal commitment to the Marxian or Lévi-Straussian corpus, but I can also see that in some ways it would be easier freely to pursue involvement, that is, political involvement in the cause of women, and to redirect one's research to fit this interest. By studying male-female relationships and the distribution of power between the two sectors of a human population one could be contributing to eventual changes in male-female images. For, given favorable social conditions, shifts in perspective could lead

to associated shifts in occupational, wealth, and status patterns, which in turn modify the central norms guiding interaction among women and men.

Even if we agree to accept some political bias in women's studies, (though not necessarily a Marxist or Lévi-Straussian bias) we are faced with problems of policy. If women's studies exists as a budding branch of sociological inquiry, then we have to press for the introduction of women's studies syllabi at centers of higher education. I would like to suggest that we set up a planning committee to explore whether there is an adequate supply of monographs on women. Most of these would presumably not be dealing with women, but would contain a certain amount of relevant information. Frontal studies are few; there is much data of a side-glance kind. Should men be involved in the teaching of women's studies? As I have suggested, some are showing an interest not just in the London Women's Anthropology Group, but in the subject of women per se.

THE ACADEMIC DIMENSION   The argument can go in one or two directions. First, it is surely inconceivable that a sane social scientist would deliberately study only "men of the X society;" so that in the end no one would study "women of the X." As the phrase goes, one studies a problem. And women may, or may not, be a dimension of that problem, i.e. the structural and historical reasons for messianism in Africa. Here, women are certainly not the central problem. As always, it is said to be the sociologist's task to locate and explain the specific in terms of the general social context, a task best performed with the aid of theory. Therefore, according to this view, since there can be nothing called women's studies, there are no theoretical principles to be elucidated.

On the other hand, there is the view that although the label "women" is a catch-all, and thus problem-concealing in the extreme, this does not prevent us from locating particular issues and generating the appropriate analytical tools. Race relations constitutes an analogous field of inquiry. Zubaida (1972:3) has argued that:

...race relations are far from being homogenous. What gives them their apparent homogeneity is their common definition as a social problem. ...it is no criticism of a field of study to say it is concerned with social problems, but it is a criticism of that field to say that it defines its own sociological problem ịn accordance with the definition of social problems prevalent in that society.

The problem that is specific to the field of women's studies is the female factor, and female awareness. Women's consciousness may not necessarily take on a corporate expression through female solidarity *vis à vis* men. Like the variables of race and racial consciousness, the female factor — e.g. women's complementarity to men, their conceptual positioning — originates in a particular category of social relationships which generates culturally defined images held by one sex of another. The sociological significance of the female factor lies in the extent to which it determines the political and cultural structure of the society. Likewise, the racial factor inspired Furnival, Smith, and Rex to develop the notion of the plural society, thus improving our understanding of the varieties of stratification.

If it is conceivable that women's studies will or does exist in its own right as a distinct area of sociological inquiry, what are the problems that mark women's studies off from other areas of inquiry?

SOME RESEARCH PROBLEMS

There are perhaps two kinds of problem which call for immediate attention: the politico-economic, and the ideological.

THE POLITICO-ECONOMIC   The political issue centres on how women fit into the male-dominated system of power in a society. We are concerned, therefore, with determining the extent to which female status is tied to that of their male partners, or is independent of it (e.g. the Muslim women of Northern Nigeria). We should also find out if a change in the resources controlled by women is of primary causal significance for the distribution of power in a society. For instance, boom conditions in the palm oil trade in eastern Nigeria during the first two decades of the century coincided with political and cultural attacks on the traditional society by representatives of church and government. Women began to acquire unprecedented sums of capital; their links with European traders was a new development, for men had been accustomed to monopolizing external trade. Later, women spear-headed the tax riots of 1929. In what kind of situation will widespread changes in stratification occur as a result, among other things, of shifts in female productivity and the division of labor? Is there a general pattern to be discerned in the causes of rebellions like the women's riots of 1929 in Nigeria, the Alice Lenshins movement of the 1960's in Zambia, and the woman's strike in Lusaka, the Capital of Zambia?

We have to investigate the external relationships of women to the rest of society, and the internal ordering of women within female status systems. What is the significance of patron-client links, women's contribution clubs and other societies, for the maintenance of female solidarity, for the reduction of individualism among women, and the development of female consciousness? Ethnographies on the Hausa, Nupe, and Ibo provide some clues. But on the whole they are vitiated by a myopic view of the nature of power, and of the stratification system (an exception is M.G. Smith's work on the Hausa). Like Nadel, writing on the Nupe, they are unable to see that women who become economically independent of their husbands are not just social deviants, or of economic interest because they trade through household connections, however secluded in their compounds, rather than in an orthodox market (Hill 1972). Rather, female autonomy affects the central system of status and power: it attacks the supports of the male-dominated system of power that Nadel, for example, describes for the Nupe of Nigeria. For Nadel, legitimate power is controlled by men, and women's status is derived from that of the men. He says the significance of powerful Nupe women traders is only perceptual, being expressed in witchcraft fantasies that men fabricate, and women can only exorcise, with the aid of male sorcerers (Nadel 1942).

While women share certain characteristics with other groupings peripheral to the established centres of power in society, the meaning of that peripherality and minority group status, and its structural consequences may well be different. For we are talking about not just one percent but 50 percent of most human populations. Men who run the political and religious cults of society have intimate dealings with women in their own sphere of dominance — the household. Women are perceived by men as a collection of dispersed and unorganized individuals in many societies; men perceive themselves, and women concur, as a group who express their solidarity through management of political and religious institutions central to power. In what ways can, or do, women structure themselves as an organized collectivity? Do they ever do so? The work of Polly Hill on the economic life of the Batagarawa Hausa of Katsına emirate, and the studies on Ibo and Nupe societies, are conducted within terms set by male-controlled values: If women participate in secret societies under female management, they do so as "the only safeguard of Ibibio women against the tyranny of their men-folk" (Talbot 1915:189). But in these studies the weapons that women can wield are exercised within the terms imposed by male managers. Here, the female factor is not studied as an unknown quantity, a category whose images of men and other women have to be unravelled.

Whereas the earlier monographs on Ibibio, Ibo, and Hausa women contain detailed descriptive accounts of women, they are remarkable for their lack of analysis. New work which follows the lines of cognitive structuralism has many conceptual gains, but loses out elsewhere. Like the older works on women, these contemporary studies may well be deficient in explaining how the observer perceives women's relationships to the wider society. Analysis then takes on a self-fulfilling dimension; we are all Azande now, equipped with our closed systems of thought.

Ardener's article (1972) on female belief among the Bakweri of Cameroon is a pioneering study in many ways. But there are faults of omission that follow from his use of the cognitive structuralist scheme.

In the first place, he neglects demographic and economic factors which go a long way to explaining why women have a large degree of economic and cultural autonomy from men. He argues that women's beliefs and self-images are concealed in those developed and managed by Bakweri men. And that it is the men who have economic power because they cultivate the lucrative cash crop, bananas. However, reanalysis of Ardener's material shows that it is the cocoyam, the woman's crop, which is the staple item of diet in the area. Women sell their cocoyams and use them for domestic consumption. How, then, did men first get the capital for banana cultivation? Surely from their women, a fact which points to female control of some sectors of the Bakweri economy. This control is not recognized as legitimate, or even admitted, in Bakweri central norms. Male unease is expressed, as it is among the Nupe, in administering medicines to women possessed by mermaids — symbols of female wildness and mobility outside the male-controlled sphere of Bakweri society.

Second, Ardener is comparing like with unlike. He contrasts the man's view of women, which is the publicly accepted stereotype among Bakweri, with the women's view of themselves. This, however, is a concealed or inner image which articulates women's independence of men through their roles as creatures of Nature. Men see women as being coinhabitants of their sphere, Culture. When they stray it is in the form of mermaids, natural agents of danger and evil, who are exorcised by public rites.

Such mistakes need not occur if we pay attention not just to belief, but to the observable facts of life "out there," and to the way in which women's values are structured by or are independent of the public, central value system of the society. Let us assume the following: both sexes are given two dimensions of being by their culture. Women, for instance, have one conceptual set of images which are molded by central system values, and one which is shaped by the values of women only. We can call this particular set of images an inner or concealed ethos. Now according to Ardener, the central (male) view of women is that they are part of Culture on the whole. But *men may also (perhaps) have an inner or concealed view of women*, a possibility which Ardener does not even consider. Likewise, women have a set of images about men which are structured by the central value system: this too Ardener ignores. Women have also a concealed or inner belief system about men and themselves as creatures of the wild which Ardener analyzes. If such a conceptual framework proves useful, we might be able to carry out detailed analyses of male-female patterns of interaction, and find out under what circumstances inner values are mobilized and under what circumstances the dominant central values take over. Such an approach would bring some additional flexibility to the explanatory models of the cognitive structuralists, and raises the possibility that in some cultures men and/or women may not have a developed inner image. Perhaps this is correlated with an absence of economic independence. Marilyn Strathern, for example, asserts that of Melpa women, Mount Hagen, New Guinea "it would be meaningless to talk of a female sub-culture" (1972:313). I wonder.

Another advantage of the inner-central image schema is that one can then assume there is a degree of autonomy between sectors of society; one is allowing for disparities and conflicts, for organizational complexity and situational selection. The study of a female factor will surely strengthen conflict theories of society, and stimulate re-examination of the concepts, "political system," "religious organization" and "myth," among others. If it becomes apparent that men only run one among several systems of power, we will have to refine and expand our currently limited idea of power.

CONCLUSIONS

1. Women's studies is possibly an intellectual hotcake, an area where new theories can be generated. It could be a rewarding area of research, a disciplinary area in its own right. Women's studies may be politcally loaded for some, but for others it would be preferable to maintain a low political profile. Their view is that change can be achieved but gradually; the slowness of the transition does not make it less revolutionary in the long run.

We should decide whether to press for courses on women now, or at a later date when more research has been published.

2. We should be aware of the deficiences in the kind of theoretical approaches to the female factor that are now so fashionable, as well

as those of earlier writers on women, or of contemporary students like Polly Hill and Marilyn Strathern. We have to assess whether a problem calls for the development of conceptual schema applicable only to research on women, or for the application of theories current in mainstream sociology. We should, finally, decide on priorities in the grading of problems that most urgently call for empirical investigation.

REFERENCES

ARDENER, E.
1972 "Belief and the problem of women," in *The interpretation of ritual*. Edited by J. La Fontaine. Tavistock.
HILL, P.
1972 *Rural house*. Cambridge: Cambridge University Press.
NADEL, S.
1942 *A black Byzantinin*. Oxford: Oxford University Press.
STRATHERN, M.
1972 *Women in between: female roles in a male world, Mt. Hagen, New Guinea*. Seminar Press.
TALBOT, D. A.
1915 *Woman's mysteries of a primitive people*. Cassel.
ZUBEIDA, S., editor
1972 *Race and racialism*. Tavistock.

Aboriginal Woman: Male and Female Anthropological Perspectives

RUBY ROHRLICH-LEAVITT, BARBARA SYKES, and
ELIZABETH WEATHERFORD

The initial purpose of this paper was to compare the findings of male and female anthropologists about Australian aboriginal women to see if there were sex-based variations. But even a cursory survey of the studies showed such marked discrepancies in both the range and quality of the data collected in the field that the analysis was extended to include the differences in the theoretical and methodological approaches, and in the concomitant ideologies.

It is generally acknowledged that an exclusively male study of a culture is usually incomplete. Male ethnographers use male informants, whether by inclination or because of cultural requirements, and observe the activities of males or those involving both sexes, but rarely those in which women alone participate. A partial ethnography is already a distorted picture, but that it is further distorted by the androcentric theory and methodology of many male ethnographers is only now beginning to be dealt with, chiefly by women anthropologists. Most of the men in the discipline find it difficult to face this reality, for it would bring into question much of the data accumulated for more than a century about non-Western cultures.

In the education of anthropologists little or no attention has been directed to eliminating androcentrism. The major focus is on expunging that aspect of ethnocentrism that involves unconscious assumptions of superiority over non-Western peoples. Yet, despite deliberate and concerted training to this end, anthropologists find it almost impossible to rid themselves of these assumptions. In his review of Castaneda's books Paul Riesman notes (1972:7) that:

The belief that all people are human has not saved Western anthropologists from feeling superior to the people they study and write about, and it has not prevented serious distortions in our picture of non-Western peoples (and of ourselves) from arising and influencing our actions.

How much more serious must be the distortions that arise from androcentrism. How is it possible for the male ethnographer, socialized from birth to his superior status in his own culture, and in no way held accountable for androcentrism, to report objectively on the relationships between women and men, and on the roles and status of women, in other cultures? Moreover, socialization into the discipline must only fortify androcentrism, since men are so obviously preferred for research grants, fieldwork, and employment.

The prototype for the androcentric approach of the anthropologist is the century-long debate over the existence of matriarchal civilizations, a debate unique for the particular emotionality of its tone. The multitude of contradictions that permeated this controversy are still with us. For example, although it is generally accepted that religious practices reflect the secular life, when the archaeological record reveals the prevalence of goddesses, the corresponding secular dominance of women is denied, despite the acceptance of masculine secular supremacy when male gods are found to predominate. And scientists who provide proof of the existence of matriarchies are stigmatized as non-scholarly.

At the same time the universality of the patriarchal system is asserted, for most anthropologists insist that even in matrilineal, matrilocal societies it is not the women but their brothers who wield political power. This flies in the face of historical evidence. The political leadership of women is well documented for many states of southeast Asia and Africa. And in the northern Andean states "the matrilineal tendencies of the circum-Caribbean area led to female as well as male warriors and rulers" (Steward 1970: 221).

The very selection of the political institution as the defining criterion of social organization is itself a projection of Euro-American society. The high status of women in many cultures was based on their crucial economic, religious, and medical roles. But such societies, it seems, may not be termed "matriarchies" because, as defined by most anthropologists, a matriarchy is a mirror image of the patriarchy, particularly of the Euro-American type in which men exercise iron control over all the the institutions. But the patriarchal concept of power, as the means of control over the mass of the people by a ruling elite, is in no way applicable to tribal peoples. As Leacock points out (1972:34), in such societies "the participation of women in a major share of socially necessary labor did not reduce them to virtual slavery, as is the case in class society, but afforded them decision-making power commensurate with their contribution."

According to Kaplan and Manners (1972:186), "the purpose for which the research and description are undertaken will determine whether an ethnographic account is couched in 'native categories' (emic terms), in the 'anthropologist's categories' (etic terms), or as is overwhelmingly the case, in some combination of the two." But in the male ethnographies of the Australian aborigines the "anthropologist's categories" predominate; the societies are represented as male-dominated, with women in a subordinate, degraded status. However, in *Aboriginal woman* and *Tiwi wives*, Phyllis Kaberry (1939) and Jane Goodale (1971) succeed in combining the "anthropologist's categories" with those of the native. Their theory and methodology seem to stem from "double-consciousness," a concept that Dubois evolved to define the special awareness of black people in a racist society (1961: Chapters 6 and 7). As women in a society that is also sexist, Kaberry and Goodale have the special sensitivity that members of subordinated groups must, if they are to survive, develop to those who control them, at the same time as they are fully aware of the everyday reality of their oppression; a quality that the superordinate groups lack. Thus, Kaberry and Goodale develop ethnographies from the actual lives and worldview of the people they study, and with a thoroughgoing awareness of the "anthropologist's categories," their theory is generated both emically and etically.

In contrast, C. W. M. Hart states (Spindler 1970: 147) that when he studied the Tiwi of North Australia, he focused on the genealogical system and deliberately ignored their mythology and subsistence techniques because they "bored" him. Pointing to the limitations of this approach, Leacock (1972:7) says: "Unfortunately, the debate over women's status in primitive society has largely ignored the actual role of women... in favor of an almost exclusive focus on descent systems." But the emic-etic perspective of Kaberry and Goodale goes beyond the particular system chosen by the male ethnographer. As Kaberry (1939:39) notes: "anthropology as a science must have its laws and abstractions, yet human beings... are apt to prove intractable to scientific manipulation."

The sensitivity of the women ethnographers to the "scientific manipulation" of people is another facet of "double-consciousness," an accurate term for a truly emic-etic perspective. This kind of manipulation is illustrated by the Aristotelian device of dichtomy, widely used by Western male social scientists to establish and perpetuate, in the case of male and female roles, status and temperament, the "natural" superiority of men and the "natural" inferiority of women. In the anthropology of the Australian aborigines, functionalists and structuralists like Durkheim, Warner, and Lévi-Strauss set up fictitious and simplistic dichotomies which arbitrarily designate men as sacred and women as profane, or men as actors and women as acted-upon objects, at the same time as women are devalued, incongruously, precisely on the grounds that they ARE actors, involved with doing. Such polarizations are tellingly challenged by Kaberry and Goodale as they focus on the revealing interactions between the quotidian and ritual activities of these people.

With the exception of Daisy Bates[1] and a few other women whose works were somehow doomed to obscurity, the data on the Australian aborigines for more than a century came from male field workers. What emerged was a view of the Australian women as pawns in a male exchange system, or as "mere drudges, passing a life of monotony and being shamefully ill-treated by their husbands" (Elkin 1939: xxii). This perspective was amazingly consistent, for, as late as 1960, *The Tiwi of North Australia* (Hart and Pilling 1960) was described by George and

---

[1] The research of Daisy Bates should be a primary source on the Australian aborigines, for she spent fifty years with them. But to date no anthropologist appears to have investigated the 94 folios of her papers at the National Library in Canberra, Australia. Although she was a member of the same racial and cultural group as the male ethnographers who studied the aborigines, Bates, as a woman, seems to have experienced the sexism they displayed toward the aboriginal women.

Before his first expedition to Australia in 1910, Radcliffe-Brown wrote Bates that her description of aboriginal social organization represented "a large amount of very valuable information which will be of immense value to us in the work we propose to do" (Salter 1972:135), and accepted her offer to participate in the expedition. Despite her own poverty, Bates had tapped all possible sources to finance the expedition, and had introduced Radcliffe-Brown to the bands she knew so well. But shortly after the fieldwork began he left her behind. He then delayed editing the manuscript which she had entrusted to him, and it was eventually lost. After his first published reports Bates wrote a friend that "some of my manuscript is being printed as new discoveries by those who had access to it. You will remember that I mentioned the Ngargalulla of the Broome district natives some years ago. I see in a recent paper that these spirit babies are Mr. A. R. Brown's discoveries" (Salter 1972:152).

In 1923 Elkin contacted Bates before beginning his expedition. But when she asked for help in obtaining a government stipend, as she was financially destitute, all she received was twenty pounds, which she refused indignantly (Salter 1972:199).

Although many high officials recommended that she be appointed as the aborigines' representative to the government, she did not get the position on the grounds that the risks involved would be too great for a woman. "For one who has lived alone amongst aborigines, wild and civilized, it was a galling decision, made worse" by the title of honorary protector, an unpaid post, "conferred on her as a consolation prize" (Salter 1972:195).

Daisy Bates continued to function productively, but there is no doubt that the discipline lost in her a most valuable ethnographer, who constantly insisted that "the native question should be looked at from the native point of view" (Bates 1938:25).

Lousie Spindler (in "Editor's note," Hart and Pilling 1960:v.) as "a case study of a system of influence and power which is based on a strange currency... woman.... Because men compete for prestige and influence through their control over women, women have the value of a scarce commodity."

Kaberry and Goodale present a totally different picture of the aboriginal women. They describe their crucially important economic roles, and show that these determine the nature of their spiritual role, refuting the male view that women are excluded from the sacred state. For Australian totemic ceremonies reflect the total social organization that the women and men have evolved in their struggle to adapt to a precarious environment.

Referring to the division of labor by sex, Ashley-Montagu (1937:23) reports that the women are nothing but "domesticated cows," while Malinowski states (1913:287) that the women are forced to do the heavier work "by the 'brutal' half of society" [and that] "the relation of a husband to a wife in its economic aspect [is] that of a master to its slave." Kaberry, however, demonstrates that the women's work is less onerous than the men's. Hunting over rugged hills and under a blazing sun is very exhausting and often disappointing, but the women forage at a leisurely pace, rest and gossip in the shade, swim in the pools to cool off, and always manage to bring food back to the camp. Women carry the burdens as the band moves from place to place in search of food, for the men must be free to use their hunting weapons. But nomadic bands travel light and the women are not unduly taxed by their loads.

The woman supplies most of the food for the family, since hunting is unpredictable and the amount of meat supplied by the man is uncertain. Foraging requires skill, patience, and an exhaustive knowledge of the environment. The woman also brings down small game and even kangaroos, with the help of her hunting dogs, which she raises and trains with care and love. According to Kaberry (1939:23):

If it was compulsory to search for food, at least they did not travel like beasts of burden, with timorous docility and bovine resignation. They were not driven forth by the men; they departed just as leisurely, chose their own routes, and in this department of economic activities, were left in undisputed sway. If it was left to them alone to provide certain goods, at least it was a province in which they were their own mistresses, acquired their skill from the older women, and served no weary apprenticeship to an exacting husband or father.

In fact, the women's work is no more compulsory than the men's. Meat is regarded as essential to the diet and "it is just as incumbent on the man to contribute this whenever possible, as it is for the woman to go out for roots and tubers" (Kaberry 1939:25).

If the husband returns from a tiring day and thinks his wife has not done her share, he quarrels with her and may try to beat her up, "but there is no question of her submissively accepting punishment for unwifely conduct" (1939:25). Every woman has her fighting stick, which she wields with great skill, and when the man is unlucky in the hunt or the wife thinks he is just plain lazy, she may attack him "with both tongue and tomahawk" (1939:26). On the whole, however, there is very real economic cooperation between husband and wife, "an expected and recognized feature of marital life" (1939:27). Both Kaberry and Goodale show that women and men sometimes go on hunting and fishing excursions together, although generally they go about their activities separately.

Kaberry suggests that the separation of the sexes during the greater part of the day is carried over into the ritual sphere. But Elkin maintains (1939:xxvi) that "both the dichotomy manifested in economic life and also in ritual life may arise from the physiological differences between men and women." When confronted by the complexities of cultural roles, many Western social scientists take refuge in the reductionist theme: "Anatomy is destiny."

Projecting the primary importance of technology in the West, Warner (1937:6) asserts that the dominant religious and social roles of the men reflect their technological skills, while the "more simple" techniques used by the women tend to "simplify their personalities" and social roles, and exclude them from the totemic mysteries. Kaberry, however, points out that the men's skills do not increase the importance of their economic activities, while the tools which the women make and use satisfy the bulk of the nutritional needs of the group. It is by virtue of their essential economic contribution that the women are respected, and assured of just and good treatment. Women have a right to their own property, and they trade many of the articles they make with both male and female partners in the system of economic exchanges. With their female partners they also exchange secret corroborees and, like the men, the women practice sorcery against undependable partners.

Many male students of the Australian aborigines, from 1840 onward, dwelt on the marital life of the women, hinting darkly at the dire fate of the young girl handed over to an old man. "Polygamy is practiced in an exceedingly barbarous manner unfit for publication," wrote Gason (1879:81). "Within these marriage classes things unspeakable may happen," said Gribble (1930:175–176). And according to Malinowski (1913:101), "the husband had a definite sexual 'over-right' over his wife, which secured to him the privilege of disposing of her." With little access to the women, how did these scholars arrive at their unmentionable conclusions?

The assumption that the prepubescent girls were sexually violated by dirty old men seems to reflect the widespread father-daughter incest fantasy among Western men. According to Kaberry, young people of both sexes have casual affairs before marriage, a commonplace in tribal societies. If a girl becomes pregnant, the man to whom she is betrothed becomes the child's sociological father, a form of insurance for the mother. But full sexual intercourse, with either lover or husband, is not permitted until after puberty. The girl's future husband begins to stay in her parents' camp before she reaches puberty, and in this transitional pre-marital period they get to know each other, so that she is accustomed to him by the time she goes to live in his territory. Both parents and young people indignantly rejected the notion that sexual intercourse took place before the first menstruation. In the myths that Kaberry collected from the various tribes, sexual relations always follow menstruation and never precede it.

The full force of the Judeao-Christian theme of female uncleanliness is projected on the aboriginal woman. Warner states (1937:394) that "masculinity is inextricably interwoven with ritual cleanliness, and femininity is equally entwined with the concept of uncleanliness, the former being the sacred principle and the latter the profane." The Murngin, according to Warner, connect the superordinate status of the males with their sacred cleanliness, as well as their technological superiority, and connect the woman's subordination with her profane uncleanliness. The ritual cleanliness of the male is made more sacred through continual ceremonial participation, which unifies the male group, while the subordinate female group is unified by exclusion from the ceremonies and by ritual uncleanliness.

Insofar as menstruation is involved with blood and the genitals it is endowed with powerful magical properties and associated with taboos. Since it is believed that the power of menstrual blood might harm the men, menstruating women keep unobtrusively out of their way. However, Kaberry reports that the men never expressed disgust for a menstruating woman. They never spoke of her as "dirty" or "unclean," nor was there a term for "dirty" which implied ritual uncleanliness. Particularly significant, says Kaberry (1939:238), is the fact that the women never think of themselves as unclean, or of menstruation as shameful, which they would do, as do women in the West, if the men viewed them that way. The women are unified not by "their ritual uncleanliness" or their exclusion from male ceremonies, but by their economic cooperation and their participation in their own secret ceremonies.

The male anthropologists insist that the men totally dominate all marriage arrangements which are entirely in their own interests. According to Hart and Pilling, Tiwi women are investment commodities, pawns in the male struggles for power. The Tiwi male view is represented in the terms of the Wall Street stockbroker (Hart and Pilling 1960:16):

As in our culture, where the first million is the hardest to make, so in Tiwi the first bestowed wife was the hardest to get. If some shrewd father with a daughter to invest in a twenty-year-old decided to invest her in you, his judgment was likely to attract other fathers to make a smilar investment.

Hart and Pilling completely ignore the benefits and powers accruing to the women in this system. Goodale (1971:52) points out that the tie between the son-in-law and his future mother-in-law is "one of the most important and enduring social relationships that either may have." In return for the promise of her future daughter, the son-in-law becomes responsible for providing for the needs and wants of his mother-in-law until his or her death. "He must supply her with all she demands in services or goods, including today clothes, tobacco, money, and the like" (1971:52). Moreover, if the son-in-law "does not serve his mother-in-law to her satisfaction, she may void the contract. A girl's father does not have the right to void such a contract" (1971:56). In the Kimberley tribes of Northwest Australia the large number of elopements and irregular marriages indicates that many young women do not meekly accept the pre-arranged marriages. Moreover, a young woman married to an old man often has a young lover.

Because of the age discrepancy between the Australian woman and her first few husbands, she is often widowed and often re-marries. But just as older men marry young women, so the woman as she grows older marries younger and younger men, and exercises increasing choice as to whom she marries. When a widowed woman outlives her brothers, her sons have the nominal right to arrange her next marriage. But even Hart describes (1960:20) Tiwi widows as "highly vocal and pretty tough old ladies who were not easily pushed around by anybody, even by their adult and ambitious sons. Whom they remarried in their old age was a matter upon which they had themselves a good deal to say." What is more, these older women not only arrange their own marriages, but also, according to Goodale (1971:57), those of their sons. "Since all contracts involve an exchange ... mothers anxious for their sons' advance might agree to exchange sons!"

Ashley-Montagu asserts that throughout Australia the physiological bond between mother and child is even less recognized than that between father and child. The Arunta woman, he says (1937:74), is merely "the medium through which a spirit-child is transformed into a baby," and much more significance is attached to "the relationships between father and child than that which should exist between a mother and the child to which she has given birth." But this appears to be a projection of the typical patriarchal denial of the female generative power.

"Primitive" peoples everywhere have an enormous respect and awe for female reproductive functions. Specifically, among the Kimberley tribes, Kaberry clearly demonstrates that the physiological relationship between mother and child is not only fully recognized, but that the mother is accorded a special respect and affection. The pregnant woman observes food taboos because certain foods are believed to injure the child within the mother's womb. The natives of South and Central Australia believe that the individual inherits the body, flesh, and blood from the mother. Children from about the age of six onward distinguish between their own biological mothers and "other mothers," such as mothers' sisters. Men who have the same mother but different fathers call each other "brother," and children have close ties with their mother's group. The mother receives a share of the gifts when her son is initiated, as well as gifts from her daughter's husband, and participates in the negotiations for her daughter's marriage. Mothers and married daughters visit and give each other gifts, and both sons and daughters care for their mother when she is old.

Ashley-Montague (1937:72) also maintains that "the actual experience involved in giving birth to a child is so minimized and the social implications of the result of the birth so magnified that the former wilts away into the obscure background before the all-embracing consequences of the latter." With no access to the rituals surrounding the woman's life crises, he somehow discovered that "childbirth among the Australians ... is a comparatively light affair for the woman.... There is no great affect normally associated with childbirth, nor is it in any way climatic" (1937:73).

This attitude, says Kaberry, typifies the male ethnographer's causal approach to childbirth and its rites. Although the Australian woman enjoys her children and the advantages that accrue from being a mother, she regards children as the consequence of marriage and not the reason for it. "Where she does bear children, they do not anchor her the more securely in a position of inferiority, nor circumscribe her activities" (Kaberry 1939:156). But women in the gathering-hunting societies deliberately space childbirths. Far from childbirth being lightly treated, many aboriginal women dislike the prospect of the pain and trouble, and the burden of carrying the baby about afterwards. A most important secret ritual is performed to lessen the difficulties of childbirth. Goodale notes (1971:145) that young wives may have several abortions "to postpone their motherhood so as not to interfere with their love life." Kaberry points out (1939:157–158) that "we cannot assume the existence of a maternal instinct prior to pregnancy or even after conception, since so many aboriginal women resort to abortion." It appears that the women in "primitive" cultures have far greater control over their bodies and reproductive functions than their "civilized" sisters.

When it comes to the spiritual life of the aboriginal women the male anthropologists are guilty of the most serious distortions. Durkheim, Warner, and Elkin all assert that only the men are sacred and make sacred progress. But Kaberry points out (1939:230) that if the men really represented the sacred element, the women would surely be cognizant of the fact and accept it. The women, however, do not regard the men as sacred; they "remained regrettably profane in their attitude toward the men." Elkin insists that the men do become sacred in the course of their secret ritual life, whether or not the women regard them as sacred. But if half the population withholds recognition of the sacredness of the other half, by what magical authority does this other half become sacred?

Many male anthropologists seem to be as bedazzled as any Western tourist by the spectacular rites of the aboriginal men. While the women participate in fewer and less elaborate rituals, the ceremonies of both women and men are closely related to their respective problems. Just as the men are mainly concerned with male rituals, so the women are involved principally with those relating to their own sex, which the male ethnographers are inclined to treat as a minor or exotic feature of native life. Spencer and Gillen, for example, describe (1927:480) women's rites in a chapter they call "Peculiar Native Customs."

The patriarchal identification of women with evil and danger is particularly marked in Roheim's denigration of the women's religion (1933: 259):

What is her religion? ... We might just as well put this question in another form and ask what are her fears, anxieties? For it is only this phase of religion that is open to women. All aspects of religion that contain any hint at a supernatural world that protects mankind ... or any element of identification are limited to the male half of the population. For a woman, religion means a supernatural or semisupernatural danger, it means demons ... or demonlike avengers or foreign tribes.

According to Kaberry and Goodale, both women and men have the same deeply-rooted beliefs in the totemic ancestors, and the egalitarian relationships between the sexes are reflected in the myths that depict male and female totemic ancestors as existing together from the first. In a Tiwi creation myth a female deity created the earth, trees, and animals, fresh and salt water; and a goddess is both the sun, which gives forth heat at mid-day, and the Milky Way at night. Unlike the patriarchal creation myths that teach men and women that a male god first created a man, the myths related by the Australian women teach them to identify with female totemic ancestors who are responsible for and protect child-birth and menstruation.

As the girl begins to approach puberty the old women chant songs to bring her to sexual maturity, and just before the first menstruation they perform secret rituals to prepare her for marriage. During the first men-struation, rituals are performed to bring the secluded girl safely through the period, and the women sing sacred songs, jealously guarded from the men, to stop the flow of menstrual blood, to facilitate childbirth and prevent hemorrhage. After childbirth rites are performed to strengthen the mother and the baby.

In Northwest Australia the men are barred from the secret corroborees in which the women participate to obtain love magic. Although some of the men oppose these events, they cannot prevent them from taking place, and the women relish the disadvantage to which they put the men. Like the male rituals, the corroborees provide the opportunity for joking and teasing, and for display and recreation. These dramatic and vivid affairs are organized and led by the middle-aged and old women. The painted and costumed dancers use their husbands' boomerangs and their own fight-ing sticks, which are endowed with magical qualities for the occasion, to simulate sexual intercourse. Many of the songs sung by the women dur-ing these corroborees, as well as at other ceremonies, emphasize the clitoris in love-making. It seems that among the Kimberley tribes the myth of the vaginal orgasm is absent.

With increasing age the Australian women become more assertive and wield more power and authority, but some male ethnographers project on them the contempt and disrespect experienced by older women in Western society. Hart, for example, usually refers to older Australian women as "ancient hags" or "toothless old hags," in contrast to his respectful references to "powerful old men." Nevertheless, the male ethnographers cannot entirely ignore the influential status of the older woman in band life, as well as in the camp. The older women teach the younger ones their economic skills, and preside over the women's rites and secret corroborees. According to Kaberry (1939:184):

Together with the old men, they are the repositories of myth, responsible for handing on tribal law and custom, and are one of the forces which make possible the stability and continuity of tribal life.

The older women take the initiative in settling disputes "when anger mounts high and threatens the peace.... Amidst the shouting, the barking of dogs, the voice of an old woman will make itself heard above the uproar as she harangues men and women impartially" (1939:184).

Summarizing the major differences between the studies of the male and female ethnographers, it is evident that the androcentrism of the male scholars results in an etic perspective which blinds them to the actual realities of aboriginal life. Androcentrism prevents the male scholars from recognizing that the natives fully acknowledge the importance of the women's economic contribution so that they are accorded commensurate roles in the other institutions. Androcentrism leads the male scholars to exaggerate the importance of political power and technology for the natives. The androcentric male scholars project on the aborigines the patriarchal notion that the physiological differences between the sexes determine all sex role differences; as well as the patriarchal concepts denying the female generative principle, attaching female uncleanliness to menstruation, asserting the subordinate status of the wife and mother, and identifying women with evil and danger. The androcentric male scholars ignore or minimize the importance of the ritual life for the women. In addition, the male scholars who are androcentric are also misanthropic, for they misrepresent the Australian men as brutal, domineering, and oblivious to the humanity of the women.

The women ethnographers, on the other hand, show us men and women living together in equal partnership, the rights, self-respect, and dignity of the members of both sexes being guaranteed. Although the men play a more important political role in intergroup relationships, the political institution is not highly developed and is geared to economic survival, in which the women play the central role. The Australian women are shown to have complete control over the reproductive function, and they are not regarded, either by the men or by themselves, as contaminating, polluting, unclean, evil, or dangerous. The women gain the same benefits as the men from their ritual experiences: emotional security during the life crises, and opportunities for drama, recreation and display. And the women ethnographers reveal the Australian men to be concerned and caring husbands and fathers.

The basic inference to be drawn from the differences between the male and female ethnographies is that many Western male anthropologists are unwilling or unable to expunge their ethnocentrism, of which the predominant elements are androcentrism and sexism. Androcentrism and sexism lead to the misinterpretation and distortion of the status and roles of women in non-Western cultures. But if the status and roles of women are misinterpreted and distorted, so inevitably must be those of men. Since the relationships of women and men interlock, the distortion of the roles of men and women leads to a distortion of the total social system.

Those women anthropologists, however, who are aware of the oppression of women in an androcentric society, and are sensitive to male misperceptions of women, bring a double-consciousness to their research which results in holistic, accurate, and objective studies. It is such women ethnographers as Kaberry and Goodale who achieve a truly emic-etic perspective.

REFERENCES

ASHLEY-MONTAGU, M. F.
  1937   *Coming into being among the Australian aborigines.* London: George Routledge and Sons.
BATES, DAISY
  1938 *The passing of the aborigines.* London: John Murray.
ELKIN, A. P.
  1939   "Introduction," in *Aboriginal woman, sacred and profane.* By Phyllis M. Kaberry. London: George Routledge and Sons.
GASON, S.
  1879   "The Dieri," in *The folklore, manners, customs and languages of the South Australian aborigines.* Edited by G. Taplin. Adelaide, Australia: E. Spiller.
GOODALE, JANE C.
  1971   *Tiwi wives.* Seattle: University of Washington Press.
GRIBBLE, E. R.
  1930   *Forty years with the aborigines.* Sydney, Australia: Angus and Robertson.
HART, C. W. M., ARNOLD R. PILLING
  1960   *The Tiwi of North Australia.* New York: Holt, Rinehart and Winston.
KABERRY, PHYLLIS M.
  1939   *Aboriginal woman: sacred and profane.* London: George Routledge and Sons.
KAPLAN, DAVID, ROBERT A. MANNERS
  1972   *Culture theory.* Englewood Cliffs: Prentice-Hall.
LEACOCK, ELEANOR B.
  1972   "Introduction," in *The origin of the family, private property and the state.* By Friedrich Engels. New York: International Publishers.

MALINOWSKI, BRONISLAW
1913   *The family among the Australian aborigines.* London: University of London Press.
RIESMAN, PAUL
1972   *New York Times Book Review.* October 22.
ROHEIM, GEZA
1933   Women and their life in Central Australia. *Journal of the Royal Anthropological Institute* 63.
SALTER, ELIZABETH
1972   *Daisy Bates.* New York: Coward, McCann and Geoghegan.
SPENCER, BALDWIN, F. J. GILLEN
1927   *The Arunta,* volume two. London: Macmillan.
SPINDLER, GEORGE D.
1970   *Being an anthropologist.* New Yort: Holt, Rinehart and Winston.
STEWARD, JULIAN H.
1970   "Cultural evolution in South America," in *The social anthropology of Latin America.* Edited by Walter Goldschmidt and Harry Hoijer. Los Angeles: Latin American Center, University of California.
WARNER, W. LLOYD
1937   *A black civilization.* New York: Harper and Brothers.

Women, Knowledge, and Power

CONSTANCE SUTTON, SUSAN MAKIESKY,
DAISY DWYER, and LAURA KLEIN

> The origins of our oppression, like the roots
> of all domination, are lost long ago. We are
> completely without memory of any alterna-
> tive.... We are background to history...
> negative to their positive... oppressed by an
> overwhelming sense of not being there....
> This inability to find ourselves in existing
> culture as we experience ourselves is true of
> course for other groups besides women. The
> working class, blacks, national minorities
> within capitalism all encounter themselves
> as echoes.... However, the problem for
> women is particularly internalized. This is
> partly a matter of history. We have no time
> or place to look back to.
>
> SHEILA ROWBOTHAM[1]

We offer this account of women's relationship to knowledge and power
in three different societies in the hope of making more visible the varied
roles that woman play. A close and complex connection exists between a
group's access to and control of knowledge and its power and authority,
its ability to make and implement decisions. Here we explore how this connection operates in societies where women's roles and statuses differ
from those traditional in Western culture. In particular, we consider how
the social location of the sexes affects their definitions of themselves, their
views of their society, and their access to the valued cultural knowledge

This is an expanded version of a paper originally presented at a conference entitled
"Women learn from women," held at Barnard College, February 10, 1973.
[1] In: *Woman's consciousness, man's world*, pages 34–36.

used to make decisions, guide action, and envision options and alternatives. Further, we discuss briefly how these social locations affect the way sex roles are symbolized in cultural ideology.

We attempt here only a preliminary exploratory foray into these complicated issues, drawing on our own fieldwork, which was carried out among three different cultural groups — Moroccans, Tlingit Indians, and black Barbadians.[2] Each of us did her fieldwork on problems other than the ones posed in this paper; consequently, we do not possess the kind of data which directly bear upon the questions we now raise. These questions did not emerge from the theoretical concerns that guided us while we were doing our field studies but from issues brought to our awareness by the contemporary women's movements in the United States and elsewhere. These issues include the problematic relationship of women to power, the nature of women's consciousness and how it has varied in other times and places, the status of women in symbolic systems, the models of reality women produce and how these compare to those produced by men. Are male political dominance and male cultural hegomony characteristic of all human societies? Is it true, as many writers currently claim, that men have been the definers of social reality, the codifiers of the cultural terms, categories, and images by which people — women as well as men — interpret their own situation? Do women not only inhabit "man-made" worlds but also operate with "man-made" ideas, images, values, and beliefs?[3] As women, and as women anthropologists, these questions have come to concern us personally and to interest us theoretically.

A theme underlying these questions is the social authorship of ideas and the circumstances that give one group the power to determine the thinking of another. This is the stuff of a sociology of knowledge. One view of the dialectic between knowledge and power assumes that knowledge is a form of power and power a means of creating and controlling knowledge.

[2]   Constance Sutton did research in Barbados in the summer of 1956 and during 1957–1958, supported by grants from the Research Institute for the Study of Man and from the Population Council. She returned in the summers of 1968 and 1969, supported by grants from the New York University Arts and Science Research Fund, the Research Institute for the Study of Man, and the Wenner-Gren Foundation for Anthropological Research. Daisy Dwyer worked in Taroudannt, Morocco, in 1969–1971. The research was supported by an NIMH grant. Laura Klein studied the Tlingit in Hoonah, Alaska, in 1971–1972, supported by a Ford Foundation research grant. Susan Makiesky carried out research in Barbados during 1970–1972, supported by a grant from the Ford Foundation Foreign Area Fellowship Program.
[3]   These questions have been formulated in a number of different but related ways in current popular and anthropological writing. See, for example, Ardener (1972), de Beauvoir (1953), Ortner (1974), Rosaldo (1974), Rowbotham (1973), Firestone (1972).

Here we rephrase this as a question of the relationship between women's social roles and their access to cultural knowledge. We do not attempt an ethnosemantic, cognitive, or symbolic analysis of the content and structure of cultural knowledge. Rather we are concerned with the distribution of knowledge among women and men and with how relations of dominance and subordination, or autonomy and dependence, affect the acquisition of knowledge and forms of consciousness that develop. Those who dominate important institutional arenas are clearly in a position to make their ideas consequential for others. This is what makes their version of reality plausible and authentic, and permits it to be imposed as a dominant ideology. Those who are subordinate and dependent are compelled to take into account the formulations of the dominant ideology. But they also produce versions of reality — complementary or contrasting. These forms of collective consciousness also interest us.[4]

But we have chosen to focus on knowledge and power for other reasons as well. Foremost among these is the fact that Western centers of knowledge and power have historically been male domains. As a result, knowledge and power have come to be regarded as intrinsically masculine attributes. It is obvious that this long history of excluding women from the citadels of learning and from prominent positions in religious and political institutions in the West has perpetuated their subordinate status, sustained an ideology of male superiority and female inferiority, and nourished the deeply-rooted cultural assumption that male cultural hegemony and political dominance are universal.

Today, though women have won entry into these institutions, the assumption that men are inherently more knowledgeable and powerful remains as a bias "deep enough in the marrow of society's bone to inspire forgetfulness" of its source while continuing to influence behavior (Stimpson 1973:304). Thus, for example, a century after Lord Byron quipped that Madame de Stael "thinks like a man but, alas, she feels like a woman," Jean Paul Sartre can say that "the wonderful thing about Simone de Beauvoir is that she has the intelligence of a man... and the sensitivity of a woman" (Moorehead 1974:26). Objective, rational, and logical thought is culturally coded as male, and terms such as "forceful" and "muscular" are used to describe ideas that are to be taken seriously, the ideas of men.

---

[4] This is the linkage between political domination and cultural domination that has been of concern to the two recent movements for equality in the United States — the Black Power movement and the feminist movement. Both groups have made the issue of becoming masters of interpretation and builders of their own culture a key political goal. Black Power advocate Stokeley Carmichael is said to have defined black power as "the power to define," while feminist literature urges that women become autonomous and self-defining.

584   CONSTANCE SUTTON, *et al.*

The latent message of these cultural codes is, then, that when a woman actively pursues knowledge or indulges in serious thought, she is acting as a man, and at some level at least, denying her own identity. This has been coded as emotional, sensuous, and nurturant — traits set in opposition to thought and action.[5]

This internalized identity conflict expresses an external social structural relationship between knowledge and authority — one symbolized in the Judaic-Christian origin myth. Here God gives to Adam the power to name all the creatures on earth, and Adam's first act is to produce the definitions by which things are known. In contrast, Eve's first act is to seek knowledge, to attempt to share God's wisdom by eating of the fruit of the tree of knowledge. This will open her eyes and make her "as God, knowing good and evil" Genesis 3:5. However Genesis underscores the danger to a woman who seeks knowledge which is possessed by the sacred male. As punishment, she is sentenced to experience pain in childbirth and to submit to the authority God delegates to her husband.

Turning to the three groups we studied, we find interesting differences in the structures of dominance and dependence and forms of knowledge and group consciousness. In Morocco we encounter a situation of marked social separation of the sexes in almost all spheres of activity, a separation that is associated with an ideology of female inferiority and with women's extreme economic and political dependence on men. In sharp contrast, among the Tlingit Indians we find an absence of marked differences in the roles of women and men; both hold important decision-making positions in their community. As with the Tlingit there is among the black rural proletariat of Barbados considerable equality between the sexes. Women and men hold positions of comparable status in the economy and the local community. But as a legacy of Barbados's slave plantation past, the community has little autonomy, and the group as a whole — women and men — has little control over economic and political resources.

We now briefly describe each of these societies and conclude with some comparisons.

---

[5] Perhaps this role conflict contributes as much to the ambivalence women reportedly experience in going through college and pursuing academic careers as does reluctance to compete with men. But this psychic role conflict exists not only for women; its counterpart exists for men who, according to Robert J. Lifton (1964), feel threatened, possibly emasculated and "seen through," as women seek to broaden the base of their knowledge.

MOROCCO

The city of Taroudannt is a regional center in the south of Morocco, one of the nation's most traditional regions. Within the historic walls of the city, 20,000 inhabitants live relatively untouched by the West. Traditional crafts, family farming, and small-scale trade are still the main occupations, and traditional patterns, such as arranged marriages and mystical brotherhood associations, continue to be prevalent. Forty years of limited French supervision of the area, followed by seventeen years of Moroccan national independence, have brought about scant change.

The city of Taroudannt thus remains a traditional world with traditional divisions (Dwyer 1973), particularly between two spheres, the public and the domestic, which overlap only minimally. The public sphere is the predominantly male arena of politics, formal religion, and business; the domestic sphere is largely the world of women, bound for the most part by the walls of the house or the limits of the neighborhood or street.

This division between the public and the domestic, the male and the female worlds, tends to seclude women within certain boundaries, and to exclude them from many activities which take place beyond. Taroudannt women are prohibited from entering the main worship area of any mosque, for example. While a small number of worship areas exist within the city for elderly women who have passed the age of seductiveness, all women are encouraged to pray in their homes. Similarly, the woman who infringes upon the male preserve of the cafe may damage her own and her family's honor. Even in the Taroudannt court, men await consideration of their legal cases within the courthouse while women are secluded in the garden outside.

One result of such seclusion is that women spend a great deal of time in one another's company, visiting with kin and friends in their neighborhoods. They congregate together, meet for advice, and sometimes work together. When they travel to outlying areas, women most often continue to be among women and thus remain secluded in a comparable female world.

The boundaries between the more public world of men and the more private world of women are maintained by formal religious ideology, as well as by more informal cultural concepts about inherent sex-linked qualities. Islamic ideology defines women as subordinate to men. The Koran states that "men are the managers of the affairs of women for that God hath preferred in bounty one of them over the other" (Arberry 1955: *sura* 4, Verse 38). The divine will is thus to be carried out by men, and women are excluded from many religious activities. Indeed, not only are women believed to be less capable religiously, but they are also considered to endanger the quality of male worship, by distracting through their sexuality and polluting through their menstruation.

This religious attitude finds expression in a legal system which, for example, formally evaluates a woman's testimony in court as having half the value of a man's. In theory, it takes two female withnesses to counter-balance the testimony of a male. In practice, the testimony of women is seldom considered seriously and more often is not even solicited.

Related to these codified notions is a set of less formally stated concepts which contrasts men's rationality and acumen with women's inherent irresponsibility and irrationality. Women share this view of themselves, but in the privacy of seclusion also consider men as ignorant and irresponsible. This view, however, remains a submerged one with little effect upon how men evaluate themselves.

Also important in restricting women are cultural notions about women's greater sexual passion and limited self control. These serve to justify women's confinement, for it is believed that if women were to move about unrestricted, they would succumb to their passionate sexual natures. Thus, unless segregated and secluded, women would threaten the honor of their kinsmen and selves.

Clearly, segregation and seclusion limit women's direct access to knowledge about economic, political, and formal religious life. And in a society such as Morocco, where people learn primarily by observing others, women's ability to learn facts and techniques is curtailed. The knowledge that is most important for functioning in Moroccan society is a knowledge of people and here too women are severely limited. They often depend upon men to establish important social contacts for them in the public domain.

In most ways, women's existence in Taroudannt is characterized by their dependence upon men. Unlike a man, a woman should not live alone, unless she has already been married and a home with kinfolk is unavailable. When a father, a son, or a brother lives in the region, the kinswoman should ideally live with him and he should provide for her support. Her economic contribution in this traditional setting is limited primarily to housekeeping, with perhaps an additional small income arising from voluntary home-centered tasks, such as sewing, spinning, and curing. Although money earned in these ways legally belongs to the woman, it is often allocated or confiscated by the family head. Only when no male support is forthcoming, or when such support proves insufficient is full-time employment in the public sphere deemed fully acceptable. As a result of these attitudes, married women in comfortable families seldom undertake full-time work.

Although class differences are not rigid in Taroudannt and although they tend to be further levelled among women, differences in the prestige of families clearly exists. Women derive their status from the men in their families, with the men's status depending upon such traits as wealth, political power, and religiosity. Initially, a woman's status is determined by her father; after her marriage it is determined by her husband. Only in cases of severe discrepancy in social rank does a woman's status affect that of a man.

Segregation, seclusion, and dependence serve to cut women off from the public world, but within their own subordinate sphere, women have considerable autonomy. Believing that the home is a woman's region and that domestic activities are predominantly her concerns, men prefer to spend their time in more male-dominated settings. Women promote the daily exodus of men by ridiculing those who center their activities in the home. Thus by virtue of male and female pressures, women remain home together, without men, for substantial time periods, and a large number of decisions about household finances and about the future of children are made by women.

Knowing many women and thus being able to relay information through a female network is a major asset for Moroccan women. In particular, women share complaints and dissatisfactions about such things as family relations, restrictions upon their mobility, and insufficiency of support, and this stress upon common problems is one basis of female solidarity. The sharing of personal information, however, remains weighted toward this negative aspect — the communication of complaints. This tendency is reinforced by notions of the evil eye, which suggest that to talk about achievements, success, and desires is to risk disaster by engendering the envy of others.

The female network, as well as the knowledge that passes through it, is used to circumvent male authority. Women can serve as transmittors for goods stolen from the family storehouse; they can be used as fictitious sources of "gifts" that are brought into the home. Young girls use a complex network of peers in order to investigate potential boyfriends, to relay letters, and to set up rendez-vous without the knowledge of their parents. So concerned are some men that such tactics and ties will be used by their wives and daughters that, to keep their women uncorrupted, they forbid contact with male and female outsiders alike.

Although girls do receive some formal education, it tends to be limited to the pre-adolescent period. At this stage, public education is permissible, for girls are thought to be not yet possessed of sexual drives that are believed to be inherently dangerous. But if they go to school, it is in a separate girls' school. At the secondary level, by contrast, boys and girls attend school together but are separated within the classroom. At this stage parents' fears about greater contact within the schools combine with their concern about their daughters' approaching pubescence, and most girls are discouraged from pursuing their education. To continue to attend school is to come into conflict with a code of behavior which stresses modesty and reserve. Girls are further discouraged because they share the prevalent view that they are more ignorant and less conscientious and so will be less successful than males intellectually.

This characterization of female abilities and potentialities is maintained by segregation, seclusion, and female dependence, all of which limit women's experience within, as well as their access to knowledge about, the wider society. Restricted in their ability to obtain or to formulate alternative self-images, Moroccan women cannot challenge the overall ideology of their inferiority. Instead they accept it and work within its bounds.

TLINGIT

In striking contrast to the separate worlds of Moroccan women and men is the situation of the Tlingit Indians living in the small town of Hoohan in the southwestern part of the state of Alaska. Although the town's 800 residents live within the political domain of the United States, they remain somewhat isolated, both physically and culturally, from centers of United States influence and have chosen to maintain their distance. The town is known in the area as a Native town and Tlingits hold the important local political positions.

The situation of the Tlingit women differs dramatically from that of the women of Morocco. Here the division between domestic and public domains, so sharply defined in Morocco, is not pronounced. Nor are the domains identified as male or female. Both women and men engage in economic and political activities in the public domain and are found at all levels of the status hierarchy. We find no marked differences between male and female spheres of knowledge and power.

The traditional Tlingit economy was highly seasonal, based on fishing. Labor was divided between men who fished during the summer and women who then processed the perishable food for year-round consumption and trade. Trade was an extremely important activity and women were traders, playing a key role in negotiations and exchanges with other groups of Indians and with Europeans (Krause 1956). Today, women and men continue to be actively involved in economic activities outside the household, and the traditional sexual division of labor still operates in the commercial realm of fishing and processing. In the new occupations of the modern economy, women have a higher rate of year-round employment than men and are preferred by white employers who view them as more reliable: unlike men, women will not quit in the summer to go fishing. They also predominate in the prestige positions of school teaching, civil service, and shopkeeping. Their importance in these occupations reinforces the traditional view that women are enterprising and more skillful than men in the handling, using, and saving of wealth.

Not only do Tlingit women and men equally occupy positions of high status in the public domain, but husbands and wives operate in this sphere independently. This may represent another continuity with the past, for traditionally rank was based on position in the matrilineal clan and was not changed by the status of the individual's marriage partner. Thus while husband and wife were usually of similar rank, significant differences between them before marriage continued after marriage. The highest rank a person could achieve was essentially set by his or her clan position. But it was not automatically reached; an individual had to demonstrate that he or she was worthy of a given ranked position, and the giving of potlatches, which involved spending a great amount of wealth, was a major way to demonstrate this worth. The literature on the potlatching that took place during the nineteenth century does not clearly specify whether women and men were differentially involved in giving or being honored at potlatches. It does, however, indicate that both sexes participated actively at various levels (de Laguna 1972).

In earlier days when the ability to give elaborate speeches, based on clan mythology, was a sign of high rank, both boys and girls were told and retold the clan stories by their grandmothers and both were repeatedly tested for competence in repeating them correctly. Women and men of high rank were both given the opportunity and expected to tell these stories in public at clan parties. The content of traditional mythology further supports the prominent participation of Tlingit women in the public spheres of town life. It depicts women as high ranking members of society and associates them with wisdom and knowledge. In traditional myths women speak well and persuasively; they resolve problematic situations for themselves and for others; and they are portrayed as sources of knowledge about important aspects of their culture, such as the potlatch and life after death.

The modern picture is similar in that highly ranked people of both sexes command respect and consideration, and both women and men achieve political influence and power on the basis of their own personal connections, some of which are derived from matrilineal kinship ties. These important networks, traced through women, interweave both male and female relatives. In the modern setting, politicking is an activity that absorbs both sexes and both are equally able to build up personal followings.

The even distribution of influence and positions of prestige and authority between women and men results from the active involvement of both sexes in the formal associations where important decisions concerning town life are made. Women hold as many official positions as men at all levels in these organizations and operate with the same principles and methods. And since the higher-level positions provide access to sources of information valued by the community, it is evident that women possess this form of knowledge to the same degree that men do and hold similar ideas about the nature of their society.

The egalitarian nature of male and female participation in public activities is reflected in a cultural ideology that assigns few differences of character or ability to men and women, and does not identify the sexes with particular domains of activity or forms of knowledge. Although as in most societies, domestic work and child care are primarily the responsibility of women, men also engage in these activities. Given the seasonal nature of the fishing cycle, the men spend much time at home in winter and during this period help care for children. There is also a free day-care center for children that operates the year round. Responsibility for children, then, is shared socially and they do not constitute a burden that limits the employment opportunities of women. Thus it is not surprising to note that 48 percent of the women, as opposed to 34 percent of the men, go to on college. Since activities are not defined in sex-linked terms, both male and female students, even at the secondary-school level, take advantage of classes in shop and home economics, as well as academic subjects.

Tlingit Indians are familiar with the culture of the encompassing white American society but are neither intimidated by its powers nor impressed by its superior technical knowledge. Proud of their own Tlingit identity, they are preoccupied with maintaining control over their community. Though increasing involvement in the United States economy and political system is increasing their dependence and subordination, they still view the larger society as a resource to be used for their own ends. The woman or man who is able to get grants or government projects for the town is more than just politically important; she or he is the recipient of community respect. "That person is one of us, you know," is the common boast.

Tlingit pride is also expressed in their preference for remaining in the community where they can maintain their cultural integrity, although economic pressures sometimes force them to move away. Thus Tlingit women and men alike have an outsider's view of the knowledge and skills of the United States which allows them to appropriate those parts that are useful to functioning in the community, without being strongly influenced by the cultural ideology of the dominant society.

This insulation from the cultural assumptions in the dominant society is, however, a relative matter. Tlingit are aware of the ways in which their own relative sexual equality contrasts with the assumptions of sex-linked differences prevalent in the larger United States society. In fact, they react defensively to outsiders who label their system a matriarchy. Women who leave the town to go to college or to work elsewhere in the United States experience directly the sex biases of the larger society, and they give this as one of their reasons for wanting to return to their town. Here they know that women as well as men can achieve success in the world of work and politics. In the Tlingit culture, then, knowledge and power are associated with rank, not sex, and rank is shared by women and men alike.

BARBADOS

In the West Indian island of Barbados, women and men of the black rural proletariat, like Tlingit women and men, are active in the world of work and the life of their communities. However, the relation between these two arenas, and their position within the island's plantation-based social structure, differs from that in Morocco and in the Tlingit town of Hoonah. For the 2500 villagers residing in the rural community of Endeavor the world of work and political power is located outside their community. The community lacks autonomy and villagers have little control over the basic resources upon which they depend for a livelihood. The island's economy remains in the hands of a resident white elite and jural-political institutions are now managed by a black middle class. In this public domain, villagers hold a subordinate position. Power is wielded by a male elite, both white and black, and is imposed upon villagers of both sexes.

Family and community life, though influenced by the activities and decisions carried out in the public domain, are organizationally and culturally distinct from it. Within the family and in the community, black Barbadians operate with cultural assumptions that differ from and sometimes oppose those guiding behavior in the public domain. The dominant ideology that prevails in this domain is identified with the political and economic elites. More relevant in the arenas of family and community life is a black folk culture that has incorporated and reworked elements of the dominant ideology.

The roles of women and men in these domains developed in the context of the island's history as an English slave plantation colony. From the beginning, enslaved African women and men were exposed to the dominant system with a brutal directness. Their relative statuses were determined by their positions within the hierarchically organized plantation community, controlled from above by members of a different race and culture.

Within the bounded system of the plantation, few areas were exempt from the watchful control of the plantation manager and his overseers. Angela Davis, writing about society in the United States, points out that the one realm of plantation life with a degree of autonomy was the living quarters of the slaves. The activities carried out in this "domestic domain" were primarily the responsibility of the slave women — an assignment reflecting both African traditions and the cultural assumptions of the white slaveowners. But the women who carried out these tasks were neither shielded nor cut-off from the world of work and public activity. They also labored in the fields alongside men, and were daily exposed to the same harsh realities. And, like the men, they acquired a knowledge of how the system worked and a consciousness of their oppressed and victimized condition. This they carried back to the home, the one haven of refuge and relative autonomy for the slave population. Here women were first among equals in devising the means and techniques for survival, subversion, escape, and outright rebellion (Davis 1971).

Thus, throughout slavery, both women and men were subjected to a system which gave them little control over their own lives but which generated a folk culture that was invisible to the dominant group (Bryce-LaPorte 1971). This folk culture served as a means of survival and as a potential base for opposing the system. Unlike the female half of Moroccan society, whose segregation and subordination have restricted their knowledge of the wider system, black Barbadians have been exposed to the dominant system with a directness that has forced them to acquire a great deal of knowledge about it. Thus there is active and continuing discussion among them of how the system works and how it can be made to work for them.

Today, as in the past, Barbadian women play active roles in both the domestic domain and in the social and economic life of the community. The central role of Afro-Caribbean women in the domestic sphere has been the subject of a voluminous literature on "matrifocality" which has emphasized both the special importance of the mother-child relationship, and the domestic authority women have. Bearing a child marks a woman's achievement of social adulthood. However, the mother role does not necessarily entail greater dependence on a man. Rather it brings responsibility and the chance for a woman to demonstrate her capabilities in effectively looking after her own and her children's interests. Nor do childcare and domestic responsibilities confine and isolate women in the home. Because these tasks are shared among female relatives, with additional help from the men and adolescents in the household, women with children frequently continue to participate actively in the public domain.

In the world of work, women and men participate on terms of equality. Although they engage in different tasks, there is also considerable overlap; the prestige of a given occupation derives from the skills required and remuneration received, not from its association with one or the other sex. In the cane fields, women and men often work together, usually with men cutting and women loading the canes. While many of the building trades are considered to be male occupations, and selling in the marketplace is a female occupation, both sexes work as bus conductors and road workers, and both are equally represented in the traditional prestige positions of schoolteacher, shopkeeper, and civil servant. The civil service and commercial establishments, which are increasingly open to blacks, employ women and men in the same capacity. But whether they will be allowed to move up at the same rate within these establishments will depend less on community-defined norms than on the policies of the national bureaucracy and the commercial establishments. It is in these institutions that male biases prevail.

As in the past, the village today is an arena that offers black Barbadians some measure of escape and autonomy from the pressures of the dominant social order. The village itself, however, is not autonomous and constitutes neither an administrative nor a socio-political unit within the wider system. Hence no positions of formal authority exist at the village level. Prestige in the village social hierarchy derives from occupation and from adherence to community-based definitions of acceptable behavior. These include not asserting authority over others (except in the parent-child context), and exercising influence by indirect means only. Though villagers show a marked preoccupation with status differences, the codes that guide their social behavior emphasize equality. In interpersonal transactions, respect is shown to others for their personal human qualities as well as for their accomplishments. The concept of dominance in social relations is not identified with either sex, but with those who hold positions of power and authority outside the village.

Coming out of a slave-plantation background, villagers of both sexes put a special premium on personal autonomy and the capacity to act in their own interests. Both women and men are admonished to not let their attachment to the opposite sex "turn them foolish." Viewed by both sexes as capable and independent, women control their own money, they own land and houses, and they act independently as legal heads of large households. Children of both sexes are encouraged to seek formal education that will allow them to attain high status positions. Achievements within this sphere are seen as based on brain power — and brain power is not attributed to one or the other sex.

Barbados' dominant cultural ideology reflects traditional European notions about male and female characteristics, and villagers of both sexes are aware of and sometimes voice these concepts. It is, however, the black folk culture, with its very different definitions of masculinity and femininity that guides interpersonal behavior within the community. Unlike the dominant ideology, this folk system of rules and meanings makes few distinctions between male and female abilities and attributes. Sex and sensuality symbolize creativity and power (in the sense of effectiveness, not dominance) but men and women are equally endowed with these qualities. Nor is sensuality thought to interfere with effectiveness in public roles; for both sexes, it is believed to enhance abilities to think and act decisively. Women's procreative powers command respect, and childbirth symbolizes women's special strength and capacity to endure pain. But the distinct qualities of masculine and feminine sexual and reproductive abilities are not viewed by either sex as a basis for different social capabilities. Rather, it is in male-female interpersonal relations that these differences are elaborated. Thus while women may complain that men are deceitful and unreliable as husbands and lovers, these attributes are not generalized to their performance in other roles. Similarly, men lament the hypocracy and untrustworthiness of women as sexual partners — but not as workers, mothers, or household heads. And both women and men are viewed as sharing the qualities of intelligence, ambition, cautiousness, and self-confidence which constitute their national self-image of "the average Barbadian."

Women and men have considerable autonomy in their patterns of socializing. Men spend a great deal of their leisure time with other men in informal cliques that meet at street corners or in the rum shops. Apart from rum drinking, a major occupation of these men's groups is talk. Worldliness and sophistication are admired, and high standing within these groups is in part attained by the ability to introduce new and esoteric bits of information on an almost unlimited range of topics. Novel and memorable ways of phrasing ideas are emphasized, for though literacy is widespread, black Barbadians rely heavily on oral traditions for transmitting knowledge and information.

Women, on the other hand, have a pattern of socializing which links them in dyadic relationships to friends, kin, and neighbors. Frequent reciprocal visiting and exchanges of favors, services, and "news" maintain rather wide-ranging networks of women within and across community boundaries. Thus even when women are not out working, their contact with women who are working continues to expose them to a wide variety of information and options.

Conversations between women and in men's informal cliques range widely over a number of topics, though current personal and political gossip evokes special interest. Sex is a prominent theme in talk among women and men. Both groups regard sex as pleasurable, desirable, and necessary for health and general well-being, and they discuss, separately and together, how to improve sexual performance and pleasure. Stylized sexual banter between women and men occurs in public and private settings, and is enjoyed by both sexes.

Politics, cricket, and the implications of national and international events are also prominent themes in village conversation. Events in England and the United States are followed with particular care, since, as a result of emigration during the 1950's and 1960's, villagers have many relatives and friends in these two countries. Their preoccupation with happenings there during the 1960's contributed toward a change in their ideas about themselves as black people and about their political system (Sutton and Makiesky 1975). A shared experience and knowledge of the wider society, together with a cultural emphasis on autonomy and independence of action, have led women and men to feel equally qualified to make their own judgements about the issues that concern them.

The received knowledge and rationales of the structure imposed by the dominant group are viewed skeptically by both women and men. From the vantage point of their subordinate position, such formal knowledge appears alien, if not sometimes inimical to their well-being. Despite this skeptisism, formal education is highly valued and viewed as a passport to achieving higher status. It is not, however, considered a source of meaningful or satisfying understandings of the social universe. More relevant for coping with social realities is the knowledge of the subculture, the folk wisdom based on experience dealing with survival, maintenance of self-respect, and how to operate with ease in the system. This knowledge belongs to women and men alike, and has today begun to serve as a base with which they can more actively confront and challenge the system that subordinates them.

CONCLUSION

The recent surge of anthropological writing on women has revealed that they play more active and influential roles in their societies than once was thought. But whether distinct spheres of activity are consistently male or female and whether female political and cultural subordination are universal are still treated as controversial issues.

It is worth noting that phrasing of these questions in such global terms reflects the strong bias in Western culture toward viewing sex differences as part of the "natural order." Even when women are treated as a social category, they are studied in terms of roles, functions, and attributes assumed to be inevitable and universal.[6] A twentieth-century concept of "universal roles and functions" thus replaces a nineteenth-century notion of "anatomy" as the explanation of female destiny. These constructs lend support to the view that women's roles are limited and relatively constant, while men have been responsible for societal evolution and change.

We have made an effort to overcome this static conception by focusing not on women's marital and maternal roles but on the varying ways that women and men relate to the knowledge and power in their society. We have used the term "knowledge" in two senses in this paper: one refers to information acquired about the workings of a society; the second, refers to a group's consciousness of its position in society and its version of reality.[7]

We started with the assumption that the socio-economic organization determines the location of the sexes in domains of activity and that this in turn affects the positions of women and men in the political and symbolic orders. The three communities discussed here are all parts of larger, complex societies involved in a world economy. As such, a division be-

[6] Prominent examples of this tendency to regard roles in terms of constants are the current oppositions between female child-rearing functions versus male leadership functions, the separation of society into a male jural-political domain and a female domestic domain, the ideological identification of women with nature and men with culture, of women with disorder and danger and men with order and authority. See, for example, Ardener (1972), Barnes (1973), Beidelman (1964), Harris (1973), Ortner (1974), Rosaldo (1974), and Tiger (1969). For a critique of these views, see Leacock (1974) and Leavitt's article in this volume.

[7] No effort was made to distinguish forms and categories of knowledge — such as pragmatic knowledge of everyday life, technical knowledge, or knowledge of wider systems of rules and meanings that constitute a 'cultural ideology. Nor have we examined how the social context of learning influences forms of knowing, except to note whether information is directly acquired or mediated by others. Hopefully, these areas will be covered in future research.

tween domestic and public spheres of activity, which develops only when domestic units no longer control their own productive and distributive activities, is a feature of all three. However, the degree of separateness of these public and domestic domains and the extent to which they are sex-linked is more varied than the literature on sex roles assumes (Rosaldo 1974).

Morocco provides the closest parallel to the Western situation but in a much more extreme form. Not only are public and domestic domains of activity sharply differentiated, but each domain is so strongly associated with one sex that sex segregation itself comes to define domain boundaries. Among the Tlingit, in contrast, the separation of the public from the domestic sphere of activity is relatively recent, a result of the encapsulation within the American political system of this formerly autonomous clan-organized group. But even as the growth of the modern wage economy sharpens domain boundaries, women and men continue to operate in both spheres, precluding the identification of these domains with one or the other sex. In Barbados, the separation of domestic and public activities is as old as the society itself and deeply entrenched. But, as among the Tlingit, the sexual division of labor cross-cuts those boundaries: women's work — though often different from men's — takes place in both arenas. It is only at the elite-controlled national level that the public and domestic domains are sex-typed and the public sphere is predominantly male.

The extent to which women have access to the public domain crucially affects the degree to which they determine their own positions in the status hierarchies of their societies. The exclusion of Moroccan women from the public domain precludes independence of action and status. Not only are women dependent on men in dealing with the larger society, but their status in society also depends on their fathers and husbands. The status of Tlingit women, on the other hand, reflects their own achievements and their kinship positions within the matrilineal clan system and is not determined by their relationship to men. Similarly, in Barbados, black women and men achieve status within their communities on the basis of their own activities in the public realms of work and community life.

In each case, the social position of women and men both reflects and reinforces cultural concepts about sex-linked character traits and capabilities. In Morocco, segregation and seclusion are viewed as necessary consequences of women's allegedly sensual and uncontrolled nature, while the ignorance and dependence produced by segregation are used further to justify women's subordination. In contrast Tlingit recognize few differences in masculine and feminine character. Their mythology does not elaborate female sexuality or motherhood as defining women's

identity or social roles, and their traditional concepts of women as competent and enterprising lend support to women's prominence in present-
day political and economic affairs. Black Barbadians highly value the
mother role, and evaluate male and female sexuality in positive terms.
Sexual differences are not thought to affect the ways women and men operate in the world outside the home, and both sexes are viewed as intelligent
and capable.

Among black Barbadians and the Tlingit, women appear to hold views
about society and themselves similar to those held by men. Similarities
in the experiences, activities, and statuses of women and men within the
public domain provide a basis for shared male and female versions of
reality and a distinct female consciousness seems to be limited in scope
and without discernible impact on women's behavior in the wider
society. Along with the men of their society, these women define their
interests in contrast to more powerful and dominant groups. But in sex-
segregated Morocco, we do find that women define their interests as
being distinct from — though not necessarily opposed to — those of men.
Although they may act to subvert male control over their lives in particular
ways, Moroccan women do not openly confront or challenge male domination.

Thus only among Moroccan women do we find a distinct female subculture, a set of ideas and experiences markedly different from those
of men. However, the separateness which fosters a distinctly female experience produces a female view that is partial, complementary, and
secondary to that of men. The exclusion of women from the larger world
prevents them from acquiring their own view of the totality of the Moroccan social universe. Hence they lack the breath of experience which is
necessary to challenge their own subordination.

This suggests, then, that the development of an alternative consciousness
depends on particular kinds of relations between subordinate and dominant groups. Black Barbadians of both sexes, like Moroccan women, are
subordinate and powerless; yet unlike Moroccan women, they have
an intimate knowledge of the system that oppresses them and possess
a group consciousness that partially counteracts the dominant culture's
notions of their inferiority. While they have used the knowledge of the
dominant society to improve their status within the system and to protect
themselves from its harshness, their own subcultural view has recently
begun to provide a basis for confronting and challenging the dominant
institutions and ideology. The Tlingit are also a subordinate group, but
their consciousness differs from that of both Moroccan women and black
Barbadians. They sufficiently control the knowledge and resources of

their community to sustain a relatively autonomous view of their culture and themselves. While this insulates them from the impact of the dominant ideology, it is not used to challenge it.

We have conducted this discussion of women, knowledge, and power at a level of generality which overlooks many questions and issues relevant to the topic. We can only hope that future research will provide more conclusive data on, for example, the content of male and female versions of reality, the culturally-specific symbolic meanings of male and female sexuality, and the range of contextually defined patterns of interaction between women and men in a given society. What our comparisons at a more general level do show is that women's marital and maternal roles do not necessarily define their status in society or confine them to the domestic sphere. Among both the Tlingit and black Barbadians, women as well as men achieve status from their activities in the public domain. The Tlingit, in fact, provide a striking example of sexual equality in the public domain. Here women are equally represented in positions of authority and decision making and take an active role in creating and shaping the public and private worlds they inhabit. And though Tlingit women do not surpass men in publicly recognized power and authority, their equality in this domain challenges the assertion that "Everywhere we find that women are excluded from certain crucial economic and political activities, that their roles as wives and mothers are associated with fewer powers and perogatives than the roles of men" (Rosaldo 1974:3). Our material suggests, on the contrary, that women are not universally subordinate in the cultural and political sphere.

REFERENCES

ARBERRY, A. J.
1955 *The Koran interpreted.* New York: Macmillan.
ARDENER, EDWIN
1972 "Belief and the problem of women," in *The interpretation of ritual.* Edited by J. S. LaFontaine. London: Tavistock Publications.
BARNES, J. A.
1973 "Genetrix: genetor:: Nature: Culture?" in *The character of kinship.* Edited by Jack Goody. London: Cambridge University Press.
BEIDELMAN, T. O.
1964 Pig *(Guluwe):* an essay on Ngulu sexual symbolism and ceremony. *Southwestern Journal of Anthropology* 20(4):359–392.
BRYCE-LAPORTE, R. S.
1971 "The slave plantation: background to present conditions of urban blacks," in *Race, change and urban society.* Edited by Peter Orleans and William Ellis. Beverly Hills, California: Sage Publications.

DAVIS, ANGELA
  1971 Reflections on the black woman's role in the community of slaves. *Black Scholar* 3(4):3–15.
DE BEAUVOIR, SIMONE
  1953 *The second sex.* London: Cape.
DE LAGUNA, FREDERICA
  1972 *Under Mount Saint Elias.* Washington D.C.: Smithsonian Institution Press.
DWYER, DAISY HILSE
  1973 "Women's conflict behavior in a traditional Moroccan setting — an interactional analysis." Unpublished doctoral dissertation, Yale University.
FIRESTONE, SHULAMITH
  1972 *The dialectic of sex.* London: Paladin.
HARRIS, GRACE
  1973 "Furies, witches and mothers," in *The character of kinship.* Edited by Jack Goody. London: Cambridge University Press.
KRAUSE, AUREL
  1956 *The Tlingit Indians.* Translated by Erna Gunthern. Seattle: University of Washington Press.
LEACOCK, ELEANOR
  1974 Review of *The inevitability of patriarchy*, by Steven Goldberg. *American Anthropologist* 76(2):363–365.
LIFTON, ROBERT JAY
  1964 "Woman as knower: some psychohistorical perspectives," in *The woman in America.* Edited by Robert Jay Lifton. Boston: Beacon Press.
MOOREHEAD, CAROLINE
  1974 A talk with Simone de Beauvoir. *New York Times Sunday Magazine* (June 2).
ORTNER, SHERRY B.
  1974 "Is female to male as nature to culture?" in *Woman, culture and society.* Edited by Michelle Z. Rosaldo and Louise Lamphire. Stanford: Stanford University Press.
ROSALDO, MICHELLE Z.
  1974 "Woman, culture, and society: a theoretical overview," in *Woman, culture, and society.* Edited by Michelle Z. Rosaldo and Louise Lamphire. Stanford: Stanford University Press.
ROWBOTHAM, SHEILA
  1973 *Woman's consciousness, man's world.* Baltimore: Penquin.
STIMPSON, CATHERINE
  1973 What matter mind: a theory about the practice of women's studies. *Women's Studies* 1(3):293–314.
SUTTON, CONSTANCE, SUSAN MAKIESKY
  1975 "Migration and West Indian racial and ethnic consciousness" in *Migration and ethnicity.* Edited by Helen Safa. World Anthropology. The Hague: Mouton.
TIGER, LIONEL
  1969 *Men in groups.* New York: Random House.

Class, Commodity, and the Status of Women

ELEANOR LEACOCK

This paper attempts neither consistent documentation nor proof. Instead it is hortatory and explorative. I want to put forth the proposition that the continued separation of woman's position from the central core of social analysis, as an "and," "but," or "however," cannot but lead to continued distortions. This might be so because of the simple fact that women constitute half of humanity. The point I want to suggest here however, is that the notion of a somehow separate "woman's role" hides the reality of the family as an economic unit, an institution as crucial for the continued exploitation of working men as it is for the oppression of women. To understand this family form and its origins is fundamental to the interpretation of social structure, past and present, and to the understanding of how to fight for and win the right of the world's people to make decisions about their future. Relegation of family forms to secondary questions about "woman's role" has hindered us in our search to comprehend the origins of class society, the dynamics of its perpetuation, and the shape of its full negation.

The same has been true of racial and national oppression, for they have also been relegated to the status of secondary issues in contemporary Marxist analysis, with serious consequences, both theoretical and political. Before developing my central point concerning family forms and their relevance to the interpretation of history, I should like to review this parallel problem briefly.

As Marx pointed out, it was the expansion of the European market

Originally prepared for and also appearing in: *Towards a Marxist anthropology: problems and perspectives*, edited by Stanley Diamond, World Anthropology (in press).

into the world market that transformed mercantile Europe into capitalist Europe. Historically, then, capitalism has been inseparable from racist brutality and national oppression throughout its history. Yet few Western scholars have chosen to explore all the ramifications of this connection. Marx unveiled the mystery of commodity production and the fetishism of money; he revealed the process whereby direct relations among people, as they labored to produce and to exchange the goods they then consumed, were transformed by the emergence of commodity production for profit, so that people's very labor became an alien force against them. In other words, Marx analyzed the nature of exploitation itself as a principle, and as a principle it was and is colorless, raceless, and sexless.

However, in the course of organizational failures and confusions, exploitation somehow became defined as centrally of whites and of men. Seduced by the divide-and-rule ploys that are constantly generated from the competitiveness inherent in capitalist structure and that are consciously reinforced by the servants of the powerful as well, scholars and self-styled revolutionaries, white and male, accepted the bribe of pitiful involvement in personal and petty oppression, and, bemused, analyzed society in their image, including the very nature of exploitation itself. The unifying power of the concept was destroyed by the hardening into dogma of a pernicious dichotomization, whereby the exploitation of the industrial worker, white and male, was pitted against the compounded exploitation and cruel oppression of the nonwhite as well as the nonmale.

The theoretical separation of class exploitation from other forms of oppression contributed to the tragic undermining of a revolutionary socialist movement in the United States following World War II. Black revolutionaries were forced to divide themselves in two, to dichotomize the oppression of their people through ritual statements that their exploitation as workers was more fundamental than their oppression as blacks. Thereby the special and powerful anger of black people was defined as inherently counterrevolutionary. I remember a black woman comrade, years ago now, saying, "I don't care what they say, FIRST I am a Negro [the term "black" being then still a term of abuse], THEN I am a worker." Her third identity, powerfully adding to the totality of her oppression, hence her potential as a revolutionary, that of a woman, she did not even express, so submerged then was such identification in the idiocies of a theoretically sterile organizational politicking. To pit national or racial oppression against class exploitation is a sophomoric sociological enterprise; it is not Marxist analysis. That people of color can fall across class lines — a few of them — has befuddled our thinking insofar as we are metaphysical and not dialectical. Class exploitation and racial and national oppression are all of a piece, for in their joining lay the victory of capitalist relations.

To pursue this line of criticism in a more academic context, consider the extent to which United States history has been written as the history of white men. The contribution from the left has mainly been to stress that the black experience must be added. Recently, some American Indians, and now women, are being tacked on as well — as if it were a matter of merely adding these extras to make the whole, rather than a matter of fundamental rethinking. Consider also how the history of capitalist development has been written as if wholly white, deriving almost totally from internal European processes. Relations with Africa, Asia, and the New World are seen as extras, as gravy, unimportant until quite late when they set off Europe's final imperialist explosion. It is agreed that the English capital which made industrialization possible was derived in major part from the triangular trade in slaves, rum, and sugar (produced in what were models for European factories, the sugar mills of the Caribbean plantations), and then the significance of that fact is forgotten. W. E. B. DuBois and Eric Williams are respectfully saluted and their work is ignored or said to be overstated (DuBois 1946; Williams 1944). It is as if the victory of bourgeois market relations over feudalism, and the "freeing" of workers to sell their labor were largely internal European developments that involved only white men. In fact it was the uniting of class, race, and national exploitation and oppression on a world scale that made the triumph of the European bourgeoisie possible. The reality was all too painfully evident to Toussant L'Ouverture when he unsuccessfully tried to win support for a free Haiti from the revolutionary French bourgeoisie, as C. L. R. James so masterfully relates (1963).

Sometimes it is argued that racial and national oppressions were in theory not essential to a victory of capitalist relations. The argument is fruitless, for historically they WERE joined. True, it was an accident of human physical differentiation that peninsular Europe was inhabited by a people who had lost much of the melanin in their skin, as it was an accident of geography that it was an area with many harbors and waterways, and relatively available coal and iron that made possible primary industrialization once the area had caught up with the ancient urban world. On another planet it might have been different. On ours, however, when it behooved energetic merchants to wring great profits from workers other than those in their own nations, color offered a convenient excuse. The first rationale for slavery was religious, since economic conflicts in Europe had been fought for so long in religious terms. "Heathens" were natural slaves. The rationale did not last long, since heathens could easily convert, at least nominally, when it was in their interest to do so. Color, and the elaboration of the "white man's burden" then became the excuse for conquest, plunder, and enslavement of non-Europeans. Racism did, and still does, serve powerfully to divide the world's workers. It befuddles the scholar as well. Were humanity either wholly "white" or wholly "black," would the early history of exploitation and oppression in the Third World be considered as somehow apart from, or as merely supplementary to, exploitation of Western workers?

I trust I have labored my point sufficiently. At present, Marxist social scientists and revolutionaries in Latin America and Africa are beginning to clarify these issues. Today there are many who recognize that it is critical to sort out true and false oppositions in joining the struggle of the world's people to bury class society before it buries us all. The point I want to make here is that the same is true when it comes to the oppression of women. And sex oppression goes further back, not just to the rise of capitalist class relations, but to the origins of class itself.

According to the happenstances of disciplinary boundaries, as they became defined in the nineteenth century, the task of analyzing the nature and origin of women's oppression has fallen to us as anthropologists. I cannot say that we have risen to the task. The dominant view today is that women have always been to some degree oppressed — the usual term is "dominated" — by men, because men are stronger, they are responsible for fighting, and it is in their nature to be more aggressive. In the United States, the position has been stated most fully by Tiger and Fox. Fox, in fact, uses the term "man" literally to mean male, rather than generically human. As "man" evolved, he evolved exogamously, writes Fox. "At some point in the evolution of his behavior he began to define social units and to apply rules about the recruitment of people to these units and the allocation of women amongst them" (Fox 1972). Referring to Lévi-Strauss, he elaborates this theory of human evolution with "we" as male, and women as passive objects of exchange:

For in behavior as in anatomy, the strength of our lineage lay in a relatively generalized structure. It was precisely because we did NOT specialize like our baboon cousins that we had to CONTRIVE solutions involving the control and exchange of females (Fox 1972:296–297).

Fox's basically biological view is gaining in popularity, containing as it it does fashionable allusions to Lévi-Strauss. However, more common among those who discuss sex roles are blunt judgements, empirically phrased, that casually relegate to the waste basket of history the profound questions about women's status that were raised by nineteenth-century writers. "It is a common sociological truth that in all societies authority is held by men, not women," writes Beidelman (1971:43); "At both primitive and advanced levels, men tend regularly to dominate women," states Goldschmidt in a text (1959:164); "Men have always been politically and economically dominant over women," reports Harris in his text (1971:328). Some women join in. Women's work is always "private," while "roles within the public sphere are the province of men," write Hammond and Jablow (n.d.:11). Therefore "women can exert influence outside the family only indirectly through their influence on their kins-men."

The first problem with such statements is their lack of historical perspective. To generalize from cross-cultural data gathered almost wholly in the twentieth century is to ignore changes that have been taking place for anywhere up to five hundred years a as result of involvement, first with European mercantilism, then with full-scale colonialism and imperialism. Indeed, there is almost a kind of racism involved, an assumption that the cultures of Third World peoples have virtually stood still until destroyed by the recent mushrooming of urban industrialism. Certainly, one of the most consistent and widely documented changes brought about during the colonial period was a decline in the status of women relative to men. The causes were partly indirect, as the introduction of wage labor for men, and the trade of basic commodities, speeded up processes whereby tribal collectives were breaking up into individual family units, in which women and children were becoming economically dependent on single men. The process was aided by the formal allocation to men of whatever public authority and legal right of ownership was allowed in colonial situations, by missionary teachings and by the persistence of Europeans in dealing with men as the holders of all formal authority (Boserup 1971).

The second problem with statements like the above is largely a theoretical one. The common use of some polar dimension to assess woman's position, and to find that everywhere men are "dominant" and hold authority over women, not only ignores the world's history, but transmutes the totality of tribal decision-making structures (as we try to reconstruct them) into the power terms of our own society. Lewis Henry Morgan had a marvelous phrase for such practice. He used it when talking of the term "instinct," but it is generally apt. Such a term, he wrote, is "a system of philosophy in a definition, and instillation of the supernatural which silences at once all inquiry into the facts" (Morgan 1963: viii). In this instance, women are conveniently allocated to their place, and the whole inquiry into the structure of the primitive collective is stunted. The primitive collective emerges with no structure — no contradictions — of its own; it is merely our society minus, so to speak.

Two examples help clarify these points. On history, take the Balonda, one of the Lunda Bantu peoples of the Congo. In his handbook of African peoples, Murdock writes of political authority among them as "vested in a headman and council of lineage or family heads within the local community," and over these, "district or subtribal chiefs with important ritual functions" (Murdock 1959:286). All are taken for granted as men. Murdock goes on to say that, although the Balonda are patrilineal and patrilocal, their Crow kinship terminology, plus a number of related practices, suggests that they were originally matrilineal and avunculocal like neighboring Bantu peoples (287–288). Murdock is a careful and conscientious scholar, and he or his assistents did, I am sure, scan the some dozen references, English and French, that he lists. Nonetheless, there is no mention of David Livingstone's encounter with the Balonda, when he was travelling through the area in 1857. At that time, women, as well as men, were chiefs. Livingstone's account of a young woman chief in her twenties, and her self-assurance both in relation to him and to the district chief, her maternal uncle, is so revealing that I am going to give it at some length.

Livingstone entered a Balonda village on the sixth of January and was brought before the chief. He wrote that a man and woman "were sitting on skins, placed in the middle of a circle, thirty paces in diameter, a little raised above the ordinary level of the ground" (Livingstone 1957:273). His men put their arms down, Livingstone continued,

...and I walked up to the center of the circular bench, and saluted him in the usual way, by clapping the hands together in their fashion. He pointed to his wife, as much as to say, the honour belongs to her. I saluted her in the same way, and, a mat having been brought, I squatted down in front of them.
The talker was then called, and I was asked who was my spokesman...
(1857:274).

This was Nyamoana, sister of Shinte, and mother of Manenko, the young woman chief. The discussion proceeded, Livingstone to his interpreter, the interpreter to Nyamoana's talker, the talker to her husband, her husband to her, the response moving back through the same chain. Livingstone wanted to go on alone to Nyamoana's brother, Shinte, while Nyamoana wanted her people to accompany the missionary. The arrival of Manenko, the young chief, and her husband, ended the argument and much to Livingstone's annoyance, Manenko was to take him to Shinte. "As neither my men nor myself had much inclination to encounter a scolding...we made ready the packages," he wrote. However, there was some delay on Manenko's part, so Livingstone seized the opportunity to leave. She intervened,

...seized the luggage, and declared that she would carry it in spite of me. My men succumbed sooner to this petticoat government than I felt inclined to do, and left me no power; and, being unwilling to encounter her tongue, I was moving off to the canoes, when she gave me a kind explanation, and, with her hand on my shoulder, put on a motherly look, saying, "Now, my little man, just do as the rest have done." My feelings of annoyance of course vanished, and I went out to try and get some meat (1857:279).

They walked, too fast for the comfort of Livingstone's men, Manenko without any protection from the cold rain. Livingstone was told that chiefs "must always wear the appearance of robust youth, and bear vicissitudes without wincing." When they arrived at the district chief's, Livingstone gave him an ox, whereupon Manenko angrily asserted it to be hers. Livingstone was "her white man," she declared and she had her men slaughter the ox and give her uncle one leg. Livingstone noted, "Shinte did not seem at all annoyed at the occurrence," thereby corroborating the correctness of Manenko's position (1857:295).

Everywhere in Africa that one scrapes the surface one finds ethnohistorical data on the authority once shared by women but later lost. However, to leave the matter at this, and argue a position of "matriarchy" as a "stage" of social evolution is but the other face of the male dominance argument. Pleasant for a change, to be sure, but not the true story. For what such data reveal is THE DISPERSED NATURE OF DECISION MAKING IN PRE-CLASS SOCIETIES — the key to understanding how such societies functioned as "collectives." The second example, from the Montagnais-Naskapi of eastern Canada, makes this point clear. Here we have more than just hints of early Naskapi scattered through various documents. Instead we have rich ethno-historical data in the *Jesuit relations*, particularly in the letters Father Paul le Jeune wrote back to his superiors in France in the 1630's (Thwaites 1906).

Elsewhere I have written of the Naskapi at length, of the fur trade and its impact on the band collective, of the emergence of the individual trap line, improperly called the privately-owned hunting territory, and of the changing position of women (Leacock 1954, 1955). The early accounts indicate a matrilocal emphasis in Naskapi society and refer to the considerable "power" held by women. The twentieth century ethnographies, on the other hand, indicate a loose structure with an emphasis on patrilocality, and infer male "authority" (Leacock 1955). Both early and late, however, considerable flexibility is reported, with no hardened formal structure. Therefore, social practices shifted without the same kind of overt recognition and resistance as, say, that among the Pueblo Indians of the Southwest who have long struggled to maintain their mores. To the ethnographers of the early twentieth century, the Indians, camping temporarily here and there in the woods in the winter, speaking their own language almost exclusively, wearing moccasins of traditional style, sharing game animals within the group, and still remembering much of their pre-metal-tool technology, appeared little changed from pre-Columbian times. In fact, however, the economic basis for the multi-family groups that lived collectively as winter units and that had links with parallel groups which could be activated in times of need, had been fundamentally undercut by the fur trade. The beaver and other furbearers had been transformed from animals that were immediately consumed, the meat eaten, and the fur used, to commodities, goods to be kept, individually "owned" until exchanged for goods upon which the Indians had come increasingly to depend. The process whereby "goods" were transformed into "commodities," although completed early in the old centers of trade, was still incomplete in outlying areas well into the twentieth century, so that the outlines of the change could be reconstructed from my fieldwork, with the seventeenth-century Jesuit records serving as the base line.

In the 1630's individuals within Naskapi society were autonomous; people made decisions about activities for which they were responsible. Group decisions were arrived at through feeling for consensus. The essential and direct interdependence of the group as a whole both necessitated this autonomy and made it possible as a viable system — TOTAL INTERDEPENDENCE WAS INSEPARABLE FROM REAL AUTONOMY. The *Relations* document the ethic of group solidarity as bound up with individual autonomy that together characterize the Naskapi. The emphasis was on generosity, on cooperation, on patience and good humor, but also on never forcing one's will on others. This ethic was enforced through ridicule and teasing, often bawdy, behind which lay the threat of great anger at injustice, and the deep fear of starvation, that might ultimately force individual hunters to abandon the group in order that someone might survive. The psychological expression of this fear was a cannibal monster—the *witigo*, and a cannabalistic psychosis.

The *Relations* also document the ethic that the Jesuits taught their converts, an ethic admirably suited to the breaking up of the band collective into families as economic units. The ethic was clearly stated: people should obey their chiefs (who should be formally elected); women should obey their husbands; a husband should take but one wife and insist on exclusive sexual rights over her; divorce should no longer be possible; and children should obey their parents. "Alas," le Jeune complained, "if someone could stop the wanderings of the Savages, and give authority to one of them to rule the others, we could see them converted and civilized in a short time" (Thwaites 1906:XII, 169). His teachings were not widely accepted, however, and his lecturing that men should restrict their wives' sexual activity so that they could be sure their children were their own, was met with a retort, "Thou hast no sense. You French people love only your own children; but we love all the children of our tribe" (1906:VI, 255). His exhortations against polygamy were similarly unpopular. "Since I have been preaching among them that a man should have only one wife," he wrote, "I have not been well received by the women; for, since they are more numerous than the men, if a man can only marry one of them, the others will have to suffer" (1906: XII, 165). The children were le Jeune's final problem. "All the Savage tribes of these quarters...cannot chastise a child, nor see one chastised," he wrote; "How much trouble this will give us in carrying out our plans of teaching the young" (1906:V, 221). He proposed a solution:

The reason why I would not like to take the children of one locality in that locality itself, but rather in some other place, is because these Barbarians cannot bear to have their children punished, nor even scolded, not being able to refuse anything to a crying child. They carry this to such an extent that upon the slightest pretext they would take them away from us, before they were educated (1906:VI, 153–155).

The "sagamores," or "headmen," were spokesmen, or intermediaries for the group; they held no formal power. "They have reproached me a hundred times because we fear our Captains, while they laugh at and make sport of theirs," bemoaned le Jeune (1906:XI, 243). They "cannot endure in the least those who seem desirous of assuming superiority over the others; they place all virtue in a certain gentleness or apathy" (1906: XVI, 165). Shamans were often people of considerable personal influence. Women as well as men became shamans at that time; this has ceased to be the case. In one incident recounted in the *Relations*, a woman shaman took over from a man who had not succeeded in reaching the gods. She began to shake the house so and "to sing and cry so loudly, that she caused the devil to come," whereupon she called upon the people to rally in war against the Iroquois. When a Jesuit Father took her task, "she drew a knife, and threatened to kill him" (1906:IX, 113–117).

Personally, I have been tempted to think of women as "natural" peacemakers; it is a role they play in many societies. Among the Naskapi, however, women joined in the protracted torture of Iroquois prisoners with even more fury than the men, in bitter anger at the loss of kinsmen dear to them. (The Iroquois were initially the aggressors.) As for the notion of women "obeying" their husbands, the *Relations* are full of arguments over this issue, with women running away from zealous male converts who were threatening to punish them for disobedience.

Reconstructed bits and pieces from the last five hundred years of North American Indian history suggest that parallel developments took place quite widely among previously egalitarian peoples. As trade, and in some cases wage labor, undercut the collective economy, chiefs and other men of influence began to play roles beyond that of spokesmen, often as entrepreneurial go-betweens in commercial matters, or as leaders of resistance, and the masculine "authority" of ethnographic accounts took shape (although doubtless often exaggerated, as largely male ethnographers recorded the views and experiences of largely male informants). Under colonial conditions, the "public" and "private" sphere became divided, as had not been the case when the "household" WAS the "community," and the "public" sphere became invested with a semblance of the female power it represents in state-organized society. However, to consider latter-day chiefs as having held ultimate authority in earlier tribal terms, is to distort the structure of societies in which relations with outside groups were not yet combined with an internal economic basis for the exercise of individual power.

At first blush, the fact that in some instances chiefly authority was undercut by the colonial usurpation of power would seem to contradict the above. However, while the great reaches of the north and northeast, down into the western plains and plateaus, constituted a huge area in which collective life was as yet unchallenged, in the southern and coastal areas of what became the United States and Canada, native American societies were developing internal cleavages prior to Columbus. I have been using the term "tribal" in an inappropriately undifferentiated manner in order to make my general point; in fact, however, the lumping of non-Western and non-Oriental peoples into a single category of "primitive," "preliterate," "tribal," etc., that is then contrasted with "civilization" has been a source of confusions which are not yet entirely cleared up. Classes, with their contradictory properties of freeing human ability and creativity through specialization of labor, while at the same time alienating the producers from control over the products of their labor, were of course developed or developing in many parts of the so-called primitive world prior to European colonialism. What is of moment in the present argument, however, is that in both egalitarian societies where chiefly authority was a matter of purely personal influence, and in stratified societies where it was based on some form of economic control over a significant part of the society's production — or whatever variation on the two principles or the combination of them in fact existed in the historic moment of any given society at the time of Columbus — at the heart of subsequent changes in group structure was the delineation or strengthening of the family as an economic unit and its separation from essential dependence on band or kin ties.

The authority structure of egalitarian societies where all individuals were equally dependent on a collective larger than the nuclear family, was one of wide dispersal of decision making among mature and elder women and men, who essentially made decisions — either singly, in small groups, or collectively — about those activities which it was their socially defined responsibility to carry out. Taken together, these constituted the "public" life of the group. These were the decisions about the production and distribution of goods; about the maintenance, building, and moving of the camp or village; about learning and practicing various specialties and crafts, and becoming curers, artists, priests, dancers, story tellers, etc.; about the settlement of internal disputes and enforcement of group norms; about feasts connected with birth, adolescence, death, and other rites of passage; about marriage; about ceremonial life, and about the extra-legal or anti-social manipulation of supernatural power; about the declaration of war and the making of peace. Even a casual consideration of any nonstratified society one knows reveals that in the precolonial context, in so far as the culture can be reconstructed; to speak simply of men as "dominant" over women distorts the varied processes by which decisions in all the above areas were made.[1]

In order to grasp the nature of the social collective from which class divisions arose, it is essential to grasp the implications of decision making as widely dispersed, with no one holding power over another by social fiat (only by personal influence). All of this is nothing new, of course, since Engels outlined the entire proposition in *Origin* (1972). It is the more surprising, therefore, that so little additional study has been made of the processes whereby the emergence of commodity production and a merchant class were interrelated with the breakdown of the tribal collective

---

[1] Although one must check for distortions in the ethnography of a group. For example, take men "exchanging" women in Australia. Older men may spend a great deal of time talking about such exchange (as to Hart and Pilling), but older women are also involved; sons are married off by elders as well; and the young people do have ways of refusing if they are dead set against the marriage. Furthermore, marriage is not that big a deal anyway, since divorce is easy, and sexual exclusiveness a foreign concept. To talk of "power" by men over women in such instances, as if it were the power of a Victorian father to consign his daughter for life to personal servitude to a man she dislikes is ethnocentric distortion.

into individual units that were economically responsible, privately, for rearing a new generation.

The male bias to which I have already alluded is part of the reason why *Origin* has not been taken more seriously. However, a good part also lies in the brevity and design of the book itself. *Origin* sets up a paradigm, a model of tribal society as contrasted with class society. Virtually all of the non-European and Oriental world are placed in the first category, and Greece, Rome, and early Germany are used as examples of the transition from collective kin-based to class-organized society. Therefore the book leaves in a very unsatisfactory state the colonial peoples who were in various stages of transition to class and state organization when their autonomous development was interrupted. Morgan's overcorrection of the Aztecs, so to speak, in his concern to clarify distinctions between Aztec rule and more entrenched state organization, was accepted by Engels, so *Origin* had little applicability DIRECTLY to New World urban societies. And the fact that Morgan, Marx, and Engels all shared an ethnocentric ignorance of Africa has limited the applicability of *Origin* to the analysis of African kingdoms. Furthermore, Engels' lack of any reference to the "Oriental" society that so interested Marx, and that subsumed, in a general way, the patriarchal societies of the East and of the classical Mediterranean that existed for thousands of years, is a further shortcoming. Finally, perhaps, Engels' work has suffered precisely because it has been so accepted, for despite its shortcomings, it is still a masterful and profound theoretical synthesis. At a time when Marx is being taken off his pedestral as a god who ordained the future, and is being seen increasingly as a man of great brilliance who armed people's hope for a better life with theoretical tools for organizing their fight for such a life, the fact that Engel's work has to such an extent been reduced to dogma has probably worked to its disadvantage. And, again, first and last, it has been relegated to the status of a "woman's book," peripheral to the scholarly domain. I cannot help but digress with an anecdote. Having sent a copy of the new edition of *Origin* with my introduction to a colleague, whom I knew was interested in many of the questions I discussed, I asked for his reaction. He thanked me for sending the book, and assured me that he had given it to his wife who was very much engrossed in it.

At present, then, we have something of a paradox. We are becoming acquainted with some of Marx's thinking about early social forms that he did not bring to publication in *Capital* or elsewhere — parts of the *Grundrisse* that predated it, and now the beautifully edited *Ethnological notebooks* that followed it. Yet these are being considered strangely apart from *Origin*, as if they somehow superseded it, as if *Origin* did not represent in the main the product of both Marx's and Engels' thinking. After all, the questions the notebooks raise — the full significance of commodity production and its early development in relation to money and then coinage, the relation between slave and free labor, between internal and external markets, between town and countryside in ancient society — were all discussed in *Origin*, along with their relation to the family as the fundamental economic unit in class society.

A recent exception is Mariarosa Dalla Costa's "Women and the subversion of the community" (n.d.), which elaborates on the economic significance of women's labor within the private confines of the family for the production of a new generation of workers. Dalla Costa also discusses distinctions between the patriarchal family and the capitalist family, as the center of production shifted from the patriarchal home to the factory. Again, however, in the contemporary academic setting in which Marxist anthropologists largely function, this is considered a "women's article."

In closing, I want to suggest the kinds of research questions that would begin to redress the imbalance I have been discussing:

1. Is the strongly institutionalized sex antagonism that is found among Melanesian and Latin American tropical forest horticulturists tied in with an early phase in the development of specialization and trade and the breaking up of the primitive collective? What are common features in both geographical areas? Are there parallels elsewhere, somewhat obscured by the happenstances of who writes about what and where? Is the formalized hostility related to incipient competitiveness over a surplus of food, at times allowed to rot in keeping with egalitarian pressures, yet beginning to operate as an independent force through trade? Is there a concomitant shift from matrilineal to patrilineal kinship? How widely was social structure affected by slaving (in Latin America the Yąnamamö apparently came out on top of neighboring peoples in this respect) or by recruitment of plantation labor (so common in Melanesia)?

2. What about the comparative study of cloth as a major form of goods that could be easily transformed into a commodity? In fact, cloth suggests itself as a perfect commodity, not only in Europe (and not only because of the first hundred pages of *Capital*), but because it is useful everywhere, and in many places essential, for everyone, while at the same time it is capable of generating a widespread demand as a luxury item that must constantly be replaced. It is readily storable, and not overly heavy for transportation, and it is very time-consuming to produce by hand. Cloth is indicated as important in the emergence of commodity production and in the delineating of the extended family household as an economic unit. Note such items as Marx's references to wives and daughters pro-

ducing cloth in the (patriarchal) Oriental household; references to traded cloth like those of de Lacerda, the eighteenth-century Portuguese emissary to Angola and Zambia (Burton 1969:79); the fact that England destroyed the Indian cloth industry when she took over that country; the discussion by John Murra on the role of cloth in strengthening the economic base of the Inca state (1962); the probable importance of cloth manufacture in the development of classes in Mesopotamia (informally, Robert Adams indicated to me that material on women as weaver-workers, and on their declining status, are available for attempting to reconstruct the early relations of class and family in this area); the importance of cloth as a trade item among the Maya (June Nash informed me that the more independent women in late Maya society were those who were weavers as well as other specialists — potters, healers, midwives, and tradeswomen).

3.   What about commodity production seen from a different vantage point, the market? The study of internal markets and external trade as they relate to the emergence of classes and the state has clearly suffered from the failure to tie in the emergence of the family as an economic unit. In West Africa, for example, data on women as internal marketers and men as external traders have too often been the focus for argument over women's status relative to men, rather than the focus for reconstruction of class and state formation. A wealth of questions awaits research in this region, where for more than five hundred years taxes from trade laid the basis for royal centers that maintained themselves along with standing armies and elaborate entourages. The historical rise and fall of these centers, the extent of urban development involved, and the nature of economic ties between these and surrounding agricultural village areas, are questions clearly related to the delineation of at least upper-class families as entrepreneurial economic units, and in many parts of West Africa kin groups ceased functioning as collectives long before colonial times. West Africa offers data on a further topic, the resistance of women to the process of their exclusion from newly-developing forms of public authority.[2]

4.   A problem of increasing interest today is the structure of those pre-capitalist class societies that have been loosely dubbed "Oriental." In the congeries of questions to do with relations between city and country-side, nature of classes, and extent of trade, the patriarchal extended family cannot be ignored as a central institution, with its upper-class and and lower-class variations.

---

[2]   For example, among the Igbo of Nigeria.

5. I could continue indefinitely, but let me end with ideology. The series of fascinating questions about concepts of omniscience and omnipotence, and absolute good and evil, that accompany the rise of classical theocracies, cannot ignore that what becomes a primary evil, sex, is represented by female temptation, not male. Are we going to leave this where Freud left it? When does the shift take place from "female" as symbolic of positive fertility to "female" as temptation to evil? Aztec theology was moving toward absolutes; are there hints of the latter aspect? When does it appear in Mesopotamia? It was very early that the law codified that women could NO LONGER take "two husbands" or they would be stoned.[3] An interesting early version of the Protestant ethic was represented by women who lived together as ascetics — as nuns, but were independent business women who produced cloth.

To sum up, as these instances illustrate, and as serious consideration of the point dictates, to relegate the analysis of changing family forms to a secondary status leaves social interpretation not only incomplete, but distorted. Furthermore, to leave out women as women, leaves out people, hence much of the dialectic that is involved in individual decision making as the stuff of social process. Such omission is conducive to mechanical determinism in the analysis of both pre-class and class society. And finally, the passing over as subsidiary of subjects concerning women, not only distorts understanding, but becomes another stone in the wall of masculine resistance that moves women to reject Marxism as not relevant to their problems. As a result, we make no positive contribution toward the woman's movement. Marx indicated that the oppression of women in a society was the measure of its general oppression. One can add, the strength of women's involvement in a movement dedicated to opposing a social order is a measure of the movement's strength — or weakness.

REFERENCES

BEDIELMAN, T. O.
1971 *The Kaguru: a matrilineal people of East Africa.* New York: Holt, Rinehart and Winston.
BOSERUP, E.
1971 *Women's role in economic development.* St. Martin's Press.

---

[3] From a 24th century BC plaque: "The women of former days used to take two husbands, (but) the women of today (if they attempted this) were stoned with stones (upon which was inscribed their evil) intent" (Kramer 1963:322).

BURTON, CAPTAIN R. F., *translator*
1969   *The lands of Cazembe, Lacerda's journey to Cazembe in 1798*. New York: Negro Universities Press.

DALLA COSTA, MARIAROSA
n.d.   "Women and the subversion of the community."

DU BOIS, W. E. BURGHARDT
1946   *The world and Africa*. New York: Viking Press.

ENGELS, FRIEDRICH
1972   *The origin of the family, private property and the state*. Edited and introduction by Eleanor Leacock. New York: International Publishers.

FOX, ROBIN
1972   "Alliance and constraint: sexual selection in the evolution of human kinship systems," in *Sexual selection and the descent of man 1871–1971*. Edited by Bernard Campbell, Chicago: Aldine.

GOLDSCHMIDT, WALTER
1959   *Man's way: a preface to the understanding of human society*. New York: Holt, Rinehart and Winston.

HAMMOND, DOROTHY, ALTA JABLOW
n.d.   *Woman, their economic role in traditional socieities*. Addison-Wesley Module in Anthropology Number 35.

HARRIS, MARVIN
1971   *Culture, man, and nature, an introduction to general anthropology*. New York: Crowell.

JAMES, C. L. R.
1963   *The black Jacobins*. New York: Random House.

KRAMER, SAMUEL NOAH
1963   *The Sumerians, their history, culture and character*. Chicago: University of Chicago Press.

LEACOCK, ELEANOR
1954   *The Montagnais "hunting territory" and the fur trade*. American Anthropologist Memoir 78.
1955   *Matrilocality in a simple hunting economy* (Montagnais-Naskapi). *Southwestern Journal of Anthropology* 11.

LIVINGSTONE, DAVID
1857   *Missionary travels and researches in South Africa*. London: John Murray.

MORGAN, LEWIS HENRY
1963   *Ancient society*. Edited and introduction by Eleanor Leacock. New York: World Publishing Company.

MURDOCK, GEORGE PETER
1959   *Africa, its people and their culture history*. New York: McGraw-Hill.

MURRA, JOHN
1962   Cloth and its function in the Inca state. *American Anthropologist* 64.

THWAITES, R. G., *editor*
1906   *The Jesuit relations and allied documents*. seventy-one volumes. Cleveland: Burrows Brothers.

WILLIAMS, ERIC
1944   *Capitalism and slavery*. Chapel Hill: University of North Carolina Press.

SECTION SIX

Conclusions

Conclusions

RUBY ROHRLICH-LEAVITT

Implicit in the data in this volume are the key questions about the inter-relationships between women's status and the nature of social systems: the preconditions for egalitarian relations between women and men; the processes that led to the present situation of male supremacy in so much of the world; the means whereby women resist oppression and struggle to re-establish, in a new social context, the equality that once prevailed between the sexes, the crucial prerequisite for a humane and just society.

Ethnohistorical data and ecologically-oriented ethnographies reveal with increasing clarity that the hunting-gathering and horiticultural societies, where the nuclear family merged with the community and decision-making was widely dispersed, engendered egalitarian relationships between women and men, as Leacock points out in "Class, commodity, and the status of women" (section 5):

The authority structure...where all individuals were equally dependent on a collective larger than the nuclear family, was one of wide dispersal of decision making among mature and elder women and men, who essentially made decisions — either singly, in small groups, or collectively — about those activities which it was their socially defined responsibility to carry out. Taken together, these constituted the "public" life of the group...with no one holding power over another by social fiat (only by personal influence).

These structures also characterized the more complex indigenous societies, ensuring egalitarian sex relationships even in such ranked cultures as the sedentary fishing clans of North America and the agricultural chiefdoms of Africa, as discussed in this volume.

The description of these societies has been the purview mainly of anthropology, but many members of the discipline have failed to perceive the realities of women's former status in non-Western societies. Since its inception, anthropology has been monopolized by men in Western cultures that until quite recently barred women from access to higher education and professional training and, as the papers in the section on "Women in anthropology" demonstrate, still discriminate severely against women. The virtual absence of women's theoretical input and of women ethnographers distorted the data that were collected, particularly those on non-Western societies. And when women finally began to enter anthropology, they were socialized in a discipline where the "male factor" was central in both theory and ethnography. Although this situation continues into the present, it is being modified by the increasing numbers of women in the discipline who, more and more, under the stimulus of the women's movement, are critically evaluating the claims and assumptions of the social sciences. Foremost is the assumption that the male supremacy typical of Western civilization is a universal fact of life. Moreover, male anthropologists, perhaps reacting to the earlier as well as the contemporary women's movements, seem to be projecting, "over and above factual reporting" on women's status in non-Western societies, the roles they want Western women to play:

male observers reading into that situation their own versions of how things ought to be (that is, women dominated by and behaving submissively toward men) — and using this interpretation to show their own womenfolk, at home, how much better off they were than they might be, and, by implication, how contented they should be with their lot (Berndt 1970:48).

The view that male supremacy is a social constant prevails in all patriarchal civilizations, along with the rationalizations that men are the physically stronger sex and women are limited, psychologically and physiologically, by their reproductive and child-rearing functions. Presented under the guise of science by most nineteenth-century social scientists, as shown by Ehrlich in "Evolutionism and the place of women in the United States" (Section 3), this type of psychobiological reductionism is periodically resurgent. Recently it has again surfaced, compounded by refinements from psychology and sociology about "instrumental" male and "expressive" female roles, reassuringly described as "complementary."

When dealing with the status of women, anthropologists have concerned themselves with "how women fit into the male-dominated system of power in a society," as Ifeka notes in "The female factor in anthropology." But women are now studying the extent to which female status is independent of the male power structure. They are examining the significance of women's societies "for the maintenance of female solidarity, for the reduction of individualism among women, and the development of female consciousness," according to Ifeka, and demonstrating that "female autonomy attacks the supports of the male-dominated system of power." They are scrutinizing the effects of power on the relationships between women and men in societies where the two sexes, the several classes, and the diverse races have differential access to socioeconomic and political power. They are finding that it was precisely such power relationships that were notably absent in the pre-class societies. The classic examples of the projection of Western values on non-Western cultures are the gathering-hunting societies in which the human species evolved and which are therefore singled out to "prove" the "naturalness" of male supremacy. These societies have been depicted as groups structured into territorial, patrilocal bands by the importance of male hunting as the basic subsistence activity. Related men are represented as "bonding" together, exercising exclusive rights over their lands, and exchanging "their" women with men in similar groups. However, recent ethnographies reveal that hunting is the main subsistence activity in only a minority of these societies, where plant foods are sparse, and that gathering, done mainly by women, provides the staple foods in most areas of the world. The principal adaptive mechanism of gatherer-hunters is free, inter-band communication, which ensures survival in times of food shortages, permits the process of fission to operate in the solution of intra- and inter-band conflict, and provides the convival companionship and variety in diet that are the basic social goals of these societies. Organized into bands that are essentially non-territorial and bilocal, gatherer-hunters reject warfare and group aggression, and value above all cooperation, egalitarianism, and personal autonomy. In such societies women and men are equal partners in communally-based subsistence and social activities (Rohrlich-Leavitt 1975).

Although the Naskapi Indians in Canada, described by Leacock, depended for their staple foods mainly on animals hunted by men, and the Australian aborigines, discussed by Rohrlich-Leavitt, et al., subsisted primarily on plants gathered by the women, sex roles were flexible in both cultures. Women also hunted, trapped, and fished; men participated in child-rearing; and women as well as men were shamans. Australian aboriginal women have been used as the prototype of the female "beasts of burden." over-worked, ill-treated pawns in male contests for prestige and power. But mythological research by women anthropologists indicates that in the pre-colonial past the women had greater authority and ritual importance than the men (Berndt 1970:46). And the seventeenth-century ethnohistorical data cited by Leacock shows "the considerable 'power' held by women" in Naskapi society. In the ethnographic present, women in these cultures are relatively autonomous in their reproductive and economic roles.

The Tlingit Indians, described by Klein in "Women, knowledge, and power" (Section 5), represent another level in human evolution, sedentary fishing peoples living in areas rich in natural resources. Prominent among such societies were the Indians of the Northwest Pacific Coast of North America who, with their surpluses of food and other materials, developed complex economic, political, religious, and artistic traditions. The culture of this area was characterized by rank based on clan position and wealth, held by both women and men, and in the Western sub-Arctic, the habitat of the Tlingit studied by Klein, the clans were matrilineal. Rank had to be confirmed by the giving of potlatches, the social mechamism for the redistribution of wealth and the occasion for oratorical displays, by both women and men, of mythological and cultural knowledge. Rank was also associated with maturity and wisdom, the ability of the individual to solve personal and group problems.

Traditionally the men did the fishing, while women processed the fish consumption and trade and also conducted the important trading negotiations with other Indian groups and later with the Europeans. Somewhat isolated from the dominant society, contemporary Tlingit are not very impressed by its ideology or technological proficiency but, encapsulated within it, they draw upon its resources. Traditional labor is divided along former lines, but women predominate in the modern prestige occupations in education, the civil service, and shopkeeping, which is consistent with "the traditional view that women are...more skillful than men in the handling, using, and saving of wealth."

In Mexico, indigenous peasant communities also maintain their traditional values to the degree that they are not fully engulfed by the dominant structures. In the Mayan village of Chan Kom, women continue to own property and keep the money they earn from the sale of their products, according to Elmendorf, the harmonious economic relations between the sexes being reflected in the symmetrical ritual roles of women and men. It remains to be seen whether the opening of the new highway into Chan Kom will succeed in finally undermining a culture which has managed to remain viable for more than four centuries of European domination. By contrast, the Nahuat-speaking peasants of Chignautla, located only a short distance from the largest market center in northern Puebla, are described by Slade as much more involved in the cash economy; the institution of marriage, as structured by the national culture, subordinates the Indian women economically, jurally, and ritually. In the tin-mining communities of Bolivia, the Chola had until very recently a "greater independence than that of the majority of the women in the world," deriving, according to Nash, from the fact that they represent 43 percent of the labor force and from the cultural and historical sense of the significance of women among Andean Indians. This is expressed in contemporary rituals to the *Pachamama*, the female generative force, which still provide a favorable climate for women to develop self-respect, strength, and courage, and to participate fully in family decision-making and important community events.

The women in the tin-mining communities formed their own organizations both outside and within the unions and also participated with the men in economic and political action, particularly in the resistance movements against the extreme exploitation of the miners. Until the social disruptions that followed the 1967 massacre in which men, women, and children were indiscriminately slaughtered, the women enjoyed the respect and support of the men. But when the unions reorganized, the influence of the dominant society finally took effect. Despite the heroic participation of the women in the men's struggles, the men did not support the women when they were fired *en masse* from the concentration pits, did not help the women in their efforts to gain the right work on the slagpile, and did not permit the women access to decision-making positions.

In Africa, the status of women can be understood only in terms of their traditional roles and not in the terms of the imposed colonial institutions. Pre-colonial women in areas that were not completely Islamicized were neither exploited economically nor dominated politically. As in other pre-capitalist societies, in Africa sex roles were interdependent, but women worked, socialized, and functioned politically and ritually mainly in concert with other women, as men associated primarily with other men. African women played vital roles as farmers, traders, potters, and weavers and controlled their own earnings. In many regions, their political roles were pre-eminent, being supported by strong women's organizations and secret societies, in which women learned to function collectively, to develop self-confidence and the ability to speak persuasively.

Okonjo delineates the position of the Nigerian *Omu*, the queen who rules the women on the same basis as her male counterpart rules the men, but who is not his wife. Okonjo also refers to the 1929 War of the Women in which almost two million women (and very few men) of the patrilocal Igbo in Nigeria organized, through the traditional women's societies,

624 RUBY ROHRLICH-LEAVITT

the first large-scale attack on British colonialism. In Sierra Leone, a country with a patrilineal bias, 95 percent of the women in all the provinces are members of the Bundu, the women's secret society which is very active and important in politics (Hoffer 1972:161). Rousseau describes the status of the women paramount chiefs in Mendeland, Sierra Leone, where the officials of the women's secret society also hold important positions in the men's secret society. Rousseau also points out that in Zaire women hold the highest political offices among the matrilineal Kongo and Lunda peoples. Leacock describes Livingstone's encounter in 1857 with an authoritative young woman chief of the Balonda, one of the Lunda peoples who once occupied the area covering parts of southeastern Zaire, Zambia, and Angola. "Everywhere in Africa that one scrapes the surface," writes Leacock, "one finds ethnohistorical data on the authority once shared by women but later lost."

In the Caribbean island of Barbados, women's status in the black rural proletariat partially reflects African traditions, female-male relationships in the village subculture being far more egalitarian than those in the dominant society, according to Sutton and Makiesky in "Women, knowledge, and power" (Section 5). Here, too, women and men have separate networks through which they exchange personal services and disseminate news and information. Although villagers take advantage of the education imposed by the dominant society, like the Tlingit Indians, they view this kind of knowledge as not very meaningful or satisfactory in understanding the universe and rely far more on the folk wisdom of their subculture for survival, to maintain self-respect, and to operate with greater ease within the system. With equal access to both kinds of knowledge, women and men increasingly use it "to actively confront and challenge the system that subordinates them."

In sum, the societies discussed above are characterized by the fact that women as well as men make decisions, either individually or in groups, for the activities for which they are responsible and, as mature, experienced adults, participate in the decisions affecting the community as a whole. In these societies women are not circumscribed by their reproductive functions; their important socioeconomic roles and human abilities are recognized and acknowledged. Very significant is the fact that women play their principal roles in concert with each other, leading lives that are somewhat separate from but parallel with those of the men. In the more complex cultures, women's political strength derives from their own organizations and secret societies, which also provide them with controls over their economic and ritual activities. In these groups, women learn to function collectively and to develop traits that ensure equality in their relations with men. Finally, women and men generally perceive themselves and each other as living in interdependence, not in competition, in societies lacking the sharp separation between public and private spheres, family and community, work and play, religion and recreation, that characterizes industrialized nations.

No greater contrast to the position of women in these societies can be imagined than women's status under Islam, the example *par excellence* of the ancient patriarchal ethos epitomized by the *jihad*. It is this institution, imperialist warfare under the guise of a proselytizing religion, which seemed to have been primary in ousting women from decision-making in the early civilizations. That a continuous state of warfare is still an important factor in preventing the realization of full equality for women is pointed out by Padan-Eisenstark in "Image and reality: women's status in Israel" (Section 4).

The Islamic archetype, as Geertz (1968) points out, is the warrior-priest-king, an amalgam of the strong man and the holy man. He is sustained in his image, as Geertz fails to point out, by the polar image of woman as profane, polluting, irrational, and weak. What invalidates Geertz' analysis is his uncritical acceptance of the kind of strength and holiness that is generated by a militaristic religiosity, and his complete omission of women and their involuntary role in upholding the Islamic structure. Early in its regime, the Russian Communist Party attempted to liberate the Muslim women in Asiatic Russia as the only way to topple the entire Islamic edifice, as Rosenthal notes in "the role and status of women in the Soviet Union" (Section 4).

At the opposite extreme from Geertz, Fanon recognizes fully that Islam is symbolized by the veil, but he glosses over the fact that at the same time the veil symbolizes the degradation of Islamic women. Revolutionary though he is, his heart bleeds for only half of "the wretched of the earth," for he represents Islamic women's immolation within the patriarchal family as voluntary and glorifies this family:

The Algerian woman's ardent love of the home is not a limitation imposed by the universe. It is not hatred of the sun or the streets or spectacles. It is not a flight from the world...The home is the basis of the truth of society (1965:66).

Women played a crucial role in achieving Algerian independence and establishing a socialist society. "They had paid for their right to equality by the suffering they had undergone by the side of their menfolk," writes Gordon (1968: 61). But within two years the Algerian woman, although legally and politically equal, was suffering economic discrimination, according to M'Rabet (1964) and was still treated as an inferior social being, "an object, a thing." It appears that socialism cannot be reconciled with Islam or any other form of patriarchy.

In Bangladesh, the suppression and oppression of women are virtually total, according to Jahan in "Women in Bangladesh" (Section 1). Secluded in the home, they are excluded from all the institutions that control their lives and are socialized in the belief that they can compensate for their existence only by producing sons and cultivating self-abnegation. But over and above the institutions that subjugate Islamic women looms the threat and practice of physical and sexual assault and humiliation. The laws passed to emancipate Muslim women in the U.S.S.R. led to a priest-headed counter-revolutionary movement comprised of men of all classes, who kidnapped, raped, and murdered the women who tried to assert their legal independence. The recent widespread rape of Bangali women by Pakistani men, their co-religionists, and the rape of Bangali women by Bangali men in the post-liberation period, reported by Jahan, show how women are victimized, even when they are passive, in societies that make them dependent on men for "protection" against other men.

In the Western capitalist societies the traditional patriarchal methods of subordinating and exploiting women are updated. As Saffioti points out in "Female labor and capitalism in the United States and Brazil" (Section 2), "In the capitalist mode of production, patriarchy reaches its most refined expression and increasingly incorporates scientific and pseudo-scientific knowledge" from the social sciences, themselves offsprings of capitalism. Social scientists continue to reap royalties and consolidate their academic niches by disseminating variations of the familiar patriarchal themes: the nuclear family is the basic social unit in all societies, women everywhere are solely responsible for child-rearing, male supremacy is an inevitable fact of life, etc.

But cross-cultural ethnoshistorical data clearly show that the nuclear family is the family form imposed by capitalism and that it differs radically from previous family systems in isolating the family from the community and in isolating women from one another. In this type of family, men are made responsible for the support of all family members, thereby locking them into their jobs, and women and children are made dependent on men, thereby perpetuating male supremacy. Men accept economic exploitation because of the free services their wives are coerced into providing in the nuclear family. The antagonism between women and men, and between parents and children, in the family hierarchy reflects the antagonisms in the class hierarchy.

But while men openly struggle against their open exploitation, women struggle against an oppression that is hidden and mystified. The servitors of the elite classes who are the most richly rewarded are those who furnish "the specific ideological coercion of women as reproducers of labor power," as Larguia points out in "The economic basis of the status of women" (Section 3), by confusing the economic functions imposed on them with their biological and psychological idenity. As child-bearers, women produce the basic human resource, and as nurturers of the present and future generations they produce labor power. Thus, as wives and mothers, women perform the most socially productive of all functions. But whether as housewives or as housewives/wage-earners, women in the nuclear family are coerced into providing "free labor to the male sex and the ruling classes," as Larguia puts it, through the mystification of mother love and conjugal love. The social functions of child-rearing and domestic work are represented by the social sciences and the commerical communications media as natural services that women should perform "freely" in the psychological sense, and "for free" in the economic sense.

These roles that women play in the individual family determine their economic and political status in the capitalist countries discussed in this volume, whether "central", like the United States, or "peripheral," like Latin America. Socialized to leave politics to the men, and with little time or energy to fight male opposition to their political participation, women rarely take part in decision-making on the issues that affect their destiny as the half of every population. Thus all the institutions are dominated by men and converge in their control not only of women's psyche but also of their reproductive functions, their economic status, and their access to the knowledge that would enable them to recognize and resist the sources of their oppression, as pointed out in "Women, knowledge, and power" (Section 5).

To maximize profits and to fulfill labor requirements as determined by the economic decision-makers, abetted by their political, legal, medical, educational, and religious servitors, women's bodies are manipulated, abused, and destroyed by anti-abortion laws. As the largest mass of reserve labor, they are pulled into and pushed out of the labor market according to the dictates of the same decision-makers. Despite the efficacy of the ideological coercion practiced on women, they are well aware of the widespread economic discrimination against them, and they opt for wifehood and motherhood as the primary form of economic security.

However, in the richest capitalist nation, the United States, they are beginning to discover that "marriage does not mean economic security, especially toward the end of life for women," according to Saffioti. The proportion of women in the economically active population rose to 44 percent by 1973, married women with children predominating, and 70 percent of the women working because of dire necessity. Married women soon discover that in a consumer society the man's salary is insufficient to cover the needs of the family, including the education of children, especially in inflationary periods. In addition, the accelerating rate of divorce and desertion in the United States, where the laws favor the male, makes increasing numbers of women the sole support not only of themselves, but of their children. Far from being economically supported, wives provide men with free services that would be extremely costly if furnished by non-wives. In addition, married women with children generally contribute all their earnings to the family. "Much of the affluence of working class, and even many middle-class, families depends on the wages of women" (Morton 1971:218).

But, as a massive reserve labor force, women constitute the lowest-paid segment. In most fields, women with the same qualifications as men earn less than two-thirds of the salaries of male workers for the same work, and the gap between their respective salaries is continuously widening, as shown by the statistics cited by Heath, Babey-Brooke, and Saffioti. In the well-paid prestige professions, the proportion of women, always very small in the United States, appears to be declining. Educated women are found primarily in the low-prestige professions that are extensions of their family roles, in which the supervisors and administrators are men. Those with less education must take tedious office jobs and work in the service occupations and in factories that are increasingly being shifted to underdeveloped countries with tax exemptions and no minimum wage laws. The new laws passed very recently to eliminate discrimination against women in the United States, and the tax-supported agencies set up to implement these laws, are largely ineffective, as Babey-Brooke points out.

With an economically active lifetime that is much shorter than that of men, and with less time and opportunity for training for advancement, married women with children are unable to accumulate pension benefits and savings for their old age. Senator Mervyn Dymally of California points out (Bianco 1974:72) that only 10 percent of all working women qualify for any kind of pension benefits in the United States. Moreover, in most states a wife has no legal right to any part of her husband's pension when he retires, regardless of how large her indirect contribution to his pension payments through her housekeeping activities and/or earnings has been. Thus, only 2 percent of women ever receive any benefits from their husbands' private pension plans. The California senator also notes that the average annual income of women 65 and over is $1,811, compared with $3,328 for men in the same age group. Saffioti points out that in 1970 women comprised 80 percent of those in the United States subsisting entirely on social security payments, and who therefore constituted the most indigent segment of the population. Given the widespread race as well as sex discrimination, minority women are far worse off than white women.

Thus, far from ensuring economic security at any time, least of all in old age, motherhood and wifehood in the United States appear to be self-sacrificing roles that mainly benefit husbands and employers. Women who never marry and who are economically active throughout their productive lifetime seem to be in an economic position that is far superior to that of married women with children.

As the hub of international capitalism, the United States also drastically affects the position of women in the peripheral regions of the system, particularly Latin America. The effect may be indirect, as on the women in the Bolivian tin-mining communities described by Nash in "Resistance as protest" (Section 2), or direct, as on the women in the tobacco-growing and needlework industries of Puerto Rico, discussed by Silvestrini-Pacheco in "Women as workers" (Section 2).

While the central capitalist societies "solve the problem of the growing difficulty of realizing surplus value through the ecological extension of the bases of their operation and by the growing penetration of precapitalist economies," as Saffioti notes, the peripheral societies "are penetrated from the outside by the capitalist mode of production," which drains off their resources. Given their high birthrate and low expansion capacity, they "generate an enormous excess of labor." And, in order to keep the number of unemployed men below the boiling point, women in Latin America are marginalized in the economy to an even greater extent than women in the central societies. The under-utilization of women's capacities in the capitalist countries, both developed and underdeveloped, as compared with pre-capitalist systems, belies the propaganda about a direct ratio between women's economic activity and socioeconomic development.

The ideological coercion of women to accept subordination and suppression expresses itself in Latin America through the dual mystique of *machismo* and the *supermadre*, as Chaney notes in "The mobilization of women" (Section 4). But the social function of the mystique is the same in every type of capitalist country, and its content is standardized, in Saffioti's words, from "international capitalism's center of dominance... through the popular distribution of 'scientific works,' television soap operas, serial stories, and comic strips, to the secondary economic, social, and cultural areas."

Thus the vast majority of women in the industrialized urban areas of Latin America — especially the Indians, Mestizas, and Cholas who leave the countryside or are dispossessed — work in the textile factories, as domestic servants, or as prostitutes, according to Sanchez and Dominguez in "Women in Mexico." Piho's study of female textile workers in Mexico City shows the degree of exploitation to which these women are subjected by employers, union officials, and family members. And Smith's description of the situation of female domestic servants in Lima, Peru, reveals the similarities in the role expectations for servants and those for women generally. It is this servant class that enables elite women to function on a professional level in a system in which the mass of women are exploited by a small number of men and women, as Kinzer indicates in her paper on professional women in Buenos Aires. The former high status of indigenous Indian women in Latin America stands in striking contrast to their subordinate and menial roles in both developed and developing countries under Western domination.

One response of women to extreme poverty in Latin America, as well as in many other under-developed countries, has long been the rejection of legal, monogamous marriage, despite their stigmatization by the middle class. Comparing the monogamous (only for women), malehead-ded nuclear family and the matrifocal household, where women live in serial consensual unions, Brown finds, in "Lower economic sector female mating patterns in the Dominican Republic" (Section 2), that the consensual union enables poor women to maximize their meager resources more easily than women in legal unions. The woman who heads her own household has much greater control over her economic resources than the woman in a legal marriage, can expel or leave an unsatisfactory mate more easily, and has a wider mutual-aid network. Dominican women in both types of household verbalized the advantages of "visiting unions," which, according to Brown, are more adaptive to deteriorating economic conditions and may therefore become more widespread. Middle-class Western women are also increasingly rejecting patriarchal marriage.

The matrilineal, matrifocal family system, as among the Nayar in India, is far more democratic than the patrilineal system, according to Westman Berg in "Sources of the matrilineal family system" (Section 4): "Men are not treated as subordinate beings, and do not acquire minority complexes.... Their status is not dependent upon the status of their 'wife' but upon themselves.... There are no double standards regarding sexual morality.... The 'husband' is not expected to work in his 'wife's' house as the wife has to work in her 'husband's' home in patriliny...."

The women's movement is scrutinizing women's status and roles under socialism as it has thus far developed in various countries. It must be remembered that the socialist states evolved out of, and were continuously beset by, civil and foreign wars (two sides of the same coin of capitalist subversion), at the same time as the economy, in each case, was being restructured. The concept that the emancipation of women and sexual equality are basic to the establishment of a just society and a socialist state is central in socialist ideology. But just as capitalist ideology proclaims that women's position improves as countries industrialize, so contemporary socialists maintain that under socialism the "full emancipation of women depends on the mechanization of agriculture and industry" (Leader 1973:57).

Comparing women's status in the most highly industrialized capitalist and socialist countries, the United States and the U.S.S.R., the major differences seem to be in the economic sphere. In the United States, women share in an exaggerated form the economic insecurity of the mass of the people. Occupying a limited range of positions from the lowest to the middle socioeconomic levels, U.S. women are largely excluded from the upper middle-class professional, managerial, and entrepreneurial categories, and are almost totally excluded from the economic elites, except in the derived status of wife. The majority of women wage-earners are married with children, and more than two-thirds of economically active women work out of necessity, belying the common supposition that in the United States women work outside the home for supplementary income or "pin money."

In the U.S.S.R., women are expected to be economically active, and are found in larger numbers than anywhere else in the world in all the professions and in every type of skilled as well as unskilled work. However, in the occupations regarded as the most important and prestigious, the top executives and those who are the best paid are men. Within the professions, women are specializing in (or being specialized into) medicine, teaching, and social-cultural work. "Increasing discrimination is forcing women to moderate their ambitions in both education and employment," according to Rosenthal. Comprising half the labor force, Soviet women earn only a quarter of all earned wages, being overly represented at the lowest economic levels. On balance, however, women in the U.S.S.R. obviously enjoy much greater economic independence and are far better represented in the professions and skilled occupations than women in the United States. If pension plans and other social benefits in the U.S.S.R. are based on length of service and amount of money earned, the number of poor older women must be far fewer than in the United States.

Politically there is less difference between women's status in the two countries. Although Soviet women are much more active on the local levels, they, too, constitute a very small proportion of the top policy makers. In both countries it is primarily men who establish the priorities and make the decisions on such matters as war and peace, consumer needs, and labor requirements. Thus it is men who control the bodies of women, the producers of labor. "It is not by chance that research in birth control has developed so slowly, that abortion is forbidden almost the world over or conceded finally only for therapeutic reasons" (Dalla Costa 1972:46). And, as Morton (1971:219) points out, "part of the rationale for the exclusion of women from so many jobs requiring training disappears when women are capable of determining when they wish to have children." It is the men in power in both the United States and the U.S.S.R. who decide whether and when to socialize child-rearing, what the extent and nature of such socialization should be, and that under any and all circumstances women are individually responsible for this function. These controls by men in turn determine women's roles in the economy and in politics in a vicious circularity.

With growing unemployment in the United States probably becoming a permanent fact of life, population decrease is encouraged through the ready availability of contraceptives and by the recent passage of pro-abortion laws. Moreover, several types of contraceptives have long been available in the United States, since the manufacture of commodities that bring a profit is not restricted. However, growing unemployment may also lead to the rescinding of pro-abortion laws as a means of pushing women out of the labor market.

The Eastern European Communist countries have labor shortages and their abortion policies, heretofore considered far more liberal than those in the United States and Western Europe, are now being reversed. According to Dornberg (1974:129), contraceptives are crude and in drastically short supply, and abortion is virtually the only effective means of birth control, except in East Germany, with deleterious effects on the health of the many women who have a number of abortions. Within the last decade Rumania, Czechoslovakia, and Hungary have outlawed abortions. In the U.S.S.R., the total abortion ban in effect under Stalin was reversed in 1955, and in European Russia the one-child family is the norm. Despite the incentives offered for bearing additional children, women consistently choose to work rather than have another child, writes Rosenthal, because an independent income brings them greater bargaining power in the family, two incomes provide a higher standard of living, and professional and skilled women experience job satisfaction. However, according to Dornberg (1974:129). the Kremlin is now concerned that the much higher birth rate in the Central Asian republics will make the Slavic peoples in the Russian republics minorities "in their 'own' countries" and "there are rumblings about a more restrictive policy" on abortion. Commenting on the reversal of abortion-on-demand laws in the Eastern European Communist countries, Dornberg writes (1974:128):

The revised abortion policy implies that a woman's body is not her own but the property of the state, and that abortion is not a right but a privilege that the government can grant or withdraw at will, dependent on an assessment of the state's economic and demographic needs.

With the entrance of an unprecendented number of women into the U.S. labor force and the extremely limited number of state-subsidized child-care facilities, child care is becoming "big business in America" (Sassen, et al. 1974: 21). The Women's Bureau of Employment Standards Administration (1972:3) states that in 1971 there were more than twelve million working mothers in the United States, "nearly all of whom worked out of economic necessity," with demographers "projecting a fifty percent increase in the number of working American women with pre-school children by the end of the decade" (Sassen, et al. 1974:21). The concern of privately-operated child-care facilities with maximization of profits leads to inferior care of children, their socialization into the sexism and racism of the system, the exploitation of personnel who are mainly women, and a great reduction in the income of working mothers.

The necessity of freeing women from child-rearing and domestic work in the nuclear family has long been recognized by the socialist theoreticians. However, Communist policies regarding the socialization of these functions and the abolition of the nuclear family are governed by the same type of expediency that is applied to the regulation of birth control. Although child-care facilities in the Soviet Union have been expanding rapidly since the 1960's, according to Rosenthal, at the present time only about a third of the pre-school children can be accommodated in nurseries and day-care centers that are overcrowded, the remainder being cared for by older female relatives such as grandmothers.

As in the capitalist countries, mothers in the U.S.S.R. are held responsible for parental and domestic duties, and even more Soviet women than U.S. women hold two jobs of which only one is financially rewarded. The expectation that Russian women will continue to suffer this exploitation, and the ideological coercion of women to maintain the nuclear family "which is incompatible with the automation of these services" (Dalla Costa 1972:35), are bluntly stated in an article by Vera Severyanova (1970:52), entitled "Should women hold managerial posts?":

...there is no post so high that it will free a woman from her family, the domestic worries, the task of bringing up her children and looking after relatives.

Because of their domestic responsibilities in both the United States and the U.S.S.R., married women with children consistently choose jobs with shorter hours, such as teaching, as Barker points out in "Women in the anthropology profession — I" (Section 4). But even such jobs leave them with little time or energy to train for advanced positions in the economy or to participate actively at all levels of political decision-making

Guettel's analysis of the relationships between male chauvinism and the "fetishization of the motherhood role" applies to all patriarchal systems, whether they be capitalist or socialist:

Fetishization of female childrearing creates a sexual division of labour in almost every sphere of life, a material difference of experience that cannot be reduced to a simple rationalization of alleged mental inferiority. Chauvinism is constantly reaffirmed by the perpetuation of the feminine childrearing 'monoploy' itself...patriarchal attitudes are in large part the result of experiencing woman first as mother and then as wife, in fetishized roles so close to immediate experience that they affect just about every aspect of the personality ...women will not actually achieve equal work in practice short of the socialization of maternity, which means that parenthood must be shared, in the sense that males and females participate equally in childrearing (1974:58–59).

The contributors to this volume not only document the exploitation and subordination of women, but also record their resistance. It must be emphasized that, before the patriarchal civilizations emerged and gradually expanded their rule over other peoples during a five-thousand-year period which culminated in the Western domination of the entire world, societies were structured to prevent groups and individuals from exploiting each other. In such societies, the family was a part of the larger community, and women functioned collectively in groups that were largely separate from but interdependent with men's groups. Women exercised control over their reproductive functions by "efficient methods of birth control, which have unaccountably disappeared" (Dalla Costa 1972:28), and were autonomous in their economic, political, and ritual activities. Thus male supremacy and women's subordination are relatively recent phenomena in human history. Resistance to these phenomena takes many forms. It takes the form of the matrifocal household and the rejection of the patrilineal family in the lower socioeconomic classes; of the one-child family of Russian women; of the single women's movement in the United States which rejects all the present forms of marriage and the family, and is evolving an ideology based on strong bonds of friendship between fictive sisters. Increasingly women understand that only through separate organizations is resistance to their oppression possible.

In "Resistance as protest" (Section 2), Nash defines resistance as "opposition to authority that has lost a basis for legitimacy in some sector of the population." Women's resistance is also "recognition...that they no longer can rely on male protectors." In Bangladesh, "the fate of the violated and other war-affected women, the vulnerable position of the women in the post-liberation period of lawlessness" to abduction and rape by their own men, writes Jahan, have finally led some women to question the legitimacy of the male-dominated system and to recognize that it not only does not protect them but that it evolved to victimize them. Feminists are now attempting to establish contact with the masses of women in Bangladesh.

Why have anthropologists who study peasant rebellions ignored the epic struggles of African women farmers against the colonial powers? Over and over again African women have used their organizations to confront the European rulers and their indigenous surrogates. In 1923, 10,000 Ibo women instigated riots in Eastern Nigeria against the British attempt to tax female farmers. In 1929, almost two million Ibo women rioted against another threat of British taxation of women. In the 1940's, organized women were responsible for the overthrow of the Ake of Abeokuta in Western Nigeria. In 1959, women farmers again rioted in Eastern Nigeria to prevent the transfer of their land to the men. Ifeka cites the Alice Lenshins movement of the mid-1960's in Zambia and the women's strike of 1971 in the Zambian capital of Lusaka.

The image of Latin American women as *conforme*, passive and dependent, concerned only with motherhood and wifehood, is belied by the militant struggles of women in Bolivia, Puerto Rico, Cuba, and Chile for their own liberation within a more humane society.

In Bolivia, the cultural significance of indigenous women is in marked contrast to the image of women disseminated by the European elites, and Indian and Chola women have a history of daring and resourceful participation in the uprisings against their Spanish rulers. In the 1930's, women in various occupations formed their own union, which became one of the most militant groups in the Labor Federation of Workers. Through their underground organization, Comando Obrero Feminino, women took a prominent part in the election of members of the National Revolutionary Movement, and the Committee of Women participated in the revolution in the streets required to bring the party to office.

Time and again the women in the tin-mining communities in Bolivia have organized their own groups of housewives and workers, besides working with the men in political and economic actions. They have used the hunger strike to focus public attention on their demands for better food supplies, their defense of the civil rights of men imprisoned for trade-union activities, and their demonstrations against the lockout of male workers. But in the last decade the men have not supported the women when they were fired *en masse* and in their efforts to get work; they have refused the women access to decision-making posts in the union.

Nash points out that the same acts of resistance have a different significance and outcome when performed by women and by men, women receiving little or no place in the new power structures that emerge with successful resistance movements. "Women's resistance," writes Nash, "shakes the very foundation of the dominant-subordinate hierarchy which has its roots in the home and family network" Or, as Dalla Costa points out (1972:25), the wage slave is afraid of losing his own slave in the house. In Bolivia, women have consistently lost power in the generally unsuccessful struggles of the past ten years. Another question that arises is how the women's loss of power has contributed to the lack of success of resistance movements. Nash concludes that women must form their own organizations for the achievement of their own goals:

Their experience demonstrates the need for separate organizations of women within liberation movements so that women's rebellious acts will not be perverted by political opportunists and their demands for change will include their own liberation.

At the beginning of the century women in Puerto Rico were actively involved in organizing the Socialist Party and the Free Federation of Workers. Although both groups recognized women's right to work and the principle of sexual equality, "few women ever occupied top leadership positions," according to Silverstrini-Pacheco. Puerto Rican women also organized demonstrations and strikes against the U.S. tobacco corporations and fought to improve workers' living conditions, as well as for the recognition of women's rights. During the depression of the 1930's, women workers played a major role in organizing strikes against the tobacco factories and the needlework industry. "The courage of the striking women facilitated the unionization of many others," writes Silvestrini-Pacheco.

When they found the labor unions unresponsive, the women in the needlework trades organized their own unions. Women workers were prominent in the demand that the Fair Labor Standards Act, establishing a minimum wage on the mainland, also be applied to workers in Puerto Rico. But this was prevented by alliances among the Socialist Party leaders, the industrialists of both Puerto Rico and the mainland, most of their Congressional representatives, and the labor union leaders. Nevertheless, as Silvestrini-Pacheco notes, "the participation of Puerto Rican women workers in labor struggles was instrumental in exposing the weaknesses of the leaders of organized labor...[and] was a major stride in the road towards their *conscientizacao para la libertad.*"

In Cuba and Chile, women figured prominently in the revolutionary and electoral struggles to achieve socialism, but always under male leadership. As Chaney notes in "The mobilization of women," male policy makers in Cuba initiated and now control the political and economic advances of women, and unless the full equality of women has the highest priority "it will be sacrificed when it competes with higher priority goals for limited political and economic resources," as has occurred generally in the socialist countries.

At the closing session of the Second Congress of the Federation of Women in Havana in November, 1974, Castro (1974:11–12) present-ed statistics on the status of Cuban women that belie the title of his speech: women comprise about 25 percent of the workers in civilian state jobs, but hold only 15 percent of the leadership posts; women con-stitute about 13 percent of the Communist Party membership, but only 6 percent of the Party cadres and officials. Although the central theme of Castro's speech is the rectification of the continuing economic and political inequality of Cuban women, at the same time he exhorts the wo-men to participate in achieving the priorities he lists as primary before they dedicate themselves to the struggle for their own liberation, which he distinguishes from the "national liberation" (1974:8–9):

It is clear that women need to participate in the struggle against exploitation, against imperialism, colonialism, neocolonialism, racism; in a word: in the struggle for national liberation. But when the objective of national liberation is finally achieved, women must continue struggling for their own liberation within human society.

In Chile, a number of outstanding militant radical women were in the vanguard of the movement that brought Allende to power. But although he "frequently asserted that his revolution would not succeed unless it incorporated women at all levels of responsibility," Allende himself always expressed his view of what women should contribute "in terms of their role as mothers or potential mothers," writes Chaney. The influence of the larger numbers of bourgeois women mobilized by the right-wing groups in the coup that overthrew the Allende regime would have been counterbalanced if the Socialist leaders had seen fit to include representatives of the masses of women in Chile in top-echelon decision-making. It has yet to be determined what part was played in the defeat of socialism in Chile by this absence of women from policy-making, and how such an absence has influenced the direction that socialism has taken elsewhere in the world.

In Europe and North America, women's resistance to male supremacy and their own subordination is taking the form of a women's movement that is a revival and extension of the movement that began in the nineteenth century. The women's movement in the United States, as described by Freeman, exists in many of the same forms in Canada and Europe. In the United States, the group that is the most highly organized is the National Organization for Women, which concentrates on equalizing, mainly by legal means, educational, economic, and political opportunities for women within the system. Although the important work of NOW — in issues centering around pro-abortion laws, child-care centers, and equal pay for equal work, which are ralllying points for women of all classes — should not be minimized, goals that are based only on egalitarian sex relationships within the system are limited, as Freeman (Section 3) points out:

To seek only equality, given the current supremacy in social values, is to assume that women want to be like men or that men are worth emulating. It is to demand that women be allowed to participate in society as we know it...without questioning the extent to which that society is worth their participation

NOW and the women's groups within the traditional Marxist organizations, though quite dissimilar in ideology and strategy, collaborate with men in a similar way for the achievement of their respective goals. These "political" women, James (1972:4) says, are easily identified:

They are the women's liberationists whose first allegiance is not to the women's movement but to organizations of the male-dominated left. Once strategy and action originate from a source outside of women, women's struggle is measured by how it is presumed to affect men, otherwise known as "the workers," and women's consciousness by whether the forms of struggle they adopt are the forms men have traditionally used.

Outside of such groups as NOW and the women of the Old Left, the women's movement has learned the lessons of history and is opting for autonomy for some of the same reasons as the black movement insists on independence from whites. Just as the traditional dominance-subordination patterns assert themselves in mixed racial groups so, as Freeman points out, "women in virtually every group in the United States, Canada, and Europe soon discovered that the traditional sex roles reasserted themselves in mixed groups regardless of the good intentions of the participants."

Moreover, many women have rejected the male-dominated trade unions and their organized parties, according to Dalla Costa (1972:32) because "the organized parties of the working class movement have been careful not to raise the question of domestic work."

Aside from the fact that they have always treated women as a lower form of life...women have always been forced by the working class parties to put off their liberation to some hypothetical future, making it dependent on the gains that men, limited in the scope of their struggles by these parties, win for themselves.

As Dalla Costa observes (1972:31), "men are too compromised in their relationship with women. For that reason only women can define themselves and move on the women question."

Women are indeed defining themselves and moving. To understand their own past and present, and to determine the nature of a future society in which they will be fully represented, women are re-examining the earlier feminist works, critically evaluating the social sciences and all forms of the humanities, and extending Marxist theory. In the United States, more than two thousand women's studies courses are being taught in the colleges and universities, and several hundred in the high schools. Women are coming to grips with the competitive elements in their socialization which hinders their collaboration with one another. They are beginning to understand the meaning of the nuclear family in the oppression of women, the power structure of sexual relationships in a sexist society, the political significance of rape and child abuse, their similarities to and differences from other oppressed groups, and the links that can be established with such groups. Political organizations are proliferating and include women's political caucuses, welfare mothers' organizations, black feminist groups, coalitions of women trade union members, women's academic caucuses, radical feminist collectives, lesbian feminist groups, the single women's movement, the wages-for-housewives movement, and international feminist collectives.

The anger and strength that are concomitants of the comprehension of their own condition have led to a women's efflorescence, an explosion of creativity in all directions. Women are writing scholarly articles and poetry about women; putting out their own newspapers, magazines, and journals; painting and photographing all aspects of women's lives; composing and playing music about and for women; putting on women's plays and street theater; making women's movies; and building up their bodies and learning to defend themselves. They are developing self-help medical and legal centers and collectives against rape and street harrassment.

These many innovative strands, which include women of all classes, races, and religions, are struggling to mesh within and across nations to create an autonomous women's movement. Such a movement would be so powerful that women would finally engage men on equal terms to transform society and to evolve new relationships between the sexes. "Autonomous struggle turns the question on its head," writes Dalla Costa (1972:44): "not 'will women unite to support men,?' but 'will men unite to support women?'" It has never been a matter of "the women question"; only "the men question."

REFERENCES

BERNDT, CATHERINE H.
  1970   "Digging sticks and spears, or, the two-sex model," in *Woman's role in aboriginal society*. Edited by Fay Gale. Canberra: Australian Institute of Aboriginal Studies.
BIANCO, LYNNE
  1974   Golden years gone rusty? *Playgirl* (October).
CASTRO, FIDEL
  1974   *The revolution has in Cuban women today an impressive political force*. Havana: Editorial de Ciencias Sociales.
DALLA COSTA, MARIAROSA
  1972   "Women and the subversion of the community," in *The power of women and the subversion of the community*. By Mariarosa Dalla Costa and Selma James. Bristol: Falling Wall Press.
DORNBERG, JOHN
  1974   "Eastern Europe: programming the population." Unpublished manuscript.
FANON, FRANTZ
  1965   *A dying colonialism*. New York: Grove Press.
GEERTZ, CLIFFORD
  1968   *Islam observed*. New Haven, Conn.: Yale University Press.
GORDON, DAVID C.
  1968   *Women of Algeria*. Cambridge, Mass.: Center for Middle Eastern Studies, Harvard University.

GUETTEL, CHARNIE
1974 *Marxism and feminism.* Toronto: The Women's Press.
HOFFER, CAROL P.
1972 Mende and Sherbro women in high office. *Canadian Journal of African Studies* 6 (2).
JAMES, SELMA
1972 "A woman's place," in *The power of women and the subversion of the community.* By Mariarosa Dalla Costa and Selma James. Bristol: Falling Wall Press.
LEADER, SHELAH GILBERT
1973 The emancipation of Chinese women. *World Politics* 26 (1).
MORTON, PEGGY
1971 "A woman's work is never done," in *From feminism to liberation.* Edited by Edith Hoshino Altbach. Cambridge, Mass.: Schenkman.
M'RABET, FADELA
1964 *La femme algerienne.* Paris: Maspero.
ROHRLICH-LEAVITT, RUBY
1975 *Anthropological approaches to women's status.* New York: Harper and Row.
SASSEN, GEORGIA, COOKIE AVRIN, THE CORPORATIONS AND CHILD CARE RESEARCH PROJECT
1974 Corporate child care. *The Second Wave* 3 (3).
SEVERYANOVA, VERA
1970 Should women hold managerial posts? *Soviet Union* 4 (241).
WOMEN'S BUREAU
1972 *Who are the working mothers?* Washington, D.C.: Women's Bureau of Employment Standards Administration, United States Department of Labor.

Biographical Notes

ANNA M. BABEY-BROOKE (1911–   ) is presently Associate Professor of English at Brooklyn College, City University of New York. She received her Ph.D. (Columbia University; English Literature) in 1938 and her D.Ac. (Doctor of Acupuncture; Taipei, Taiwan) in 1964 — the first American woman to earn the doctorate in Acupuncture. She has worked on various union committees of the City University of New York (CUNY), especially for affirmative action on Discrimination Against Women; she is the elected President of the Queens Chapter of NOW (National Organization for Women); currently is President of one foundation and Treasurer of another; and has authored nine books.

DIANA BARKER (1941–   ) was born in Trinidad. She studied Natural Sciences and then Archaeology and Anthropology at the University of Cambridge. After teaching science for some years, she was a graduate student in Social Anthropology at the University College of Swansea, and she is currently Visiting Lecturer in the Department of Sociology at the University of Essex. Her special interests are in ritual, folk religion, courtship and marriage, the position of women, and the political economy of the family in industrial societies.

KARIN WESTMAN BERG (1914–   ) was born in Uppsala, Sweden, and received a Ph.D. from the University of Uppsala in the History of Literature (1962) with a dissertation on Almqvist where she introduced the method of literary sociology which analyzes images of women in literature. She continued that type of study in a critical seminar outside the university for eight years, which resulted in two books (*Sex roles in literature from antiquity to the 1960's*, 1968; *Sex discrimination past and present*, 1972). She was Associate Professor at the University of Uppsala 1967–1972, started a research project on Fredrika Bremer in 1968, and was invited on a lecture tour to U.S. universities in 1973. In 1974, she introduced interdisciplinary women's study courses in Swedish universities and became international correspondent to SIGNS: Women in Culture and Society. Recent publications include: *Feminist criticism in Scandinavia past and present*, 1974; *Source book of Swedish feminist authors*, 1975 (in collaboration with T. Lundell, Ph.D.).

SUSAN E. BROWN (1945–   ) A native of Bridgeport, New York, she received her Ph.D. in Cultural Anthropology from the University of Michigan (1972). Her major academic interests concern advocacy research for the Hispano communities of the urban United States, Ibero-American studies, and female perspectives on the study of culture —in this she is dedicated to the correction of male bias in anthropology.

JANET M. BUJRA (1940–   ) was born in Huddersfield, England, and is now a Lecturer in Sociology at the University of Dar es Salaam, Tanzania. She received her B.Sc. from the London School of Economics, and her M.Sc. and Ph.D. from the School of Oriental and African Studies, University of London. She has done research on politics, urbanization, history, and sociolinguistics in Kenya, and has taught at the American University in Cairo as well as at the University of Dar es Salaam.

ANN PATRICIA CAPLAN (1942–   ) studied at London University, completing her Ph.D. in Social Anthropology in 1968. She has carried out research in a Muslim village on the coast of Tanzania (resulting in several published articles as well as *Choice and constraint in a Swahili community*, Oxford University Press, in press) and in a Hindu village in the mountains of Nepal (several articles and *Priests and cobblers: a study of social change in a Hindu village in western Nepal*, Chandler, 1972). She is at present (1974–5) carrying out fieldwork on women's organizations in Madras City, India. Her regional interests are East Africa and South Asia, and research areas include kinship, the sociology of Islam and Hinduism, and social change.

ELSA M. CHANEY, Associate Professor of Political Science at Fordham University, Bronx, New York, completed her work in 1971 at the University of Wisconsin, Madison, with a doctoral thesis on the political role of women in Peru and Chile. She has since pursued this interest in several articles and as collaborator in the organization of a conference and a summer seminar on "Feminine Perspectives in Social Science Research in Latin America" held this past year in Buenos Aires, Argentina, and Cuernavaca, Mexico. During 1975 she was engaged in a study of working mothers and role conflict with Latin American colleagues in Lima, Peru. Her recent articles include "Women in politics in Latin America: the case of Peru and Chile" in *Female and male in Latin America* (edited by Ann Pescatello; Pittsburgh: University of Pittsburgh Press, 1973); "Old and new feminists in Latin America," *Journal of Marriage and the Family* 35 (2) (May 1973); "Women and population: some key policy, research and action issues," in *Population and politics: new directions in political science research* (edited by Richard L. Clinton; Lexington, Mass.: D.C. Heath, 1973); and "Women in Allende's Chile," in *Women in politics* (edited by Jane Jaquette; New York: Wiley, 1974).

DELIA DAVIN (1944–   ) obtained a B.A. in Chinese Studies from Leeds University in 1968. She continued her studies in Hong Kong, Tokyo, and Paris. In 1974, she received her Ph.D. from Leeds for a thesis on women in Chinese society. Since 1972, she has been a Lecturer in Social and Economic History at York University. She is spending 1975–6 in Peking. She is the author of *Women and the Party in revolutionary China* (Oxford University Press, in press) and various articles on related subjects.

ANA ELIZABETH DOMÍNGUEZ-PEREZ (1934–   ) was born in Guadalajara, Jalisco, Mexico. She graduated at the Feminin University of Mexico where she is now Professor of Science. She also teaches at the National University of Mexico (UNAM). Her interest and points of view on women's issue had been expressed through articles and conferences as well as her performance as coordinator in different events. Some of her works are: "Women in the Latin American reality" (1967); "Women's role in church and society" (1967); "Femininity in Mexico" (1971); "Women of the Americas face a changing world" Interamerican Seminar (1972); and "Women and society" (1973).

DAISY HILSE DWYER (1945–   ) is Assistant Professor of Anthropology at Columbia University. She studied at Yale University, where she received her doctorate in 1973. Her primary fields of interest are law, ideology, and other mechanisms of social control, both psychological and political. In her fieldwork in North Africa, she has particularly examined modes of social control and conflict resolution between the sexes.

CAROL EHRLICH (1934–   ) is Assistant Professor of American Studies at the University of Maryland, Baltimore County. Her teaching and research interests include the social psychology of sex roles; theories of power in the contemporary American women's movement; the politics of mental health; radical movements in twentieth-century America; the politics of mass media; and the interaction of science and culture (evolutionary theory, the nature of human nature). She is also executive co-producer of The Great Atlantic Radio Conspiracy, a nationally syndicated radio program of Left political commentary, and is a director of Research Group One, a radical social science research collective.

MARY LINDSAY ELMENDORF (1917–   ) is Visiting Professor of Anthropology, World Campus Afloat, Chapman College, Orange, California and freelance consultant to AID, the Ford Foundation, and others on the roles and status of women, with special interest in development. She received her Ph.D. in Humanistic Anthropology and has had extensive experience in applied anthropology in Mexico and elsewhere. She has served on the faculty of Hampshire College, Goddard College, and Chapman College and has been a consultant on field studies to New College. She has served on national and international boards and is a Fellow of the American Anthropological Association and a member of AAAS, Society for International Development, Latin American Studies Association, and other professional societies. Her special field of research is the peasant woman as she relates to the pressures of modernization.

JO FREEMAN (1945–   ) received her B.A. with honors in Political Science from the University of California at Berkeley in 1965 and her M.A. and Ph.D. in Political Science from the University of Chicago in 1972 and 1973. She currently teaches at the State University of New York, College at Purchase. During her years in Chicago she was a founder of the Women's Liberation Movement and editor of its first national newsletter. She has since lectured widely and written extensively on women and the Women's Liberation Movement. Her published works include: *Women: a feminist perspective* (editor, 1975) and *The politics of Women's Liberation* (1975).

KATHRYN G. HEATH (1910–   ), Assistant for Special Studies in the U.S. Office of Education, has her B.A. in Economics and Ph.D. in Public Administration from The American University, while her M.A. in Personnel and Guidance is from Syracuse University. She is the author of

Ministries of Education: their functions and organization, prepared with the cooperation of 69 national governments. For more than 30 years she has worked to promote equal opportunities in education and employment, beginning with the poor and expanding her efforts to encompass minorities across the country and women around the world. She represented the U.S. Department of Health, Education, and Welfare on the U.S. Delegation to eight sessions of the U.N. Economic and Social Council when reports of the U.N. Commission on the Status of Women were being debated.

CAROLINE IFEKA-MOLLER (1939–) is a Lecturer in Social Anthropology at the University of London. She carried out fieldwork in eastern Nigeria 1965–1967 on leadership and cognitive structures in prayer-healing churches. Main research interests are: the sexual division of labor in pre-capitalist and capitalist formations; the impact of capitalism on indigenous structures in West Africa; and the place of religion in colonial formations. Recent publications include: "Factors facilitating conversion to Christianity in Nigeria" (1974); "Female militancy and colonial revolt in Nigeria" (1975).

ROUNAQ JAHAN (1944–) was born in Dacca, Bangladesh. She graduated from Dacca University, Bangladesh, in 1963 and received her Ph.D. from Harvard University in 1970. She was a Research Associate at the Southern Asian Institute of Columbia University 1969–1970 and at the Center for International Affairs, Harvard, 1971–1972. At present she is an Associate Professor and Chairman of Political Science Department, Dacca University, Bangladesh. She is the author of *Pakistan: failure in national integration* (New York: Columbia University Press, 1972) and co-author of *Divided nations in a divided world* (New York: McKay, 1974). She has contributed a number of articles in journals. Her major research interests are problems of political development in the Third World countries and status of women.

NORA SCOTT KINZER is Professor of Sociology at Purdue University, Westville, Indiana.

LAURA F. KLEIN (1946–) was born in Nova Scotia, Canada. She received her Ph.D. in Anthropology from New York University in 1975. Her dissertation, based upon fieldwork in southeastern Alaska, is entitled "Tlingit women and town politics." Her special interests are in cross-cultural studies of women, politics, and modernization.

ISABEL LARGUIA is an Argentine writer presently living in Cuba.

ELEANOR BURKE LEACOCK (1922–   ), Professor of Anthropology at City College, City University of New York, received her Ph.D. from Columbia University. She has conducted research on American Indians (editor, with Nancy Lurie, of *North American Indians in historical perspective*, 1971); on education and other urban subjects (*Teaching and learning in city schools*, 1969, and editor of *Culture of poverty: a critique*, 1971); and on problems in social evolution and the status of women (editor, with introduction, of Lewis Henry Morgan's *Ancient society*, 1963, and editor, with introduction of Friedrich Engels' *Origin of the family, private property and the state*, 1972).

SUSAN R. MAKIESKY received her B.A. from New York University in 1967 and is completing her doctoral dissertation in Anthropology at Brandeis University. She has done research in the West Indies in Antigua and Barbados on social and political change. She was Visiting Lecturer in Sociology at the University of the West Indies (Cave Hill Campus) in 1971–1972 and was an Instructor in the Anthropology Department of New York University during 1972–1973. She is currently Senior Research Scientist in the Anthropology Section of the Biometrics Research Unit, New York State Department of Mental Hygiene. Her special research interests include migration and ethnicity, political anthropology, Caribbean studies, and the anthropology of women.

AMELIA M. MARIOTTI (1946–   ) is a Ph.D. candidate at the University of Connecticut, Storrs, Conn. Her areas of concentration include urban anthropology, economic anthropology, sociocultural change, and sub-Saharan Africa. Her dissertation topic is "The incorporation of African women into wage employment in South Africa, 1920–1965."

JUNE NASH (1927–   ) was born in Ipswich. She received her B.A. from Barnard College in 1958, and an M.A. and Ph.D. in Anthropology from the University of Chicago in 1953 and 1960. She has been Professor of Anthropology at City College and the City University of New York since 1972. She has served on the Board of the American Anthropological Association, the Committee on Latin American Studies of the Social Science Research Council, and is now serving on the Guggenheim Foundation selection committee for Latin American scholars.

KAMENE OKONJO (1931–   ) was born in Nigeria. She received her

M.Sc. in Economics from the University of Erlangen-Nuremberg in 1961. She is on the staff of the Institute of African Studies of the University of Nigeria, Nsukka, as a Research Fellow. She is currently on a short leave of absence from the University of Nigeria, and is working on her thesis for her Ph.D. in Sociology at Boston University, Boston, Massachusetts. She is especially interested in women and their roles in the developing countries of the world. Her thesis is on "The role of women in social change in Nigeria." She has held key positions in women's organizations in Nigeria, including the chairmanship of the Nigerian Association of University Women, Nsukka. She has read papers at conferences and given talks to international women's groups in Europe. Her latest paper, read at the American Political Science Association Meeting, 1974, and soon to be published, is on "Political systems with bisexual functional roles: the case of women's participation in politics in Nigeria."

DORIT PADAN-EISENSTARK (1925–   ) was born in Germany. She recieved her B.A. in 1963, her M.A. in 1968, and her Ph.D. in 1973 in Sociology from The Hebrew University of Jerusalem. Her research interests and publications are in the fields of social stratification, social mobility, sex roles, and sociology of the family. Her recent publications include: "Girls' education in the kibbutz" (1973), "Ideological factors in the selection of a reference group in a cooperative community in Israel" (in collaboration with H. Hacker, 1974), and "Role system under stress: sex roles in war" (in collaboration with R. Bar-Yosef, 1974). She acts as chairperson of the Behavioral Sciences Department at the Ben-Gurion University of the Negev.

VIRVE PIHO (1924–   ) received her M.A. in 1962 at the National School of Anthropology and History in Mexico City with a dissertation about the life and labor of the female textile worker, published as a book in 1974 by the National University of Mexico. Since 1963, she has occupied a research position at the National Institute of Anthropology and History, and since 1971 she has been Professor for Precolumbian Studies at the School for Foreign Students at the National University of Mexico. In 1973, she recieved her Ph. D. in Anthropology at the same university with a dissertation about social ranks in Aztec society. Her numerous publications refer mostly to Aztec culture.

RUBY ROHRLICH-LEAVITT was born in Montreal, Canada. She received her M.S. in Speech Pathology from Adelphi University and her Ph.D. in Anthropology from New York University. She is Associate Professor in the Social Science Department at the Borough of Manhattan Community College, City University of New York. Her publications include: *The Puerto Ricans: culture change and language deviance* (Viking Fund Publication in Anthropology 51; and "Women in other cultures," in *Woman in sexist society: anthropological approaches to women's studies, a module* —edited by V. Gornick and B. Moran).

BERNICE GLATZER ROSENTHAL was born in New York City. She studied History at City College of New York and the University of Chicago and received her Ph.D. in Russian History at the University of California at Berkeley in 1970. Now Assistant Professor of History at Fordham University Bronx, New York she teaches Twentieth-Century Russia and Modern European Intellectual History. Publications include: "Love on the tractor: women in the Russian Revolution and after" (1974), "Nietzsche in Russia: the case of Merezhkovsky" (1974), and *Dmitri S. Merezhkovsky and the Silver Age 1890–1917: the development of a revolutionary mentality* (1974). Now working on a second book on the reorientation of Russian culture before the Revolution, she also plans a comparative study of women in socialist societies.

IDA FAYE ROUSSEAU is currently Fulbright Professor at the National University of Zaire, Lubumbashi Campus, on leave from Morehouse College (Atlanta University Center) in Atlanta, Georgia. She received her M.A. in Sociology from the University of California, where she is presently a candidate for the Ph.D. in Sociology. She has spent three years in Zaire and two years in Sierra Leone. It was there that she conducted the research for the article in this volume.

HELEIETH IARA BONGIOVANI SAFFIOTTI (1934–   ) was born in Brazil. She received her Ph.D. in 1967 in Sociology. She is currently Full Professor of Sociology at the University of Araraquara and has been Chairman of the Department of Social Science three times. Her publications include 22 articles on various subjects (of which 8 are about women) and two books on women. One of the books — *Women in class society* — will soon be published in English by Monthly Review.

AURELIA GUADALUPE SÁNCHEZ MORALES (1941–   ) studied social and developmental sciences in Mexico and Santiago, Chile. She has participated in two socioeconomic studies of industrial enterprises in Mexico, one study on unemployment in Mexico City, and twenty socioreligious studies on various areas in Mexico. These studies have provided her with the opportunity to become closely acquainted with most of the country. Currently she works with CIDAL (Coordination of Initiatives for the Human Development in Latin America) as Director of the Team on Permanent Employment, which position has occasioned business trips to all the countries of Central and South America.

BROOKE GRUNDFEST SCHOEPF is currently Associate Professor of Sociology at the National University of Zaire, Lubumbashi, and a staff member of the Rockefeller Foundation. She received her Ph.D. from Columbia University in 1969 with a study on "Doctor-patient communication and the medical social system." Her interests in social theory link research efforts in the areas of medical anthropology, development studies, and women.

BLANCA SILVESTRINI-PACHECO (1947–   ) was born in San Juan, Puerto Rico. She did her undergraduate work at the University of Puerto Rico and her graduate work at the University of Louvain, Belgium, and at the State University of New York at Albany where she received her Ph.D. in 1973. At the present she is Assistant Professor of History at the University of Puerto Rico and is the Associate Director of a major research project on the Puerto Rican society at the end of the nineteenth century. Her main research interest is the social history of Latin America and at present is also working with changes in roles and functions of the family in Puerto Rico during the twentieth century.

DOREN L. SLADE (1945–   ) began her study of anthropology at the George Washington University and received her B.A. in 1966, continuing on for her doctorate in Social Anthropology at the University of Pittsburgh. After completing two years of fieldwork in a Nahuat Indian community of Mexico's Sierra de Puebla, she recieved her Ph.D. in 1973 with a dissertation on the political economy of the community's religious system. Before becoming the Andrew Mellon Postdoctoral Fellow in Anthropology at the University of Pittsburgh in 1974, she taught at Queens and Lehman Colleges of the City University of New York.

MARGO L. SMITH (1943–   ) Educated at Indiana University, she is currently Associate Professor of Anthropology and Director of the graduate Social Science program at Northeastern Illinois University. She is author of several articles on domestic service in Peru.

CONSTANCE R. SUTTON received her M.A. in Anthropology from the University of Chicago in 1954 and her Ph.D. in Anthropology from Columbia University in 1969. She is Associate Professor in the Anthropology Department of New York University, where she has taught since 1960. During 1971–1972, she was Chairwoman of the Anthropology Department at New York University's University College of Arts and Science. Her field research has been in the Afro-Caribbean region, where she studied plantation workers in the late 1950's. She returned to the West Indies in the late 1960's and early 1970's to carry out follow-up studies on political and ideological change. Her monograph, *Protest and change in Barbados*, focuses on changing forms of political protest. Her current research interests include migration and ethnicity and women's models of social reality. She has served on committees of the American Anthropological Association, is a Danforth Associate, and is a member of New York University's Affirmative Action Council

BARBARA A. SYKES received her B.A. from Goddard College in 1970 and her M.A. in Social Anthropology from New York University in 1975. She has dual British and American nationality, and her interest in anthropology was awakened by her upbringing in North and South Africa, Europe, the United States, Mexico, and Asia. She joined the women's movement in the 1960's, working for the repeal of abortion laws. Her anthropological and feminist interests quickly fused, and she is entering a career in international aspects of population planning, using work-related research toward her doctorate. She is also a published journalist, poet, and photographer and has participated in an intensive summer of learning ethnographic film-making at the Anthropology Film Center in Sante Fé, New Mexico, under an NHF grant.

ELIZABETH WEATHERFORD (1945–   ) grew up in Memphis, Tennessee. She received her B.A. from The New School for Social Research in 1970 and is currently working on her doctorate in Cultural Anthropology. She is on the faculty of Richmond College of the City University of New York and the School of Visual Arts, New York City. She has published articles on the artistic roles of women in both traditional and avant-garde contexts.

Index of Names

Index of Subjects

Aba Commission Report, 37
Abeokuta Native Authority, Nigeria, 38
Aboriginal woman (Kaberry), 569
Adire (dyed cloth), 35
Africa, 4, 19, 31–52, 392, 472, 494–495, 536, 561, 603–604, 612, 614, 619, 623–625, 635. *See also* Names of individual countries
Agriculture, 9, 17–18, 31, 35, 79, 98, 100, 107, 129, 134, 151, 160, 249, 461–462
Ainu, 516
Ake, 635
Akwete, 35
Alake, 38
Alaska, 582, 588–591
Algeria, 270
Alice Lenshins movement, Zambia, 562, 635
All Pakinstan Women's Association (APWA; later, Bangladesh Mohila Society), 24–26, 28
Alpha Gamma Delta social fraternity, 163
American Anthropological Association, 159
American Anthropologist (journal), 532
American Association of University Women, 333, 354, 371
American Education (journal), 327, 346
American Federation of Labor, 256
American Historical Association, 538
American Journal of Sociology, 300
American Political Science Association, 346, 538

American Sociological Association, 538
American Sociologist (journal), 346
American Women: 1963, 338
Androcentrism, 567–568, 578–579
Angola, 44, 614, 624
Anjuman-e-Khawatein-Islam (Muslim women's organization, Bangladesh), 24
Anjuma Falah Muslim Kawateen (women's organization, Bangladesh), 27
Anthropology, 247, 300, 362–363, 390, 392, 414, 529–616, 620–621, 634; androcentrism in, 567–568, 578–579; asexual role of fieldworker in, 535–555; careers of graduates in, 547; cognitive structuralists in, 559, 565; degree evaluation by sex in, 547–549; demographic factor in, 564; "double-consciousness" in, 569, 579; ethnocentrism in, 567, 578; "female factor" in, 534, 559–566; husband-wife teams in, 556–557; in Mexico, 96, 111, 147; "male factor" in, 534, 567; marital status of women in, 556–557; men in, 533, 547, 552, 555, 567–568, 570–576, 578–579, 620–621; pragmatism in, 559; problems in sex-segregated societies in, 534; research money by, sex in, 549; research questions in, 613–615; sex bias in studies on, 567–580; student-teacher relationships in, 543–544; women in, 529–616, 620–621, 634; women Ph.D's in, 532–533, 538, 548–549; women researcher's self-evaluation in, 552, 553;

Mayordomias, 131, 135, 141, 144–145
Mazahua Indians, 96
Mbangala, 44
Mehr, 15–16
Mejoras, 480
Melanesia, 392, 613
Melpa, 565
Men: agricultural, 134; as economic provider, 152–153, 263; as household heads, 137, 158; Bangali, 3, 14; careers of, 18–19, 25–26, 131–132, 138, 234–235, 561; Cuban, 477; "dominance" of, 319–323, 605, 634; economic status of, 61, 131–134, 142–144, 152–158, 234–235, 264, 288–289, 322, 561, 585, 623; education of, 8, 25; in anthropology, 533, 547, 552, 555, 567–568, 570–576, 578–579, 620–621; inheritance of, 140–141; Islamic, 3; Israeli, 493, 502–503; as labor power in Brazil, 81; legal status of, 586; life expectancy of, 69; marginality of, 149; marital status of, 134–137, 139–140, 142–144, 147–148, 152–161; Maya, 122-123; Mexican, 129–148; Pakistani, 4; political status of, 129–137, 144–148, 264, 563, 578, 589–590, 606, 621, 623; ritual rank of, 133–137; salary differential from women, 71–76, 105, 192, 363, 394–395; social status of, 131, 134, 585, 590–591, 592–595, 621; support of Chinese Women's Movement by, 457
Mendeland, Sierra Leone, 624
Mesopotamia, 615
Mestizo, 96, 100, 112, 117, 165, 630
Mexico, 56–57, 89, 95–127, 187, 199–245, 393, 622, 630; birth control in, 120–121; cargo system in, 131–136; conquest of, 97–98, 200; Federal Labor Law in, 201, 206; labor unions in, 207–212; marriage patterns in, 119, 129–148, 230–239; religion in, 239–240; rural migration to cities in, 104–105; Social Security in, 207, 214–215, 217, 225
Mexico City, 95, 106–107, 199–245, 630
Milpas, 114, 130–132, 138–139
Moi Moi, 33
Montagnais-Naskapi, 607–610
Monterrey, Mexico, 100, 107
Morelos state, Mexico, 95
Morocco, 3, 535, 582, 584–588, 597–598; education of women in, 587–588;

French supervision in, 585; legal system in, 586; male status in, 585–588; seclusion of women in, 585–588; sexual segregation in, 585–588, 597
Mukti Bahini, 21
Mundo, El (Puerto Rican newspaper), 255, 256
Muslim Family Laws Ordinance, Bangladesh, 16
Muslim League, Bangladesh, 20
Mutterrecht, Das (Bachofen), 508, 510
Myuomba, 44

Nahuat language, 130
Naior, 17
Narodnoe khoziastvo SSR, 446
National Business Women (periodical), 337
National Education Association of the United States, 344
National Federation of Business and Professional Women's Clubs, 333, 336
National Institute of Mental Health (NIMH), 582
National Liberation Front, 477
National Organization for Women (NOW), 279–280, 344–345, 347, 369, 376, 379–382, 638–639
National Revolutionary Movement, Bolivia, 165–166
National Women's Political Caucus, 350
Nayar, 425–426, 508, 516–525, 630
Netherlands, 63, 76
Neue Deutsche Mercur, Der (magazine), 522
New Economic Policy (NEP) (USSR), 433–434
New Guinea, 565
News and Views (journal), 346
New York City/State Commissions of Human Rights, 362–369
New York Times, 270
New York University, 367
New York University Arts and Science Research Fund, 582
New York Women's Anthropological Caucus, 129
New York Women's Bar Association, 71
Ngbabandi, 43–44
Nigeria, 4, 31–40, 562–563, 614, 623, 635; *Omu* in, 623; War of the Women (1929) in, 623–624; Women's Riot of 1929–1930 in, 623–624

Women's Bureau of Employment Stan-
dards Administration, 633
Women's Equity Action League (WEAL)
347–348, 369, 376
Women's Federation, 459–462, 465, 467
Womens' Liberation Movement (WLM),
375–387, 390–391, 398–419
Women's Rights Organization, 526
Women's Voluntary Association (WVA),
Bangladesh, 27–28
Women that speak out (Zentina), 104

Xocoyol, 223

Yenan, China, 466
Yoruba, 34
Young Catholic Working Women (JOC)
Lima, Peru, 173–174
Yugoslavia, 73

Zaire (originally Congo Free State), 4,
41–52, 624
Zambia, 44, 562, 614, 624, 635
Zhenotdel, 434
Zhenshcina i deti V SSR, 444, 446
Zonta Club, Bangladesh, 27–28